THE WESTMINSTER SERIES

General Editor: W. A. J. FARNDALE

VOLUME 4

TRENDS
IN SOCIAL WELFARE

THE WESTMINSTER SERIES

General Editor: W. A. J. FARNDALE

TRENDS
IN SOCIAL WELFARE

Edited by

JAMES FARNDALE

Senior Lecturer in Hospital Administration
City of Westminster College, London

PERGAMON PRESS

OXFORD · LONDON · EDINBURGH · NEW YORK
PARIS · FRANKFURT

Pergamon Press Ltd., Headington Hill Hall, Oxford
4 & 5 Fitzroy Square, London W.1

Pergamon Press (Scotland) Ltd., 2 & 3 Teviot Place, Edinburgh 1

Pergamon Press Inc., 122 East 55th St., New York 22, N.Y.

Pergamon Press GmbH, Kaiserstrasse 75, Frankfurt-am-Main

First edition 1965

Library of Congress Catalog Card No. 64–17192

PRINTED IN GREAT BRITAIN BY
THE ANCHOR PRESS, LTD.
TIPTREE, ESSEX

1728

Contents

v

Section XI—The Churches in Welfare

List of Contributors

APPLEBEY, MARY, O.B.E., J.P., General Secretary, National Association for Mental Health, 39 Queen Anne Street, London, W. 1.

ARCHER, PETER, Editor, *Social Welfare and the Citizen* (Penguin), Arvika, 21 Clements Road, Chorleywood, Herts.

BACH, FRANCIS, M.A., D.M., D.PHYS. MED., Physician to the Rheumatics Unit, St. Stephen's Hospital, Chelsea; Vice-Chairman, British Rheumatism and Arthritis Association.

BARGH, J. H., D.P.A., F.I.S.W., Barrister-at-Law, Director of Welfare Services, Glamorgan County Council, Greyfriars Road, Cardiff.

BEGLIN, M. F., Director of Welfare Services, City of Bradford Welfare Office (P.O. Box No. 62), 22 Manor Road, Bradford, 1.

BENTLEY, J.G., 25 Mannock Road, London, N.22.

BLYTH BROOKE, C. O. S., M.D., D.P.H., Barrister-at-Law, Medical Officer of Health, Finsbury Health Centre, Pine Street, London, E.C. 1.

BOVAN, COLONEL R. W., Chief Secretary, Salvation Army Men's Social Services, Middlesex House, 110–12 Middlesex Street, London, E. 1.

BOWDEN, JEAN, Author, Editor and Journalist, Member of the British Red Cross Society, 14–15 Grosvenor Crescent, London, S.W. 1.

BOYCE, WALTER E., County Welfare Officer, County Council of Essex, 73 Springfield Road, Chelmsford, Essex.

BRAMALL, MARGARET E., M.A., A.M.I.A., General Secretary, National Council for the Unmarried Mother and her Child, 255 Kentish Town Road, London, N.W. 5.

BRAYSHAW, A. J., J.P., B.A., Recently General Secretary, National Marriage Guidance Council, 58 Queen Anne Street, London, W. 1.

BUCKE, MARJORIE, Secretary, National Old People's Welfare Council, 26 Bedford Square, London, W.C. 1.

BURDEN, G. S., B.SC.(ECON.), General Secretary of the British Epilepsy Association, 27 Nassau Street, London, W. 1.

BURROWS, J. H., B.SC.(ECON.), Staff Lecturer in Sociology, Department of Extra-mural Studies, University of London, W.C. 1.

BURT, J. S., Barrister-at-law, Director, Family Welfare Association, 296 Vauxhall Bridge Road, London, W. 1.

COLLIGAN, J. C., C.B.E., Director-General, Royal National Institute for the Blind, 224–8 Great Portland Street, London, W. 1.

DONNISON, D. V., Professor of Social Administration, London School of Economics and Political Science, Houghton Street, London, W.C. 2.

DUNBAR, ELSA, C.B.E., Women's Voluntary Service For Civil Defence, 41 Tothill Street, London, S.W. 1.

FARNDALE, W. A. JAMES, PH.D., F.H.A., Barrister-at-Law, Senior Lecturer in Hospital Administration, City of Westminster College, London, S.W. 1.

FRANKLIN, REV. GORDON A., Secretary of the Shaftesbury Society, Shaftesbury House, 112 Regency Street, London, S.W. 1.

GRAHAM, W. L., General Secretary, Elderly Invalids' Fund, 34 King Street, London, E.C. 2.

GREET, REV. KENNETH G., A Secretary at the Department of Christian Citizenship of the Methodist Church, 1 Central Buildings, Westminster, London, S.W. 1

GREGORY, J.T., D.P.A., A.I.S.W., Chief Welfare Officer, London Borough of Southwark, Welfare Department, 1 Queen Anne's Gate Buildings, Dartmouth Street, London, S.W. 1.

GUTTMANN, L., C.B.E., M.D., F.R.C.P., F.R.C.S., Director, National Spinal Injuries Centre, Stoke Mandeville Hospital, Mandeville Road, Aylesbury, Bucks.

HAWKINS, ANN, B.SC.(ECON.)—C.A.B. Liaison Officer, Family Welfare Association, 296 Vauxhall Bridge Road, London, S.W. 1.

HENHAM-BARROW, M. A., Secretary, Southern Regional Association for the Blind, 14 Howick Place, London, S.W. 1.

HOBMAN, DAVID, Information Officer, National Council of Social Service, 26 Bedford Square, London, W.C. 1.

HODSON, RT. REV. MARK A., Lord Bishop of Hereford, Chairman of the Church of England Council for Social Work, The Bishop's House, The Palace, Hereford.

JOHNSON SMITH, G., M.P., The House of Commons, London, S.W. 1.

JONES, DR. T. SEYMOUR, M.B., CL.B., M.R.C.S., L.R.C.P., D.P.H., Divisional Medical Officer, Lancashire County Council, County Divisional Health Office, Parsons Lane, Bury, Lancs.

JORDEN, F., County Welfare Services Officer, Royal County of Berkshire, 7 Abbots Walk, Reading.

KEIGHLEY, REV. D. A., Formerly Secretary, Social Responsibility Department, British Council of Churches, 10 Eaton Gate, Sloane Square, London, S.W. 1.

KIERNANDER, B., M.B., M.R.C.P., D.M.R.E., D.PHYS., M.ED., Honorary Medical Adviser to the Cheshire Foundation Homes for the Sick, 7 Market Mews, London, W. 1.

LIDBURY, W. L., D.B.E., Formerly Regional Controller, London (North) Region National Assistance Board, Friars, Parsonage Down, Dunmow, Essex.

LLOYD JACOB, F. L., Barrister-at-Law, Secretary of the London Central Consultative Committee on the Welfare of Old People, and a Principal Officer of the Welfare Department, London County Council, The County Hall, Westminster Bridge, London, S.E. 1.

MacQUEEN, IAN A. G., G.B.E., M.A., M.D., D.P.H., F.R.S.H., Medical Officer of Health and Director of Welfare, Health and Welfare Department, City of Aberdeen, and Lecturer in Public Health, University of Aberdeen, Willowbank Road, Aberdeen.

PARFITT KLEIN, J., Formerly on the editorial staff of *The Times*, 18 Onslow Gardens, London, N. 10.

PARKER, R. A., B.SC.(SOC.), PH.D., Lecturer in Social Administration, London School of Economics and Political Science, Houghton Street, London, W.C. 2.

PAVITT. L. A., M.P., The House of Commons, S.W. 1.

PERCEVAL, R. J., Director of Field Work, National Council on Alcoholism, King Edward's Mansions, 212A Shaftesbury Avenue, London, W.C. 2.

PHILLIPS, MARY, A.A.P.S.W., Tutor in Social Work Training, College of Commerce, Unity Street, Bristol, 1.

PHILP, A. F., Secretary, Family Service Units, 207 Marylebone Road, London, N.W. 1.

PRENTICE, R. E., M.P., The House of Commons, London, S.W. 1.

PRIDHAM, JOAN, Secretary, Natinal Citizens' Advice Bureaux Council, 26 Bedford Square, London, W.C. 1.

PRINCE, J., Health Services Correspondent, *Daily Telegraph*, Fleet Street, London, E.C. 4.

RICHARDSON, M., M.A., Welfare and Youth Officer, Jewish Institute Advisory Centre, Adler House, Adler Street, London, E. 1.

ROBERTS, J., F.C.C.S., F.I.S.W., Director of Civic Welfare, Civic Welfare Offices, Broughton Road, Salford, 6.

ROSS, HELEN M., M.A., Previously Chairman of the Committee of the Presbyterian Settlement, London, 1955-61, 64 Wildwood Road, London, N.W. 11.

SALATHIEL, T., Formerly of the L.C.C., 21 Mead Crescent, Sutton, Surrey.

SIMPSON, REV. W. W., M.A., Advisory Secretary, Central Churches Group, National Council of Social Service, 26 Bedford Square, London, W.C. 1.

SLACK, K. M., Lecturer in Social Administration, London School of Economics, Houghton Street, London, W.C. 2.

SOMERSCALES, T. L., F.C.A., Secretary, Joint Committee of the Order of St. John of Jerusalem and the British Red Cross Society, 12 Grosvenor Square, London, S.W. 1.

STEVENS, C. P., M.B.E., M.B., Director of the Spastics Society, 12 Park Crescent, London, W. 1.

TILLEY, M., Formerly Training Secretary, Church of England Council for Social Work, Church House, Dean's Yard, London, S.W. 1.

TINTO, T., F.S.A.A., D.P.A., F.I.S.W., Principal Welfare Services Officer, Corporation of Glasgow, 23 Montrose Street, Glasgow, C.1.

TODD, F. JOAN, B.A., A.A.P.S.W., Psychiatric Social Worker, 26 Longfield Road, Shaw, Oldham, Lincs.

USDANE, W. M., PH.D., Professor of Education, San Francisco State College, V.S.A. Fulbright Research Senior Scholar and Visiting Professor at the London School of Economics and Political Science, 1962–63. Now Chief, Research Division Vocational Rehabilitation Administration, Department of Health, Education and Welfare, Washington, D.C.

VARAH, REV. CHAD., M.A.(OXON.), Founder of "The Samaritans", Director of the London branch, Rector of St. Stephen Walbrook, City of London, E.C. 1.

WATERHOUSE, REV. H. O., S.J., Priest-Director, Catholic Social Guild, Plater Hall, Boars Hill, Oxford.

WEDDERBURN, DOROTHY COLE, Senior Research Officer, Department of Applied Economics, Sidgwick Avenue, Cambridge.

WESTMORELAND, J. E., M.B.E., M.S.M.W.O., Honorary Secretary, Society of Mental Welfare Officers and Mental Health Officer, City of Nottingham, 136 Mansfield Road, Nottingham.

WINTOUR, ELEANOR, 3 Cochrane Street, London, N.W. 8.

WOODHILL, G. W., Brigade Secretary, St. John Ambulance Brigade, 8 Grosvenor Crescent, London, S.W. 1.

Contributors from public authorities wish to state that their authorities accept no responsibility for any statement or expression of opinion contained in their articles in this Symposium. The views expressed are entirely their own.

List of Plates*

* Plates 1–15 provided by courtesy of the London County Council.

Editor's Introduction

THIS is a sequel and companion volume to *Trends in the National Health Service* and forms the fourth part in a series of books known as the Westminster Series. This series, on the hospital and social services of our country, is intended for the general public and students at home and abroad, as well as for those already connected with these services. The writers of the series are all closely connected with the social services. It is not intended that these books should present only a rosy picture of the present-day situation, and they should therefore include some informed criticism. However, the main intention is to give a description of some of these services, showing their growth and recent development and the more important trends. The services, which now form part of our Welfare Society, have not grown overnight nor are they necessarily unique to this country.

Trends in Social Welfare may be used as a handbook for social workers, students and people who have a general interest in welfare as a whole, but it is hoped that, apart from this, it will also be interesting to the general reader.

This book is also for the busy person, including the professional man or woman who, though not necessarily engaged in work for these services, may find this will serve as an introduction or guide to certain of our welfare services. The fact that the articles which make up this guide are signed by many interesting contributors demonstrates their authenticity and authority.

Welfare is one of the most difficult subjects to cover adequately because of the vastness of the field. Obviously, in outlining trends in modern social welfare, the line must be drawn somewhere, but it is believed that the contributors to this volume have given a fair outline of many statutory and voluntary welfare services—including examples of co-ordination and co-operation, and present and future trends. Much care has been taken to include as many aspects as possible, but it must be remembered that some subjects are dealt with, or will be covered, in other volumes in this series.

The "Triple Alliance"

The reader will be reminded here of many of the present human social needs and the quiet suffering and often desperate plight of many people, together with the steps being taken by the central and local authorities and voluntary organizations to meet that human need. Throughout the symposium, this "triple alliance" has been illustrated, as articles on the work of central government, local authorities, and voluntary organizations are often included together, side by side, especially in parts dealing with services for the Elderly, the Deaf, the Blind, the Handicapped and in the Mental Health Field, and so on. In this way, it is hoped that the reader will get an overall picture. The "triple alliance" reports some of its activities and hopes to enlist the sympathies and interests of the reader for the human needs portrayed, as much more remains to be done for the welfare of certain members of our society.

Social Welfare

"Social welfare" embraces a wide field and a large number of services. This symposium began with a suggestion that, as the welfare services are of such importance, and hospitals rely to such an extent on them for the continued care of their patients, a sequel to the symposium on the National Health Service should follow, dealing almost entirely with the welfare services. This volume therefore includes a description of some of the services provided, especially by the local welfare authorities, but excludes the National Health Service except for reference to some of the services of local health authorities. It also excludes education, services for youth and children, and services connected with the courts and penal system. However, the scope of the symposium was widened to include some aspects of social security, or "the cash services" as they are sometimes termed, and sections on Family Welfare, Moral Welfare and the Churches in Welfare. It was therefore decided to describe the volume as *Trends in Social Welfare*, which is wider in scope and covers more social services than the original proposal for a volume on the welfare services.

Social Workers

Many of the problems surrounding the recruitment, selection and training of social workers and their eventual deployment have been considered by some contributors, who leave little doubt as to the sort of social worker and administrator who makes the best social service. Some of the recommendations of the Younghusband Report and the action taken on that report are considered, but the question is still being asked—Are good social workers born or made?

When a house is in need of repair, be it a small job or a repair to the major superstructure, there are two ways of tackling it. A patch or prop can be put up which will cover the weakness but will never repair it. The patch or prop must always remain. Alternatively, a scaffolding can be put around the house and, slowly but surely, the house can be underpinned or thoroughly repaired until the scar is completely obliterated. When the scaffolding is removed the house is like new again.

So it follows with welfare work of all kinds—instead of a crumbling house, read a person or a family. Some well-meaning person without training or experience in social work can come along to do a patch-up job, or become a prop to cover the damage. Obviously, though, the well-trained experienced social worker will realize that, though the job may take longer, by using a scaffold the person or family in question can eventually become rehabilitated —like new again!

General Aspects of the Social Services (Section I)

The symposium begins with articles describing the growth, development and some general aspects of our social services and the modern Welfare State. The history and growth of some of the services is traced by Peter Archer; a stocktaking is made by John Burrows, and he also discusses some of the services in our Welfare Society. John Prince, in his article, considers that in certain fields, such as the services for the elderly and housing, the Welfare State is still a goal and not an achievement. Kathleen Slack shows the importance of voluntary effort and illustrates the various forms which it may take in this country. Professor Donnison, in his "Report on Social Work", also makes the point that our social services have a long way to go before they justify the claim of this country to be a Welfare State, and that our expanding society must accept responsibility for helping those who come to grief in it, social work being one way of providing that help. Professor Donnison, in his "Postscript", describes some of the action taken on the Younghusband Report which led to the Health Visiting and Social Work (Training) Act of 1962, the establishment of two councils—one for health visitors and the other for social workers, and the establishment by charitable trusts of the National Institute for Social Work Training. In interesting, stimulating and thought-provoking articles these contributors set the scene for a detailed examination of some specific social services. In the opening articles, and indeed throughout the book, the need for many of the social services is, first of all, shown, and then how that need is being met. The Ten Year Plan for Local Health and Welfare is introduced and featured. One contributor considers that this plan should have come before the Hospital Plan. This comment shows the importance of the Plan for Local Health and Welfare. In view of this importance, descriptions and comments on the Plan have been given by both Conservative and Labour Members of Parliament.

One of the basic principles underlying the Hospital Plan (see Volume 3 in this series) is that, where illness or disability occurs, the aim will be to provide care at home and in the community for all who do not require the special types of diagnosis and treatment for which only a hospital has facilities. The adequate development of community services, particularly in the fields of mental health and the care of old people, is vital to the success of the Hospital Plan.

Local Authority Welfare Services (Section II)

There is an emphasis in Section II, and throughout the book, on some of the work of local welfare authorities, or, where combined with health, with the work of local health and welfare authorities. It should be noted that these services do not need to be combined. Many would prefer them to be administered separately, and indeed there are twice as many chief welfare officers concerned with welfare alone as medical officers of health who are in charge of both local health and welfare. Irrespective of whether there is lay or medical direction of the local welfare services, many local authorities have a Welfare Committee in addition to a Health Committee.

A detailed description and discussion of the Ten Year Plan for local health and welfare is also given here, and from it the reader will no doubt be able to learn a great deal about the operation and extent of these services. Functional aspects of the work of local welfare authorities, such as services for the Blind, the Handicapped and the Deaf are discussed in separate sections of the book.

In this section are given some examples of the overall work of welfare authorities in Lancashire, in Essex and in Scotland. Attention is also directed to the need for co-operation and co-ordination between social services, as, for example, between local authorities and hospital authorities, and also between local authorities and voluntary organizations.'

Many services grew up out of the old Poor Laws, the first of which was passed in 1601 in the reign of Queen Elizabeth I, as Peter Archer reminds us in the opening chapter. There has in the present century been a complete break with the old Poor Laws, and in the reign of our present Queen Elizabeth II the modern Welfare Society has grown to fuller development. Yet however much these laws are scoffed at now, it must be remembered that they were established under very difficult circumstances and have made a wonderful "corner-stone". The Relieving Officer was not always the villain many imagine but was often the link—mentor and friend who helped with every problem and did not refer people from one social worker to another—a man who tended to think of people for what they were, not pigeon-holing them as "cases". Power was in these men's hands, and, as far as they were able, they used it to benefit the needy and dispense the limited charity at their disposal.

Until 1929 the Boards of Guardians were the controlling bodies administering the "welfare services". The Guardians controlled the amount of money the Relieving Officer (who was a statutory official) could issue and were also responsible for admissions into workhouses and hospitals. Then, in 1930, under the Local Government Act, 1929, the control was handed to the Public Assistance Committees of the local authorities and remained there until the advent of the National Health Service Act, 1946, and the National Assistance Act, 1948. The welfare services have thus broken away from the old Poor Law, since the National Assistance Act, 1948, brought the Poor Law to an end. Relief from economic distress may now be obtained as a right and not as a form of "charity", a point which needs to be stressed and which is rightly emphasized by more than one contributor.

Voluntary Social Services

Side by side with the growth of the local authority services has been the marvellous work carried out and often pioneered by the voluntary bodies during this time and, indeed, right up to the present day. Many of the voluntary associations have been approached to contribute articles typifying their work. These articles highlight the real co-operation which exists between them and the statutory bodies, although there is room on both sides for greater co-operation. In spite of our Welfare State there is hardly a social service which does not also have the support and co-operation from voluntary organizations, and in almost every section of this book there is an article by way of illustration of their supporting and complementary work.

Many of the social services had their origin in the voluntary services, and, although the State has assumed statutory responsibility for most of the social services, there is still a continuing and vital need for voluntary organizations and volunteers. Voluntary organizations have pioneered many of our social services because they are better able to experiment and follow up new ideas. They are more suited to certain types of social work, but they have, however, the disadvantages of lack of adequate finances, overlapping and rivalry. In addition they are sometimes based on a leading personality, which is a bad thing, as, when that person retires, the voluntary organization is apt to suffer a setback.

Voluntary organizations provide services independent of government control although they may receive financial aid, and they may employ salaried staff. The part they play in the development of our social services has always been important. A strong voluntary organization movement such as we have in Britain is one of the correctives to a possible bureaucracy in a Welfare State.

There is a need to distinguish between voluntary organizations and volunteers. A volunteer is a person who gives his or her service voluntarily and without payment of any kind. There is a need for further development and organization of volunteers in many branches of the social services, including the hospitals and services for the elderly. There are opportunities for volunteers in many directions, such as serving as members of local welfare authorities or of committees of hospital authorities, serving with the Women's Voluntary Services, the Red Cross or St. John Ambulance Brigade, or in helping the elderly by domiciliary work, just to mention a few examples.

Voluntary organizations are also concerned with bringing about improvements to our social services. Their informed and constructive criticism can be a valuable stimulus and corrective to any tendency to inertia or complacency on the part of the public social services. In a similar way, voluntary organizations should be receptive of criticism of their services. There is a need for "work study" in both public and voluntary social services.

Social Security (Section III)

Section III describes some of the cash services which form an important part of our social services. Services for the elderly, for example, have to rely upon adequate national insurance, including pensions, and on national assistance. Such social security schemes have relieved all classes of people of much worry and hardship.

In 1942 Lord Beveridge presented to Parliament a report in which he focused attention on the five main causes of unrest or five giants on the road to reconstruction. They were poverty, disease, ignorance, squalor and idleness.

Social insurance, fully developed, may provide income security. Want or poverty is being combated by the National Insurance Acts, the National Insurance (Industrial Injuries) Act, the National Assistance Act, and the Family Allowance Act, all of which form part of our Welfare State.

It is typical of the history of this country that the Government should have set up the Beveridge Committee in 1941 to investigate social insurance and allied services at a time of the war when it had little certainty that there would be any social services for much longer or that the Committee's recommendations would ever be implemented. The Beveridge Report arrived at an opportune time when there was the special national unity of the war years.

The National Insurance Act was a direct outcome of the Beveridge Report, and its aim is to make provision against loss of earning power due to sickness, childbirth, unemployment, old age and death. The National Assistance Act partly acts as a safety net. It cannot be too strongly emphasized, as pointed out by Mr. Lidbury in his article, that national assistance can be claimed as a right, and that acceptance of it should no more be regarded as a stigma than is acceptance of the other social services paid for from public funds, such as family allowances or education.

It is difficult for those who have experienced only the special conditions of the post World War II period, to imagine the implications of life without the social insurance and assistance now enjoyed. It is often argued that state provision against poverty has made the British people materialistic, morally flabby, unwilling to save, and to provide for themselves and their dependants. This is not true of the majority, but the risk is there, and this must be regarded as a challenge and not as an excuse to put the clock back.

Social security schemes have come to stay. They are large and expensive, costing at least £1700 million a year, which is about twice the cost of the National Health Service. A service of such size and cost deserves a place in any book on social welfare, and, of course, it also justifies its place because it helps to prevent human misery and to provide income security for all.

On this subject especially, policy decisions should be based, as far as possible, on a study of empirical data rather than on abstract theorizing. That is one reason why the contributions from Reg Prentice, M.P.,* and Mrs. Dorothy Wedderburn are of such importance. They are not only clear-cut descriptions of part of the social security system at work, but they analyse many of the factors to be taken into account in assessing its adequacy, especially in relation to pensions.

Specific Services (Sections IV–X)

Services for the elderly, blind, deaf and other handicapped people, as well as those for mental health and moral welfare, are all described. Many of these fine articles show what profound knowledge and sympathy is felt by the contributors for these people without appearing over-sentimental or too ruthless. Articles such as the one by Mr. Francis Jorden on the Welfare of the Deaf are good for reference purposes, as well as being enlightening and readable.

Under the heading of "Housing and Family Welfare" (Section V) the connection will be readily understood on an examination of the contents of this section, including as it does important articles on Housing—What Next?, Homeless Families, Temporary Accommodation for Homeless Families, the work of the Family Welfare Association, Family Service Units, and Marriage Guidance.

Services for the Elderly

In country districts and in villages of only two or three thousand inhabitants, the aged are usually safe enough.

In towns and cities, however, the problem of discovery is acute, and a large number of elderly people who need the help of an existing service do not receive it simply because no one knows of their need. Attempts are

* Who has since been appointed Minister of State, Department of Education and Science

being made in several towns to attack this problem and some take the form of giving old people who live alone a sign or card which may be exhibited from a window if assistance is urgently needed.

In respect of services for the elderly, the main problems which beset old people may be classified broadly as inadequate income, unsuitable housing, lack of occupation and loneliness. These problems are being dealt with by a bewildering variety of organizations—but to the forefront are, of course, the local welfare authorities, which have a duty under the National Assistance Act to provide residential accommodation for the elderly, and the local Old People's Welfare Committees which co-ordinate some of the services for the elderly. Then there is the provision made by the National Insurance Schemes, and supplemented by the work of the National Assistance Board, which has the responsibility for meeting the needs of all those whose wants can be provided for by grants of money. Articles have therefore been included on these and related aspects which come under the general heading of "social welfare", although the emphasis throughout is on a simple description, with some analytical comments on present and future trends of the services provided from statutory sources, and some illustrative articles from some of the main voluntary organizations.

The partnership between the State and the voluntary organizations has been demonstrated by including descriptions of some of the voluntary effort in the same sections as a description of work by the State, especially in the sections on the Elderly, the Blind and the Handicapped.

The Churches in Welfare (Section XI)

Churches of several denominations were invited to contribute articles to the last section on The Churches in Welfare. Throughout the ages the religious bodies have dispensed "welfare" in various forms, although their welfare work, of course, takes in the wider field of spiritual as well as social ministrations. These articles show that they are still making an important contribution to our present-day welfare society in the form of social service.

Attention is directed, for example, to the promising work of the Central Churches Group of the National Council of Social Service. As pointed out, the "country parsons" of all denominations have an important role to play in interpreting the new social services to the man in the street and in showing him how he can take advantage of what they offer. Practical examples are given of the Fish Scheme at Headington (p. 474) which, with many other local projects, owed its inspiration to a Christian Stewardship Campaign in a local church. One is impressed with the all-round value of these "Stewardship" campaigns, and it is envisaged that much useful voluntary service could be made available by the churches harnessing some of their Stewardship or Planned Giving resources of time, talents and money to local needs, in the service of the elderly, such as the Meals on Wheels Service, visiting the sick in body or in mind at home and in hospital, as well as in the service of the deaf, the blind and other handicapped people. The Bishop of Hereford so rightly points out that the skilled worker cannot function alone; the ordinary people must not contract out of neighbourly social care on the grounds that they are unskilled. More trained people are required in the social work field and the churches can help to give their members the sense of vocation towards this work, which has already caused many to take it up.

The Social Responsibility Department of the British Council of Churches, the Christian Citizenship Department of the Methodist Church, the Social Services of the Salvation Army, and similar organizations, are guiding and directing their members in the effective presentation of the Christian social witness, and, in many practical ways, are pointing to and filling gaps in the social services of the State. Inquiries such as the one undertaken by the Birmingham Council of Churches, the results of which were published in "Responsibility in the Welfare State", draw attention to needs which can be met by the local churches.

As a Protestant, I am impressed with, and interested in, the extent of the Roman Catholic Welfare Services and also the welfare work of the Anglo-Jewish Community.

There has in recent years been a movement towards world-wide Christian Unity and it is evident from articles that this movement is reflected in the field of voluntary social services by many churches and religious bodies acting in unity to meet many and various human social needs.

Some of the social services now taken over by the State had their origin in voluntary services, and it is also true that many voluntary services were initiated by the Church and were and are influenced by people with religious and charitable motives. The important contribution which the churches are making directly and indirectly to the development of our social and welfare services may not generally be realized. Part of their direct contribution (although small in relation to the whole) to present-day social welfare is vividly portrayed in the section of this symposium on "The Churches in Welfare", and part of their indirect contribution in the articles on voluntary organizations. For example, with regard to the work of the Samaritans (p. 403) Dr. Richard Fox, in an article in *The Lancet* (1962, 1105), has written: "For many the Samaritan movement symbolises much more than a telephone service for would-be suicides; it could represent a tremendous resurgence of practical Christianity."

Many Shades of Opinion

The Editor has endeavoured to be impartial and independent, both politically and with regard to the administration of some of these services, and to present many shades of opinion or schools of thought. For example, on the important Ten Year Plan for local health and welfare services articles were invited from Members of Parliament of the Conservative and the Labour parties. Geoffrey Johnson Smith (Conservative M.P.), gives an introduction to the Ten Year Plan, and this is followed by a critical examination of the 1963 Plan by Laurence Pavitt, a Labour member of Parliament.

The importance of welfare work carried out locally under the direction of both medical officers and lay welfare officers is recognized by contributions from representatives of both.

Voluntary organizations have been given, as a whole, almost as much space as the national and local authorities which operate parts of the Welfare State. The importance of voluntary effort is fully recognized, and, even in a Welfare State, it is interesting to note the development of new voluntary organizations, such as the Elderly Invalids' Fund, the National Council on Alcoholism, the Samaritans (formerly known as the Telephone Samaritans), and the rapid development of war-time or post-war voluntary organizations such as the Cheshire Foundation Homes for the Sick, the Women's Voluntary Services and many bodies providing homes or housing for the aged.

Every effort has been made to quote full references and to condense aspects of the relevant Acts into simple lay terms understandable by all.

Hospitals Rely on Many Social Services

Here are some of the social services which may be of importance to hospital patients both before and after hospital treatment. The hospital service, described in previous volumes in this series, cannot work in a vacuum, and well organized and co-ordinated social and welfare services are needed to support its patients not only on discharge, but sometimes whilst they are still in hospital. Hospitals, therefore, take a great interest in the social needs as well as medical needs of their patients.

These are some of the services on which many are lecturing to medical, nursing and other students, and especially to hospital administrative and clerical staffs studying for the professional examinations of the Institute of Hospital Administrators. When the students take up their studies it has been my experience that, although they may know the names of some of these services, very few have a wide and detailed knowledge of this wealth of national, local and voluntary effort available for those in need, and of our great heritage in this respect.

As these articles were sent to me to read, my eyes were often opened to new fields of activity, and I have learned a great deal about the vast range of some of these services. It may be that readers will also find in this book something new to them—perhaps a service which might meet the need of someone known to them.

And yet this is only a part of this wide field of activity and service, a selection of some of the services which make up the social welfare system. Some other aspects of our social services are dealt with in other volumes in this series which I hope will be read as a whole.

I would like to record my thanks and appreciation to all those who have provided original articles or agreed to the reproduction of work they had already published. I would also thank many who have helped me in the preparation of this symposium. Amongst those who have assisted me have been Mr. Walter Boyce, Chief Welfare Officer of the Essex County Council, and Miss Irene Roberton of the Welfare Department of the London County Council, to both of whom I was first introduced when visiting the United Nations Study Group on the Care of the Elderly, at Nottingham University in 1962. It was due especially to their help, encouragement and assistance that invitations were issued to many of the contributors. Miss Roberton has put in a great deal of work in the preparation of this volume, and given me the benefit of advice based on her wide experience and practical approach both as a social worker and as an administrator in the Welfare Department of the largest local authority in the country (the London County Council). I also wish to acknowledge the advice and assistance given by Mr. F. L. Lloyd Jacob, Principal Officer of the Welfare Department of the London County Council.*

> The reader may wish to be reminded that under the London Government Act, 1963, the new Greater London Council from 1 April 1965 takes over many of the London County Council's powers and duties, but its health, welfare and children's services are transferred to the new London Boroughs created by the Act. There are 12 such Boroughs (and the City of London) covering the L.C.C. area. These take the place of the previous 28 Metropolitan Borough Councils and there are a further 20 new London Boroughs replacing the local authorities previously covering the suburban districts now brought within Greater London. The Greater London Council's area includes that previously controlled by the London County Council and the Middlesex County Council, and parts of Kent, Essex, Hertfordshire and Surrey and the County Boroughs of East and West Ham and Croydon. The Greater London Council will therefore be responsible for the major services over a wide area, such as certain housing and town planning, highway services, and powers under the Town Development Act, licensing and other public control functions, the larger parks and open spaces, whilst the new and enlarged London Boroughs will amongst other local services be responsible for public health and personal health services, children's services and welfare services. A new and separate authority, the Inner London Education Authority, will, at least until 1970, continue to discharge the L.C.C.'s education functions.

The co-operation of many people has made the publication of this volume possible, and I hope they will all be rewarded in its usefulness to those who are actively engaged in serving, studying and developing the social services

* These officers and other contributors from public authorities have assisted me in their personal and not official capacities. As such we in no way commit our employing authorities to any statement or expressions of opinions which are, of course, entirely our own.

and to the people whom they help, both in this country and other countries. It is a privilege to take a part in making more widely known some of these services and in describing some of the very fine work being carried out to help those who are in need. Some of the contributors are modest; they are certainly not smug or they would not criticize themselves so severely for the gaps and shortcomings in many of the services; but I am sure the reader will discern through these pages the hard work, industry, thought and often sacrificial service behind the efforts of national and local authorities and voluntary organizations working for the benefit of those in need and for the public good.

May this book also be a tribute to their service and devotion to their allotted task of alleviating the sufferings of others, so far as it is possible for them to do so with their present resources.

London 1965 JAMES FARNDALE

SECTION I
GENERAL ASPECTS OF THE SOCIAL SERVICES

1. The Growth of the Welfare Services

Peter Archer

Editor, *Social Welfare and the Citizen* (Penguin)

THE STORY of social welfare is the history of a double process. In the beginning society knew no conscience beyond the individual consciences of its members. Such of them as were inclined to charity could spare some of their resources to alleviate misfortune, and it would be the misfortune of those whom they might select. First, then, is the process by which the group imposes its collective conscience alike upon the just and the unjust. The other process consists in widening the circle of recipients, from those whose plight obtrudes upon the giver, and touches his generosity, to all who experience a need.

The processes overlap at the point of prudence, for many of us are at one time able to set something aside, at another in need of help, and a private granary or a secret stocking is less reliable than a future preserved in common with others. A community is more secure than any of its members. These processes are the development of civilization, which is another name for interdependence and communication. But always there are those who cry that interdependence will kill self-reliance, that it will be abused, and that, deprived of whips and carrots, the donkey will work no more.

"Labourers of old", complains the *Mirour de l'Omme*, probably written in about 1375, "were not wont to eat of wheaten bread; their meat was of beans or coarser corn, and their drink of water alone. Cheese and milk were a feast to them, and rarely ate they of other dainties; their dress was of hodden grey; then was the world ordered aright for folk of this sort...." This diagnosis of the world's evils in the prosperity, and consequent expectations, of the lower orders, has worn well for 600 years.

The uneventful existence of the Middle Ages had been shattered by the Black Death, and the consequent discovery of the labouring population that their reduced numbers had given them a scarcity value. In 1349 the Statute of Labourers insisted that all who were able-bodied and without other means of support should work for an employer in their own parish at rates prevailing before the Plague, thus imposing probably the earliest wage-freeze. The Statute also declared it an offence to give alms to the able-bodied, who would therefore be compelled "to labour for their necessary living". This is possibly the first recognition in statute law of a distinction which has ever since dominated social administration, the distinction between

3

the deserving and the undeserving poor. Relief of need on rational principles would be impossible without it, though its purpose disappears when poverty is regarded as conclusive evidence of being undeserving. At its inception, the distinction coincided with physical capacity. To be able-bodied and poor admitted of no excuse.

For 200 years the purpose of the legislator and the administrator was the twofold one which has frequently functioned as a substitute for compassion: to keep the unfortunate away from the public view, and to safeguard law and order against demonstrations. Those wandering unemployed outside their own parishes were whipped, branded, sent to the royal galleys or, as a merciful alternative under Henry VIII, set in the stocks for three days.

In 1553 Nicholas Ridley, Bishop of London, preached a sermon before Edward VI on charity to the poor. It resulted in the appointment of a committee to consider what provision should be made in London. The report provides an excellent analysis, and a model which many later commissions would have done well to emulate. It divided the poor into three categories: children in need of care, the sick and impotent, and the sturdy and idle. They pointed out that provision already existed for deprived children in Christ's Hospital, formerly the Church of the Grey Friars. The impotent poor were cared for in St. Bartholomew's Hospital. For the third group, they proposed to erect a "house of occupation", where they could be employed in useful labour. And they persuaded Edward to give them his dilapidated palace at Bridewell. So was established the first workhouse, on what is now the Embankment, behind St. Bride's.

There were complaints that children from the "dunghill", when nourished in the hygienic conditions of Christ's Hospital, sickened and died, and that disabled vagrants, brought to St. Bartholomew's, seized the first opportunity to run away to their vagrancy. The extent of this, or even the truth, we shall never know. But other cities were sufficiently impressed to emulate London.

An Act of 1597 gave legal force to practices which were already being followed. Overseers of the Poor were to be appointed in each parish, consisting of the churchwardens and four householders. Under the supervision of the justices, they were to levy upon the inhabitants or landholders a sufficient sum to provide relief for the impotent poor, and to purchase materials upon which the able-bodied poor could be set to work. In 1601 these, and other scattered regulations, were codified in the Poor Law Act.

The Elizabethan Poor Law embodied two basic principles; there should be no relief for the able-bodied without setting them to work; and each parish was responsible for its own poor. The former principle was admirable in conception, financially and psychologically, but its sponsors had not read Keynes. Producing goods which no one could afford to buy merely resulted in the unemployment of those who were already producing them. And it was left to Daniel Defoe,* in the early eighteenth century, to point out that, demand remaining equal, an extra piece of cloth produced in Bishopsgate entailed one piece the less required from Colchester. He also insisted that begging was an occupation which would attract labourers away from industry if it were lucrative, and hence argued that giving alms to beggars was a disservice to the nation. Unfortunately, Defoe's solution was to leave them to find work for themselves or to die like men in the army.

The second principle of the Elizabethan Poor Law, its administration through the parish, proved disastrous in the next two centuries. The resources available, and the enthusiasm with which they were employed, varied widely from area to area. The relief which a pauper might expect depended upon the chance of his birthplace. Not that this was an accidental effect of the system. Giving powers to local authorities entails the freedom to use them well or badly. The rights of a free people include the right to make disastrous choices, or not to choose at all.

For most parishes, a principle aim of policy was to ensure that never should they relieve a pauper who was properly chargeable to another parish. Disputes between parishes were argued at Quarter Sessions and, as a final resort, in the Privy Council. Rules became increasingly technical, and the legal profession benefited more than the poor. A determination to save every penny of public funds may be more expensive than a more generous spirit.

In 1661 there was passed the Law of Settlement and Removal, empowering parish overseers, upon a justice's warrant, to remove forcibly any new-comer to the parish unless he could satisfy them that he and his family were never likely to become a charge on the rates. It was not necessary that he should actually have applied for relief, or even contemplated doing so. England became a land inhospitable to strangers, and a poor man was imprisoned within the parish of his birth.

In 1696 the City of Bristol secured a private Act combining nineteen parishes, under an authority known as the Corporation of the Poor. The Corporation quickly discovered that, by erecting a common workhouse and insisting that able-bodied applicants for relief should reside there, the cost of relief could be considerably reduced. Not that the workhouse was in itself a profitable venture. Indeed, the cost per head of workhouse relief was greater than that of out-relief. But the prospect of entry into the workhouse was such that most applicants would face near starvation before applying. Thus the lazy were suitably deterred, and if the deserving suffered in the process, this was a price felt to be worth paying by those who had not themselves to pay it.

The revulsion from the workhouse is hardly surprising, though Bristol's administration was better than most. It was felt that a separate institution for each class of pauper was uneconomical. The old, the children, the diseased,

* "Giving alms no charity."

the insane, and the newly born babies, were crowded together. Normally, the overseers discharged their duty by contracting with a private individual, who kept the poor in the workhouse and fed them, at a fixed price per head. Poor relief was therefore a profit-making occupation, and the sole aim was economy. Year by year workhouses became dirtier and more rat-infested until the workhouse gates became a symbol of hopelessness, where the spirit and the will to work of those who were compelled to enter were crushed for the remainder of their lives.

Bristol's example was quickly followed in other towns, and amelioration came only in the closing years of the eighteenth century, when the Government was faced by the prospect of a long war with France. Not for the last time, the national need for loyal and well-nourished cannon fodder gave the nation's people an existence more worth fighting for. It was not only Hegel who thought of the State as more real than its members.

In 1795 an Act was passed protecting law-abiding persons from eviction under the Law of Settlement and Removal unless they actually applied for relief. In the same year the Berkshire justices, meeting at Speen, resolved to deal with the rise in the cost of living, which had outdistanced wage rates, by instructing overseers to grant supplementary relief making up wages to subsistence level. The so-called "Speenhamland Act" was soon followed throughout England.

The social services have still not recovered from the effects of this resolution. Faced with a situation in which a family could find itself starving even while its bread-winner was in employment, the authorities might have chosen between a number of courses. They might, by a system of price control, aided by subsidies, have reduced the cost of living. They might have adopted a national wages policy, fixing a legal minimum. Instead, they imposed a burden on public funds. And it was a cardinal maxim of administration that public funds should not be squandered. Naturally the maxim applied only against the poor. The sanctity of public funds was not such as to protect them from a burden which might properly have been borne by employers or merchants.

Its consequences were threefold. First, the justices, with a high degree of care and responsibility, worked out a scale of needs varying with the price of bread and the size of the family. It was a commendable piece of work, but it established in social administration the concept of a subsistence minimum, the lowest income which would enable a hypothetical careful housewife, with a good knowledge of dietetics and time to shop carefully, to keep a family on a monotonous diet in a badly furnished house. Secondly, it enabled employers to pay wages below the minimum necessary to live, and thus presented them with their labour on a subsidized basis. Just as in the present century the "safety net" of National Assistance provides an argument for holding down rates of insurance benefits, so the industrialists of the early nineteenth century were able to point out that no one was actually starving, or at least not obviously so. Finally, the workman who applied himself industriously to keeping his family was no better off than the shirker and the wastrel. There is no greater destroyer of incentives than the means test.

The system continued until the Whig reforms of 1832. Meanwhile, the rulers of the country justified their indifference by citing Malthus, who had demonstrated to their satisfaction that unless the growth of population was restricted by starvation, the poor would increase in numbers until they outdistanced the means of subsistence. Poor relief (like aiding underdeveloped countries) therefore defeated its own object.

In 1832 a Royal Commission on the Poor Laws was appointed. Its Report was largely the work of two of its members, Nassau Senior, an Oxford professor, and Edwin Chadwick, formerly secretary to Jeremy Bentham. It was embodied in the Poor Law Amendment Act, 1834, which repealed the Elizabethan Poor Law. It brought Poor Law administration under a central authority, consisting of three Poor Law Commissioners. They were to group the parishes into unions, each under an elected Board of Guardians. Thus the disadvantages of local administration were at least alleviated, since the unit was a more substantial one. And they were subjected to supervision on behalf of the Central Government.

Chadwick, who had hoped to be a commissioner, was made Secretary to the Commission, and spent the next seven years quarrelling with his superiors and intriguing against them for the ear of the Cabinet. But the subject of their quarrels was not a matter of principle, only a question of how rigorously they should apply the principles on which they all agreed. The Report had recommended that the Speenhamland system be discontinued and, wherever possible, relief was to be administered in a "well-regulated workhouse". This meant that it was to be on the principle of "less eligibility". The pauper's situation was not to be "made really or apparently so eligible as the situation of the independent labourer of the lowest class". Where indoor relief was impossible, at least half of the relief was to be in food. This steered the money away from the gin palace, but did so at the cost of restricting choice and discouraging responsibility.

Chadwick's complaints were twofold. The principle was not applied quickly or consistently enough. (In fact outdoor relief continued to be granted on a large scale.) And the entire family was accommodated in a single workhouse, whereas he wished to implement the Report's recommendation that special workhouses be maintained according to the sex and classification of the inmates. In effect, he was prepared to see the family broken up in order to ensure that children should be protected from the vice and disease of the well-regulated all-purpose institution.

The old system of contracting out maintenance was abandoned, and there grew up in the unions a body of salaried officials. Even before the Act some parishes had provided medical treatment for the poor. The Act of 1834 gave statutory recognition to the practice, and the Commissioners encouraged the appointment of salaried medical officers in each union. Admittedly in many unions the post was given to the doctor who submitted the lowest tender for the job.

In the next fifty years it was gradually borne upon the authorities that a well-constructed ladder is a better investment than a capacious safety net. If living conditions and medical services were improved, there would be fewer sick paupers in need of relief. If provision was made for education, there might be less complaint about the ignorant, dissolute, and feckless habits of the poor. If facilities existed for casework, difficulties might be set right in the early stages, and frauds on the services were less likely to remain undetected.

Some of these services grew out of private charity. In others, nothing could be effected without legislation. Hospitals provided by religious orders had nursed the sick since the twelfth century, and in places even earlier. But while their charges lived in the filth and darkness of their courts they worked against an impossible handicap. London had aqueducts and sewers in the twelfth century, though they were regarded rather as labour-saving devices. Regulations of fourteenth-century London provided: "No man shall cast any urine-boles into the street by day or night afore the hour of nine of the night."* But it was only in the eighteenth century, with unfolding medical knowledge, that hygiene became associated in the public mind with health. Even then the effect was that the rich withdrew to the West End, where they proceeded to pave and drain the streets, leaving the East End to its squalor.

An epidemic of typhus in 1837 led to a request from the Government (urged by Chadwick) for a report by three eminent doctors. This was an early application of the principle that social policy should be preceded by diagnosis. Most influential was the report of Dr. Southwood Smith, who showed that houses in the East End were practically impossible to keep clean, and epidemics were virtually incessant. Their reports were presented to the Home Secretary by the Commissioners, with a letter (doubtless drafted by Chadwick) pointing out the financial burden imposed upon the poor rates by the sickness and death of bread-winners. There followed a public campaign, a Select Committee of the House of Commons, a Royal Commission, a series of delays and, finally, with the news that a cholera epidemic was sweeping Europe, the passing in 1848 of the Public Health Act and the Removal and Diseases Prevention Act. There was set up the Board of Health, and there followed a slow series of measures, opposed by vested and vociferous interests, to clean up water supplies, instal sewerage and drainage, provide refuse removal, supervise the supply of food, and control the practice of medicine.

* Quoted by Barnes, *The Slum: Its Story and Solution*, P. S. King & Son, Ltd., 1931.

Meanwhile it came to be recognized that private building could not provide housing for the lower income groups at rents within their means. In 1851 Lord Shaftesbury secured the passing of an Act to Encourage the Establishment of Lodging Houses (i.e. dwelling houses) for the Working Classes (though only one local authority, Huddersfield, could be prevailed upon to implement it). At the same time Octavia Hill was demonstrating that the question who were the deserving poor was usually asked too early, since tenants were often found to deserve good housing only when they were given a chance to live decently. From managing "Paradise Place", a few cottages bought by Ruskin, she began a movement to provide clean, well-ventilated, and even attractive houses, and to combine this with casework.

It was in the nineteenth century, too, that something was done to combat the ignorance which had descended on the poor since the Church and the colleges of Oxford and Cambridge had closed their doors to them at the end of the Middle Ages, and the grammar schools had selected their pupils by ability to pay. By the eighteenth century they were regarded as safe only while their eyes were closed.

"Consider only", invited Dr. Stebbing in a sermon preached in 1732, "what we are to expect if once the religion of Fine Gentlemen shall come to be the religion of the Poor. Do you think that this freedom of thought would not everywhere produce a corresponding freedom of action? Would your homes be safe from being plundered, and your daughters secure from violence? Would poor men do the duties of poor men, and bear the burdens which God has laid upon them with patience?"* He was referring to a proposal to teach poor children to read the bible.

But in 1780 Robert Raikes opened his first Sunday School. In 1816 Henry Brougham introduced into the Commons a Bill to provide for public education. It was defeated because the Church of England and the Dissenters could not agree on the religious tests to be imposed upon teachers. (Even the Act of 1870 was finally achieved, as Tenniel declared, by "reducing the fractions to their lowest common denomination".) But in 1833 the Government set aside money for providing schools on condition that at least half the cost was met locally, and that the application was recommended by the British and Foreign Bible Society or the National Society. In 1853 a People's College was set up for adults in Sheffield, to be followed by the founding of Working Men's Colleges in various parts of the country by the Christian Socialists. And it became clear that, far from wallowing in their ignorance, many of the poor were crying out for learning for themselves and their children.

The disabled were rescued from a lifetime of begging by such institutions as the Liverpool School for the Blind, founded in 1791; the Society for the Indigent Deaf, formed in 1792; and a variety of homes where the feeble-minded were trained, and where cripples were taught to overcome their disabilities.

* Quoted by Slater, *Poverty and the State*, Constable & Co., Ltd., 1930.

In 1819 Thomas Chalmers had organized poor relief in Glasgow on a basis of rehabilitation by casework. In 1859 Louisa Twining formed the Workhouse Visiting Society for casework in the workhouses. In the same year the Jewish Community in London founded the Metropolitan Board of Guardians to minister to the needs of Jewish immigrants and those fallen on misfortune. And in 1869 the Charity Organization Society was formed to co-ordinate the relief which was already threatening duplication and diffusion of effort. With the Artisans' Dwellings Act, 1875, and the Education Act, 1870, the principle was established that certain types of provision were "social services" for which the community, through the Government, recognized responsibility.

By the beginning of the twentieth century it was clear that not even the statistical man of the social scientists, or the electoral man of the politicians, lives by bread alone. Human needs are various, but many of them may be grouped into administrative patterns. The welfare services had extended far beyond the mere relief of poverty. The feeling was growing that there was no limit set by nature to the activities which might be carried on by public authorities. Which human needs might best be met by public provision, and what proportion of the national income should be devoted to each, are questions to be decided by political debate. "It will be seen, then," remarks a recent pamphlet, "how absurd is the suggestion 'to take the social services out of politics'. The social services ARE politics."* When, in 1908, Asquith presented his budget with an item for financing the new scheme of non-contributory old age pensions (payable, subject to an income limit, to those found to be deserving) he remarked that this was "only one of a group of questions the settlement of which, although it cannot be simultaneous, should as far as possible be harmonious and self consistent".

It was at this stage that public charity fused with a different strain, that of thrifty self-help. It was a strain which had begun with the mediaeval guilds, some of which preceded the Norman Conquest, had continued through the trade unions, the trade clubs and the friendly societies of the eighteenth century, and in the nineteenth swelled into a multitude of dividing societies, deposit societies, collecting societies, death-and-divis, and insurance companies. From an average of 97 per society, when Eden published his *State of the Poor* in 1797, some of them had grown to the size of the Hearts of Oak, which in 1872 contained nearly 33,000 members.†

Lloyd George examined the social insurance scheme which Bismarck had established in Germany in 1880, and in 1911, after a violent political storm, he secured the passing of the National Insurance Act. The Act introduced public provision, independently of a means test, for those whose earnings were interrupted by sickness or unemployment. Sickness benefit was available

---

* *Reflections on the Social Services*, Socialist Union, 1958.
† See Raynes, *Social Security in Britain*, Pitman, 2nd edition, 1960.

to all manual workers, and to non-manual workers earning not more than £160 per year. Unemployment benefit applied only to specified trades. Benefits might have been financed from general taxation, or from a special social security tax. By either method the burden would have been borne according to ability to pay. The British people preferred to pay for their own benefits, by means of a funded insurance scheme. There was a feeling, too, that a fund was safe from future public economy cuts as payments from the Exchequer would not be.

Social security in Britain paid a high price. First, it was half a century before it was thought possible to demand contributions higher than could be afforded by the lowest-paid worker, and it was confined to benefits correspondingly low. A modest experiment with graduated contributions and benefits was introduced with some hesitation in 1959. Secondly, benefits were dependent on the payment of certain contributions, and those who were sick or unemployed for long periods, and were often in greatest need of benefits, failed to qualify. Thirdly, there was no scope for varying the conditions of benefit according to the cost of living, changing trends in the employment of older workers, or the size and needs of families. And the administrative cost of fixing stamps to cards, counting them, and tearing them up, has lain heavily on social security ever since.*

But it was an enormous step forward. Here was a scheme offering financial benefits, where the beneficiaries were not defined by reference to a means test. For they were invoking a contract. True, there was an element of redistribution, but it was not so obviously the rich helping the poor as the healthy helping the sick, the employed helping the unemployed, the fortunate at any given time helping the unlucky.

That the State should concern itself in the affairs of those who were not paupers was a bitter draught for many. A correspondent wrote to *The Times*† pointing out that all manual workers were within the scheme, including the affluent shipyard worker. "Such a man is in no sense of the word fit to be considered an object of charity or a suitable case for Government help." The leader writer agreed, but added regretfully: ". . . no line has ever been drawn, there is no machinery for drawing it, and any attempt to draw it would raise such a howl from a pampered class that no politician would dare to face it."

The Poor Law (euphemized in a less-insensitive age, after 1906, to "Public Assistance") was no longer the hub of the welfare services, but a subsidiary service to mitigate their oversights and mistakes. The argument is not closed. The contributors to *Crossbow* (April–June 1963) have urged that any element of redistribution should be directed where it is most needed, and that this entails restoring National Assistance to a primary position. Indeed,

* And see Abel-Smith, *The Reform of Social Security*, Fabian Society, 1953.
† 10 June 1911.

there are still those who object to any redistribution by legislation. A correspondent wrote to *The Times* in 1958:*

> Diffusion of property may result from self help; from human kindness; from normal economic development; or from forcible transfer. The welfare state has been based on the last of these and has stemmed the operation of the other three; of self help by providing security at the expense of others and thus diminishing incentive; of human kindness and economic development by taxation on a scale which has baulked normal expression.
> ... Philosophers so far apart as Aristotle and Herbert Spencer have expressly condemned the dispossession of the rich for the benefit of the poor. And these are far from being alone in warning of the tyranny of state organized force.

Yet during the last hundred years there has emerged the idea that social responsibility for the good life, like the good life itself, is indivisible. The Local Government Act, 1888, attempted to gather the scattered local services under a single system of authorities, as the creation of a Local Government Board in 1871 had been intended to do for central welfare provisions. Not that satisfactory co-ordination has been achieved, but to speak of the need for co-ordination is to recognize something in common between the relief of poverty, health visiting and town planning. The Beveridge Report declared it an aim of social welfare to curtail, and ultimately to abolish, the "five giants"—poverty, disease, ignorance, squalor and idleness. And as the welfare services have expanded, particularly since 1946, the self-labelled middle class has partaken substantially, though sometimes half-ashamedly, of the benefits. The beneficiaries of the Welfare State are socially respectable and electorally overwhelming.

The services are breaking away from the concept of an arithmetically calculated minimum, although rates of benefit are not. Those which are used only by limited and less vocal groups (like old people's homes) are most at the mercy of meanness and prejudice. But the National Health Service of 1946, like the sewerage system of the previous century, was not intended as a minimum provision, for those who could afford nothing better. A municipal orchestra is not a second-rate substitute for those who cannot pay for a better one.

And if National Assistance or medical services are sometimes abused, like such older-established public services as the police force, and such newer ones as municipal playing fields, the solution lies with improved techniques of administering and supervising them. There is room for argument as to how, or even whether, a particular welfare service can most conveniently be administered by public authorities. But he who would live independently of them all would set thimself apart from the human race. It is no accident that Defoe wrote *Robinson Crusoe*. When the poor cry it is comforting to be all right, but when the bell tolls for the welfare services, it tolls for Jack.

* 22 September 1958.

2. A Stocktaking of the Social Services

JOHN H. BURROWS
Staff Lecturer in Sociology
Department of Extra-Mural Studies, University of London

The Rationale of the Welfare State

During the dark days of World War II Beveridge produced in 1942 his now famous *Report on Social Insurance and Allied Services*. In this he reviewed the inadequacies of previous social legislation and drew up a blueprint which has since been transformed into an edifice which we call for want of a better term "the Welfare State". What Beveridge did in his Report was to demonstrate the destructive role which the giant evils of society play in an industrial society such as Britain if allowed to go unchecked. No society, least of all our own, can afford to ignore these evils—want, idleness, ignorance, squalor and disease. A healthy, well-educated society, and one from which the anxieties of insecurity and want are kept at bay, is the best guarantee of its own survival.

In Britain we have reached the conclusion over the years that the best way to advance our social welfare is through a body of statutory social services, aided and enriched by voluntary agencies. Other countries may prefer to rely on private enterprise or provision through churches, trade unions or other institutions—the actual machinery will be determined by historical forces and cultural factors. Nevertheless, no matter what the ultimate arrangements are, expenditure on the social provision will be regarded as sound national investment—in terms of our own experience the Welfare State is wealth-producing.

Social Costs of Industrialization

This point needs constantly to be borne in mind whenever criticisms are made about the range and quantity of expenditure on the social services. There are some observers who believe that the Welfare State should be self-liquidating and that people should be taught how to do without it. All these views are tinged with moral judgements—that too much welfare corrodes the fibre of society and undermines individual responsibility. What these commentators lack is a sense of historical perspective, because what they recommend is a return to the kind of society which existed in Victorian Britain. Perhaps the best antidote to these attitudes is a brief reference to a now forgotten government inquiry on Physical Deterioration published in 1904.

In a sense this Report is a crushing indictment of the kind of society which existed in the nineteenth century—acquisitive, self-satisfied, alternatively treating poverty as a crime or something to be alleviated by charity. It was largely indifferent to the social costs of uncontrolled industrialism— low expectations of life, appallingly high rates of infantile mortality (250 per 1000, for example, amongst illegitimate births in Sheffield) and the steady deterioration of the physique of the nation. The origins of the inquiry were the high rates of rejection of recruits to the army, for physical reasons. during the Boer War, amounting to 40–60 per cent in different places, Graphically and systematically it revealed the low standards of medical care, the inadequacies of much of working-class housing and the pervasiveness of poverty in what was thought by many politicians to be the richest society in existence.

The Contribution of Social Research

Although this was the first time a government report had laid bare the grosser facts of social pathology, there had been previous inquiries which had come almost to the same melancholy conclusions. Charles Booth, a wealthy Liverpool shipowner, set out in 1883 to disprove the allegations of a marxist critic, Henry Hyndman, that there was a great mass of unrevealed poverty in London, the heart of a rapidly growing British Empire as it was then called. With the aid of Beatrice Webb and other skilled social investigators, Booth eventually published by 1903 seventeen volumes on *Life and Labour of the People of London*. One of the memorable parts of the study was a map showing the distribution of poverty in the capital—this geography of hunger revealed that 30 per cent of Londoners were living in poverty. Added corroboration came from another survey by B. Seebohm Rowntree, this time of York, and published in 1901 as *Poverty: A Study of Town Life* and reaching virtually the same statistical conclusions.

These inquiries were the first of a line which have produced verifiable facts about social conditions. Without these researches it is doubtful whether public opinion would have been prepared for new steps in social policy. After all, thirty-seven bills had been presented in Parliament between 1896 and 1905 to introduce a modest pension for old people, but the characteristic response had been much along the lines of the Liberty and Property Defence League, "The streets of our towns and villages would be swarming with vigorous old men whom the state had taken away from honest toil to become loafers at the expense of the community."

The Roots of Social Policy

Facts by themselves have never been enough to arouse the social conscience, they have to be fired by the emotion and protest of social reformers. Fortunately, there has never been lacking in our history men and especially women impelled by a single-minded devotion to one or other cause— Elizabeth Fry and prison reform, Florence Nightingale and nursing, Josephine Butler and her struggle for equal moral standards between the sexes. Nearer our own time was Eleanor Rathbone who, since the first publication of her book, *The Disinherited Family* in 1922, had battled for some measure of state financial support for the family.

Another element in the emergence of the Welfare State has been the influence of politics. With the widening range of democracy, first in 1867 then in 1884, it was inevitable that the great mass of the population would have to be wooed for their votes—their chance came early in the twentieth century with the emergence of an independent working-class political movement— the Labour Party as it became in 1906, and the Liberal Party victory in the General Election in the same year. School meals, school medical inspection, old-age pensions and a modest system of insurance against unemployment and sickness were all established within the next six years. No longer would the State be regarded as a kind of night watchman but instead it would play an increasingly active role in promoting the well-being of society.

The Social Services Between the Wars

In many ways the inter-war years 1919–39 remain a blot on our social history, though there are some exceptions. The promise "Homes for Heroes" heard during the "Khaki Election" of 1918 had somehow or other to be redeemed, and eventually led to an innovation in social policy—the housing subsidy. A new term entered the English language as a consequence, and council houses came into existence. The Education Act of 1918, though it ended the so-called "half-time system" which permitted bright boys and girls to combine schooling with employment at the age of eleven and introduced the compulsory school-leaving age of fourteen, was otherwise a disappointment. Its original proposal for day-continuation classes unhappily remained a dead letter. What else has to be recorded of the twenties and thirties is largely a doleful story of mass unemployment and the ineffectiveness of the measures to tackle the problem. For the unemployed man it meant a wearisome encounter with a complexity of administrative procedures—there were all kinds of benefits, transitional, unemployment insurance, the Poor Law, Public Assistance and Unemployment Assistance. To his vocabulary were added new phrases such as "the means test", "the dole", "food tickets", the "bureau"—in practice all of them unpleasant, but the lot of millions of able-bodied men and women until 1939.

New Perspectives Since World War II

No wonder then that new ideas soon germinated during World War II. This was a period of total war and common suffering; hurriedly new schemes of medical relief and assistance had to be devised for the whole nation. Moreover, men and women on national service, mindful as many of them were of the inter-war years, were unlikely to accept a post-war world moulded in the same image. The Beveridge Report was hailed as the promise of a new order and before the war had ended, drafts were being made for legislation to implement its findings. The Education Act of 1944 can now be seen as making a distinct break with the attitudes and traditions of the past and the forerunner of a new social policy.

In the past the social services had largely been concerned with working-class aspirations and needs—the various insurance schemes, for example, were mainly for those in manual employment. Local authority hospitals were largely for the same social group, whilst middle-class patients were expected to pay something for their medical care either in voluntary hospitals or with their private doctors. One of the great achievements of the post-war Welfare State has been to make its benefits available for all members of society, irrespective of class or employment. Comprehensiveness and universality are the features of the social services today. When it comes to estimating who have been the greatest beneficiaries of the Welfare State, there may be something in the view it is the middle classes, now freed from the anxieties of doctors' bills and school fees, so frequently a burden before the war.

Public Reaction to the Social Services

But whether one section or other of the community has benefited more from the Welfare State is, in many ways, an irrelevant issue. Nevertheless, some consideration has to be made of the impact of the social services on the community. When it is remembered that the amount now spent on them works out at over £50 a head, it is perhaps strange how little is known about public reaction to this expenditure. Consumer research is a well-established practice in private enterprise; indeed, no self-respecting manufacturer would launch a new line without some preliminary assessment of its likely popularity. Yet how much is spent on this type of inquiry in the social services? The answer is, unfortunately, very little; perhaps it reflects the attitude that the men in Whitehall know best, and that there is no need to find out what patients, clients, parents and other users of the social services think about their range and quality.

The nearest approach to this kind of appraisal was made by Political and Economic Planning amongst a sample of married women with children in Leicester and reported in *Family Needs and the Social Services* (1961). It might be thought that their views would not necessarily reflect the population at large, possibly so, but they and their families are the most important "consumers" of the social services. Of the sample 99 per cent used the National Health Service, 84 per cent the various benefits of the National Insurance Scheme, 74 per cent the educational system, 61 per cent family allowances, 25 per cent council housing and 12 per cent National Assistance. When asked which service had helped them the most during the previous year, the National Health Service received 82 per cent of the replies, education 8 per cent, family allowances 5 per cent, and the rest an insignificant number of answers.

Research such as this should be directed on a more intensive basis to all the services and to all groups of consumers. Without social research of this kind mistakes may well be made in the expansion of the social services which is now being planned. The National Health Service is a good case in point—hospital plans have been announced for the expenditure of over £700 million over the next ten years—new hospitals are to be built by the score, old concepts such as the small cottage hospital will disappear. Yet how much is known of patients' views on a whole range of highly relevant topics—for example is there a preference for the large ward or the smaller unit of 2-4 beds?

Financial Pressures

With the steady increase in the cost of the social services, after allowing for the increased demand from a growing population and inflationary pressures, there have been various demands for limiting expenditure. The National Health Service comes in for much criticism on this account, with allegations of waste and abuse. That expenditure soared in the early years of the service is all too true, but this was as much a reflection of pent-up demand for medical care, from wigs, artificial limbs to false teeth and spectacles as it was a consequence of bad mistakes in assessing likely pressures. By 1951 the first charge for prescriptions was introduced, and since then the principle has been extended elsewhere to welfare foods as well as the rates for some kinds of National Health Service treatment being increased. A ceiling has to be imposed on all aspects of government expenditure, but in the case of the National Health Service decisions are being made all the more difficult by the ever-increasing pressures on the service and by the continuing advances in medicine. The maternity services are a case in point. The Hospital Plan for England and Wales, published in 1962, contained forecasts made two years previously for the number of births likely to occur in 1971; the first estimate was 818,000, the revised one in 1963 was 891,000.

Introducing Competition in the Social Services

What is more open to debate is the idea that there should be an element of competition in the social services—the suggestion being that market forces should be allowed to operate. Certainly in the field of medical care there has been a marked growth of private arrangements with $1\frac{1}{2}$ million individuals privately insured for health services. People clearly prefer these arrangements for a variety of legitimate reasons, extra comfort and the choice of doctor, for example. Proponents of the extension of this system further argue that competition ultimately improves the quality of the provision in the public sector by offering a yardstick of efficiency. Whether, in fact, improvements in the public sector automatically result from the demonstration of superior standards in the private area may well be an unverified hypothesis. Enough is known about the quality of public school education for it to be regarded as a better product in many people's eyes, if only because of its smaller classes, but over-large classes still abound in state schools and will continue to remain there in the foreseeable future.

The problems of introducing a "market" in the social services have received some consideration by the Institute of Economic Affairs. A sample of just over 1000 male married heads of households between the ages of twenty-one and sixty-five were asked various questions and the results published in *Choice in Welfare* (1963). Between a half and three-fifths of those surveyed believed that individuals should be allowed to contract out of the public social services. There was, moreover, some support of up to 40 per cent for the idea that those who so opted out and made their own private provision for the education of their children and medical care should be compensated by reduced National Insurance contributions and lower taxes. Whether this would ever be politically feasible or, indeed, desirable, is open to debate; moreover, the survey has been criticized for the kind of question it asked and the scope of the sample. Nevertheless, it raises several important issues.

Choice or Universality

The first question of some magnitude is whether the principle of universality should be abandoned. If people can pay for their private arrangements does this mean that the social services should be restricted to the needy and be backed by tests of means and needs? The idea that there should be some measure of choice is clearly a matter of vital concern in a democratic society. Ideally, the choice should not rest on the size of the individual's purse, but should be a first principle of our social policy.

Whilst these are matters for legitimate debate, there can be little doubt that more needs to be done to improve the relations between those who provide the various social services and the recipients, in their guise as client, patient, parent or ordinary citizen behind the counter. An interesting development over recent years has been the development of pressure groups to improve the quality of various services—societies for the advancement of state education—an association for the improvement of the maternity services and a patients' association. Are they to be regarded as private busybodies or are they a reflection on the existing machinery for representation of the public's views?

To answer this question would lead to a lengthy inquiry into the committee system in our central and locally provided services. In the hospital service, to take one case in point, some 10,000 members of the public give their time and energies, unpaid and largely unacknowledged by the world at large, to manning its various boards and committees. Advisory and appeals committees exist in similar profusion in National Assistance and National Insurance and so on throughout the educational service, child care, welfare and the rest. One can only marvel at the devotion of this largely anonymous empire, though this should not inhibit further discussion of the system of administration to which it gives rise.

The Necessity of Voluntary Action

As the present volume clearly demonstrates, the voluntary social services have had and will doubtless continue to play an important role in the social provision. Many of them have a long ancestry, and those which have remained the longest in the field have never hesitated to adjust their structure and functions to the changing pattern of the times. By doing so they have continued to pioneer new developments and to bring resilience and flexibility to our social policy. The danger to which the voluntary society is perhaps especially prone is that of duplication and overlapping. Fortunately, where there is goodwill between the statutory service and the voluntary body, problems of co-ordination are resolved in a friendly manner.

Demographic Trends and their Likely Consequences

Looking to the future of the Welfare State, what are the kinds of problems and issues likely to become pressing as the years go by? Apart from the costs of the services which inevitably will show a steady increase, the other most important influence will result from changes in the population. One of the great bogeys just before and after World War II was that of the declining population. Demography, the study of population trends, is still far from being an exact science, but just how far estimates can vary is seen from comparing figures in the Beveridge Report with most recent ones both of the actual and expected rise of Great Britain's population.

	Estimated population of Gt. Britain Beveridge Report, Table XI	Actual	Forecast of the Registrars-General and Government Actuary's Department
1951	47,501,000	50,225,000	—
1961	47,192,000	52,925,000	—
1971	45,980,000	—	57,487,000
2001	—	—	72,369,000

The population of Great Britain will inevitably increase as a result of recent trends and instead of us becoming an ageing community, the average age will remain low; there are likely to be as many pressures, as we have seen in the maternity services, as in the welfare of the elderly. Two other forces are also at work—women are marrying earlier, and, because of the surplus of single men of marriageable age over single women, a greater proportion of them are marrying. Gradually the pool of single women is drying up, and problems of recruitment in nursing, social work and teaching—conventional careers in the past for these women—are becoming more intractable. Added to this is the increased demand for all these kinds of workers. The government plans for the expansion of the community services, published in 1963, envisages the addition of several thousand more social workers, whilst the fulfilment of the proposals of the Younghusband Report on social workers in local health and welfare authorities that the untrained worker should eventually disappear, will add to the problems.

New ideas will have to be adopted if this expansion in numbers of trained social workers is to become a reality over the next decade. Further opportunities will have to be made for the large-scale recruitment of married women, and it may even be necessary to have an emergency training scheme similar to the one which was so successful in bringing many new recruits to teaching after the war.

Priorities in Social Policy

Finally, one of the most urgent needs is for a closer definition of future priorities in social policy. Inevitably the amount of national resources in terms of manpower and money which can be allocated to the social services has to be limited, and it is clearly desirable to ensure the best return from this expenditure. Only further research and inquiry into the aims and methods of social policy can ensure how this objective can most purposely be attained, but so far little has been undertaken.

If an estimate has to be made of the broad lines of future development, then clearly there should be a drive to expand those services which actively promote *positive* welfare. To explain this further—so much of social expenditure deals with problems after they have occurred: the neglected family, the disabled worker or the patient with an illness which might have been avoided. Anything which prevents the outbreak of the various forms of social pathology is to be preferred to curative, remedial measures. Services to improve the environment—good housing; measures to support family life, higher family allowances, maybe; greater emphasis on preventive medicine—these should rate high in the social priorities during the next decade or so.

3. Fiction of the Welfare State

JOHN PRINCE

Health Services Correspondent, *Daily Telegraph*

WHAT happened in the severe winter of 1962–3 must surely have shattered the last illusion of the most sanguine that Britain was a Welfare State. It has never been that for most of the 8 million citizens of pensionable age, more than 2 million of them aged 75 or over. A million or more lived, and sometimes died, alone.

In the freezing months of 1962–3 their lot was grim indeed. Hospital and family doctors reported to the *British Medical Journal* and the *Lancet* cases of old people dying from hyperthermia or abnormally low body-temperatures. Many could not afford coal. Others, unable to obtain delivery, were too frail to fetch any for themselves. They were found dead or collapsed in their unheated homes. Some the hospitals were able to revive and restore to health.

Professor Peter Townsend concluded his enlightening study of homes for the aged, published in November 1962, *The Last Refuge*, with these words:

> At a time when we stand perhaps on the threshold of a new era in social policy we are in danger of being stigmatized by future generations as grudging, indifferent and parsimonious to those among us who are unable, because of chronic illness, disability, poverty, loss of family or inadequacy of housing, to stand up to the rigours of a competitive society.
> We look back with horror at some of the cruelties perpetrated in the 1860's, just as our descendants, a hundred years hence, will look back with horror at some of the cruelties we perpetrate today. It may be worth reflecting, if indeed a little sadly, that possibly the ultimate test of the quality of a free, democratic and prosperous society is to be found in the standards of freedom, democracy and prosperity enjoyed by its weakest members.

If that test be applied, the Welfare State is still a goal, not an achievement.

Workhouses Still

Certainly Britain is no Welfare State for the old people who were the subject of Mr. Townsend's survey, many living out a dreary last spell of existence in the century-old workhouses whose doom was pronounced in 1948. It is no Welfare State for many other old people, managing on small pensions and lacking human relationships, help, heat, suitable meals, safe and convenient premises. It is no Welfare State for the unemployed and their families. Nor for the homeless, with families torn apart, mother, father and children being housed separately.

"Welfare," says my *Pocket Oxford Dictionary*, "person's or society's prosperous or satisfactory condition." So far, so good. It goes on: "*w. work*, efforts to make life worth living for workmen, etc." That "etc." has become all-important. By combining with his fellows, the working man has won his battle for a share of welfare in return for his contribution to the national wealth. But he still needs, if he can, to avoid unemployment or serious illness if he is not to know misery. But true welfare is lacking or poor in quality for many sections of society: mentally subnormal children and adults, many of the sick, whether of mind or body, the increasing number of older people, many young people wanting to marry and set up an independent home together, and young parents unable to provide a home for a growing family.

In our sophisticated and interdependent society, welfare is all or it is nothing. The grim winter of 1962–3 illustrated how fundamental is welfare's aim, how wide its field. Within days we were down to the level of a developing country. We needed warmth and were given power cuts. Those same power cuts impeded hospital work. In London and many other centres admission to hospital was restricted to emergency cases. The hospitals were filled largely with old people suffering from chest and heart conditions, many of them victims of the dilatory attack by the Government and many local authorities on the menace of air pollution.

At home the sick languished in chilly rooms and pleaded in vain for coal or boiler fuel. Children were sent home because their schools were cold or their outside lavatories were frozen up. Pipes froze and burst, and thousands were without water.

Priorities

To return to our definition: for millions life was indeed scarcely worth living. Needless to say, the shocking travelling conditions endured daily by millions worsened with the weather. We were barely a civilized community let alone a Welfare State.

About this time, in February 1963, Professor P. M. S. Blackett, of Imperial College, London, speaking in Geneva at the United Nations conference on putting science and technology to work in the developing areas of the world, said that the danger of relying on wonder drugs and neglecting the plumbing was very real. Not more than a fraction of mankind had a sewage system up to the technological level of civilized man 5000 years ago.

Here Professor Blackett went to the heart of the matter. This surely is where welfare starts. The sick, like the poor, will always be with us. But a more adequate investment in power stations and gasworks, better homes, especially of the smaller, convenient type suitable for aged individuals and couples, more rational plumbing, more home helps, nurses, health visitors and meals on wheels might well reduce the need for hospitals and drugs.

In Ibadan, Nigeria, I saw one of the finest hospitals it has been my privilege to visit, University College Hospital. But Ibadan, a city with nearly a million people, lacks modern drainage and water supplies, and disease is rife. The hospital performs magnificently, but can cope with only a fraction of the sick who daily besiege it at 5 o'clock each morning. Here, undoubtedly, adequate sewage and water-supply systems would in the long run reduce the burden on the hospital. Yet in Ibadan, Lagos and other towns in Africa, skyscrapers and night clubs multiply while drainage and water supplies remain rudimentary, and the infant mortality rate appalling.

But we need not go to Africa or South-East Asia to find people who have to live without running water, baths or main drainage. In *The Ageing Country-man*, published in February 1963, Dr. H. C. Miller, a Shropshire family doctor, told of old patients who had lived most of their lives in picturesque but draughty cottages lacking lighting, piped water and sanitation.

"The pathetic eagerness", he wrote, "with which many old country people are coming forward to apply for tenancies of newly-built council bungalows and flats reflects the dissatisfaction felt by so many with their present sub-standard housing conditions."

Similar conditions are rife, too, in our industrial towns, grim relics of the Industrial Revolution. It is no good looking to the new property millionaires or to the building societies for amelioration of these conditions. And we, as represented by the State, are so slow in clearing the slums, housing the homeless and providing bungalows and flats in which the aged could maintain independent lives.

Never so Good?

In the war we were offered "Blood, toil, sweat and tears", and it proved a winning recipe. But it gave way to "I'm all right, Jack" and "Never had it so good". Betting shops, bingo halls and skyscraper office blocks proliferated, but hundreds of thousands lacked decent homes, and not one new general hospital had been completed since before the war.

Goodwill and voluntary helpers abounded. The limiting factor was lack of resources.

When the National Health Service was introduced in July 1948, the hospital service inherited a run-down system in bad repair. Many of the 3000 hospitals were over a century old. Little maintenance work had been possible during the war years. Administrators and doctors at many hospitals were ashamed to show foreign colleagues around. Yet for years capital expenditure remained at less proportionately than was spent before the war, and hospitals were plagued by lack of money to carry out day-to-day maintenance work.

We had to wait until 1962 for the Government's rebuilding programme, and even this was considerably less than had been urged some years earlier by Mr. A. Lawrence Abel and Mr. Walpole Lewin in a report adopted by the British Medical Association. But, belated though it was, did the hospital programme come at long last a little too soon? Ought not the Ten Year Plan for local authority health and welfare services to have come first?

All the talk now is of home and community care, which is impossible without local supportive services. It is agreed that a person is, where it is possible, far better off at home, if not in a home. Prevention is better than cure. For most people a spell in hospital is a rare and isolated episode. Tarrying in bed unduly does no one any good, and the aim now is to make a stay in bed and hospital as short as possible. Home, the presence and help of loved ones, the familiar environment, are better than the finest hospital once the acute need has been met.

For lack of maternity beds mothers and their babies are chased out of hospital in a day or two. Increasingly, the mentally ill are to be cared for within the community. Mr. Powell (then Minister of Health) envisaged a substantial closing down of psychiatric hospitals within the next decade or so. Several hundred smaller general hospitals are to go. All this and maintenance of the independence of an increasing proportion of old people in their own homes cannot possibly be achieved reasonably without a massive extension and strengthening of the local authority services.

Inadequate Provision

Care of the aged is a combined operation by families, friends and neighbours, voluntary bodies, the Government and local authorities. It is more than doubtful whether the Government and many local authorities are doing enough. Against the need, the provision made would seem to be meagre in the extreme. There are wide variations in the provision made between different areas. Thus gross expenditure per 1000 population on home helps varies between £30 and £600. Where one area employs one home help per 10,000 population, another has thirteen. In one district help is given in fifteen cases per 10,000 population, in another in 120.

It thus pays to be an old person in an active, pioneering borough such as, for example, Rotherham, which has long led in such services as home helps, night visiting, home meals, laundry, nursing and chiropody.

A valuable co-ordinating and inspiring role is filled by the National Old People's Welfare Council, which celebrated its 21st birthday in 1961. It has a fine record of achievement behind it, and the tasks facing it grow steadily bigger year by year. It was one of the good things to come out of World

War II. Established by the National Council of Social Service in 1940, its first chairman was Miss Eleanor Rathbone, pioneer woman M.P. and a famous warrior for many good causes. Represented on it are more than fifty voluntary bodies and government departments—Health, Labour, Education, Pensions and National Insurance and Housing and Local Government, plus the National Assistance Board.

The number of nurses employed in the home nursing service has risen steadily since 1948, but, compared with the need, the total in 1961 in England and Wales, 10,442, would seem to be far too small. Health visitors are devoting more of their time to old people, but there are only the equivalent of 4571 whole-timers, and the calls on them are many.

Home Helps

Home helps are doing a magnificent job, but again the service scarcely matches the need. In 1961 there were 2605 whole-time helps (plus 592 organizers) and 49,822 part-time helps (with 190 part-time organizers). They assisted in 328,275 cases, but these included maternity, tuberculosis and other cases as well as the old; and there are a million house-bound old people to start with. Seventy-six per cent of the cases in which help was given were old age and chronic sickness; 11 per cent, maternity cases; 1 per cent, tuberculosis; 12 per cent, problem families and the rest.

The net cost of the service in 1960–1 (the cost to the authorities after deducting payments by people using the service) was greater than the individual cost of all but one of the local authority services—the ambulance service. The cost of the service exceeds £11 million a year. But residential care for the old would cost more.

The Ministry of Health annual report pays tribute to "the voluntary work done by home helps for the families they serve, such as looking in at week-ends to make sure that old people are comfortable". Recent information suggests that this spirit is infectious. Examples have been given, in Middlesex, of the interest shown by the husbands of home helps. An elderly lady had tripped over some loose linoleum and the home help thought that new linoleum ought to be laid. She brought her husband along and he not only laid the linoleum, but decorated the room as well. On one occasion the home-help organizer, harassed by increased needs and staff shortage during an epidemic, was visited by the husband of one of her home helps with the news that his wife was ill, but that he would himself manage in his wife's place and had already visited her charge that morning to light the fire and get the breakfast.

Net expenditure of local authorities on health visiting exceeds £5 million a year and on home nursing it is around £9 million a year. Estimated expenditure on accommodation for the aged and infirm in 1962–3 was £25,111,000.

The Ministry knows the needs. In commending its hospital plan to local authorities it said: "Services for the elderly should be designed to help them to remain in their own homes as long as possible." This might have been expressed more felicitously perhaps—out of sight out of mind?—but the drift is clear.

One good, if belated, move was that from 1959 local authorities were permitted to provide chiropody services. Chiropodists are thus enabled to keep many more old people mobile.

Housing*

The National Corporation for the Care of Old People in its 15th annual report said: "The Corporation regards housing, at least for the aged, as one of the social services", a view with which there will be wide agreement. It goes on to highlight another grave failure. "Progress", it says, "in the numbers of housing units suitable for, but not necessarily allocated to, the aged is not being made, and in 1961 the number of one-bedroom dwellings built by local authorities in England and Wales was some 2000 less than in the previous years." The 1962 figures show an increase of 4700, but the total of 28,900 is only about half the estimated annual requirement. In some instances the Ministry of Housing and Local Government reduced the numbers of dwellings for old people proposed by some local authorities.

In dealing with the future the same report describes housing for old people as "one of the crying needs at the moment. For the fact is that only about half the estimated annual requirements for dwellings for old people are now being built and in some places even existing contracts are being reduced."

On the individual old person's financial need, the report dismisses as mere palliatives such items as cheap travel, cinema seats, fuel and milk and free television and radio licences. They lessened "the force of any case for increased retirement pensions".

> For although it is obviously misleading to suggest that old age and poverty are synonymous, yet the standard of living of many retirement pensioners is low and it is worth noting that of the 1,844,000 people on National Assistance weekly allowances at the end of 1961 about 70 per cent were persons of pensionable age and in addition there may well have been some who though eligible for it did not claim it.

In my experience the Corporation is here being over-cautious. Many old people, fiercely and, I think, wrongly "independent", do not apply for the National Assistance grant they could well do with. We must all drive home the lesson that in these days of unending inflation there is nothing wrong in turning to the help we are providing communally.

* For further details on housing, see the chapter by Dr. Parker, Section V, p. 219.

There will be wide acceptance of the Corporation's conclusion. Protesting that it is not so foolish as to claim that the care of the aged should always rank as top priority, it ends:

> On the other hand, we shall be profoundly disappointed if there are no signs of completely new thinking about this integral part of our national life, and we trust that one result of such new thought will be to wipe out once and for all a certain tendency to wait until all other needs, regarded whether rightly or wrongly as "pressing", have been met and then, but only then, to see what is left in the till for old people.

In May 1963 the then Minister of Housing and Local Government, Sir Keith Joseph, produced a ten-year housing plan. But it made no specific new proposals for assisting the aged. Indeed, one's first reaction was that the new programme was inadequate to the need. Further study of the plan and the comments of those intimately concerned with the housing problem only confirm this view. Sir Keith announced a new target figure of at least 350,000 houses a year and, to do him justice, he emphasized the phrase "at least". His programme, he said, would produce nearly 1000 new houses every day plus at least 500 older houses modernized. These are fine figures and represent welcome help to many families. But was Sir Keith aiming high enough? All slums, he implied, would vanish within ten years (excepting perhaps those in the main centres of urban squalor). His programme, he said, would bring within the reach of "nearly every citizen in the land" either a modern or a modernized house. But will it? How many does "nearly every citizen" leave out?

Sir Keith admitted an existing housing shortage of 500,000 to 1 million houses. The household growth in the next twenty years would be $2\frac{1}{2}$ million. The annual housing need, simply to keep pace, was 125,000. The slum problem is massive and terrible in the misery and ill health it is responsible for. Ranging from the true condemned habitations to those which are also unfit, probably ought to be condemned and would be pulled down but for the pressing need of any kind of shelter, slum clearance, according to those qualified to say, requires replacement of 2 to 3 million houses. And this is no static total. Every year more of the older houses fall into the slum category. Even if slum-type houses needing replacement are put down at no more than 2 million, they alone would require 200,000 new houses a year if the slums are to be cleared away in ten years. It was clear, therefore, from the start, that the sooner Sir Keith got his new legislation through and the sooner he raised his target above 350,000 the better. We are, it seems, well down in the list of countries as far as annual production of new homes is concerned.

Perhaps, again, it is a question of readjusting our priorities. Surely in any civilized country, and certainly in a so-called Welfare State, tolerable housing conditions should rank high.

An interesting feature of Sir Keith's programme was a proposal to establish a Housing Corporation as a government agency, with the task of building up the housing society movement. It was to be provided with £100 million from the Treasury.

The Building Societies Association was to recommend its members to support this new drive. The Minister hoped "we shall work up to 15,000 houses a year". Again one is forced to ask: Is this adequate and to whom will they be available?

The New Plan

Slowly, after our long winter of discontents, came the spring of 1963 and the long-awaited ten-year, £220 million plan for developing local health and welfare services for the sick and old, mothers and children, and the mentally and physically handicapped. The scheme was announced by the Minister of Health, but it was in reality the sum of the individual plans of 146 local health authorities. It was complementary to the Hospital Plan. Later in the year, Mr. Powell promised, there would be a report on the part to be played by the family doctor—and if increased community care is to be achieved his will be a major role.

The fourth partner in the promised comprehensive and integrated health and welfare service, the voluntary worker, was not overlooked. In a message to local authorities Mr. Powell said: "With the further development of care in the community there will be even more scope for voluntary effort than in the past."

Under the plan, expenditure on the health and welfare services will rise from £111 million in 1962–3 to £163 million in 1971–2. The Minister explained that about half would be found by the ratepayer and half by the taxpayer. Actual cost of the programme may work out at more. The Minister suggested that some authorities should increase their proposed provision of homes for the old, health visitors, home helps, etc. And plans are to be revised annually.

Workhouses to go

The Minister urged quicker elimination of the old workhouses. Some 20,000 out of 34,000 places were to be closed by 1972. "This rate of progress is not fast enough", he said. The scheme envisages a 45 per cent increase in staff.

Places in old people's homes will rise from 90,448 in 1962 to 132,923 in 1972; junior places in training centres for the mentally subnormal from 16,407 to 23,031, and adult places from 11,259 to 27,795; hostels for the subnormal will increase from 47 to 464; and centres and hostels for the mentally ill from 41 to 314. Health visitors will increase from 5269 to 7607; home helps from 25,478 to 37,083; home nurses from 7704 to 9790; midwives from 5261 to 6509; and social workers from 2943 to 4879. Where is Mr. Powell— or, more to the point, the local authorities—to find all these people? It was somewhat surprising to find that there are to be 1225 new maternity and child welfare clinics. But many will replace temporary or unsuitable premises. And the Minister was able to show that increasing use is being made of the clinics. Summing up, he said: "The health service can now walk into the future on two firm legs, knowing broadly the direction in which it is proceeding." Maybe; but only if (1) adequate funds are provided by the Government and (2) training and pay and conditions are improved sufficiently to attract the additional workers of all kinds who will be needed. And the continuous, determined leadership of one wanting the best possible health and welfare service will be needed if the professional and voluntary workers and buildings essential to the plan are to be forthcoming and the programme translated from paper into a shining new way of life for some of the most needy, distressed and deserving of our fellow citizens.

Family Care

One reassuring note in reports on care of the old which I have read recently is the testimony given of the time and energy devoted by younger relatives to the care of aged fathers, mothers, grandparents, uncles and aunts. Dr. Miller, for example, in the book mentioned earlier, *The Ageing Countryman*, says that young people work hard to care for their old and ailing relatives. He gives many moving examples.

> There is a feeling abroad that the younger generations of today [he says] are unwilling to face their responsibilities towards the old and failing members of the family, and that they often display a distasteful impatience to get the old people out of the way— into a "Home", into a hospital—no matter where. My experience in the country has been the very reverse of this.

But failure to provide sufficient housing, both for families and for old people, does not make the young people's task of caring for the old any easier. Neighbours, too, Dr. Miller and other investigators have found, play a noble part in making life bearable for old people. Which brings us on to the neighbourliness represented in the mass of voluntary work done for the old. There are probably between 80,000 and 100,000 active workers in voluntary services for the old. It is an impressive number, but not excessive against the need.

I am sometimes asked how people can take up voluntary service. I suggest doing something for the old or joining a league of hospital friends. Many hospitals have these leagues and depend on them for amenities for both patients and staff which state funds are quite insufficient to provide. If your local hospital has not got its league of friends, I tell my inquirer, you could start one.

Many towns now have their Old People's Welfare Committees. They can find work for willing hands, and the National Old People's Welfare Council runs training courses for new-comers.

Loneliness is a major trial for old people. Death removes treasured relatives and friends and many old people find themselves deprived of all personal relationships. Visiting and a leisurely chat can make a lonely old man's or woman's day. Voluntary visiting services are increasing. They have a practical value, too. They ensure that an isolated old person is not left to lie ill or to die alone. In need a family doctor or other helper can be alerted. There is a need both to strengthen services for the aged and to do much more to make known what services are available. Shopping and preparation of meals are valuable services for the old. Too many exist on tea and bread and jam. Lack of protein food lowers their resistance to disease.

Sir John Charles, in his final report in 1960 as Chief Medical Officer to the Ministry of Health, said of old people: "Their response to a proper diet is often dramatic." Many old people with mental infirmity, he said, recover remarkably when introduced to decent meals.

Thus the mobile meals services run by Women's Voluntary Services and others are invaluable. But much more needs to be done. It is estimated that not more than 0·3 per cent of the old receive two meals a week from these sources. Darby and Joan clubs bring companionship and pleasure to many old people.

Youth's Part

Most encouraging is the fact that youth organizations are playing an increasing role in caring for the old. Many young people are regularly carrying out valuable practical tasks—shopping, cleaning, decorating, changing library books, repairing shoes and wireless sets. Youth fellowships take religious worship to old people who are house-bound.

In St. Marylebone I came across an outstanding example of teaming-up between old and young. A fifth of the borough's population is over 65 years of age. A group of Methodist students redecorated an old couple's home and repaired their television set. Soon they had a regular service going, and a succession of drab rooms were redecorated.

This task and privilege of extending a helping hand and companionship to the old will not grow less. More and more of us are surviving to the Psalmist's three score years and ten and beyond. We dare not, in the name of self-respect and the good reputation of this country as a pioneer in social service, allow these extra years to peter out in loneliness and squalor.

4. Voluntary Effort

KATHLEEN M. SLACK
Lecturer in Social Administration, London School of Economics

WHATEVER the merits or otherwise of voluntary social services, organizations and workers in the field of social welfare, it is clear that as far as the foreseeable future is concerned, both their number and their importance is likely to be maintained and quite possibly increased. Over the last half century they have proved to be both tough and resilient and have withstood the different tests of war and peace, depression and affluence, absence and introduction of social legislation.

Status

Some part of their traditional or conventional justification may have proved, as will be suggested later, to be rationalization, but they have achieved a status and even a sanctity which it would now be difficult effectively to challenge, even were such a challenge thought to be desirable. Indeed, they were described in 1959, in the report of the Working Party on Social Workers in the Local Authority, Health and Welfare Services, as "an integral part of the health and welfare services".

The final award of merit may be said to have been conferred upon them by the Minister of Health in 1962 in circulars addressed both to hospitals and local authorities: *A Hospital Plan for England and Wales, Voluntary Help in Hospitals* and *The Development of Local Authority Health and Welfare Services*. The first of these initiated conferences between representatives of hospital authorities, local authorities and national voluntary organizations on the scope of voluntary provision in the development of the hospital and local authority services. It was later stated that there was general agreement on that occasion that there was scope for a considerable expansion of voluntary effort in hospitals; and Hospital Management Committees and Boards of Governors were asked to take the initiative by considering ways in which greater use could be made of help from voluntary bodies.

In the circular addressed to local authorities, reference was made to the necessity *inter alia* of consulting voluntary organizations providing health and welfare services on *all* aspects (author's italics) of plans for the future development of local authority services. Voluntary organizations were referred to as already doing much valuable work and it was stated that there were fields in which voluntary work was particularly effective and where it could develop further. Examples given were mobile meals, occupational and recreational clubs, and holidays for the elderly and handicapped; services which local authorities were themselves empowered directly to provide under the National Assistance Act, 1948, (Amendment) Act, 1962.

This suggests that the Minister was not at heart persuaded that voluntary work would be able to develop sufficiently in fields regarded, for unspecified reasons, as those in which it could be particularly effective. This well illustrates the fact that whilst voluntary bodies and voluntary workers may be looked upon as making a valuable contribution to social welfare, they are not competent, singlehanded, to meet need as a whole, either in general or in particular.

Limitations of Voluntary Effort

Limitations of voluntary effort were, in fact, specifically referred to in one of the Ministry's circulars. In this, reference was made to common agreement between representatives of local authorities and voluntary bodies that the spread of work then being done by voluntary effort was uneven, either because local authorities had not asked for more, or because voluntary help had not been available. To these two reasons can be added others equally, if not more, cogent. For example, unevenness of services provided by voluntary bodies is frequently due to insufficient funds, the failure to appoint or to obtain full-time, salaried staff, or the lack of local initiative, knowledge or energy.

The representatives of the national voluntary organizations claimed, however, that their local bodies would not fail to respond to a call for more voluntary workers, and expressed confidence that an increased number, both of reliable and able people, would be forthcoming. In the light of this assurance, local authorities were asked by the Minister to consider existing arrangements for securing co-operation with and amongst the voluntary organizations in their areas and how these could be improved or extended to ensure regular consultation. Without this, it was stated, local authorities might remain unaware, on the one hand, of the help voluntary organizations could give them, and fail, on the other, to inform the latter of the help they could provide, without which they would not be in a position to provide and train volunteers for the particular tasks for which they are needed.

The reason for this observation was obscure, as many voluntary bodies had long been providing training courses for voluntary workers for the "particular tasks for which they are needed"; voluntary youth workers, marriage guidance counsellors, old people's welfare workers, and citizens' advice bureaux personnel—to name but some. Official recognition of the fact that voluntary workers require training was, however, a welcome sign of the times, in keeping with the view of the Working Party already referred to, which concluded that selection and training of voluntary workers was essential if they were to give their services knowledgeably and acceptably, and in order that they might recognize when a more highly trained worker was required.

Terminology

Throughout the circulars referred to above there is clearly apparent an unfortunate but common confusion. The voluntary organization or voluntary body, the voluntary worker or volunteer, voluntary work, voluntary effort, voluntary help, voluntary provision, voluntary service and voluntary services, are variously used as if interchangeable, and as though there were no possibility of different meanings being attached to them. But any assessment of the place and value of voluntary effort, to use an all-embracing term, requires a clear distinction between voluntary service and voluntary services, and between the voluntary worker, or volunteer, and the voluntary organization, each of which has different roles to perform. To use these and other terms indiscriminately is but to confuse both thought and action. Certain definitions are essential and they have, in fact, been suggested in more than one standard work.

The following definition is chosen from Madeleine Rooff's *Voluntary Societies and Social Policy*:

> The terms voluntary organisation, voluntary society, voluntary agency, or voluntary association, in the context of the social services are used . . . to cover those bodies which provide some form of social service, which control their own policy and which depend, in part at least, upon financial support from voluntary sources.

From such a definition it follows that the voluntary social services are those provided by and on the initiative of voluntary organizations, that is to say, other than under statute by central or local government departments, although grant aid may be given by such departments towards their provision and/or administration.

A voluntary worker or volunteer—as distinct from a voluntary organization—is neither more nor less than a person who gives help, whether as an amateur or as a professional, or whether to a local authority or to a voluntary body, without a wage or salary. That is to say he gives voluntary service, not to be confused with the voluntary services. He is free to reduce, withdraw, or terminate his help at any time and is governed by no conditions of appointment or legal contract of service. Any exercise of control over his work rests upon goodwill or upon the personal authority of the staff of the organization whom he serves. A voluntary worker in another role may be a paid employee of some other body, or a retired person, or a housewife, a local councillor, or still be receiving full-time education. The status "voluntary worker" depends solely upon the giving of social service, free from financial reward, for the furtherance of the social welfare of some person, group or the community as a whole.

Using the Voluntary Organization

From the foregoing it is clear that for a local authority to make use of or assist a voluntary organization is not the same thing as for it to make use of a voluntary worker. To the first it can in many instances, and to an increased extent since the war, entrust public funds by way of grant aid. This is so, for example, in the case of voluntary youth organizations or adult community centres, under the Education Act, 1944. It is so in the case of voluntary organizations providing facilities covered by the Physical Training and Recreation Act, 1937. It applies to voluntary organizations concerned with the welfare of the old, under Part III of the National Assistance Act, 1948, as amended in 1962, and likewise to voluntary organizations designed to promote the welfare of the disabled. The Local Government Act, 1948, makes possible grant aid to voluntary bodies providing information and advice services. Many other instances of a like nature could be given.

Such assistance of voluntary organizations opens the way for a local authority to use one or more of them as its agent in the provision of welfare services, of assuring itself that their standard of work is high, and of furthering experimental work without saddling the ratepayer with long-term or uncertain commitments. The use of voluntary workers is not necessarily involved in this procedure at all. Whether or not they are recruited is left entirely to the discretion of the organization receiving grant, which may or may not take the view that only trained and salaried staff meets its particular needs.

The voluntary social services, being those provided by voluntary bodies, include, like them, many financed in part out of statutory funds, for example, Marriage Guidance, Family Welfare, Citizens' Advice Services. Over the years the voluntary social services have preceded, accompanied and supplemented the statutory services. Their justification and value do not depend upon their being more personal, more concerned, more efficient, less official or more appealing to their users than statutory services, as is often claimed. The appointment under statute of trained caseworkers in child care, probation, mental health, prison welfare and residential work has shown such arguments to be invalid. And further appointments by local authorities, in their health and welfare departments, of social workers trained in courses following the recommendations of the Working Party are likely further to substantiate this view.

The value today—whatever may have once been the case—of the voluntary organization and the voluntary services alike, lies not in a difference of quality of service but in their being channels for the goodwill and interest of the private citizen who wishes to take a direct part in social welfare, in their freedom and ability more easily to pursue controversial goals, to experiment and explore new areas of need, to act quickly in crises, and to encourage the extension or improvement of their statutory counterparts and, to this end, to co-operate and not to compete with them.

Using the Volunteer

For a local authority to use a voluntary worker or volunteer as distinct from a voluntary organization, is for it to use the services of a person, not a corporate body. This has the advantage of economy, of freeing its own manpower, of permitting more time to be spent on purely personal and friendly contacts than a salaried worker may rightly give, and harnessing the goodwill of individual local people. But it has the disadvantages of a lack of contract or conditions of service which control selection, standards of work, deployment and, if necessary, termination of employment. Voluntary workers as a whole, whose number is virtually beyond assessment, are without doubt making a substantial contribution to the furtherance of social welfare, but individually they are persons possessed of the virtues and the failings of mankind in general. These have to be weighed in the balance in making use of voluntary workers, whether such use is by a voluntary organization or a local authority. Not to do so is to court a lowering or further unevenness in standards of service. The voluntary worker cannot be used anywhere and everywhere. He should be allocated to work for which he has the interest, ability and time to perform properly, and he must be ready, if necessary, to work under or be guided by the professional.

Trends in Voluntary Effort

Five trends in voluntary effort can be distinguished as features of the present century. The first is the reduction in emphasis on the meeting of material needs, no longer so necessary by reason of the assumption of State responsibility for greater numbers of people in more areas of need than has hitherto been the case. This is so clearly evident that further elaboration should not be required.

Of the other four trends, the first is the steady increase in the number of voluntary organizations. The evidence of this is contained in the last (1965) edition of the Handbook and Directory of the National Council of Social Service, *Voluntary Social Services*. This lists all the voluntary social service organizations of which it has information. It shows that in the three twenty-year periods 1900–19, 1920–39 and 1940–59, 23, 23 and 31 new national voluntary societies were formed (77 in all), excluding those solely serving Scotland, Wales and Northern Ireland. Only those services are included in this number which promote, or include in their activities in one way or another, the promotion of individual or group health or welfare, whether physical or mental. That is to say, educational organizations, urban or rural preservation or improvement societies, professional associations, standing conferences, animal welfare organizations, those concerned with the promotion of peace, religion or particular social standards, such as abstinence or the regulation of sexual behaviour, are excluded. Such a dividing line between one aspect of voluntary effort and another is, to some extent, arbitrary and open to dispute, but a line must be drawn somewhere if the subject is to retain any kind of manageable proportions.

Compared to the 77 new voluntary welfare organizations formed between 1900 and 1959, the Directory lists only 43 of a similar nature formed prior to 1900, of which 31 were formed between 1860 and 1899. In other words it is clear voluntary effort in social welfare is a phenomenon of the last 100 years, in particular of the last 50 years, and still further the last 30 years. It is, of course, possible that some voluntary societies were formed but dissolved prior to the dates given, but if so it is unlikely that they were sufficiently large in number or importance to invalidate this conclusion.

It is possible to argue that the increase of the last sixty years is not wholly desirable, being the result in part of duplication or splintering of voluntary effort, with a consequent danger of confusion or even competition between societies concerned with the same area of human need. The welfare of the physically disabled or handicapped is one such area, where since 1900 no less than nineteen national voluntary societies have been formed, concerning themselves either with those suffering from one specific disability or with those suffering from physical disabilities as a whole. It is open to question whether such proliferation is, in fact, the best way of promoting the welfare of the disabled.

The same can be asked of the seventeen organizations concerning themselves in one way or another with the welfare of children—a question which would appear to be justified by the establishment, in June 1962, of a National Bureau for Co-operation in Child Care.

The second trend in voluntary effort which is less obvious than the increase in the number of organizations but is, nevertheless, important, is the establishment of societies designed to further the mutual assistance and support of like persons in like need. This aspect of voluntary effort was emphasized by Lord Beveridge in his discussion of the work of the Friendly Societies in his Study, *Voluntary Action*.

More recent examples of self-help is Alcoholics Anonymous, which is "a fellowship of men and women who share their experience, strength and hope with each other, so that they may solve their own problem and help others to recover from alcoholism". There is also the British Association of the Hard of Hearing, which is composed of, as well as for, those who suffer from impaired hearing. There is the Haemophilia Society to provide a fellowship for haemophilics; the British Polio Fellowship "to associate sufferers from polio in fellowship for the encouragement and development of their interests and abilities"; the Multiple Sclerosis Society, which, in local groups, arranges "mutual help and comradeship". All these, and certain similar organizations, were formed in the 1930's, 1940's or 1950's, and although still relatively few in number are examples of a healthy development of self-help as distinct from the provision of one group for another which, however necessary, carries with it the danger of benevolent paternalism.

Thirdly, the last fifty years have seen the foundation of the large Trusts dispensing substantial funds for the furtherance of the work of voluntary organizations; for example by grant aid towards research, experimental work, the initial costs of the establishment of new ventures, or other objects falling within the terms of the foundation's constitution. These Trusts include the Calouste Gulbenkian Foundation, the Carnegie United Kingdom Trust, the City Parochial Foundation, the Isaac Wolfson Foundation, King Edward's Hospital Fund for London, the King George's Jubilee Trust, the King George VI Social Service Scheme, Nuffield Provincial Hospitals Trust, and the National Corporation for the Care of Old People. The means at their disposal is potentially and actually of the greatest importance to the present and future development of the voluntary organization and the voluntary services, making possible social research and experimental projects far beyond the normal financial scope of voluntary effort, and unlikely to attract adequate statutory support.

Finally, there has been a trend towards the establishment of international voluntary organizations and services. Voluntary effort has in recent years widened its geographical boundaries, crossed national frontiers and concerned itself with the welfare of the political prisoner, of the refugee, the starving and the underprivileged abroad rather than at home. Examples of this international aspect of voluntary effort are to be found in the work of "Amnesty", the British Council for Aid to Refugees, the Ockenden Venture, the Oxford Committee for Famine Relief, the Save the Children Fund, and the Danilo Dolce Trust. All these, as also International Social Service of Great Britain, International Voluntary Service, and Voluntary Service Overseas, were products of the 1940's and 1950's. They reflect the tensions and the challenges of the post-war world, and they illustrate the fact that at its best voluntary effort can and does attract support, both of money and manpower, of those of compassion, vision, energy and ability.

There is no reason to assume that the trends noted above will form a continuing pattern of voluntary effort. There is no finality in social welfare.

Constant changes take place, new pressures are exerted, new problems emerge as old ones are solved. All that can be said with any degree of certainty is that the voluntary organizations, providing the voluntary social services, and the contribution of voluntary workers and volunteers giving voluntary help or service, are likely to be permanent features in one form or another of British social welfare.

5. Report on Social Work*

D. V. DONNISON
Professor of Social Administration,
London School of Economics and Political Science

THOSE who regard social work as the sticking-plaster on the sore parts of society will be depressed at the sight of a 400-page blue book on the subject, published a dozen years after the great reforms that were to free the country from ignorance, idleness, want and squalor. At the end of the war it was recognized that social workers would be needed to carry out specialist jobs within the big statutory social services. But many thought that old-fashioned general social work, or family casework, would wither away as soon as a comprehensive range of services had been set up to meet all the principal human needs. Had not the Webbs made it plain long ago that the poor arrive at their poverty "along one or other of three roads—the road of Neglected Childhood, the road of Sickness or Feeble-mindedness, and the road of Unemployment"? In the Welfare State the roads to ruin would be blocked.

A lot has happened since then. There has been the rediscovery of "the family" and "the community", and the recognition of the support and comfort people gain in times of trouble from their relatives, friends, and neighbours. In hospitals for children the "Bowlby revolution"† is taking place. Mental hospitals have been getting patients back into the community at a rate never known before, and greater efforts have been made to help the mentally ill and defective in their own homes. The local authority children's departments are coming to regard child care not as an end in itself, but as one part—preferably a temporary part—of the help they can give to families that have difficulty in looking after their children. Juvenile delinquency and truancy are increasingly looked upon as manifestations of tangled relationships within the family. Old people's welfare committees, home helps, and other services have been set up to enable people to look after themselves at home.

These attempts to keep people out of institutions and provide more comprehensive help for them in their own homes will go much further. For a hundred years the Poor Law institutions were designed to frighten the poor

* Reprinted with the permission of the editor and author from *Political Quarterly* **30'** 357–66 (Oct.–Dec. 1959, No. 4).

† That is, reforms of medical care and hospital routine designed to minimize the ill effects of separating young children from their parents.

into fending for themselves, and it is not surprising that a lot of people have gained a horror of institutional life. If many families still look upon it as the final betrayal to allow grandma to go into a home or a mentally sick brother to be "put away" in an asylum, then those who would help these people must go out and find them in their own homes.

The specialist services have found that human needs do not come in neat specialist packets. Deaf children may be educationally backward, and if all the family's attention is directed to them their brothers may become uncontrollable and their mothers frantic. To do its job properly each service has had to take account of other needs besides those it was set up to meet.

Moreover, the State is responsible for providing for everyone in the last resort, and the provision may have to be made in very expensive and lengthy fashion—through national assistance, or in mental hospitals, prisons, special schools, children's homes, and "Part III Accommodation".* A family of five recently evicted from a council flat for failing to pay its rent cost the local authority £50 in rent arrears, and the price of caring for three children until they reach the age of 18. Such cases are quoted to justify the development of "preventive" services and the appointment of more social workers on the plea that they will save money and prevent scandal.

The Social Worker

Meanwhile, social workers themselves have begun to take a more comprehensive view of their responsibilities. Anyone who starts thinking of people, families and their needs "in the round", rather than concentrating on the provision of specific services (finding people jobs, getting boys into clubs, procuring wheel-chairs, and arranging convalescent holidays) is faced with a whole new world of opportunities and anxieties. The growing knowledge of human motives and relationships provided by the psychiatrists has been seized on by social workers for application in their own trade. It may be, too, that the social workers' "clients" now demand more sensitive treatment and a more comprehensive service: they are probably getting it elsewhere, to judge from the growing interest in "human relations" shown by teachers, personnel managers, salesmen and others. Social workers have gained increasing power to develop their work in their own way. The creation of the children's departments brought trained social workers to the chief officers' table in town hall dining-rooms. Committee members responsible for social work agencies increasingly leave their professional staff to make decisions about individual cases.

* Residential accommodation provided under Part III of the National Assistance Act, 1948.

The Younghusband Report

Thus within a dozen years administrative necessities, professional pressures, changing attitudes to people in need and the growth of knowledge about human behaviour have created a demand for social work that the Charity Organization Society itself could not have foreseen. And now from the deliberations of the Working Party on Social Workers in the Local Authority Health and Welfare Services has emerged a report—the Younghusband Report*—which recognizes these developments, examines their implications within one field of social service and calls for major changes in the recruitment, training and deployment of social workers in this field.

The Younghusband Committee found that the great majority of social workers in these services have no systematic training. No estimates could be made of the extent of the needs these workers are supposed to meet. Their departments are undermanned, salary scales are low, opportunities for training and promotion are few, and field workers spend an inordinate amount of time in travelling, writing their own letters and reports, and doing odd jobs of irrelevant kinds. Meanwhile the passing of the Mental Health Act† means that frightening new responsibilities are soon to be thrust upon them. If something is not done quickly, much of the big talk about "community care" will amount to no more than Welfare State jargon for expressing the old-fashioned Poor Law view that people should fend for themselves.

The Committee proposed radical reforms. Social work in these services should no longer be divided into categories that owe more to historical accident and administrative convenience than to the nature of the human needs to be met or the kind of skills required. There should be three kinds of social workers. Experienced workers with a university qualification in the social sciences and further professional training are required to provide a casework service for those needing the most skilled help with personal and family problems, and to act as advisers and supervisors. Though there are far too few of them, such people are already being trained by the universities, the Home Office and the Institute of Medical Social Workers. Next there is needed a large body of social workers capable of providing systematic help with less complex problems. For these workers, who will constitute the backbone of the service, there should be a two-year full-time training leading to a national certificate of sufficient standing to be recognized as qualifying its holder for certain appointments, promotions, and salary scales. This training would be given in colleges of further education with the help of local social services in

---

* *Report of the Working Party on Social Workers in the Local Authority Health and Welfare Services,* H.M.S.O., 1959.
   † Enacted in 1959.

which the students would do supervised practical work. A National Council for Social Work Training* would be set up to get it going, to work out criteria for the selection and assessment of students, and to gain the help of local authorities, hospitals, technical colleges, universities, and other bodies. Finally, there should be a third group of "welfare assistants" who would be responsible, after a systematic in-service training, for straightforward visiting and the provision of material help and simple services of various kinds.

The feature of this scheme that makes it a landmark in the development of social administration is the fact that the Working Party has cut its way through the jungle of the health and welfare services—family casework, the home-help service, the services providing care and after-care (residential and domiciliary) for the sick, the aged, the mentally ill and defective, the blind, the deaf, and the handicapped—and has emerged with the discovery that no matter which of these fields it is practised in, social work faces much the same problems and requires much the same aptitudes and training. The Young-husband Report states the case for social work as a profession.

To most people outside the social services this conclusion seems boringly obvious. It was accepted long ago in America, France and most of the Commonwealth countries. But in this country social work has been regarded as one aspect of the administration of a social service, rather than as a distinctive profession with its own body of knowledge, its own methods and codes of behaviour. In this setting the conclusions of the Younghusband Report are going to upset a lot of hallowed traditions.

The Need for Training

Their first and most obvious implication is that social workers must be trained. Clerks who seem good at dealing with people, insurance salesmen with experience of knocking at doors, young ladies with a family tradition of good works, and university graduates with some knowledge of the social sciences—all these may make good social workers, but they must be given training first. And it is local government and the social services generally that must give it. To many local government departments it will come as a new idea that they too—like the armed forces and many industrial firms— should train those who are to work for them. When the costs of training schemes and the costs of employing better qualified workers are added up there may be some second thoughts about "community care". Many forms of institutional care only look expensive today because the alternative is so cheap—and sometimes so nasty.

If social workers are given an adequate training, many voluntary organizations may have to choose between providing a second-rate service or going

* The body established by the Health Visiting and Social Work (Training) Act of 1962 is called the Council for Training in Social Work.

bankrupt in the attempt to match the State's improved standards. The next ten years will show which of them can make the grade. A strange relationship has grown up between the State and the voluntary social services. Apart from a few unsinkables with a strong public appeal, like the N.S.P.C.C., most of the voluntary organizations now fall into three groups. There are those which draw a large part of their incomes from the State; the residential institutions for children, delinquents, the old and the convalescent led the way, but casework agencies such as the Family Service Units are now following the same pattern. There are those whose chief function is not to provide a service but to get better services from the State—for example the British Legion, the Howard League, and the old age pensioners' associations. And there are those that retain voluntary forms while relying so heavily on statutory direction and finance that they can often be regarded as *ad hoc* (and extremely valuable) agencies for enabling the State to do more than its legislation permits—for example the W.V.S. and the old people's welfare committees. The Younghusband Report stresses the need for voluntary services, but its recommendations may eventually force them to rely even more heavily upon the State, and thus blur still further the distinction between a statutory and a voluntary body.

The most important implication of the Report is one that its authors could only hint at. "A number of witnesses", they say, "commented on the difficulty of limiting their evidence to social workers in the health and welfare services, since this would be considering only certain aspects of the total picture. . . . In their opinion, a comprehensive review of the training and employment of social workers in the whole field of the social services was required in the light of experience gained since 1948." If such a review is ever made, it may well produce for social work as a whole conclusions very similar to those the Younghusband Committee reached in its own field. The differences between the work done by probation officers, child-care officers, hospital almoners and others are no greater than those found among social workers in the health and welfare services. In child care and probation, standards of training are better, but not uniformly good; and the almoners and psychiatric social workers have only been able to maintain their standards by refusing to expand their services further than the exiguous supply of trained workers permits. (A hospital can be run without social workers, but children's departments and the probation service cannot—if they do not get enough good workers they must make do with bad.)

Despite the shortage of social workers in every branch of the social services, and the inadequate numbers (smaller now than in 1950) being trained in the universities,* and despite the major developments that have

---

* The number of social workers being trained at the universities is now (1965) increasing, but remains far below the demands of employers and the demand for training amongst qualified candidates.

taken place since the war, no attempt has been made to review the whole situation. There has been no scarcity of committees and working parties: social workers in the probation service, the youth service, mental hospitals, schools for the maladjusted, marriage guidance agencies, and the children's service have each in turn been investigated. But the administrative boundaries and the departmental and professional rivalries that bedevil these investigations make it impossible to resolve the major problems that reappear in each of these fields. How long must the social services go on bidding against each other for the few trained workers available, before they set up a comprehensive system of training and recruitment? How necessary is it for social workers of various kinds to have a university training, and how can the few who get it be most effectively deployed? Should each social service meet a wider range of human needs, or should one of them become a general "family welfare service", calling on specialist help from the others when it is wanted? What do the people who get all this help think of the services provided? For which human problems does social work provide an essential form of help, and which can be resolved by better housing, higher pensions, more jobs? Questions of this kind can barely be asked within the terms of reference of the investigations that have been made so far.

But if the Younghusband Committee's recommendations are acted upon, other services cannot be insulated from their effects. It will be impossible to exclude their staff from the training courses that lead to the national Certificate in Social Work. Health visitors, National Assistance Board officers, N.S.P.C.C. inspectors and many others have shown themselves anxious to learn the kinds of things the Committee wants to see taught in these courses. The proposed "National" Certificate was presumably named with this in mind. Soon the probation service and the children's departments will have to decide whether to recognize the qualification or whether to try to get all their staff trained at university level. The Committee recommend that an independent body should be set up with support from charitable foundations to develop training methods and provide a national centre for discussion, experiment and research in social work.* This body would not be confined by departmental or professional boundaries. To some extent it could make up for the lack of a professional body representing all branches of social work.

Many of the Committee's recommendations will be disputed and most of the disputes will be productive, for the Committee has focused attention on the big issues. Whether its recommendations are accepted or not, there will henceforth be a "post-Younghusband" flavour to all discussions of social work and social administration.

* The National Institute for Social Work Training, established as a result of this recommendation, is mentioned in the Postscript to this article

Health Visitors

So far the Report has been attacked from two quarters. The first assault could have been predicted before the Committee started work. At the end of the last century "health visitors" were appointed by voluntary organizations in the larger cities to teach mothers how to keep their children healthy. In time they were required to have nursing qualifications and a special public health training. They became an important part of the staff of every medical officer of health, and in conditions of overcrowding and unemployment, when rickets, vermin, and "summer diarrhoea" were commonplace among children, they probably saved many lives. In happier times their functions have changed, but still remain a little uncertain. One of the many post-war inquiries into separate branches of the social services dealt with the training and recruitment of health visitors, and concluded that this group should become the general practitioners of the welfare business. The Younghusband Committee could neither repeat this inquiry nor dispute its findings. Its Report pays brief respects to "doctors, health visitors, nurses, teachers, and others", recognizes that confusion sometimes occurs between the functions of health visitors and social workers, but says that this should be cleared up once an adequate training is provided for the latter. An appropriate passage is selected from the health visitors' report to show that health visitors should give expert advice and refer to other workers those cases that need something more than advice. To make the point cruelly clear, they then quote from a health visitor's log book:

> Tuberculosis contact visit. Diabetic mother, father disabled and on National Assistance, family problems. Contacts well. Daughter and husband are separated, two children in the care of the local authority. Another daughter will not keep her house or children in order. Two school children are bed wetters. Advised mother on best way to cope with each situation.

Health visitors, frustrated already by the shelving of their own report, have not taken kindly to this treatment. Medical officers have reported that all social work should be reserved to their own departments. What ought to be done? Some people regard the health visitors as an anachronism that should be allowed to fade away. But a force of 8000 highly trained women, backed by the prestige of the medical profession, does not wither easily. Their future may become clearer if it is remembered that they are not second-rate social workers but first-rate health teachers, capable of playing an important part in the National Health Service. Some general practitioners are already asking health visitors to help them in their surgeries and visit patients on their lists. In time, many over-worked doctors may welcome the help they can get from health visitors and other staff of the local authority health departments.

The Skills Required

The second attack upon the Younghusband Report has come from an altogether different quarter. It can be illustrated most forcefully and entertainingly from the pronouncements made by Lady Wootton in her recent book on *Social Science and Social Pathology*. She asserts that social workers are altogether too sensitive about their professional status, too intent upon the glorification of their "human relationship skills", too ready to assume that all human problems have a psychological origin, and too complacent about social injustice and the squalid surroundings that many of their "clients" have to live in. The Younghusband Report, she argued in a recent broadcast, reflects these tendencies only too clearly. What social workers really need is "good manners, ability and willingness to listen, and efficient methods of record keeping". For ordinary people in difficulty they should make arrangements, provide information and procure material help. When dealing with "those who fail to conform to currently acceptable standards of behaviour . . . the plain fact is that in these cases social work is only undertaken with the object of changing people's behaviour in a particular direction".

These criticisms contain too much truth to be disregarded. Indeed, many of them have been made by social workers themselves. But the anxiety of social workers to secure a professional training and professional status cannot be understood merely from a perusal of the literature (particularly the more pretentious American literature that forms the bulk of Lady Wootton's armoury). Take two of the many cases quoted in the Younghusband Report:

> The mother of a single man recently discharged from a second admission to mental hospital, telephoned to the mental welfare officer to say that he was violent and refused to work. She appeared to be an aggressive, accusing woman who resented her loss of income whenever she had to look after her son. The mental welfare officer could find no clear evidence of delusions or violent behaviour . . . the mother required casework help either to accept the son, whom she was trying to push back into the mental hospital, or to make alternative living arrangements for him.

> A large family where all the children wet the bed and the home was very dilapidated; the father appeared to be an immature person who did not keep his jobs or get up in the morning. A home help gave the mother practical assistance in keeping the home clean but the other problems were not being tackled. Some time later . . . one organization . . . offered to "deal with the father". Thereupon he disappeared, the mother felt obliged to go out to work, and the home help was stopped. Later a court action was brought against the mother for neglect and the children were scattered into nurseries or received into care.

Most of us claim to have "good manners, ability and willingness to listen, and efficient methods of record keeping", but would we feel equipped to help such families? Yet it is families of this kind who come to social workers

when doctors, psychiatrists and others with a recognized professional training have washed their hands of them.

Unifying the Service

Moreover, it is not knowledge and skills alone that social workers aspire
to. Not so far behind them lie the traditions of old-fashioned charity and the
Poor Law—the expectation, still lurking in many committees, that social
workers should help the "deserving" and make the undeserving aware of
their disapproval ("dealing with" ineffective fathers). To these pressures are
now added the demands of those who administer the big statutory social
services—administrators who are responsible in the main for serving the
"normal" population that knows its rights, obeys the rules and accepts expert
advice when it is given. To these administrators social workers often appear
to be a handy instrument for coping with the ignorant, helpless, hostile and
feckless—the grit in the administrative machine. Social work will extract
rent from spend-thrift tenants, get awkward old ladies into institutions, move
recalcitrant patients out of hospital (and persuade resentful mothers to care
for their unbalanced sons without any nonsense about "alternative living
arrangements"). Many of the social workers upon whom these pressures are
directed are young and inexperienced; many of them are isolated in departments where they have little contact with other social workers. It would not
be surprising if some of them fell into the habit of gossiping about the private
affairs of those whom they help, if some resorted to bullying and threatening
people who do not conform to their own patterns of behaviour, and if some
were content to satisfy (or fool) their committees rather than maintain the
standards that most social workers would expect. The creation of a united,
self-respecting social work profession with recognized codes of behaviour
and standards of practice may help to protect us all from this kind of
thing.

Our social services still have a long way to go before they justify Britain's
claim to be a Welfare State. But it is already clear that full employment,
decent housing, good education, and a good health service are not enough. If
we also want opportunities for all to make the best of their talents—opportunities to leave the neighbourhoods, friends, and families among whom they
were born and seek their fortune in new places and new jobs—we must
recognize that for some the strain will prove too great. Institutions for the
homeless, mental hospitals, prisons, old people's homes, and children's
homes, all contain a high proportion of people who lack close ties with
friends and relatives. An expanding, changing society must accept responsibility for helping those who may come to grief in it. Social work is one way
of providing that help.

Postscript*

It took three years for the Government to act on the recommendations of the Younghusband Committee, but developments are now proceeding apace. The Health Visiting and Social Work (Training) Act of 1962 established two Councils under a single chairman to supervise, develop and co-ordinate the recruitment and training of health visitors and social workers in the local authority health and welfare services. Both Councils are also empowered to carry out or assist in research dealing with questions relevant to their functions. Each has just over thirty members, seven of whom belong to both Councils, and Sir John Wolfenden was their first chairman.† Goodwill and close collaboration appear to be growing between these bodies.

Several training courses for social workers were set up in anticipation of the 1962 Act, others have since been started and more are being planned. By the autumn of 1963 there were nearly a dozen courses in operation, following fairly closely the pattern outlined in the Younghusband Report. The demand for training among experienced social workers is keen, local authorities are increasingly willing to give their staff up to two years' paid leave of absence for training, and there appears to be a growing interest in social work training of all kinds among the public at large.

National Institute for Social Work Training

The Nuffield Foundation and the Joseph Rowntree Memorial Trust established a National Institute for Social Work Training in 1961. The principal of the Institute (Mr. Robin Huws Jones) was vice-chairman of the Younghusband Committee, and Dame Eileen Younghusband is a part-time member of his staff. The Institute is already providing courses in social work and administration for older and more experienced staff in the welfare, mental health and child-care fields. Among its other activities are the provision of short-term fellowships for trained and experienced workers who may become tutors to "Younghusband courses", and the organization of regular "consultations" between local authority members, officials and social workers concerned with welfare services of various kinds. Thus the Institute does not confine itself to the fairly narrow sector of the social services to which the Council for Training in Social Work is limited. It aims to become a centre of training, research and discussion, serving the whole field of social work.

The foundations have been laid for a major development that could change the face of social work in Britain. But those who will have to build on these

* A further note by Professor D. V. Donnison.
† Later suceeded by Sir Charles Morris.

foundations face some thorny problems, a few of which can be briefly noted here.

The money for the new training courses must be found by local authorities, with no direct support from the central government. The Home Office already contributes in various ways to the training of probation officers and child-care officers, and the Ministry of Health contributes to that of almoners and psychiatric social workers. But in the local authority health and welfare services, where the shortage of trained staff is even greater, a whole new system of training must be launched without such help. It will not be surprising if some conclude that this field is still to be treated as the poor relation of the social work family.

Meanwhile, the development of community care services for the mentally disordered, and the growing numbers of elderly people in our population, both make increasingly heavy demands on the services surveyed by the Younghusband Committee. As some of the most skilled and experienced workers are withdrawn from these services to become tutors and supervisors to the new training courses, standards of service in some areas will almost certainly fall—at least until the output of the two-year training begins to make itself felt.

Renewed efforts are being made—and with some success—to increase the output of trained workers for the child care and probation services. But the relationship between these forms of training and the new "Younghusband courses" has yet to be worked out. Moreover, the types of training to be provided for the local authority health and welfare services have not been settled. The courses started so far follow the two-year pattern, leading to a nationally recognized certificate. Nothing has yet been done about the training of "welfare assistants", and it is unlikely that firm decisions can be taken on this proposal until the future extent and standard of the two-year courses is clarified.

The two-year courses themselves will not be easy to establish in colleges unaccustomed to this form of education. There will undoubtedly be great pressure on those running such courses to adopt the heavy programme of lectures, with scant tutorial supervision and field training, which is familiar in colleges of further education but peculiarly inappropriate for social work training.

University departments of social studies, many of which were originally established to train social workers, may find that a rapid growth of training outside the universities (combined, as it may well be, with a growth of research on social administration carried out in government departments and full-time research institutes) calls for a re-examination of their own functions.

But such problems are an inevitable part of social change, and major changes must be made if the developments now afoot are to achieve the hopes of those who laid the groundwork for them.

References

1. MINISTRY OF HEALTH, *A Hospital Plan for England and Wales*, Cmnd. 1604; *Voluntary Help in Hospitals, The Development of Local Authority, Health and Welfare Services*, Circulars (62) 29 2/62 and 7/62.
2. Report of the Working Party on Social Workers in the Local Authority Health and Welfare Services, 1959.
3. NATIONAL COUNCIL OF SOCIAL SERVICE—Voluntary Social Services, *Handbook and Directory*, 1960.
4. M. P. HALL, *The Social Services of Modern England*.
5. BARBARA N. RODGERS and JULIA DIXON, *Portrait of Social Work, A Study of Social Services in a Northern Town*.
6. EILEEN YOUNGHUSBAND, *Social Work and Social Change*.
7. D. V. DONNISON *et al.*, *Social Policy and Administration*.
8. BARBARA WOOTTON *et al.*, *Social Science and Social Policy*.

SECTION II
LOCAL AUTHORITY WELFARE SERVICES

6. The Local Authority Services

LAURENCE A. PAVITT
Member of Parliament

LOCAL health and welfare authorities are the bodies responsible for providing in England and Wales those health and welfare services which fall outside the hospital service and the general medical services administrated by Executive Councils. Collectively these services are sometimes known as local (or environmental) health and welfare services, or simply as community care. There are 146 local health and welfare authorities, comprising all the county councils and county boroughs of England and Wales. Their statutory duties to provide these services derive from a number of Acts of Parliament, the principal among them being the National Health Service Act of 1946, the National Assistance Act, 1948, and the Mental Health Act, 1959.

The majority of the local authority welfare services are provided under Part III of the National Assistance Act, 1948, covering residential and temporary accommodation and welfare services for all kinds of handicapped persons. The welfare authorities are required to set up a Welfare Committee or Sub-committee to deal with such matters, and there are, in fact, 177 chief welfare officers responsible for the day-to-day administration of these services. Welfare authorities exercise their functions in accordance with schemes approved by the Minister of Health, but have considerable autonomy in carrying them out. The dividing line between health and welfare functions is sometimes blurred, since some local authorities choose to exercise both functions through a single joint committee. Further complications arise when we come to a service like special housing for old people, which could come under the heading of either welfare or housing. Within certain statutory limits local authorities are free to make whatever organizational arrangements suit them best.

The list of services a local authority is required to provide under the heading of health and welfare is a long one. Home nurses and midwives, health visitors, social workers, home helps and mental welfare officers are among the staff they must employ .They must organize after-care of patients discharged from hospital, especially those suffering from psychiatric disorder; they must provide hostels, sheltered workshops, training centres for the mentally and physically handicapped, old people's homes and, occasionally, health centres. They must organize ante-natal and post-natal care in maternity and child welfare centres. They run the ambulance services. They may provide chiropody and laundry facilities for the elderly. This catalogue is by no means exhaustive.

It will be seen that the health and welfare services provide for certain special categories of need, notably the elderly, the handicapped, mothers and babies, as well as providing occasional services for the generality of the population, such as ambulances and after-care. It may be convenient to consider the services under these headings.

The Elderly

By far the largest problem facing local authorities is that of the elderly. It is a problem that has been accentuated by population trends that were not foreseen early enough, and not sufficiently taken into account in forward planning. With developments in therapeutic techniques, and in particular the discovery of antibiotics, the individual's life-span all over the world has been significantly increased. Certain diseases which in the past killed off vast numbers of old people every year have succumbed to the discoveries of modern medicine. In consequence the number of old people, and the proportion of old people in the population, have been steadily rising since the war, in Britain as elsewhere. The actual number of persons over 65 in England and Wales is expected to increase by $7\frac{1}{2}$ million, or about one-third, in the next twenty years. The problem of caring for the old has been further complicated by the chronic housing shortage in the big cities and the urban areas generally. Families with young children often found it impossible to continue to look after the grandparents in conditions of acute overcrowding, and yet were unable, owing to the housing shortage, to move into larger accommodation which would have permitted the three generations to remain under one roof. It is commonly alleged that younger people today are far more prone than was the pre-war generation to offload on to public authorities responsibility for looking after the old folk. The more likely explanation is a practical rather than a moral one, namely that the price of looking after the grandparents may well be the endurance of intolerable conditions for the young children.

Whatever the explanation, local authorities have been confronted with unexpected difficulties in providing accommodation and other facilities for old people. These were intensified by the emergence in the post-war period of the Welfare State and the consequential demand for a higher standard of care than had previously been looked upon as adequate. The inevitable result has been that with rare exceptions, local authorities have been unable to discharge satisfactorily the largest single task they had to perform.

Part III of the National Assistance Act, 1948, placed upon local authorities the duty of providing residential accommodation for old people who for

various reasons are unable to provide it for themselves. The Act as a whole
sought to replace the old charity-based Public Assistance with a statutory
service to which those in proved need had every right of access. But where
residential accommodation was involved, the new service inherited the old
buildings, the public assistance institutions and the workhouses which for
too long continued to constitute the main provision. These buildings, for the
most part spartan, cheerless, indestructible, vast, with no semblance of a
home atmosphere, almost defied modernization. The better local authorities
did what they could, but the result was never satisfactory.

But all the time the problem was growing in size, with more and more old
people to be accommodated. Most authorities built old people's homes of a
very different character, relatively small, intimate, homely and—by earlier
standards at least—well-furnished. Numerically, however, those resident in
the old Public Assistance institutions still formed the majority throughout
the 1950's. The total number of local authority residential places was 76,000
in 1961, including some 5000 places in homes run by voluntary organizations.
In many areas it became progressively more difficult to get old people into
local authority homes of any kind.

The Home Help Service

For those who cannot, or do not need to, enter old people's homes, there
is a range of supportive services designed to make it possible for them to live
in the community at large. The Home Help Service, when it is adequately
provided and efficiently organized, can be an invaluable aid not only to old
people but to mothers with young babies, to invalids and handicapped persons as well. Home helps number rather more than 50,000 for England and
Wales, and all but about 5 per cent of them are employed on a part-time
basis. Three-quarters of their work is devoted to helping old people, and this
proportion covers about a quarter of a million households.

The Home Nurse and the Health Visitor

The home nurse and the health visitor make a substantial contribution
between them towards maintaining old people in their own homes. Roughly
half the home nurse's time is taken up with looking after old people, and this
represents more than 14 million visits in a year to about 430,000 elderly
folk. The health visitor and the social worker are available to supplement the
work of the home (or "district") nurse.

Supportive Services

Since 1959 local health authorities have been empowered to provide chiropody services for old people. Some authorities provide the service themselves, while others delegate it to voluntary organizations and meet the net cost. Laundry services for old people are provided by only a minority of local health authorities. Another important service which enables elderly persons to remain outside institutional care is the delivery of hot cooked meals to their homes. The "Meals on Wheels" Service, as it is invariably called, was started as a voluntary effort by the Women's Voluntary Service. Amending legislation in 1962 made it possible for local authorities to provide meals on wheels themselves, and to subsidize voluntary organizations for this purpose.

The Physically Handicapped

Local authorities are required to make a variety of provisions for the physically and mentally handicapped. Physical handicap covers those who are blind, deaf or dumb, either wholly or partially, as well as "persons who are substantially and permanently handicapped by illness, injury or congenital deformity". The needs of this group may include employment, residential accommodation, skilled help with personal problems of adjustment and recreational facilities. The size of the problem is indicated by the numbers registered with local authorities under the different headings. In 1961 the total for England and Wales was rather more than 250,000, of which nearly half were wholly or partially blind, about one-seventh wholly or partially deaf (including the deaf and dumb) and the remainder classified as generally handicapped. Almost half the total were aged 65 and over.

Local authorities themselves provide residential accommodation for about one in ten of the physically handicapped, and by far the greater part is for the elderly. Voluntary agencies supplement this provision, on behalf of the local authorities, to a modest extent. The main responsibility for the employment of the physically handicapped falls upon the Ministry of Labour, but here, too, local authorities may provide occupation centres for those who are unable to follow normal employment. They also cater for the social needs of this group by means of clubs and social centres.

The Mentally Disordered

The mentally disordered in the community produce a different, and perhaps a more difficult, problem for the local authorities. Their responsibilities towards the mentally disordered are of long standing; until fairly recently some of them were merely permissive, while others had long been mandatory duties. Authorities were required to provide services for the subnormal (previously known as the mentally defective) persons in the community, including training centres for both adults and children. Where mentally sick persons were concerned, they were permitted under the National Health Service Act, 1946, to provide after-care facilities.

The extent to which these responsibilities were discharged by particular authorities varied between very wide limits, but it would be true to say that few indeed undertook more than the barest minimum—even where the task was mandatory. With the passage of the Mental Health Act, 1959, and the making of a new Regulation by the Minister of Health, local authorities' responsibility for the mentally disordered* was re-defined, expanded and made mandatory. Among their additional duties is the acceptance of statutory guardianship over a proportion of the mentally disordered persons in the community.

One of the premises underlying the Mental Health Act, and the Report of the Royal Commission on the Law relating to Mental Illness and Mental Deficiency on which the Act is largely founded, is that there are many patients in mental hospitals who could well live in the community if only the necessary supportive services existed outside. Ideally, community mental health services, as they are collectively called, should embrace hostels for the subnormal, for ex-mental patients and for the elderly confused, training centres for the subnormal, occupation and training centres for the mentally ill who cannot yet return to normal employment, and visiting services carried out by trained social workers and psychiatric social workers.

Since in most areas the foundations for such a service are rudimentary, if that, it is not surprising that progress has been slow in the few years that have elapsed since the Mental Health Act came into operation. Capital for construction or adaptation of buildings and training facilities for the many skilled staff needed are perhaps the basic requirements. At least a start has been made.

Local Services for Mothers and Babies

The services for mothers and babies are relatively well established. They aim at providing ante-natal and post-natal advice and care, often in maternity and child welfare centres whose work is supplemented by the health visitor. There are at present around 6000 child welfare centres, and rather more than 5000 health visitors employed by local authorities. Where a baby is born at home the local authority assumes added responsibilities, including the provision of the domiciliary midwife, of whom there are some 7500, and home nurses and home helps where required. Some local authorities provide day nurseries where children below school age can be looked after while the mother is at work, or when she is ill. The present number of day nurseries, less than 500, is barely a third of the war-time figure.

* "Mentally disordered" is the new term used in the Mental Health Act to include the mentally ill, the subnormal and the severely subnormal.

The Ambulance Service

Lastly there are the services for the population in general. One of the most important of these is the ambulance service which meets the needs of hospital patients, accident cases and the chronic sick and others living in the community who require out-patient treatment or transport to and from training centres. There are in all some 5300 ambulances operating from nearly a thousand stations. Though the provision of ambulances was made a statutory duty of local health authorities by the National Health Service Act, 1946, there are some who consider that the ambulance service should be the responsibility of hospital authorities, since they are the main users of the service.

Conclusion

It will be seen that local authorities are responsible for a wide variety of services. Some try to provide the whole range in full measure; others may wish to maintain only the barest minimum of services. Before the system of General Grants was introduced in 1960, most of the services attracted a specific grant, varying in percentage, from the Central Government. Today, the health and welfare services have to compete, not always successfully, with other important local authority services for a fair share of the General Grant. By any standards these services must be improved and expanded. In a subsequent Chapter (p. 66) we shall consider in 1963 Ten Year Plan for the health and welfare services and examine how feasible these Ten Year Plans are, and how far they go towards matching the likely demands of the community in ten years' time.

7. The Ten Year Plan for Health and Welfare— An Introductory Note

GEOFFREY JOHNSON SMITH
Member of Parliament

THE Plan for the development of the health and welfare services of local authorities in England and Wales cannot be mentioned without reference to the other side of the coin, the Ten Year Plan for the development of the hospital service. With the adoption in 1962 of this Plan for the development and modernization of the hospital service, the National Health Service entered a new phase. It marked the end of a post-war period when existing hospitals were extended and modernized. To make the service truly match up to modern needs, new hospitals were needed, and, more than that, hospitals had to be located in areas where changes in the size and structure of the population made only too clear how obsolescent was the structure of the hospital service itself.

If the N.H.S. as a whole was to be given a "new look", it was obvious that these developments could not be looked at in isolation. There were all the other health and welfare services with their clinics, training centres, home nurses and social workers, which were complementary to the work of the hospitals themselves. They, too, demanded a plan over a period of ten years on equally comprehensive lines. Administrative reasons and logic alone did not create the demand. The concept of care in and by the community had undergone a change since the forties and early fifties, and the time had come to put the new ideas into practice.

There were several influences at work: there had developed a growing appreciation in official quarters of the role of voluntary organizations. The increased welfare responsibilities taken on by the State in the immediate post-war years were seen by some people to lead to the inevitable decline of amateur, part-time help. The image of "Lady Bountiful" patronizingly conscious that she was dispensing charity to the "poor" was an anathema to them. This spirit had no part in the modern Welfare State. The citizen could, and should, look to the provision of health and welfare services as a right; and it was the function of the State to provide them.

Much to their surprise the voluntary organizations did not wither away. Side by side with a growing understanding of the limitations of state provision, there was also a growing recognition of the status of social work and the need to have more and better-trained workers. This, in turn, grew out of the increasing appreciation that community care did not mean mass care often in large institutions run along authoritative lines. To be, at the same time, efficient and humane, welfare services had to be tailored to individual needs, to individuals who should not be segregated from society but encouraged to form part of it.

What focused attention on this trend was the Report of the Royal Commission on Mental Illness and Mental Deficiency, which expressed the conviction that the care of the mentally disordered was primarily the responsibility of the community (acting through its local authority health services) rather than of the mental hospitals. "Community care" and integration into the general life of society was to be the aim rather than segregation.

The implications of this Report and the Mental Health Act which followed are enormous. What goes for the mentally sick (who occupy some 50 per cent of our hospital beds) goes for others in the need of care, the old for instance. At the end of 1961 some 47 per cent of the elderly people in England and Wales were accommodated in former public assistance institutions. These are grim-looking places, far too large and impersonal, and the vast majority can never be adapted. Under the health and welfare plan 24,000 of the 34,000 places will be closed by 1972. This will reduce the proportion of elderly people living in these institutions to 11 per cent.

The Plan for the development of health and welfare services was published in April 1963, and accepts the concept that each local authority must undertake responsibility for increased community care. It seeks to accelerate the expansion of services designed to meet the needs of three broad groups of people: mothers and young children; the elderly; the mentally and physically handicapped.

The aim of all the health and welfare services is not just to help the afflicted but also to forestall illness and disability by preventive measures. Care within the community should be either at home, at specially designed centres or, where necessary, in residential accommodation. This work is to be supported by the family doctor. Indeed, he is the essential link, since he can call to his aid the services of the hospitals or of the local authority whenever he thinks fit.

The Plan embodies the proposals of all the 146 local health and welfare authorities of England and Wales. No attempt was made to enforce uniformity. Each authority has independent responsibility in its own area. The purpose of the Minister of Health was to bring these plans together so that he and the nation could see precisely what was involved. Assessments of future needs are, of course, constantly subject to change. The plan therefore is not definitive and so each local authority has been asked to revise their requirements annually, carrying them forward a further year on each occasion so that plans for the decade ahead will always be in view.

The idea of an annual review makes sense both administratively and financially. I have already implied that there are gaps in our social services which exist partly because we do not allocate enough resources and sometimes because we do not deploy our resources wisely enough. To measure the size of a gap and the existence of new ones entails a continuing analysis of the changing nature and incidence of need.

Spelled out in more detail, what does the Plan mean? First, its provisions for mothers and young children. In 1960 800,000 babies were born; for 1970 the estimate is 900,000. Thus, to cope with the increase, and to develop higher standards, some 1250 new maternity and child welfare clinics will be built. To meet the needs of the clinics for more staff, the Plan calls for about 8600 health visitors, the equivalent of one health visitor for every 100 children born every year. These health visitors, working in co-operation with both family doctors and hospitals, are, in the opinion of many people, of growing significance. Secondly, the aged. Since the Second World War many local authorities have turned to building single-bedroom homes for the elderly. This means they will have to find more home nurses, home helps and chiropody services as well as ensuring the expansion of the "Meals on Wheels" Services pioneered by voluntary organizations. Therefore the number of home nurses is expected to go up from 7000 to nearly 10,000, and of home helps from over 50,000 to 75,000.

There will, of course, be those old people who are too frail, or too handicapped, to live on their own. For them, as I mentioned earlier, smaller residential homes will be built.

Thirdly, there are the mentally and physically handicapped. In their case the aim is to make them feel that they are wanted and needed and that they can make a useful contribution to society. Their special requirements create the need for a tremendous variety of special services. For those who are hard of hearing, the companionship of clubs can do much to compensate them for the isolation which deafness brings. Under the Plan, purpose-built comprehensive centres, where there are both recreational as well as occupational activities (an elderly or partially handicapped person seeking only recreation may be encouraged to shake off his spirit of defeat or lethargy on seeing others doing craft-work), will increase by 185.

The heartless attitude to the mentally subnormal which fear and suspicion have fostered in the past should be entirely swept away thanks to more enlightened public opinion. It is good to note that the capacity of training centres for mentally subnormal children will go up from 13,000 places to 27,000. At similar training centres for adults there will be an increase from 10,600 to 30,000 places.

It has not been my purpose to look for flaws and shortcomings in the plans drawn up by the 146 local authorities, but I think it would be appropriate at this stage to place a few question marks over them which others will go into in greater detail in this book. An interested layman, like myself, can wonder, for instance, whether or not the Plan fully comprehends the need for providing sufficient hostels for those people who have been discharged from psychiatric hospitals but still need more care and time in which to be able to adjust to life within the community.

Another doubt—a wider one this time—concerns the role of social workers. At long last people are beginning to recognize the importance of this role. I hope, though, that as the case load expands, we will resist any trend towards breaking down their work into a series of highly specialized compartments. It is no reflection on those who work in our hospitals to say that hospital life can appear to be almost callous and impersonal. Mrs. Smith in the corner of Ward 10 can be the "heart" or the "kidney" complaint—an incurable just playing out time as strength slowly ebbs from her body, an object of medical curiosity. Returned to the care of a small clinic and her family doctor, within the ambit of friends and neighbours, Mrs. Smith can more easily be seen as a whole personality. It is the social worker visiting a person at home who can see the individual against this background. A social worker with general training should be quick to spot when a kind word, a letter written, a relation contacted, can do as much good, if not more, than all the potions of modern science. Mrs. Smith must be able to call upon specialist services, but the "key" figure is the social worker with a background of general training.

I will conclude by making two general points. First, can we afford the Plan? Secondly, how sure can we be that the present structure of local government will be able to carry it out? There can be no doubt that the Plan is something which is attainable.* Bearing in mind the £600 million Hospital Plan, an additional £200 million for health and welfare services over the last decade is not a sum which even at the present modest rate of growth of our economy† we cannot afford; it is not, in other words, "pie in the sky". It is not based on the assumption that our economy will grow at any faster rate than it has over the past five years. As national income rises, so the amount spent on these other social services can increase without absorbing any higher proportion of the country's resources.

The rate of expansion which can be greater than that proposed under the Plan will depend on the extent to which the public "wills" it. It seems that there is a strong and lively interaction between public demand, public consciousness of a particular social need and the creation or expansion of a service to meet that need. This is why it is so important that local government should be able to shoulder the huge burdens of running these personal and human services. They are community services, and if they are seen to be run by, for and with the community, the interaction I have referred to should

---

* The Plan has now been carried forward to 1974, and over the 10 years to 1973–4 involves the spending of £226·5 million.

† The £600 million Hospital Plan in the 10 years to 1972–3 is also subject to annual review. Their latest revision (May 1964) estimates expenditure over the next 10 years to 1973–4 at £750 million.

maintain impetus. But in carrying out their tasks it is reasonable to suppose that local authorities will have to consider reforms affecting their size and their functions.

Some local authorities may be too small, others will have to consider pooling their resources for some of the more expensive specialized services, and one wonders just how capable the local authorities are of making adaptations and to what extent Parliament itself is conscious of the urgency of this problem.

This Plan is, when all is said and done, a bold venture. Our health service has been described by an American social historian, Professor Almont Lindsay, as "magnificent in scope, and almost breath-taking in its implications". Not least of these implications, as we can see now, is the growing emphasis on the welfare services as an integral part of a properly designed health service. Preventive medicine increasingly comes to mean something more than, say, the handing out of pills, the fixing up of the body by clinical methods. Welfare implies the responsibility for the whole man, mental and physical, and an acceptance that the purpose is to enable man to live as best he can within, and not outside, the community. The Plan does us all a service by emphasizing the increasing value of local welfare authorities up and down the country. With the Hospital Plan and the Health and Welfare Plan, we enter a new phase, the scope of which is a challenge to our ingenuity, but above all, to our humanity.

8. The Ten Year Health and Welfare Plan— A Critical View

LAURENCE A. PAVITT
Member of Parliament

IN APRIL 1963 the Conservative Government produced a White Paper (Command Paper 1973) embodying a Ten Year Plan for the development of the health and welfare services of the local authorities in England and Wales. This is clearly regarded as a companion document to the Hospital Plan published rather more than a year earlier, which sets out the development plans of hospital authorities over the next ten to fifteen years. There are, however, marked differences in the scope and nature of the two White Papers, and in the role played by the Ministry of Health in their production.

In one respect at least the Health and Welfare Plan has been generally welcomed. For the first time local authorities have been forced to look, more or less objectively, at the services they provide under these two headings, and to consider in what respects and to what extent the services should expand in the next decade. The Plan has another virtue in that it enables comparisons to be made, among local authorities themselves and by the public at large, between the services provided in different parts of the country. Self-examination is always a useful exercise.

Widespread Variations

The first thing that must strike anyone who studies the Health and Welfare Plan is the very wide variations over the whole range of services that exist between different authorities. Nor do these variations follow any expected pattern. It is obviously easier to provide services of any kind for a compact, urban population than for one that is more sparsely distributed over a wide area. This might lead one to expect better all-round services from the boroughs than the counties, with their longer lines of communication and their relatively lower rateable values. Such a distinction may be discernible in the community mental health services, but it does not appear to operate generally. Other factors, indeed, work in the opposite direction. Certain needs will be greater among a rural population with less ready access to hospital facilities. The county authority may have to provide more home nurses and midwives than a town population would require.

66

It is therefore difficult to discover any general rule which can explain the wide variations in the provision of health and welfare services. A few examples will serve to illustrate the point. The average number of places in homes for the elderly per 1000 of population is 16·1 for England. Barnsley provides 36·4 and Middlesbrough 32·6, while Staffordshire is content with 9·2 and Blackpool with 7·2, the ratio between the extremes being 4½ : 1. In the case of home helps the ratio is 18 : 1. The average number per 1000 population is 0·55; Rotherham employs 1·18 per 1000, Plymouth only 0·08. Among home nurses the provision varies between narrower limits, as one might expect. The average is 0·17 per 1000, Eastbourne and Rotherham's figure is 0·3, while Bradford, West Hartlepool and the Soke of Peterborough manage with 0·1, a ratio of 3 : 1. The employment of social workers varies in the ratio of 8 : 1. Oldham, Bootle and Barnsley have 0·16 per 1000, Northampton and Hertfordshire only 0·02, the average figure for England being 0·06. When one comes to places in hostels and centres for the mentally disordered, it is impossible to present in statistical form the gap between the extremes, since so many authorities make no provision at all in one or more categories of service.

One might have expected to see a narrowing of these gaps and at least a move in the direction of a more uniform standard of services for the country as a whole, when one comes to examine the targets for 1972. In fact the variations will be hardly less striking in ten years' time. A general expansion is certainly forecast in the Plan, and some laggard authorities have recognized the need to do better in future, but many will be as far behind the national averages in 1972 as they are today.

Lack of Preparatory Work

This end result is largely inherent in the White Paper, which is not a plan at all in the accepted sense of the word. In order to show this it is necessary to examine the basis and origins of the Ministry's White Paper. Once the decision was taken to draw up a development programme for local health authorities on similar lines to the Hospital Plan, the Ministry of Health might have taken one of two courses. It could have laid down certain standards to which each authority should in general conform by the end of the ten-year period, making due allowance for local variations in need. For example, guidance could have been given as to the appropriate number of home helps needed per 1000 of population, or the number of places in homes for the elderly. Alternatively, when the individual plans of the local authorities had been studied, they could have been referred back by the Ministry for reconsideration of those aspects of the services which were likely still to be inadequate at the end of the period. In fact, the Ministry appears to have taken neither course. No initial guidance was given to local health authorities, who were asked merely to provide statistical information about certain of their existing services, and to indicate what expansion, if any, they anticipated between now and 1972. The resulting programmes, with only minor revisions at the Ministry's instance, were collated and published as the Appendix (of 320 pages) to the White Paper (of 48 pages). The White Paper itself sets out in 162 paragraphs to amplify the information provided, to cover the bare statistical bones of the Appendix, and to set out certain considerations which would have been most useful to the local authorities if they had been set out in advance. These paragraphs cannot, however, conceal that the White Paper falls far short of the national plan it purports to be.

Need for Co-ordination and Research

The opening paragraphs of the White Paper stress the interdependence of the hospital services, the local authority services and the general practitioner

Yet little or no co-ordination, or even consultation, with either the hospital or the general practitioner services is apparent. Nor does there seem to have been much liaison even between adjacent local authorities in drawing up their plans. These appear to have been concocted by each separate authority in a vacuum.

One good reason why more guidance was not made available to the county boroughs and county councils is that all too little information existed upon which such guidance could have been based. Apart from a few local studies, no central research has been carried out into future—or even present —needs in any of the fields covered by the White Paper, nor into the possibilities of adequate numbers of trained staff coming forward to meet future demands. The need for such research is obliquely touched upon in paragraph 9 of the White Paper. One incidental virtue of the document is that its production will stimulate, and to some extent facilitate, the required surveys.

Perhaps the fundamental weakness of the White Paper lies in its failure to introduce any new concepts of community care. The Plan tacitly accepts, and is based upon, the existing pattern of health and welfare services. The assumption that this pattern is not only right for today but will remain appropriate to the needs of the 1970's does not command general acceptance. Many believe that a more radical reassessment of the whole structure of the community services will have to be undertaken as soon as sociological research has provided the tools for this purpose.

Does the Plan Match the Need?

The White Paper provokes two major questions. Are the planned develop ments likely to be adequate? Are the objectives likely to be reached by 1972? In the light of such information as we have at present the answers to both are bound to be speculative to some extent. It is always difficult to prove or disprove that services of this nature are adequate to meet needs, since needs are often hidden where no services, or only rudimentary services, exist. Nowhere is this more true than in the mental health services, where often the provision of a new service appears almost to create a demand for it. The real explanation is that many people who suffer from the milder forms of mental disorder, and who would benefit from special care or treatment which is not readily available, contrive to get by without it, often causing distress to themselves and their families. Some break down completely in the end and become psychiatric in-patients. One of the functions of a community mental health service is to prevent people from becoming psychiatric casualties of this kind. Where no service exists it is quite impossible to measure the extent of this particular need. There are, however, other functions of this service which are more capable of assessment. It is known that there are many thousands of subnormal patients in hospital today who could live in the community if the necessary supportive services—hostels, training centres and social work support—were available in sufficient quantity. Similarly, our mental hospitals contain a large number of elderly patients who are mildly confused, if that, and who do not need the medical and nursing care that only a hospital can provide. They could be more suitably cared for in special hostels run by the local health authority, if such places existed. There is no indication in the White Paper that either category will be sufficiently catered for by 1972. Indeed, hardly any authorities are planning special homes for the elderly mentally infirm. Though rather more provision is being made for the subnormal, the great majority of those who could now leave hospital will still be there ten years hence.

The Needs of the Elderly

Many who have studied the Hospital Plan and the Health and Welfare Plan consider that neither proposes sufficient provision for the elderly. They believe that in both documents the Ministry of Health has seriously underestimated the seriousness and the size of the problem. If the critics are right, and the statistics appear to be on their side, there will be in ten years' time a serious deficiency in accommodation for old people in general hospitals, in chronic sick hospitals, and in local authority welfare homes. It is true that, through new construction and the abandonment of many of the large "workhouse" type of homes, accommodation will be of a better standard, but the White Paper itself points out that in 1972 no less than 14,000 old people (11 per cent of the total) will still be accommodated in the former public assistance institutions. In this respect at least, the Ministry has asked local authorities to think again, and to aim at eliminating all these institutions by 1972 or thereabouts.

It is not only in the provision for residential care for the elderly that the Plan is likely to fall down. In many, perhaps the majority of, areas the services required to maintain old folk in their own homes—those provided by home helps, home nurses, health visitors and social workers—are clearly going to be insufficient. The White Paper quotes the Registrar-General's estimates of the expected increase in the number of old people in the next twenty years—32·5 per cent in those aged 65 and over; 40·5 per cent in those aged 75 and over. Yet there is little evidence that the figures have been brought forcefully to the attention of the local authorities, still less that they have acted upon them in compiling their development programmes.

Will the Targets Be Achieved?

Leaving aside for the moment the adequacy or otherwise of the Plan, what are the chances of its targets being achieved? This will depend in the main on two factors: first, upon the determination of each authority to press ahead each year with its programmes and find the necessary money from its rate income and from the General Grant; and, secondly, upon the availability of substantially increased numbers of trained staff.

It cannot be said that the outlook is wholly encouraging on either count. No local authority is committed to fulfilling its projected programme, nor could it be. In most instances it would probably be unfair to dismiss the programmes as no more than pious hopes, but among medical officers of health there is a good deal of scepticism about the chances of reaching their stated targets. They have perhaps seen too many worthy schemes postponed on account of financial stringency in the past.

Shall We Get the Trained Staff?

Doubts must also exist whether sufficient trained personnel will be forthcoming. Table 10 of the White Paper sets out the estimated numbers of different categories of staff called for by the Plan. In many instances the proportionate increases are considerable. In approximate percentages we shall need 270 per cent more general-trained and 180 per cent more university-trained social workers in 1972 than are employed today; 50 per cent more home helps; 50 per cent more health visitors; 25 per cent more home nurses and midwives; and 200 per cent more welfare assistants. The total increase required for England and Wales will be about 37,000, or nearly 50 per cent. These are considerable numbers for staff of good educational standard, most of whom will require a training of some years' duration. Only recently was any action taken to implement the Younghusband Report on Social Work

Training, and the number of courses for general training so far established will hardly provide the social workers required.

Even if training facilities were adequate, the question arises as to the chances of attracting sufficient men and women into a field where the work is exacting and the remuneration unspectacular. It is true that opportunities for employment in industry are bound to diminish as automation progresses, leaving more men and women free to pursue a career in other fields, of which the social services must be one. But the social services are undermanned today and no one can be sure that the expected increase in recruits will do more than keep pace with the expansion of the services. In any event a special type of recruit is needed for much of this work, and there are competitive demands from other forms of public service for the same recruits.

There seems to be a strong argument for a national manpower survey to determine the size of the pool on which the various forms of public service will be able to draw in the future, and if necessary to suggest some kind of quota system to ensure that staffing requirements are realistically expressed. Until such a survey is carried out, it is impossible to say whether or not the manpower targets implicit in the Health and Welfare Plan can be achieved.

At Least a Beginning

The development of community care is of sufficient importance to warrant a searching and critical examination of the Ten Year Plan for which so much has been claimed by its authors. No apology need be made for pointing out some of its defects. At the same time it must be acknowledged that an important beginning has been made. The Minister of Health has stressed that this document, like the Hospital Plan, is flexible. It will be revised annually and can be adapted to changing needs. Much adaptation will undoubtedly be necessary, and already the Minister has recognized one important lacuna in the Plan by requiring local authorities to state their intentions, at the first annual review, as to the provision of special housing for the elderly.

It will be argued in favour of the White Paper that local authorities are masters in their own house and that the Ministry of Health does not seek to dictate to them. In the eyes of many this doctrine has been carried to extremes. Guidance from the summit is essential if an intolerable variation of standards is to be avoided. Such guidance and advice can be given without dictation and without the imposition of rigid criteria over the whole of England and Wales. Local differences can be respected and allowance made for them, but a minimum standard of service must be demanded of all authorities in the interests of the population as a whole.

9. Reorganization of Welfare Services in Essex*

WALTER E. BOYCE

County Welfare Officer, County Council of Essex

SINCE the National Assistance Act in 1948 set up welfare services to replace those formerly provided under the Poor Law system, there has been a continual process of development and expansion. Most of this growth has taken place unobtrusively, but the trend in recent years towards community care in the social services has tended to emphasize the importance of the role of the welfare services.

The publication of the Younghusband *Report on Social Workers in the Health and Welfare Services,* the Minister of Health's request to local authorities to prepare plans for the development of the health and welfare services during the next ten years, and also the various proposals for the reorganization of local government in the Greater London area and other parts of the country, have all heightened interest in these services and the varying ways in which local authorities have organized them to suit local conditions.

The Essex County Council in 1962 undertook a review of their welfare services to ensure that they are efficiently organized after the very rapid expansion in the last few years and would be able to meet the demands arising from the further development proposed in the Ten Year Plan. As a result, a reorganization of area administration has now been completed, which is designed to meet not only the present needs but also to provide a sound basis of administration for the development proposed over the next ten years.

Essex has a population of about 1,900,000, of whom some 900,000 live within the densely populated Greater London area. Many parts of the County, including two new towns, are expanding quickly, but there are also rural areas adjoining the counties of Hertfordshire, Cambridgeshire and Suffolk where different problems arise.

The full range of welfare services under the National Assistance Act for the elderly and infirm, homeless families, the blind and other handicapped persons, have been delegated to a Welfare Committee, with a separate Welfare Department under a designated principal county officer, the County Welfare Officer.

* Adapted from articles in the *Municipal Journal.*

Review of Development Since 1948

In its review the Welfare Committee trace the development of the services since 1948. Residential accommodation for the elderly and infirm, administered directly by the Committee, has increased from three small homes in 1948 to the present figure of forty-two homes, and a total of 2900 residents are being cared for in these homes and in homes where agency arrangements have been entered into. Four or five purpose-built homes are now being opened each year, and it is anticipated that the Committee will have seventy-eight small homes, accommodating up to sixty old people in each, at the end of the ten-year development period in 1972.

Five of the old institutions shared with the Hospital Boards have already been replaced, and the remainder of this type of accommodation will have been evacuated by 1967–8. In addition, plans have been made to provide accommodation to meet such special needs as the younger physically handicapped and the elderly mentally infirm.

To assist old people to remain independent in the community for as long as possible, and also to relieve the heavy demand for places in the Welfare Committee's homes, the Committee have been working very closely with the county district authorities on the provision of special housing for old people. The Committee's officers have assisted in the preparation of these special housing schemes, and substantial financial aid has been given to the housing authorities to meet the cost of welfare facilities provided for the elderly tenants. For the same reasons, the Committee have given considerable financial support to voluntary organizations providing a wide range of services for old people living in their own homes, and a very close liaison has been built up with local Old People's Welfare Committees and their officers.

The provision of temporary accommodation for homeless families has presented many problems of special difficulty since 1948. In addition to providing units at which some eighty-five families can be provided with temporary accommodation, the Committee has developed a family case-work service. This service, at the present time, is undertaking preventive work with 380 families who have been referred by housing authorities as in danger of eviction. It also undertakes rehabilitative training for families in temporary accommodation and supervision of families who have been re-housed by housing authorities under a two-year rent guarantee scheme.

Services for the blind, including a placement service, have continued to grow slowly since 1948, and are responsible for helping more than 4000 blind and partially sighted persons registered with the Welfare Department.

Services for the physically handicapped have developed more recently. The number of handicapped persons registered has increased from 2500 in

1959 to 4400 at the present time, and considerable further expansion is anticipated in the Ten Year Plan. Officers undertaking duties similar to those carried out by the Home Teachers of the Blind now visit the handicapped in their homes and give instruction in handicrafts, issue aids and gadgets and give advice and help with structural alterations in the homes of the handicapped to permit them to become more independent. Provision of occupational centres, to which handicapped persons can be taken in special transport, is being developed. These centres are intended primarily to provide a wider social contact for the severely handicapped people who attend, but they also provide them with a source of pocket money from the sale of handicrafts or from light out-work undertaken for industry. Four centres of this kind, each accommodating 40–60 persons per day, are now operating, and a further sixteen are proposed in the Ten Year Development Plan.

In the County, work for the deaf has been undertaken entirely under agency arrangements by voluntary organizations. The Committee now propose, with the full agreement of the voluntary agencies, to provide directly a domiciliary service for the deaf similar to that provided for the blind and the handicapped. This will allow the voluntary organizations, with continued financial support from the County Council, to concentrate their activities on the spiritual and recreational work amongst the deaf.

Requirements of the New Area Organization

In the light of all these developments, and those flowing from the Health Visiting and Social Work (Training) Act of 1962, the County Council decided that reorganization of their area administration should be undertaken, and that the main objectives of the new administrative pattern should be: First to provide an adequate local organization to maintain contact with all the individual persons looking to the local authority's welfare services for assistance. Secondly, the new organization should provide for the coordination in the local offices of all the fieldwork undertaken in the various welfare services, which had tended to grow up independently as specialist services.

It was also thought to be of the greatest importance that the organization should be such that the knowledge and skill of the trained social workers coming into the service from the universities and from the new two-year training courses could be utilized to the best advantage. It would also be important that the staff establishment should provide an attractive career structure to aid the recruitment of persons of the right calibre, and to give the trained social workers, administrative staff and welfare assistants reasonable prospects of promotion to more senior and responsible posts.

Such a local organization, on which a team of social workers with a wide range of interests would be centred, would provide a focal point to facilitate the vital co-operation with other social services, such as the hospitals, housing departments, health services and voluntary organizations.

The New Area Organization

To meet these requirements it was decided that the following changes should be made. First, that the size of the areas into which the County was divided for welfare purposes should be substantially reduced. The County has now been divided into seven new areas, the size of these areas outside the Metropolitan part of the County varying according to acreage from 120,000 to 300,000 people, but in the Metropolitan area, in view of the proposed changes of the local government structure, a higher population figure of approximately 450,000 in each of the two areas was accepted.

It was decided that the duties to be undertaken in the Area Welfare Offices should, in addition to the day-to-day supervision of residential accommodation, include the supervision and co-ordination of the casework undertaken for all the welfare services in the area. This included the services for the blind, the physically handicapped and the family casework for homeless families, which had, up to that time, been supervised centrally.

To carry out these duties it was decided that the staff establishment at each of the Area Offices should include an Area Welfare Officer, an Assistant Area Welfare Officer and a sufficient number of social welfare officers and welfare assistants to provide approximately one officer for each 120 of the total caseload in the area. Provision has also been made for the administrative and clerical assistance required for the day-to-day supervision of the old people's homes in the area, and to carry out duties of a purely clerical nature for the social workers.

As part of the plan for recruiting and training more social workers, it was decided that a scheme of in-service training should be introduced as part of the headquarters organization of the Department. This training, primarily intended for the newly recruited welfare assistants, would also be used, where necessary, for existing staff at present undertaking specialized social work duties. To undertake this work an additional post was created at the Department's Headquarters Office for a Senior Social Worker to be responsible for the organization of training.

On this basis the establishments tabulated overleaf were approved for each of the new welfare areas.

The Committee recognize that it would be some years before there would be sufficient social workers trained under the new arrangements to fill all the above posts, but existing officers have been placed in the social welfare officers' grade, in accordance with recommendations of the National Joint Council. When the reorganization was introduced, these officers continued to carry the type of caseload they previously had, but with a reduction in

Area	Area Welfare Officer	Asst. Area Welfare Officer	Social Welfare Officers	Welfare Assts.	Administrative and clerical
Metropolitan West (pop. 440,030)	1	1	12	2	10
Metropolitan East (pop. 429,910)	1	1	12	2	10
Forest (pop. 226,260)	1	1	6	1	6
South-East (pop. 314,540)	1	1	9	2	7
Central (pop. 179,450)	1	1	6	1	6
North-West (pop. 127,730)	1	1	5	1	6
North-East (pop. 177,680)	1	1	8	2	6

caseloads, the recruitment of more trained social workers, and with experience and training within the new organization these existing officers are gradually taking over a wider range of responsibilities.

These new arrangements have now been in operation for a few months, and already a considerable number of members of the public, general practitioners and other social workers have commented on the advantages of having the co-ordinated welfare services in their area. In addition, it has been possible to attract young people of good educational standards into the service as welfare assistants, with a view to their eventual training as social welfare officers. A number of these, and also some of the more experienced officers, have been accepted for the two-year training courses for general social work, and have been seconded to undertake the training course whilst still in the employment of the County Council.

10. Local Authority Welfare Services in Scotland

THOMAS TINTO
Principal Welfare Services Officer, Corporation of Glasgow

THE local authorities responsible for the welfare services in Scotland are the counties, the four counties of cities—Glasgow, Edinburgh, Dundee and Aberdeen—and the large burghs. The large burghs are, broadly speaking, those burghs with a population of more than 20,000. There are in Scotland thirty-three counties, two pairs of which—Perth and Kinross, and Moray and Nairn—are combined for certain purposes, and twenty large burghs.

It has been felt in many circles that the area and resources of some of the authorities are too small to provide a standard of services in keeping with national trends and acceptable to public opinion. The Scottish Development Department presented to Parliament in June 1963 a White Paper (Cmnd. 2067) on the *Modernization of Local Government in Scotland*, which suggested among other things that the local health and welfare services might be administered by new enlarged counties and the counties of cities. There will no doubt be much discussion before Parliament introduces legislation for the proposed modernization.

Residential Accommodation

Under Section 21 of the National Assistance Act the local welfare authority has a duty to provide residential accommodation for persons who by reason of age, infirmity or any other circumstances are in need of care and attention which is not otherwise available to them.

Local housing authorities have a duty to provide housing for the population and the Regional Hospital Boards have the duty to provide hospital accommodation, including long-term accommodation for those in need of it.

The welfare authority's residential accommodation falls between those two authorities. At the border-line between housing responsibilities and the welfare authority's, one of the most interesting developments in Scotland was the provision of cottage homes for elderly people at Crookston in Glasgow by the Corporation of Glasgow Welfare Committee (now the Health and Welfare Committee), a development which took place between 1934 and 1939. They were built adjacent to a large residential home from which services are provided. Eight blocks were built, four of eight houses, two of sixteen and two of twenty, providing on two floors seventy-two houses for single persons and thirty-two for couples, accommodating a total of 136 old people. Each cottage has a sitting room with an open bedroom off it, a kitchenette and bathroom, completely furnished and equipped. Radio is provided; they are heated by electricity, with one open solid-fuel fire. The residents are issued with food to provide their morning and evening meals. Dinner at midday is cooked in a central kitchen and is served in day rooms which accommodate a maximum of thirty-six residents. Television is provided in the day rooms. These cottages are part of the Corporation's residential accommodation for those in need of care and attention and the residents in the cottages represent the fittest of those accommodated under Section 21 of the National Assistance Act. They therefore represent accommodation provided on the welfare side of the border-line between housing authority and welfare authority.

At the other end of the scale there is the border-line between welfare and hospital. The needs of old people on both sides of this border-line are more pressing as they cannot all be provided with adequate care by the domiciliary services. On the hospital side of the border there is the geriatric hospital or long-stay unit. On the welfare side the old person is described as "frail ambulant" and the type of home sometimes referred to as "frail ambulant unit". The division of responsibility between the hospital and welfare authority has been set out in Scotland in the appendix to the Department of Health for Scotland, Circular No. 60/1958, printed at the end of this article.

In order that the community might be served best by its welfare homes and hospitals for the aged, it is most important that there should be good and reliable co-operation between the local authority welfare officers and hospital geriatric physicians. An interesting example of this co-operation exists in Glasgow where a geriatric physician visits regularly a home for fifty frail ambulant residents and is able to give advice on residents who could benefit from specialist geriatric treatment in hospital and can also refer confidently to the local authority patients fit for discharge from hospital, in the full knowledge of the suitability of the residence for the old person (reported in the *Lancet*, 28 April 1962, p. 903, Dr. N. H. Nisbet).

Frail ambulant accommodation is more expensive to maintain as 24-hour staffing is always necessary.

While some residential accommodation in Scotland is in former Poor Law institutions, variously modernized, most of it is provided in houses adapted for the purpose or in more recent years in purpose-built homes. The adapted house has the disadvantage of few single rooms, limited ground-floor accommodation and is not always suitable for the installation of a lift. On the other hand, the external architecture and sometimes the internal as well is more in keeping with older people's ideas of domestic design which is not always possible in purpose-built homes. A Commonwealth civil servant studying social work in Glasgow, after visiting adapted and purpose-built homes, observed: "When I get back home I am going to build two old houses and adapt them." Mainly because of expense it has not always been possible to provide single bedrooms for all residents, but recently Stirling County Council Welfare Committee has been given approval by the Central Department for the building of a Home for 26 residents, 20 being in single rooms and 6 in double rooms, a separate toilet being provided for each room.

Voluntary organizations have made a substantial contribution in the provision of homes for the aged, including the Church of Scotland, the Roman Catholic Church, the Salvation Army, the Jewish community and Earl Haig Fund. There are also one or two old private Trusts which provide homes, and where a home in England is considered to be particularly suitable for any resident, Scottish local authorities do agree to their being accommodated in them, e.g. the Royal Alfred Homes for Merchant Seamen, voluntary homes for the aged deaf and blind.

Residential accommodation for the younger infirm and disabled has presented different problems. No local authority in Scotland has its own home for the disabled. Such accommodation has been provided by voluntary organizations and among them are the Epileptic Colony (Bridge of Weir), Cheshire Homes and such homes as the Searchlight Home at Newhaven.

Temporary accommodation provided under Section 21 (1) (b) of the National Assistance Act for those who are in urgent need thereof, being need arising in circumstances which could not reasonably have been foreseen or in such other circumstances as the authority may in any particular case determine, is not in such demand in Scotland as it is in London and in other industrial areas in England and is usually provided when required in Scotland in former Poor Law institutions.

Residential services for the disabled are frequently associated with the welfare services for the disabled. For example, at Largs in Ayrshire the Scottish Branch of the British Red Cross Society have for some years had a home for young disabled persons where there has been a regular programme of rehabilitation. The endeavour has been marked with considerable success and the next stage has now been reached when the Red Cross have now built there a sheltered workshop with a hostel attached and the young disabled there are accommodated under the local authority's welfare services provisions under Section 29 of the National Assistance Act.

Recently the Church of Scotland opened in Glasgow a hostel for epileptic young men who may come from any part of Scotland and who, it is hoped, will be able in Glasgow to have industrial training and employment.

Welfare Services for the Disabled

The Blind

The blind section of the disabled were the first disabled persons for whom local authorities had the responsibility of providing welfare services. In

Scotland the home teacher service, which is the main service for the blind in their own homes, is provided by voluntary organizations as agents for the local authorities, except in Glasgow and Stirlingshire, which two authorities employ their own home teachers, but even in those two areas there are the additional facilities made available by the Mission to the Outdoor Blind for Glasgow and the West of Scotland which provides the home-teaching service for the other authorities in the south-west of Scotland.

There are five sheltered workshops for the blind in Scotland—in Inverness, Aberdeen, Dundee, Edinburgh and Glasgow. The first four are operated by voluntary organizations, and the Glasgow workshop, which is the largest, is administered by a Joint Committee made up of representatives of seven counties, the County of the City of Glasgow, and fifteen large burghs.

The Glasgow workshop employed, at 1 April 1963, 317 journeymen and women, of whom 30 were sighted-disabled persons, and 46 trainees, of whom 9 were sighted-disabled.

The organization and activities of all the workshops for the blind will be affected by the organization which has been established following upon the publication of the *Report of the Working Party on Workshops for the Blind* (H.M.S.O., 1962). The Minister of Labour has established a non-profit making Limited Company named Industrial Advisers to the Blind, Limited, to provide advisory service for workshops for the blind (including any necessary surveys and investigations) and developing a trading service to sell workshops' products and buy raw materials for them. The Minister also intends to carry out a review in consultation with the company of the likely need for capital development in the workshops during the ten-year period from 1 April 1963.

The placement service for the placing in open employment of blind persons has for some years in Scotland been provided by the Ministry of Labour, while in England and Wales this placement service was provided by voluntary organizations. In terms of Ministry of Labour Circular 14/8/63 the Minister of Labour has provided the placement service for the whole of the United Kingdom as from 1 October 1963.

The Deaf and Dumb

In Scotland the services for the deaf and dumb are principally provided by voluntary organizations, supported by the local authorities. The co-operation is very real; for example, in Glasgow holiday accommodation for the aged deaf and dumb is provided by the Corporation of Glasgow.

The Generally Handicapped

Probably the first needs of handicapped persons are for housing conditions in which they can live the most normal lives and, in common with other authorities throughout the United Kingdom, in Scotland local authorities provide adaptations and gadgets in the homes of the disabled. Important in this connection is co-operation with the hospitals, particularly with the orthopaedic and neurological departments of the hospitals, in order that suitable domestic arrangements can be made prior to the discharge from hospital of severely disabled persons. At times questions arise as to the provision of medical equipment for domiciliary use by patients coming out of hospital and the following are the principles that have been agreed and are set out in the Department of Health for Scotland Circular 23/1960:

(a) Appliances which must be "tailor-made" to individual patients should be the responsibility of the Regional Hospital Board.
(b) On discharge from hospital special equipment required by a patient without which he would have to remain in hospital for treatment should be supplied by the Regional Hospital Board.
(c) Items of home nursing equipment recommended by the general practitioner (other than those prescribable on Form E.C. 10) should be supplied by the local authority.

(i) Invalid chairs (for outdoor and indoor use and with or without commode facilities)

Supply on a permanent basis is the responsibility of the Regional Hospital Board. The Regional Hospital Board will also supply on a temporary basis where, in the opinion of the hospital authorities, the items are required for the continuation of treatment begun in hospital.

(ii) Spinal carriages
(iii) Hospital-type beds with mattresses
(iv) Self-lifting apparatus

The principle (b) above should be applied.

(v) Crutches

Either the Regional Hospital Board or the local health authority might supply as appropriate; for example, crutches used in the hospital and fitted to individual patients' needs might be issued on loan by the Regional Hospital Board.

Many local authorities provide clubs where the centres of population make this possible. The employment situation in Scotland has made it more difficult to provide paid homework for the disabled on any large scale but it has been possible in a limited field. This is a field in which co-operation with voluntary organizations has been most successful and yet there are those who think that there are probably too many separate organizations dealing with different disabilities. In Glasgow we feel that advantage should always be taken of the personal interest that many of its citizens have in particular disabilities and we therefore co-operate gladly with all the voluntary organizations. For example, in one of our welfare services centres, Laurieston House, which is close to the centre of the town, Glasgow Corporation provides facilities for clubs run by a variety of voluntary organizations, i.e. the Scottish Epilepsy Association, the Multiple Sclerosis Association, the Muscular Dystrophy Group, the Scottish Society for Mentally Handicapped Children, and the Disabled Drivers Association. A troop of handicapped Girl Guides also meets at Laurieston House.

The Department's special transport is available for taking disabled persons to their clubs and for outings. In this connection we have found smaller 12-seaters to be the most desirable. Larger buses lose too much time collecting the disabled persons and 8–10 persons represents about the maximum number who can be collected and returned home and still have a substantial part of the day available for the main activity.

Sheltered workshops for the generally handicapped have been later in development than the blind workshops, but we have in Scotland Remploy factories and also sheltered workshops provided by the Red Cross and the Scottish Epilepsy Association. Recently Stirling County Council and Falkirk Town Council opened a small sheltered workshop under their joint control. The Scottish Council for the Care of Spastics, whose activities have been developing considerably recently, have in the west of Scotland a training and works centre on one of the industrial estates outside Glasgow. Sheltered employment has also been provided by the old-established Cripple Aid Societies.

In order that the services for the disabled might be made available to those in greatest need, we have in Glasgow an after-care service which operates in co-operation with the Education Service and Youth Employment Service, under which all physically and mentally handicapped children leaving special school are interviewed by our after-care officers and provided with the appropriate services. Similarly, we are building up relations with the hospitals, as referred to earlier, in respect of patients who will require disabled welfare services on discharge from hospital, and contact with general practitioners is also being intensified.

Services for Old People

Under Section 31 of the National Assistance Act, 1948, as amended by the National Assistance Act, 1948, (Amendment) Act, 1962, local authorities have power to make arrangements for the provision of meals and recreation for old people and may employ as their agents for this purpose voluntary organizations. The Meals on Wheels Service is probably the best-known service under this section of the Act, and grants are also given to a variety of voluntary organizations providing these services.

One of the more interesting recent developments has been the setting up of the Glasgow Retirement Council which has as its main purpose the promotion of education for retirement and occupational activities on retirement. This Council was set up following a conference called by the Lord Provost of the City in October 1957, and each year courses on preparation for retirement are run as day-release courses at one of the further education colleges in Glasgow. Courses are run separately for men and for women, and are attended by men and women approaching retirement. Each course meets for an introductory evening and on one day per week for seven successive weeks.

In addition to these courses the Retirement Council, which has enjoyed financial support from the National Corporation for the Care of Old People and from the Corporation of Glasgow, have been able to set up a number of crafts and hobbies centres which, along with the study courses, are also supported by the Corporation of Glasgow Education Committee.

The kind of services for the care of old people which is being aimed at in Scotland is illustrated in the Memorandum issued by the Department of Health for Scotland, now the Scottish Home and Health Department, which concludes this chapter, and acknowledgement is made to that Department who have agreed to the reproduction of this important circular on one aspect of the welfare services in Scotland which is receiving increasing attention.

Care of the Elderly

Memorandum of the Scottish Home and Health Department*

This memorandum gives a brief account of the services required for the adequate care of old people, whether these are provided by the statutory authorities or voluntary agencies, and attempts to sum up present experience of the problems and of the lines on which solutions may be found. It is hoped that the memorandum may help both fieldworkers and authorities to see how their own duties and powers link up with those of others. The service for the elderly—best regarded as one service, not as several—depends on finding the cases requiring help and advice, and this can only be done by regular and active visitation. The family doctor is in a very favourable position to initiate services, but important work in maintaining health and initiating needed services can be done also by the health visitor, as a key preventive fieldworker of the local health authority service. There is ample scope for more voluntary effort but the best value from voluntary work is obtained where there is full co-operation between statutory and voluntary services.

Old people prefer to live their lives in their own way. This desire for

---

* This memorandum on the care of the elderly was issued by the department of Health for Scotland, June 1956. (Now the Scottish Home and Health Department.)

independence has to be respected, and they should be helped to go on living in their own homes. The growing proportion of elderly in the population makes it essential also to take measures to prevent or postpone the stage at which care in a hospital or in a welfare home becomes inevitable. There should normally be no admission of old people to hospital unless they need the medical or nursing treatment which can be provided there and there alone. Only those who cannot do without the care and attention of a welfare home should go there.

A kind but brisk outlook is proper to welfare work for the elderly and three principles are suggested:

    (i) Keep them in their own homes.
   (ii) Get them out of their homes.
  (iii) Give them the feeling of security.

Under the first head are included the various measures to provide meals for old people who live alone and who cannot or will not cook for themselves. If old people do not receive proper and regular nourishment they become liable to deteriorate physically and perhaps mentally, and thereby become a direct charge on the hospital or welfare service. There are various ways of providing meals for old people who need them; some can best be persuaded to go out for meals, but for some it is better that meals should be brought to them in their own homes. The aim should be to provide at least three cooked meals per week. (The National Assistance Board may be prepared to assist financially in appropriate individual cases where the old person has incurred extra expense.)

   (a) Frequently old people are helped through good neighbours from whom they may receive a meal or with whom they may share a meal. This method has much in its favour.
   (b) Lunch clubs are popular in many places. They form an excellent way of bringing old people together and of helping them to spend a pleasant hour or two. The meals themselves can be drawn from private caterers or made on club premises.
   (c) Some organizations have a very useful arrangement with the school meals service. They collect meals at cooking depots and deliver them to old people's houses in insulated containers. Other organizations have similar arrangements with works canteens.
   (d) Others again have made arrangements with private caterers whereby old people attend at a restaurant and hand over a voucher in their name. This arrangement is useful to cover holiday periods when school kitchens are closed.

The main responsibility for providing meals for old people still lies with voluntary organizations who have already done splendid work in this connection, but further advances, on some such lines as those suggested, are needed, and voluntary organizations and local welfare authorities would do well to seek the co-operation of each other. It is important, of course, to see that this service goes only to those who need it (on other than financial grounds) and it is advantageous if medical advice is available either from the general medical practitioner or from the local authority. (It is a sound principle that an old person should contribute to the cost of meals.) Dependence on outside organizations for meals should not be overdone: there are elderly people, who, for various reasons, have ceased to prepare meals for themselves and who can be encouraged to develop a revived interest in cooking to the benefit not only of their physical condition but also of their self-esteem.

Recreation

Getting people out of their homes means bringing them into the life around them. To areas which have a strong community tradition, as for example many mining areas have, this may come more easily than to others. Clubs and hobby centres are a help; a recreation in which old people are able to be active themselves is more effective than one where they are simply spectators. Anything they can do for others is good; they like above all to know that they are not forgotten and are wanted.

Visitation

To give them the feeling of security is important for their happiness. Here the various domiciliary services of the local authority join with the work of the voluntary agencies. Loneliness can be the bane of old age and many old people are immensely encouraged by a regular visit from some friend. This is one of the attentions to which the voluntary agencies devote themselves. Perhaps the secret of bringing happiness to old people is to understand them and be willing to listen to their tales. Many who visit elderly people have found it rewarding but it is not a job that can be hurried. Three are as many as any one individual can expect to visit regularly. There is much to be said for encouraging people on retirement to take up this valuable work for those who are rather older than themselves.

Domiciliary Services

Where local authorities exercise to the full their powers and duties as local health authorities under the National Health Service (Scotland) Act, 1947, and their welfare powers under the National Assistance Act, 1948, a very comprehensive range of domiciliary services can be provided, particularly if there is full co-operation with voluntary bodies.

Health Visiting

In recent years the post-nursing training of health visitors has been widened to include more about the elderly and much more about requirements for emotional health and social well-being. Health visitors can help old people in five main ways:

(a) They can do much to maintain the physical and emotional health of persons still reasonably fit (e.g. by advice on diet, exercise, rest, budgeting, and cultivation of leisure interests, and removal of needless fears and worries);

(b) They can advise the elderly about the various services and allowances available;

(c) They are in a favourable position to set in motion services (e.g. home nursing, domestic help or simple visiting) to meet particular needs though this does not imply that health visitors are the only people who can initiate services;

(d) They can play a useful part in the after-care and rehabilitation of those who are recovering from illness; and

(e) They can secure information which will be of great value in fixing policy to meet the local needs.

Home Nursing and Home Help

The home nursing and home help services of local health authorities bring help to many old people who fall ill or are otherwise in need of help. These services have been steadily expanding over the past few years and do much to avoid the need for many old people to enter hospital or a welfare home.

Laundering and Nursing Requisites

Local authorities, especially in the towns, have other ways of assisting with illness or helplessness of long duration. They can use their powers relating to prevention, care and after-care to provide facilities for laundering bed linen where the full burden is beyond what the householder can undertake. Authorities without a laundry of their own may make arrangements with a commercial laundry or there may be a hospital laundry able to help. Local health authorities under these powers may also provide nursing requisites beyond what the nurse will need for carrying out her duties. Ingenious contrivances (such as tripod walking-sticks and long-handled shoehorns) exist for the use of old and sick people themselves, and the Scottish Branch, British Red Cross Society will be glad to advise any local authority that is interested.

Welfare Services

For old people disabled by blindness, deafness, or some other infirmity, local authorities, in pursuance of their powers under Sections 29 and 30 of the National Assistance Act, can help by advising on matters relating to statutory and voluntary services and on domestic and personal problems, and by providing (a) physical help in houses (e.g. handrails in passages or bathrooms, ramps), (b) library, wireless and other recreational facilities, (c) holidays and outings, and (d) tuition in handicrafts.

Health Clinics for Examination of Old People

In co-operation with the Regional Hospital Board two authorities provide health clinics for examination of old people to which general practitioners can refer elderly patients, not the sick so much as old people who have troubles or difficulties which might lead to ill health. These clinics are "preventive" as distinct from the curative work carried out on the frail elderly in the geriatric unit of a hospital, but a geriatric specialist attends whenever his services are required in particular cases. The aim is to provide a place where people getting on in years can go for consultation and advice about the problems which advancing years inevitably bring, e.g. what plans to make against retirement. One of these clinics sees four new people a week and each is given a detailed assessment designed to ensure that preventable disabilities are not allowed to develop. There would seem an opportunity here for other authorities to experiment on these lines; no two preventive clinics need be alike. More study of the needs and circumstances of older people, particularly those approaching retirement, could be of great value. These clinics include chiropody and physiotherapy as part of their regular service.

Chiropody

Chiropody as a service for old people probably ranks second only to visitation in the amount of general good it can do. Numbers of old people are rendered partially or almost entirely immobile for the lack of this service. Immobility brings in its train other physical and mental problems and the object of providing meals, physiotherapy, etc., for old people can be defeated if the elderly are allowed to become progressively more housebound as a result of lack of proper care of their feet.

Many old people make their own arrangements with private chiropodists. Some voluntary organizations (in particular, the Scottish Branch of the British Red Cross Society and the local Old People's Welfare Committees) operate excellent chiropody schemes which are assisted by grants-in-aid from the local health authority. As with meals for the elderly, it is wise that the old person participating in such schemes should make some contribution towards the treatment. Old people should be seen and referred to the chiropodist either by the general medical practitioner or by a medical officer of the local authority; otherwise demands are liable to become excessive.

Chiropody is a provision which should be made available to all residents in old people's homes.

Physiotherapy

The power of physiotherapy to help in restoring capacity to the elderly might well be made the subject of further investigation at geriatric clinics and elsewhere. In the hospital service physiotherapy is provided under specialist supervision; and local health authorities may themselves provide physiotherapy in connection with welfare homes under appropriate medical guidance. It seems possible that certain residents at welfare homes might, after physiotherapy treatment, be restored sufficiently to live at home again with relatives. Local authorities might discuss with the regional hospital board the possibility of arranging for mobile units to call at welfare homes.

Discharge from Hospital

Old people are sometimes said to be afraid of going into hospital because they think it means goodbye to their own homes. In fact, experience has shown that many of the old people accepted as in-patients in the geriatric wards of a hospital specially equipped to treat and rehabilitate them can now be made well enough to go home if the relatives can look after them and the home conditions are adequate. Help can sometimes be arranged through voluntary agencies towards preparing conditions for home-coming. Also, if the hospital authority can keep in touch with the relatives and undertake to accept the patient back into hospital if he falls ill again, they will usually find that the relatives, if they can, will play their part. It is important that the relatives should feel they will have the hospital always behind them in case things go wrong.

Short-stay Service in Hospital or Welfare Home

Sometimes the hospital or welfare home can give the relatives a much needed rest by taking the old person off their hands for a week or so. Friendly arrangements of this sort, if they succeed in preventing a breakdown of home care, are obviously to the advantage of all.

Activity in Welfare Homes

Too little responsibility and too much regimentation seem to be the main things to avoid in welfare homes. Old people do not take kindly to having their lives run for them, and prefer to have the opportunity to do things themselves, even though they may not seem very actively inclined. There is always room for ingenuity in bringing old people out of themselves; at one home a common interest was noticeably absent until the introduction of a small bagatelle board happily broke the ice. The problem of finding something to occupy the minds and hands of male residents in particular must remain difficult so long as they have not developed hobbies in their earlier years.

Respective Responsibilities of Hospital and Welfare Home

Hospital and welfare authorities have sometimes found it difficult to agree on their respective duties towards elderly people. The criterion is to be found in the help that an old person needs. If it is primarily the medical, nursing and other hospital services, he should be in hospital; if it is simply care and attention on account of frailty and neither active hospital treatment nor continuous nursing is needed, he should be in a welfare home. Any definition can only be a general guide; the proper care of old people depends much more on co-operation and goodwill between the authorities than on strict adherence to defined obligations. One method of achieving co-operation is for a hospital consultant and the medical officer of health (or a senior member of his staff) to have honorary status on the local authority and hospital staff respectively, with consequent freedom of access to institutions and records, and to consult together on doubtful cases. Everyone concerned should understand that movement of old people between the hospital, on the one hand, and a welfare home or the patient's home, on the other, need not always be towards hospital.

Subject to what is said above, some definitions of the respective responsibilities are set out in the following appendix also issued by the Department of Health for Scotland.

Hospital Authorities*

Apart from the acute sick and others needing active treatment, who clearly require hospital admission, the responsibility of the hospital authorities normally covers:

(i) those who require more or less continuous nursing care or supervision, whether they need medical treatment or not;

(ii) continued care of the elderly sick who have completed active treatment but who still require rehabilitation in hospital or for some other reason are not yet ready for discharge to their own homes or to a welfare home;

(iii) care of senile, confused or disturbed patients who cannot, owing to their condition, live a normal community life in a welfare home;

(iv) care of the person (accidents apart) who has lost control of bowels or bladder.

The hospital authority cannot be expected to be responsible for providing

* Quoted from the Appendix to the *Memorandum on the Care of the Elderly*, issued by the Department of Health for Scotland.

all medical or nursing care needed by elderly persons, however minor the illness or however short the stay in bed.

Welfare Authorities*

The elderly person who is in need of care and attention which he cannot be given at home or be expected to obtain for himself elsewhere in the community, is a responsibility of the welfare authority, who should undertake also:

    (i) care of residents in a welfare home during minor illnesses which may involve a short period in bed but not medical or nursing care beyond what is normally undertaken by the general practitioner and district nurse in a patient's own home;

  (ii) care of the infirm old person who may need help in dressing, toilet, etc., and may need to live on the ground floor because he cannot manage stairs; this will include the senile whose senility does not require continuous nursing care or supervision;

 (iii) care of the resident who is not expected to live more than a few weeks in circumstances where if in his own home he would have stayed there, e.g. because he cannot benefit from treatment or nursing care beyond what could be given to him at home.

    All these are persons for whom any necessary nursing care would be given by relatives with the help or advice of the district nurse if they were living in their own homes. In welfare homes care of this kind is given by the staff with the help where necessary of the domiciliary nursing service.

The authority cannot be expected to be responsible for giving prolonged nursing care to the bedfast but welfare homes over the next decade should concentrate rather, it is suggested, on the frail.

---

* Quoted from the Appendix to the *Memorandum on the Care of the Elderly*, issued by the Department of Health for Scotland.

11. Co-ordination and Co-operation in Providing Welfare Services

T. SEYMOUR JONES

Divisional Medical Officer, Lancashire County Council

VERY many organizations are involved, directly or indirectly, in providing a variety of social services for the benefit of the more handicapped members of the community. The provision of social services must be geared to the various needs of the community, some members of which are physically handicapped. Others are mentally handicapped, either temporarily or permanently as a result of mental illness or mental subnormality. Some are both physically and mentally handicapped and may also be suffering from blindness or deafness. Indeed, any permutation of these various handicaps can be found in some members of the community.

The provision of various services for the amelioration of the problems and difficulties of those in the community who are in need is shared by local health authorities, local housing authorities, hospital authorities and a variety of voluntary organizations.

Because some services are provided either by local authorities or by hospital authorities as a statutory requirement, in cases where these authorities have no legal power, or only permissive powers, many of the gaps in social services are filled by voluntary organizations. It is imperative that there be as perfect co-ordination as possible between the various bodies providing the services, to avoid duplication and overlapping with resultant waste of time, effort and money, in order to give as full as possible a service to the individual. It is now intended to study these services in more detail and in relation to the various organizations involved.

The Welfare Committees of county councils and county boroughs have a relationship to the County District Housing Authorities and Housing Committees. This is different in the two cases because of two-tier and one-tier local government organization. Ideally, there should be very close co-ordination and co-operation between the Welfare and Housing Committees of a county borough in providing the right kind of housing and residential accommodation for the elderly, but this is not always so. Jealousy exists between committees and departments, which means that in some cases only lip-service is paid to such co-operation. This failing is so marked in some areas that there is no consultation as to what type of housing is being

91

provided. (Housing is complementary to residential accommodation provided under the National Assistance Act, 1948.)

The situation as it affects county councils is rather different, for they are the health and welfare authorities, while the constituent county district councils are the housing authorities. There must be the utmost co-operation and goodwill between the county councils and county district councils if the various residential accommodation services are to be really complementary to each other.

Special Housing for the Aged

It is now some years since the first groups of specially designed buildings were started in Lancashire. These housed those old people who, despite many handicaps, could live an independent life provided that they had the overall care and supervision of a person who acted as a part-time resident warden. These schemes, of which there are many versions, consist of a group of purpose-built bungalows, bed-sitting rooms, or flatlets, with a resident warden. He or she keeps a watchful eye on the residents, and is ready to call in whatever service is necessary to enable the elderly to live to the end of their days in their own home with as much independence as possible. These individual dwellings are connected to the warden's residence either by a call-bell system, or by an intercommunication system, so that the warden can speak to every member of her large "elderly family" without leaving her own house.

These are the basic requirements; but in addition many schemes provide one or more communal rooms with a small kitchen attached, used by the residents for social activities. This room provides a centre for talks, pastimes, games, birthday parties, watching television and many other activities. Some of the schemes have provided laundry facilities so that the elderly can do their own washing with the latest labour-saving devices under the supervision of the warden. Many welfare authorities have helped financially to provide these schemes, but what has taken place in the large industrial County of Lancashire is of continuing interest. There are 109 county districts in the Administrative County of Lancashire and all are responsible for providing in their own area suitable housing for the needs of the community. In the past, emphasis has been placed on providing homes for young families, but today it may be said that housing authorities are particularly occupied in providing houses to accommodate those who used to live in slums, and in providing bungalows, bed-sitting rooms, flatlets, etc., for the completely independent elderly, as well as the special groups of housing under the supervision of the part-time warden. In this case the provision of call-bell systems, communal rooms, laundry, and the salary of the warden, is the financial responsibility of the welfare authority.

By the end of 1962 fifty-two county districts had submitted seventy-five schemes which, when completed, will provide 1768 units of accommodation. Already 1048 units are in use, and experience up to now shows that about 75 per cent of the accommodation is occupied by a single person and 25 per cent by two people, mainly elderly couples. It is anticipated that schemes approved by the end of 1962 will provide accommodation for approximately 2210 elderly persons.

An interesting fact which has emerged from the provision of these special housing schemes is that the occupants end their days in independence. This is a result of the supervision of the warden coupled with the great assistance given by the home help service and the home nursing service, together with friendly visiting by voluntary workers of the various Old People's Welfare Committees. The need to transfer the residents in these units to permanent accommodation provided by the County Council in hostels for the aged occurs only on rare occasions.

Bungalows have been built close to a home for the aged for thirty-five residents on a common site in delightful surroundings. The residents are cared for by the warden of the hostel through her staff, who provide 24-hour care for those elderly who can still live independently. There is frequent inter-visiting between the residents in the hostels and those in the bungalows.

Another six similar schemes are planned. The County District Council will build a small group of bungalows on a common site where the County Council will provide a hostel for the aged. It is hoped that future developments may provide a hot midday meal in the dining room of the hostel for the bungalow residents.

Domiciliary Services for the Aged

There are other ways in which co-operation between county councils, county district and voluntary organizations is proving invaluable. At the moment the County Council makes an annual grant to the County Old People's Welfare Committee to help organize services for the elderly. The county districts in their turn make grants to their local Old People's Welfare Committees to provide local services, clubs and meals on wheels. Meals on wheels in the majority of cases are provided by the W.V.S.

The 1962 amendment to the 1948 National Assistance Act augurs an improved standard of co-operation between the various partners. The future holds new development in the provision of day clubs in Lancashire either by the County Council or County District Council, separately or jointly. This means that the provision of a building and of equipment will be made by the local authorities, and that the help to organize day clubs for the elderly will be provided by voluntary organizations who can provide the volunteers to help run these clubs. It is also hoped that from these day clubs will develop the provision of lunch clubs for the elderly.

Good as the Meals on Wheels Service has been in the past, in general it has not been able to provide for the full needs of the elderly, especially those living alone, for whom it is desirable to provide at least one hot meal a day to keep them in good health. Speaking generally, elderly people need three to four good hot meals weekly to keep them in a reasonable state of health.

It is hoped that the lunch club will provide meals not only for those able to get to the club by independent means, but also for those needing transport. As well as providing a nourishing meal, it will give isolated folk the opportunity to meet friends and contemporaries.

There will, however, still be a place for the Meals on Wheels Service in an even more expanded form than at present, to meet the needs of those elderly who are completely homebound. The problem of providing the elderly in rural areas with meals could be solved in part by having mobile kitchens or by the invitation of the elderly into a neighbour's house for a hot meal. If necessary the cost of the meal could be subsidized by local authorities or voluntary organizations.

During the past fifteen years co-operation between the local health and welfare authority and a wide variety of voluntary organizations has developed in order to provide the best possible care for those in the community who are aged, physically handicapped, mentally handicapped or chronic sick.

In Lancashire, for example, great efforts have been made to co-ordinate the work of the County Council and of voluntary organizations whose main interest is the care of the elderly.

In each of the seventeen Health Divisions a Welfare Sub-committee has been set up; this consists of representatives of the County Council, Divisional Health Committees, County District Councils and the Old People's Welfare Committees from each County District, along with the consultant geriatrician of the Regional Hospital Board, and the local representatives of the National Assistance Board.

The function of this Welfare Sub-committee is to co-ordinate all the efforts of local authorities and voluntary organizations in providing services for the care of the elderly living in their own homes. The statutory services provided under the National Health Service Act and the National Assistance Act are under the day-to-day control of a Divisional Medical Officer who has the assistance of a Divisional Welfare Organizer in co-ordinating these services.

The Divisional Medical Officer has at his disposal a variety of statutory services to provide for those members of the community whose needs demand them. The Divisional Medical Officer is the co-ordinating officer for all services, such as home helps, home nursing, health visiting, social welfare workers, and residential accommodation, ambulance service, etc., so that any person can be provided with one or more of these services as required.

As 95 per cent of the elderly are living in the community either in their own homes or with relatives, the demand on the statutory services is substantial.

The various domiciliary schemes in operation in Lancashire have been expanded very rapidly in the past nine years to meet the demands of the elderly and to enable them to remain in their own homes (where they want to be) till the end of their days in as much independence as is compatible with their physical and mental conditions. The services most in demand are those of the home help and the home nurse.

In 1954 the Lancashire County Council employed 1428 part-time home helps who devoted 71 per cent of their time to the care of the elderly. By the end of 1962 3784 home helps were employed and 82·6 per cent of their time was taken up with caring for the elderly. Year by year demand increases for more home helps, and the allocation of their time devoted to the care of the elderly is also increasing.

The home nursing services of the Lancashire County Council employed 329 nursing staff in 1954 and 39 per cent of their time was taken in caring for those over 65 years of age. This work has developed materially so that by the end of 1962 there were 463 home nurses who had spent 51·4 per cent of their time with the elderly.

Similarly, the health visiting service has been called upon to take more and more interest in the elderly. The number of visits paid by health visitors to the elderly has increased from 6070 in 1954 to 48,314 in 1962.

The County Old People's Welfare Committee has played a great part in recent years in co-ordinating the activities of churches, W.V.S., Rotary, Round Table, Red Cross, St. John Ambulance Brigade, etc., which provide services for the elderly. This was achieved by the setting up, in most county districts, of an Old People's Welfare Committee which organizes a rota of voluntary visitors to visit those elderly in the community whose main affliction is that of loneliness. The value of regular visits to elderly persons living alone can hardly be overstated. Such visits keep the elderly in touch with the rest of the community.

The number of Old People's Welfare Committees has increased from 80 in 1954 to 166 in 1962. These committees are responsible for co-ordinating all voluntary effort in each area and provide a valuable link with the statutory services.

There are sixty-four full-time day clubs in being in the Administrative County Area and these, together with another 250 clubs which usually meet once a week, provide a meeting place for those elderly who are fit and mobile. This helps them maintain an interest in everyday things which is so important to their well being.

Another aspect of co-operation has been the pioneering work of many Old People's Welfare Committees in providing a chiropody service for the elderly. Although the Lancashire County Council is responsible for this service now, some Old People's Welfare Committees act as agents of the County Council in organizing this service for the elderly. During 1962

40,215 aged persons received chiropody treatment either by direct County Council services, or through the agency of the voluntary associations.

Day Care for the Aged

A new development in the care of the elderly in the community was recently begun with the provision of a day care centre attached to a new home for the aged. The County Council decided to provide for twelve elderly people to come to the centre daily. They would have their own sitting rooms and would have a hot lunch and tea before returning to their homes.

Many of those selected for this day centre were living alone and needed the support of the day centre on two, three, or more days per week. This service, it is felt, will enable them to continue to live in their own homes where circumstances might otherwise have compelled them to seek permanent residential accommodation.

Others were living with relatives and their entry into the day centre on one or two days a week allowed the daughter or daughter-in-law a respite from the care and supervision of an elderly relative. It also enabled her to go out shopping or visit her own friends, free from the worry of wondering if the elderly person were safe and secure.

If this new venture proves a success, the County Council would be encouraged to develop the day centre idea. Day centre facilities linked with homes for the aged would give relief to hard-pressed relatives and might diminish the overall need for full hostel care.

Co-operation with Regional Hospital Boards

The successful prosecution of such schemes as the above demands the full co-ordination and co-operation of the welfare authorities and the Regional Hospital Boards. In the main there is good co-operation between the local consultant geriatrician and the welfare department, in the exchange of elderly persons requiring the appropriate services, whether it be hospital or residential accommodation.

Though an adequate and efficient geriatric service has not been built up in every area, experience throughout the country shows that there should be a unit in the geriatric department for the correct assessment of the disabilities and needs of the elderly patient. There should be units for intermediate and long-stay patients who require rehabilitation and a feeling of confidence before returning to their own home or a home for the aged.

A certain number of aged patients will need permanent hospital treatment because their disability is such that, although it is not likely to yield to medical and nursing care, they are too handicapped to return home or to live in a communal home.

Over the past ten years there has been a marked change in the physical condition of elderly persons admitted to homes for the aged. In the early years, those admitted to residential homes tended to be able to do most things for themselves. This is no longer true and gradually more old people, infirm and frail both physically and mentally, have gained admission.

In a survey carried out in the Lancashire County Council residential homes for the aged at the end of December 1961, 2376 old people were being cared for. It was found that 23 per cent of all residents required help in washing and dressing, etc. Twenty-four per cent were incontinent, 12 per cent were mentally confused. Of those who were mentally confused it was thought there were none for whom it was justifiable to seek hospital care.

There is a great need for the closest co-operation between geriatric departments and homes for the aged to ensure that cases of incontinence are assessed and stabilized before being returned to residential homes. Elderly persons suffering from permanent incontinence and intractable mental confusion should be the responsibility of the hospital authority.

It seems to be the view of some hospital administrators and perhaps a proportion of consultant geriatricians that if the hospital services cannot provide any further relief to an elderly person then the welfare authority should be responsible for them. This implies that the geriatrician has not an interest in those elderly for whom treatment is of no avail and the further implication is that the welfare authorities should be responsible for the incurably chronically sick. This is certainly not the view expressed by the Ministry of Health in their memorandum and directives. Furthermore, if the local health and welfare authority is to fulfil its defined function and provide the home services so urgently needed, then the hospital must provide more long-stay beds for the intractable geriatric and psycho-geriatric patient.

Welfare Services for the Blind

The voluntary organizations which have provided services for the blind in this country have been in existence for over 150 years. It was not until 1920 that statutory authorities were given the responsibility to provide services for the blind. Welfare authorities usually delegated their obligations, such as home visiting, workshops for the blind, home workers, social centres, handicraft centres and general social welfare to the many voluntary societies for the blind which had been set up over the previous 100 years. Many of these continue to do very good work.

In the last twenty years over 70 per cent of those on the register were notified for the first time as being blind at 70 years of age or over.

Blindness among young adults has greatly diminished, thus reducing the demands for instruction in Braille or Moon.

The majority of the blind are elderly and need as many of the services as old people who can see. These services can usually be provided by the general social welfare worker.

At present the majority of home teachers for the blind are working directly from a voluntary agency as specialized visitors. This tends to restrict opportunities for contact, which is so desirable, with other social workers such as health visitors, home help service, and general welfare social workers.

If the Younghusband Report is to be carried out as far as home teachers of the blind are concerned, then future development would be towards the integration of services for the blind with those for general welfare of the elderly. Home teachers would become part of the welfare team of workers.

There is real need for a qualified home teacher of the blind to be a member of a larger team of social workers who care for the elderly, the physically handicapped, etc. The qualified home teacher would be called in to use his or her specialist training in helping those who have recently become blind, to adjust to their new situation. After this stage, unless the blind person needs Braille or Moon teaching, the general welfare social worker should take over.

Services for the Physically Handicapped

Before the passing of the National Assistance Act in 1948 there were comparatively few voluntary organizations interested in the specific problems and welfare of the physically handicapped in this country. Recently a large number of voluntary organizations has developed which deals with the special problems of groups of people afflicted by a certain disease. Whilst these national bodies have been set up, there are few local voluntary organizations to help the physically handicapped, and the development of services for them has been left mainly to the welfare authorities. Although there are few local voluntary organizations there is much co-ordination and co-operation between the various statutory authorities and the voluntary organizations.

A very interesting instance of this co-ordination occurred recently in Lancashire. Some time ago a man and woman, both severely handicapped with paraplegia following poliomyelitis, were residents in a home run by a voluntary organization for persons having had poliomyelitis. After a while this man and woman were married, and the husband was employed as a clerk at a nearby works. Later a son was born to the couple, and the voluntary organization applied to the housing authority of the wife's birth-place, which was in Lancashire, to provide suitable accommodation. As a result of this approach a conference was called of the County District Council (Housing Authority), the County Council (Welfare Authority) and representatives of the voluntary organization. The outcome of this conference was that the County District Council offered a ground-floor flat; the adaptations which were necessary to make the flat habitable by two physically handicapped persons, both in wheel-chairs, were paid for by the County Council, the

County District Council and the voluntary organization, on a sharing basis. The husband gave his wife a great deal of assistance in caring for their son after his return from work each day and at the week-end. Help in decorating and furnishing the flat was provided by a number of voluntary organizations. A telephone was installed by the County Council so that the wife would not feel isolated during the day whilst her husband was at work, and could get in touch with various services in an emergency. Once the family was installed in the flat, the home help service was provided daily, and various voluntary workers have given freely of their services. All this co-ordination of effort has meant that two very severely handicapped people are able to live as near as possible independent lives.

The National Health Service Acts of 1946 and 1948, the National Assistance Act (and other social legislation) brought into being the so-called Welfare State. Many felt that the Welfare State would mean the end of voluntary effort in regard to the hospital service and community services in general. It was thought that the State, with its great resources in money and manpower, would render superfluous the spirit of voluntary service which had existed in Great Britain for many centuries. This, however, has not proved to be the case. Today the picture is brighter than it has ever been, with much more voluntary assistance available to help the hospital service, the elderly, the physically and mentally handicapped, the blind, the deaf and any other unfortunate member of the community. Various organizations have rapidly developed, each of which has the specific object of helping a particular sub-group of those who are disabled in some way. There are far too many splinter groups intent on caring for a very small section of people suffering from a specific handicap. The great need today is to co-ordinate all the efforts of individuals and the multiplicity of voluntary organizations in order to bring the maximum benefit to all who are in any way handicapped. This voluntary effort must be diverted into the right channels so that it can fully co-operate with the statutory authorities for the greater benefit of the community as a whole.

There is an equal need for statutory authorities to explain what services they want undertaken by voluntary organizations, so that these are given a sense of purpose. It would be much better if the statutory authorities were to provide the necessary buildings and equipment for the appropriate services, whilst voluntary workers give their time, enthusiasm and energy to help run these services. All too often much of the effort of voluntary workers goes into the problem of raising money. This can overshadow the actual service given to people in need.

From the study of all these services, this major need emerges: co-ordination, which will lead to greater efficiency; there is still much to be done.

12. Local Government and Voluntary Organizations

C. O. S. BLYTH BROOKE

Medical Officer of Health, Metropolitan Borough of Finsbury

FROM time immemorial charitably minded persons have given of their substance to those in need by way of personal gifts, by appointing almoners to distribute their bounty or by adjuring others in whom they had confidence to dispense their benefactions. Similarly, by their testaments they have made bequests to this end. Before the Dissolution of the Monasteries, most of the offerings for charity were distributed by them, but after this the church-wardens were often nominated for this purpose, as were numerous Trusts whether known as such or not. These were the forerunners of the voluntary organizations of today.

In the nineteenth century the consciences of many good-hearted persons, such as the Earl of Shaftesbury, were deeply moved by the unhappy plight of large numbers of poor living in intolerable conditions, and they joined with others like-minded to found new associations for the relief of suffering of all kinds. This practice has continued ever since, for although the miseries due to poverty of the last century no longer exist, their disappearance has made more apparent other forms of suffering, and so the number of charitable societies still grows.

The needs to provide, for which the societies were founded, have been great, and often almost as soon as their work was started they found that the calls upon their resources far outstripped the funds available. In order that their efforts should not suffer and might even expand, local authorities began to support their endeavours by financial aid in the form of grants. This process of grant aid was extended more widely when charitable subscriptions fell, and voluntary helpers on whom the societies greatly relied became less freely available, on the one hand, and when local government came to assume greater responsibility for the welfare of the community, on the other hand.

Unfortunately, a vicious circle was often created: the more grant aid that was given, the greater was reliance placed upon it as a source of income and the more did the public and benefactors regard local authorities as responsible for carrying on the services. In consequence voluntary contributions decreased and the greater became the need for further grants. This development was accelerated by the changing social conditions, with more calls on the public for voluntary subscriptions leading to greater difficulties in the collection of funds, and with more ready sanction being given by Parliament and public opinion to local government concern in health and social welfare.

Eventually grant aid came to form the principal financial support of some societies, and then the local councils often wished to assume more responsibility in regard to the expenditure of the money, and to attach conditions to their grants. In this way some associations first became agents for the councils. Some councils then felt that they could carry out their intentions and fulfil their responsibilities more satisfactorily if they had the direct management, and so, finally, the associations lost their identity and their work continued as part of the Council's functions in the ordinary way. Such an evolution developed years ago with the maternity and child welfare services, and is taking place today in relation to home nursing and the care of old people.

Nevertheless, much social work is still carried out by voluntary organizations and this will probably continue for many years.

Under present legislation local authorities are required to provide a number of health and welfare services, and may provide others. The provision may, in most cases, be made either by the authority, by the agency of a voluntary organization, or by making a grant to it. In certain instances only the last alternative (with or without the approval of a Minister) is permitted.

The expression "voluntary organization" is given slightly varying interpretation in a number of Acts of Parliament, though the ordinary meaning is substantially the same in all. The simplest is that contained in the National Health Service Act, 1946, where voluntary is stated to mean "not carried on for profit and not provided by a local or public authority". In most cases, if not in all, it is a charitable body and registered under The Charities Act, 1960.

It is governed by its constitution and may only use its resources for the purposes set out, but, as these are usually in wide and somewhat vague terms, it may do this in whatever way it thinks fit. The members of the governing body are to be regarded as trustees of the monies they hold, and must use them in accordance with the equitable principles of trusteeship, that is, as a reasonable and sensible man would with his own money, for the purposes established, but are not restricted in any way as to the manner of their application.

Because of the freedom thus allowed to them to attain their purposes, the mode of operation of voluntary organizations is very flexible, and can be frequently changed without formality, and neither need it follow precedents or predetermined methods. They are, therefore, most suitable for pioneering experimental projects of every kind, when the exact lines along which these would be best developed are nebulous, and can only be settled by trial and error, and may fail altogether to answer the needs for which they were established.

For similar reasons they are particularly suited to deal with the small and more personal needs of those whom they endeavour to help, and also because formalities may be reduced to a bare minimum the approach to these people may be of a close personal and informal type.

Voluntary organizations are also more economical of both money and labour in their overhead expenditure, as administration is generally less detailed than that required by local authorities; there are no necessities to maintain elaborate records or to conform with the complicated methods of local government accounting.

A very great and often forgotten value of voluntary organizations is in their very appeal to the public for funds, for thereby many persons are made aware of the sad predicament possibly of large numbers in unfortunate circumstances, of which previously they had no conception at all. It can also arouse the sentiments of love of our neighbour, of our desire to succour him in time of trouble, and of our concern for the weak and defenceless. These organizations form an outlet and vehicle for practical expressions of such feelings, and the act of giving, whether in money or personal services, enhances the feelings themselves. And in regard to nearly all forms of social work, whatever a public authority considers it right to take upon itself, there must surely be further ways in which help may be given, as the needs of the "fatherless and widows" are without limit, and the innate desire of all Christians to help their fellow beings cannot thereby be killed.

The efforts of a voluntary association may be directed to one or more particular section of the community, without intending thereby any real discrimination of a religious or racial nature. The association may be concerned with special needs of a particular group, or the members of a group may wish to help the more unfortunate ones among them. This can be of advantage, however, to the whole community for whom it would be impossible, on such an extensive scale, to administer the assistance needed, and at least some obtain the desired help. It may still be appropriate for a local authority to assist financially provided they bear in mind the proportion of the inhabitants they are assisting, and are agreeable to help similarly other groups as and when practicable. It would not normally be right, on the other hand, for the authority itself to directly administer a scheme to help one section except as preparatory to a more expanded project.

Although at one time most of the fieldwork undertaken on behalf of voluntary organizations was by unpaid persons, who gave either freely or sparingly of their services, yet in recent years less voluntary help has been available. They have been forced to employ salaried workers in order to cover the increasing amount of work that has fallen on them to carry out. These paid workers have generally less security, a smaller salary and fewer other benefits such as superannuation, than they would secure if employed by a local authority. Despite these facts this service tends to attract the best type, especially of women, for it gives greater individual scope, and freedom from administrative control; many dedicated individuals feel that in receiving only a low salary and in dispensing voluntary funds, that they are themselves taking part in a voluntary, perhaps missionary, effort. Improvements in the salaries of such workers in recent years have, however, reduced, but not abolished, these considerations.

But the work of voluntary organizations suffers from a number of drawbacks which are not inconsiderable. The most frequent among them is shortage of money leading to the dissipation of time and energy of staff in the collection of subscriptions and failure to complete projects embarked upon. Some drawbacks are also associated with certain features already mentioned, which have their advantages. Thus little time on administration may cause muddle and unreliability in the services rendered, and similar results arise from workers whether paid or voluntary who, through lack of training and supervision, do not realize the necessity of efficiency and dependability in regard to details. The freedom enjoyed by voluntary organizations of conferring their benefits on whom they, for one reason or another, consider most deserving, in spite of its advantages, does open the door to the abuses of unfair selection through faulty information and personal prejudices.

Although the low salaries and other conditions usually given to the paid worker attract some of the best individuals, it has to be admitted that it also excludes some very worthy persons who, on personal grounds, must seek higher emoluments. It has also, unfortunately, to be conceded that the charitable nature of the services given enables helpers with a tendency to condescension in their temperament to show it in their dealings.

Many of the advantages of direct local government provisions appear from the comments already made, and others, include a less danger of disruption through temporary absence of helpers, as there is usually staff available engaged in other duties who may be diverted as occasion arises. Channels for complaints, which allow possible abuses to be checked, are more readily available.

A particular advantage of immediate local authority control of any service is to enlarge the social conscience among all groups of the community. At the same time it may deflect some, and even those who have duties as relatives, from helping those in need, by salving their sense of moral obligation in the concept that the State is responsible.

The most important consideration ought clearly to be the reactions of those that any service is designed to help, and in this respect by far the most significant factors are the personality of and the approach by the worker irrespective of the authority or association whom they represent. One is happy to state that in both cases the majority are considerate and of an understanding disposition.

There are some few recipients, or would be recipients, of help who are only too ready to accept anything from anybody, and are often loud in their demands for what they think to be their right, but many more are reluctant and occasionally even resentful of receiving help of any kind from anyone. They may feel that it destroys their independence and injures the dignity that they have in self-reliance; they may hate the idea of being beholden to anyone or to the State. It may be difficult for them to appreciate that it is part of what is paid from their rates and taxes or is given in love by their neighbours. Generally the latter is the better understood and voluntary efforts more readily appreciated.

Our welfare services vary in their administration from place to place, and to an outsider are most complicated, but nevertheless out of the confusion there is a very real and intensive ministration to social needs in this country, and they are more satisfactory than any bureaucratic scheme could be, however tidy in its administration.

It is to be regretted that it is not uncommon for jealousies and recriminations to occur between the various voluntary organizations themselves, and between them and the local authorities as a result of suspicion and misunderstanding. In the latter case it may be partly due to fears that local authorities may wish to control directly all voluntary activities, and to establish all social provisions as rights to which all are entitled, which might gradually oust all voluntary endeavour and personal and family responsibility. On the other side, implicit trust may not be forthcoming in the efficiency and cover provided for the whole population by the organizations. These fears are frequently either exaggerated or altogether unwarranted.

It is probably inevitable, where many bodies are involved, that there should be both gaps in the services provided and overlapping as well: the latter may, however, be beneficial as it can ensure a wide extension and any competition between the bodies involved may stimulate greater efficiency.

Co-operation and co-ordination is in the interests of all but is sometimes difficult to establish. Co-ordinating committees (such as local councils of social service and Old People's Welfare Committees) quite often play a useful part.

A friendly relationship between the parties is the first step towards co-ordination and may be achieved to some extent by the acceptance by a voluntary organization of the nomination of one or more representatives of the local authority as members of its Committee of Management. If the parties can agree for an officer to share actively in both administrations, an even closer link can be established.

In the country at large at the present time, many social services are carried out by voluntary organizations often with the aid of a small (occasionally somewhat larger) grant by the local authority.

An increasing number are being carried out by local authorities directly or by the agency of a voluntary organization. The latter arrangement may be regarded as very felicitous as it embodies nearly all the advantages of a voluntary character and permits safeguards in the conditions that a local authority may attach to any agreement.

The Ministry of Health in a number of circulars issued in recent years has paid tribute to the work of voluntary organizations, and has urged the utmost collaboration between them and local authorities.

SECTION III
SOCIAL SECURITY—CASH SERVICES*

* *Editor's Note:* Since this section was written a Labour Government has been elected. An act has been passed increasing the basic scales of benefit and further legislation is likely to bring about changes in the social security service. The policies and principles discussed in the section are still relevant, although some of the details may, of course, be changed by future legislation.

Full details of the current schemes of social insurance including pensions, are given in leaflets, which may be obtained free of charge from the local offices of the Ministry of Pensions and National Insurance.

13. Trends in National Insurance

Member of Parliament

THE PRESENT social insurance system in Britain is still based largely on the post-war legislation of the Labour Government, which implemented the Beveridge Report. In recent years a lot of the assumptions of that period have been challenged on all sides.

The Labour Party has put forward proposals for a major advance in social insurance standards based on a new set of principles. The Conservative Government has introduced a graduated element into contributions for pensions, while keeping most of the Beveridge system intact, but they have been urged by some of their backbenchers and by other critics to alter the system by introducing the means test principle on a larger scale.

In this article I want to examine the various proposals for altering our present National Insurance system. Before doing so, it may be useful to sketch in briefly the history of recent years and to see what the present system amounts to.

Historical Perspective

National Insurance is a product of the twentieth century. In Victorian times there were few social services of any account and no national insurance at all. There was a repressive and humiliating Poor Law, but *laissez-faire* ideas precluded anything in the nature of retirement pensions, unemployment or sickness benefits.

In the present century there have been two main periods of advance. The first was in the years 1906 to 1914, when the Liberal Government of the day introduced the first old age pensions and insurance against sickness and unemployment. These were improved and added to in the inter-war years, but up to 1939 there was still an incomplete patchwork of social insurance. Some people were covered for all the main forms of benefit, some for certain benefits only and some not at all. There was no National Health Service and there were no family allowances.

The second major period of advance occurred under the Labour Government of 1945–51. The Beveridge Report issued during the war had proposed

* Since contributing this chapter Mr. Prentice has been appointed Minister of State, Department of Education and Science in the 1964 Socialist Government.

a comprehensive National Insurance scheme whereby everyone would pay a compulsory weekly contribution and then be entitled, without any means test, to weekly benefits for retirement, widowhood, sickness or unemployment. This was enacted in the National Insurance Act, 1946, which was based on the Beveridge proposals, but with rather higher benefits than he had suggested. Its stable companion was the Industrial Injuries Act, which replaced the old Workmen's Compensation Acts by a comprehensive insurance system against industrial accidents and industrial diseases. In the same group of legislation were the Family Allowances Act, 1945, the National Health Service Act, 1946, and the National Assistance Act, 1948.

National Assistance was intended as the "long stop" of the system. The most common causes of hardship were to be covered by National Insurance and the retirement pensions, etc., were intended to be at a sufficient level for subsistence. The assistance part would then come into the picture to supplement these benefits when there were unusual circumstances, e.g. if an old age pensioner had to pay an exceptionally high rent, or when there was hardship caused by something outside the National Insurance field—such as desertion of the family by the bread-winner.

In practice it has never worked like this. Pensions and other benefits have never been sufficient to live on. Despite a number of increases in the rates of benefit, the system has been undermined both by the rising cost of living and by the rising prosperity of the whole community, in which the pensioners have some right to share. The basic rates have never been deemed sufficient, and therefore supplementation by the National Assistance Board has become a regular feature of the system. Of some 5 million retirement pensioners, about 1 million draw supplementary pensions from the N.A.B. It has been estimated that perhaps another half-million are entitled to do so, but are too proud to apply.

Apart from changes in the rates of contribution and benefits which have occurred fairly regularly, there have been certain changes in the machinery of National Insurance of which the most important was in the National Insurance Act, 1959, when the graduated element was introduced. The description which follows is a brief summary of the present position. The figures for contributions and benefits are those which were in force in June 1963, following the increases which occurred in the preceding weeks.

National Insurance Today

Contributions

Since 1961 (when the 1959 Act came into force) the contribution paid by an employed person has varied with his income unless he is contracted out of the graduated part of the scheme. An employer can contract out his employees if he is operating a pension scheme which meets certain tests. For men who are contracted out there is now a weekly contribution to the National Insurance fund of 16s. 1d. a week. The employer matches this with a contribution of 15s. 4d. For women the contribution is 12s. 11d. plus 12s. 8d. from the employer.

Those who are in the graduated scheme pay as follows: there is a basic contribution of 13s. 8d. from men and 11s. 5d. from women (the employer paying 12s. 11d. and 11s. 2d. respectively). To this is added $4\frac{1}{2}$ per cent of everything earned between £9 and £18 a week, with another $4\frac{1}{2}$ per cent from the employer. The maximum graduated contribution is therefore 7s. 8d. a week for those earning £18 or more.

Self-employed and non-employed persons are outside the graduated scheme. The self-employed pay 18s. 8d. (men) and 15s. 4d. (women). The non-employed pay 14s. 11d. (men) and 11s. 7d. (women).

Benefits*

The standard weekly rates of benefit are now £4 for a single person and £6 10s. for a married couple, with certain increases for dependent children. These apply to retirement pensions, to sickness and unemployment benefits, and to widows' pensions.

There are certain other payments paid under the Act, i.e. maternity benefits, guardians benefits and death benefit.

There are no automatic pensions for widowhood. There is a widow's allowance for the thirteen weeks following the loss of the husband. After that there is a pension in cases where there are dependent children, or the widow is over fifty, or she is incapable of self-support.

So far as retirement pensions are concerned, the flat rate will be supplemented in future years as the graduated system begins to "bite" according to the value of graduated contributions paid in. For every £15 paid in respect of a male contributor (half by him and half by his employer) in the form of graduated contributions, he earns a "unit" which will increase his pension by 6d. a week. For a woman each unit costs £18 contributions, because she has the expensive habit of retiring five years earlier than the man and living longer! This additional pension will remain at a very modest level, i.e. only a few shillings a week for many years to come.

Industrial Injuries and War Disabled

A small part of the contribution goes into a separate Industrial Injuries Fund, and special rates of benefit are paid to those injured at work and to those who contract certain prescribed industrial diseases. There are benefits while off work of £6 15s. a week (single) and £9 5s. 0d. (married) for

* The rates shown on this page are the higher benefits provided under the National Insurance Act 1964.

a period of up to six months and disability pensions after that, which are paid according to the degree of disability. There are supplementary benefits for those who suffer a loss of earning power, those who are unemployable and those so badly disabled as to need constant attendance. There are also rather higher rates of widows' benefits for people killed at work than those paid under the main National Insurance scheme.

War pensioners receive disability pensions and supplementary benefits on almost exactly the same terms as the industrially disabled. These pensions are provided for by a special Royal Warrant outside the scope of the National Insurance Acts and they are paid directly from the Exchequer.

Finance

Apart from war pensions, all the benefits I have described are paid out of the National Insurance Fund, or the Industrial Injuries Fund. These funds are financed by the contributors and their employers, plus an Exchequer contribution on the following basis:

(1) National Insurance

The Exchequer supplement to flat-rate national insurance contributions:
  (i) for employed persons not contracted out of the graduated scheme, one-quarter of the flat-rate contribution income from employers and employed persons;
 (ii) for employed persons contracted out of the graduated scheme, one-quarter of the flat-rate contribution income that would be paid by employers and employed persons if the latter were not contracted out;
(iii) for self-employed and non-employed persons, one-third of the contribution income subject to a minimum annual payment of £170 million.

(2) Industrial Injuries Insurance

The Exchequer supplement to industrial injuries contributions is equal to one-fifth of the contribution income from employers and insured persons.

(Quoted from the White Paper, *Proposed Changes in the National Insurance Schemes*, January 1963.)

The limit of £170 million was only made possible by the introduction of the graduated scheme, whereby the additional contributions performed a rescue operation for the Exchequer. The graduated pensions are deliberately less in value than the contribution would justify. The extra burden which is borne by contributors in the £9 to £18 a week range of income would otherwise have led to very much larger contributions and to the undermining of the insurance principle altogether.

There are two basic reasons for this. One is the increase in pension rates on several occasions. All these increases have, of course, been paid to existing pensioners, whose contribution rates were geared to the old rates of pension. In other words, the existing pensioners are all drawing pensions larger than their own contributions ever justified from the actuarial point of view.

This process began in 1948 when the existing pensioners were blanketed in without ever having contributed to the new fund.

The other reason is that medical science is keeping elderly people alive longer, so that the number of recipients of retirement pensions is larger than was originally anticipated, and will grow larger still in the future.

It is this financial problem which has been one of the mainsprings of all the discussion about national insurance in recent years.

The other mainspring has, of course, been the desire of many of us to see a much better deal for the retired people, the chronic sick, etc. Their living standards are so very much behind the rest of the community. Many other countries who lagged behind our standards in 1948 have now overtaken us and are paying much higher pensions and other benefits. Our present affluence has been built up partly by the existing generation of pensioners in the past. They are entitled to a larger share of the national cake. Therefore there has been a search for a new way forward.

Labour's National Superannuation Statement, 1957

The first fruit of the fresh thinking on this subject was the publication in 1957 of a Labour Party policy statement *National Superannuation*. It had been preceded by a good deal of discussion in the Labour Movement, and the Fabian Society had already published the results of a study made by a group of members of the Transport and General Workers Union in Woolwich, which had commended itself to the Working Party established to study the matter by the Labour Party. This Working Party was under the able chairmanship of Mr. R. H. S. Crossman, and its members included Professor R. Titmuss and his assistants, Dr. Abel-Smith and Mr. Peter Townsend, all of them social scientists at the London School of Economics. This "skiffle group of professors", as they were scornfully described by the then Minister of National Insurance, provided a lot of the ideas adopted in the statement.

The policy statement began with the objective of improving the living standards of the retirement pensioners (and, of course, the other groups of National Insurance, but the main argument concerned the pensioners, who are the biggest group). For the reasons mentioned above it rejected the hope of doing very much on the basis of the flat-rate scheme. So long as there was a flat-rate contribution, progress would be limited to what the poorest contributor could afford. The statement went on to identify the "two nations" in old age. One group enjoyed the security of pension schemes associated with their work. Some of these schemes were generous, some very modest, but those workers who had some kind of superannuation, about a third of the working population, enjoyed a great advantage over those with none at all. Government policy was helping to widen this advantage, by making tax concessions for superannuation payments, which amounted every year to a larger total than their contribution to the National Insurance Fund.

The best way forward was therefore to establish a National Superannuation scheme. Everybody not covered by a satisfactory scheme at work would contribute a percentage of their earnings. There would also be contributions from the employers and the State. There would be contracting out by workers covered by schemes which came up to the level of the State scheme.

This meant that everyone would be covered by a superannuation scheme, either at work or the proposed State scheme. It also meant abandoning the Beveridge system of flat-rate contributions and benefits. There would be higher contributions and higher pensions for the better paid. Wage-related pensions were felt to be more appropriate in the second half of the twentieth century. Flat-rate pensions had been appropriate when we were simply concerned with guaranteeing a subsistence level, but now the proper objective was to avoid a sudden drop in living standards on retirement. There was, however, to be some element of levelling out within a general objective of "half-pay on retirement". The scheme proposed more than half-pay for the lowest paid and rather less than half for the higher paid.

Another very important feature of the policy statement was the idea of an annual review of all pensions—the existing flat-rate ones as well as the future wage-related ones. This would keep them in line with the movement of wage rates. In other words, the pensioner would get an increase, not only if the cost of living went up, but also if the general level of incomes went up. He was entitled to his share of any increase in national prosperity.

"Provision for Old Age"—the Government White Paper, October 1958

Eighteen months after the Labour Party statement, the Government published a White Paper covering much of the same ground. It, too, was concerned about the trend of National Insurance finance and the limitations of the flat-rate system. It also drew attention to the part played by occupational schemes in helping people provide for their old age. It also came down in favour of graduated contributions and graduated pensions.

But there was a fundamental difference between these proposals and those of the Labour Party. The Labour statement had envisaged national superannuation on an ambitious scale, so that every worker could build up a substantial pension in the way that a minority can already do through their occupational schemes. The Government rejected this and proposed a modest graduated element, so as to rescue the finances of the National Insurance Fund and avoid an ever-increasing subsidy from the Exchequer. In paragraph 32 their view was summarized: "For the State to go further would be to arrogate to itself the individual's right to dispose of his income in what he thinks the right way, and would seriously undermine the individual sense of responsibility for his own affairs."

This led to the type of contributions and pension rates described above. The White Paper proposals were enacted in the National Insurance Act, 1959, and came into force in April 1961. They were slightly amended in 1963.

In order to achieve the financial objective, the graduated element in the pension was deliberately kept below the actuarial value of the contributions. The estimate of the Government Actuary provided that the income from graduated contributions will always be more than double the expenditure on graduated pensions. For instance, in the year 2001, after forty years operation of the graduated scheme, there would be an income of £537 million from that part of the contribution and an expenditure of £199 million on the graduated part of the pensions.

This scheme was criticized by the Opposition as a "swindle". The Government argued that the extra money taken from the graduated contributor went towards the flat-rate benefits. If it were not found in this way, it would have to come from the Exchequer, i.e. out of one pocket instead of the other. To this the counter-argument was that a subsidy from the Exchequer would be fairer, rather than putting the extra burden on those in the £9 to £15 wage bracket (amended in 1963 to cover people up to £18 a week).

More Discrimination?

When the new system resulting from the 1959 Act came into force in 1961, there was also a modest rise in pension rates and there was another one in 1963. But these rises were on a small scale and have been partly cancelled out by the increased cost of living. They have not had the effect of raising the level of pensioners' living standards very much. Meanwhile, as the rest of the population has become better off, there has been a widespread feeling that the poverty facing many elderly people and some sick people and widows ought to be more drastically tackled.

One line of argument that has been heard from some quarters, including many Conservative backbenchers, is this: why give all-round pension increases when lots of pensioners do not really need them? Why give a higher pension to thousands of elderly people with private savings and investments? If the increases could be confined to those with little or no other source of income, they could be on a larger scale.

This is in many ways an attractive argument. There is a limit to what can be demanded in terms of taxes or national insurance contributions from the lower paid worker with a family to keep—particularly if the money is to go for increases in pensions for people better off than himself. Why not concentrate the extra money where it is most needed?

But how? The only available answer has been to make increases in National

Assistance rates rather than in National Insurance rates. Each applicant must prove a need and the extra money would go to those who were genuinely without other means of support.

The main objection to this has been the reluctance of people to undergo a means test. Every social worker and every M.P. has met elderly people who cannot bring themselves to apply for National Assistance. They feel it is a form of charity and that there is something degrading about it. This attitude is, of course, entirely wrong. They are entitled to a supplement from the N.A.B. to which they have contributed in the past as taxpayers, but many of them will not see it that way. As already stated, it has been estimated that perhaps half a million pensioners are entitled to assistance, but fail to apply. Among these people is to be found the worst poverty in Britain today.

This, then, is the dilemma. On the one hand, selective improvements, based on a means test, will fail to help many of the very poorest, who reject the indignity, as they see it, which is involved in this method. On the other hand, there is a limit to what we can afford by way of all-round increases when the burden has to be spread over the contributors. This dilemma has hitherto faced the Labour Party as well as the Government. The National Superannuation scheme would have provided a long-term solution, but it would not have done sufficient for existing pensioners or for those due to retire in the next twenty years or so, as they would not have built up very much entitlement under the scheme.

New Frontiers for Social Security

It is this dilemma which led the Labour Party to make further studies which have recently resulted in the publication of another policy statement—*New Frontiers for Social Security*. As a member of the study group this time, sitting at the feet of Dick Crossman and Professor Titmuss and his "skiffle group", I can testify that we went very carefully and thoroughly over the whole field of national insurance. We reviewed, for instance, the effect of the 1959 Act upon our proposals for National Superannuation. Fortunately, the machinery now established can be adapted to more ambitious proposals, and it was possible to be fairly clear about the kind of amendments we would need to make.

We also reviewed the place of sickness and unemployment benefits in the scheme and we proposed that they, too, should be wage-related, at least for the first year's absence from work.

But our central problem was the one referred to in the last section. How to manage a really substantial improvement for the existing pensioners and those who will retire before the National Superannuation scheme begins to "bite"?

This led to the important new proposal which has been called the Income

Guarantee. This would cover all retired people and those on widows' benefits. A minimum income will be fixed below which nobody in these groups will be allowed to fall. When the actual income, including the flat-rate pension, falls below this level, an income supplement would be paid to bring it up to the guaranteed level. This would happen automatically and without a personal test of means. It would be done in a simple income return on the lines of the simplified tax returns already in use. The only "means test" would be in the form already familiar to every income-tax payer.

The level of the guarantee would in the first year be substantially above the current pension rate, and it would be increased by annual increments to the point where it would lift the great majority of pensioners out of the National Assistance level—all except those with unusually high rents, or some other special burden, for whom National Assistance would be there as an alternative.

The statement also contains an important modification of the proposals for National Superannuation. The entitlement to pension rates would be built up more quickly by doubling the value given to the contributions of the over 50's during the early years of the scheme. The aim would be to ensure that a married man with average earnings will qualify for a half-pay pension if he retires at any time after the scheme has been in operation for seven years. This means that the liability incurred by the State for the income guarantee will decline rapidly and will disappear after a transition period.

A further step would be the abolition of the N.A.B. and its merger with the Ministry of Pensions and National Insurance in a new Ministry of Social Security.

Conclusion

It will be seen that the thinking of both the Government and Opposition has undergone a number of important changes in recent years. Both have had to re-think previous policies, and it cannot be said that the process is necessarily complete. The basic fact behind this is that the prospect of economic growth opens up the possibility of better living standards and greater dignity in the lives of those millions of people unable to earn their living, whether because of old age, widowhood, sickness or unemployment. The way in which the rest of us face up to our responsibility to this section of the community is one of the biggest domestic issues of the day.

14. Financial Provision for the Aged

DOROTHY COLE WEDDERBURN

Senior Research Officer, Department of Applied Economics, Cambridge

POVERTY among the old is no new phenomenon. The great pioneers of the social survey in Britain, Booth and Rowntree, found in their studies that the old figured prominently among the poor. Recent attempts[1] to assess the nature and extent of poverty in present-day affluent Britain have again found that the poverty of old age is a real problem. To understand why this is so I shall first consider the development of state financial provision for the aged.* Secondly, I shall consider state provision in the total picture of financial resources available to the old. Thirdly, I shall try to identify the main problem groups among the old, and finally I shall consider the implications of this picture for the future of pension policy.

The Development of State Provision

At the end of the nineteenth century, among the aged poor there was complete destitution—no income, no resources, the workhouse. As Rowntree remarked: "in 1899 a person too old to work and having no private sources of income had as a rule to choose between two alternatives—either to live, often as an unwanted guest, with a married son or daughter, or to go into the workhouse."[2] By the inter-war period the situation had changed. Non-contributory old age pensions, payable at 70 to all whose means were proved low enough, had been introduced in 1908. In 1925 the principle of contributory old age pensions, payable as of right to those who satisfied the contribution conditions, was introduced for manual workers. Thus by the time that Rowntree carried out his second poverty survey in 1936, most old people had a pension on which, as he put it, they "can manage to live". The important thing was that in 1936 this pension, even when supplemented by Public Assistance (the old "means test"), left the recipient below Rowntree's poverty line and a long way below it at that. It was in no sense a "subsistence" pension.

The Beveridge Report of 1942 argued that: "Any Plan of Social Security worthy of its name must ensure that every citizen, fulfilling during his working

* This chapter was written in 1963, and all statistics are the latest then available. Since this chapter was written, the retirement pension was increased in March 1965 to £4 for a single person, and to £6 10s. 0d. for a married couple. National Assistance scale rates were increased in 1965 to £3 16s. 0d. for a single person, and £6 5s. 6d. for a married couple.

life the obligations of service according to his powers, can claim as of right when he is past work an income adequate to maintain him."[3] It went on to say: "This means providing as an essential part of the plan a pension on retirement from work which is enough for subsistence, even though the pensioner has no other resources whatever; some pensioners will have no other resources. It means also providing a pension which is not reduced if the pensioner has other resources." The Report's proposals were based upon three principles: (i) universal coverage, (ii) benefits available to all on satisfaction of the contribution conditions, and (iii) flat-rate subsistence benefits. The National Insurance Act, 1946 (which followed the Beveridge Report), provided for the compulsory insurance of everyone over school-leaving age and under pensionable age. But, in the event, the flat-rate benefits payable under the Act, and which included retirement pensions, were fixed, in real terms, below the pre-war Rowntree poverty line. The subsistence principle was abandoned *de facto* at the outset.

Since 1948, when the National Insurance Act came into full operation, the level of the retirement pension has been raised six times, the last increase being in May 1963. But prices have increased over this period too. Has there been an increase in the real value of the pension? Broadly speaking until 1958 the increases were only enough to keep pace with the increase in prices. But since then the increases have been such as not only to ensure that benefits "keep abreast of the cost of living but that pensioners should share in rising standards"[4]. The basic retirement pension now stands at £3 7s. 6d. a week for one person, £5 9s. 0d. for a husband and a dependent wife.[5] Comparing this with the equivalent at today's prices of the minimum subsistence income which Rowntree calculated as necessary for a retired person in 1936, we find these rates are between a fifth and a third higher. The pension today is above pre-war subsistence levels; it has built in a floor and eliminated poverty among the old as it was known before the war.

But as Beveridge himself wrote in 1942: "What is required for reasonable human subsistence is to some extent a matter of judgement: estimates on this point change with time, and generally in a progressive community change upwards."[6] Current dissatisfaction with the present levels of retirement pensions, which is still widespread, spring from the feeling that *pre-war* subsistence standards are inadequate. Our society is much wealthier than pre-war by any measure· If we consider simply one measure that is *per capita* personal disposable income, this is 25 per cent higher in real terms than pre-war. The retirement pension, then, in the last seventeen years has scarcely kept pace with the general increase in prosperity. It has certainly not, as many would argue it should, increased faster.

Not everyone became entitled to a retirement pension in 1946. But as a result of the generous terms by which new contributors to the scheme were given entitlement to full pensions in 1958 after paying only ten years' contributions, today the great majority of people over retirement age (65 for men and 60 for women) have a right to a pension, and nearly three-quarters of them are actually drawing one. There are $7\frac{3}{4}$ million people in Great Britain over pensionable age, and 6 million of these are retirement pensioners. Over 400,000 are men and women who have postponed retirement and are earning increments to their retirement pensions, and 700,000, it is estimated, are women 60 and over married to men who have not yet reached retirement age. A tiny group, some 100,000, all over 70, are receiving non-contributory pensions under the Old Age Pension Act, 1936. These are pensions administered by the National Assistance Board and payable subject to a test of means with a maximum rate of 28s. 4d. per week for a single person. The remainder of those people over retirement age, one-half to three-quarters of a million, have no entitlement either to a retirement or to a non-contributory pension.[7]

The great majority of the existing retirement pensioners are receiving the standard full rate of pension. About 5 per cent are receiving less than the full rate, usually because they have failed to satisfy the necessary contribution conditions. Just over a fifth receive increments to the basic pensions. At the moment most of these increments have been earned by continuing to work and to pay contributions past retirement age. The average increment earned in this way is 7s. 6d. a week. Since the middle of 1961 another kind of increment has begun to make its appearance as a result of the introduction of the graduated pension scheme through the National Insurance Act, 1959. That Act provided for the payment of graduated contributions equal to $4\frac{1}{4}$ per cent of earnings, by employer and employee, on a limited band of earnings. The accumulated units of contributions earn extra pension. The amounts of extra pension, however, are small. To give an example, a man paying the maximum graduated contribution for eight years will have earned only an extra 12s. 6d. a week by the time he reaches retirement age.

The situation has now reached a point where there are 150 different rates of retirement pension in payment.[8] This means an immense complication of the scheme in administrative terms, and yet the actual money value of the increments earned is small. There is no consistent philosophy underlying the level at which the basic pension or the increments are fixed other than generalized statements about "sharing in prosperity". Mr. Niall Macpherson, as Minister of Pensions and National Insurance, is reported as saying: "Our philosophy is to make a foundation payment and then add to it in accordance with need. We aim to provide an insurance benefit at a level which takes account of contributions that the great majority of contributors can reasonably be asked to pay."[9] In the House he said: "To estimate what a subsistence level universally applicable throughout the country should be is virtually impossible."[10]

The result of this abandonment of any subsistence basis for the determination of the level of retirement pensions has been that throughout the whole of the post-war period another major source of state provision for the aged has been the National Assistance Board. The Board is empowered to lay down scale rates to meet "needs". Where an applicant's resources as determined by the Board fall short of his "needs" a payment is made. Since 1948 the percentage of retirement pensioners receiving supplementation from the Board has never fallen below a fifth and at times has been as high as 27 per cent. In recent years it has been some 23 per cent.[11] Other old people without retirement pensions, but whose income from other sources leaves them below the scale rate, have also had help from the Board. Sixty-eight per cent of the recipients of weekly allowance from the Board are past retirement age. Of all people over retirement age a fifth have help from the Board.

The scale rates for requirements other than rent (in most—although not all—cases, rent is met in full in addition to the scale rate) have been increased ten times since July 1948. As with retirement pensions, many of these increases have simply served to restore the value of the scale rate which had been eroded by rising prices. Again, of recent years, however, there has been an improvement in real terms. The scale rate (excluding rent) for a single householder is £3 3s. 6d., and for a couple £5 4s. 6d.[12]

The Total Picture of the Financial Position of the Old

In the frequent discussions about the levels of the retirement pension, commentators, including Government spokesmen, have frequently stated that no retirement pensioner has to live on his pension alone. As Mrs. Thatcher, the Parliamentary Secretary to the Minister of Pensions, said in a debate in March 1962:

> The question is often asked whether anyone can be expected to live on the retirement pension of 57s. 6d. or on the National Assistance scale of 53s. 6d. The obvious answer is that no-one is expected to, because there are other resources available. Of the 5½ million pensioners today, many have private resources or are members of occupational pension schemes and are receiving benefits from them.

Others, including critics of the Government, have argued that there are retirement pensioners too proud or too ignorant to apply for the National Assistance to which they are entitled, or with such small amounts of income from these supplementary sources, like private pension schemes, as to be virtually dependent upon their retirement pension.

Only in the last year or so have the facts become known, as a result of a national survey of the economic circumstances of old people which I carried out in 1959–60.[13] Although the *levels* of pension and National Assistance scale rates have been raised since the information was collected, there is no reason to suppose that the data obtained from the survey about the proportion of old people largely dependent upon the State for their income, in one form or another, are invalid.

The first striking fact to emerge from the survey was that 46 per cent of all people over retirement age derive most of their income from the government retirement pension, from the National Assistance Board, or from the two combined. If we consider retirement pensioners alone, the percentage rises to over 53 per cent. In precise terms "most of their income" means that in addition to the sources named, these old people have no more than £1 a week from any other source. The great majority also have negligible savings.

This means that in addition to those retirement pensioners receiving National Assistance, or old people receiving nothing but National Assistance, there are as many old people again who have their standard of living (in so far as this depends upon the income available to them as of right) determined by the current levels of state benefits. Two groups can be distinguished here. The first is a group, representing half as many again of all old people who are at present receiving National Assistance, who are entitled to it but for one reason or another are not drawing it. The second is a group without entitlement to National Assistance, but whose small incomes from part-time jobs, from pensions from previous employers and so on, act rather as a substitute for National Assistance, than as a substantial elevation of their total level of income.

This particular estimate of the number of old people with entitlement to, but not receiving, National Assistance has been criticized, mainly on two grounds. The first has been that the size of sample was such that a relatively large margin of error attaches to the estimate. In fact the sampling error is not so large. But if we say that at the moment we know that a fifth of all individuals over retirement age are receiving National Assistance, the minimum estimate of the percentage with entitlement, and not receiving it, is another 7 per cent of all old people. But the sampling error could also mean that as many as another 11 per cent were entitled. The actual figure given by the survey is 9 per cent.

The second criticism is not of the statistic but of its interpretation. The argument runs that the low level of income which these findings imply tells us nothing about the poverty of old people because many of the poorest are to be found living with their children and, it is implied thereby, enjoying a higher standard of living. It is true that the small but not insignificant group of old people who have no resources at all, other than their retirement pension, are all to be found sharing house with others. But of the whole group with entitlement and not receiving help from the Assistance Board, some two-thirds are keeping house alone, or with a husband or wife only. Such an argument, however, raises important issues of policy which go beyond the immediate question of National Assistance. Should the adequacy or otherwise of the income levels of the old be judged on the basis of how they choose to live— on their own or sharing house with family or friends? It would appear from the way in which the operation of the means test was reformed by the

National Assistance Act, 1948, that public opinion in this country was no longer prepared to tolerate any system which laid upon the family a legal duty to support its dependent old. The only recognition given to the advantages which might accrue from sharing a house is that a lower scale rate is applicable to a non-householder, and he is assumed to contribute only a reasonable share of the total rent of the household. Similarly, when the recipient of National Assistance is a householder but has children or others living with him he is again assumed (since 1959) to receive from the other members of the household only a "reasonable contribution to the rent".

A final decision on this issue must in part be a personal value judgement. But more evidence has now become available to strengthen the case for considering only the independent money income of the aged. In this country some 46 per cent of all those old people with surviving children are keeping house with at least one of them. This by no means ensures that they are prosperous. As my study showed, when the child is a single woman her own income may well be quite small and possibly reduced by having to care for her aged parent. On the other hand, it is clear that for large numbers the subsidy from young to old in the joint household can be considerable. But in these cases the psychological as well as the economic needs of the old have to be considered. At a time when many find their growing physical dependency a source of great worry, the knowledge that they are also financially dependent—unable, as they put it, to pull their weight on the income side—may be the last straw.

Why, then, do not old people—both those living alone and keeping house with others—with entitlement—apply for National Assistance? Sometimes the answer lies in their ignorance. Old people may be unaware that a hundred or two pounds in the bank or living with a child does not make them ineligible. Of recent years the publicity given to the workings of the National Assistance Board has in part helped to counteract this. I have also argued that simplification of the regulations which govern the determination of "resources" for the National Assistance Board would also help.[14] At the moment there are certain quite arbitrary distinctions between *kinds* (rather than amounts) of resources which are quite unjustifiable. The easier it is for people to see whether they are entitled, and how their entitlement is arrived at, the more likely are they to apply. But over and above all this it must be recognized by policy makers that there is a deep-rooted aversion to "asking for help", or "charity" as it is often called, and having "to plead poverty", which is how the means test is all too often seen. It might be thought that this was a special problem for the present generation of the old, who have vivid memories of the slump, and the "Public Assistance" as it was administered in the thirties. But it seems that they have passed on their aversion to their sons and daughters. We find young men and women who are sick or widowed doing all they can to avoid having to apply for National Assistance. The dilemma which this deep-rooted feeling creates for those who, quite rationally and logically, when faced with scarce resources, wish to concentrate help on those "who need it most" is a problem to which I shall return.

At the other end of the scale to those who are primarily dependent on the State for their income is a sizeable group who can be regarded as very largely independent of it. Of all the retirement pensioners in my sample 20 per cent had income from other sources which more than doubled their income from their state pension. This is some evidence of the existence of "two nations in old age", although the nation of those primarily dependent upon the State is by far the largest. Then it must also be remembered that for the quarter or so lying between these two extremes, income from the State is still very important.

The Main Problem Groups Among the Elderly

If we examine more closely the dependence of the elderly upon state financial provision we find that there is a wide difference between the position of single and widowed women, on the one hand, and of men and married couples, on the other. The women are in all respects worse off. Fifty-eight per cent of them have less than £1 a week income from sources other than the retirement pension and/or National Assistance. Only 40 per cent of the men are in this position and just over a fifth of the couples. Thirty per cent of the single and widowed women over retirement age are receiving National Assistance, 20 per cent of the men, but only 11 per cent of the couples.

In my survey the median income of those couples who had retired was more than twice that of the women. This is a much bigger difference than that allowed for in the retirement pension itself. The retirement pension for a couple is 1·6 times that for a single person. The explanation of the rest of the difference lies in the much greater diversity of resources available to the couples than to the women. The couples more often have employment income (even those who have retired from full-time jobs); they more often have pensions from a previous employer; they more often have income from property or from investments. But not only do they more often receive income from these sources, but the amounts which they receive from them are, on average, larger than the amounts which the women, also with income from these sources, are receiving. The same is true of assets.

The reasons for the relative poverty of the women are twofold. First, even without directly wage-related state pensions, financial position in old age is to a considerable extent dictated by past work experiences or by continued ability to work. Although the post-war period has seen what amounts to a revolution in the extent to which married women work, the proportions are still low compared with those of men in equivalent age groups. According to official figures, in 1961, in the age group 55–59 94½ per cent of males were working, but only 61 per cent of single and 31 per cent of married women. Despite the great drop for all, the difference continues in the group over 65. Twenty-seven per cent of the men were in the working population, but only 6 per cent of the single and of the married women.[15] So long as women are supplementary earners the consequences of lower pay for women are not fully realized. It is when the full responsibility for upkeep of the home falls upon their shoulders that their vulnerable economic position becomes apparent. The other way in which past work experience affects income in old age is through occupational pensions. In my survey I found that very nearly a half of all the single and widowed men in the sample, and of the husbands in couples, had some sort of pension from their previous employer. A fifth of the *single* women (who are, of course, the women most likely to have a record of continuous employment), but only 2 per cent of the widows, had such pensions by virtue of their own previous employment record. Perhaps even more significant, only 4 per cent of the widows had pensions from the former employers of their deceased husbands.

The second factor, making for the relative poverty of the women, is that so many of them are in fact widows. In Britain in 1961, again according to official sources, single and widowed women were 6 per cent of the age group 30–39, 8 per cent of the age group 40–49, 13 per cent of the age group 50–59 but 41 per cent of the total population over 65.[16] In my survey 60 per cent of the widowed women had lost their husbands more than ten years ago. Thirty per cent of them had lost their husbands before they were 50, and another 30 per cent between 50 and 60. In this situation it is not surprising to find that many of these widows had little opportunity to accumulate even a small amount of savings; or if they had, to find it run down as they adjusted to the much lower income with which they were faced upon the death of their husbands.

The vulnerable position of women is of very great importance not only for the formation of policy today, but also in assessing what is likely to happen in the future. It is often argued that, to the extent that there are problem groups in terms of poverty and low income among the elderly it is a temporary phenomenon, to be accounted for by the fact that the elderly today are a generation whose working lives were profoundly affected by the inter-war years of depression. The financial position of the elderly in the future will be quite different, it is said, because they will be the generation of post-war affluence. Their savings will be higher, and increasing numbers of them will have occupational pensions.

Our analysis of the problem of poverty in old age as a woman's—particularly a widow's—problem, immediately throws some doubt on this thesis, unless very firm steps are taken to safeguard widows' rights in occupational pension schemes. Apart from this, however, it seems doubtful whether there will be any dramatic increase in the number of beneficiaries of either sex from employers' pension schemes, at least in the next ten to fifteen years (and we can scarcely attempt to forecast in the field of pensions over a much longer period!). The information we have about the coverage of such schemes at the moment is most inadequate. There may be as many as 10 million members.[17] But membership at a point of time is not the end of the story. A member of a private occupational pension scheme who changes his job either voluntarily or because he is dismissed, may have his pension rights at the very least interrupted, at the worst reduced, to the maximum provided by the present State scheme. We cannot, therefore, tell from figures of coverage what proportion of workers will arrive at retirement age with the right to an occupational pension or how much that pension will be. A parallel study of a group of people between the ages of 50 and retirel ment age, which I made at the same time as the survey of the over-retire- ment age group, suggests that the percentage with rights to occupationa- pension will not be significantly higher among people retiring during the next few years than among those already retired.

As for savings, the evidence from this same pre-retirement age group sug- gests that they were unlikely to reach retirement with significantly larger amounts of savings than their older counterparts. A feature of some im- portance here is that to save out of income (without assistance from em- ployers) amounts of capital which are large enough to make a real difference to the level of financial resources in old age requires a big effort. It is interes- ting at this point to compare the position with the United States. If it is argued that higher real incomes during working life mean greater oppor- tunities to save for old age; and if it is agreed that the American aged have by and large enjoyed a higher standard of living than their English counter- parts, then the similarities in respect of ownership of assets and receipts of income from assets require some other explanation which it is difficult to supply. Almost exactly the same percentage of the aged in both countries (a third) are without assets, and without any significant income from assets.[18]

The Implications for Future Pension Policy

There has probably never been so much discussion of pension policy in this country as in the last few years. Some of it has, of course, stemmed from the more general problems of how to finance pensions, with which this essay is not concerned; but much of it has undoubtedly been provoked by the obvious inability of our present pension system to guarantee a socially acceptable standard of living to the old. Much as present levels of retirement pension represent an improvement over the past they are still, as we have seen, not more than a third higher than Rowntree's pre-war poverty standard. We have only to remind ourselves of the stringency of the standards which Rowntree adopted, particularly for the old, to feel that even 30 per cent above that standard is not likely to be a wholly acceptable measure of "subsistence" today. Such discussions of pension policy have centred on three key problems: they are the principles by which the levels of pension should be determined; the problems of, what I will call, "equity"; and the problem of choice and alternatives to state schemes.

(a) The solution to the problem of determining pension levels has been sought in the principle of "wage relation". This has taken two forms. One is simply a device for ensuring that what may be a flat-rate benefit keeps pace with increasing real national income by expressing the flat rate as a percentage of some national average wage. In 1952 the I.L.O. adopted a convention which recommended that benefits payable under national pension schemes should not be less than 40 per cent of the average earnings of an unskilled worker.[19] The second form is to link benefits in some way to the past earnings record of the individual worker. This has always been a feature of the German pension system. The pension reform of 1957, in that country, in addition to extending this principle, also introduced a neat device for ensuring that pension levels increased with real income. The individual's past earnings' record is expressed in terms of current levels of earnings and pensions actually in payment may also be increased if there is a real increase in earnings.[20]

These are useful techniques. The political philosophies used to justify the method of wage relation are diverse. But the main logic lies in the view that hardship and poverty are relative to the past income experience of the individual. To minimize this hardship on retirement the individual is called upon to accept not more than a specified percentage reduction in his income. There are a number of problems raised by this argument. The most important, in the context of the present discussion, is that the principle does not wholly avoid the concept of "subsistence", unless we are prepared entirely to ignore the consequences of the system in terms of the actual levels of income produced in retirement. For it may well be that a fixed percentage of the lowest earnings in the society would produce an income level below that which would be socially acceptable. The old problem of a minimum income below which people should not be expected to live will arise again.

This is a particularly important problem in view of what we have seen of the position of single and widowed women among the old. They are likely to decline as a proportion of the total over-retirement age group over the next ten to twenty years, but not dramatically, and will still not be below a third. If we are expecting to depend upon the work records of women for calculating their entitlement to pensions we must bear in mind that while women's wages remain at levels some one-half those of men's, any percentage of former earnings which may produce acceptable levels of pension for men may well not do so for women. In addition we have seen that the breaks in married women's work records are likely to be such as to produce unacceptable bases for calculating their entitlement to pension when they become widows. Steps must be taken to guarantee the position of widows via their husbands' earnings record. But the simple principle of wage relation alone may not suffice, or even continue to be acceptable. On what basis can we judge what the drop in income should be in widowhood?

Finally, it must be remembered that schemes for the wage relation of pensions depend upon the building up of rights based upon contributions made during working life. They are schemes largely for the future. Each one faces the problem of how rapidly such rights shall be allowed to build up, and how and to what extent existing pensioners are to benefit. Without special steps being taken, the bulk of pensioners for a long time to come will not be benefited.

(b) The position of existing pensioners immediately raises the problem of "equity". Our examination of the evidence showed that, on the one hand, about one-half of today's pensioners do have their level of total income almost wholly determined by levels of state benefit. Moreover, a substantial proportion have to submit to an investigation of their means which by and large is very unpopular. At the other extreme there is also a not insignificant proportion, perhaps a fifth, who are quite well off without the State, but who are nevertheless receiving a retirement pension. It is argued by many that because there is this group who "do not need it" and in view of the considerable cost of raising the pension by any substantial amount for all 6 million pensioners, more reliance should be placed upon a test of means to identify those who really do. In this way help can be concentrated where it is most needed.

Here is the dilemma, to which we referred earlier, between the means test as a device to identify those really in need in order to give them substantial help, and the means test as a hated symbol of loss of status in a society which ostensibly sets great store by "independence" and self-help. Indirect devices for singling out a group broadly coterminous with those whose need is greatest have been suggested—for instance higher pensions for the single and widowed or higher pensions for the over-seventies.[21] Another possibility is now widely canvassed on both sides of the political fence.[22] It rests for support on the view that the income-tax system is not seen by people as a means test. This is so, not least because it does not single out a particular group for attention, but applies to all citizens in society. In this situation, it is argued, let supplementation of retirement pensions, or even retirement pensions themselves, be administered and paid on the basis of the information supplied in income-tax returns. Not only would it be possible then to pay more to the poorest, but it would also avoid some of the administrative waste at present involved in paying retirement pensions to the richest and then taking back a large part, in income and surtax.

(c) Finally, does the examination of the financial resources of today's pensioners shed any light upon the current controversy between the advocates of state provision for old age, on the one hand, and of freedom of choice to make individual private provision, on the other?[23] Our examination of the evidence lends little support to the view that genuine "self-provision", i.e. through the accumulation by the individual of savings, or insurance policies during his working life which will provide him with income in old age, can, in any way, be considered a real possibility for the great majority in the foreseeable future. The only *genuine* alternative to a state scheme which has so far emerged is the system of occupational pension schemes as run by employers. We have seen that these are already an important source of income for certain groups over retirement age, and although there are good reasons for supposing that there are serious limitations on their extension in the future, they have to be reckoned with.

But the question then arises how far can such occupational pension schemes be regarded as "individual" provision? There is all too little evidence available about the operation of such schemes. But it appears that only in the minority of cases does the worker have any choice about whether or not he belongs to such a scheme; and in even fewer cases does he have much influence upon the nature and kind of benefits offered by it. There is frequently substantial discrimination between groups of workers (i.e. between works and staff or between age groups) in the value of the benefits offered. The choice, if there is one, seems to lie between compulsion by the State and compulsion by the employer with, in the latter case, the State acting as a long-stop to protect those groups not covered or covered inadequately by employers' schemes.

References

1. PETER TOWNSEND, The meaning of poverty, *The British Journal of Sociology*, Vol. 13, No. 3. DOROTHY COLE WEDDERBURN, Poverty in Britain today—the evidence, *The Sociological Review*, Vol. 10, No. 3.
2. S. ROWNTREE, *Poverty and Progress*, Longmans, 1941.
3. *Social Insurance and Allied Services*, Cmnd. 6404, H.M.S.O., 1924.
4. MR. NIALL MACPHERSON, House of Commons, 28 Jan. 1963.
5. From 27 May 1963.
6. *Op. cit.*, Cmnd. 6404.
7. MINISTRY OF PENSIONS AND NATIONAL INSURANCE, Retirement and Contributory Old Age Pensions and Widows' Benefits, *Abstract of Statistics* for the years 1959 and 1960.
8. MRS. MARGARET THATCHER, House of Commons, 13 Mar. 1962.
9. Policy and caution, *New Society*, 18 Oct. 1962.
10. MR. NIALL MACPHERSON, House of Commons, 26 Nov. 1962.
11. *Report of the National Assistance Board for the Year Ended 31st December 1961*, Cmnd. 1730, H.M.S.O., 1962.
12. From 27 May, 1963.
13. DOROTHY COLE with JOHN UTTING, *The Economic Circumstances of Old People*, The Codicote Press, 1962. The evidence which follows is from this interim study or from data to be published in the main report of the survey.
14. *Ibid.*

15. *Economic Trends*, H.M.S.O., Sept. 1962
16. *Ibid.*
17. ARTHUR SELDON, Contracting out of State Pensions, *The Times*, 23 Jan. 1963.
18. ETHEL SHANAS, *The Health of Older People*, Harvard University Press, 1962.
19. *Official Bulletin of the I.L.O.*, Vols. 34–35, I.L.O., 1952.
20. KURT JANTZ, Pension reform in Germany, *International Labour Review*, Vol. 83.
21. COLE with UTTING, *op. cit.*
22. See, for instance: CHRISTOPHER CHATAWAY, Pensions: A New Approach, *Crossbow*, Vol 4, No. 14. *New Frontiers for Social Security*, The Labour Party, 1963.
23. See, for instance: ARTHUR SELDON, Beveridge 20 years after, *New Society*, 14 Feb. 1963. BRIAN ABEL-SMITH, Beveridge II: Another viewpoint, *New Society*, 28 Feb. 1963.

15. The National Assistance Board

... and distribution was made
unto every man according as he had need
(Acts iv. 35)

WILLIAM L. LIDBURY

Formerly Regional Controller, London (North) Region,
National Assistance Board

Introduction

The chief duty of the National Assistance Board is to provide financial assistance to people in need. It was in 1948 that the Board, under the National Assistance Act of that year, were made responsible for administering a single scheme of financial assistance which would provide for all those in need.

The 1948 Act was the culmination of earlier Acts, starting with the Unemployment Assistance Act, 1934. Under the 1934 Act the Unemployment Assistance Board was set up to administer a new social service covering practically all able-bodied unemployed people who normally worked for wages, making provision for their welfare as well as for the payment of cash allowances on a basis of need. These allowances included where necessary the supplementation of unemployment benefit payable under the unemployment insurance scheme. Nearly 800,000 unemployed men and women were assisted by the Board as soon as the 1934 Act came into force.

At the outbreak of war in 1939 the number of unemployed men and women declined rapidly, but in 1940 the supplementary pensions scheme was launched, providing weekly payments to contributory and non-contributory pensioners on a needs basis. The number of supplementary pensioners ultimately rose to over $1\frac{1}{2}$ million, and the introduction of the new scheme and the decline in unemployment at the time meant that the Board was no longer concerned wholly or even mainly with unemployment problems; the Board's title was therefore changed to the Assistance Board. It became the National Assistance Board under the 1948 Act. This change marked the completion of the long process of liquidating the old Poor Law.

The fact that assistance from the Board is available only on a test of need distinguishes it from other branches of the country's social security system, such as the benefits received in return for National Insurance contributions and family allowances.

The Board itself consists of a chairman, a deputy chairman, and not less than one nor more than four other members; at least one of them must be a woman. All are appointed by the Queen on the advice of the Prime Minister. They may not stand for election to the House of Commons or sit as a Member of Parliament. When matters affecting National Assistance arise in the House of Commons they are dealt with by the Minister of Pensions and National Insurance. The expenses of the Department, including both the cost of assistance grants and the salaries of the staff, are met by the Exchequer in the same way as the expenses of other Government departments; the staff are civil servants. The day-to-day work of dealing with applications and issuing allowances is carried out at local area offices, of which there are 437.

What the task of helping all those in need means today may be judged by the fact that at any one time about 2 million people are receiving weekly allowances, of whom 85 per cent are old or sick; a year's total of applications is nearly 3 million. Interviews at the local offices and in applicants' homes number about 14 million. The cost of these allowances, including about £15 million for administrative expenses, is over £210 million a year, and the money is voted by Parliament and paid from taxation. Nevertheless, old prejudices sometimes die hard, and a pensioner with memories of the days of the Poor Law may still regard applying for a supplement to his pension as "asking for charity" and in some way hurting his self-respect. However understandable, this is quite wrong. Acceptance of the help the Board can give should no more be regarded as involving a stigma than does acceptance of the other social services paid for from public funds, such as family allowances or education.

The National Assistance Act, 1948

The Board's duty to assist is set down in the National Assistance Act in the following words:

> It shall be the duty of the Board in accordance with the following provisions of this part of this Act to assist persons in Great Britain who are without resources to meet their requirements, or whose resources (including benefits receivable under the National Insurance Acts 1946) must be supplemented in order to meet their requirements.

The Act goes on to limit this very general definition by saying that assistance cannot be granted to people in full-time employment, or to their dependants. A person directly involved in a trade dispute is also disqualified from receiving assistance, though help can if necessary be given for his wife and children. There is, however, an overriding power to assist anyone, whether they would otherwise be disqualified or not, in the event of a real emergency.*

* An example of such an emergency was the very serious flooding along the east coast and in the Thames Estuary during the night of Saturday, 31 January 1953, when thousands of people became temporarily homeless. The floods came in most places without warning. The local authorities were under statutory obligation to supply shelter and food to the victims and the National Assistance Board, under their emergency arrangements, made 9000 payments to meet immediate necessities such as clothing and footwear.

An application cannot be accepted from anyone below the age of sixteen; the Act makes parents responsible for their children below that age. If a parent requires assistance, the needs of any children will be included in his allowance; a family living together is dealt with as a group and one allowance only is paid, usually to the husband.

The Basis of the Board's Allowances

The position is then that anyone over the age of sixteen who is not in full-time work and is in need can apply to the Board for help. How does the Board's officer decide whether an allowance can be paid and, if so, how much? The rules for deciding whether assistance is needed are laid down in the National Assistance (Determination of Need) Regulations. The original Regulations were made in 1948, but they have been amended from time to time; the Board submits new draft Regulations to the Minister of Pensions and National Insurance, who in turn submits them to both Houses of Parliament for approval.

The Regulations lay down weekly sums called scale rates for needs other than rent. Under amending Regulations approved by Parliament the scale rate for a married couple from 29 March 1965 is £6 5s. 6d. a week, £3 16s. 0d. for a single householder, £3 7s. 6d. for anyone else over twenty-one years of age, and amounts for children which vary according to age. There are specially higher scale rates for the blind and for persons who have suffered a loss of income to take treatment for respiratory tuberculosis. Broadly speaking, the grant payable is calculated by taking the appropriate sums for the applicant, his wife, and any children under sixteen living with him, adding a rent allowance and then deducting their resources, less whatever amounts the Regulations say are to be left out of account. The amount by which resources fall short of needs is the amount of the grant which is paid.

Rent Allowances

If the applicant is a householder, the rent allowance to be added to the scale rates mentioned above will provide for reasonable rent, and rates if they are paid separately or, if he owns the house he lives in, for such outgoings as rates and any mortgage interest, together with an allowance for insurance and repairs. Rent under this definition is allowed in full in over 98 per cent of all current cases. If a person is not paying rent himself but is living as a member of someone else's household, his rent allowance will usually be his share of the rent up to a limit of 15s. a week.

Treatment of Resources

Most resources* are taken fully into account, e.g. sickness and unemployment benefit, retirement pensions and family allowances, but certain other income is ignored up to a total of 30s. a week in all, e.g. the first 15s. of charitable payments and superannuation payments and of sick pay from a friendly society or trade union, and the first 30s. of disability pensions, disablement benefit, and maternity allowances, are all disregarded up to a total of 30s. a week. In addition, the first 30s. plus half the next 20s. of any earnings of the applicant (or his wife) are disregarded unless he is fit and of working age and therefore required to register at the Employment Exchange, when the amount disregarded is limited to 15s. a week. With the exception of blind people, a householder's resources are taken to include a contribution towards the household expenses from any self-supporting member of his household, e.g. a son or daughter in employment and living at home. This contribution is never more than such member's proportionate share of the rent, and if his earnings are low, it may well be less.

Discretionary Powers

The Board's officers have a discretionary power under the Regulations to adjust the grant otherwise payable where there are special circumstances. The scale rates are intended to cover all normal day-to-day requirements apart from rent, but where a person has additional necessary expenses which he cannot meet from his own resources, extra provision can often be made for them. For instance, an elderly person may have to send laundry out, or may be arthritic and need more heating than most people during the winter. A person who is sick may have to follow a diet more costly than a normal one, or may need to build up his strength during a period of convalescence. Full use is made of these discretionary powers, and in about a million cases —about half the total number of weekly allowances in payment—the allowance is increased under this discretionary power by varying sums averaging about 8s. 10d. a week, at an annual cost of about £23 million. Lump-sum

* *Capital assets:* Where there are capital assets, the weekly amount of the grant will not be affected if the value of the capital is less than £125; but no grant will ordinarily be payable if the value of the capital exceeds £600. If the value of the capital is between £125 and £600, the grant otherwise payable will be reduced by 6d. a week in respect of each complete £25 in excess of £100.

The term capital assets means all money, bank allowances, investments and house property owned by the applicant, wife or husband, and dependants; but the capital value of the house in which the applicant lives is entirely disregarded.

No account is taken of the first £375 invested in "war savings" by each person included in the assessment. Broadly speaking, war savings consist of money invested with the Government since 2 September 1939.

grants may also be made where someone urgently needs help for such things as clothing or bedding; over 300,000 of these are made in a year at a cost of over £1,200,000.

Other Adjustments

An allowance may also have to be adjusted in quite different circumstances; for example, when a man is receiving help from the Board because he is unemployed, the Regulations require that he should not be made better off by way of assistance than when he has a full-time job, since he would otherwise be positively discouraged financially from seeking further employment. In such a case there may be several children and also a substantial rent; under the Board's normal assessment calculation, which would include the appropriate scale rates for each of the children, the man's income whilst unemployed could exceed his income when working; it is therefore necessary to reduce the allowance to an amount below his normal earnings.

Special Cases

A word should perhaps be said about certain people whose circumstances are rather out of the ordinary.

(1) *Hospital Patients*

If one of a married couple who are receiving a grant has to go into hospital, their income is generally kept at the same level as before for several weeks. Where a patient in hospital has nothing for personal expenses or cannot keep up the rent of his home, he will usually be able to get an allowance from the Board. But in psychiatric hospitals provision for personal expenses is made where necessary by the hospital.

(2) *Persons in Homes*

In old people's homes provided by local authorities under Part III of the National Assistance Act and by voluntary bodies which have made arrangements with a local authority, anyone who cannot pay the minimum charge may apply for help from the Board. He will ordinarily be given a grant sufficient to put him in a position, with any other resources, to meet the minimum charge and have 16s. 0d. a week left over for pocket-money.

National Health Service Charges and Fares to Hospital

Anyone receiving a regular weekly grant from the Board can get National Health Service prescription charges* refunded by obtaining a receipt from the

* With effect from 1 February 1965, charges for prescriptions and surgical appliances supplied under the National Health Service were abolished. Help with the charges which remain for dentures, dental treatment and glasses can still be obtained from the Board, as explained above.

chemist (form EC 57) and taking it along, together with his order-book, to a post office. Grants can also be made to meet charges under the National Health Service for glasses, dentures and surgical appliances and for dental treatment. If necessary, help can be given before the charge is met. A person whose income is at or very near the level of National Assistance, whether or not he is in full-time work, may also be able to get grants towards these expenses. A patient can also apply to the Board if the cost of fares to attend hospital, a clinic or a convalescent home for treatment is a cause of hardship. For a person already receiving an allowance from the Board, the hospital will pay the fares on production of the order-book, but other people whose income is roughly at assistance level may seek help through the Board's officer.

How Assistance Is Given

Apart from unemployed people, who should apply through the Employment Exchange, all that a person who wishes to obtain help has to do is to complete a simple form (O.1) obtainable pre-addressed and franked at any post office or local office of Ministry of Pensions and National Insurance and send it in to the Board's area office. If he prefers just to write, he will find the address of the Board's office on the post office notice board. When the form or letter is received, a member of the office staff will call within a few days to discuss his position and see whether any allowance can be paid. Of course, anyone in urgent need of help because of some emergency can go along to the office, where a payment can, if necessary, be made straight away. But in the ordinary way there is no need whatever to call at the Board's area office.

How Payment Will Be Made

When the officer calls, he will ask the applicant about his own resources and those of his wife and dependent children, about the make-up of the household, the rent he has to pay, and whether he has any special expenses. The facts are written down and read over to the person applying, who is then asked to sign the statement as being a true account of his circumstances. If an allowance is payable, a book of weekly orders is sent to him; this book can be cashed at the post office along with his pension, if he has one. But if he is registered at the Employment Exchange for work, the allowance will be paid there. Arrangements can be made for a pensioner to cash his pension and supplement at any post office he chooses.

The recipient of an allowance is asked to let the Board's officer know at once if at any time his circumstances or those of his dependants alter in any way, so that the allowance may be adjusted. A special form for this purpose, already franked and addressed, is provided with the order-book.

A person who is house-bound through age or infirmity can appoint a deputy to collect the allowance. If, through mental disorder or for any other reason, he is altogether incapable of managing his own affairs, the initial application can be made on his behalf by a third party acting as his agent; this agent would also deal with subsequent visits made by the Board's visiting officer.

Special Arrangements for Welfare

The Board's officers are concerned not only with providing financial assistance for those who need it, but also with the welfare of those to whom they are giving help. Under the National Assistance Act, 1948, the National Assistance Board are required "to exercise their functions in such manner as shall best promote the welfare of persons affected by the exercise thereof". By means of the regular home visits, usually made every half-year for the purpose of reviewing the allowance, the visiting officer is able to see for himself the welfare needs of each applicant. He is able to put the applicant in touch with any other local services which he may need or be glad to make use of, such as the home help service or an old people's club or friendly visiting service in the case of old people. Furthermore, the visiting officer, with his comprehensive knowledge of the friendly help and advice which the specialist voluntary societies can provide, is able where necessary to put the applicant in touch with someone who would try to help in solving his personal problem; the complications and difficulties which so often arise in family life are often unravelled and eased by this co-operation.

It is not necessary to wait for the next visit of the Board's officer if a problem develops before the next visit is due. The form which is provided for letting the office know about any changes in circumstances can also be used simply to make contact with the Board's officer at any time. If the person would like an officer to call to discuss something which is worrying him, all he has to do is to say so on the form and send it in; even if he posts the form without writing on it, it bears his reference number, and an officer will call. As a further safeguard for an elderly person living alone, the officer will ask at the first visit whether he would like someone to act as a friend to get help or to get in touch with the Board if for any reason, such as illness, he is not himself able to do so. If the applicant agrees, the officer will visit the friend, explain the Board's interest, and leave a franked and addressed form with him so that he can let the office know in the event of any emergency. The Board's officer keeps in close touch with the other local statutory and voluntary organizations who are concerned with people's welfare, and where there is a committee to co-ordinate the work of the different bodies he attends their meetings.

Advisory Committees

The Board are required by the National Assistance Act to establish Advisory Committees throughout the country to advise them on general local matters and on difficult individual cases. There are seventy-seven committees which, for the purpose of dealing with individual cases, are divided into subcommittees associated with each of the Board's local area offices. Committee members are drawn from a wide field and include such persons as local councillors, representatives of employers and workpeople, voluntary and professional social workers from many different organizations, ministers of religion, housewives, teachers, lawyers and doctors.

Appeal Tribunals

The National Assistance Act provides that a person who is dissatisfied with the decision of the Board's officer about assistance—whether it should be granted, the amount, the manner in which it is paid, or the conditions of payment—shall have the right of appeal to an Appeal Tribunal. The tribunals are independent; they have the same discretionary powers as a Board's officer and their decisions are binding on both the Board and appellants. Each tribunal consists of a chairman and two other members. The chairman is selected by the Minister of Pensions and National Insurance from a panel of persons appointed by the Lord Chancellor (in Scotland the Lord President of the Court of Session). One of the two members is appointed directly by the Minister, and the other is drawn from a panel of persons nominated by the Minister to represent workpeople. There are 151 local appeal tribunals.

The Question of Abuse

Whilst the Board's main concern is to provide help where it is needed, they must also see that their services are not abused. When necessary, they prosecute people for fraud or attempted fraud and also for "persistent refusal or neglect to maintain", i.e. where an able-bodied person is persistently idle when he should be working and supporting himself or his family. Where such a person is not receiving unemployment benefit the Board's officer may, with the prior consent of the Appeal Tribunal (and as an alternative to prosecution), make a condition of his receiving assistance that he should attend a course of training or attend one of the Board's re-establishment centres.

When a woman who is either a separated wife or a mother of an illegitimate child is given help by the Board, the husband or father becomes liable for maintenance under the National Assistance Act, and steps are taken to see that he complies with his liability so far as he is able to do so; he can, indeed, be prosecuted. The value of payments obtained from liable husbands and fathers is over £6 million each year. There is also a saving of public funds where action by the Board's officer leads either to a reconciliation or to regular payments from the man large enough to remove the need for further assistance from the Board.

Reception Centres

The Board are responsible under the National Assistance Act for providing temporary board and lodging in reception centres for persons without a settled way of living, and to influence such people to lead a more settled way of life. There are about twenty-five of these centres, some of which are administered by local authorities on the Board's behalf. The average total number of casuals accommodated nightly at these centres during 1963 was 1306. The level has varied little over the past 4 years.

Re-establishment Centres

Subject to the approval of the Minister of Pensions and National Insurance the Board may set up re-establishment centres where men who have been unemployed for long periods may be restored to the habit of working. There are now two residential re-establishment centres and one non-residential centre.

Non-contributory Old Age Pensions

The Board also adminster non-contributory old age pensions paid under the Old Age Pensions Act, 1936. Such a pension is payable to a person who is not receiving a retirement pension or a widow's pension who had reached the age of 70 before 30 September 1961, or who, if blind, has reached the age of 40. An applicant is required to satisfy conditions about means, nationality and length of residence in the United Kingdom. The maximum weekly amount of pension payable is 28s. 4d. About 79 per cent of these pensions are being supplemented by allowances payable under the National Assistance Act.

By reason of the age limitation, and because most people on retirement now qualify for a retirement pension, the number of non-contributory pensioners has been declining for many years and is now only 95,000; of these, about 77 per cent are over 80 years of age.

Legal Aid

The Board have also been made statutorily responsible for inquiring into and assessing the financial means of people applying for legal aid in civil proceedings under the Legal Aid and Advice Acts, 1949 and 1960, and the Legal Aid (Scotland) Acts, 1949 and 1960.

Administration

One of the requirements of the National Assistance Act and Regulations is that the Board shall set up local offices. There are 437 area offices in the field, grouped under eight regional offices in England, a central office in Scotland and another in Wales.

The Board's area office is a base from which the home visits mentioned earlier are organized; these visits number over $7\frac{3}{4}$ million each year. In rural parts, a journey to an area office could be a long one and quite expensive. These home-visiting arrangements are therefore a great boon to pensioners and others who would otherwise have to make such a journey.

Over 6 million callers each year are interviewed at the area offices and supplementary stations—usually persons in temporary or sometimes urgent need, or who are seeking information. The order-books for the payment of assistance are prepared at the area office and posted to applicants and the records are also held there.

The Board Annual Report

The National Assistance Board present a Report to the Minister of Pensions and National Insurance each year. This Report describes in an interesting and logical way the main events in the carrying out of the Board's functions during the year; it summarizes and explains how the money is expended and distributed and it gives some valuable and interesting statistics. It also includes an account of a selection of interesting welfare cases.

The Report is a primary source of material for students and others about contemporary problems and it shows how these problems are being dealt with. It is presented each year in June and copies are obtainable from Her Majesty's Stationery Office.

16. The Edge of Poverty*

Jo Parfitt Klein

Growing out of the ancient Poor Laws, our National Assistance programme
has burgeoned into a complex combination of regulations and subjective
judgements. How and why it distributes £180 million among 4 million poor in
the affluent society is a matter of intense public interest

FROM a spacious sixth-floor room in one of the barrack-like new office
blocks of London, the panoramic view happens to include a striking prospect
of the statue of Justice smiting the sky above the Old Bailey. It is quite an
apt coincidence. For in this room, once a month, the six members of the
National Assistance Board come together to review their own scales of
justice for the poorest citizens of the Welfare State.

This task, always huge, has grown to mammoth size since 1948, when the
National Assistance Act swept away the remains of the Poor Law and entrusted the new Board with care of the needy. The House of Commons was
told then, by the Parliamentary Secretary to the Minister of National Insurance: "It would be inappropriate to wish the National Assistance Board
an active future. Our hope is that the extensions of insurance, and eventually
a rising level of prosperity for all, will in the long run leave it with little to
do. But for some time to come it is likely to remain responsible for providing,
in whole or in part, the maintenance of more than 1,000,000 people."

Like many calculations made in those stirring, post-Beveridge days, that
one proved to be a little wide of the mark. Two years later, some 2 million
people including dependants were being assisted. Today the number is
officially reckoned at about $2\frac{1}{2}$ million but if account is taken of the turn-
over in recipients of assistance during the course of the year, it might be
nearer 4 million a year. Far from being simply an emergency stick for people
unsupported by other forms of insurance, National Assistance is an indispensable prop for the large numbers of men and women whose pensions or
benefits alone are not high enough to support them.

The proportion of weekly assistance grants paid to supplement pensions
or benefits now stands at just over 70 per cent. Nearly 60 per cent of these
grants are for reinforcing retirement pensions alone. Thus we are back at the
position observed by Beatrice Webb thirty years ago: "The pension provided
for old age is so low that many aged persons who have led respectable and
hard-working lives find themselves compelled to seek extra assistance from

* Reprinted from *New Society*, 23 December 1962, with the permission of the editor and
author.

the Poor Law." We have abolished the Poor Law. The modern system of means-tested assistance bears no comparison with its harsh forerunner. But the fact remains that many elderly men and women do not enjoy having to ask the State for extra money as a gift in contrast to drawing benefits earned as a right.

What is the alternative? Of some $5\frac{1}{2}$ million retirement pensioners in the country, roughly one-fifth receive National Assistance. The proportion has remained fairly constant over the last ten years. An all-round pension increase high enough to relieve these Assistance pensioners of the necessity to seek extra help would be a financial impossibility. If pensions were raised to £4 a week for a single person and £6 8s. 6d. for married couples with proportionate increases in war pensions and industrial injuries benefits, this would cost the Exchequer £130 million: equivalent to an increase of fourpence in the standard rate of income tax. Insurance contributions would have to go up by 6s. a week for women, 7s. for men. Such an increase would be impracticable for other reasons. It would not apply to the 530,000 people on Assistance who for one reason or another are not entitled to insurance benefits. It would not abolish, but only reduce, the need for assistance of retirement pensioners without other resources. And it would give a great deal of extra money to a great many pensioners not in need of it. By contrast, the essence of the National Assistance scheme is that every shilling spent— £182 million in 1962—goes to those who really want extra money, and to each person according to his or her need.

To say this, however, begs the crucial questions: what is need, and how do you determine the different needs of 4 million different people?

Under the 1948 Act, the Board is required simply "to assist persons in Great Britain who are without resources to meet their requirements or whose resources (including benefits receivable under the National Insurance Acts, 1946) must be supplemented in order to meet their requirements". Specific guidance on how this is to be done is laid down in separately published statutory regulations setting out the various weekly sums—scale rates—for use in computing the various needs and resources of different categories of people.

These scale rates represent the theoretical framework for determining need. In practice, the Board's officers must work out a different piece of arithmetic for every single person assisted. This is done by adding to the appropriate scale an allowance for rent, and then deducting from the resulting total that person's resources, some or all of which are wholly or partially disregarded. In addition, officers are empowered "where there are special circumstances" to give extra grants to meet the cost of a wide range of extra needs such as home help, laundry, or special diets.

Since 1948, when the scale rates were 24s. for a single householder and 40s. for a married couple, they have been raised ten times—to 76s. 0d. and

117s. 6d. As explained above, no one is expected to live at this level. There is an additional allowance for rent, and other allowances are available for other needs. But the scales are the fulcrum on which the system turns. They prescribe the general sums according to which the millions of particular sums are worked out. They define the modern poverty line.

In one sense, this line is impossible to draw. It is impossible, that is, to define subsistence except on the negative, rock-bottom basis of what it takes to prevent a man from starving, freezing or going naked—the old means test approach involving what George Orwell called "a disgusting public wrangle about the minimum weekly sum on which a human being could keep alive". But legislators have to draw lines somewhere and the scale rates selected in 1948 reflected recommendations on subsistence levels made in the Beveridge report six years earlier and based on surveys of pre-war spending patterns.

The initiative for proposing increases in the rates to the Government lies with the Board, who must decide whether the time has come to recommend an improvement, and how much. In arriving at these vital decisions, their first concern is to maintain the purchasing power of the rates. They are not tied, in doing this, to any master index of their own creation, or to any other specialized index reflecting the special needs of their clients, most of whom are old, sick or house-bound. To discover how the rates are bearing up against inflationary pressure, they review them in relation to official measurements considered relevant for the purpose. The rates are compared with the Retail Price Index as it stands and with this index adjusted in various ways to reflect the spending habits of people on Assistance. The index is reweighted, for example, to take account of heavier expenditure on food and fuel, lighter spending on transport and entertainment compared with the rest of the population. Comparisons are also made with average earnings, wage rates, consumer expenditure figures, and even disposable income per head (the yardstick introduced by Mr. Tony Lynes in his recent pamphlet on *National Assistance and National Prosperity*). In addition to this broad statistical review, the Board also studies first-hand accounts of how its clients are faring provided by reports from local officers all over Britain.

Should the Board decide to recommend an increase, its proposals have to be presented to the Minister of Pensions in the form of draft regulations which must be approved by both Houses of Parliament before the new scale rates can come into force. Debates on these occasions reveal two fundamental conflicts of opinion.

First, there was bitter disagreement between the Government and the Opposition about the validity of the methods used in determining increases in the rates. The Socialist case, which rests largely on researches made by Mr. Lynes and Professor Richard Titmuss, is that the Retail Price Index is a wholly inadequate measuring stick for the purpose and that a different index, reflecting more precisely the spending habits of low income households, would give a different, more sombre picture of the financial position of those on National Assistance over the years. This is emphatically refuted by the Government, who stick to their argument that the purchasing power of the scale rates has never lagged behind the R.P.I. and that the use of any specialized index would not necessarily give any substantially different effect.

But the essential conflict lies deeper: has the level of the scales been raised high enough in relation to the general standards enjoyed by the rest of the nation? And on this question there can never be agreement, because all approaches to it are inevitably subjective and the result is a head-on clash of value judgements which are tinged with political convictions or prejudices. Such value judgements are not confined to politicians. Old ladies on Assistance are full of them. Most are over 70, veterans of hard struggles to bring up large families in the years between the wars. Their view of today's Assistance grant is conditioned by their memories of yesterday's dole. "I know what hunger is, I can tell you", said an 83-year-old widow. "My husband went off in 1914 and left me with six children. Used to take them round the West End looking for cheap food: you could get a good bit of meat in those days for threepence. It's different today. Not that you can afford to do yourself very proud. But you can manage all right on the Assistance. You can manage." And another woman with much the same family history: "I've always been used to scrimping so it doesn't worry me as much as it does some of the younger ones. If you go gently, you can scrape along all right."

Is it right that old people should have to call into play the pinchpenny skills of yesterday in order to manage on the Assistance grants of today? In 1959 the Government evidently decided that it was not right, for in that year the White Paper accompanying an increase in the scale rates expressed a significant change in official thinking. Its first sentence ran: "Her Majesty's Government and the National Assistance Board have been considering the position of those on National Assistance and have reached the conclusion that the time has come when it is right to move to a higher standard, so giving them a share in increasing prosperity."

For the first time in eleven years of National Assistance as conceived in 1948, the principle was conceded that it is not enough for the scales merely to keep their money value: the poor must also be given a stake in national prosperity.

Increases since 1959 continued to maintain the purchasing power of the scale rates, and the increases made in 1963 gave a further improvement in the real value.

One of the things which gives a certain air of unreality to discussions in Parliament about National Assistance is that such debates are necessarily concerned mainly with top-level decisions of principle. In practice, the quality of this financial rescue service also hinges on millions of decisions made at local level by officers of the National Assistance Board up and down the country. They are the field campaigners in the state war on want. And it is their interpretation of rules and regulations made at the top which, to a large degree, dictate how the poor shall live.

In their exercise of this awe-inspiring responsibility, officers must rely for general guidance on statutory regulations and the 1948 Act, which instructs them to do their work "in such manner as shall best promote the welfare of the persons affected". Another important provision is that if a person urgently needs help, it must be given without heed for any of the regulations which might otherwise rule it out.

The statutory guidance goes only so far: it lays down the scale rates and specifies the types and amounts of income or capital which must be ignored when balancing needs against resources. But it also enables separate allowances to be made over and above the basic scales. In deciding what these shall amount to and whether people are entitled to them at all (except for rent, which must always be allowed) officers are left remarkably free to use their own judgement.

A rent allowance is added to the appropriate basic scale for a householder according to "what is reasonable in all the circumstances". Then, important extra grants called "discretionary additions"—because they are given at an officer's discretion—can be used to supplement weekly assistance allowances "where there are special circumstances". Yet another type of grant, made as a single payment to meet an exceptional or temporary need, is given, again, according to what is "reasonable, having regard to all the circumstances of the case".

Everything depends on how N.A.B. officers interpret these deliberately vague phrases. The only outside check on their decisions is through one of the independent appeals tribunals set up under the Act, whose members are not appointed by the Board. But the practical value of these is limited in the sense that many who seek assistance are too feeble, sensitive or plain dim to dream of appealing. Otherwise there is no one outside the department, not even the Minister of Pensions, who can interfere with an officer's decisions in any given case; although he is, of course, subject to internal supervision.

All this is fundamental to a system which must have plenty of stretch in it. It must be flexible enough to cater for a tremendous diversity of human needs, and also to ensure that in meeting those needs, Exchequer money is not handed out indiscriminately. This means relying on the rules to prescribe the minimum level of help in straightforward cases and on the judgement of local officers to adjust this level where they think fit in the light of their first-hand knowledge of different people's circumstances.

In practice, nearly 99 per cent of the $1\frac{1}{2}$ million householders paying rent or rates and receiving weekly assistance allowances do have their full rent paid, the average amounts varying from 29s. 1d. a week in London and the south to 18s. 1d. in Scotland. Figures provided in the annual reports of the Board show that the discretionary additions are given to about half the people drawing weekly allowances; the average amount of these additions in 1963 was 8s. 6d. per week. Most of these payments are made to cover the cost of special diets, laundry, domestic help and exceptional fuel needs— highly important extras for the old, sick, disabled or house-bound men and women who comprise the majority of people assisted.

In addition to the regular weekly allowances, officers make grants to meet exceptional needs, mostly to cover the cost of replacing clothing, bedding or household equipment, and they also make single payments for temporary needs, mainly to unemployed or sick people or to women separated from their husbands. During 1962 there were 223,000 grants for exceptional needs, and 1,800,000 payments to meet a temporary need.

All these figures, and a great many others given by the Board in its annual reports, are useful as far as they go. Unfortunately they do not always go far enough to give the interested public a complete picture of the way the Board and its officers use the administrative freedom entrusted to them by Parliament.

Some of the resources disregarded in calculating Assistance allowances.

Maximum Disregarded Capital

	£	s.	d.
War Savings	*375	0	0
Other Capital	124	0	0

* *Savings above this limit are reckoned at 6d. a week for every £25 up to a maximum of £600.*

Maximum Disregarded Weekly Income

	s.	d.
Friendly society or trade union sick pay	15	0
Superannuation	15	0
War wounds or disability pension, workmen's compensation, etc.	30	0

(*The total maximum disregarded on all incomes from these sources is 30s. a week.*)

	s.	d.
Earnings of old people not registered for work	30	0

(*plus half the next 20s.*)

Suspicion of harsh treatment flourishes on lack of information. It is not enough for the Board to present these aspects of their work in the form of averages, percentages and totals. Only by knowing much more about the particular circumstances in which particular people are granted particular sums of money is it possible to judge the general fairness or otherwise of the system.*

In other directions the Board has in recent years made fruitful, if belated, progress in improving its information services. In the press and elsewhere, much has been done to publicize the National Assistance scheme as widely as possible for the benefit of people still ignorant of its existence, suspicious of its workings, or terrified of applying because of their too vivid memories of "going on the parish" and the harsher means tests of the thirties. More important still, serious efforts have been made to improve the quantity and quality of training given to the Board's field staff—about 13,000 in all, based on over 430 area offices throughout Britain.

As a department, they are older than their colleagues elsewhere: in 1959 in the Civil Service as a whole, 33 per cent were 50 or over, compared with 45 per cent on the Board, and there has since been little change. Many joined the Board when it was first set up in 1948 after years as relieving officers under the Poor Law. And although a certain amount of young blood comes into the department every year, most new entrants are also men or women mature in years transferred from other departments, such as the Post Office or the Ministry of Pensions, with experience of meeting the public face to face.

Because of this high age structure, the Board has a remarkably high turn-over of staff: each year about one-tenth of the current staff retire, resign, or are transferred elsewhere. And this in turn means a very heavy annual training programme. Formal training is done at the Board's headquarters and practical training, including day to day instruction on the job, at individual area offices, where it is the responsibility of the managers.

To be effective, this training must aim at turning out not simply good Civil Servants but also imaginative connoisseurs of human distress. For because of the complexity of National Assistance regulations, whether people receive their dues over and above the basic scale will often depend entirely on the tact and perception of local officers. But not all their clients are sweet old ladies, like the one who told me: "My gentleman says if everyone was like me, his job would be a pleasure!" They also have to treat with sick, irritable, slow, stupid, dishonest, angry or abusive people; and with mentally mixed up people. Here, the most significant development, and one with great possibilities for the future, are the special part-time university courses in human relations for Board officers, conducted by university tutors, usually people experienced in psychiatric social work.

* *Editorial footnote:* Since this article was published the Board have provided in their Annual Report for the year 1962 much additional information on the circumstances of people receiving assistance. The 1962 Report is considerably longer than previous reports and includes nearly double the number of statistical tables.

National Assistance Basic Weekly Scale Rates for Requirements Other than Rent, 1948–63

	1948 5 July		1950 12 June		1951 3 Sept.		1952 16 June		1955 7 Feb.		1956 23 Jan.		1958 27 Jan.		1959 7 Sept.		1961 3 April		1962 24 Sept.		1963 27 May	
	s.	d.	s.	d.	s.	d.	s.	d.	s.	d.	s.	d.	s.	d.	s.	d.	s.	d.	s.	d.	s.	d.
ORDINARY RATE:																						
For husband and wife	40	0	43	6	50	0	59	0	63	0	67	0	76	0	85	0	90	0	95	6	104	6
For a single householder	24	0	26	0	30	0	35	0	37	6	40	0	45	0	50	0	53	6	57	6	63	6
For other persons:																						
aged 21 or over	20	0	22	0	26	0	31	0	33	6	36	0	41	0	46	0	49	6	51	6	55	0
18 to 20	17	6	19	0	22	0	26	0	27	6	29	0	31	6	36	0	38	0	40	0	43	0
16 and 17	15	0	16	0	18	6	21	6	22	6	23	6	26	0	30	0	32	0	34	0	37	0
11 to 15	10	6	12	0	13	6	16	0	17	0	18	0	20	0	23	0	24	0	25	6	28	0
5 to 10	9	0	10	0	11	6	13	6	14	6	15	6	17	0	19	0	20	0	21	0	23	0
under 5	7	6	8	0	9	6	11	0	12	0	13	0	14	6	16	0	17	0	18	0	19	6
SPECIAL RATE:*																						
For a single householder	55	0	58	6	65	0	77	0	82	0	87	0	96	0	107	6	112	6	120	0	120	0
For husband and wife	65	0	68	6	75	0	89	0	95	0	101	0	110	0	112	6	127	6	136	0	145	0

* For the blind and those who have suffered loss of income during treatment for tuberculosis.

These courses were pioneered at London University in 1958 by Mr. Eugene Heimler, county psychiatric social work organizer for Middlesex, to whom the scheme owes its inspiration. Other courses of a similar nature have been or are being given at Birmingham, Bristol, Cardiff, Durham, Exeter, Glasgow and Nottingham. Their aim, in Mr. Heimler's words, is to produce "men able to recognize in themselves the things their clients are suffering in more dramatic form: men who remain in the role of National Assistance Board officers but who can sometimes take off the mask and let their clients see them not just as official providers of cash but as people willing to help with other problems".

But these courses have so far reached only a very small proportion of the staff. It will obviously be a very long time before the full potentialities of such advanced training can be realized. Meanwhile, one can only judge the way Board officers behave by asking their public. Among the dozens of men and women I spoke to, only two were indignant at the way they had been treated—and these were people who seemed to have a permanent grudge against the world. More important, there is the evidence of Dorothy Cole's interim study, with John Utting, of *The Economic Circumstances of Old People*, based on 400 interviews. This reports the "overwhelming impression" that those people receiving National Assistance were satisfied with the way it was meted out to them.

Social or voluntary workers and others in touch with the Board and their clients reported the same impressions to me, except for a psychiatrist and a health visitor. Both of them knew of mentally disturbed people who had brusquely been shown the door by one of the clerical officers who deal with personal applications for assistance made over the counter at the local office. A telephone call to the superior officer secured the necessary help for these people; but the real damage in such cases cannot be so easily cured. Once snubbed, a person may never ask again. At any rate the Board is aware of this problem and their training for clerical officer receptionists includes the use of tape-recorded situations "to prompt self-criticism".

Because of the sheer weight of work carried by Board officers, it would not be surprising if such incidents were more numerous. Office managers, the most senior members of the field staff, are in charge of areas where anything from 2000 to 7000 regular allowances are in payment each week. In addition, personal callers to the office asking for single payments to help them over a bad patch have to be dealt with. Most applications for this sort of help come from unemployed men, and the stream of callers can quickly become a flood if a local factory closes down or there is a strike in the district. (A man on strike, although disqualified from receiving assistance for himself, may apply for a grant to maintain his wife and family, and to cover his rent.) It is a tough job to keep the machine running smoothly in such emergencies, especially as there is no room in this branch of the Civil Service for that useful word "pending": appeals for assistance have to be met promptly.

For administrative convenience, an area is split into several sub-areas, each containing about 1000 persons or families receiving weekly allowances, and each in the charge of an executive officer with general responsibility, under the manager, for these cases and any new ones that may arise. It is the executive officer who usually undertakes the crucial first visit to a person's home to decide whether he or she qualifies for a weekly allowance, and how much it should be. If an allowance is granted, the new applicant is visited again within three months of its issue and thereafter about twice a year, to check whether there has been any change of circumstance calling for an adjustment in the allowance.

This important review visiting is done by clerical officers, who are expected to visit and report on about twelve to twenty people a day in a fairly typical sub-area. To encourage vigilance on certain basic points, the clerical officer carries with him a form filled in after the first visit by the executive officer. Among details noted are home conditions, general state of health—including arrangements for medical care—and the name and address of a friend or relative who can be reached in an emergency if a man or woman is living alone. Officers also have to say whether a person is chronically ill, deaf or mentally feeble and, where necessary, report on household management, good or bad; attitude to work; and any signs of self-neglect or neglect of children. Frequently a person needs help from one of the local statutory or voluntary welfare organizations, and liaison with these bodies is an important and valuable part of Board officers' work.

But if there is general admiration for the way in which most officers administer assistance, there is also concern, by no means confined to left-wing critics, about whether even the most generous interpreters of the regulations are able to do more than soften the edges of poverty. All are agreed that vast advances have been made in humanizing the system. There is perhaps less agreement on whether the general financial level of assistance has kept pace with the changed economic and social conditions of the affluent sixties.

In this connection, possibly not enough attention has been paid to the composition of the Board itself, which should, in theory at least, set the tone of the vast administrative complex it controls. Members of the Board are appointed for a fixed term by the Crown on the Advice of the Prime Minister. Is it not courting accusations of political prejudice to appoint an ex-Conservative M.P. as chairman? Is it advisable for the Board to be so top-heavy with years that not one of its six members is under 50 and half are nearly 70?

For in drawing up National Assistance scales there is always the danger that these will be seen merely as improving on abuses of the past without at the same time allowing for trends of the present which will develop into problems of the future. In a society where an increasing proportion of the population will be aged men or women dependent—if inflation continues to erode pension rates—on National Assistance for survival, the whole financial framework so far evolved may have to be radically revised to take account of rising concepts of need.

17. The Finance of the Social Services

W. A. James Farndale and J. G. Bentley

The term finance of the social services covers a wide field, and it may be analysed at national and local levels for both public and voluntary social services, at inter-departmental levels, and at personal levels. Competition for the resources of the community between public and private sectors and between one public social service and another is strong, and the collection and

TABLE 1

Distribution of Social Service Expenditure between Public Authorities (£m.)

	1937/38	%	1954/55	%	1960/61	%
Central Government (direct)	128	26·7	920·6	44·3	1325·2	38·85
Local authorities	221	46·1	587·8	28·3	1029·1	30·15
National Insurance Fund	130	27·2	568·4	27·4	1055·9	31·0
Total	479	100·0	2076·8	100·0	3410·2	100·0

distribution of social finance may be studied in the terms of its national economic consequences or may be approached from the viewpoint of social welfare to determine the effectiveness with which the collective services and benefit payments achieve their aims. The main considerations made below are: (1) a general outline of the control of sources of revenue and of the distribution of expenditure, (2) external economic factors influencing social service expenditure, (3) a consideration of income redistribution.

The Control of Revenue and Expenditure

Financial responsibility for the current income and expenditure of the social services has moved largely from the hands of local authorities to the Central Government, a change which took place during and after the war. Approximately three-quarters of the revenue is raised by Central Government taxation, the remainder being raised by insurance contributions from private employers and employees together with a much smaller contribution from local rates. The Central Government finances its own direct responsibilities, e.g. the National Health Service, and also has to meet an annual statutory contribution to the National Insurance Fund, which, although a separate department of the public accounts, is closely linked with Central Government finance and has become partially dependent on Exchequer grants.

Local authorities spend more than they raise, the balance being provided by grants from the Central Government. The percentage of total current expenditure controlled by local authorities has fallen from virtually 100 per cent in 1890 and 46 per cent in 1937–8 to 30 per cent in 1960–1. Prior to 1959 specific grants were payable by the Central Government towards the cost of local education, health and welfare services. The Local Government Act, 1959, provided for replacement of many of these specific grants by a general grant. When allocating the general grant the Minister of Housing and Local Government takes into account previous expenditure and the need for developing services formerly aided by specific grants, and he has the power to reduce the general grant payable to any authority if he is satisfied that it has failed to achieve or maintain reasonable standards in the provision of services.

The statutory legislation creating public responsibility for the social services is administered by the Ministries of Health, Pensions and National Insurance, Housing and Local Government, by the National Assistance Board and by Local Authorities. The division of expenditure between the principal services may be seen in Table 2. Three services—health, education and retirement pensions—account for over two-thirds of the total expenditure.

TABLE 2

Current Expenditure by all Public Authorities (£m.)

		1954/55	%	1960/61	%
Education	Local authority services	389·3	18·7	730·2	21·4
	Other	42·7	2·1	81·5	2·4
Health and Welfare	Health	512·4	24·7	837·7	24·5
	Welfare	118·6	5·7	144·6	4·2
Benefits and Assistance	National Insurance	568·4	27·4	1055·9	31·0
	Other	341·5	16·4	438·8	12·9
Housing		103·9	5·0	121·5	3·6
Total		2076·8	100·0	3410·2	100·0

Source: *Annual Abstracts of Statistics, 1962.*

The National Health Service*

The sources of finance of the health service vary slightly from year to year as modifications are made (e.g.) in charges to patients, but generally the Exchequer meets about 75 per cent of the cost and about one-sixth is met by health insurance stamp contributions. The percentage provided by stamp contributions and patients' charges has shown a slow but definite increase over the last decade, whilst the proportion met wholly by the Exchequer has shown a slight decline (Table 3).

TABLE 3

National Health Service (England and Wales) Sources of Finance (£m.)

	1949/50	%	1955/56	%	1960/61	%
Exchequer wholly	305	78·6	423	79·1	559	69·1
Rates wholly	14	3·6	22	4·1	—	—
Exchequer and rates jointly	—	—	—	—	67	8·2
Transfers from N.I. Fund contributions	36	9·3	36	6·7	102	12·6
Patients' charges	4	1·0	26	4·9	36	4·5
Superannuation contributions and transfer values	21	5·4	27	5·0	44	5·5
Miscellaneous	8	2·1	1	0·2	1	0·1
Total	388	100·0	535	100·0	809	100·0

Source: *Ministry of Health Statistics.*

The gross cost of the health service in England and Wales has risen rapidly from £388 million in 1949–50 to £809 million in 1960–1. This covers the hospital, specialist and ancillary, general medical, pharmaceutical, general dental, supplementary ophthalmic, and local authority health services. The services are available to all, fixed charges being made for dentures, spectacles and various appliances, whilst a charge of 2s. was made per item of medicine supplied on a prescription.

General practitioners who join the service (approximately 20,000 out of 21,000) are remunerated by a capitation fee for each patient included on their lists, but are left free to take fee-paying patients if they desire. Hospital staff are remunerated by salary from Exchequer funds. Wages and salaries account for approximately 60 per cent of current hospital expenditure, which is more than twice the cost of fuel, maintenance and medical supplies combined (Fig. 1).

* See also "Trends in the National Health Service", Volume 3 in the Westminster Series (Pergamon Press), Chapter No. 32 on the Hospital Plan by Dr. L. S. Carstairs for discussion on capital expenditure.

round Floor/Storage Page Slip

ON _____

_____ TIME _____

<u>CALL NO</u>.

E _____

_____

/DATE _____

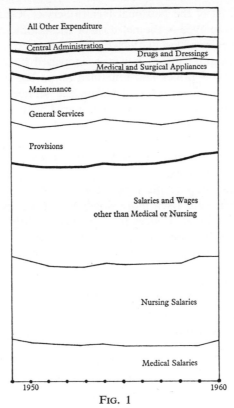

All Other Expenditure

Central Administration

Drugs and Dressings

Medical and Surgical Appliances

Maintenance

General Services

Provisions

Salaries and Wages
other than Medical or Nursing

Nursing Salaries

Medical Salaries

1950   1960

FIG. 1

Shares in total hospital expenditure, 1949–60. Reprinted from *Hospital Costs in Perspective*
by permission of the Office of Health Economics.

Source: *Ministry of Health Annual Reports*.

Factors which have contributed to rising costs in the health service include:

(1) The increase in the numbers of persons receiving treatment.
(2) The growing amount and complexity of work being performed by
    the professions supplementary to medicine.
(3) Medical advances.
(4) The organization of, and external competition for, female labour,
    leading to demands for higher wages.
(5) The increased number of staff employed.
(6) The decrease in the value of money.
(7) Public criticism leading to improved services.

The influence of the extension of services and decreases in the value of
money, which affects different services to a varying degree, is well illustrated
by the findings of the Guillebaud Committee (Report of the Committee of

Inquiry into the Cost of the National Health Service, Cmnd. 9663). During the period 1949–50 to 1953–4 the net cost of the health service rose by £59 million, which, when revalued at 1948–9 prices, revealed a true rise in costs of £11 million. The population, however, increased by 2 million, thus the cost per head at 1948–9 prices had remained about the same from 1949–50 to 1953–4. The trend of expenditure within the service changed. Hospital expenditure increased by £71 million compared with an increase of £11 million for local authority services. The cost of executive council services fell by £24 million mainly because of increased charges to patients and a reduction in dentists' earnings, measures which were found necessary in the effort to stabilize rising costs.

Subsequent to the Report the proportion of total expenditure absorbed by the hospital service has risen more slowly whilst the proportion absorbed by the general practitioner services has declined slightly. The tendency for hospital expenditure to rise more rapidly than total expenditure and national income has been observed in many other countries including Canada and the U.S.A.

The Local Authority Services

Table 4 shows the nature of government grants to local authorities for the social services and also the range of services covered by local authorities.

TABLE 4

Nature of Central Government Grants to Local Authorities (£m.)

	1954/55	1960/61
EDUCATION		
General Education Services	212·7	—
School Health Services	5·3	—
Scholarship, students' maintenance and training allowances	11·3	—
HEALTH		
National Health Service	23·5	—
WELFARE SERVICES		
National Assistance	0·5	—
Industrial rehabilitation, training and employment of disabled	0·4	0·6
CHILD CARE		
Approved Schools	0·6	1·0
Services under 1948 Children's Act	7·4	—
WELFARE FOODS		
School Meals	37·1	58·9
HOUSING	57·5	80·3
GENERAL GRANT	—	496·5
Total	356·3	637·3

Source: *Annual Abstract of Statistics, 1962.*

The local authorities, after taking into account Central Government grants and income from rents and trading activities, raise the balance of the revenue they require by levying rates which are a local property tax. Property is valued and given a "rateable value", then the rate in view of local needs is fixed at a value in the pound to provide the required revenue. For example, if the property in an area has a rateable value of £2 million and the local authority requires £1 million, the rate will be fixed at 10s. in the pound.

A proportion of the rates are levied for the local health, welfare, housing and education services, the remainder being levied to meet the cost of other public services, e.g. highways, police, fire protection and libraries. The distribution of expenditure between the services is decided by the local authority,

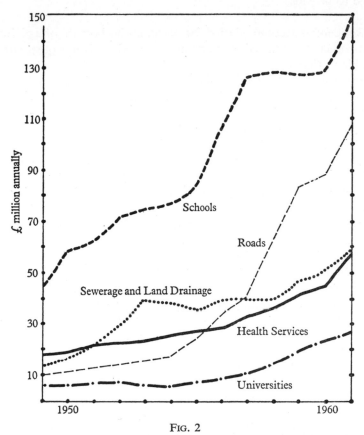

FIG. 2

Gross fixed capital formation in education, health, roads, and sewerage and land drainage, United Kingdom, 1949–61. Reprinted from *Hospital Costs in Perspective* by permission of the Office of Health Economics.

Source: *Central Statistics Office; National Income and Expenditure*, 1962.

Note: Expenditure on land is excluded; both private and public expenditure are included.

and varies from area to area, but usually a large proportion (about 50 per cent) is spent on education. A significant feature of the education services since 1950 has been the high rate of capital expenditure compared with the other services (Fig. 2). By retaining control of education and housing, local authorities have remained in control of most of the capital expenditure on the social services, although for major works they may find it necessary to raise loans through the Central Government.

The main local authority welfare services are provided under the National Assistance Act, 1948, Part III of which deals with residential and temporary accommodation and with welfare services for handicapped persons. These services are provided by county and county borough councils who are required to provide:

(1) Residential accommodation for persons who because of age, infirmity or other reason need care and attention which is not otherwise available to them.

(2) Temporary accommodation for persons who find themselves homeless due to circumstances which could not reasonably have been foreseen, e.g. fire or flood.

Residents are liable to contribute towards their own maintenance. Husband and wife are liable to maintain each other, and parents to maintain their children, but not children their parents.

Local authorities must fix a standard maximum charge for accommodation. A different standard charge may be used for each home or type of home. The charges are calculated each year on the basis of costs in the preceding year, and usually the costs of all homes in a local authority area are pooled in doing this, but the costs of old (i.e. pre-1948) establishments and new homes may be separated.

The standard charges are used as maximum charges to residents. Persons who are unable to afford these are assessed in accordance with their resources, and when deciding how much an individual shall be charged the local authority must ensure that he is left with a prescribed amount for his personal needs which in 1965 was fixed at 16s. 0d. per week. There is also a minimum charge of £3 4s. per week, and if necessary the National Assistance Board will make an allowance to bring a person's income up to this whilst still allowing him to retain the minimum of pocket-money.

The future development of local authority health and welfare services is tentatively covered in a report on the Ten Year Plan for development of community care announced in April 1963 (Cmnd. 1973). Plans for the development mainly of services for the elderly, mentally disordered, physically handicapped and mother and child, which were submitted to the Ministry of Health by 146 local authorities, envisage an increase in annual revenue expenditure from £111 million in 1963 to £163 million in 1971–2. Capital expenditure of £220 million is planned over the next ten years, an average of £22 million a year, compared with capital expenditure of £3 million in 1949–50 and £16 million in 1961–2. An increase of 45 per cent in staff is proposed in order to meet the growing demand for the services, particularly the need for care of the elderly. The number of persons aged 65 and over is expected to increase by 32·5 per cent over the next twenty years. The majority of these persons will live in their own homes and approximately 10 per cent are expected to be in need of the home nursing service. The number of home nurses is expected to average 0·19 per 1000 of the population by 1972. The Ministry also recommends replacing all residential accommodation provided for old people in former Public Assistance institutions.

Under the plan a total of 103 centres for the mentally disordered are proposed by 1972, and for the physically handicapped 185 centres for re-habilitation, employment and occupation are to be provided. An increase in the number of child welfare clinics from 5985 in 1961 to 6926 in 1972 is expected, but only five local authorities plan to provide more day nurseries. The number of children cared for by private day nurseries and registered daily minders doubled between 1955 and 1961, whilst two-thirds fewer day nursery placcs are being provided by local authorities now than at the end of the war. The statistics given in the new plan do not include the contribu-tions which will be made by voluntary organizations.

The Finance of Voluntary Organizations

Finance frequently operates as a limiting factor in the activities of voluntary organizations who are having to increase the numbers of salaried professional staff they employ to compensate for the fall in the numbers of people able to give full-time unpaid service. Regular income has thus become vital for the conduct and maintenance of regular services, and this is more difficult to raise than are funds for special occasions, e.g. earthquakes, floods and other natural disasters, which are accorded great publicity and have a much stronger emotional appeal.

The regular income of voluntary organizations comes from subscriptions, donations, income from investments and grants from public funds and charitable trusts.

Redistribution of income through taxation has resulted in smaller dona-tions from private individuals, and the place of the great patrons is now being taken by charitable trusts and also by large industrial and commercial organizations with some notable exceptions such as the benefactions of the late Lord Nuffield.

The larger charitable trusts include the Carnegie United Kingdom Trust, the Nuffield Foundation, the Pilgrim Trust, the National Corporation for the Care of Old People, the Isaac Wolfson Foundation, the Calouste Gulbenkian Foundation, and in London the City Parochial Foundation and the King Edward Hospital Fund for London. Grants from charitable trusts are valuable in encouraging voluntary organizations engaged in experimental and pioneer work.

Regular patrons of voluntary organizations who have paid tax at the full standard rate may increase their contribution by entering into a covenant to pay a fixed sum annually for a period exceeding six years, usually a seven-year covenant. The charity may then obtain from the Inland Revenue the tax paid in relation to the subscription. A greater amount of aid may thus be given to the voluntary organization without additional cost to the patron.

Grants from public funds may be made to voluntary organizations by either Government Departments or local authorities, and these grants are a recognition of the work of voluntary bodies in a field which interests the statutory authorities. The voluntary bodies have an important part to play in the development of community care (see later parts of this book), and progress in this field will be greatly influenced by the degree of co-operation achieved between voluntary and statutory bodies.

Voluntary organizations also have large fund-raising activities, for example, flag days, Christmas card funds, broadcast appeals and other methods.

Charities Aid Fund

An interesting and promising development is the Charities Aid Fund, which in a recent year distributed over £1 million to voluntary and charitable organizations named by the 8000 companies, societies and persons who make regular contributions to the Fund. The Fund was established by the National Council of Social Service to promote and facilitate the distribution of money to charitable organizations. The majority of funds are obtained under deeds of covenant whereby income tax is recovered and the total is distributed at the discretion of the donor who will be given advice if required on current trends and needs in voluntary and charitable social work. The money can be passed on in the name of the donor or anonymously, and the donor can vary his list and donations annually if he wishes.

The service is being used by many thousands of subscribers, including companies and clubs, such as Rotary Clubs, enabling their giving to be increased by recovered tax. It may benefit organizations for the advancement of religion, advancement of education, relief of poverty, the provision of facilities for recreation and leisure-time occupations, which are in the interest of social welfare, and has been used by schools and colleges for a variety of appeals, and by churches in their local stewardship campaigns.

Concerted Voluntary Giving

New methods to encourage the average citizen to assist in financing voluntary organizations are by:

(a) Community Chests, which usually involve a once-a-year appeal to raise money for a number of charities, promising freedom from local appeals for the rest of the year.

(b) Organizations such as "United Voluntary Organizations" which started in Liverpool and, at an early stage, collected weekly contributions from 60,000 staff in 550 firms and distributed the sum so collected annually. The U.V.O. has now extended to other cities and towns, and has proved to be a useful way of local people making regular weekly donations, and ensuring a fair distribution to deserving local charitable causes.

Concerted and planned voluntary giving by groups of local people could well develop into an important method of financing some social services.

Economic Factors Influencing Social Service Expenditure*

The social services compete with other public services and private industry for the real resources of the community in the form of labour, goods and capital (Fig. 3). The increase in the proportion of the national income devoted to the social services from approximately 6 per cent in 1937–8 to 17 per cent in 1960–1 has given rise to much adverse comment. Figures of this nature exaggerate the increase in demand made on national resources by the social services, for expenditure in the form of social security benefits represents only a *transfer* of income from one section of the community to another, and a large proportion of health service expenditure provides services which were formerly purchased directly by individuals.

The nature of this concern over rising costs depends on whether one considers the social services a drain on the national economy and objects to the demerits of the taxation system or whether one considers provision of comprehensive services more desirable than individual prosperity and a prerequisite for an efficient working population. To pursue either point of view too far may be misleading. The pattern of social service expenditure since the war has been formed by the competitive assertions of the exponents of these opposing points of view.

In the health service success in combating certain diseases has resulted in economies to employers and the National Insurance Fund from reduction in absenteeism formerly caused by these diseases, and similarly improved

* See Fig. 3 for diagrammatic representation of some economic factors.

methods of treatment have allowed more intensive use of hospital resources, but the claim made at the inception of the health service that control of disease would result in self-limiting expenditure, due to decreased or static need for medical care, has proved false.

Due to "medicated survival" and new discoveries, our concepts of disease and the pattern of disease have changed, leading to a demand for higher standards of treatment and extension of services, particularly for the elderly. The criterion of "the need for care" has not been able to act as a limiting factor in expenditure as it has itself become a changed concept.

External economic factors have, however, limited expenditure. The greatest pressures on British governments since the war have been towards maintaining full employment, gaining a favourable trade balance and promoting national prosperity. Those aspects of economic policy which promote these aims without conflicting with concepts of equality, may be considered as an unclassified social service. Fear of damaging inflation and competition for resources during a period of industrial expansion and full employment plus the desire to avoid the dis-incentives of increased taxation were factors which influenced political decision to restrict expenditure by imposing a ceiling on health service expenditure and by paying social security benefits well below subsistence level.

Central Government revenue from taxes automatically compensates for inflation, but the percentage of revenue devoted to the social services is decided politically. Revenue from rates is inelastic and increases only if the rate is raised by the local authority. Any proposal to increase expenditure to compensate for inflation has, therefore, first to overcome strong public and political opposition.

In contrast, private and to a lesser degree public, industries are relatively free to compensate for inflation by raising prices, and thus there is always a tendency for the social services to be placed in the least advantageous economic position, a state of affairs for which the term "social imbalance" has been coined.

During 1962–3 a series of events occurred which went some way towards restoring a more favourable state of balance from the point of view of the social services. Industrial production necessitates consumption, and when in 1962–3 a decline in consumer spending, due partly to localized unemployment and increased personal savings, created a gap between the two, a vicious circle of unemployment, less spending and more unemployment began to develop. Significantly, authorities in depressed areas had for a considerable time been advocating, along with other measures, increased public expenditure, mainly in the form of capital expenditure, to relieve localized unemployment and to improve local facilities to attract new industries from more prosperous areas. When the general decline in consumer spending aggravated the situation, they were joined by political groups who in addition

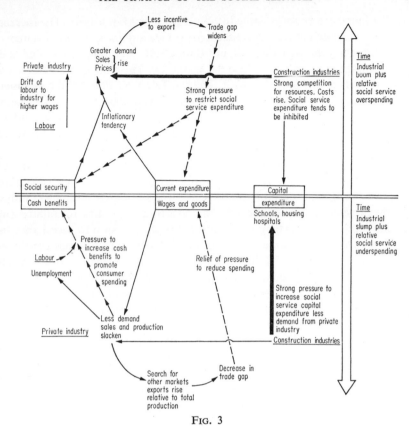

FIG. 3

A Guide to economic factors influencing social service expenditure as seen
through the eyes of laymen.

advocated an increase in social security cash benefits on the grounds that
they would increase consumer spending power. J. K. Galbraith, in his influential work *The Affluent Society*, had already gone further in advocating
"cyclically graduated compensation", i.e. unemployment benefits to be
paid at a variable level depending on the number of unemployed.

Galbraithian theories were much in evidence during the parliamentary
debates on social insurance and unemployment during November 1962.
To choose a specimen quotation:

> How can we reconcile the idea that those who are leading industry are entitled to
> as much as they can get whilst nurses, teachers and doctors must be restrained. Step
> up unemployment pay by £1 million a week . . . make a great difference to the un-
> employed and provide some additional demand for industry.

In January 1963 the Government announced an all-round increase in
social security benefits and pensions at an increased cost of £227 million a

year. The increased benefits came into operation in March 1963. The increase in insurance contributions designed to provide an increase in revenue of £187 million a year was delayed until June 1963, an unprecedented step taken to inject spending power into the economy. The balance of the cost was met from Exchequer funds. In April 1963 the Ten Year Plan for development of community care was announced with the proviso that it was to be carried out "subject to economic conditions".

Prolonged restriction of social service expenditure has resulted in wages and salaries of certain grades of employees falling behind in relation to those for industrial posts which offer better protection against inflation, and this has contributed to the shortage of qualified personnel. Buildings and equipment have become outdated, resulting in lower standards of efficiency than may otherwise have been achieved. The resulting strain has stimulated two potentially important developments, one being the decision to investigate the possibility of applying modern management efficiency techniques developed by business organizations to the health service by the formation of an Advisory Council for Management Efficiency* in May 1959. The Council's work has included recommendations on the hospital capital programme, where attention has been drawn to the use of standardization, repetitive units and the need for designs which will allow flexibility to meet future needs. Consideration has also been given to organization and career structure, recruitment and training, the use of incentive schemes and methods of preparation and presentation of statistical material which provides an essential tool in tackling many hospital service problems. There are now more than 125 work study officers in the hospital service, the pace of change is increasing, and there are many signs of promise for the future.

Another development, which is still very much in its infancy, is the decision of the National and Local Government Officers Association to press for the replacement of the present central control by a National Health Authority patterned on the lines of the authorities which control nationalized industries and other public undertakings, for example the Gas and Electricity Councils. The avowed aim is to reduce Treasury control of the Whitley Council negotiating machinery, but also envisaged is a longer career structure and a promotion ladder which would lead to more persons with practical hospital experience reaching positions in central authority. The plan, which will meet strong opposition, may by its very existence lead to reduced resistance to union demands over salaries and conditions of service.

Income Redistribution

Expenditure on the social services designed to reduce individual hardship

* Now reconstituted as an Advisory Committee for Management Efficiency in the Health Service.

due to the causes of primary poverty, to provide "essential services" and to reduce inequality, falls into three main groups of payments:

(1) Transfer payments in the form of cash benefits.
(2) Expenditure on provision of collective services in kind.
(3) Subsidies.

Transfer payments comprising social security benefits, pensions and family allowances provide additional unearned income for those receiving them. Their effect on production depends on how near they fall to the recipient's income margin where he begins to prefer increased leisure to additional income. The recipient is free to spend or save the additional income, but the recent increase in benefits was based on the assumption that it is spent. In discussion of equality, increases in the *net total* of personal income changing hands must be distinguished from increases in *total* social service expenditure on transfer payments. The proportion of transfer expenditure met from insurance contributions is important because this is a regressive, i.e. unequal, form of taxation falling on employers and employees, and as the cost of retirement pensions is rising there is a strong case for financing these benefits out of general taxation.

Collective services are provided in kind and aim at providing optimum well-being and opportunity for personal development. They are financed from general taxation with the exception of education, for which approximately 40 per cent of the cost is met from rates which are also a regressive form of taxation. The case for a centrally financed education system has been presented with much less force than that for a centrally financed insurance fund because ratepayers are much less organized than employers and trade unions, and professionally interested groups are dubious of the virtues of central control.

Subsidies reduce the price of certain "necessary" goods, for example school meals and welfare foods, to those making use of them, and thus promote equality if we accept the supposition that those with the lowest incomes make the greatest possible use of them.

Studies of income redistribution have revealed that there is considerable vertical redistribution of income from higher to lower income brackets, but the extent to which persons benefit is decided by their consumption habits rather than their income. To illustrate this we may compare the position of a bachelor in private accommodation with that of a married man with the same income living in a council house receiving family allowances for several children who attend a state school and enjoy subsidized meals.

The issue of equality often dominates political debate on social service expenditure, the merits of the services and their needs for finance being lost in the wrangle over which sections of the community should foot the bill.

An impartial investigation, to determine the proportion of the national income which should be allocated to the public services in general and the proportion of this it is desirable to spend on the social services, would provide authorities with a more acceptable limit to expenditure.

Regional Government

Proposals have been made in several quarters, and also by Mr. John Vaizey, Fellow of Worcester College, Oxford, and Director of the Acton Society Trust, at a Conference organized by the 1963 Campaign for Education, for a form of regional government for education, health and welfare and other social services. Many of our local authorities are too small to manage and control these services. A larger authority could be given additional powers of raising money and imposing taxes, and so would not have to rely entirely on Central Government for financial support and direction of regional services.

Summary

The Central Government controls approximately three-quarters of expenditure both by direct expenditure and indirectly through the National Insurance Fund and local authorities to whom it makes grants. Local authorities, however, control the major part of capital expenditure. Three services—health, pensions and education—dominate expenditure.

The aim since the war has been to provide the best possible, rather than minimum essential, services, but because of the danger of inflation, political attempts have been made to restrain expenditure at a time when the demand for services has been increasing. These attempts were only partially successful. Despite restricted expenditure, inflation occurred, and because other sectors of the community compensated for it by raising prices, the social services were placed in a disadvantageous economic position which only began to improve when certain forms of expenditure were increased to combat rising unemployment.

Wages and salaries which form a large proportion of expenditure have fallen in relation to those for other occupations, and this has stimulated interest in efficiency studies and union attempts to reduce Treasury control of expenditure.

Whilst a wide scope of services is socially desirable, it is unlikely that sufficient revenue will be provided to meet all needs because of the adverse political and economic effects of increasing taxation. An impartial investigation to decide methods of achieving an optimum balance between the public and private sectors of the economy would be a better guide to future planning of the finance of the services than political debate which is often too strongly influenced by the issue of equality.

References

1. GALBRAITH, J. K., *The Affluent Society*, Hamish Hamilton, 1958.
2. HABENBUCH, W., *Social Economics*, Nisbet and Cambridge University Press, 1958.
3. MINISTRY OF HEALTH: (1) *Health and Welfare: The Development of Community Care*, Cmnd. 1973. (2) National Health Service Advisory Council for Management Efficiency (England and Wales), *Second Report*, Circular H.M. (63) 71.
4. OFFICE OF HEALTH ECONOMICS, Hospital Costs in Perspective, 1963.
5. PEACOCK, A. T., *Income Redistribution and Social Policy*, Jonathan Cape, 1952.
6. SEALE, J., Assumptions of health service finance from *Trends in the National Health Service*, edited by W. A. James Farndale, Pergamon Press, 1964.
7. *Report on Control of Public Expenditure*, Cmnd. 1432, 1961.

SECTION IV
SERVICES FOR THE ELDERLY

PLATE 1. External view of local authority purpose-built small home

PLATE 2. Local authority purpose-built home showing integration with modern developments

PLATE 3. Dining room in a purpose-built small home

PLATE 4. Sitting room of a local authority adapted home

PLATE 5. New resident arriving at a local authority home. Welcome to the home

PLATE 6. Being shown to her room

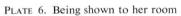

PLATE 7. A typical bedroom

PLATE 8. Being introduced to the residents

PLATE 9. Making herself at home

PLATE 10. In the garden

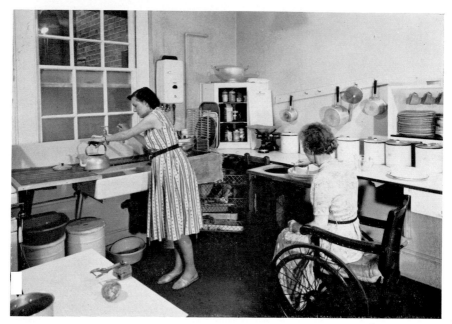

Plate 11. Social rehabilitation—kitchen at a Day Welfare Centre

Plate 12. Adapted cutlery—specially useful for paralysed and rheumatic cases

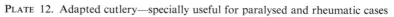

18. Welfare Services for the Elderly

F. L. LLOYD JACOB

Barrister-at-Law, Secretary of the London Central Consultative Committee on
the Welfare of Old People, and a Principal Officer of the London County Council
Welfare Department

Introduction

Few services are of more immediate interest, in the wider concept of the
social services of this country, than those provided for the welfare of the
elderly. Nor are the principal reasons for this difficult to give. First, we all
have a personal interest because in the ordinary way we shall ourselves
qualify, in the fullness of time (if we have not already done so), for inclusion
in that section of the community.

Secondly, it is reliably predicted that old people in the state retirement
age groups will form an increasing proportion of the total population of
this country as the years go by. The 1961 census indicated that nearly 15
per cent of the population were aged 65 years or over, and it is expected that
by 1971 the percentage is likely to be nearer $16\frac{1}{2}$.

Thirdly, there is this further important factor. The older generation in
this country have lived through two devastating world wars and endured
severe recurrent industrial depressions during their lifetime and, in so far as
the community has now attained a noticeably improved standard of living,
it is no less than our duty to try to ensure that the declining years of those who
bore the burden during those difficult times are made as tolerable and comfortable as our economic circumstances permit.

It is against this general background, therefore, that we need to view the
welfare services provided for elderly people, to assess their adequacy, to
indicate the deficiencies and to point the way for improving them.

In considering this subject it is important early on to refer to what is still
a relatively common misconception. This is that, where there is no financial
need, there is no need for help from the welfare services. It is true, of course,
that money—if one has enough of it—can still open most doors. It is also
axiomatic, I think, that the possession of means imports an obligation to
pay for, or contribute towards, the cost of services received. But it certainly
does not mean that the benefits of organized welfare services should be
exclusively reserved for the poor—nor is there any statutory basis for so
doing.

The statutory authority for providing these welfare services stems almost exclusively from the provisions of the National Assistance Act, 1948—an enactment which is one of the foundation stones of what has come to be known as the Welfare State. This Act starts off—in Part I—by abolishing the Poor Laws of this country. Part II of the Act sets out the responsibilities of the National Assistance Board which—in the context of this article—provide for monetary grants (almost invariably receivable weekly) to people in need either by way of full maintenance or, more usually, by way of supplementation of National Insurance benefits such as the state retirement pension. Part III of the Act sets out the responsibilities of local welfare authorities (county councils or county borough councils), and it is to this part of the Act that we must look for the authority for most of the welfare services for the elderly. Before considering this in detail it is appropriate also to mention that the National Assistance Act also contains a Part IV, comprising some general and supplementary provisions, and there are also a number of schedules of an explanatory or interpretive character. Part IV of the Act contains an important provision* requiring the local authority to register (and inspect) all old people's homes which are privately managed or run by voluntary societies. Registration can be refused, or withdrawn, if certain minimum standards are not complied with.

Returning now to consideration of Part III of the National Assistance Act, 1948, it is convenient to deal separately with the two broad divisions into which the services naturally fall. These are (a) the provision of residential accommodation in old people's homes—Part III accommodation as it is technically known—and (b) the provision of domiciliary services—welfare services for old people living in their own private household.

Residential Accommodation

Local authorities are required to provide residential accommodation for old people who are in need of "care and attention which is not otherwise available to them" and to have regard to their welfare by providing "different descriptions" of accommodation for "different descriptions" of people. In providing this accommodation, local authorities may, and indeed invariably do, make arrangements with voluntary societies having residential homes of their own, for the admission thereto of suitable old people, and the residual cost is met by the local authority. This is a useful addition to the local authorities' own residential home provision which is usually so arranged as to provide separate accommodation for different classes of people, e.g. for the blind and for other handicapped people, for the senile and for very infirm old people as well as for the relatively few active old people who need admission. The requirement "in need of care and attention not otherwise available to them"

* Section 37, National Assistance Act, 1948.

needs some further explanation. At the one extreme, it imports that the old people are no longer able to live independently and manage for themselves with the help, if need be, of the domiciliary services described later in this article. At the other extreme, it stops short of requiring hospital medical and nursing care which, of course, is the responsibility of the National Health Service to provide. In practice, it is often a fine point to decide whether hospital treatment is really essential, and not infrequently the unavailability of an immediate hospital bed leads to a request for admission to an old people's home. It is not, however, the function of local authorities to provide medical services of this nature although, on humanitarian grounds, old people are often *retained* in old people's homes even when they have reached the "chronic sick" or bed-fast stage and, strictly speaking, have become the responsibility of the Regional Hospital Boards, rather than disturb them, in the evening of their lives, by transfer to strange surroundings and amongst strange faces. Similarly, elderly hospital patients are not infrequently retained a little longer in hospital than is medically necessary in order to provide time for them to be suitably accommodated in an old people's home in the district of their choice.

Old people face a major upheaval in the pattern of their lives on giving up independent living and entering a communal home. There is a certain intrinsic finality about it. It is thus not easy for old folk to adjust themselves happily to a different environment, to make new friends and to be tolerant of the idiosyncrasies of their fellow residents. A long span of life inevitably engenders a feeling of remoteness, that the world is passing one by, particularly in swiftly moving times such as we have experienced in this century.

It is worthwhile, therefore, to consider in some detail how old people come to go into residential homes and what their life is like once they are in. It is comparatively rare, in my experience, for old people by a logical process of thought to come to the conclusion that it is time for them to enter a residential home. Such cases do occur, of course, but much more frequently the decision is brought about by circumstances such as a deterioration in health, the death of the partner, or domestic difficulties of the relatives with whom they are living. At an advanced age, even a notice to quit may suffice, particularly where private accommodation is difficult to find. It is at this stage that whatever agency is involved—the old person's doctor, the hospital almoner, the clergyman, the relative, friend or neighbour—approaches the local welfare authority on behalf of the old person, and the process of admission is set in motion. The first step is the visit by a welfare officer for a friendly talk, a sympathetic appraisal of the need and an assessment of the degree of urgency. At this stage, too, an endeavour is made to decide the type of residential accommodation likely to be needed and in what locality. From then on the appropriate arrangements are made, such help as is needed in disposing of household effects is given, and the old person is ultimately received, together with the usual few treasured possessions, into the old people's home. In the absence of a relative or friend, the Welfare Officer usually accompanies the new resident to the home.

The emphasis now is upon making the new resident feel at home, and the current trend of providing a single bedroom for each resident (double rooms for married couples or friends) does much to facilitate this. Personal reception by the Matron of the home is the usual course, since the total numbers in any of the modern small homes are by no means excessive, the average throughout the country probably being 50–60 residents. A "welcome" leaflet is often handed to the new resident in the first hour or two, which can conveniently incorporate information such as meal times and a few pleasantly worded "do's" and "dont's". Although residential homes are nowadays run with a complete absence of restrictive regulations, it is important for the Matron to know if one of her elderly residents is going to be back late from a visit; the usual thing is for the Matron to ask to be told if it will be after dark or after 9 p.m. The emphasis must necessarily be upon consideration for others—respect for the feelings of the other residents and a due regard for the responsibility of the Matron for the safety of each old person in her home. In many homes, those residents who are fairly active are encouraged to pursue hobbies—knitting is a great favourite, which is not surprising since women outnumber men in these advanced age ranges by about 4 to 1. Some residents undertake small jobs about the home, such as making communal purchases from the local newsagent and tobacconist, helping with the dusting, laying tables or sorting the linen. In return, a monetary "reward" of up to 15s. weekly can be allowed,* which is a useful addition for those of limited means to the minimum spending money allowance. Even without the prospect of reward, the opportunity of doing useful small but necessary jobs about the home engenders a feeling of "belonging" in the little community within the four walls of the home. And it is the knowledge of being accepted in this way which is so essential before old people can really happily settle down to communal life.

A material factor is, of course, the question of cost, because in all but a small minority of cases this falls to be met in one way or another by the community. The average weekly cost in a local authority's old people's home is of the order of £7 17s. 6d. per person towards which, from the week of admission, a "minimum charge" of £3 4s. weekly (usually from the state retirement pension or National Assistance grant) is payable. In all cases, however, a balance of at least 16s. 0d. weekly, for personal spending money, must be available. A higher charge, up to the total cost, is payable by those possessed of adequate means. A cost of this order, however, is infinitely less than even the most economically run hospital and understandably so because the emphasis is upon "care and attention" and not upon medical or surgical treatment.

* Section 23 (3) National Assistance Act, 1948, and Ministry of Health Circular 87/48.

Domiciliary Services

It is important to remember that the average age of the residents in old people's homes is now between 75 and 80 years. We all know that people are living longer nowadays, but what seems to be more important is that not only are more people living to the 70's and 80's but they are, on the whole, enjoying a healthier and more active old age because of the advances in medicine, improved surgical techniques, preventive treatment, health supervision and so on. The direct result of this improvement in health and activity is that old people are now generally able to stay in their own homes for much longer than was once the case; they are more active in relation to their age, and such infirmities as they do suffer are not now such handicaps as they once were because of the help provided by "meals on wheels", district nurses, "home helps" and other domiciliary services. This is a good thing because old people are nowhere so happy as in their own homes. But when old people can no longer carry on independently and have to seek admission to an old people's home for their remaining years they have, more often than not, reached an advanced stage of infirmity. This is increasingly so in cases where old people have been living with sons or daughters who have helped them along until the burden has become too much for them. Thus the provision of residential accommodation for old people over recent years has been more and more for the seriously infirm. In 1962 the London percentage of infirm old people (and this is probably also true of the country as a whole) was no less than 73 per cent of the total residents of the old people's homes.

In parallel with this, much more attention is being paid nowadays to the housing requirements of old people. Experience has shown that purpose-designed accommodation can do much to enable old people to continue to live independently in the community even though, because of their years, they are to some extent "at risk". This is a calculated risk and worth taking if it brings contentment to the old people. However, the risk can be, and often is, minimized by "good neighbour" arrangements, by warden/caretaker services for grouped old people's dwellings whereby, in return for a small salary or retainer (which can be paid by local authorities), an active resident of one of the dwellings keeps a watchful eye daily on the others. Perhaps one of the most imaginative arrangements, on these lines, is that which is progressively being developed in London (and probably elsewhere) whereby, within the curtilage of the site of an old people's home, a number of old people's flatlets are erected. The residents of the flatlets maintain themselves independently, but the Matron of the home collects their rents and keeps an eye on them; they can take a cheap midday meal in the home and go in and out as they please to watch the television or just for company and, most important of all, if the time comes when they can no longer manage for themselves, admission to the home with which they are already familiar does much to dispel the fear which most old people have of "going into a home".

Mention has already been made of the domiciliary services which help to keep old people reasonably well and happily living independent lives. In considering them in greater detail it is important to remember that, since they are an admixture of voluntarily-run and statutory services, the pattern is by no means uniform throughout the country. However, in most of the urban conurbations, as well as, no doubt, in many rural areas, the services available are on the following lines.

Meals Services

These invariably take the form of a hot midday meal served in an old people's social and lunch club or, in the case of house-bound old people, delivered to their door. The latter have come to be generally known as "meals-on-wheels" and the Women's Voluntary Services (W.V.S.) have been very active in setting up kitchens and arranging delivery services. The lunch clubs often open on weekdays from about 11 a.m. until 3 p.m. or so, and provide opportunities for social activities, for a game of cards or dominoes or for a sing-song, and serve as a focal point around which other activities such as outings, competitions, talks and the practice of handicrafts are arranged. Many of the clubs are associated with their local church, others with social settlements, women's institutes and similar bodies. In many areas, Old People's Welfare Committees have been formed to further these activities. Local authorities have a permissive power to help in this work; until recently, they could make grants to voluntary organizations providing "meals or recreation" for old people.* Many local authorities in fact make quite substantial grants and, not infrequently, have sought representation upon the Old People's Welfare Committee or other relevant voluntary organization. As a natural result of this and because of the increasing importance of this work in the interests of old people, recent amending legislation† now enables local authorities to provide a comparable meals and recreation service for old people either as a local authority service or in conjunction with voluntary organizations. These powers, however, are still permissive only, and inevitably this means that there will be wide variations from district to district. The local authority grants in London, which may also be made by the London metropolitan boroughs and city councils, are aimed at providing a nourishing freshly-cooked midday meal on payment by the recipient of 1s. to 1s. 2d. a meal, representing about one-half of the actual cost of production.

Home Help and Chiropody Services

This is a service for sick people, again permissive only, and is run by

* Section 31, National Assistance Act, 1948.
† National Assistance Act, 1948, (Amendment) Act, 1962.

local authorities under health powers.* In practice, however, it is found that old people form the majority of cases needing the service. It is really a kind of domestic service; the home helps are employed by the local authority and are sent round to people's homes to clean up, do some cooking or shopping, and generally to help out for an hour or two. Sometimes they go each day, sometimes two or three times a week. People who can afford it are expected to pay according to their means, but it is usually those who have little money who need the help. The usefulness of a home help service in regard to the elderly is becoming more and more recognized and this is likely to lead to a noticeable expansion of the service throughout the country. Another local authority "health" service† which, in practice, largely benefits old people, is the provision of chiropody treatment. This again is a permissive provision, so that the pattern varies from district to district, and an added complication is that much has been developed by voluntary effort (usually through old people's welfare organizations) because there was an estoppel, until comparatively recently, upon further health service expenditure outside hospitals for this purpose. The usual arrangements are for local clinics to be set up, occasionally in conjunction with the lunch clubs, where the foot ailments of old people can be attended to. Such an arrangement is to be preferred to a home-visiting chiropody service which is wasteful of the chiropodist's time —particularly as there is a shortage of qualified chiropodists. This again is a most beneficial service since relatively few old people have escaped the usual foot troubles to which perhaps the tendency in the past has been to devote inadequate attention. The restoration of a painless mobility is a boon, indeed, to the old folk.

Recreational and General Welfare Services

As has been mentioned earlier, these are ancilliary to the meals services; they cover an extensive range, and in addition to the purely recreational activities, include such services as occasional home-visiting, assistance with shopping, library-book changing, organized holiday arrangements, advice on domestic and financial matters, boarding-out schemes and "workrooms for the elderly". Almost all are provided either by, or in close co-operation with, the local voluntary old people's welfare organizations, and their range reflects the individual (and perhaps haphazard) growth of local interest in the problems of old people. Three of these services merit further explanation. Summer holidays, whereby groups of old people go away together to seaside hotels and boarding houses—usually at either end of the accepted holiday season and at reduced rates—are increasingly being organized, and this is extremely valuable work. Boarding-out schemes are as yet in their infancy; the idea is to "place" lone old people in private accommodation as paying

* National Health Service Act, 1946, Section 29.
† National Health Service Act, 1946, Section 28.

guests much as children in care are boarded-out. Clearly a successful placing can be most rewarding, but experience suggests that the requisite matching-up is time-consuming and successes are elusive. It is early to make a considered appraisal but it can, I think, fairly be said that boarding-out is unlikely, numerically, to make much contribution in the field of old people's welfare. Workrooms for the elderly, a field in which the Employment Fellowship (formerly the Winter Distress League) has been most active in sponsoring schemes in the last decade, is now an established feature in some districts. Schemes provide for groups of elderly people to attend a workroom by the half-day, day or on several days according to local arrangements. An organizer, usually a salaried employee, is in charge and controls the seeking of orders for outwork from local industry, arranges deliveries and the payment of rewards to the elderly workers. The measure of the reward varies, but probably 1s. an hour (and usually a maximum of 15s. a week) is about the average. Since the activity is diversionary only and not industrial in the true sense, the amount earned is not the only criterion of the value of these arrangements, acceptable though the additional income usually is to most state retirement pensioners and those dependent on National Assistance benefits. Modest earnings of this nature are disregarded in computing National Assistance grants. The feeling of being useful, of producing something, of being a worker again, is an invaluable morale builder. Indeed, solely on economic grounds these schemes would be difficult to justify, particularly as only the smallest fraction of the total of old people is ever likely to be found diversionary occupation of this nature. For these reasons it seems to be an activity better arranged by voluntary bodies whenever sufficient voluntary help is forthcoming. It is important to remember, however, that local authorities now have power* to provide, or to help in providing, recreational services for old people, and that there is authority for the inclusion therein of "workrooms for the elderly".

Conclusions

Having now completed this survey of the services available to old people, it remains only to consider their adequacy and the directions in which improvements might be made. First, the point can legitimately be made that there is little justification for the wide variations between district and district which can still be discerned in regard to the domiciliary services. This may be inevitable where the powers given to local authorities are permissive only, but few will deny that it is regrettable. In particular, the Meals on Wheels Service for home-bound old people is clearly inadequate since it is only in the rarest cases that there is any weekend coverage at all. That being said, however, it is true to say that immense advances have been made, since the

* National Assistance Act, 1948, (Amendment) Act, 1962.

end of the last war, in recognizing and trying to meet such obligation as the community owes to the old folk. It is perhaps in regard to housing and the residential provision that some further thinking and research might prove most rewarding because there are certainly two aspects which, to my mind, are at present inadequately provided for—and, in this connection, it is important to remember that it is common throughout the country for local authorities to have quite lengthy waiting lists for admission to old people's homes. The first aspect is the need, against the background of the rapidly increasing proportion of old people in the community and, I should add, the increasing difficulty of finding suitable staff willing to cater for their needs in residential homes, for a large—a very large—increase in the provision of purpose-built housing specially designed for old people, so that more and more of them, with the help of the domiciliary services, both statutory and voluntary, will be able to live their own independent lives for longer and longer.

The ideal housing design should ensure that with a minimum of effort (and a maximum of the right built-in equipment) the old folk can rub along comfortably. Much research has already been done in this field: instances which come to mind are the correct siting of gas and electricity meters, no high curtain or other fittings, safe heating, the avoidance of steps and the use of those ingenious cooking stoves which automatically shut off the gas if the burner is not lighted.

The second aspect is perhaps more controversial since it trespasses in the field of what is properly a welfare and what is properly a health responsibility. And it is this. Once medical science—including, of course, the geriatric services specially designed to get old people back on their feet—have done all that is humanly possible and it is clear that particular old people are going to be bed-fast for the rest of their lives, would it not be infinitely preferable to provide for them some form of intermediate accommodation completely divorced from the customary regimen and specialized routine of hospital life? The clinical environment, the daily hospital "drill" conditioned by the timing of the doctor's ward visit and not by the comfort of the patient, the sleeping draught during the night to combat wakefulness instead of the more acceptable cup of tea, indeed the whole panoply of hospital resources; surely these are inappropriate for the terminal care of chronically bed-fast old people. How much more desirable it would be (and how much less expensive) to provide accommodation of a more homely type with, of course, the requisite nursing facilities, geared to providing a serene and peaceful quietude in which life can draw gently and imperceptibly to its close.

19. A General Review of Services for the Elderly

IAN A. G. MACQUEEN

Medical Officer of Health and Director of Welfare, Health and Welfare Department,
City of Aberdeen, and Lecturer in Public Health, University of Aberdeen

Introduction

Although four old people in every five have little need of social welfare services in the normal sense of that phrase, those who require help so outnumber the combined totals of other groups in need as to determine the pattern of the social services. For example, in the City of Aberdeen there are 140 blind persons below pensionable age (and 220 blind old people), 140 problem families, 150 illegitimate children born each year, 450 persons of working age on the register of physically handicapped adults, and 23,000 pensioners of whom 4650 are deemed in need of services. To understand the trends not only in services for veterans but in welfare services generally, it is therefore important to have a numerical picture of the elderly population.

In the thirteenth century Roger Bacon wrote of old age as beginning at 35 and described persons over 60 as senile. During the next 700 years there was gradual prolongation of life and of vigour, but as late as 1901 only 5 per cent of people in Britain were over 65 years. With the conquest of most infectious diseases, the introduction and expansion of services for maternity and child welfare, the spread of health education, the partial abolition of primary poverty and improvements in medical and nursing services and in their availability, the demographic picture has altered completely. By 1931 7 per cent of Britain's population was over 65 years, by 1950 11 per cent, and by 1963 about 14 per cent. On the quite unscientific basis of present pensionable age—65 for men and 60 for the stronger sex—we had 1 pensioner in every 7 inhabitants by 1955 and will probably reach 2 in every 11 by 1980.

Historical Perspective

In the last fifty years there have been three overlapping phases of social services for veterans—the era of bare subsistence, that of sentimental support at the dawning of community responsibility, and that of maintenance of health and well-being.

In the era of bare subsistence (broadly until about 1948) the normal policy was to provide beds in the poorest hospitals for the elderly sick, Poor Law institutions—with separation of married couples—for the frail aged, and a pension of 10s. a week for persons deemed capable of maintaining an independent existence. Organized and unorganized charity helped those judged to be sufficiently needy and subservient enough, but the underlying philosophy—seldom overtly expressed—was that anyone who had the temerity to survive beyond working age should either have saved for retirement or produced dependants who would be legally bound to maintain him. The policy, economically sound but ethically unjustifiable, and obsolescent by 1939, was rendered untenable by smaller families (and therefore fewer available younger relatives), increased mobility of population (offspring and parents far apart), more women at work (and fewer available for unskilled home nursing), more surviving veterans, decline in the value of money (so that the provident found their savings inadequate), decrease in incomes of charitable organizations, and rising demand for insurances (with allowances as a right).

Inevitably the dawn of public responsibility—legal onus on the community, not on dependants—led to an attitude of sentimental support. Lloyd George[1] wrote:

> How we treat our old people is a test of our national quality. A nation that lacks gratitude to those who have honestly worked for her in the past, while they had strength to do so, does not deserve a future, for she has lost her sense of justice and her instinct of mercy.

For a dozen years (1946–58 roughly) hospital services dominated the health stage: while politicians and health workers demanded more and more hospital beds, the army of doctors, nurses, ancillary staff and domestics grew year by year. In the local authority field a similar philosophy obtained: welfare authorities replaced voluntary bodies as the main owners of hostels; and between 1948 and 1958 some 1200 additional hostels were opened in Britain, while—until about 1955—services with a preventive slant (like facilities for employment of veterans, health-visiting and chiropody) lagged behind. Provision of more and better hospital and hostel accommodation was a human policy, but to leave hospitals and hostels in the central position and to ignore the preservation of physical and emotional health and social well-being would ultimately have led to economic collapse. The increased birth-rate following the reaching of marital age by the "bulge" children born in 1945–7 is necessitating more midwives, more health visitors and more school teachers, and, if simultaneous substantial increases had continued in staffs of geriatric hospitals and old people's homes, there would have been insufficient adults available for productive work.

There appeared in the 1950's and reached a peak in the early 1960's a shift of emphasis—from simple support of the frail and diseased to counselling and casework for those not yet incapacitated, from hospitals to health visitors and health education, from hostels to housing and home helps, and from acceptance of the "functionless interregnum"[2] between retiral and death to provision of opportunity for continued work and encouragement of leisure interests. The change was gradual and did not imply neglect of supportive and rehabilitative services. Moreover, the swing to maintenance of health and well-being occurred at different times in different areas, and official reports in the 1950's showed a curious ambivalence: e.g. the Younghusband Report[3] of 1959, while usefully stressing the need for qualified social workers in various fields, was in many respects less orientated to the preservation of physical and mental health than was the Jameson Report[4] of 1956.

The Idea of Maintaining Health and Well-being

The recrudescence of prevention began in part with the National Health Service Acts (England and Wales, 1946, and Scotland, 1947): both Acts had a section on prevention, care and after-care, another section expressly extending the work of the health visitor, and a third establishing the home help service; and the Scottish Act gave local health authorities power to conduct research. These Acts came into operation simultaneously with the National Assistance Act, 1948, which charged welfare authorities with, among other things, the duty of providing hostels.

Several publications in the early 1950's are heralds of the dawn or the first light of the new day. In 1950 the Department of Health for Scotland[5] stressed the role of the health visitor (a health teacher and medico-social worker dedicated to prevention rather than support) in social work for the elderly; a year later the Scottish Health Services Council, in a report, *What Local Authorities can do to Promote Health and Prevent Disease*,[6] emphasized the economic advantages of prevention, and in respect of the elderly expressly indicated the need for study of the origin of diseases of old age and the value of health advice by health visitors; and in 1952 these and other points were elaborated in another report, *The Ageing Population*.[7] About the same time Langton, Superintendent Health Visitor of Salford, published in the *Nursing Times* some penetrating articles on health maintenance in the elderly, and two years later Lamont's lucid analysis of the health visitor's role in the care of the aged[8] set the pattern for that aspect of the social services: her work was quoted extensively in *Hansard*, summarized in a Report of the Ministry of Health,[9] and later paraphrased in a circular of the Department of Health for Scotland.[10] Meanwhile the administrative head of Scotland's governmental health and welfare services had publicly declared that

> The health services and social services will have failed and failed disastrously if it ever becomes necessary to maintain a very large number of old people either in chronic hospitals or in Eventide Homes.[11]

and had suggested that the Medical Officer of Health—whom he defined as "essentially a sociologist with clinical insight"—should be no less interested in old people than in children.

After an initial partial failure at Ramsgate a preventive clinic for old people had opened at Rutherglen (to be later followed by others); the British Medical Association[12] had singled out the elderly and the handicapped as two of the seven groups in which "the health visitor can play a most important part"; the Guillebaud Committee[13] of financial experts had advocated amalgamation of Health Departments and Welfare Departments in the interests of efficiency and economy, and had given the health visitor pride of place in each of their references to the elderly; a Royal Society of Health prize-winning essay on amalgamation of health and welfare services[14] had attracted widespread attention; some local health authorities had begun to provide chiropody (e.g. Aberdeen in 1952); the professional education of health visitors was undergoing a revolution following the creation in 1948 of a separate profession of health visitor tutors with an obligatory higher qualification; the Jameson Committee[4] was working out proposals for a national policy on health visiting and the Younghusband Committee[3] was preparing its enormous report on social work and usefully differentiating persons requiring help into those with uncomplicated needs, those with complex problems requiring systematic help from trained workers and those with problems of special difficulty; and the Phillips Committee[15] had already reported on the financial aspects of the ageing population.

Roughly simultaneously there were produced various fact-finding surveys on the needs, problems and attitudes of old people—first broad exploratory studies such as those of Sheldon in Wolverhampton, McCoubrey and MacQueen in Caithness, and Wallace in Aberdeen, and then more detailed studies of particular facets, e.g. Richardson's study of retired men.[16] Shaw's analysis of causes of social breakdown in veterans,[17] Macfie's investigation of the nature and effects of the preventive and social work carried out with old people by health visitors,[18] and Rae's study of the attitudes of persons in municipal and voluntary hostels.[19] Equally important, clinical knowledge of diseases of the aged was advancing rapidly, and geriatrics and gerontology were benefiting not only from the contributions of specialists in these fields but also from those of experts in adjacent territories: a useful outline is that of Hobson.[20]

A recent development of major importance was the creation, under the Health Visiting and Social Work (Training) Act, 1962, of National Councils to supervise the professional education of appropriate workers.

Modern Trends

Before describing services, as existing in 1964, it may be useful to indicate eight important modern trends.

(1) There is a tendency to encourage whole-time or part-time employment

beyond the age of retirement: illustrative examples are the proviso that persons may earn increased pensions by remaining at work after reaching the age of 65 (male) and 60 (female), the extension of the age of obligatory retirement from various professions, and the starting (in Finsbury as early as 1951) of sheltered workshops in which old people can work at slower pace for reduced remuneration. In recent years, however, the prevalence of unemployment has largely blocked this trend in Scotland, northern England and south Wales.

(2) There is a shift of emphasis from the institution to the home—a realization that most veterans are happiest in the privacy of their own homes with their own furniture around them, and that it is often better (as well as cheaper) to provide appropriate domiciliary services than to provide more hostels. To quote the Ministry of Health:

> The key to the problems stemming from an ageing population lies with the preventive and domiciliary services; the extension of communal accommodation, as the only measure, will not prove a solution.[21]

(3) In respect of local authority services there is a double trend. (a) The shift of emphasis to domiciliary work, recommendations by bodies like the Guillebaud Committee,[13] and increasing appreciation of the fact that an old person may (like a baby) be unwell today, well tomorrow and ill on the next day, have led in some areas to amalgamation of Health Departments and Welfare Departments, under the aegis of the Medical Officer of Health. (b) As welfare officers qualified mainly by experience retire, there is in other areas a tendency to replace them by officers with a professional qualification in social work. At present amalgamation seems the dominant policy in Scotland and northern England, while segregation predominates in the south. A penetrating discussion by a leading medico-social worker[14] who is neither a Medical Officer of Health nor a Director of Social Welfare may be mentioned; and it may be noted that, while amalgamation is advantageous to the client and also saves public money, a unified health and welfare department need not lack suitably qualified staff for each branch of its educative, preventive, medico-social and social work.

(4) A vast expansion of the home help service began in the 1950's and is still continuing; and the chiropody service—a later starter in most areas—is also in process of extension.

(5) For generalized domiciliary fieldwork with old people—both for health maintenance and for social counselling—there is a widespread tendency to rely mainly on the district health visitor. This tendency is strengthened by shortage of personnel (since it is extravagant to have two professional workers traversing the same street and even entering the same house if one would suffice) and by the growing co-operation between health visitors and general practitioners.[22] It should, however, be noted that, although the health visitor is a well-qualified officer with five years of full-time professional education, she carries out a wide range of duties; so there should be

available to her some workers of narrower—and hence more intense—specialization on whom she can call at need, just as the general practitioner can call on the medical or surgical consultant. While the pattern is only emerging it would seem that some of the specialized workers will have a social science qualification and others will be health visitors who have concentrated on particular subjects or groups.

(6) Throughout the whole of social, medico-social and preventive work there is a trend towards multiplication of specialities, not unlike the trend in medical work a generation ago. An inevitable corollary of the two trends last mentioned is a dwindling place for the unqualified worker.

(7) Many changes are taking place in old people's homes. In about 70 per cent of local authority areas, hostels on the lines of private hotels or superior boarding houses have already replaced the old Poor Law accommodation. As services to maintain health expand, the average age of admission to hostel is rising and the average degree of frailness of residents is increasing, with repercussions on staffing needs. In addition it is becoming common for hostels to reserve a few places for short-term admissions, e.g. old people who normally live with relatives but cannot accompany them on holiday.

(8) The role of voluntary bodies is altering. Just as in the past voluntary organizations engaged health visitors, organized child welfare clinics and employed home nurses, but in due course passed these functions over to local authorities, so today there is a dawning recognition that the bodies which led the way in building old people's homes and employing caseworkers should begin to think of transferring these buildings and workers to local authorities, thereby leaving themselves free for tasks which statutory bodies are not empowered to undertake or are reluctant to tackle.

Some Services to Maintain Health and Well-being

In the outline that follows pensions and allowances under the National Insurance and Assistance Acts are not discussed in detail; but it should be noted that the maintenance for old people of a standard of living just above subsistence level has been accepted as a community responsibility, that each increase in scale rates in recent years has been in large measure nullified by subsequent increases in the cost of living, and that, despite the statements of some pensioners, the scales have on the whole tended in recent years to be just high enough to cover necessities with carefully budgeted expenditure. While health services (e.g. health-visiting, home nursing, chiropody and home help service) are discussed along with welfare services, no rigid demarcation is attempted because (a) the boundaries of after-care (health) and social support (welfare) are undetermined, and (b) an individual may need medico-social counselling (health) in January, temporary accommodation in a hostel (welfare) in February, a home help and a chiropodist (both health) in March, care of property (welfare) while in hospital in April, and home nursing (health) in May.

Since shelter is—like food and clothing—a primary need, we must as a preliminary ask the question—hostel or home? Decision whether an old person should be admitted to a hostel must depend partly on his desires (most veterans preferring to stay at home as long as possible but a minority seeking the comfort and companionship of a hostel), partly on availability of relatives and their willingness to help (without legal obligation to do so), and partly on the cost of necessary domiciliary services (e.g. home help, laundry service and calls by health visitor or other medico-social worker). Broadly someone who on a long-term basis needs half the working time of a home help is about the point at which accommodation in a hostel becomes less costly than domiciliary provisions, but for an elderly couple it is cheaper to keep them at home unless they require full-time help.

Housing

"Some old people are virtually prisoners in their own homes and it is difficult for them to get exchanges to ground-floor rooms. Others live in family houses now larger than they require."[23]

Timely rehousing may well prevent or postpone the need for institutionalization. An old woman with moderately severe arthritis and her husband with considerable cardiac disability may live happily for years in an easily run, ground-floor flat, whereas if left on the fourth floor of a tenement building they would, within weeks, have to be admitted respectively to a hostel and a hospital, with disruption of their companionship and considerable cost to the community; a widow in danger of collapsing under the strain of maintaining a six-roomed house may not need any help if given the opportunity to transfer to a special-purpose house.

Britain has an insufficiency of special-purpose houses, ground-floor flats and "granny plus" houses (with a self-contained flatlet with communicating door). It is often suggested that 10 per cent of new housing should be allocated to small units, including 7 per cent for old people.[24]

Establishing Personal Contact

Contact is necessary for two reasons. To take the simpler one first, a person in need should have a method of getting in touch with the services that may meet the need. In specially built houses adjacent to hostels a series of alarms has been tried, but is not practicable in the ordinary community. Lights to display in windows at night or signs to exhibit during the day can indicate to undesirable characters that a house is occupied by an old person living alone. In most cases we have to fall back on neighbourliness—asking a neighbour to note whether a blind is drawn at dusk and pulled up in the morning, and to take appropriate action at need.

More complex is the establishing of contact with old people not yet actively seeking advice on health maintenance and social well-being but often capable of being considerably helped by timely counselling. To wait until clinical or social emergency causes the veteran to make contact is futile, since by then the thing that might have been prevented has occurred. Some local authorities have introduced a voluntary register: while any old person can himself ask to be placed on the register, names are usually submitted by relatives, neighbours, friends, clergymen, doctors, nurses and lawyers, the source of the information remaining confidential. When a name reaches the department, an appropriate visitor—usually the district health visitor—calls, mentions some of the services in a friendly chat, and asks the veteran whether he wishes to be placed on the register, in which case he will be visited from time to time and will be eligible for other services at need. Despite the notorious independence of the elderly, in the area where the writer works 99 per cent of notified persons welcome the visits and accept inclusion on the register. It has been claimed, probably rightly, that a high acceptance rate is associated with the initial caller being the health visitor for the locality, known and respected in the particular street.[25] The refusers are simply told that, if they ever change their mind, they can contact the department whose services will be available to them; and for the 99 per cent of acceptances the visitor completes —not necessarily at one visit—a detailed record of their personal and social circumstances with an assessment of their needs, and places the old person on her own list, to be visited at her discretion.

Professional Visitation

Whether professional visiting should normally be undertaken both by a health visitor for guidance on physical and emotional health and by a welfare officer for advice on social problems is perhaps still the subject of argument, although it has to be remembered that the Jameson Report[4] includes social advice among the health visitor's primary duties, that the Younghusband Committee[3] expressly accepted the findings of the Jameson Report, and that the Department of Health for Scotland in a valuable circular about the care of the aged[10] included the following paragraph:

Health visitors can help old people in five main ways:
(a) they can do much to maintain the physical and emotional health of persons still reasonably fit (e.g. by advice on diet, exercise, rest, budgeting, and cultivation of leisure interests, and removal of needless fears and worries);
(b) they can advise the elderly about the various services and allowances available;
(c) they are in a favourable position to set in motion services (e.g. home nursing, domestic help or simple visiting) to meet particular needs (though this does not imply that health visitors are the only people who can initiate services);
(d) they can play a useful part in the after-care and rehabilitation of those who are recovering from illness; and
(e) they can secure information which will be of great value in fixing policy to meet the local needs.

Again, a Working Party set up by a Regional Hospital Board[23] has concluded:

> Adequate visiting by health visitors can do much to maintain the physical and mental health of many elderly people, and health visitors can also play an important part as social advisers and in initiating or co-ordinating social action. The Working Party endorses what has been said in many authoritative reports about the clamant need for adequate health visitor staffs.

Three points on which the guidance of appropriate qualified visitors is particularly important may be selected for special mention. (1) *Guidance on budgeting, catering and diet.* At the period of life in which income often falls sharply the need for skilled counselling about expenditure of limited money is obvious. Moreover, in addition to having restricted incomes, many old people living alone deem cooking a needless chore and tend to live largely on bread and butter and the inevitable cups of tea until lowered resistance leads to illness. Again, people who have retired from occupations involving heavy manual work often eat too much, through persisting habit, placing excessive strain on heart and kidneys. Yet again, it is far from unknown for excessive eating to follow bereavement and to accompany loneliness and loss of interests. (2) *Counselling on measures to reduce the likelihood of accidents.* In Britain as a whole, home accidents are a leading cause both of death and of disability in old people, but are in large part preventable. In one area systematic study of aetiology, planned visiting by health visitors and some group education not only reduced the overall incidence of domestic accidents in the community by more than a third but also made all types of accidents except falls rarities in old people.[26] (3) *Maintenance of emotional health.* The removal of needless fears, the alleviation of loneliness, the explanation of services available at need, and the preservation of morale in the elderly perhaps constitute the biggest task of medico-social workers. The job must, of course, start in the senescent, not in the aged.

Whatever workers tackle these important duties, they must be adequately qualified and numerous enough to do the jobs thoroughly. Where a health visitor alone acts as general purpose health educator and social counsellor for the people in her district (with, of course, the co-operation of the family doctor in the case of households in which illness exists), she should be able to devote about 10–12 per cent of her working time to the elderly, and it has been suggested that a reasonable staffing standard is one health visitor for every 2200 population:[27] the Jameson Committee's proposed minimum[4] of one per 4300 was widely criticized in 1956 as too low, did not take full account of "welfare" functions as contrasted with "health" functions, and has also been completely outmoded by new duties devolving on health visitors in recent years and by new appreciation of the complexity of health maintenance, especially in the psycho-social field.

Where separate workers—health visitor and welfare visitor—are employed for health maintenance and social counselling, it is important that the welfare visitor should be adequately qualified and that each of the two workers should have some insight into the functions and skills of the other. The total staff required will necessarily be larger, since no amount of organization can prevent all duplication of effort and since frequent discussions are needed to minimize the likelihood of conflicting advice.

Certain elderly men are best visited by members of their own sex or are reluctant to accept advice from women. One or two areas have begun to employ for such individuals male health-visiting officers[28] who have nursing and medico-social qualifications, like health visitors.

The case for a small number of specialized officers (to act as consultants) has already been mentioned.

Voluntary Visiting

There are obvious limits to the average frequency of professional visiting, and the vast majority of old people will see their health visitor or welfare visitor only once in several months. While voluntary visitors cannot without professional training offer guidance on complex matters, they can nevertheless be of great value in relieving loneliness and making old people feel "wanted", and they can also help with shopping, mending and exchange of library books. To be of real value the visiting should be sufficiently frequent to establish and maintain rapport. Probably the commonest error is for the enthusiastic beginner to undertake to visit more veterans than his leisure and inclination will really permit. The ideal is for two visitors each to visit the same two old people, so that during any absence of one visitor (e.g. summer holidays or illness) neither veteran feels friendless. Visiting may be arranged informally or through Old People's Welfare Committees.

Where communications from relatives are few an occasional letter or picture postcard from the voluntary visitor who is temporarily absent can give very real pleasure, as can a small birthday or Christmas gift. Visits, letters and gifts should not, of course, cease if the veteran later has to be admitted to a hostel or hospital. Where eyesight is failing, an offer to read aloud is often received with gratitude.

Professional visitors should bear in mind that, with a little tact, it is often possible to induce one lonely old person to act as voluntary visitor to another, ostensibly for the benefit of the second but actually in the interests of both.

An obvious (but often overlooked) point is that a visitor should try to establish the names and means of contacting various "official" sources of help well in advance of actual need. Circumstances may well arise in which the visitor would feel it desirable to pass a message to, say, the general practitioner or the health visitor without the veteran being made aware of the fact. A working knowledge of the services of the area is also useful to a voluntary visitor.

Chiropody

Unremedied foot defects cause people to become needlessly house-bound, with reduction of interests and impairment of mental health, difficulties in shopping and damage to diet, lack of exercise and insufficiency of fresh air. Chiropody is therefore an important preventive service. In an area with well-developed services for old people, Wallace,[29] in a sample of 1005 veterans, finds health visitors' calls the commonest need and the commonest unmet need (20 in each hundred requiring them and 8 receiving them) and chiropody the second commonest (15 in each hundred needing treatment and 8 getting it). In view of the relative frequency of diabetes and certain other conditions the general practioner should, of course, be asked to state, before chiropody is undertaken, whether he raises any objection.

Staffing requirements are hard to calculate—partly because in most areas chiropody is a young service, partly because relatively less treatment will be needed if chiropody is started before damage has progressed far, and partly because a man who at first has to be treated frequently at home may in a few months be able to walk to a clinic and require only occasional treatment. However, one full-time chiropodist for every 6000 veterans is certainly not excessive.

Health Education of Veterans

Although group education in health is commonly considered applicable mainly to prospective parents, parents of young children, school pupils and adolescents, it can also be important for hale and hearty persons recently retired or approaching retirement[30]—helping to prepare them for retirement, to foster pleasurable and healthful use of leisure, to maintain emotional and physical health, and—in case of disability—to live to its limits. To give a single example to illustrate the need, despite all that has been written on the role of focal sepsis in the creation of ill health, in many areas it is still nobody's task to advise an apparently healthy veteran to visit a dentist.

Formation of groups for health education at the period of increasing leisure is relatively easy. In some towns pre-retirement classes are organized under the auspices of the Education Department, but mostly health education is regarded as a Health Department function. For all purposes (including the elderly) it has been suggested that each local health authority should employ on the staff of its Medical Officer of Health at least one well-qualified Health Education Officer with status and remuneration no less high than those of the heads of other sections of the Health Department,[31] and that, using health visitors as the main educators and health education officers as organizers and advisers, the American standard of one officer for every 50,000 total population might be appropriate.[32]

The Equivalent of "Well-baby Clinics"

Clinics for routine overhaul of elderly persons not consciously suffering from any illness can facilitate identification of disease at a much earlier stage than if no medical action were taken until the individual himself consulted his general practitioner because of symptoms, can serve as useful centres for counselling on measures for preservation of health, can act as places to which health visitors and social workers refer persons about whom they are in doubt, and can serve to some extent as centres for social contact and social activities. They have also important potentialities for research: while research in geriatrics may be largely a matter for hospitals, research in gerontology—the causes and processes of senescence—must be carried out on persons in whom the process is not yet too advanced; and in particular study of the influence of nutritional, emotional, psychological and socio-economic factors in hastening or retarding the ageing processes and the diseases of old age can be successfully undertaken only by persons with medico-social as well as clinical skills, and with knowledge of the conditions in the home, the office and the factory. From the point of view of research the tragedy of the early 1960's is that areas with gerontological clinics seldom have adequately developed medico-social staffs to investigate and follow up, while areas with sufficient health visitors and other domiciliary workers do not yet have clinics.

Other Services

At the age when relatives, spouses and contemporaries are dying and work contacts are ceasing, loneliness is a very serious problem. Apart from voluntary and professional visiting, recreational clubs and luncheon clubs are useful. Under Section 31 of the National Assistance Act local authorities are empowered to contribute to the funds of organizations providing recreation or meals, and in most areas finances are adequate but clubs are popular only with a minority: the figure of 16 per cent of pensioners has been quoted as the membership in Liverpool, for example, and even this figure may reckon twice individuals who are members of two clubs.

Another sphere for voluntary bodies is arranging "boarding out" schemes for persons too frail to live alone but not necessarily so enfeebled as to need admission to a hostel. Exeter and Plymouth have been pioneers here.

Provision of facilities for continuation of work beyond the normal age of retirement and for carrying out full-time or part-time work at a slower pace than in an ordinary factory is important, both for old people and for the community [33, 34] with its increasing load of veterans. Social workers mostly advocate gradual rather than sudden cessation of work (although in many occupations there is still a fixed age for retirement), and persons in employments demanding considerable speed or physical strength are often advised to change their jobs while still young enough to learn new skills (though the current amount of unemployment must be considered before such advice is given).

Some Supportive Services

Services for maintenance of well-being and for help of those who have to some extent ceased to be clinically or socially well merge into each other, so the division between this and the previous section is not rigid.

Home Helps

Where a widow or spinster can almost manage to live independently but finds the heavier parts of housework difficult, provision of domestic help for two or three mornings weekly may enable her to remain happily at home at far less cost to the community than if she entered a hostel. In most areas the home help section already rivals the ambulance section as the most expensive single component of the local authority health and welfare services, is still increasing rapidly and will probably continue to grow as the population ages—although in some areas it is becoming very difficult to find more available women of working age. In 1962 there were in England and Wales 53,000 home helps (50,000 of them part-time) and 800 home help organizers;[35] and about 76 per cent of the time of home helps was devoted to the elderly.

It is impossible to specify a staffing standard for home helps, because the number needed to some extent varies inversely as the strength and success of the services for health maintenance. As a very rough guide here are figures for a city containing 23,000 pensioners: 4500 need medico-social visiting and 3300 need chiropody (these needs being not completely met), and 2400 need home nursing at some time during the year while 1250 need home help (these needs being virtually met in full); 80 per cent of the total time of the home help service is devoted to the elderly; and of the old people receiving domestic help 35 per cent have it for one half-day per week, 38 per cent for two half-days, 25 per cent for three, and only 2 per cent for more than three half-days.

The charge made to recipients of domestic help service varies (according to income) from full cost down to a minimum (in some areas as little as 1s. for each half-day) which in necessitous cases can be reclaimed from the National Assistance Board.

Where Health Departments and Welfare Departments are separate home helps are normally appointed by the former, the powers being contained in the National Health Service Act. Desiderata for appointment include—experience of housework, personal cleanliness and honesty. Where practicable, home helps should be given a short course of instruction, including, for example, the use of different appliances (since an electric cooker may present difficulties to a woman previously accustomed only to gas), nutritional and dietetic needs of old people, food hygiene, accident prevention, the mental reactions of veterans (if only to lessen indignation when an absent-minded and suspicious old person accuses a home help of the theft of an article or suddenly uses bad language) and the available medico-social services.

There is much variation in the type of supervision of home helps. Clearly medico-social skills are required for assessment of cases to receive help, ability in personnel management is desirable for direction and control of a considerable number of workers, and knowledge of the psychology of the aged is useful for dealing with complaints. In urban areas perhaps the best plan is to have as head of the section a health visitor or almoner with personal experience of house management (e.g. a married woman or a widow), assisted by a few practical supervisors who are themselves promoted home helps; and in rural districts the health visitor or "combined" health visitor/district nurse normally acts as local organizer and supervisor.

Home Nursing

For persons requiring skilled nursing to a lesser quantitative extent than would justify admission to hospital the need can be met by the daily (or twice daily) visits of the district nurse. Description of her functions is not within the scope of this book, and the same applies to the functions of the general practitioner with whom she works in close association; but to prevent confusion the distinction between the district nurse and the health visitor must be made clear. While both are qualified nurses, the district nurse is essentially concerned with the treatment of the sick, and is in fact the domiciliary counterpart of the hospital ward sister or staff nurse; the health visitor, with the same nursing background, has spent a further year in acquiring skills in health teaching, prevention of disease and medico-social work, and she is essentially concerned with the preservation of physical and psycho-social well-being—so much so, indeed, that the Royal Society of Health has described her as "the spearhead of the social services".

For old people who are gravely ill but desire to die at home, and for others whose relatives are becoming exhausted through a series of disturbed nights during a temporary illness, some local authorities provide a night nursing service. Supplied in moderation and with discretion this can be very valuable; but, if developed unreasonably, it could become an expensive and inefficient substitute for hospitals.

Home nursing services are provided free of charge, and local authorities are also empowered to lend sick-room equipment without charge.

Mobile Meals Service

Where a medico-social visitor or a general practitioner finds that the nutrition of an elderly person is becoming defective and is incapable of being improved by information about available financial allowances, guidance on budgeting or purchasing, or emphasis on need for adequate diet, the answer is not necessarily a home help or admission to a hostel. The mobile meals service, supplying a hot, cooked meal twice a week, with usually enough to be warmed up for a second meal, may well make the difference between malnutrition and good nutrition.

The service is an excellent example of co-operation between voluntary and statutory bodies. Normally the local authority provides vehicles and containers, a voluntary organization (e.g. the W.V.S.) organizes the service, distributing the meals by unpaid workers who carry the containers from van to houses, and the cost of each meal is shared between the local authority and the recipient. Unfortunately, in many areas the number of volunteers is inadequate, and it is not uncommon to find a county borough with 500 persons deemed to need meals and only 100 receiving them. Consequently there has been a tendency in recent years for local authorities to seek to undertake the job directly, using paid workers, and sometimes utilizing the staff and equipment of the school meals service.

The luncheon clubs mentioned earlier are a useful variant for veterans whose movements are not unduly restricted.

Boarding-out of Old People

"It is regarded as worthwhile to advertise for persons willing to take suitable old age pensioners as boarders. In particular, married nurses might be encouraged to give a home to the frailer type of elderly persons."[36] Boarding-out schemes, sponsored by voluntary bodies, have worked well in a few areas, provided that the "foster children" can be assured that the old people will be removed to an appropriate institution if they come to need special care and attention. It must be admitted, nevertheless, that there is in the average community much less enthusiasm for boarding-out old people than for similar boarding for deprived children.

Other Domiciliary Services

While the home help service and the mobile meals service are in the main applicable to old people living alone or living with other veterans (e.g. elderly married couples), many veterans reside with younger relatives; and there is a tendency for the public, while blaming younger adults who—often for sound reasons—decline to have members of the older generation living with them, to ignore the needs and problems of households with frail old people. Where they cannot properly be left alone a sitter-in service (whether on a voluntary or on a paid basis) may be the only means by which an unmarried daughter can obtain temporary relief from the strain of looking after her mother for twenty-four hours a day on seven days a week, and the only means whereby a married couple can ever get an evening out together. In addition to improving the mental health of the relatives, such a service provides a refreshing change of companion for the old person.

In cases of frequent or even occasional incontinence a laundry service can be of very real value. It is sometimes possible to utilize a hospital laundry for the actual washing, with the local authority providing the bags and transport.

To reduce the likelihood of stiffened joints and disuse atrophy of muscles there is a case for the development of a domiciliary physiotherapy service. In addition it should be remembered that a person suffering from physical or mental handicap should not by reason of age cease to be eligible for services appropriate to his type of disability.

Hostel Accommodation

While retirement pensions and unemployment benefit are provided under National Insurance Acts, some of the main provisions of the National Assistance Act, 1948, relate to financial allowances for the needy, welfare services for the handicapped and residential accommodation for persons incapable of looking after themselves by reason of age, infirmity or other circumstance. In the last fifteen years most local authorities have closed or modernized the grim, forbidding institutions of the pre-war era. The modern residential hostel for old people is a pleasant building with the atmosphere of a private hotel and with a minimum of rules and regulations. In the early post-war years shortages of accommodation necessitated the adaptation of old buildings, with in many cases the creation of dormitories with 3–5 beds; but in modern hostels the majority of the rooms are single, and this trend will undoubtedly continue, since (1) something like 90 per cent of old people outside hostels do not share bedrooms otherwise than with a spouse, (2) married couples seldom seek admission to hostel (perhaps because the disabilities of the two individuals normally differ and the couple tends to remain a functionally efficient unit) and (3) the single and the widowed express an emphatic preference for rooms of their own. Admission to hostel is normally made on a basis of need, not income, although a person in residence has to pay in accordance with his means.

The border-line between home and hostel depends—as already indicated—partly on the old person's preference, partly on the presence or absence of relatives willing to lend a hand, and partly on cost to the local authority. Certainly an individual who will need for a long period more than the half-time services of a home help is a case for admission to hostel. The border-line between hostel and hospital is more related to nursing than to medicine: while occasionally need for treatment more skilled than could be given by a general practitioner may necessitate admission to hospital, the usual criterion is nursing more skilled or more continuous than could be given in an ordinary home by relatives with the district nurse paying a couple of visits daily. A hostel, in short, is not a nursing home, although it should be able to cope with minor illnesses. In this connecton it should be noted that the employment of a qualified nurse as matron does not alter the position: to provide one nurse constantly on duty it would be necessary to employ four full-time nurses (to cover 168 hours in each week) together with a fifth nurse to take over during the holidays and illnesses of each of the four.

Suggested standards for hostel places vary from $2\frac{1}{2}$ to 5 per 100 pensioner (or roughly 4–9 per 1000 total population), but with adequate domiciliary services for maintenance of health and well-being these standards would almost certainly be too high. As yet, however, few areas have adequate staff of preventive and medico-social workers, so the need for hostel places i greater than it otherwise might be. In the city where the writer works, th health visiting and health education services are fairly well developed, th proportion of hostel places is approximately 2 per 1000 of population, an the active waiting list is fairly small.

The optimum size of a hostel is about 30–36 places. Smaller hostels ten to be expensive and larger ones to acquire the characteristics of institution Having regard to the gradual but steady tendency for the entry age to ris and the degree of frailty to increase, a staffing ratio of not less than one mem ber of staff for every three residents is recommended. This is, of course, very much lower ratio than obtains in hospitals and implies that seriously i residents will be transferred to hospital.

In large towns with a number of hostels the rival claims of locality an compatibility have to be considered. Many elderly people prefer to enter hostel in their own district so that they can visit friends and be visited b them; on the other hand there are advantages in allocating particular hostel to social or occupational groups. Whichever policy is adopted it is desirabl to have in each populous area one hostel—not uncomfortable but les "luxurious" and run on less permissive lines—for people who are habituall anti-social in their ways of life.

Accommodation for Limited Periods

As suggested earlier, there is also a need for short-stay accommodatio either in ordinary hostels or elsewhere, e.g. for people living alone an temporarily requiring some care although not ill enough to need admissio to hospital, or for people normally living with relatives who are at the tim either ill or going on holiday. A parallel problem in pleasure resorts is th of persons who live in lodgings or boarding houses for about nine months c the year but are required to vacate their accommodation during the seaso of summer visitors

Crucial Points

The community has a moral responsibility to make decent provision fc those who were the workers of yesterday, but the sheer magnitude of th elderly population renders it imperative that the provision be effected wit reasonable economy. Fortunately, however, humanity and financial economy can to a considerable extent march together. The demand for very expensive hospital accommodation for the elderly sick and for quite dear hostel accommodation for the frail aged can be reduced considerably by provision of domiciliary supportive services which are in most cases much cheaper, and the need for all three can be greatly lessened by the development at very limited cost of adequate domiciliary services for the preservation of health and social well-being: as in so many other parts of the health and welfare field, prevention is both pleasanter and less expensive than treatment or palliation.

References

1. LLOYD GEORGE, D. (1944), Foreword to E. M. Sampson's *Old Age in the New World*, London.
2. TITMUSS, R. M. (1954), *The Times*, 29 Dec.
3. Report of Working Party on Social Workers in *L. A. Health and Welfare Services* (1959), H.M.S.O.
4. *An Inquiry into Health Visiting* (1956), H.M.S.O.
5. DEPARTMENT OF HEALTH FOR SCOTLAND (1950), Circular E.C.S. 75A/1950.
6. SCOTTISH HEALTH SERVICES COUNCIL (1951), *What Local Authorities Can Do to Promote Health and Prevent Disease*, H.M.S.O.
7. *Ibid.* (1952), *The Ageing Population*, H.M.S.O.
8. LAMONT, D. J. (1954), *The Medical Officer*, **92**, 162.
9. MINISTRY OF HEALTH, *Annual Report for 1954*, Part 2, p. 198.
10. DEPARTMENT OF HEALTH FOR SCOTLAND (1958), Circular 60/1958.
11. HENDERSON, SIR G. K. (1952), *Health Bulletin of Department of Health for Scotland* (x) **3**, 43.
12. BRITISH MEDICAL ASSOCIATION (1955), *Evidence to Working Party on Health Visitors*, par. 17.
13. *Report of Committee on Enquiry into Cost of National Health Service* (1956), H.M.S.O.
14. LAMONT, D. J. (1957), *The Nursing Times*, **43**, 1210.
15. *Report of Committee on Economic and Financial Problems of Provision for Old Age* (1954), H.M.S.O.
16. RICHARDSON, I. M. (1956), *Scottish Medical Journal* (1) **12**, 381.
17. SHAW, P. H. S. (1958), *Journal of the Royal Society of Health*.
18. MACFIE, M. (1959), *The Medical Officer*, **101**, 147.
19. RAE, W. J. W. (1962), *The Medical Officer*, **107**, 3317.
20. HOBSON, W. (1956), *Modern Trends in Geriatrics*, London.
21. BOUCHER, C. A. (1957), *Ministry of Health Survey of Services Available to the Chronic Sick and Elderly*, H.M.S.O.
22. ROYAL COLLEGE OF NURSING AND COLLEGE OF GENERAL PRACTITIONERS (1961), *The Health Visitor and the Family Doctor*.
23. NORTH-EASTERN REGIONAL HOSPITAL BOARD, *Report of Working Party on Care of the Aged* (1957), p. 1.
24. HALL, M. P. (1960), *The Social Services of Modern England*, 5th ed., London, p. 283.
25. LAMONT, D. J. (1958), *Rehabilitation*, **26**, 36.
26. MACQUEEN, I. A. G. (1960), *A Study of Home Accidents in Aberdeen*, Edinburgh.
27. *Ibid.* (1956), *Public Health*, **70** (1) 12.
28. *Ibid.* (1962), *Public Health*, **76** (2) 89.
29. WALLACE, J. M. (1958), *Rehabilitation*, **25**, 19.

30. LAMONT, D. J. and MacQUEEN, I. A. G. (1958), *The Medical Officer*, **100**, 279.
31. SCOTTISH ASSOCIATION FOR MENTAL HEALTH, *Annual Report for 1960–61*, p. 19.
32. MacQUEEN, I. A. G. (1962), *The Medical Officer*, **108**, 231.
33. WELFORD, A. T. (1958), *Ageing and Human Skill*, Cambridge.
34. *Old Age in the Modern World* (Report of Third Congress of International Association of Gerontology) (1958).
35. NEPEAN-GUBBINS, L. (1962), Address to Institute of Home Help Organizers meeting at Cambridge.
36. NORTH-EASTERN REGIONAL HOSPITAL BOARD, *Report of Working Party on Care of the Aged* (1957), p. 2.

20. Residential Accommodation

M. F. BEGLIN

Director of Welfare Services, City of Bradford

IF ONLY Parliament could supply a magic wand with each new piece of legislation, and thereby enable local authorities to create overnight the full effect of the long-term provisions contemplated by the legislator! Alas, this cannot be done, even though many expect the local authorities to attempt this.

When the National Assistance Act of 1948 received Royal Assent, the country was still licking its wounds from the Second World War, and, perhaps to satisfy the clamour for social change, the appetite for which had been whetted by the Beveridge Report, was piously writing into the Statute Book the ultimate hopes it had for this "land fit for heroes". Residential accommodation suitable for the differing needs of different classes was envisaged,* although, as far as can be seen, few, if any, surveys had preceded the Act, properly to determine the need, or to pave the way for practical development. In truth the Act was introduced without sufficient preparation and it is little wonder, therefore, that development has not been spectacularly rapid. The reports of the Committee stage of the Bill in *Hansard* reveal how vague were the notions of the Bill's long-term effects.

That so much has been achieved is greatly to the credit of members of Welfare Committees and their officers, who have had many difficulties to overcome and many frustrations in their endeavours. In the ten years from 1950 to 1960, 28,943 extra bed-places were created, and the number of small homes provided rose to 1105. The Ministry report for 1961† indicates that of seventy-five homes for the elderly or infirm opened that year, fifty-five were new buildings. It is the greater pity, then, that recently the first large-scale survey to be published concerning residential care‡ places emphasis not on the excellent start made, but on the continued existence of some former institutions, and so may cause people to panic into a hasty alteration of the now successfully established pattern of residential care. In the initial stages, shortage of steel, building restrictions and financial "squeezes", all plagued the enthusiast. Far more frustrating, however, was the necessity to catch up

---

* Paragraph 50 of Ministry of Health Circular 87/48.
† Report of the chief Medical Officer to the Ministry of Health 1961.
‡ *The Last Refuge—A Survey of Residential Institutions and Homes for the Aged in England and Wales,* by Peter Townsend, Routledge & Kegan Paul, 1962.

on the back-log arising from waiting lists. Who knew with certainty what the future needs would be? Did we, or could we even be expected to know the major shift in emphasis likely to take place within a few years? What we did know as a stark fact was the number of tragic cases on waiting lists desperately needing shelter. Ministry advice* was (whilst recommending homes for 30–50 people), with regard to the larger establishments, to alter the names of existing premises and cover up the unsightly bricks with plaster and gay paint and thus lull ourselves into believing things had changed. Circulars still talked of the anti-social, and it is now apparent that the Ministry was as unprepared as anyone else. There were the first whisperings of the phenomenal increase likely to take place in the numbers of elderly in the community.†

Early Beginnings

Homes of 30–50 beds were the order of the day. Thus to clear one institution of 350 beds the forward-looking Welfare Officer could see that ten new sites and buildings were needed, and this before one *extra* bed could be provided. Adapt old houses, they said! Welfare officers, keen to apply the new spirit, rushed hither and thither, delighting estate agents and buying who knows how many pigs in pokes! The irony is that ten years later, because of increasing infirmity of residents, these adapted houses are far less satisfactory than the former premises and are becoming extremely expensive to maintain. The higher proportion of infirm residents is reflected in the increasing number of night attendants employed, and the realization that lifts are now necessary in adapted buildings. Some financial experts were not impressed by the necessity for all this change, and frequently one heard it murmured "The Country can't stand it"—"There's a limit to the purse"—"This is all expensive experimenting" and such "wise" opinions. The task of providing adequate standards of residential care for old people was openly regarded in some places as Empire-building on the part of the Welfare Officer!

A start had been made before 1948 in certain areas, notably at Bradford where, in 1905, twenty-eight cottages were provided by the welfare authority enabling two old people to live in each, while having main meals and other supporting services in a central administration block. The same authority had provided two small hostels before the Act came on to the Statute Book. Slowly a few authorities obtained permission to erect hostels built for the purpose, and though mistakes were made, lessons were learned, so

---

* Paragraph 12, Ministry of Health Circular 49/47.
† Registrar-General's *Quarterly Return for England and Wales*, Fourth Quarter, 1962 projects increases in the elderly population from 5602 thousands in 1962 to 7425 thousands by 1982.

that today we have the "ideal" layout and pattern translated into building notes right down to the last nut and bolt.* All this effort had necessarily to be devoted to creating *extra* beds and easing the waiting lists on the principle of the "greatest good to the greatest number". Only patching and painting, in the main, could be undertaken at the old institutions, although some authorities admittedly tried to improve conditions by reducing numbers, providing new furnishings and erecting sick bays. The most encouraging development was the evidence of an enlightened attitude by members of the Welfare Committees and their staffs. Thought was given to the many small considerations which tend to make a resident's life a happy one. At conferences, meetings and group discussions, one constantly heard of the qualities of the new matrons and the new ideas being introduced. The National Old People's Welfare Committee pioneered courses of training, and many local authorities supplemented these with local in-service training. As a result, tables for four (two ladies, two men) replaced the long dining tables. Care was now being taken, on admission, to make a new resident really welcome; matrons started encouraging the more active to escort the infirm, and one authority even introduced blue crockery for the boys and pink for the girls, though it must be admitted it was really to try and check which sex was responsible for breaking most! Welfare officers were determined that old people should not be forced to enter a hostel at the whim of relatives and neighbours. They insisted that if the old people were to have a chance of settling happily, they must enter of their own free will and in the belief that they had chosen to make the hostel their home.

The Extent of the Demand

In 1948 and the years immediately following, the intake of residents contained a high proportion of reasonably active folk who could not find a suitable bungalow or flat and who were welcomed in the new small homes to help establish an atmosphere akin to the seaside boarding house. As time and resources permitted, a few from the old institutions were introduced into the new homes and it was hoped to absorb them all eventually. Unhappily, demand exceeded supply, and the warning notes of hard-pressed G.P.s and coroners had to be observed, with a result that the beds in the former institutions were filled as quickly as transfers took place.

Development in the field of residential care was not taking place in isolation. Hospital authorities, who began to concern themselves with geriatric treatment more than with the care of the chronic sick, were seeking a more rapid discharge of cases of the type which for generations had been regarded as a hospital responsibility. The National Assistance Board and Superintendents of Reception Centres were encouraging the elderly wayfarer to lead a

* Local Authority Building Notes 1 and 2, S.O. 32/510/1 and 32/510/2.

more settled form of life. Improved home visiting by local authorities and Old People's Welfare Committees constantly revealed the plight of hitherto undiscovered cases requiring care. In each of these instances, partly because an adequate supply of suitable flatlets, etc., was not available, the Welfare Department was asked to accept them on to already swollen waiting lists. The Mental Health Act* envisaged the discharge of thousands of long-term, elderly "burnt out" mental cases—where? To residential accommodation.

Could the housing authorities be expected to give flats to people who had spent many years in mental institutions and whose outlook was thereby dulled? Could the elderly cripple after minimal geriatric in-patient care return to live alone without vastly expanded domiciliary services? Was the old tramp likely to appeal to a landlord as an ideal tenant? Hardly. Therefore residential accommodation was sought by ever-increasing numbers.

Financial Limitations

Yet the need for economy was uppermost in the mind of many Finance Committees, and to cater for those new classes of residents as well as to replace the former institutions was an expense not enthusiastically welcomed. The "anti-Empire-building brigade" frowned on long-term plans since they hoped to continue, in the absence of a plan, only to meet current pressing needs. The direction of the Minister in 1962 that each local authority should prepare forward-looking ten-year plans has at last armed the Welfare Officer with the ability to plan the abolition of former workhouses. Few will be slow to seize and use this opportunity. The days of the workhouse are now truly numbered.

Border-line Sick Cases

Whilst it can be said that some who entered hostels in 1948 were comparatively fit, even by 1954 such was not the case, since the Phillips Committee (Cmnd. 9333) observed

> that since the accommodation is limited Local Authorities are bound to have regard to the urgency of the need of those deserving admission and, as a result, a high proportion of the residents in these homes are old or infirm. Such people require a certain amount of nursing and special care and while it can be argued that the physical standards of admission to these homes are too high, it would clearly be undesirable if homes intended for relatively able-bodied residents should become another form of chronic sick hospital.

Until 1957† local authorities had no clear guidance about where to draw the line of demarcation between themselves and the chronic-sick hospital.

* 7 & 8 Eliz. II, ch. 72, Mental Health Act, 1959.
† Ministry of Health Circular 14/57 and H.M.C. Circular (57) 86, *Geriatric Services and the Care of the Chronic Sick*.

The medical man's decision in any particular case that the person was more suited to a hostel than to hospital had to be accepted. Understandably, therefore, many border-line chronics were forced upon "the Welfare" and admitted at the very time when Welfare Departments were desperately trying to make hostels a substitute for normal home life. In what normal home do you expect to find yourself sleeping in the same room as the confused incontinent or bed-fast? In a survey undertaken in the summer of 1962 by a Bradford doctor* working almost full time in residential accommodation, 190 consecutive admissions were investigated. One-third of all were found to be "mentally confused". The definition of "mentally confused" was those who were disorientated in time on admission. The doctor found that this type of person usually became disorientated in place within a period of six months and was thus far more liable to wander. This condition arose despite medical attention during the period of residence. The same doctor examined all the residents at one large establishment and selected those in the following few categories:

(a) Confused but no trouble.
(b) Wandering type.
(c) Socially irritating to others.
(d) Disgusting habits.

One hundred and thirty-six people, that is, rather more than one-third of the total, fell into these categories, only sixty-six being in category (a).

It can be seen that the picture has changed completely since 1948, and a totally different concept of residential care has emerged. The report of the Chief Medical Officer of the Ministry of Health (1961) comments on the increasing infirmity of residents and the altered emphasis on the types of cases admitted today.

The Future

Is the present image necessarily the correct one? Peter Townsend, in his *Last Refuge*, feels that "communal homes of the kind which exist in England and Wales today do not adequately meet the physical, psychological and social needs of the elderly people living in them". He bases his view on the results of a survey undertaken in a sample of old people's homes, and upon the reaction of the residents. Naturally many residents gave as their opinion that they would prefer still to be living in their own little house. Of course they would, but comparing their present circumstances with the conditions under which they formerly lived it becomes clear in the majority of cases that their interests are being better served in residential care.

The publication mentioned advocates the transfer of approximately 40,000

* Bamford, N. (unpublished).

old people now in care, some 30,000 to new dwellings to be erected as sheltered housing over the next ten years, and the remainder to communal accommodation managed by Hospital Management Committees. This is not realistic. Experienced welfare officers, familiar with the plight of many of these residents before admission to hostel, will be alarmed at the possibility of their returning to the community, and perhaps quickly deteriorating to a worse state than before. The domiciliary support services could not expand sufficiently to give adequate support to such people, without being so costly in manpower and finance as to be prohibitive. The transfer of communal care to the hospital machine, with its emphasis on medical care and its clinical approach, would not be in the best interests of the aged. People who need residential care ought to be kept, not in a state of medicated senility, but in an atmosphere of social well-being, encouraged to live as normally as they did at home.

The Ten-Year Plan

The ten-year plan for local authority development of residential accommodation, contained within the complete Health and Welfare Development Plan (published as Cmnd. Paper 1973),* reveals that the Minister of Health firmly agrees with the present pattern of residential care. Unlike Peter Townsend,† he does not advocate either a diminution in the number of places to be provided in residential homes or a transfer of this type of accommodation to the hospital service.

On the contrary, the Minister indicates that local authorities propose to increase the number of homes for elderly or physically handicapped from 1711 as at the end of March 1962 to 2890 by 31 March 1972. This will result in 136,618 bed-places being made available at a cost of some £120 million. The Minister does not seem to be completely satisfied that even this expansion will be sufficient, since he urges authorities to re-examine their proposals, and where they are based on a provision of less than 18 beds per 1000 of total elderly population to bring the provisions up to this standard.

Cmnd. Paper 1973* illustrates clearly the task it has been, and will be in the future, to keep pace with growing demand alone. The elderly population of England and Wales rose from $4\frac{3}{4}$ million in 1951 to $5\frac{1}{2}$ million in 1962 and is estimated to reach $6\frac{3}{4}$ million at the end of the ten-year period in 1972.‡ In his publication *Elderly People,*§ D. C. Marsh showed that some 10 per cent of the elderly living at home are house-bound because of illness or infirmity, and this fact, coupled with many other considerations rendering

---

* *Health and Welfare. The Development of Community Care*, Cmnd. 1973 H.M.S.O.
† *The Last Refuge*, by Peter Townsend.
‡ *Registrar-General's Quarterly Return (England and Wales)*, Fourth Quarter, 1962.
§ *Elderly People*, by D. C. Marsh. *A Survey of Social Circumstances in Two Areas of Nottingham* (Nottinghamshire O.P.W.C., 1955).

the elderly at risk, reflects the continuing demand for residential care as the numbers of elderly in the community rises.

It appears that the long-term objects of the National Assistance Act may stand a chance of being fulfilled by 1972, just a quarter of a century after the Act received Royal Assent. If only Parliament could supply that magic wand!

21. Co-ordination of Services for the Elderly through Old People's Welfare Committees

MARJORIE BUCKE

Secretary, National Old People's Welfare Council

MANY people of retirement age live independently. Some manage with the help of family and friends. Others who need help are less fortunate, having outlived their friends or their relatives live far away. Of $7\frac{1}{2}$ million people of pensionable age today less than 4 per cent live in hospitals and residential homes. Of the rest 10 per cent are estimated to be house-bound, and probably over 1 million live alone.

As by 1982 there will be an additional 2 million people of pensionable age, it is small wonder that the care of older people now makes one of the greatest demands on the social services. Among those elderly people who need help, and an estimate of the proportion has been put at 20 per cent, some need occasional assistance of a simple kind, but others need constant care in a variety of ways.

Our services are now infinitely better, and our approach to social problems shows more regard to human dignity than at the beginning of the century and even twenty years ago. But there is still avoidable loneliness, suffering, and even neglect among the old, and still a tendency to plan for "the old" as a category rather than for elderly people as individuals.

It is sometimes suggested that in our so-called "welfare society" there can be little if any scope for independent or voluntary action, and that the National Health Service Act, the National Insurance Act and the National Assistance Act, together with the Housing Acts, cover every eventuality. But this is not so, because:

(a) Some of this legislation is permissive and not mandatory, so that services vary considerably in scope and extent in different parts of the country; and it is not always realized that even welfare authorities do not have unlimited powers.
(b) Existing legislation is administered by many different agencies, such as Central Government Departments through local offices, various local authorities, Regional Hospital Boards, Executive Councils, etc. Their work is not as closely co-ordinated as it should be, and individual elderly people may not get the services they need.

206

(c) Some of the statutory services are not extensive enough to meet all needs. There are, for instance, shortages of geriatric beds, of beds in old people's homes, and of home helps and home nurses. There is also a considerable shortage of social workers.

For these reasons voluntary organizations have an important part to play not only in supplementing the statutory services but also in rendering personal help or pioneering new services, for which they are particularly suitable. Voluntary organizations concern themselves with the care of the elderly in a variety of ways. (Voluntary services for old people, particularly residential homes run by voluntary societies, existed even before the three main Acts came into force between 1946 and 1948.) Some societies are national with local branches, others are independent local bodies.

This is where Old People's Welfare Committees (or councils or associations—the function is the same) come in. An Old People's Welfare Committee is not just another organization. It is the key organization which brings together in its area all those who are concerned with the care of the elderly. In other words, it fulfils an urgent need by linking together the many different statutory and voluntary agencies which have a duty or concern or opportunity to help the elderly. It is independent, representative of medical and social interests, and of all religious denominations and politics. It is not, therefore, meant to be a subsidiary part of a county, or borough, or other council, but naturally includes (or should do) adequate representation of *all* local authority departments which have powers to help, as there is ample work for all to do in harmony, and not in any sense of competition.

The area of an Old People's Welfare Committee usually corresponds with local county and regional government boundaries: it may be that of a major or a minor local authority, or of a large parish or a group of parishes, or it may be a region of considerable size. There are well over 1500 local committees in addition to county and regional committees in England and Wales. Local committees, but not county committees, have been widely developed in Scotland. In Northern Ireland a committee of the Council of Social Service for Northern Ireland carries out most of the work direct, but there are also a few local Old People's Welfare Committees.

Old People's Welfare Committees—primarily conceived as co-ordinating bodies—find they are often obliged to pioneer a specific service on a co-operative basis, using the personnel of several voluntary organizations. Social clubs, lunch clubs, boarding-out schemes, personal services for individuals, forming housing societies, answering numerous queries for accommodation, acting as a focal point for advice or to show where help can be found, are all part of a committee's stock-in-trade. Visiting organized by a variety of bodies needs co-ordination to make sure nobody who wants a regular visit is left out. These functions and others, described in *Old People's Welfare*

Committees: Why they are Needed, can only be provided adequately with staff, and an office open daily. Many volunteers want or are wanted to help—and courses under the King George VI Social Service Scheme are designed to equip them to use their few free hours to best advantage. But not enough county and county borough committees, nor smaller areas, have as yet an annual income sufficient to employ adequate or trained staff to carry out their necessary work.

In 1949, 1950 and 1959 the Government of the day issued special circulars concerning Old People's Welfare Committees to local authorities. In one year, 1950, following the issue of Circular 11/50, the number of committees grew from 510 to 831, many as a result of local authority initiative. These committees have continued to increase in number, to improve in efficiency, to influence—often unobtrusively—understanding between authorities and organizations, whether central or local, and between individual officers with a common cause if not outlook. Planning and working together has undoubtedly also speeded up the development of services, prevented much overlapping, and revealed gaps.

Unfortunately, this progress has sometimes been slowed down, and in some places never started because of the resistance (often passive) of local personalities, or the attitude of a voluntary society or an authority. Ministry of Health Circulars 2/62 and 7/62 issued in 1962 make it clear, however, that in planning health, welfare and hospital services for ten years ahead, there is no room for complacency, or for isolationists, if every old person is to be helped according to need. The circulars insist that it is the responsibility of Old People's Welfare Committees and all they represent to gear their organization to the needs of the community, and not just provide what their present organization can give. This means that in future co-ordinating committees must not be reluctant to seek adequate financial help from official sources and from the public to carry out their proper functions.

It is their job not only to co-ordinate but also to pioneer services to fill gaps inevitably left by the authorities. It was through Old People's Welfare Committees and their affiliated organizations that chiropody services for the elderly were first provided, and a few areas this is still a grant-aided voluntary service, although local authorities mainly now provide it themselves. The committees encourage the development of clubs, day centres for the house-bound, sheltered workshops, holiday schemes and many other ventures to relieve loneliness and give a sense of purpose to elderly people, particularly those who live on their own. Carefully selected volunteers not only offer friendship to lonely old people but discover needs and see that they are met. They may be for domestic help, or meals, short-stay care in a home, or for small personal services such as assistance with shopping; or for redecoration of a room, a service often undertaken by a team of young people. With the steady increase in the number of the elderly in the community, neither statutory nor voluntary services are yet sufficient nor efficient enough to do all that should be done. As joint action expands, Old People's Welfare Committees (and this means all their constituent bodies) will assist in providing better facilities for the care of the elderly who may be in need of some help.

References

1. *Report of the Committee on the Economic and Financial Problems of the Provision for Old Age* (Phillips Committee), H.M.S.O., 1954.
2. MINISTRY OF HEALTH CIRCULARS 51/49; 11/50 (65/49 Department of Health in Scotland); 11/59; 12/61; 2/62; 7/62.
3. MINISTRY OF HOUSING AND LOCAL GOVERNMENT CIRCULARS 18/57; 33/59; 10/61; 55/61; 43/64.
4. *Age through the Ages*, N.O.P.W.C.
5. *Statutory and Voluntary Services*, leaflet version of Wall Charts, N.O.P.W.C.
6. *Old People's Welfare Committees: Why they are Needed—How they are Started—What they Do*, N.O.P.W.C.
7. *The Organization of a Visiting Service by an Old People's Welfare Committee*, N.O.P.W.C.
8. Annual Reports of National Old People's Welfare Council and of local Old People's Welfare Committees.
9. *Age is Opportunity* (plus Supplement 1964), a handbook on all aspects of ageing and a guide to practical work, containing a bibliography of relevant publications, N.O.P.W.C.

22. Elderly Invalids' Fund

W. L. GRAHAM

General Secretary, Elderly Invalids' Fund

HOSPITALS, residential homes and domiciliary services which the State provides for any needy members of the community irrespective of age may appear at first sight to be all-embracing. So far as elderly people are concerned, however, there are three distinct groups who must often seek the help they need outside the statutory services.

The first group consists of those who must wait indefinitely for help or may even be denied it altogether because their needs, usually of a medico-social nature, are less serious than those of other applicants for the services which are already fully extended.

In the second group are those who are admitted to hospital and benefit from treatment there, but are not sufficiently restored to be able to be discharged home or to a residential home. They themselves have no wish to spend their remaining years in large hospital wards, and their stay there delays the admission of others who need treatment.

The third group includes those who receive adequate care in their own homes, but must have alternative arrangements made for them when their relatives want a holiday.

The solution to the problems of most people in these three groups probably lies in a service that is provided privately or by a voluntary organization. Such services, however, usually have to be paid for. This may be no hardship to many, but elderly people on retirement pensions or other small fixed incomes cannot consider such costs.

It is, however, often because of ignorance of what is available or how it can be obtained or paid for, that elderly people in these groups go without the help they need. This could probably be arranged without much difficulty if an application or inquiry were made to the right quarter.

The Elderly Invalids' Fund, which was founded in 1954, is designed to help these three groups. First, it helps financially. Elderly people who are unsuitable for care at home and do not need treatment in hospital are helped to pay nursing home fees which they cannot afford. This help is related to the need of each case. It may be arranged on a permanent basis, which gives the feeling of security so important to the elderly. It may be given temporarily to allow an elderly invalid to be cared for during some domestic crisis or while relatives have a holiday. Many of those giving devoted care are on call day and night, sometimes for several years. This imposes a strain that is too great for the most willing and robust relative to bear continuously.

The Fund receives many applications and inquiries which are outside its charter. In these cases it tries to make introductory contacts in order to save the disappointment, embarrassment and even despair which fruitless applications can cause those who are wanting help.

Secondly, the Fund helps by giving advice and information. For this a service has been established for the use of doctors, almoners, welfare workers and private individuals. A number of organizations have similar services already, but as, when people want help or advice, they turn to sources they know or to which they are recommended, the establishment of a number of information agencies is to be encouraged. But no organization should answer on behalf of another. What inquirers want most of all is to be told where their particular difficulty can be solved. This may involve much questioning before the nature of the problem becomes clear, after which the appropriate organization can be approached.

The majority of inquiries received by the Fund's Information and Advisory Service are for details of homes that would be suitable for invalids of various kinds. A register is kept of homes in England and Wales and those in the London area are visited from time to time by the Fund's staff. For homes further afield the Fund relies on information it receives from agencies in the areas where the homes are situated.

The following is a typical illustration of the kind of application the Fund receives. Mr. X at the age of 80 had both legs amputated. Though he made a good recovery, the hospital decided that he would never learn to use artificial limbs. His future therefore presented difficulties. His wife, who was also 80, was in failing health, and even with the help of the domiciliary services, was unable to give him the considerable care he needed. The E.I.F. found that the patient had followed a trade of which there was a benevolent fund. Through this the weekly sum needed to pay the fees of a nursing home was arranged and the patient was admitted to a home which was near enough for his wife to visit him. The Fund would have paid the fees if there had been no benevolent fund to help him.

A very frequent problem that the Fund is asked to solve is the one where a daughter, dependent on her salary, finds her invalid mother is demanding more time than her work allows her to give, or it may be that disturbed nights leave her unfit for her day's work. By keeping abreast of developments and trends the Fund is often able to suggest some service that is available locally which will be satisfactory to both patient and relative. There may, for instance, be a day hospital or day centre where the patient can be looked after during working hours. Or perhaps there is a Good Neighbour Service which will see that the patient is never left alone. It is possible in various ways to overcome difficulties which at first seem unsurmountable when full details of both patient and local services are known.

The E.I.F. is trying to support and supplement the statutory services, not replace any of them. Therefore it keeps in close touch with the hospital and local authorities as well as with voluntary organizations. This has resulted in the co-operation which is essential to the speedy solution of problems of old people and their relatives.

23. Workrooms for the Elderly

C. O. S. BLYTH BROOKE

Medical Officer of Health, Finsbury Health Centre

MANY elderly suffer from the most acute misery in the realization that they are not wanted by others, and have no part in the life that flows on around them. Most feel an inward urge to remain a true component of the society of mankind, and to serve it if only in a humble capacity. Some are able to do so by assisting in the care of grandchildren, in the nursing of sick relatives or friends, or in countless other domestic ways. Some find outlets for the urge in voluntary work in connection with religious, social or political organizations. But there are many others who have no friends or relatives who need their help, and who have not the strength, education, ability or possibly personality, to embark on neighbourly visits or the promotion of particular tenets. If remunerated employment under protected conditions is available, they will readily find a way to give service to the community, for the accepted view today is that real work receives its financial reward. As pensions and allowances rarely allow for more than the basic needs, any small additional money earned may well also be a godsend.

Sheltered employment, especially in industrial centres, can be a modern counterpart of the lighter duties of the homestead, which in former times engaged the ageing members of the family in their rural surroundings. It can fulfil to some extent the spiritual and psychological yearnings of the ageing which are often forgotten in an enthusiasm to supply their more obvious bodily requirements; they are not met by a life of leisure or the usual forms of recreation. It can also overcome some of the loneliness which is so often encountered among the elderly.

There can be no question of the joy found by the elderly in participation in sheltered workshop schemes, and this alone must have a profound effect on their physical and mental health, but the going to work and the work itself have a further far-reaching favourable influence on the preservation of health. The decrepit state of senility in which the body has lost most of its former strength, and the mind most of its faculties, is as much dependent on a failure to use them as on the inherent process of senescence and the supervention of disease. All functions of body and mind rapidly degenerate if not exercised, and require to be used regularly to moderate degree in order to preserve them from deterioration. This applies to the ageing as to others. The appropriate stimulus is required to initiate any form of activity, and as a result of the changes that occur in the process of ageing, the stimulus needed must be stronger than before. This is no more true of any organ than of the brain. Regular employment and attendance at a work centre furnishes an incentive to the use of body and mind, and encourages their exercise.

These theoretical considerations have been amply substantiated by the thirty to forty sheltered workshops which, following the successful outcome of the pioneer scheme in Finsbury (commenced under the joint sponsorship of the Employment Fellowship and the Finsbury Borough Council), have been established in the past decade.

The Finsbury workshop consists of a specially constructed prefabricated building, including four well-lighted workrooms, a store-room, a rest-room, a display room, office, small kitchen for making teas, and cloakrooms. It was opened by the late Lord Horder in 1954, but work was started in 1951 in less suitable accommodation. Some centres have, in fact, found it possible to operate satisfactorily in church halls, and almost any type of accommodation available.

In this workshop 100–120 elderly persons are employed for two hours, five days a week, in two shifts, of approximately equal numbers, one in the morning and one in the afternoon. This is probably about the optimum size, though much smaller units can well operate satisfactorily; much larger units are not normally required, as more persons are not likely to be living within the area from which it is reasonably accessible.

A full-time organizer and an assistant organizer are employed. Generally this type of work is better undertaken by a woman. She needs first of all to have a real interest in the old people themselves, and much tact and patience in dealing with them. But she must also have a suitable personality for approach to business executives, a tidy mind for dealing with orders, accounts and wages, much common sense in dealing with a multitude of minor administration matters, and ability herself to learn quickly, so as to be able to teach others how simple factory or business processes are carried out, as well as to be able to check with attention to details, that work carried out is fully satisfactory. An interest and knowledge of handicrafts is also an advantage. Voluntary assistants may be found in most districts to help the organizer in various ways.

The work carried out by the elderly in the various schemes varies very considerably; most of it is generally on behalf of local or other firms who are able to deliver and collect the work as required, and depends on its nature as to what can be supplied from time to time, and, of course, on the skill and aptitude of the workers, which in most cases is minimal. It is essential that all work attempted should be well done and finally checked before return to the firm, as otherwise confidence in the scheme will be lost and work difficult to obtain. It is also essential that a fair charge be made for the work done for the firm on the basis of the payment that would be made to an ordinary employee working at a reasonable speed at the trade union rate, together with a small additional charge towards overhead expenses. Many commercial firms are willing to support schemes in this way, partly on humanitarian grounds, and partly because it provides a pool of additional labour which they may be able to utilize in the event of extra demands. It may be desirable to undertake some work normally given out as homework in order to preserve a continuity of supply at times such as the period immediately after Christmas when other firms are not able to find suitable work, but payment cannot be expected above the rates usually paid, which are very low.

A few examples of the work carried out in the centres are: packing all sorts of small articles, covering library books, weighing and packaging wool, addressing envelopes, inserting circulars in envelopes for mailing, assembling the parts of drop bottles, etc.

In addition it is sometimes possible for goods such as aprons, night-shirts, fancy articles, dolls, etc., to be made for direct sale either privately, in a bazaar held as occasions arise, or in other ways. This involves an appreciable risk and adds to the work of administration, but can sometimes yield good financial results.

A fair wage must be paid to the workers, not but that many of them would gladly play their part without it, but because otherwise they would not appreciate the value of their work, and in consequence not derive the full satisfaction in it which is the purpose of the schemes. This wage must not be less than that actually earned, though as the average speed is usually low, it may be much less than that normally earned by younger people. It is often rather above this, the difference being met by subsidies. A flat-rate payment to all, irrespective of output, is commonly about 1s. 3d. per hour.

The participants are limited to those of the pensionable ages who are not able to find employment otherwise; the majority are usually in the 70's but even those in late 80's may derive much benefit. Priority should be given to those who, on social or mental grounds, are most in need of occupation. The workshop is probably best treated as a separate service, but close links with the health and social services for the elderly are clearly an advantage.

The benefits are exhibited most often in the changed and cheerful character of the old people, and their improved tidy and clean appearance resulting from them regaining their self-respect. They themselves credit their happiness to the help it gives them to pass the time, which otherwise seems long and weary, and to the fact that it makes them feel important. By providing them with a purpose in life and hope in the ability to look forward to the next day, many of the elderly have their lives transformed from a negative existence in mental desolation to one of active participation in the world around. There can be no doubt of the value of a workshop to the health and especially the mental health of the ageing.

T.I.S.W.—Q

Work centre schemes have been widely inaugurated by voluntary organizations (sometimes established specifically for the purpose), and depend on subscriptions from Trusts and individuals together with grants made by local authorities under Section 4 of the Physical Training and Recreation Act, 1937, or with the consent of the Minister of Housing and Local Government (which is readily given) under Section 136 of the Local Government Act, 1948.

It has also been suggested by the Minister of Health in a circular that schemes could be operated by county or county district councils, under the National Assistance Act, 1948, (Amendment) Act, 1962, directly or through the agency of a voluntary organization, as well as by means of a grant.

The total cost of a scheme depends on local considerations, but should not exceed about 10s. a week for each elderly person employed, and may be very much less.

The Employment Fellowship, Drayton House, Gordon Street, London, W.C.1, is willing to help with advice and, in some cases, with financial aid, in the inauguration of new schemes.

In connection with these schemes it may be noted that about a dozen larger firms have established workshops somewhat similar to those described, to assist their own retired employees.

SECTION V
HOUSING AND FAMILY WELFARE

24. "Housing—What Next?"

R. A. PARKER

Lecturer in Social Administration,
London School of Economics and Political Science

IN SPITE of the fact that shelter is a basic human need, housing has never formed an integral part of the social services of this country. Of the $14\frac{1}{2}$ million dwellings in England and Wales, 45 per cent are owner-occupied, 30 per cent rented from a variety of private landlords, and only 25 per cent let by local authorities. Conventionally, only this last category, constituting a mere 5 per cent of the stock of houses before the 1914–18 War but growing in importance since 1919, is considered part of our welfare provisions. Nevertheless, all types of housing have been considerably affected by social policy since the end of the last century.

Although housing cannot be regarded as a comprehensive social service, the nature of government intervention in this field has been, to a greater or lesser degree, determined by "welfare" considerations. At different times the emphasis has rested upon different aspects, but broadly speaking the State has acted directly, or indirectly through the local authorities, to control or influence standards, cost, quantity, distribution and allocation.[1] It has been possible, albeit at times with more optimism than accuracy, to refer to a government's "housing policy".[2]

This century, for example, has seen the introduction of rent control in the private sector, at least two clearly distinguishable slum clearance drives, the development of planning control and the extension of the local authorities' housing responsibilities from the "working classes" alone to all in housing need. There have been subsidies to private enterprise builders, subsidies to local authorities, tax allowances for interest repayments on mortgage loans, improvement grants available to any owner whose property lacks certain basic amenities, rent tribunals, specialized council housing for old people, attempts to control overcrowding, and so forth.

The Standard of Housing

Today there are a number of discernible trends, with welfare implications, which are beginning to affect housing policy and are likely to shape its future. Perhaps one of the most important and potentially far-reaching is the renewed interest in the quality of our housing. This has taken several forms.

219

There is, for instance, an increasing concern about the vast numbers of old houses which, lacking modern amenities, in poor repair, or monotonously packed together in the centres of nineteenth-century industry, no longer provide homes of an acceptable standard. It remains impossible to judge the precise extent of this problem, for no comprehensive survey of the condition of our housing has ever been undertaken, but there are probably some 6 million houses (45 per cent) built before 1900 and a third of these are over a hundred years old.

Two policies have been adopted for dealing with this problem of worn-out sub-standard housing. Since 1956 the attention of the local authorities has been directed to slum clearance and away from building to meet other general needs. The progress made since the initiation of this latest "drive" seems impressive (286,000 dwellings were cleared or closed in the five years 1957–61),[3] but against the backcloth of the total size of the problem it is inadequate. For instance, to ensure that in twenty-five years' time there are only as many century-old houses as now demands about 200,000 clearances a year—a trebling of the present rate. Clearly the replacement of unfit and obsolete houses will become a growing public issue as the level of housing aspiration continues to rise. To achieve a programme in which 200,000 or more clearances occur each year will require some major reconsiderations of policy and administration. The White Paper produced in May 1963[4] gives no indication that a programme of this size is in view. It points out that "according to the estimates of local authorities made in and since 1956, there are still 600,000 slums to be cleared. The aim is to clear these within the next ten years in all but the largest conurbations."[5] This will represent an average annual rate of something less than 60,000 in England and Wales and Scotland—a reduction in fact on the annual rates of the last few years.

Essentially the rate of clearance is determined by the rate at which alternative housing is made available for those displaced from the slums. As the responsibility for rehousing these families rests squarely on the local authorities under the Housing Act, 1957, this is primarily controlled by the rate of new building undertaken by councils in the appropriate areas or made available to them in new towns[6] or in expanded older ones.[7] Clearly the local authorities will have to increase their rates of building: private enterprise can contribute little, for prices are beyond the means of many families[8] and it is unusual to find such developments on a sufficiently large scale in or near the areas of greatest social squalor.

What stops local authorities building more and what steps will need to be taken if their contribution is to be expanded? There are several answers. The building industry of this country is already employed at near full capacity, and much of its activity has been focused on construction other than that for the local housing authorities. Areas with the greatest problems of replacement and urban renewal are also confronted by other housing problems, such as overcrowding, eviction, medical re-housing and long general waiting lists, which compete for each new allocation. Some authorities claim that the difficulties of raising capital at rates of interest sufficiently low to keep the rents of the new houses within the reach of ordinary families has deterred them, while others face undoubted problems of constricting local government boundaries, land scarcity and high prices. Many have difficulty in recruiting and retaining sufficiently able technical staff. It has also been suggested that some of the smaller authorities have failed to think and plan on a really ambitious scale because of their customary and traditional levels of activity.

Really great strides, however, are unlikely to be made by local councils in isolation. They will find their task easier against a general expansion in the building industry and the more widespread adoption of new techniques. They will need the benefit of generous government aid in the fields of finance, technology and research. A start has been made on the last of these with the Ministry of Housing and Local Government's development group, already responsible for some experimental building. However, not only will the maintenance of high levels of local authority building demand clear leads from Central Government, but in all likelihood greater co-operation between many of the 1400 housing authorities themselves.[9] It may even be necessary for building to be planned and administered on a regional basis so that the economies and advantages of large-scale operation can be achieved. The bigger contractors would certainly be more interested in the large continuous contracts which could be offered. Once completed the homes could be passed to the local councils for allocation and subsequent management.

There are at least two undesirable possibilities inherent in the rapid expansion of the slum clearance programme. First, that in attaining an increase in quantity the quality of new building will receive insufficient attention; and secondly, that this particular aspect of the housing problem is solved at the expense of others. There are good historical reasons for this fear, for in the past policies have either encouraged the addition of new houses without replacement or replacement without addition. These two activities have never been carried out at the same time satisfactorily: they have tended to be regarded as alternatives. In future we should plan for them to be pursued simultaneously, since the demand for houses to meet the needs of the additional households created by population growth (some $2\frac{1}{2}$ million between 1951 and 1961),[10] more and younger marriages, greater longevity, and the desire of many single people to have homes of their own cannot be ignored.

Raising Standards by Improvements

A policy, complementary to slum clearance, has also existed for some years. This rests upon the relatively short-term solution of improvement. Owners have increasingly been encouraged to instal basic amenities where these are lacking and offered grants to help them meet a substantial part of the cost. Facilities for such schemes have existed generally since 1949, but certain changes were introduced in 1954[11] which made the grants much more attractive. As a result the number of grants rose but remained at the 30,000 to 40,000 a year level until other changes occurred in 1959.[12] By 1961 the number of improvement grants had reached 130,000 a year. Even this achievement, however, can hardly be regarded as a satisfactory basis for a crash programme to make houses at the end of their useful life into acceptable homes.

The difficulties surrounding this policy seem to be closely related to the nature of the ownership of these older houses. Because the pre-eminent housing institution of the nineteenth century was private landlordism, the great majority of the houses which cause most concern are owned by private landlords, who, for reasons which are only beginning to be understood,[13] are unwilling to apply for such grants. In fact most grants have gone to owner-occupiers. It seems unlikely, therefore, that the majority of old dwellings will be improved by measures such as this while the private landlord remains the principal owner. Nevertheless, in the 1963 White Paper[14] the Government remained optimistic about the effectiveness of this policy, claiming that the aim is to secure the improvement with or without grants of most of the older houses worth improvement (estimated at between 2 and 3 million) within the next ten years. This means an average rate of improvement of between 200,000 and 300,000 a year.

One solution, stoutly defended in a recent publication of the Alliance Building Society,[15] is for these houses to be purchased by owner-occupiers who, as experience has shown, will be anxious to improve them. Providing landlords are ready to sell and potential purchasers able to buy, this is certainly something which will encourage a greater use of improvement grants. However, one hesitates to laud a development which must hang a weighty millstone around many necks. Such houses will be bought mainly by those who can afford nothing better, and thereafter they are likely to be rushed from one maintenance and repairs crisis to the next by the age and physical deterioration of their homes. Perhaps a more acceptable solution, short of actual clearance, is for the local authorities to take the initiative by acquiring, either by agreement or compulsion, such accommodation and themselves improving it with the help of the exchequer grants.[16] In fact, over 40,000 improvement grants were made to local authorities in 1961—representing some 30 per cent of the total. Of course, since 1954 councils have also been able to become landlords of sub-standard property well before it is due for demolition, so that in the meantime the houses could be made reasonably tolerable for the families who were obliged to live in them and wait until their turn came to be re-housed.

If, as an interim device for raising the quality of the older housing, we wish to encourage large-scale improvements, it seems clear that an increasing number of old privately rented dwellings will have to pass to the local authorities. This is already occurring, and if it continues the result will be a considerable reduction in privately rented accommodation already eroded by clearance and sale while the local authority and owner-occupation sectors continue to grow. The not-too-distant future may well see us approaching a situation in which people are either owners of their accommodation or rent it from their council. The widespread administrative and political implications of such a development still remain to be calculated.

New Housing

The trend of renewed interest in quality has not been restricted to existing older houses alone. There has also been a sharpened interest in the quality and standard of new housing. In 1961, for instance, an important document was produced by a sub-committee of the Central Housing Advisory Committee[17] which investigated this whole question. The recommendations, which it stressed were minimal, suggested standards more generous than those commonly accepted today and particularly emphasized the need for greater overall space, radically improved systems of heating, more storage facilities, a garage to each house, better ventilation and insulation against noise.

In many ways the problem of the standard of the housing which we build now and in the near future poses difficulties as great as the improvement of the old. Hundreds of thousands of houses a year are needed for replacement; as many more to cope with the growth of new households (estimates have been suggested of 400,000 a year in all). If we face the future with the intention of meeting such needs adequately *and* achieving radical improvements in the present low level of standards in new houses, any government will be faced with a fundamental housing problem. This will be the problem of encouraging both these developments, seen by many as almost irreconcilable, and making sure that people are able to meet any rise in cost which ensues. It may well be that standards can be raised and, by gaining economies from new techniques and large-scale production, costs kept reasonably steady. It is more likely, however, that the cost of housing will rise as a result. The financial problem which this poses is not unfamiliar. It was exactly the problem of setting acceptable minimum standards, but the inability of the poorest members of the community to pay for them which prompted first the activity of philanthropic housing associations in the later nineteenth century and then launched the local authorities as institutions for building to let in 1919 with the aid of the then new system of housing subsidies.

The Financing of Housing

The future will have to see a comprehensive and far-reaching review of the financing of the whole field of housing if the trend towards high standards, now becoming evident, is to grow into anything more. The cost of housing was reviewed in the 1963 White Paper which suggested "a complete overhaul of housing subsidies" (para. 76, p. 15), but from what follows it becomes apparent that subsidies are narrowly defined to include only those plainly visible in the financing of local authority housing.

But the systems of financial help which operate to reduce the cost of housing are today anything but plainly visible; they are the confused results of the piecemeal policies of the past. It is impossible to determine which sections of the population are benefiting or which are being unduly penalized. Many regard the council tenant as the privileged householder benefiting at the expense of his fellow citizens. This is an over-simplified view. The owner-occupier, for instance, buying his house with the aid of a loan, can offset a proportion of the interest repayments, and if he has raised the money through endowment assurance, a proportion of the premiums, against his taxable income. Likewise, as already pointed out, "gifts" can be claimed from the Government to help with the costs of certain improvements. Similarly, although the 1957 Rent Act freed many privately rented dwellings from rent control and increasingly frees others as tenancies change hands, private tenants have for many years (on and off since 1915) been protected from the full blast of "economic rents".

One possible development which might well overcome some of these problems of standards and cost is the growth of co-operative housing associations. Such housing institutions—well established in Scandinavia and other parts of Europe, but virtually non-existent in this country—appear to have the Government's blessing, for the Housing Act, 1961, empowered the Minister to advance up to £25 million to encourage their development. As he pointed out in the debate on the Bill: "One type of housing association which I greatly hope may spring up as a result of the Bill is . . . the co-operative housing association, in which a group of would-be occupiers form themselves into a body to build and then to manage collectively houses or flats in which the members themselves will live."[18] Since such a body is not profit-making, can borrow over a much longer period than the individual, and can gain certain advantages through the pooling of insurance, repairs and maintenance costs, the price may be kept sufficiently low to allow standards to rise. A recent P.E.P. pamphlet summarized the financial advantages thus: "For a given annual commitment and a given down payment, the housing association member can afford a higher capital cost than the owner-occupier. Here is a way to a much needed raising of housing standard."[19]

The previous Conservative Government, however, appeared to put its main faith in private enterprise building,[20] particularly for sale, as the keystone of future developments. It is accepted that this cannot touch anything but the fringe of the clearance problem even though private developers are becoming increasingly interested in schemes for the comprehensive replacement of the centres of some towns. If, however, private enterprise building for sale is to meet effectively at high standards the additional housing needs created by increased rates of household formation, other changes will have to take place which may alter its basic character. For example, it is no longer justifiable to allow large numbers of new houses to spring up unplanned. They can no longer be built outside the framework of a general plan which includes considerations of land use and price, commercial and industrial location, or communications. The interdependence of such factors and housing has been cogently illustrated by the wave of homelessness in and around London; by the extension of commuting suburbia in the wake of better systems of transport in the south-east, and by the overall "drift to the south" of which so much has been recently heard.

Planning, based one hopes on adequate research, will have to be a cardinal feature of future developments in housing. Government intervention will continue to be necessary whether in promoting higher standards and greater output, modifying the cost, or influencing location.

What Types of Houses?

As well as these issues the question of the "types" of houses to be built will have to be seriously considered. For example, it seems unlikely that our present housing institutions, particularly in the private sector, can take sufficient account of this without some considerable modification. At the moment, for instance, the building societies, by their loans policies, encourage building suitable in the main for families. But the pattern of housing need is changing. Many of the households in need in the next decade or so will be the newly married younger couples, the elderly who live longer and are less inclined (or encouraged) to live in homes or with relatives, and the single. None of these groups is well served by the present credit institutions. Since loans for house purchase are made primarily on the life and income of the purchaser, young couples and old people will find difficulty, and the spinster may well be asked to look around for a male guarantor or be refused altogether. Should these groups, however, solve such financial problems, they will find it somewhat difficult to discover accommodation small enough or appropriate to their needs. Where, for example, can the old person *buy* at reasonable cost a small convenient bungalow with purpose-built equipment and planned to meet their declining physical ability? Certainly the local authorities have increasingly built to meet the needs of this latter group, but few instances exist of the ageing owner-occupier being able to transfer to a council purpose-built dwelling without financial penalties. Likewise what provision is made by any housing institution for the unmarried mother, the bachelor or the spinster?

The obvious needs, both now and in the future, for greater flexibility in housing type may be satisfied by some of the possible developments in industrialized building. Essentially, as a recent Civic Trust conference report explains, this is "prefabrication and mass production, that is the construction in large numbers of building elements before they are brought together on the building site".[21] Such techniques are not new, but their development has been restricted by a number of related factors. The limited scale of building operation (there are still many small projects and many small building firms) has played a part; so has opposition within building unions; there has until recently been little encouragement from government or the traditional financing bodies, and a certain stigma still attaches to the notion of a prefabricated house. Such housing has been regarded as "second rate", stop gap or inflexible. There need be nothing "second rate" about factory-made components, and there is potentially much greater flexibility in the use of standardized interchangeable components: a flexibility which may begin to match both the changing needs for housing type and the previously ignored changes which occur in the life-cycle of any normal family. The only sort of flexibility available today if a family's housing needs change is movement: in future addition or subtraction of component units may be easier and cheaper.

Conclusion

Both the present and the future pose difficult housing problems. Two which can no longer be treated as separate issues are the improvement of quality and the expansion of production. Even these monumental problems, however, cannot be solved outside a more general framework which includes the additional and related difficulties of financing housing; reorganization within the building industry, particularly in regard to scale and technology improving and initiating housing research of all sorts and the reconsideration of the nature and function of the traditional housing institutions. The concurrent solution of such a variety of interrelated problems which affect the welfare of every individual in a way we are but gradually fully appreciating will only be achieved by comprehensive and accurate planning, backed up by the political conviction that solutions must be found.

References

1. BOWLEY, MARIAN, *Housing and the State*, Allen & Unwin, 1945.
2. DONNISON, D. V., *Housing Policy Since the War*, Occasional Papers on Social Administration, No. 1, Codicote Press, 1960.
3. *Report of the Ministry of Housing and Local Government*, Cmnd. 1725, 1961.
4. *Housing*, Cmnd. 2050, May 1963.
5. *Housing*, Cmnd. 2050, May 1963, para. 11, p. 3.
6. The New Towns Act, 1946.
7. The Town Development Act, 1952.
8. NEEDLEMAN, L., A long-term view of housing, in *Economic Review* (National Institute of Economic and Social Research), No. 18, Nov. 1961.
9. In England and Wales the housing authorities are the county boroughs, the municipal boroughs, the urban district councils and the rural district councils. There are only a few examples of formal consortia of authorities being set up, for example one in Yorkshire (3 authorities) and one in the Midlands (10 authorities). (See Cmnd. 2050, para. 22, p. 4.)
10. General Register Office Census 1961, England and Wales, Preliminary Report.
11. Housing Repairs and Rents Act, 1954.
12. Housing and House Purchase Act, 1959.
13. CULLINGWORTH, J. B., Housing policy and the private landlord, *Guardian*, 24 March 1961.
14. *Housing*, Cmnd. 2050, May 1963.
15. *Four Million Decaying Houses*, a report compiled by the Alliance Building Society.
16. ALLAUN, FRANK, Putting baths in old houses, *Guardian*, 13 Feb. 1963.
17. MINISTRY OF HOUSING AND LOCAL GOVERNMENT, *Homes for Today and Tomorrow*, 1961.
18. WADDILOVE, LEWIS E., *Housing Associations*, P.E.P. Planning, Vol. 28, No. 462, 21 May 1962, p. 113.
19. WADDILOVE, LEWIS E., *op. cit.*, p. 141.
20. See, for example, the Government White Paper *Housing in England and Wales*, Cmnd. 1290, 1961, and White Paper *Housing*, Cmnd. 2050, 1963.
21. Civic Trust Conference, 29 Mar. 1963, *Industrialized Building*, introductory paper.

Bibliography

ALDERSON, STANLEY, *Britain in the Sixties—Housing*, Penguin Special, S. 211, 1962.
CULLINGWORTH, J. B., *Housing Needs and Planning Policy*, Routledge and Kegan Paul, 1960.
CULLINGWORTH, J. B., *New Towns for Old*, Fabian Society Pamphlet, 1962.
DONNISON, D. V., COCKBURN, CHRISTINE, and CORTLETT, T., *Housing Since the Rent Act*, Occasional Papers on Social Administration, No. 3, Codicote Press, 1961.
GREVE, JOHN, *The Housing Problem*, Fabian Society Pamphlet, 1961.

25. Homeless Families

JAMES ROBERTS

Director of Civic Welfare, City of Salford

Duties of the Local Authority

A definite duty is placed on county and county borough councils to provide residential accommodation for persons who because of age, infirmity or other circumstances are in need of care and attention. The National Assistance Act of 1948, which, when introduced, was acclaimed by the national press as the "Old People's Charter", lays down in Section 21 (i) (a) the type of care which is necessary.

There is a further obligation resting on local authorities under Section 21 (i) (b) of the same Act. This refers to the provision of temporary accommodation for people who are in urgent need of it in a crisis or in any special situation with which the authorities may have to deal. When the Act was passed it was thought that most of the emergency powers from this section would be used to meet need caused by emergencies such as fire, storm or flooding. This need might be great if there were a large number of people requiring short-term accommodation whilst temporarily homeless. Furthermore, the difficulty of housing evicted families, which formerly rarely arose, has become a major problem.

Necessary Services

Residential accommodation under the first part of Section 21 provides an adequate substitute for a normal home whilst meeting all reasonable needs of people requiring care and attention. These include clothing, additional amenities in the way of tobacco, sweets, etc., which the resident perhaps is unable fully to provide out of his own resources, and other facilites such as recreational activities, books and periodicals, religious worship. In temporary accommodation people may not need a full range of these services.

Major catastrophies causing large-scale distress are fortunately rare. They usually arise in certain areas: flooding on low-lying coastal stretches, fires in densely populated industrial areas, gas explosions in towns where gas lighting is still a feature of slum-clearance properties. In such emergencies residential accommodation of a temporary nature usually only extends to a night or two until the victims are able to make new arrangements. Im-

228

provised arrangements are often made, which are copied from the experience of the Rest Centre Scheme successfully operated during the Second World War.

Failure to Meet Obligations

A recent Annual Report of the Ministry of Health on health and welfare services stated that all local authorities have not yet provided temporary accommodation which will care for a family as a whole; nor have they recognized the importance of skilled help and supervision if progress is to be made with families who have little prospect of early re-housing.

Government circulars, conferences, talks between corporate bodies, reports of sociologists, etc., are constantly concerned with this social problem. In the fifteen years since the 1948 Act fashioned the blue print of welfare services, a specific solution has not yet been found. Some authorities still have not made use of the emergency assistance provisions that are available under Section 21 (i) (b) of the National Assistance Act, 1948.

Homeless Families

Temporary accommodation is mostly given to homeless families involved in eviction proceedings. Many such people either cannot or will not move a finger to help themselves and are quite content to lean on the official services to act and think for them. There has, however, been a minority of people who have received notice to quit through no fault of their own. Their misfortunes include termination of tenancy with cessation of employment, death of a tenant, overcrowding conditions, condemnation of property, etc.

Keeping a family together is an essential aim with which no one would disagree. It is equally important to promote services to provide rehabilitation and, where possible, to prevent such situations of distress. This is especially required where the woman in the home fails to accept simple domestic responsibility.

Co-ordinated Achievement

In July 1960 the Home Office, in collaboration with the Ministries of Health and Education, issued a circular advising local authorities to appoint an officer responsible for co-ordination of all services dealing with the prevention of neglect or ill-treatment of children. This should have provided the impetus to design adequate preventive measures which would mitigate the demand for temporary accommodation or, in cases of excess demand, eliminate it entirely.

If co-ordination of this kind was a real practical effort on the part of all departments dedicated to a single end—the preservation of family unity in the home—the resulting action could be most effective.

A fine example has been provided by the Frimhurst Recuperative Home, Surrey. Here whole families, including fathers, are accepted, completely removed from the atmosphere of neighbourly disapproval. In addition, many admirable schemes have been undertaken by progressive local authorities. Their welfare services have established units of separate accommodation where efficient supervision is maintained. Qualified officers of special experience assist these families, frequently categorized as "problem families", where in many instances voluntary workers are making a useful contribution.

It has been argued, however, that successful rehabilitation of needy families can be better obtained by co-ordinated services applying maximum *preventive measures* when the conditions and atmosphere of home life are leading towards a situation which might involve eviction and subsequent temporary accommodation.

Measures for Rehabilitation and Prevention

It is necessary to insure that such activities are directed to overall rehabilitation and training. For example, mothers of homeless families should be trained in home management. If a personal contention from extensive experience may be permitted, it is suggested that far too often the description "problem families" is too loosely used. It would be better to refer to "problem fathers"; too little attention is paid to educating the father in his proper acceptance of marital obligations as head of the family. It is often seen that the root cause of a woman's deterioration or inability to cope satisfactorily with domestic affairs is the man's continual neglect of his wife and children, even at times his unwillingness to work, or addiction to gambling, alcoholism, etc.

Where experiments have been carried out to stop a man's undesirable habits in an early stage, success has consistently been achieved. This depends upon the co-ordinating officer and the use of methods to prevent neglect of children in their own homes.

Where families show themselves unable to care or pay for proper accommodation, rehabilitation is achieved by an efficient team. In combined operations welfare, children, education, health and housing departments are all concentrated on re-housing within a minimum period. At the same time they draw on the facilities of a family advice centre, potential evictions are prevented, and the actual demand for temporary accommodation is kept very low.

Future Policy

Great disasters as a result of floods, aeroplane crashes, gas-main explosions, collapse of old property, which produce large-scale evacuation and leave thousands temporarily homeless, are comparatively rare; cases of evicted families are always occurring. All emergencies demand a state of constant readiness in every city and county borough to ensure fulfilment of the Act. The warning tone of the Ministry Report on the potential deficiencies regarding family care is timely. It should not be disregarded by areas where administration is faulty. It cannot be ignored if the aims of the Welfare State are to be maintained, and if it is to remain sensitive to social problems which could respond to correction, but will otherwise disrupt family life.

There is no clearly defined statutory obligation requiring either welfare or housing authorities to provide immediate accommodation for people where circumstances could reasonably have been foreseen. It is incumbent upon such bodies to use the powers which they possess to establish these facilities; the alternative is that families may be without shelter. It is appreciated that arguments can be put forward concerning local responsibility or financial cost. All these should be quashed in order to abolish what could become a grave defect in the social system in which this country has some justifiable pride.

Recent legislation has, however, eased the situation considerably through the Children and Young Persons' Act 1963, and particularly the Protection from Eviction Act 1964. Under the latter, eviction without a County Court Order is a criminal offence, and according to a Ministry of Housing and Local Government statement at the end of January 1965, homelessness, caused by eviction, had declined generally from the effective date, 17th December, 1964, based on informal estimates made in London, Birmingham, Manchester and Liverpool.

Local Authorities have a statutory *duty* placed upon them, under the Children and Young Persons' Act 1963, to make available such advice, guidance and assistance as may promote the welfare of children, by diminishing the need to receive or keep them in care under the Children Act 1948 and permissive powers to include provision to extend assistance in kind, or, in exceptional circumstances, in cash, which will undoubtedly have immense preventive effect in dealing with the problems of homeless families.

26. Temporary Accommodation for Homeless Families

M. F. BEGLIN

Director of Welfare Services, City of Bradford

PROVIDING temporary accommodation for homeless families gives rise to some of the most difficult problems which face a local authority. The term "homelessness" embraces not only the blameless victim of accident, but even the defiant anti-social; thus the innocent victim of unlawful ejection can find herself side by side with the culpable engineer of his own misfortune. Each seeks, sometimes demands, help.

Can a social worker overlook the needs of either? Is there any justification for treating only the cream and ignoring the skim? Is it reasonable to devote supporting and rehabilitative services only to the former, and leave the latter to an indefinite period of communal care in institutional premises?

Housing authorities have slum clearance programmes, long waiting lists of applicants for lodgings and they need to consider special classes who merit re-housing for reasons of health. They are often not in a position to help; so it is understandable if they are unwilling to provide housing for people who have been evicted from their homes through their own fault, when some applicants have endured overcrowding or hardship for long periods with patience and restraint.

Legislation

The National Assistance Act, 1948, the Children Act, 1948, the Housing Act, 1957, and Children and Young Persons Act, 1963, all contain authority to deal, to a limited extent, with the problem. The Children Act would place some children in care and deprive them of parental support. To keep the family together and avoid the damaging consequences of a broken home is generally regarded as of paramount importance, hence few authorities rely upon the power contained in Section 1 of the Children Act as follows:

> Where it appears with respect to a child or person under seventeen years . . . that his parents or guardians are, for the time being, or permanently, prevented from providing for his proper accommodation . . . and the intervention of the local authority is necessary . . . it shall be the duty of the local authority to receive the child into its care.

By Section 48 of the Housing Act, 1957, a local authority by whom an

232

area has been declared to be a clearance area may postpone the demolition of any houses on land purchased by or belonging to the local authority within that area. Thereafter the houses may be patched and brought up to a standard, which is adequate for the time being. In given circumstances such action will attract housing subsidy. The Ministry of Housing and Local Government Circular 55/54, in referring to unfit houses where action of this nature is intended, states:

> These houses may also serve to form a pool of accommodation available for families who are homeless, and for the re-housing of families now occupying temporary accommodation provided under the National Assistance Act.

Despite the fact that Section 21 (1) (b) of the National Assistance Act, 1948, imposes a duty to provide only for persons whose need arises "in circumstances which could not reasonably have been foreseen", progressive authorities have endeavoured to deal with each of the different categories of people rendered homeless, thereby attempting to resolve the social evil. In so doing these authorities have not been content only to provide a temporary shelter but have taken action to train such people for a new way of life. A combination of the powers contained in the National Assistance and Housing Acts is thus used to provide a useful social service. Care in former institutions is avoided and is replaced by a progressive policy of house training followed by a probationary period under limited visiting supervision.

Causes

A true study of the factors leading to homelessness would be both interesting and informative. Some of the factors are apparent and can be found amongst the following:

(1) Inability to budget for weekly rent and other commitments.
(2) The high level of rentals and interest charged.
(3) Low incomes competing with high rentals, and the substantial deposits necessary for purchase of older property.
(4) Deliberate withholding of rent to force a landlord to execute repairs.
(5) Overcrowding aggravated by the birth of a further child.
(6) Matrimonial discord.
(7) Ignorance or poor ability in housecraft.
(8) Inability to control children's misbehaviour.
(9) Landlord requiring accommodation for his own or family's needs.
(10) "Tied cottage" transactions where employment ceases.
(11) Death of contractual or statutory tenant leaving lodgers unprotected.
(12) Unauthorized sub-tenancy discovered by landlord.
(13) Work-shyness on the part of the husband.
(14) Excessive drinking, smoking or gambling.

These are reasons often given by applicants, but one wonders whether some of these causes would operate if it were not for the present-day practice of large houses being under-occupied by old people, and the apparent unwillingness on the part of householders to accept children into lodgings. It must also be admitted that local authorities have inadequate facilities for preventing homelessness.*

Size of the Problem

Whilst perhaps small in number compared with all those people seeking housing, the homeless present a substantial problem. The incidence of homelessness is not uniform throughout the country. The Midlands, London, industrial cities and the south coast towns appear to have a greater problem than the rest of the country. Indeed, on 30 December 1960 there were only nine persons in the whole of Wales provided with temporary accommodation, whilst several northern boroughs appeared to be free from this worry. The total accommodated on this date was 6473, of whom 809 were in London, 115 in Croydon, 101 in Southampton and 51 in Portsmouth. Totals have been high since 1948, but dropped to 4500 ten years later. Since then they have been steadily increasing. Unless determined action is taken to halt the increase and to deal with those at present in temporary accommodation, this problem may remain indefinitely. Such a position clearly should not be tolerated and legislators and social workers need to give this matter serious study.

Prevention

Because of administrative practice it can happen that families are accepted into temporary accommodation, particularly by night, without adequate investigation into the necessity for admission. There is, in this procedure, a pious hope of sorting things out the next day, but this is seldom done. A spirited attempt to provide an alternative solution has been found to be in the best interests of the family and the community.

Ideally, where the circumstances of the family are known, or can be made known, to the social worker, steps can be taken when the trouble begins to try to overcome the main difficulty. It must be admitted that few authorities have the staff capable of providing long-term casework. They have neither the clear power to operate a preventive service,† nor the authority to supply financial and other material assistance. It happens from time to time that debts have to be cleared before a start can be made on re-training the family, pawned items need to be redeemed or household belongings replaced; yet

* Since submitting this article Local Authorities have been given powers under the Children and Young Persons Act, 1963, to take certain preventive measures.

† This criticism may be met to some extent in one course by the operation of the Children and Young Persons Act, 1963.

the social worker can only seek help from charitable sources in these circumstances. The cost of providing such help would, in many cases, be only a fraction of the cost of receiving the family into care, yet this step has to be taken for want of resources.

Every avenue of hope should be explored before deciding upon admission. The possibility of help from relatives, friends or neighbours can too easily be overlooked. It is sometimes very effective to return an "ejected" family to their former household in the early hours of the morning and impress upon the tenant that the local authority will not lightly permit him to eject a family without due period of notice. The fact that a local authority cares about the family and cannot so easily be put upon, will sometimes influence a relative's sense of responsibility.

Where adequate warning is given, a case conference of the interested officials may well produce a possible solution and will certainly prevent one officer from carrying the whole problem single-handed. The need to find employment for the husband may be a first step, and an approach to sympathetic employers through a local male charitable organization can sometimes be more effective than an official employment inquiry. Help of marriage guidance counsellors, the Citizens' Advice Bureau (e.g. where hire purchase debts are involved), or help of the domestic science staff of the authority, will perhaps be necessary after obtaining the applicant's consent.

Training

There will be some for whom no immediate solution other than admission to temporary accommodation can be found. In these cases it is essential to use the accommodation as a means of enabling the family to make a fresh start. The cause of their homelessness must be discovered and appropriate help or guidance given. Smaller authorities, particularly county boroughs, should find this easier to effect than the larger county councils, if only because they are both housing and welfare authorities. For the blameless victim of eviction little is needed apart from re-housing, but "queue jumping", where the applicant has not the requisite priority, may well prove a difficulty. To offer such a family a "patched" house might be the solution, since the normal applicant for re-housing would not be anxious to obtain this type of dwelling. Having served the requisite period of time in a "patched" house to qualify for normal council house priority, the family can be treated in the same fashion as all other housing applicants—with the understanding that occupation of a "patched" house should not be regarded as a tenancy which would debar a person in those areas where the local authority decide to give priority only to lodger applicants.

For those families with a basic defect, systematic re-training is desirable and may be achieved in the following manner.

Families should be admitted to a small hostel where communal living can be provided for three to six families with resident supervision. They should be taught how to live together, and how to share a home, since often inability to do this has been their downfall, and for many this type of living will be their only prospect for some time to come.

Mothers should accept maximum responsibility to buy, prepare and cook their own food, to care for their own children and to carry out the other jobs which a responsible mother does for her family. Any attempt to replace this responsibility by providing kitchen staff, nursery nurses, etc., is over indulgent and will never help the mother to cope on her own. The premises and their contents should be as much as possible like those of similar families in the district. Expensive labour-saving devices should be avoided, since to train a mother in the use of washing machines, spin dryers and vacuum cleaners, etc., may render her unable or unwilling to do certain household tasks by hand when she finds herself re-housed and unable to afford these luxuries. The accent should rather be placed on improvisation, and the opportunity should be taken to instruct the family in making attractive household items by using inexpensive materials. (How often has one seen illustrations of a most attractive bedside cabinet constructed from spare wood with Fablon tops and gaily curtained fronts?) Families should be encouraged to save for the cost of basic necessities when they are re-housed, thus avoiding the necessity for borrowing equipment or needing help with weekly hire-purchase charges.

The rent or charge for the accommodation ought to compare with council house rents or the average price of furnished accommodation in the neighbourhood; otherwise, when a family finds an offer of alternative accommodation is made they may be put off by the higher cost.

The points which cause disagreement or friction when families share a house are usually to be found in the services which form part of the communal aspect of the building. It is to deal with such matters that training is usually needed. They include the responsibility jointly to keep clean the halls, staircases, landings or doorsteps; to contribute to the cost of heating or lighting communal rooms and domestic hot-water supply; to leave the communal kitchen or dining room clean and tidy after use; and to preserve the peace. Those mothers who have spent long periods in institutions, where food has been supplied and the children looked after by staff, may have forgotten how to do even the simplest household jobs. So, too, may those wives who have lived with relatives who did such things for them. People like this may need to be taught ordinary household jobs such as cooking. Here a resident female member of the staff with practical ability will be invaluable. If communal cookers were used mothers would be obliged to work out amongst themselves a rota for using the cookers and dining rooms according to the needs of their families. They should all contribute fuel for the main fires, each family taking a day, or week, in turn. Electricity repayment meters in the bed-sitting rooms can be calibrated to compensate for the cost of lighting halls, staircases, etc., but it is not advisable to operate shared gas equipment on a prepayment meter basis because of the danger of accidents. Under such an arrangement, families would learn to share dining facilities and accept mutual responsibility for cleaning shared rooms. Set times can be agreed for bathing and laundry, and other arrangements formed to make shared living more comfortable. Where domestic defects or lack of budgeting sense have led to non-payment of rent, families should be given guidance about how to deal with their housekeeping allowances.

If the opportunity to obtain rooms arises, a family re-trained to this standard should not be a problem for a new landlord. In this re-training the father must not be forgotten, and should be helped to keep his job, to take an interest in his family, to accept his share of responsibility, and not be allowed to feel that he has fulfilled his role once he has handed over the housekeeping allowance to his wife and supplied the children with their weekly pocket money. Some men have pleaded that they were unaware that their wives had mounted debts. This should never be the case.

Fathers may benefit from attending night school, as may many mothers, particularly where they study cookery or household management. Other supporting services can be brought in at this stage to try to ensure that after a period of not longer than three months the family is fitted to move on to intermediate accommodation in a "patched" house. Pressure should constantly be maintained on the families themselves to search for alternative housing.

Intermediate Housing

Families who have benefited from the re-training period at a hostel may still not be acceptable to many housing authorities, who will justifiably feel that they ought to wait almost as long as other applicants for a new council house. It would not be desirable, however, to keep these families longer than three months in a hostel, since the discipline necessary there is somewhat strict. Moreover, a family will only be prepared to co-operate fully with the staff until familiarity with their surroundings makes them resent authority. Room must be available for new entrants who should not be allowed to come into contact with, or under the influence of, the more hardened cases. A "patched" house provides an avenue of graduation from close supervision to complete independence, and also provides an immediate form of accommodation for blameless applicants. The districts selected for these houses must be carefully chosen, because environment will influence the development of the families. To return a family to a district where arrears or neglect are commonplace is to court disaster.

People transferred to such houses should be subject to limited supervision only, and the supervision should be so unobtrusive that neighbours would not notice it. The weekly visit of the rent collector may suffice. Where a Family Service Worker or Welfare Officer has to visit, he or she can act for all other interested parties, thus giving the family the chance to lead as normal a life as possible. A constant procession of visitors to one house would soon lead the neighbours to treat the family as unusual and would prevent the family from developing independently. This does not mean that supporting services will be unnecessary, but where they are very necessary one worker should carry them out.

It is sincerely hoped that after a year or two in such accommodation a family would readily be accepted by a Housing Committee. Such a system may not work everywhere, but it ought at least to be considered. The welfare authority has no statutory obligation to perform this service of re-training, but where it does so, it will undoubtedly bring satisfaction to the individua and to the community as a whole.

27. The Family Welfare Association

JOHN S. BURT

Director, Family Welfare Association

A STUDY of the history of the Family Welfare Association over nearly a hundred years is, in fact, a study of the development of welfare services in the United Kingdom.

Under the formidable title of The Society for Organizing Charitable Relief and Repressing Mendicity, the Association came into being to combat the appalling conditions prevailing in the 1860's; Gladstone, Lord Shaftesbury, Ruskin, Cardinal Manning and Octavia Hill being among its supporters.

However, with Poor Law relief available to aid the needy, and numerous charities already in existence, it might be asked what call there was for the formation of such a Society. The need was twofold:

(i) To press for discrimination in the giving of charity.
(ii) To establish that the provision of material relief did not in itself provide the solution to a sufferer's problems.

The former involved the Charity Organization Society (as it came to be called) in the unsavoury task of running to earth and exposing bogus and dubious charities and, later, the promulgation of a list of those known to be reputable and deserving. The latter was giant seed, had they known it, for from it grew what proved to be the first fruits of a Family Casework Service. The principle established was that help and guidance was needed in the running of homes and care of families; a process that enabled people to learn how to help themselves and become useful and self-reliant members of the community.

Out of these earliest ideas has grown the pattern of modern family casework. Its spread has been swift and wide; to the Commonwealth and, through the Family Service Association of America, to the United States. There, indeed, the work now surpasses anything like it in the United Kingdom.

This thread of family casework has run right through the history of the Association. But there have been many other activities, particularly those that concern themselves with pioneer action. For instance, it was involved in the founding of the first Labour Exchange, the appointment of the first Hospital Almoner, legislation on housing, mental health, hire purchase and the setting up of the Citizens' Advice Bureau movement.

239

Besides racial characteristics the maintenance of family life depends upon a number of factors. The basic necessities of life—such as food, clothing and shelter—are accepted in this country today as the right of everyone, and if an individual is not in a position through disability of any kind to provide them himself, arrangements are made for them to be provided by the community. But to exist at bare subsistence level is hardly conducive to a free and healthy life, and a man seeks more than this for himself and his family. The rise in the standard of living in the last twenty years, while opening up new horizons to the average wage-earner, has brought in its wake many problems. For example, the growing custom for both parents to work. While enabling many luxuries to be provided, this has reacted against many of the old-established ideas about family life. The home-coming of a child to an empty house cannot but have its effect, and may well be a contributory cause of the rise in juvenile delinquency.

While the Family Welfare Association—so re-named in 1946—provides many other services, such as a department dealing with homes for old people, the publication of the *Guide to Social Services*, etc., its Family Casework Service remains at present its largest activity. This is provided by seven area offices which cover twenty-six of the metropolitan boroughs of London, and these are primarily concerned with the problems which give rise to stress in a family.*

Whereas in the 1870's much of its activity had its inception in the meeting of material needs, today the meeting of these by the Welfare State has enabled the caseworkers to concentrate more directly upon the psychological stresses that can disrupt the family. The removal of pressures engendered by material distress has enabled deeper-lying tensions to rise to the surface, and in many cases it is with these that today's family caseworker is concerned.

Some of the problems most commonly met with arise from marital discord, parent–child relationships, one-parent families, handicapped or isolated people, the elderly, and economic difficulties. Such people needing help are referred by other social workers, members of other professions, personnel and welfare departments of industrial concerns and by private persons.

The service is provided by trained professional workers, who bring to bear upon each case a skill based on their knowledge and experience. As long as fifty years ago it was accepted that, as in other responsible professions, social workers required the attainment of certain standards of training. To like people and wish to help them is not enough—it is no more appropriate for untrained workers to interfere with people's lives than for unqualified persons to prescribe for them in the event of sickness. In training, the caseworker studies the causes underlying family conflicts—and learns how to

* Arrangements have been made for the reorganization of areas to meet the circumstances created by the London Government Act, 1963.

establish a close relationship with the clients without falling for the temptation to give advice based on "snap judgement".

The underlying principle of family casework is to attempt to help clients become aware of the reality of the situation, and thus to "help them to help themselves". The service is confidential and fills gaps in the present statutory services. Indeed, it is part of the task of the caseworker to show the clients how to make use of the statutory services available to them. The effects of family stress are not only manifested in the home, and many a discerning employer is quick to realize that an employee with private problems is one whose productivity is falling off and with whom absenteeism is likely to increase.

The results of casework are difficult to assess in terms of success. It is virtually impossible to say that, but for certain support and help, a family would be on the rocks of despair. The study of factors leading to disaster indicate that the timely help of a caseworker might well have saved the situation. Similarly, it is impossible to assess the result of the work in terms of saving to the community. Children in care, unpaid debts, delinquency—all these are costly to the State, and any help given which averts such results of family failure must stand high on the credit side. But what is most important is the long-term effect of family casework and its benefit to succeeding generations. Such benefit must accrue, for a secure and happy home life cannot but influence the development of the character of young members of the family.

A final word about training. The skill and knowledge at the disposal of those seeking help is also placed at the disposal of those training to follow on in the field of social work. Every year approximately a hundred students of social work receive their practical training at the various area centres of the Association throughout London.

28. Family Service Units

A. F. PHILP

Secretary, Family Service Units

FAMILY SERVICE UNITS is a voluntary organization aiming to meet the needs
of families whose many pressing problems may lead to the neglect of their
children or the break-up of their homes. Such families fail to profit from the
help of the usual social services and are often called "problem families".

Although they may be a problem to society, society is often just as much
a problem to them. Adverse social circumstances, poverty, bad housing and
unemployment combine with personal handicaps such as physical or mental
illness, low intelligence or an unsatisfactory childhood, so that the parents
have immense difficulty in reaching the standard of family and social life
that the community demands. Repeated experience of failure reinforces their
feeling that there is very little they can do about their situation. Disharmony,
debt or delinquency become part of the pattern of their lives and may eventually cause the total disintegration of the family. Suspicion, apathy and
aggression prevent the parents from using the social services constructively.
F.S.U. provides a service which breaks through these barriers and fosters
the strengths that will enable the family to re-establish itself.

The special needs of these families have to be considered in planning help
for them. Interviews usually take place in the home because, apart from the
parents' reluctance to seek help for themselves, the demands of young children and other practical difficulties prevent them from travelling to see social
workers in an office or clinic. The F.S.U. worker's approach is informal and
friendly. The parents may feel hopeless and hostile; they may have come to
anticipate nothing but rebuffs from society and its representatives. The worker
attempts to show his belief in and respect for them in spite of their failures.
This is possible as he tries to appreciate the problem as the family sees it and
to find an area where they feel some need for help and support; he shows an
understanding of the parents' feelings and of the problems that beset them
so that they no longer seem alone in their struggles. The consideration that
is offered to them helps to restore their self-respect and their confidence in
their ability to lead happier and more acceptable lives. The interest and trust
of the F.S.U. caseworker can give the family a new experience of society,
enabling them to face the outside world with less suspicion and hostility.

These families need tangible services. They may have become so bewil-
dered and discouraged that they need help with tasks which most other

people take in their stride: the problem of getting the children to school or redecorating a room may be too great unless there is someone to give a friendly hand; their relationship with their creditors is such that negotiations concerning payment of debts need to be made with the aid of a third person who can see the situation sympathetically but objectively; they need help to complete an application form for re-housing or to make a hospital appointment. The concrete expression of the worker's willingness to help and his clear appreciation of the practical difficulties are vitally important to the parents. They show his genuine sympathy and concern for them. Where they can participate with him in some effort for the family welfare, they can gain a real sense of achievement which can be a first step towards further improvement.

The worker visits frequently. He gets to know the parents well and begins to see their strengths and limitations clearly, so that all help, whether it comes from F.S.U. or through the co-ordination of other services, can be made appropriate to the family's needs. He supports them through the many crises which may endanger family stability, such as threats of eviction, court appearances, illness, mental breakdown, the death or desertion of their partner in marriage. He helps them to manage in the way best suited to them, without creating difficulties for themselves and others.

Often the worker will need to call upon other services, such as the National Assistance Board, the Home Help Service, the Education or Children's Departments. Most of the families have permanent handicaps such as low income, ill health or mental instability, and they will always need a great deal of support from the social services, although it is hoped that eventually they will use them appropriately and constructively. F.S.U. has no resources of its own for giving financial or material aid beyond a small supply of clothing and equipment which most Units keep for use in times of special need. The Units do, however, provide evening activities and summer holidays for the children in the families; they, like their parents, are often unable to take advantage of the usual provisions or they need special attention from adults to offset some of the unsatisfactory experiences they have had.

The F.S.U. worker has only a small caseload, normally about fifteen families. This enables him to give a good deal of time to each family, visiting at least once a week and several times, or even daily, during periods of particular difficulty, and occasionally he may have to spend several hours giving practical help. He must also see that his efforts and those of other workers in touch with the family are properly co-ordinated and that specialist help and advice is obtained.

Families are normally referred to Units by other social workers who recognize that the family is showing signs of breakdown and needs intensive help which they cannot give because of their large caseloads or specialized functions. When F.S.U. begins to work with a family, other social workers

usually reduce their visiting and co-operate with the F.S.U. worker in pur-
suing a common policy. Where for some reason, such as pressure of work,
the Unit is unable to accept a referral, the Unit Organizer will try to help the
referring worker find other ways of assisting the family.

A Unit usually works with a family from two to four years. Success is
difficult to measure. The majority of families show improvement and some
come to manage alone very adequately. A small number seem unable to
respond to help and may eventually be evicted or broken up. In some
families there are bonds of affection that suggest that the children will be
given a better start in life if the family can remain together, although the
parents seem unlikely to change very much. In such cases, F.S.U. will
continue to visit for many years, preventing the situation from deteriorating
to a point where the break-up of the family is inevitable. In these families
the later development of the children has justified this long-term work.

Family Service Units was formed in 1947 to develop work started during
the Second World War and now has a casework staff of over ninety men
and women workers. The majority have a social science qualification; in
addition they have at least six months' preliminary training in F.S.U. Workers
have opportunities for individual supervision of their casework and there are
also arrangements for further in-service training. All Units have been
approved as training agencies for social science students and the demand
made on them to provide experience for students from universities and professional social work courses is greater than can be met. Some local authorities
also send to F.S.U. for training newly appointed workers who will be specializing in family casework within their departments.

At present there are fourteen Units, four in London and ten in other
large English cities. The work is financed partly from voluntary contributions
and partly from local authority grants, two Units being wholly maintained
by their local authorities. Most Units work in the older central areas of the
cities, but the work is spreading to local authority housing estates and to
some more rural areas. Each Unit has a large measure of autonomy under
its own Local Committee but all are united under a National Committee
with a National Headquarters. The National Office is responsible for recruitment and general policy concerning personnel, training and the development of the work. It also brings the Units together to discuss mutual difficulties and to collaborate in further developments.

A Unit may have from two to eight workers, under the direction of a
Fieldwork Organizer. The staff works together as a team, assisting one another
in the work, sharing problems and developing new approaches. There are
regular staff meetings where matters affecting general policy or the problems
of particular families are discussed. Although each worker is responsible for
his own caseload, he is able to use other workers and the total resources of
the Unit to help his families. The Unit Centre is usually an old house, in or

near the area where most of the families live. It provides a homely, friendly atmosphere where families will feel welcome to call. Coming to the Unit Centre, even at the invitation of the worker, may be a family's first step towards looking out into the community instead of remaining wrapped up in its problems and sense of hopelessness.

Some families become very dependent on the Unit for a time: it may be the only place where they feel certain of understanding if things go wrong for them, and so Units try to arrange that, where practicable, a worker is always available to talk to them. As they overcome some of their difficulties and have better relationships with others, they become more independent of the Unit workers. Their problems are no longer overwhelming and therefore frightening, tending to increase because there seems so little hope of any improvement. Through their relationship with the F.S.U. worker and the help given to them, the parents find a new confidence in themselves and a greater capacity to care for their children.

List of Units with Addresses and National Address

Birmingham Unit
398 New John St. West,
Birmingham, 19.
Tel.: ASTon Cross 4341–2.

Bradford Unit
20 Edmund St.,
Bradford, 5.
Tel.: 26061.

Bristol Unit
42 Knighton Rd.,
Southmead, Bristol.
Tel.: 693155.

Leeds Unit
66 Marsh Lane,
Leeds, 9.
Tel.: 24333.

Leicester Unit
54 Highfield St.,
Leicester.
Tel.: 26895.

Liverpool Unit
56 Grove St.,
Liverpool, 7.
Tel.: ROYal 7765.

Manchester, Salford and Stockport Unit
296a Upper Brook St.,
Manchester, 13.
Tel.: ARDwick 2212.

Oldham Unit
25 Radcliffe St.,
Oldham.
Tel.: MAIn 7468.

Sheffield Unit
88 Upper Hanover St.,
Sheffield, 3.
Tel.: 21533.

York Unit
82 Bootham,
York.
Tel.: 53846.

East London Unit
71 Vallance Rd.,
London, E. 1.
Tel.: BIShopsgate 0442.

Islington and North London Unit
36 St. Mary's Grove,
London, N. 1.
Tel.: CANonbury 8017.

Kensington and Paddington Unit
36 Colville Terrace,
London, W. 11.
Tel.: BAYswater 6357.

South London Unit
20 Heygate St.,
London, S.E. 17.
Tel.: RODney 9292.

National Office: 207 Marylebone Rd., London, N.W. 1. Tel.: PADdington 0218.

29. Marriage Guidance

A. J. BRAYSHAW

Recently General Secretary, National Marriage Guidance Council

SINCE the Second World War there has been widespread recognition of the great importance of early childhood influences upon adult behaviour. This has focused public interest on family relationships. While divorce rates are only a rough indication of trends, the number of petitions (for dissolution and nullity) filed in England and Wales reached a peak of 48,000 in 1947, and (with some fluctuations connected with the financial provisions for legal aid) declined to about 26,000 in 1958 and 1959, since when the figure has risen to 34,625 in 1962. Among those marriages where the wife is still of child-bearing age, as many (or more) are ended by divorce as by death; and the Royal Commission on Marriage and Divorce, which reported in March 1956, showed that each year in Great Britain some 20,000 children under the age of 16 are affected by the divorce of their parents. It is against this background that the modern service of marriage guidance has special importance.

The main effort in this new field of voluntary social service has come from about 115 Marriage Guidance Councils linked together in the National Marriage Guidance Council with headquarters at 58 Queen Anne Street, London, W.1. (Scotland has its own National Council.) The movement was started in 1938 by the late Dr. Herbert Gray with a group of doctors and social workers. Ten years later the official Denning Committee (which first recommended grants for the development of marriage guidance work) described the movement as "the most striking civilian development of recent times". Similar work is undertaken for Roman Catholics by the Catholic Marriage Advisory Council, which has thirty-six local centres; and by the Family Discussion Bureau which is a section of the Tavistock Institute of Human Relations, and which does specialist work at a Centre in London. These three organizations, which all maintain exacting standards, especially of selection and training of marriage counsellors, are recognized and grant-aided by the Home Office, the grants amounting in 1963–4 to £30,000 to the National Marriage Guidance Council and £8000 to each of the other two organizations. These grants are largely intended to ensure a high standard of work, and they may be compared with the fact that the taxpayer contributes some £3⅓ million a year as the cost of providing legal aid and advice in divorce and other domestic cases.

These new services have two main fields of endeavour: education and preparation for marriage, and help to the married in overcoming any difficulties that may endanger their marriage. The educational side is probably the more important in the long run, but the remedial side has so far been more fully developed. The following outline relates to the work of Marriage Guidance Councils, though that of the Catholic Marriage Advisory Council is conducted in broadly similar ways.

"Marriage counsellors" are voluntary part-time workers who are much more rigorously selected and trained than any other voluntary social workers. They are married men and women, mainly in early middle age, who have been sponsored by one of the local Marriage Guidance Councils, have then passed a selection board arranged by the National Council, and have taken its training. At the residential selection conference, fourteen candidates meet five selectors including a psychiatrist over two days in a succession of interviews and other selection procedures. Only about half the candidates are selected for training, for this service needs special qualities of temperament. Counsellors must have high principles, yet real tolerance and freedom from prejudice; sympathy and insight, yet unwillingness to take sides. They must be at once tender with others and tough with themselves, since they will inevitably meet many disappointments.

Although American agencies often argue whether a Master's Degree is sufficient for marriage counselling, or whether a Doctorate should be required, this voluntary service in Britain has a different approach. It regards marriage counselling as being more concerned with insight and emotional support than with the intellectual solving of a puzzle. Husband and wife who come in marriage troubles do not need to have the sensible or kind course pointed out to them. Usually they see this clearly enough. The trouble is that they cannot follow it because of prejudices, blind spots or emotional blockages, often connected with their childhood influences. The task of the marriage counsellor is to help people to gain insight into themselves and their partners, their motives and their needs, in order that they may grope their own way to their own best solution. It is found that in training marriage counsellors it is necessary not only to give them a certain amount of essential information, but also to help them in turn to understand their limitations, prejudices and blind spots, which would otherwise hinder their attempts to help others.

There is a stream of suitable volunteers willing to become marriage counsellors, who are prepared to face all the hurdles erected in their path, and if they surmount them, to give devoted and selfless spare-time service in work that cannot but be anxious, difficult and time-consuming. In England, Wales and Northern Ireland, the Marriage Guidance Councils now have over 800 active counsellors, for although twice this number have been selected and trained since the Second World War, there is a normal retiring age of 65, and inevitably some drop out for other reasons.

Besides enforcing all sorts of safeguards for the confidential nature of their work, the Councils insist that those who want help in overcoming marriage problems should come themselves to seek it. They come because they have heard of the service or have been encouraged by a doctor, minister, lawyer, probation officer or advice bureau. The help the counsellors offer is not what is commonly supposed. It is not in the main "giving advice", still less imposing a solution or apportioning blame. Essentially it is an attempt to befriend husband and wife and patiently to help them work their own way through to their own acceptable decisions. The counsellors are not indifferent. They want to see bitterness healed and children assured of love and security in their own homes. But this is sought not through directives but through helping people better to understand themselves and each other, so that they resolve their own difficulties.

In the counsellors' training great stress is laid on the limits of their competence and on the symptoms or situations that need referring to skilled professional help. This is provided in each council by a panel of doctors, psychiatrists, spiritual advisers, lawyers and social workers generously offering their services, appropriate arrangements having been agreed with the legal and medical professions. Particular care is taken that in medical matters there is co-operation with the family doctor whenever the patient is willing.

The number of couples seeking help increases each year. In 1963 these numbered more than 16,250, one or both parties being seen privately and alone —and often repeatedly—by a marriage counsellor. In the same year, some 14,000 cases were closed, representing couples who between them had more than 19,000 children under the age of 16. Though it is inherently difficult to devise tests of the success of such a service, careful research shows that between a third and a half of all these couples say subsequently that they have been substantially helped either in surmounting their troubles or, it may be, in learning to live with them. Much depends on couples facing any marriage difficulty promptly when it arises. Even the most tragic and irretrievable situations have a beginning somewhere. There is much more hope if they are tackled early than if they are left to become embittered by years of strife— and, perhaps, by solid ranks of relatives.

It is, however, in education and help for couples before marriage that most important future developments lie. Many marriage troubles would never arise if couples had embarked on married life with a fuller understanding of its responsibilities and rewards. There is a clear need for education for marriage and family living to be developed in its widest sense, through the schools, through youth clubs, through sound publications and mass media, and in specific preparation for marriage.

Originally, the chief contribution of the Marriage Guidance Councils lay in organizing talks and discussions for engaged couples, often with remarkable success. There is no attempt to tell young couples what they should think or do. The aim is to encourage them to think and decide jointly for themselves. Several aspects of marriage are well known as likely causes of difficulty, such as differences of religious belief, ignorance and insensitiveness about sex, family intentions, money and the whole question of the wife working outside the home, and relationships with in-laws. Such things are unlikely to cause trouble if couples sort out their own ideas, so that they enter marriage of one mind, united on the things that matter.

Small friendly groups of engaged couples usually meet three or four times at weekly intervals. In big towns meetings are usually arranged at a central place where they can meet over refreshments after working hours. A doctor may start the discussion one evening, a clergyman on another, a marriage counsellor on a third. In these informal discussions young people help one another to view aspects of marriage in perspective. Other groups meet around the fireside in the home of some suitable happily married couple, who initiate the talking.

However, engagements are short and busy nowadays, and the education workers who are similarly selected and trained for their task find even greater opportunities with work among young people in clubs and schools and colleges, where they are invited to go. During 1963 more than 50,000 young people were reached in this way by speakers who are not merely concerned with sex education, but rather with preparation for the responsibilities of life, including sex. Wherever possible, these education workers prefer to initiate discussion among small groups which have many advantages compared with the platform speaker giving a set address.

However, this great and growing effort cannot reach more than a small proportion of young people. Hence, the National Marriage Guidance Council has published many inexpensive booklets which are not concerned with marriage troubles, but are designed to help ordinary sensible young couples to make the most of marriage by offering suggestions about wedding etiquette, budgeting, home making, starting a family, the early years of marriage and—the most recent—ways of helping grand-parents too. The Council's Book Shop publishes a periodic list of recommended books, which is sent free to inquirers enclosing a stamped addressed envelope, and the Council's publications now have a very wide circulation.

Marriage Guidance Councils now exist in almost all the large centres of population. These are voluntary organizations depending on voluntary service, and deriving most of their funds from subscriptions and donations, though local authorities almost always make contributions. Nearly all of these Councils are in need of help, not only in funds but in personal service, especially from those willing to face selection and training as marriage counsellors or educational workers. The address of any Marriage Guidance Council may be found in the telephone directory, or can be obtained from the National Council at 58 Queen Anne Street, London, W.1.

SECTION VI
SERVICES FOR THE BLIND

PLATE 13. London County Council sheltered employment for sighted-disabled persons at St. Pancras, London

PLATE 14. Blind instructor teaching a newly blinded person to operate a telephone switchboard

PLATE 15. Deaf–blind person receiving nstruction at one of the Social Rehabilitation
Centres

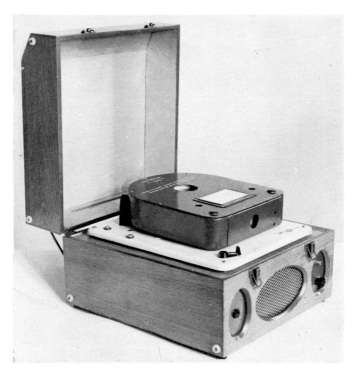

PLATE 16. The revolutionary new Tape Talking Book Machine, developed by the Royal National Institute for the Blind in cooperation with St. Dunstan's, which, utilizing eighteen sound tracks on a half-inch, provides twenty-one hours of reading time. Within the cassette—seen here in position on the play-back unit—the driving gear, play-back head and tape are housed, thus preventing damage and ensuring consistently high quality of reproduction

PLATE 17. The Braille-marked micrometer—one of a range of precision measuring instruments specially developed by the Royal National Institute for the Blind for use by blind workers in industry—by means of which a trained blind operator may measure to an accuracy of one ten-thousandth part of an inch

30. Services for the Blind

Trevor Salathiel

Formerly of the London County Council

BLINDNESS has been recognized as a severe handicap from Biblical times, yet it was not until the latter part of the eighteenth century that real efforts were made to ameliorate the condition of those who suffered the disability.

We know that in the year 1329 an asylum was established near London Wall by a London mercer as "A Shelter for 100 blind men". Some 200 years later, in 1528, the Clothworkers Company of the City of London commenced its grants of pensions to needy blind people, and it is interesting to note that this Livery Company still grants some thousands of pounds each year in such pensions.

The Poor Law Act of 1601, probably the best-known piece of Elizabeth I legislation, made the parish responsible for its own destitute people, and it became the duty of the community to provide for the blind along with the old, impotent and others not able to work. For nearly another 300 years, apart from further Poor Law Acts, there appears to have been no other legislation relating to the welfare of the blind until the 1870's when, in a typical British manner, there crept into one of the Customs and Inland Revenue Acts a section which read:

> Nothing in the Dog Licences Act, 1867, or in this part of this Act shall render a licence necessary in the case of a dog kept and used solely by a blind person for his or her guidance or render such person liable to any penalty in respect of a dog so kept and used.

Although this small concession by the Government is noted as being exceptional for the time, there had already, during the preceding 100 years, grown up a considerable volume of social services for the blind.

In Paris in 1771 a French philanthropist, Valentine Hauy, saw a group of blind men at an annual fair, dressed by an innkeeper in a ridiculous manner, decorated with peacock feathers and asses' ears, being held to ridicule by the crowds. He was so shocked at this outrage to humanity that he devoted himself to devising methods of teaching the blind.

Having first taken for tuition blind youths whom he found begging in the streets of Paris, he founded the first school for the blind (Institution Nationale des Jeunes Aveugles) in 1784, and also invented and commenced the printing

253

of embossed type. This establishment attracted the attention and support of Louis XVI who encouraged Hauy to publish an account of his methods, which appeared in 1786 under the title *Essai sur l'Education des Aveugles.*

The work started by Hauy was taken up in Britain by Gall in Edinburgh and Alston in Glasgow, and schools for the blind were established in Liverpool, Bristol and Southwark in the last decade of the eighteenth century and commenced the monumental work of welfare of the blind which voluntary societies of this country may well be proud.

One of the greatest problems which these early schools encountered was the lack of a good method by which the blind could communicate in writing. Hauy had himself evolved a system of raised printing which could be used by his students to read articles and instructions, but was not suitable as a means for them to communicate with others or to record their thoughts. Weissenberg in Germany and Gall in Scotland also devised systems which were adopted by some schools but were displaced by the method invented by Dr. Fry of London in 1837, whose alphabet consisted of ordinary capitals without their small strokes. The Royal Society of Arts of Edinburgh had offered a gold medal for the best method of printing for the blind which was won by Dr. Fry a few years before Dr. Moon of Brighton brought out his system, which partially retains the outline of the Roman letters. Dr. Moon's letters, which are easily read without very lengthy tuition, are still taught to those people who lose their sight late in life and who do not feel able to undergo the intensive training required to learn an entirely new method of reading. These systems were known as line types and proved extremely valuable in the teaching of the blind people, but the real break-through came when Louis Braille, a student at the Paris school founded by Valentine Hauy, invented an alphabet in which characters are formed by an arrangement of dots. The signs are purely arbitrary and consist of varying combinations of six points placed in an oblong (similar to the dots on a domino piece) of which the vertical side contains three and the horizontal side two points. Each letter consists of from one to six raised dots arranged in two parallel lines and numbered 1 and 4, 2 and 5, and 3 and 6. These six dots or points can be permuted to give sixty-three different signs, and so, in addition to the letters of the alphabet, the signs can be used for figures, punctuation marks and contraction of commonly recurring words or combinations of letters. The writing is done with a small stylet on a special board which has a series of perforations on a metal band which keeps the writing straight. As the dots are made by pressing the stylet on to the paper, the raised letters so formed will be read by feeling the reverse side of the paper, it follows that the letters must be reversed and written from right to left.

Dr. Moon's line type and Braille point system have both survived the test of time, and to these names in the annals of welfare of the blind should be added that of Dr. Armitage, the founder of the British and Foreign Blind

Association (now the Royal National Institute for the Blind) whose unremitting efforts brought the Braille system for literature and music into general use in this country in the 1860's.

During the early Victorian era a considerable number of associations for the welfare and teaching of the blind came into existence. Most of them were connected with religious organizations and, as was customary in those days, they had particular links with denominations, and set out to improve the lot of those blind who belonged to the denomination which had founded the society.

The need for greater assistance to enable the blind to support themselves was apparent, as it was found that the schools which had been set up to educate blind children were rarely able to train them to a standard where they could earn a living in ordinary employment, and some associations had provided workshops where their former pupils could be employed under special conditions. Other societies started homeworker schemes under which the blind who had learnt a craft at school could use it at home, receiving help in obtaining materials and in the marketing of the finished articles. The number of blind people who were able to benefit by these schemes was very small, probably not more than 10 per cent of those who wished to be trained and employed.

To their other good works the blind welfare associations added the very valuable establishment of a "lobby" for the blind, and constantly pressed the Government to help in the work. So great was this pressure that a Royal Commission was appointed in 1886 to report on the condition of the blind in the United Kingdom. Among its recommendations was one that schools and special workshops should be set up in every large centre of population, but, although the Report excited interest in the problems of education, training and employment of the blind, the Government did not implement it or provide the necessary funds. However, voluntary effort and funds enabled many more special workshops to be opened, and a number of societies made a practice of arranging for regular contact to be kept with the blind, teaching crafts in the home and helping generally with advice and monetary grants. This pattern of welfare for the blind continued for many years. During this period the study of ophthalmology had made considerable strides, mainly due to the establishment of the School of Ophthalmology in Vienna University which attracted students from all over the world who on their return to their own countries continued the study of preventive measures.

A few months before the outbreak of the First World War in 1914, the House of Commons debated:

> In the opinion of this House, the present system of voluntary effort in aid of the blind people in the country does not adequately meet their necessities, and that the State should make provision whereby capable blind people might be made industrially self-supporting and the incapable and infirm maintained in a proper and humane manner.

This was carried without a division, and a Committee was set up to investigate the condition of the blind and to make recommendations.

The Committee's Report was followed first by the assumption of responsibility by the Ministry of Health for the welfare of the blind, with government grants to workshops for the blind and the registration of blind people, and in 1920 by the passing of the first Blind Persons Act. This Act set out the definition of blindness as being "so blind as to be unable to perform work for which eyesight is essential", it gave old age pensions to blind persons at the age of 50 (altered to 40 by a later Act), and it gave some rules relating to the method of deciding which local authority should assume the duty of providing the necessary services.

Following the coming into operation of the 1920 Act, a really comprehensive service for the blind became possible, and it evolved out of a partnership between the Central Government, acting through the Ministry of Health, the local authorities and the voluntary societies. The Ministry set up the standard of what was required, but in the main the voluntary societies did the work, meeting a large part of the cost from their own funds but obtaining considerable grants in aid from local authorities for those of the services which they provided on an agency basis. As local authorities were thus having to provide funds for services over which they were unable to exercise full control, a number of them from time to time decided to discharge directly their functions under the statutes relating to the welfare and education of the blind.

During the First World War St. Dunstan's was established and has since grown into the splendid organization for blinded ex-Service men and women which accepts responsibility for their welfare, training and employment. Between the wars considerable advance was made in the arrangements for the prevention of blindness, particularly the steps taken to ensure that sight was not lost from inflammation of the eyes due to infection at soon after birth. Ophthalmia neonatorum, as this inflammation is called, was once the cause of blindness in almost a quarter of all cases, but by the beginning of the Second World War it had almost ceased to appear on clinical reports. Facilities for education of blind children were improved, and an increased number of them attained a high degree of scholarship and entered the professions, although it still was difficult for any blind person to find employment other than in one of the special workshops or under a "homeworker scheme". During the Second World War, however, the Royal Institute for the Blind, St. Dunstan's and some local authorities, at the request of the then Minister of Labour, introduced blind workers into a variety of industries where, but for the War, they would not have been considered for employment. This service, which became known as "Placement", opened a new era in welfare for the blind, as it was found that there were many occupations, some of them skilled or semi-skilled, which blind people could follow as well as could their sighted friends.

Organized welfare work among the blind is now the responsibility of county councils and county borough councils and, under the National Assistance Act, 1948, they were required to submit to the Minister of Health a scheme for his approval. These schemes covered all the welfare work for the blind undertaken by the appropriate local authority, including arrangements for the ophthalmological examination of persons losing their sight, for their subsequent registration and classification, the facilities for home teaching, training and employment in special workshops or the blind person's own home or in normal industry, and the promotion of their well-being in a variety of ways.

The statutory definition of blindness is still "so blind as to be unable to perform any work for which eyesight is essential". This definition is vague and the decision now usually depends on a test of visual acuity, with focus properly corrected and with regard to the field of vision. It is therefore not necessary to be completely sightless in order to be registered as "blind". It must be remembered that there are degrees of blindness: total blindness means that a person cannot distinguish light from darkness; some technically blind people can see vague shadowy outlines and patches of colour, others can see a very small patch of scenery very clearly but all the rest is blank, or to some any outline is distorted. A very large proportion of people who are technically blind have, in fact, some vision.

When a person has been examined by the ophthalmologist for registration, the result of the examination is entered on a form of certificate (known as a B.D. 8) together with how long he has been blind and, if possible, some family health history. All this information is looked upon by the authorities as strictly confidential, but it is extremely valuable in indicating the methods to be adopted in the rehabilitation and training to follow. Registration is not compulsory, but in order to be eligible for any of the benefits of the welfare service a person must be so registered.

A key figure in the welfare services for the blind is the home visitor, who almost always holds the certificate of the College of Teachers of the Blind. She is the first contact a blind person has with the welfare services, and so important is her role that some of her duties should be enumerated. They were listed in one of the schemes approved by the Minister of Health to include:

1. The discovery of blind persons and the ascertainment of their needs.
2. The visitation of blind persons in their houses or elsewhere within the administrative county.
3. Teaching blind persons wherever practicable to read embossed literature.
4. Instructing blind persons in simple pastime occupations in their homes or elsewhere and in methods of overcoming the effects of their disabilities.

5. Generally assisting in promoting the welfare of blind persons.
6. Advising blind persons of all available social services.
7. Paying particular attention to those blind persons who are also suffering from some other form of handicap, the nature of which is such as to increase the disability of blindness.
8. Assisting in the management of social centres and classes for blind persons.

There are some 100,000 blind persons in England and Wales of whom about 7 per cent are babies or children of school age, and about 30 per cent between the ages of 16 and 65. It therefore will be seen that the services need to be of a number of kinds to provide for all. Different techniques are required in dealing with those who are born blind or lose sight at a very early age and those who have received a sighted education and possibly worked for some years before becoming blind. It is obvious also that the very old who have lost sight gradually over a number of years will not require training so much as comfort, company and confidence.

The home visitors will be able to advise and help the parents of the very young children to train them to become almost normal members of a household. Children whose knowledge of the world around them is acquired through hearing, touch, smell and taste attain an amount of independence which is remarkable if not restrained by the hands of too solicitous relatives, and, in due course, the child can go to a sunshine home and then to a school where he will have a normal education. Although it is usual for blind children to attend residential schools, parents are not now expected to pay for them, as the residential accommodation in the school is looked upon as part of the education facilities.

The question of employment on leaving school is considered carefully by the education authority and the Youth Employment Service, and nowadays there is a considerable choice as to the type of work for which training can be given. The Royal National Institute for the Blind has set up an establishment in Surrey known as "Hethersett", where children brought up in schools for the blind can be introduced into the somewhat more robust sighted world. Pre-vocational training is given, and the school leaver can be helped in deciding what form of employment he would like to follow and to which he is most suited. Local education authorities from all parts of the country send suitable youngsters here and pay the fees.

For those who become blind between school-leaving age and 65 there are now many occupations in ordinary employment which can successfully be followed after a period of training.

At the time of registration as blind, coming as it may after months or even years of hospital treatment, with alternating hope of recovery and fear of blindness, a person is often emotionally upset and requires considerable help in facing the future. It is generally agreed that at as early a stage as possible all newly blinded persons should have the opportunity of attending a special rehabilitation course. There are differing views as to the respective advantages of residential and non-residential establishments for this purpose. Two forms of rehabilitation are available—industrial rehabilitation, which is directed towards the resettlement of the blind person in employment, and social rehabilitation, which helps the newly blind in the ordinary processes of living. For industrial rehabilitation, the Ministry of Labour accepts responsibility for the fees payable to the body responsible for providing the centre, but the local authority will usually contribute towards the cost of social rehabilitation at a special centre or may itself provide one. During rehabilitation consideration will have been given to the type of employment which is likely to be most suitable for the blind person.

The handicap of blindness can largely be overcome, although much depends on the individual. A man does not change his nature when he becomes blind, but his adjustment to his new circumstances is necessarily related to his normal habits and activities. It may be that his previous employment was such that, with small adjustments in practice, he can again follow it, or it may be found that an entirely new line has to be followed.

There are today in England and Wales some 6500 blind people in ordinary employment and the professions performing some hundreds of different kinds of jobs including masseurs and physiotherapists, carpenters and joiners, typists, telephonists and farmers. If training is necessary, it is provided, if there is a likelihood of the trainee succeeding. Sometimes it is found that, for one reason or another, ordinary employment is not the most suitable, in which case the special workshop, which has been mentioned earlier, will take both blind men and women for training and employment under sheltered conditions in one of the traditional trades such as mat, brush, basket or mattress making or machine-knitting or chair-caning.

The Ministry of Labour pays for the training and also grants a maintenance allowance to the blind person during training, but when the trainee has completed his training, which might last for three or more years, he is rarely able to earn more than 50 per cent of the wage which a sighted worker would earn in a similar trade.

Over the years, as a result of negotiations between the National League of the Blind (the blind worker's trade union), the workshops and the local authorities, it has become the practice for blind workshop employees to be paid as a minimum wage, wages within the scales of the Joint Industrial Council for Manual Workers. To pay such wages, the workshops, although they sell more than £2¼ million of goods per annum, could not carry on without financial support from the local authorities, who are in turn grant-aided by the Ministry of Labour to the extent of 75 per cent of their expenditure for this purpose (with a maximum of £240 per annum per blind employee).

It is clear that, possibly because the trades practised in these sheltered industries are outdated, this method of providing employment for the blind is very costly and quite unprofitable.

By far the largest number of blind people are over 70 years of age, and, of these, their loss of sight in a great many cases has been due to cataract or glaucoma. As has been said, their needs are mainly for comfort and companionship, and the home visitor is assiduous in providing these, together with advice about the many techniques which enable a blind person to perform the ordinary tasks of daily living. Many clubs at which the unemployable blind may meet and have social contact exist in all parts of the country, and at many of them tuition is given in various handicrafts.

For the future, what are the trends? Enormous advance has been made in recent years in eye surgery. Where previously it was thought that surgery for the removal of cataract must be delayed until the cataract was "ripe", it is now possible to repair the eye at a very early stage in the growth of the cataract. Many of those who a few years ago would have to suffer partial or almost complete blindness from this cause will in the future have good vision restored to them almost as soon as the condition is recognized.

Considerable research has been done and is continuing on the chemical composition of the fluids of the eye, and with the increase in knowledge of the chemical processes which increase the vitamin content of these fluids there is great hope of much sight being saved. Great credit must be given to the generosity of the charitable Trusts which have recently endowed a "chair" for the study of the medical aspects of the prevention of blindness.

When serious steps were taken to eliminate ophthalmia neonatorum, the number of blind babies was noticeably reduced. There was an upward surge in the incidence of blind babies during and after the Second World War caused by a new disease called retrolental fibroplasia. It appeared and existed for some ten years until, after great research, it was found to have been caused by an excess of oxygen being used in the oxygen tents which were instrumental in saving the lives of so many prematurely born babies at that time. Once this was discovered, new rules were made about the correct amount of oxygen to be used in such circumstances and the disease was defeated, unfortunately not before some hundreds of children were blinded.

We have recently had experience of the dangers to eyes and limbs of babies whose mothers had had recourse to the thalidomide drugs, but except for such unfortunate incidents there is a real prospect that the number of children without sight will diminish each year.

Regarding employment for the blind, the Ministry of Labour recently set up a Working Party to "review the employment facilities provided in workshops for the blind". The Working Party published its Report late in 1962, and found that there was still a need for sheltered workshops for the blind but that "a central organization should be established, as a non-profit-making limited liability company without share capital, employing a paid staff, which would serve as an advisory organization to the workshops for the blind and undertake commercial operations on their behalf". In all there are twenty-three recommendations in the Report, some dealing with the training of new entrants and others with a re-formed wage structure in the workshops. One of the most important says: "There should be a co-ordinated programme of capital development aimed primarily at introducing new forms of productions in place of the traditional handicrafts." The Report envisages considerable expenditure on this reform of sheltered workshops of which a large proportion is expected to be provided by the Ministry of Labour, but also lays it down that workshops should only employ those blind persons who, while they cannot be placed in ordinary employment, are capable of doing work of substantial economic value. The implementation of this Report will go a long way to attaining the aims of the Central Government following the passing of the Disabled Persons (Employment) Act, 1944, that the Ministry of Labour should assume responsibility for all aspects of the rehabilitation, employment and placing of the adult blind.

This short survey of welfare of the blind beginning with the days of Edward III and including the days when George III was on the throne and Sir John Fielding, the blind magistrate and half-brother of the famous novelist, quelled the riot of "Wilkites" in Palace Yard, to these days when the promotion of welfare for the blind is admittedly the duty of local authorities and of the Central Government, has, I hope, given full credit to the splendid work in this field by the voluntary societies over some hundreds of years. There is still a large field of service in which their money and enthusiasm can be used, particularly in the realms of "social" as opposed to "welfare" work. The "comfort" and "company" which so many of the aged blind require could well be provided by voluntary workers, and the author has a personal view that if the voluntary societies concerned with the welfare of the blind would follow the example of the more enlightened ones and devote their considerable assets to research into the prevention of blindness, there might be possible an era in which, but for wars, accidents and acts of God, the handicap of blindness would disappear. In the meantime it should be remembered that we who have our sight should never treat the blind as though they were abnormal specimens of humanity, never talk to a blind man as though he were deaf or imagine that the mere possession of sight implies superior knowledge. Sound and touch are a blind man's "sight", and except for this he is just the same as you or me.

31. Social Welfare for the Blind

M. A. HENHAM-BARROW

Secretary, Southern Regional Association for the Blind

Organization of Services for Blind and Partially Sighted Persons

The social services of this country for blind people are, quite rightly, acknowledged as being the best in the world. Plans throughout the years have been so well laid and integrated that the ramifications of welfare for the blind are vast. In practice, however, these follow a simple triple alliance with the obligation to provide services being shared between the State-local government and voluntary enterprise, with local statutory and voluntary bodies working together in co-operation, and their activities knitted together by Regional Associations who, in turn, are responsible to the Minister of Health.

From the earliest times blindness has been recognized as not only a medical but a social problem, and during the last two centuries this recognition has increased further. For well over 200 years we have been fortunate in having outstanding people both blind and sighted with a deep understanding of the problems concerning a person unable to see, and on the basis of this great voluntary and pioneer work legislation has resulted, for the State has increasingly interested itself in the lives of the blind population, and the "triple alliance" was created by legislation of 1920–48. This plan works very satisfactorily, although arrangements for working it vary from county to county, for while it is the statutory obligation of local authorities to provide services, it has always been part of the essence of the system that there are no exact boundary lines between the spheres of official and private energies. In some areas the local authority deals directly with the services through its Welfare or Public Health Departments; in other areas, the local authority has entered into an agency agreement with the local voluntary association and leaves the work entirely to them by payment of grant; in other areas, again, the local authority deals directly only with certain aspects of the services and leaves varying responsibilities such as the running of homes, arrangements for holidays, etc., to voluntary associations. The position generally is, therefore, that local authorities can, and do, provide services to the limit of their scope, supplemented by voluntary enterprise.

In discharging the duty placed upon them by government enactments to make available services for the blind, every county council, county borough

262

council and local authority with delegated powers provide for education, training and employment, and finally, homes and welfare services for the aged, and a blind person registered with a local authority is secure in the knowledge that he can look to this authority to arrange for whatever services he requires, whether national or local. All this stems from the Blind Persons Act of 1920, which made it a statutory obligation for the community to look after its blind members, and which position was reaffirmed by the National Assistance Act, 1948, and the comprehensive organization of welfare for the blind can best be shown in the chart printed on pp. 264–5. This was first published in 1949 by the Southern Regional Association for the Blind and enumerates the various Government Departments responsible for services to blind welfare, indicating how local authorities, voluntary associations, regional and national bodies form the intricate pattern of services.

Certification for Registration

Before a person can be admitted to the local register, evidence of blindness has to be produced, and to obtain this evidence local authorities arrange for examination by an ophthalmologist (Ministry of Health Circular 4/55 2 March 1955), who completes a uniform and confidential form approved and supplied by the Ministry of Health which is known as Form B.D. 8 and which is the standard form used for this purpose throughout the country. If the ophthalmologist can say that the person "is so blind as to be unable to perform any work for which eyesight is essential" (the official definition of blindness, see M.O.H. Circular 4/55), the person can be admitted to the register of the blind and included in the local authorities' schemes of welfare for the blind under Section 29 of the National Assistance Act, 1948. If, however, the ophthalmologist can only say that the person is not at present in that category but:

(a) "is substantially and permanently handicapped by congenitally defective vision", or
(b) "suffers from defective vision of a substantial and permanently handicapping nature caused by illness or injury",

the person is placed on the register held by local authorities for partially sighted persons which services will be described later in this article.

Collation of Forms B.D. 8

All certificates of blindness and partial sight (Form B.D. 8) completed in this country are sent by the responsible local authorities to its Regional Association for submission to Professor Arnold Sorsby, M.D., F.R.C.S., of the

T.I.S.W.—T

CHART OF ORGANIZATION OF BLIND WELFARE

(Published by the Southern Regional Association for the Blind)

1. Government Departments

Ministry of Health (Hospital, Specialist and Health Services, Welfare Services, Provision of Accommodation).

Department of Education and Scie⟨ (Education and Training).
1. Inspectorate.

1. Advisory Committee on the Health and Welfare of Handicapped Persons.
2. Inspectorate.
3. Regional system of devolution includes inspection and advice under National Assistance Act.

2. Local Authorities

and

Local Authorities are responsible for certification and registration of all blind persons; welfare services; provision of necessary accommodation; registration of Homes and Charities for disabled persons.

L.A. Education Committees are ⟨ sponsible for the education of chi⟨ and training of adolescents (w⟨ general education is also provided⟨

3. Voluntary Associations

Local Voluntary Associations may have statutory duties, in whole or part, delegated to them by Local Authories which include:
1. Registration;
2. Provision of H.T. Services;
3. Clubs and Social Centres.
4. Local and other Voluntary Societies may provide services and amenities additional to those given by the Local Authority.
OR
5. May receive financial contributions towards cost of providing Homes and maintaining residents in them.

1. Sunshine Homes (R.N.I.B.)
2. Special Schools and Training Ce⟨ for the Blind provided by L.A.s ⟨ V.A.s as part of a Blind Instituti⟨ as a separate establishment (an⟨ R.N.I.B.).

4. National and Co-ordinating Agencies

* Regional Associations (advisory and consultative bodies co-ordinating work of L.A.s and V.A.s).

Inter-Regional Committee confers upon regional matters in order to achieve uniformity throughout the country.

National Voluntary Agencies

1. Royal National Institute for the Blind.†
2. National Library for the Blind.
3. Royal Normal College (Academy of Music and training school for shorthand/typing.)
4. Jewish Blind Society (serves the Jewish Blind).

Special Agencies for the Blind

1. Guide Dogs for the Blind Association.
2. St. John's Guild (Church of England Society).
3. National Deaf-Blind Helpers League.
4. British Wireless for the Blind Fund.
5. Greater London Fund and United Appeal for the Blind. (Money-raising societies.)

Professional Bodies

1. College of Teachers (Exam⟨ Board for Home Teachers ⟨ Blind; Teachers of the Blind; Instructors of the Blind).
2. National Association of ⟨ Teachers.
3. National Association of ⟨ shops for the Blind.
4. Association of Blind Cha⟨ Physiotherapists.

istry of Labour (Train-
and Employment).

at. Advisory Council on
Employment of the Dis-
d (B.P. Committee).
ocal Disablement Ad-
ry Committees.
.R.O.s and B.P.R.O.s
al Labour Exchanges).
egister of Disabled Per-
at Local Labour Ex-
ges.
ehabilitation Centres.
employ Ltd. (employ-
t factories).

ning and employment
agements for adults.
rvision of L.A. Shelter-
mployment schemes, ap-
ed blind training and
loyment establishments.

ind Instns. Training
workshop establish-
s—municipal or volun-

ome Workers schemes
y voluntary agencies or
authorities.
acement in Sighted In-
y in conjunction with
s or agency, or special
ment officers (and see
I.B.).
ehabilitation Centres
I.B.).

Ministry of Pensions and
National Insurance (Insurance Benefits and Pensions).

1. National Insurance Ad-
vistory Committee.
2. Industrial Injuries Advisory Council.
3. Office of National Insurance Commissioner.
4. Pensions for ex-service
men and women and war
widows.
A. Welfare Service.
B. Local Appeal Tribunal.
C. Pensions Appeals Tri-
bunal.

Direct contact with individual registered blind persons.

1. Voluntary Pension Societies for the Blind (offer
additional assistance in the
form of pensions and grants
to blind persons).
2. St. Dunstan's undertake
all duties in respect of blind
ex-service men and women,
except provision (through
local authorities) of wireless
licences.

National Assistance Board
(Finance: Blind Old Age
Pensions: Supplementary
Financial Assistance).

1. Local Advisory Com-
mittees.
2. Local Appeal Tribunals.

Direct contact with in-
dividual registered blind person.

General Post
Office.
1. Wireless and
television
licences.
2. Special postage
rates for em-
bossed literature.

---

nizations for Blind Persons
nal League of the Blind.
nal Federation of the Blind.

NOTES

* Maintain Central Register of Blind Persons.
Training Courses for Home Teachers. Refresher
Courses. Conferences. Research into Certification
of Blindness. Collation of Data supplied by
agencies.
 † Provides **inter alia**: Publication of books and
music in embossed types, apparatus for the blind,
Sunshine Homes, higher education schools,
homes for the blind, placement services, professional training.

ABBREVIATIONS

R.N.I.B.—Royal National Institute for the Blind.
L.A.—Local Authority.
V.A.—Voluntary Association or Society.

Ophthalmological Research Department of the Royal College of Surgeons
and Royal Eye Hospital, for scrutiny into causes and prevention of blindness. Valuable statistical evidence is provided, therefore, and the analysis of
the information contained in the forms of examination provides data un-
paralleled in its comprehensiveness, collated on a uniform basis over a
period of years. Since registration, whether of the blind or partially sighted,
can be obtained only on confirmation by a recognized ophthalmologist, the
available data allows for a full and accurate analysis of the causation of
blindness and emphasizes the fact that the increase shown since 1948 in the
number of people registered does not necessarily represent an increase in
the incidence of blindness but focuses attention on the age groups.

Statistics and Registration Local and Central Registers for Blind and Partially Sighted Persons

The first necessity for administering the 1920 Blind Persons Act was to
have a register of the blind in each area, with a central register to check overlapping and to safeguard the interests of odd cases likely to fall between two
stools. The growing interest of the State had, in fact, recommended the
compilation of a central register as early as 1918, when it was realized that
in order to obtain some idea of the size and scope of the problems it was
hoped to solve by legislation, such a central register was essential. With the
passing of the 1920 Act, however, when the local authorities became responsible among other things for the keeping of registers of blind persons
resident in their areas, the State ceased to keep this central register and it has
been the duty of the Regional Associations for the Blind to keep these, as
agents for the Ministry, ever since. (Particulars of functions and scope of
Regional Associations follow.)

Today, under the National Assistance Act, 1948, local authorities are still
obliged to keep a register of all blind and partially sighted persons within
their boundaries, and the maintenance of a live register remains the foundation of welfare services, giving, as it does, the need for extension or reduction
of present and potential provisions. By maintaining a central register at
regional level, special trends and requirements can be pin-pointed, and it is
possible to watch the rise or fall in age groups, and by relating these to the
new cases registered each year to form some conclusions as to the changes
and whether they are due to such things as better ascertainment or to increases in blindness, or reflect an improvement in services. It is also possible
to anticipate what further provision might be necessary to meet nationally a
service which locally would be uneconomic, because of the small numbers
involved.

The Minister of Health publishes, annually, statistics for the blind covering
England and Wales. These the Ministry gains from three regional register

in England and an independent return from Wales. The regional registers are prepared from information collected from local authorities by means of monthly and annual returns. The detail in which the regional registers are kept provides an overall picture in age groups of services to be supplied for the entire blind population, covering the pre-school child, education, training, employment, special provision for the blind with additional handicaps, residential accommodation, services for the aged and manpower within the field of social work.

There are nearly 100,000 persons registered as blind in England and Wales, and about 70 per cent of new registrations at the present time are over the age of 70 years, with the 80–90 age group being pretty considerable. It does not follow that everyone on the blind register is without sight. They possess varying degrees of vision from complete lack of sight to possession of certain visual acuity coming within the definition of blindness for registration purposes. The statutory definition for the purposes of registration as a blind person under the National Assistance Act, 1948, is that the person is—and here I quote—"so blind as to be unable to perform any work for which eyesight is essential", and a very important point here is not whether the person is unable to pursue his ordinary occupation or any particular occupation, but whether he is too blind to perform *any* work for which eyesight is essential.

The Function and Government of Regional Associations

There are three Regional Associations in England and these are:

The North Regional Association for the Blind.
The Southern Regional Association for the Blind.
The Western Regional Association for the Blind.

Similar functions are carried out in Wales by the Wales and Monmouthshire Regional Council. In Scotland the Scottish National Federation for the Welfare of the Blind is occupied in very much the same way but has different terms of constitution and membership.

Each Regional Association is an autonomous body and is governed by representatives from every county council, county borough council and voluntary association within the area covered by the regional boundary. The Associations have similar functions but vary in their *modus operandi*, and for the purpose of this article the work of the Southern Region is used as an example. This Association covers an area of 28 counties, containing 67 local authorities and 74 voluntary agencies and is governed by a General Council which is mainly composed of elected representatives of local authorities, on the one hand, and of voluntary associations, on the other. From the General

Council, an Executive Committee is formed, which in turn is broken down to other committees who meet on matters of education, finance, general purposes, the needs of the deaf–blind and any other *ad hoc* committee needing to be formed. The Regional Associations are registered as charities under the National Assistance Act and operate as voluntary associations. They are, however, unique in that they are non-fund-raising bodies, and work to an assured income divided evenly between an Exchequer grant and grants on a blind population basis from local authorities within the area covered by the region. The Exchequer grant is paid in respect of services including the maintenance of the central registers; certain advisory services and the publication, by local authority areas, of statistical information about blind and partially sighted persons. The local authorities' grants are paid under the National Assistance Act, 1948, in return for advisory, consultative and practical services dealt with in more detail in the following paragraphs. Certain income is also derived from the voluntary societies within the region who are affiliated to the Association and pay a nominal affiliation fee.

The Regional Associations have as their objects and activities the promotion of the welfare of blind and partially sighted persons, the furthering of prevention of blindness, and one of their chief duties is to maintain contact with and facilitate co-ordination between the local authorities and voluntary associations in the region. The regional body provides a focal point in its area for the whole of blind welfare services and an important function is to arrange conferences to promote discussion between statutory and voluntary bodies, thus providing a "neutral" platform for discussion and information on subjects both of a general nature and specific subjects or branches of the work. The publication of such conference reports contributes considerably to circulation of informed opinion.

The way in which the Regional Associations can best offer help to the local authorities and voluntary associations they serve, must of necessity shift in emphasis in the light of current national requirements. At the time of the 1920 Act—when they were known as Counties Associations—they naturally guided their constituent voluntary societies in the new statutory obligations coming into effect. The same applied in the 1940's at the time of the Beveridge Report and emergence in 1948 of the Welfare State. Their advisory and consultative services in helping to interpret with local authorities the new enactments prevailing were then in constant demand. The advisory and consultative service continues to be widely used in all its aspects, and to meet the demands of the mental climate now prevailing for training in social work, *ad hoc* training and refresher courses have been developed which are designed to give administrators, field welfare officers, and senior social workers concerned with welfare services for the blind some insight into the special problems of blindness. This has enhanced the contribution to welfare for the blind by workers with different levels of training, while improving, at the same time, staff relationships.

These *ad hoc* courses, designed to meet the need of present trends, are additional to those organized regularly each year and which have developed to help local authorities and voluntary associations with the staffing of their welfare services. The training and recruitment of home teachers of the blind has always occupied an important place in regional work, and here it is perhaps helpful to describe the home-teaching service which is the link between the blind person and statutory benefits. Home teachers are employed by all county councils and county borough councils under their welfare schemes, and are teachers of the skills needed by blind persons to enable them to function in a seeing world. They are personal and professional counsellors needed to give information and assistance in developing attitudes to cope with the seeing world. They help the community to understand the handicap of blindness, and how to accept blind people as responsible contributing citizens. The home-teaching service has, therefore, three main functions—teaching, social rehabilitation and public relations.

The training and refresher courses extensively used annually by the constituent bodies of the Southern Region are:

Non-residential Courses:
One-year training course for the certificate of home teaching.
Two-day courses on the nature and prevention of blindness. This is open to all working in the field of welfare for the blind and education. Includes clinical demonstrations, and lectures by ophthalmic surgeons upon the structure and functions of the eye; the prevention and main causes of blindness.

Residential refresher courses of up to one week for:
Qualified home teachers of the blind;
Supervisors of home teachers;
Matrons and wardens of homes for the blind*
Junior staff of homes*
Deaf–blind and social rehabilitation.

* Open also to staff of homes for sighted people in which some blind people are accommodated.

The Inter-Regional Committee of the Regional Associations for the Blind

The Regional Associations have formed an Inter-Regional Committee in order to meet together for discussion on matters of national importance and for co-ordination of policy. The Committee, in itself, has no executive functions, and recommendations made are referred back to its constituent organizations. The Committee, which meets regularly, was formed in 1942 by the Regional Associations and Regional Council in Wales and were joined by Scotland early in 1947. The Committee is made up of three representatives from each of the following organizations:

> The North Regional Association.
> The Scottish National Federation.
> The Southern Regional Association.
> The Wales and Monmouthshire Regional Council.
> The Western Regional Association.

Ophthalmic Referee Service

Written into the schemes for welfare for the blind adopted by county councils and county borough councils under Section 29 of the National Assistance Act is the security of using a special ophthalmic referee service in the event of dispute in certification. The Regional Associations are used in this way when an independent opinion is required in cases of certification or de-certification of blindness or partial sight being questioned. Each Regional Association has a panel of consultant ophthalmic surgeons and, upon an appeal being received from a registering authority, the Association arranges an independent consultation and pays the fee incurred. This service confers considerable benefit on the constituent bodies of the Regional Association and the blind in its area.

Welfare Provisions for Partially Sighted Persons

There is no statutory definition of partial sight, but the Ministry of Health has advised that a person who is not blind within the meaning of the Act but who suffers from defective vision as quoted in and (a) and (b) on p. 263, is within the scope of the welfare services which the local authority is empowered to provide for blind persons, although this does not apply to other benefits specially enjoyed by the blind, e.g. additional assistance grant and the blind pension at 40 where applicable.

Certain criteria has been provided by the Ministry as a general guide when ophthalmologists are determining whether a person falls within the scope of the welfare provision for the partially sighted as well as in recommending the appropriate type of school if a child under 16. (Ministry of Health Circular No. 4/55 quotes visual acuity recommended for registration purposes.)

In looking at the historical background of services for the partially sighted it is well to remember that before the National Assistance Act, 1948, there were no statutory powers under which general welfare services could be provided for any group of handicapped people other than blind. The

Blind Persons Act, 1920, did not provide for the partially sighted, and the only provisions which could be in any way applied were public health measures relating to the prevention of blindness. Voluntary organizations for the blind, however, kept observation registers of people threatened with blindness, mainly so as to ensure that people likely to go blind received treatment whenever possible and that their eyesight did not hopelessly deteriorate for lack of someone to help and advise them as to what they should do.

The National Assistance Act, 1948, made a statutory link between blind and partially sighted welfare services and, in 1948, when welfare services generally were being set up, it was thought that home teachers of the blind were the most appropriate people in the social work field to look after them because of the knowledge home teachers had of certification, registration and services available for the blind, and what it meant to be threatened with deteriorating sight. Subsequent experience and development of welfare services for handicapped people generally since 1948 has led to a reappraisal by the Advisory Committee of the Ministry of Health of the position of the partially sighted, and much thought as to the psychological effect of close association with blindness upon those partially sighted people who are never likely to go blind.

These considerations, together with services now available for the partially sighted under the Education Act of 1944 and the Disabled Persons (Employment) Acts, 1944 and 1958, combined with the view of the Younghusband Working Party that a home teacher of the blind will on occasions "not be acceptable to someone clinging to the hope of improvement of restoration of sight" and that "efforts should be made to build up the services for the partially sighted", led to the issue of Ministry of Health Circular No. 4/63 (15 March 1963). This circular makes suggestions for giving effect to certain recommendations and amendment of schemes for promoting the welfare of partially sighted persons, and this step in 1963 can be regarded as important for the partially sighted as the Blind Persons Act of 1920 was for the blind. This circular under the National Assistance Act, 1948, could mark the beginning of a much-needed expansion of statutory services for people handicapped by partial sight.

Welfare Provisions for the Double Handicap of Blindness and Deafness

The problems of deaf–blind people differ from those of the seeing deaf and the hearing blind, for the sense of touch is the only link that a deaf–blind person has with the outside world. Their problems of communication are different from the seeing deaf, for they cannot see to read the visual sign language used by the deaf neither can they hear, as can the blind, and receive aural stimulus through speech. As a result of this, they tend to get much more cut adrift from their environment.

Every county council and county borough council in the country include in their welfare schemes provisions for the care of the deaf–blind. Blindness is regarded as the primary handicap for registration purposes, thus making available the whole range of services and statutory benefits that registration brings, including the home-teaching service. Despite this provision under the National Assistance Act, 1948, services for the deaf–blind are not as full as could be desired.

In 1951 the Minister of Health's Advisory Council for the Welfare of Handicapped Persons issued a report on the special welfare needs of deaf–blind people. This report included among its suggestions that the Regional Associations should further develop special courses already established, which were designed to give home teachers an understanding of these special needs. This has been done over the past ten years, and in the Southern Region (with a total blind population of 53,000 of which 1300 are deaf–blind and 2700 hard of hearing blind) these have taken the form of residential courses of one week at which trainee home teachers and qualified home teachers live side by side with the deaf–blind for whom the local authorities pay to attend these courses. In this week of social rehabilitation it has been shown that communication is the greatest need, and that a major problem is constantly revealed as being one of acute loneliness, calling for each deaf–blind person at all levels of social development to have someone upon whom they can count for mental stimulus through communication.

It is a vital necessity that they establish means of communication with the outside world, in order to escape from the isolation engendered by their double handicap, and there are two standard and very easy methods of talking to a totally deaf–blind person. One is the simple method of tracing block capital letters on the palm of the hand of a deaf–blind person, and the other is an adapted tactile form of the well-known manual alphabet for the seeing deaf.

Most deaf–blind people can reply through speech, but in the absence of sight and hearing the sense of touch plays a paramount part in "receiving" the alphabet. It is as important, too, for the deaf–blind person to be encouraged to reply through speech in order to conserve this faculty, otherwise speech deteriorates and the person rapidly becomes a person with a triple handicap. Copies of specially printed leaflets giving these two manual alphabets can be obtained from the Southern Regional Association for the Blind.

Some of the larger of the local authorities—where the number on their registers warrant it—employ full-time specialist home teachers for the deaf–blind and also run special holidays, over and above the usual holidays for the blind. Others, where numbers do not warrant it, use the regional social rehabilitation courses for holidays for individual deaf–blind, and the Regions adapt their courses accordingly. As the deaf–blind become more and more prepared to participate in local social activities as a result of their attendance at the courses and local deaf–blind socials and classes which are being organized in increasing numbers (many by the deaf–blind themselves), so they are participating in the holidays arranged at local authority level for the blind.

Special homes are organized nationally, and a national organization for the deaf–blind, run by the deaf–blind themselves, has existed since 1928. A local authority in the West Country has been running a Guide Help Service for the deaf–blind as a result of the Western Regional refresher courses, and there is evidence that the success of this is prompting local authorities in other areas to do the same.

Altogether there is an upsurge of interest and an accumulation of benefit resulting. The problem, however, is far from solved, and although the numbers are small numerically, they are great in human unhappiness.

Conclusion

A fact with which a newly blinded person will always be confronted is that despite adjustment to his handicap, he will continue to live in a world in which blindness is regarded with considerable emotion and sentiment.

From the foregoing article, however, it can be seen that trends in social welfare for people who cannot see have moved steadily forward over the past hundred years towards concerted efforts on the part of central and local government and voluntary societies to relieve the problems of blind people and help them to become—as they are today—useful citizens accepted without curiosity into the everyday world. Well-organized services exist through the "triple alliance" referred to, which can be swung into motion and bring help in any problem affecting any age group of the blind community.

32. The Royal National Institute for the Blind

J. C. COLLIGAN

Director-General, Royal National Institute for the Blind

THE SERVICES of the Royal National Institute for the Blind, which is by far the largest single voluntary organization for the blind in the world, are many and varied. Briefly, they consist of the provision of national services to the 110,000 blind of the United Kingdom in the sense of the performance of those things which cannot best be done by some other purely local voluntary organization or statutory authority. In this way it fits smoothly into the pattern of the highly integrated partnership in welfare for the blind which is singular in this country.

The organization was founded in 1868 by Dr. Thomas Rhodes Armitage with the primary object of finding a universally acceptable system of embossed reading for the blind. In those early days it was known as the British and Foreign Blind Association, but the scope of its work grew so enormously over the years and included so many other activities besides the publication of embossed literature that in 1953 it was awarded a Royal Charter and became known by its present title.

The Institute is governed by a Council of whose members about a quarter themselves are blind. This Council represents every aspect of welfare for the blind—local and national interests, blind and sighted voluntary workers and official agencies. It relies for its financial support upon the charitable public and seeks to eliminate overlapping and competitive appeals by unifying its collections with those of local agencies and assisting local societies and institutions engaging in progressive work for the blind in their own areas. The blind themselves play a considerable part in the administration, organization and routine work of the R.N.I.B., and its work owes much to their intelligence, first-hand knowledge, ability to enlist help, technical knowledge and manual dexterity.

The production of embossed literature in Braille and Moon type has continued to be the largest single factor in the emancipation of the blind, and the Institute has for long been the largest publishing house for the blind in the British Commonwealth, producing books covering every field of literature educational textbooks, music, newspapers, magazines and periodicals. Its total output, amounting to some 640,000 volumes annually, includes Braille editions of the *Radio Times*, *National News Letter*, *World Digest*, and a

Braille News Summary designed for those 3000 people in this country who are known to be deaf as well as blind.

Another leading activity is a Talking Book Library run by the R.N.I.B. in co-operation with St. Dunstan's. Originally based on recording on gramophone-type discs it now increasingly comprises tape reproducers using multi-track tape recordings involving the use of eighteen separate sound tracks on a half-inch tape, giving in all a maximum playing time of twenty-two hours for each tape cassette (Plate 16). These "books" are recorded in the Institute's own recording studios by first-class professional readers; selection of titles is based on a careful analysis of the literary tastes of library members, and availability is at present some 1000 books with an average of some 200 new titles added each year. Membership of the library, which is on a single inclusive "rental" of £3 per annum, is now over 14,000 and expanding rapidly, with two libraries in operation, one serving the needs of the south and the other the northern half of the country.

In addition, there are in existence Students' Libraries in Braille and Talking Books where special works are hand-transcribed or individually recorded to meet the needs of blind students.

The development and supply of apparatus and appliances for all kind of domestic use and for means of livelihood, including Braille writing machines and appliances, a variety of adapted games, mathematical boards and instruments, embossed maps and globes, rules and measures, micrometers and gauges for engineers (Plate 17), clocks, watches, white sticks, domestic utensils, and a huge variety of miscellaneous articles: all these are undertaken by the Institute and supplied to the blind at heavily subsidized prices.

In the field of education the Institute is responsible for six Sunshine Home Nursery Schools for the care and training of blind babies and children, including one establishment for those who are deemed to be ineducable but trainable. It also maintains two schools, Condover Hall near Shrewsbury and Rushton Hall near Kettering, for children who have other handicaps additional to their blindness and who need education according to their interests and aptitudes rather than on conventional lines. At Condover there is also a unit for the education of deaf–dumb and blind children. At Worcester College for Blind Boys and Chorleywood College for Blind Girls the R.N.I.B. provides higher grammar-school education for children of intellectual promise, often in preparation for a university career. At these schools students enjoy all the amenities of public school life: the well-balanced curriculum, out-of-door sports in pleasant surroundings, the comradeship of club, guild and team, and a close relationship between teachers and pupils. A comparatively recent development has been the establishment near Reigate of a Vocational Assessment Centre for adolescents from other schools for the blind where young people may combine a choice of future work with a closer integration into sighted society.

Technical and professional training is provided at a Training College for blind shorthand-typists and telephonists and at a School of Physiotherapy (which is the only one for the blind in the Commonwealth).

Although blindness is increasingly becoming one of the attendant disabilities of old age, there are still some 1200 people annually who lose their sight during working life. It is principally, though not wholly, for them that the Institute maintains its Rehabilitation Centres at Torquay and Bridgnorth where courses of pre-vocational training (in conjunction with the Ministry of Labour) and social rehabilitation are provided. For those who are likely to be re-absorbed into commerce or industry, it is a logical step to the commercial or professional training centres or to the Letchworth Government Training Centre in light engineering.

The R.N.I.B. takes considerable pride in the part that it has played in ensuring that Britain has a higher percentage of its blind employed than any other country in the world, the majority in ordinary industrial or commercial occupations. The Institute's industrial placement service has placed at normal-sighted rates and conditions of work almost 6000 blind people. This service, which has been conducted entirely through the efforts of blind or near-blind placement officers, in the belief that the blind can best appreciate both their capabilities and limitations, has recently passed to the Ministry of Labour as a national employment service, leaving the voluntary organization still free to fulfil its proper function of pioneer and experimental work with particular emphasis on commerce and the professional field.

Residential accommodation for the blind is normally regarded as a local rather than a national service, but nevertheless the R.N.I.B. is involved in the provision of certain homes of a special character for holidays, convalescence, geriatrics, and for those who are deaf–blind. In addition to nine homes of this character it provides three residential hostels for blind persons in training or employment.

In addition to the foregoing the Institute concerns itself with research into every aspect of blindness—educational, occupational and technical. It watches over legislation which may affect the lives of the blind. It maintains contact with organizations for the blind in all parts of the world both through the World Council for the Welfare of the Blind and the Royal Commonwealth Society for the Blind. It administers several societies of great importance to the blind, e.g. the Guild of Blind Gardeners, the British Wireless for the Blind Fund, the Sir Beachcroft Towse Ex-Service Fund, and several important pension funds and charitable trusts.

It is perhaps in respect of prevention of blindness that it has made the most important advances in recent years. In 1962 its Prevention of Blindness Committee, which for a number of years had been assisting smaller research projects in this field, set up under the Institute's trusteeship a British Foundation for Research into Prevention of Blindness, which has already established two important research units—one at the Royal Eye Hospital to investigate the genetic causes of blindness amongst children (particularly those with additional handicaps) and the other at the Royal College of Surgeons for active investigation of the problems of clinical tissue preservation and biological research into eye transplantation. With the assistance of a most distinguished scientific advisory panel it is already assessing a number of further important research projects which it will sponsor as funds become available.

The foregoing briefly summarizes the way in which the Royal National Institute for the Blind, working with the blind and for the blind, seeks to help them to help themselves.

PLATE 18. Steps before adaptation

PLATE 19. Steps after adaptation and ramped access after improvement

PLATE 20. Aerial view of Stoke Mandeville Hospital

PLATE 21. The Fearnley Cup awarded in 1956 to The Stoke
Mandeville Games for the Paralysed

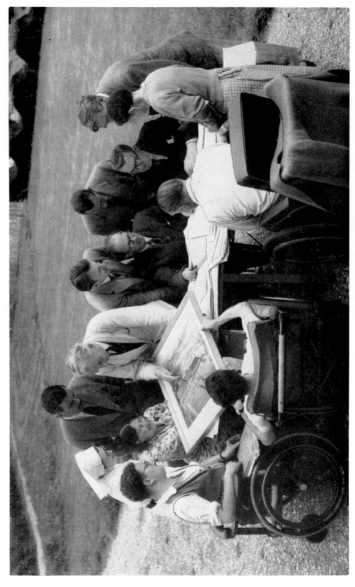

PLATE 32. Residents at Le Court, the first Cheshire Home, collaborating with an architect in the design of a new building

PLATE 33. A view of the workshop at Athol House, the Cheshire
Home in Dulwich

PLATE 34. The experimental kitchen at Athol House, the Cheshire
Home in Dulwich

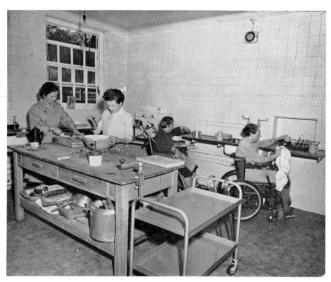

SECTION VII

SERVICES FOR OTHER HANDICAPPED PEOPLE INCLUDING THE DEAF

33. Services for the Physically Handicapped

J. T. GREGORY

Chief Welfare Officer, London Borough of Southwark

PROLONGED and nationwide discussion of the Beveridge Report during the Second World War produced in 1945 a climate more insistent on social reform than any other in our history, far more radical than that after the 1906 election, to which it bore some resemblance. Of the Acts passed in the immediate post-war period, which provided the foundations of the Welfare State, none expressed the determination of the time to achieve social security instead of relying as previously on the relief of destitution, more than the National Assistance Act, 1948. The prevailing mood was simply expressed in Section 1 of that Act when it stated that the "existing poor law shall cease to have effect". Thus ended a long process of disintegration that had been heralded in 1909 by the Minority Report of the Royal Commission on the Poor Law.

Few social services could have had a more promising beginning than those for the physically handicapped that this National Assistance Act introduced. Until then there had been no statutory authority responsible for providing services for physically handicapped people other than the blind, for whom comprehensive services had been steadily developed ever since the Blind Persons Act, 1920, made county and county borough councils responsible for preparing and submitting to the Minister of Health for approval schemes for welfare services for the blind. Procedurally the National Assistance Act followed the same pattern, though at first with less insistence. The Ministry of Health published a circular, concurrently with the Act, which interpreted the spirit of the post-war legislation thus:

> The guiding principle of the welfare service should be to ensure that all handicapped persons, whatever their disability, should have the maximum opportunity of sharing in and contributing to the life of the community, so that their capacities are realized to the full, their self-confidence developed, and their social contacts strengthened. The provision of skilled advice and help will in most instances be the pre-requisite to the achievement of this aim.

Schemes for the Handicapped

Though it was not at first mandatory on local welfare authorities to submit schemes for the Minister's approval, most local authorities had done so by

1960 when the Minister made it compulsory on the few laggard authorities to conform. However, preparing and submitting a scheme is one thing and applying it in a progressive spirit is another. Every scheme includes both mandatory and permissive clauses, the former involving less cost—the maintenance of registers, generally giving assistance, advice and guidance, arranging for voluntary workers to visit, trying to facilitate the admission of handicapped people to places of worship or entertainment and so on. The more practical services—the provision of aids, adaptations in the home, arrangements for sheltered homework, transport facilities, holiday schemes and hostels—remain permissive, and many of them are still not widely applied, some scarcely at all. Though the results throughout the country are undoubtedly uneven, a great deal has been learned and much progress made since the Act came into force.

Social Workers in Short Supply

Local welfare authorities—county and county borough councils—must employ welfare officers in order to carry out their welfare responsibilities in such numbers "as the Council may from time to time determine". This may mean little or it may mean a great deal. Certainly caseloads are much too heavy though the best welfare authorities are making conscious efforts to reduce the number of handicapped people a domiciliary visitor is expected to be responsible for; but the overall shortage makes it almost impossible at this stage for any authority to be adequately staffed. Though the arrangements resulting from the Younghusband Report are beginning to produce some social workers trained under the new national training scheme, it will be many years before there are sufficient numbers of social workers trained by this means to satisfy the expanding demand for their services. A welfare officer can provide personally only a fraction of the comprehensive services that are now beginning to be available, but he is an important channel of communication about the wider range of services, and if he is given too large a caseload and can visit handicapped people in his district only at infrequent intervals, he obviously cannot be available whenever his advice is needed or set in motion the kind of help required.

Team-work

In a fast expanding service, when staff are in short supply, it necessarily follows that standards of staff are uneven in quality. While most local authorities pay lip service to the need to recruit suitably qualified staff, in fact few authorities are able to attract them in sufficient numbers because there are not enough of them. A welfare officer with years of service in the field but unqualified is rarely able to undertake a two-year Younghusband course that the new arrangements demand, especially if he has family commitments. The four-year university extra-mural courses, with but little modification, could have contributed large numbers of welfare officers of good standard during the next twenty years while the programme of full-time social work-training is being built up, but these longer spare-time courses seem to have received little official encouragement. Another important factor must be faced. It is inescapable that many of the tasks with which a welfare visitor for the handicapped is faced have a practical content which university training does not equip them to provide. Nobody could reasonably expect a Younghusband course to include training in practical problems like designing aids, adapting homes, running social rehabilitation and work centres and teaching crafts. Technicians able to carry out these functions are of equal importance to handicapped people and should be allotted an equal place in the future services. There is a need to create a team approach to the problems of the disabled which, regrettably, is attracting too little attention.

Publicity

There was a very real fear when the Minister of Health approved the first schemes in 1952 that the welfare authorities responsible for the new services would be overwhelmed before they had had an opportunity to learn what was required of them. Publicity was not courted, therefore, but now that, after thirteen years of ascertaining the needs of the physically handicapped, local authorities are aware of what is required of them they could now well publicize what can be done to help. There are far too many disabled people who remain unaware of the services that are available for them.

Work in Open and Sheltered Industry

Most handicapped people want to make their own contribution to society, and the most obvious way of responding to this desire for independence is by giving them an opportunity to work. Since the Disabled Persons (Employment) Act, 1944, came into force, the Ministry of Labour has been excellently equipped organizationally to encourage the seriously disabled to seek work and employers to give them a chance to find it. One of the weaknesses of the requirement that firms employing more than twenty workers have to employ a quota of disabled persons from the Ministry's register is that while those with minimal handicaps are freely offered jobs, there is difficulty in placing the seriously handicapped. The whole range of services provided by the Ministry of Labour under the 1944 Act was conceived in a generous mould. Sheltered workshops for the employment of disabled persons under protected conditions are administered by both statutory and voluntary bodies which receive financial assistance from the Government in many ways—by capital grants towards the cost of the initial project or subsequent improvements, training allowances (according to family circumstances) for the trainees and training fees for the establishment responsible for training, usually the workshop concerned, which also qualifies for deficiency grant of 80 per cent of the net annual loss per head with a maximum of £265 (which is under review). Voluntary organizations often receive from the local welfare authorities further deficiency grants equivalent to the net loss not covered by the government grant in respect of workers for whom the local authority has accepted financial responsibility. Only one condition has to be met—the worker has to be approved by the Ministry and the local authority as capable of making a significant industrial contribution; this is difficult to express in practical terms, but a minimum earning capacity of about one-third of that of an able-bodied worker may be taken as a rough guide. Resulting from a re-commendation of the Piercy Committee (Cmnd. 9883, November 1956) statutory responsibility for sheltered employment for the disabled was transferred from the Ministry of Health to the Ministry of Labour under the Disabled Persons (Employment) Act, 1958.

Nowadays, starting a sheltered workshop demands from the management considerable financial resources and from the disabled workers the ability to work a full week for a full week's wages. Not all seriously handicapped people are capable of this degree of effort, but those who are not should not be deprived of an opportunity of making a somewhat less extensive effort, so alternative arrangements have to be devised for them. Homework schemes have not been organized by local authorities on the scale of those introduced in the past for the blind, and it is preferable, if at all possible, for the seriously disabled to be conveyed from their homes by some means or another so that they can meet other people as badly off as themselves but in a constructive atmosphere; they benefit enormously from such social contacts. In some localities groups of badly handicapped people are organized for carrying out outwork for local industry and it is usually the welfare authority's task to organize this. Work centres are developing after the fashion of the more well-known workshops for the elderly, payment on a piecework basis being made to the workers by the firms, through the local authority, as a rule on a co-operative basis. Competition for this kind of industrial outwork is intensifying continuously as the work is eagerly sought by work centres for the physically handicapped, workshops for the elderly, training centres for the mentally handicapped and by mental hospitals for their patients. There is an urgent need for these ventures to be sponsored by leading firms and trade unions in each locality and encouraged on a national basis by employers' and trade union organizations. There must always be an insistence on a fair price for the piecework but, nevertheless, it is quite impossible for a week's wages to be earned by the disabled workers employed, and the main emphasis should always be on the social benefit to be derived from what is, after all, diversionary occupation and not normal employment.

Fortunately social insurance regulations, though untidy, fit in well with these arrangements. For those on national assistance, 30s. a week can be earned without loss of benefit while half the next 20s. earned can also be retained. Provided a doctor will testify that the work is medically beneficial, a disabled person on sickness benefit can earn up to 40s. a week, but there is stricter control over the maximum additional earnings permitted to those few recipients of national assistance who are subject to an earnings rule and are obliged to register at the employment exchange, the limit then being only 15s. a week. There is no limit for a person in receipt of a retirement pension, but a disabled person receiving unemployment pay may not receive more than 6s. 8d. per day and in certain circumstances, according to a recent ruling, payment of unemployment pay may be disallowed.

Handicrafts for the Most Seriously Disabled

Many are so seriously disabled that this kind of occupation is out of the question and for them the objective must be less ambitious—an enjoyable means of passing the time. But for some even here there are chances to supplement social insurance benefits by taking advantage of the handicrafts tuition that is available and becoming so skilled that either by their own efforts or with the help of the sales organization often run by the welfare authority (from which materials can usually be purchased cheaply) they will be able to dispose of their products and make a modest profit.

Powered Invalid Carriages

Whether it is for a full week's work in a sheltered factory or for two of three hours a week diversionary occupation in a social centre, the seriously disabled have to have means of travelling between their home and places or work. The best way of providing transport for the disabled is on an individual basis, and this is done by the Ministry of Health by the issue on free loan of powered invalid carriages through its local appliance officers. These vehicles are usually restricted owing to short supply to those who are employable but unable to get to work by public transport or by other means. Normally the invalid carriages are petrol-driven, an allowance for petrol being given by the Ministry, but electrically driven vehicles are available on special medical grounds (e.g. for some arthritics) which are determined by the hospital, whose recommendation as to eligibility and the most suitable type of vehicle is essential before application for any kind of invalid carriage can be considered.

Transport to Clubs and Classes

For those ineligible for the issue of an invalid carriage or too disabled to be able to drive one, some local welfare authorities provide specially designed coaches with a tail-lift by which it is possible to transfer a chair-bound person from pavement level into the coach. Those who have access to such a service have found their horizons broadened beyond their wildest hopes—instead of being virtually a house prisoner for seemingly endless years it suddenly becomes possible to attend clubs, places of worship, evening classes, cinemas and theatres (where special provision is made by some managements for the accommodation of chair-bound persons) and to go on outings and holidays by the sea. Although these special coaches are expensive to provide initially and to run, large numbers of them are required in order to make a serious contribution to the well-being of the handicapped, but hitherto few only have been commissioned. In urban areas it takes as long as two hours to collect and convey to a club twelve passengers, and much ingenuity is needed in the preparation of the coach-journey schedules to ensure that the vehicles are used to the maximum to do the valuable work for which they have been provided. They are sometimes made available by local authorities to voluntary organizations which cater for the needs of the handicapped, and so contribute towards the success of the clubs and other activities organized by those bodies.

Social and Rehabilitation Centres

Where the welfare authority runs social or day centres for the handicapped, the main function of the coaches is to convey disabled persons to and from them. The purposes of the centres are manifold; often rehabilitation courses are arranged at which the disabled can be taught to cope with their difficulties in daily living. To call them rehabilitation courses is perhaps misleading as it suggests that a time will come when further rehabilitation will be unnecessary, but the welfare authority is a residual authority and it cannot expect a time limit to be set to an individual's need for its services. As the activities at the centres are not very dissimilar from those practised in the occupational therapy department of hospitals, it is possible for handicapped patients at hospitals who have reached the end of their useful medical treatment to be transferred to the day centres (where they exist) by arrangement with the hospital doctor who, if he is wise enough to see the value of this kind of co-operation, might well act as unpaid, unofficial consultant, assessing the condition of those applying for admission to the centre. So far as the hospital is concerned, this is merely enlightened self-interest, for it makes way for someone on the hospital waiting list to be given treatment in the hospital.

Aids to Daily Living

Every social rehabilitation centre should have a limited stock of the more commonly used aids so that those who attend can be shown how to use them if they are needed. Thousands of types of aids and gadgets have been devised during the last ten years and it is necessary to guard against issuing them as a routine when more simple and satisfactory alternatives can be found. Often this may mean learning new methods of tackling day-to-day tasks that used to be simple before disability made their achievement impossible; many difficulties can be resolved by a re-organization of working technique or by rearranging a kitchen or other workplace. Here, again, it is the duty of the welfare authority to advise what adaptations are possible in the home to help the handicapped person look after himself, and to assist financially whenever resources are inadequate; this includes helping to interest ex-service and other organizations in the problems of individuals for whom they may have some special responsibility and, where necessary, raising funds. In some areas exhibitions of aids have been organized by the British Red Cross Society which acts as agent for the distribution of the many excellent and inexpensive aids designed and produced in the Ministry of Labour Government Training Centres. The Sir Geoffrey Peto Travelling Exhibition of Aids is sent on tour during the summer months by the Central Council for the Disabled, and the City of Westminster has a permanent exhibition of aids at its excellent social and rehabilitation centre at Victoria where handicapped people and those concerned with their problems may inspect a collection of aids and try them out.

Providing a Home

Sometimes major adaptation of a home becomes necessary, particularly in the case of paraplegics who are taught at the Stoke Mandeville Spinal Injuries Unit, for example, to overcome their difficulties in a way that a few years ago would have been impossible. Though ready for discharge to their homes and to a job, they cannot leave hospital until the adaptations are carried out, and it is essential for hospital and welfare authorities to co-operate with one another to ensure that the work is completed at the right time. It would be wrong to gloss over the problems involved—obtaining the landlord's consent to the work, undertaking to reinstate the premises when vacated by the disabled person should the landlord desire it, obtaining plans from the architect and competitive estimates from builders, and endeavouring to raise funds to pay for the work from voluntary bodies and, of course, from the welfare authority itself. So it is not altogether easy to conform with a hospital timetable, and early joint planning is called for.

Holiday Schemes

Holiday schemes for the physically disabled are being developed rapidly. The London and Middlesex County Councils before they went out of existence each sent away more than 750 handicapped persons each year to privately run holiday homes on the east and south coasts, neither County Council having yet opened a holiday home of its own. There are problems met in running holiday homes that cannot easily be solved. Normally the maximum holiday period is from April to the end of September because, even with our uncertain climate, the summer months are preferred. But this time of the year coincides with an acute labour shortage in seaside resorts when high rates of pay have to be offered which may be passed on to the holiday-maker when holidays are organized commercially but with which a local authority cannot compete. Labour is plentiful during the winter months when holidays on the coast are not popular. Nevertheless, with an imaginatively designed and run holiday home, centrally heated to withstand the vagaries of our climate, enjoyable holidays could be provided at any time of the year. The Woodlarks Camp at Farnham has shown how much enjoyment seriously handicapped scouts and guides can derive from the kind of camping holiday that able-bodied youngsters enjoy, and the Winged Fellowship Holidays started by the W.V.S. at the City Parochial Charities' camp at Chigwell, Essex, have both demonstrated that there is plenty of excitement for the disabled outside the routine type of seaside holiday and that there are reserves of goodwill in every locality that can be tapped to help make a holiday a success.

The end-of-season use of holiday camps at St. Mary's Bay, Gorleston, and Squires Gate has also successfully demonstrated a type of holiday so much enjoyed by the handicapped, possibly just because it is the kind of holiday that able-bodied people enjoy. By now most local welfare authorities will underwrite a holiday of this kind to ensure that disabled people without the means of paying for a holiday can nevertheless benefit from one or another of the schemes. Each year pressure increases on the few holiday homes whose proprietors specialize in the holiday needs of the handicapped, and before long local authorities will have to consider providing suitable holiday accommodation and care themselves in order to meet the growing demand.

Co-operation between Voluntary and Statutory Bodies

Because of the complex of voluntary and statutory authorities concerned with helping the disabled face up to their problems, the rate of progress made will depend on the level of co-operation that can be developed. Luckily there are few fields in which the desire to promote mutual goodwill exists in greater strength than in this branch of the social services. Much depends on whether the right or wrong methods of seeking co-operation are employed. In the social resettlement conferences organized by many hospitals co-operation was raised to new levels, for social workers and administrators from outside the hospital found common ground with the hospital team. While a great deal of ground can be covered in this way and individual patients helped to plan their future, the most important value of these conferences is often not in the direct benefit gained by the small handful of special cases it is possible to discuss, but in the creation of a climate of goodwill around the hospital staff, social workers and organizations represented. This advantage persists for a long time, and much more can then be achieved by letter-writing and telephone communication.

All kinds of attempts have been made to weld the voluntary and statutory organizations in common action, some more successful than others. In Birmingham the voluntary organizations have always had the closest and friendliest relationship with the welfare authority; in London the L.C.C. took the initiative to establish a Consultative Committee representative of voluntary organizations and the local authority departments most concerned with the welfare of the handicapped—education, health, housing and welfare —but achievement has not matched the opportunity, largely because the voluntary bodies have been too timid to advance their ideas, but in some areas these attempts at co-ordination are entirely lacking. The Standing Conference of Voluntary Organizations—organized by the Central Council for the Disabled—gives to many voluntary agencies catering for the handicapped an opportunity twice a year to exchange points of view with one another and with representatives of government and local government departments. These conferences provide a useful launching-pad for new ideas and the chance to re-examine old ones. The Ministry of Health sought in 1962 to encourage more voluntary work in connection with the Ten Year Plan for the health and welfare services, this being seen by the Government as an essential part of the improved community services it looked for. Such a development can only be brought about with maximum co-ordination of effort and by first establishing where the line of demarcation between voluntary and statutory effort runs, for, if this can be established, future relationship between the two branches would then develop free from the mutual suspicion and rivalry with which past efforts have frequently been bedevilled. The Piercy Report had something to say on this theme which indicated a possible basis of agreement, suggesting that the most fruitful fields for voluntary effort are pioneering new services and carrying out personal services for those in need of them. Many voluntary agencies appreciate the advantages of co-ordination and co-ordinating bodies already exist (perhaps too many of them!). If the plans now unfolding for the development of the social services during the next ten years are to achieve even part of what they promise, a streamlining of the work of both voluntary and statutory services must be brought about so that they each complement the efforts of the other to ensure that the handicapped may be helped to play the fullest possible part in the life of the community.

It is a far cry from the pioneering work of Dame Agnes Hunt, already started at the end of the last century, and of Sir Robert Jones on medical rehabilitation during the First World War, but the principles they sought to emphasize have now been generally accepted. The Piercy Committee confessed its inability to measure the size of the problem accurately because there were no reliable records of the numbers of substantially and permanently handicapped persons. We must continue to expand and improve the services—both as part of the Ten Year Plan or otherwise—until we are quite sure that the benefits they offer are within the reach of every disabled person needing them.

34. Welfare of the Deaf

FRANCIS JORDEN
County Welfare Services Officer, Royal County of Berkshire

The purpose of Social work is to help individuals or families with various
problems, to overcome or lessen these so that they may achieve a better
personal, family or social adjustment.

(Younghusband Report)

WHAT disability can produce such complex personal problems as those arising from deafness? It may be true that many infirmities are more severe,
that more personal help may be needed, and the cost involved in providing
services much greater, but invariably the solutions are arrived at by much
simpler processes than is the case with those afflicted with total or nearly
total loss of hearing. As a deformity, deafness is unique. Surely this is recognized by its being singled out, with blindness, for special consideration in the
legislation relating to the social needs of the disabled.

Perhaps in this world of glamorized advertisement, publicity of the more
prosaic deficiencies of man have either been overlooked or looked over. It
seems that today fewer understand the meaning of deafness. Little has been
written about its effects and the means of combating them, except works of
a professional nature dealing with medical aspects or teaching techniques,
which reach a very limited reading public.

This is unfortunate, for progress is undoubtedly urged on by pressure of
public opinion, and the often heard cliché of the work for the deaf being the
"Cinderella" of the social services is perhaps no less true because it is hack-
neyed. It reflects the frustrations of those in this field of welfare, and certainly
the effort and finance put into welfare work for the deaf falls far short
proportionately of that devoted, for example, to the blind.

Comparisons such as this must only be viewed objectively, for they point
to one of the difficulties in the struggle to develop fully a satisfactory and
rewarding service. There are other obstacles which may be much harder to
negotiate.

In the first place the word deaf means many things to different groups of
people. In its simplicity the term "deaf and dumb" was precise and offered
to all at least an interpretable meaning. With progress it has been possible to
teach some who are deaf to speak, thereby demonstrating that no one was
dumb in fact. Only the inability to hear and so imitate articulate sound prevents others from speaking. The expression "dumb", which has become

291

corrupted in modern usage, is no longer used. Instead the teacher of the deaf uses three classifications:

(a) Those whose hearing is only very slightly defective.
(b) Those whose hearing is seriously impaired but can hear with the aid of some mechanical or physical device.
(c) Those who are totally deaf to speech no matter how much the speech is amplified.

To the otologist, who recognizes the above definitions, deafness means much more, and his classifications are based on distinctions between congenital and acquired deafness; conductive (i.e. obstruction of the external canal) and perceptive (i.e. defect of the perceiving apparatus), operable and non-operable conditions. The site and cause of the obstruction in the case of conductive deafness determines what remedial action can be effected. In the case of perceptive deafness the causes are customarily classified in chronological sequence, hereditary, pre-natal and peri-natal groups.

The audiologist defines deafness in terms of measurement of hearing capacity in decibels and in relation to tones and frequency.

Between these groups there is and has been a close working relationship so that in full understanding of what each other means they are able, on assessment of deafness, to plan for the educational future of a child.

Whilst recognizing broadly these classifications, the social worker has, until recently, broken down the groups of deaf between:

(a) Those deaf from birth or early age, including partially deaf;
(b) the hard of hearing.

The most recent development in classification has been the acceptance by the Minister of Health in Circular 25/61, of a further differentiation under (a) above between:

(1) *Deaf without speech*. Those who have no useful hearing and whose normal method of communication is by signs, finger spelling or writing.
(2) *Deaf with speech*. Those who (even with a hearing aid) have little or no useful hearing but whose normal method of communication is by speech and lip-reading.

This seemingly simple revision (although not coterminous) brings a common understanding with the educationalist, and can lead to better working relationships between the teacher of the deaf and the social worker, who has an important part in the teamwork approach to the problem of the individual deaf person.

As surgical techniques improve and advances are made in the field of electronics, we can look to more being able to be classified in the groups with less defective hearing. There is, unfortunately, no evidence at present that the group (a) in the foregoing paragraph will be eliminated. The persuasiveness of adverts for hearing aids apparently assuring us that deafness is a thing of the past, often misleads the general public into thinking that a person who uses a language of signs is too difficult or obstinate to use an aid.

When the difficulties of classification of deafness are eliminated the way is open to surmounting the next obstacle, the co-operation between the teacher of the deaf and the social worker. Here, perhaps, the lack of a common concept has led to the controversial issue of education by the oral system or a combination of oral and manual language, and in consequence two groups of workers aiding the deaf are pulling in different directions. The deaf are bound to be the ones to suffer. The future progress in the welfare of the adult deaf depends to no small extent upon the solution to this impasse.

It is not the intention of this paper to enter the controversy as a participant, but in considering the trends in welfare for the deaf some reference must now be made to the existence of this issue and its effects upon social workers and upon the deaf themselves.

The responsibility for the welfare services for the adult deaf rests squarely on the shoulders of the local authorities under Section 29 of the National Assistance Act, 1948. In discussing the trends of welfare for the deaf, however, one cannot ignore the essential fact that a human being is a complete entity. Social work involves the whole process of living and not merely isolated periods through life strung together for administrative convenience. Although in many stages of life the social worker has no cause to interfere, he must always seek the co-operation of others to give purpose to his own function, and in turn must be able to play his part as a member of a team.

The greatest advances in the welfare of the deaf for a century have occurred in very recent years. Thanks to the work of Sir Alexander Ewing, to Lady Irene Ewing, Miss Edith Whetnall, Dr. Mary Sheridan and others, some successful research projects have led to one of the most hopeful breakthroughs in the early diagnosis of deafness. Through the years the uncertainty of ascertainment of deafness in children had led to their passing their most formative years in an uncomprehending silence, making the task of the teacher more difficult later on. It also led to many children being certified as mentally deficient, for a frustrated child almost inevitably becomes a maladjusted one.

Today, by means of careful screening of risk groups, and by skilful application of new testing techniques, it is possible to discover the existence of hearing loss in a child of only a few months. It is also possible, by the improvement in electronics and in the methods of audiometric registry, to assess with reasonable accuracy the degree of deafness, and so make possible the use of a hearing aid. It is not unusual to fit aids to babies under the age of six months. Not only this, but the continuing established work of maternity and child welfare services greatly assists in the prevention of congenital deafness.

The early diagnosis gives to the otologist the opportunity of studying the causes and site of the affliction, and therefore of early consideration of remedial treatment. Dr. Ballantyne, in his book *Deafness*, gives a comprehensive account among other things of modern surgical techniques. He illustrates, for example, the success of the modern operation of stapes mobilization and its replacement, as a first choice surgical treatment of otosclerosis, of the fenestration operation which was more serious and had at best only a three in four chance of success.

The advantages gained by medical research must not be lost in the long-term care of the deaf. Although there are hereditary causes of deafness, nevertheless a high proportion of totally deaf children are from hearing parents. The problems facing these parents on finding their child with this disability can produce many reactions which, if not corrected by skilful guidance, may have detrimental effects physically and psychologically on both parents and child. Here again the experiments of the Manchester University Department of Education for the Deaf have pointed to a pattern of parent–child clinics attached to the audiology units or working in close association with them. The development of the normal parent–child relationships during the first few years of life, which do more to produce a stability of temperament and a quicker comprehension of language, plays an essential part in social adjustment. It must be noted that the mere hearing of speech, either with or without an aid, is not nearly so important as the understanding of language. The use of peripatetic teachers and health visitors with special training in the problems of deafness has already shown that this system of parent–child advising is able to work beneficially. At this stage, too, there is a place for the social worker to co-operate with and be complementary to the health visitor, particularly in dealing with parents who are themselves deaf.

Let it be said that these processes, explained in detail in the Ministry of Health memorandum which accompanied Circular 23/61, are still in a stage of development. No one would yet claim that there are no difficulties, or that everything works like clockwork in practice, or even that it operates on a nation-wide basis. The importance of the trend is that it has transpired in a period of less than ten years after a century of comparative stagnation. It must lead to a reduction in the number of children classified as totally deaf.

Twenty-five years ago a deaf child could not hope to be admitted to a special school before the age of 7. Today children are taken at the age of 2. This may seem a tender age to be separated from mother, but it does provide the opportunity of the earlier acquisition of speech and the habit of lip-reading.

The type of education any individual child receives makes its mark on that person for the remainder of life. The normal child, however, has by far the greater chance of remedying an unfortunate schooling in later life. To the deaf child allocation to the wrong system of schooling can have much more disastrous results, for errors are much more difficult and sometimes impossible to correct. The assessment of children for educational purposes by a team consisting of medical officer, otologist, educational psychologist or teacher of the deaf, which again in recent years has become recognized practice, offers the best guarantee against wrong placement. Once again, the social worker has a place in this team for education is a part of the welfare needs of the individual, and its end product will eventually be the charge of the social worker in later life. In the work for the deaf the teacher in turn must recognize himself as having social work responsibilities. As with the health visitor the social worker must work in co-operation with and be complementary to the teacher.

Depending upon the degree of hearing the following educational facilities are available:

The school for the deaf.
The school for the partially deaf.
The unit for the partially deaf in the ordinary school.
Peripatetic teaching.

The decisions of the team will, however, be influenced by other considerations such as wishes of parents, health of child, residence of child in relation to school and other factors. It is an individual solution for every child, and should not be a conclusion arrived at as a block pattern, for example by assuming that with aids all children can attend ordinary schools. A deaf child has greater scope for advanced studies than ever before. Since the Second World War a few have gained university degrees. Obviously these opportunities are available only to the deaf of the highest intelligence, and the balance is inevitably in favour of the partially hearing. By inclination and scope the bias of studies is with technological subjects where possibilities of good level employment are greater. This trend is encouraged by the training at the Mary Hare Grammar School and Burwood Park School. Unfortunately, some of the advantages are offset by the disagreements between teacher and welfare worker, for the older missioner has tended to denigrate the higher education schools whilst the teacher feels that the missioner is reactionary in his approach and fails to consolidate the benefits of higher education when it comes to placement in employment.

It would seem that a higher proportion of deaf in, for example, America hold down senior positions than is evident in Britain, but without more detailed consideration it may be unwise to arrive at a conclusion. It is much more to the point that the two workers helping the deaf in their various ways should arrive at an agreed purpose.

The majority of the more severely deaf attend special schools based more or less at secondary modern level. All but one are completely oral schools, i.e. communication is by speech, and the technique of lip-reading is taught and practised. As may be expected, the child of ordinary intelligence experiencing difficulty with comprehension, and undergoing exacting speech, and lip-reading training, is considerably behind the ordinary hearing child on leaving school at the age of 16.

With the totally deaf child who proves to be an "oral failure", the comparison may not be as favourable. This position is the hard core of the welfare workers' complaint about the education system, for he claims that under it school-leavers have a very limited vocabulary, do not and sometimes cannot read and are conscious of their classification as failures. He calls for the introduction of manual language in schools as soon as it is realized that a child is unable to make progress with speech and lip-reading. He claims that when a school-leaver comes to take his part with other adolescents and adults at centres and institutes he reverts to signing and eventually loses what speech he had. Even those retaining speech do tend to lose their aptitude to some degree. Once again, whoever is right in this controversy, the deaf are most certainly the sufferers. This situation cannot be allowed to continue, for one of the consequences is that teachers not infrequently advise children and parents against attending centres where, with the right approach, much could be done to overcome the disadvantages of being deaf in a hearing world.

At this stage in the life of a deaf child he passes out of the care of the educationalist (if not out of his interest) but he can still play an important role in further education. The educationalist has played his part for some 12 or 14 years and for the next 60 years of a deaf person's life responsibility for his well-being, so far as it lies with the State, rests on the welfare authority.

From 1835 when the first society for the adult deaf was founded in Edinburgh until the 1930's, the missions for the deaf and dumb carried out alone the development of services providing essentially for spiritual care, placement in industry and social recreation. Starting in the large towns they spread to the adjacent smaller centres of population until today there are some eighty centres in the country as a whole. The National Institute of the Deaf, now the Royal National Institute, was formed to co-ordinate their activities, and in the late 1920's Regional Associations were instituted to act as liaison links between the National body, the missions, the local authorities, schools and hospitals. Eventually in 1933 the Minister of Health urged local public assistance authorities to make use of powers under Section 67 of the Poor Law Act of 1930 to make contributions to the missions. Some authorities complied but the principle was to make grants for placement work and the sums calculated on a capitation basis were small. Even after the passing of the National Assistance Act in 1948 such grants were continued in many cases at the same level.

Although Section 29 of the National Assistance Act gave power to authorities to carry out welfare services for the deaf, it was not until his Circular 32/51 that the Minister instructed local authorities to submit schemes showing how they intended to perform this function. Once approved the scheme was mandatory, but it was not compulsory to submit a scheme, and some authorities did not do so for some years after 1951. The general provisions of the schemes were in the main repetitions of Section 29, and included the power to appoint a voluntary organization as agent for carrying out the work. The great majority of authorities took this latter course, a few appointed their own welfare officers with specialist experience of the deaf. The circular laid down that the qualifications for such officers should be

> persons holding a diploma or certificate in social science or a similar qualification in social work of a comparable character, or persons as respects whom the Council are satisfied that they enjoy a special aptitude for the work, possess a broad knowledge of the social services and some experience in the field of welfare, and have an understanding of the problems of deafness and the principles of deaf education.

There were at that time no training facilities for an adequate number of welfare officers, and whilst a knowledge of the manual language could quickly be gained, proficiency in its use and an understanding of the deaf could only come after two or three years in close touch with the deaf. It was inevitable that agency relationships should have been entered into with the local deaf missions, with, however, a new formula for financial assistance. The Minister had encouraged the co-operation with voluntary bodies and so far as the institutes were concerned this involved pooling their own income with that provided (sometimes still on a capitation basis) by the local authorities. This pattern has continued to date.

As has been said, the missions were started more than a century ago. They have never been able to raise adequate funds from charitable sources to allow for the accumulation of capital, and many of the smaller societies experienced a hand-to-mouth existence. Fund-raising was often almost the major function, measured in time, of the missioner. It is the last task that should be required of a welfare officer when the number of these is all too few. The buildings which house the missions are, for the most part, old, geared to a different age and unsuitable, in spite of much effort on the part of the deaf themselves to improve the amenities. In a modern age they can be dowdy and dismal, and the general routine of activities sometimes seems to have remained unchanged through the century. Whilst this criticism is not comprehensive of every institute it does appear that too often Management Committees either through lack of finance or leadership have been content to accept for themselves the very scourge of deafness itself, isolation.

Nor are the local authorities without blame, for ten years, whilst such splendid progress has been made in other spheres, they have satisfied themselves with paying the smallest reasonable grant and either paid lip service to the wonder of co-operation or sat back, without interest, and allowed their agents to carry on. Those authorities who undertook a direct service fared no better, they fell into the same pattern as their predecessors or ignored the missions and concentrated purely on casework. At the time when experiments and new ideas were called for so much was lost.

General criticisms are always unfair to some, so it is desirable to single out as one example of progress the co-operation between Bristol City Council and the Bristol Institute for the Deaf, which has resulted in a fine new centre for the deaf. The building, purpose-designed, includes special acoustic properties and induction-circuit wiring, but more important still it is used daily by the deaf and it is the centre from which the Assessment Clinic works. It points to the possibility of development along lines which will make such buildings in fact centres for the deaf, where all services can work together and where deaf of varying severity can meet; where the periodic testing of the partially deaf and hard of hearing as visualized in the Younghusband Report can be undertaken; where continued speech training, lipreading and further education can be provided under conditions similar to those available in the most up-to-date schools; where spiritual care is available; where social workers are on hand to give help and guidance and where with teachers of the deaf they can overcome the prejudices of the past in their common purpose. Only then can welfare services keep in step with the progress which is being made in the field of medical care and education for the deaf.

Developments along these lines may not be possible nor even desirable in every place where missions now exist. Some existing buildings may be sufficiently sound to adapt for wider use, although in many ways new buildings can create the break from the more unfortunate of the associations with the past without necessarily losing that which was good. It is clear that the voluntary organizations will not have the necessary capital to undertake building on this scale. Local authorities must be prepared to meet the cost and may well see in it the opportunity to revise their existing agency arrangements. Perhaps it is fair comment to indicate that to date, on this most important service, the authorities have contributed proportionately little in comparison with the sums expended on welfare for the blind. Nor need the missions be put out over apparent loss of an agency. Their pioneering of the services has been completed, a new field of research waits to be explored. Their work, founded on spiritual care, could go on, their co-operation in providing many forms of cultural and recreational facilities would be welcome, indeed it is encouraged by the Minister in many circulars, and their funds, perhaps handsomely augmented by proceeds of realizing real estate could greatly assist the deaf.

County authorities having problems of the deaf in rural areas already accept the association of those deaf with centres in the nearby towns, and they could be encouraged to co-operate with other counties and county boroughs in the development of these projects. In this way the welfare services would gain the respect and co-operation of the health and education authorities and enable themselves to give effect to the future development of their services for the deaf, the partially hearing and the hard of hearing as visualized in Circular 25/61.

Buildings are, of course, of importance but, as in every other field, the quality of social work, which after all is the ultimate objective, is paramount. This can come from an adequate number of trained and experienced personnel. The Younghusband Report made the point that the aim should be to establish a high standard of service and to make use of special knowledge and skill without establishing a separate service. It also suggests that a proportion of local authority welfare officers should acquire real fluency in communication. In this the Report is recommending that the social problems of the deaf be dealt with in exactly the same way as the hearing person is helped. There appears, therefore, possibly some discrepancy between this view and that which must follow from the interpretation of Circular 32/51, an extract of which was quoted earlier. The requirements of the latter qualification "having an understanding of the problems of deafness and the principles of deaf education" calls for prolonged contact with the deaf, more experience in fact than could possibly be acquired by the superficial fluency in communication referred to in the Report. Further, the welfare officers whose duties are considered in Circular 25/61 must be social workers with additional specialized training if they are to gain a thorough understanding of the deaf and the principles of deaf education. It may well be that the Department of Education for the Deaf at Manchester University could assist with this training. In spite of a proportion of welfare officers in the general field acquiring a knowledge of methods of communicating with the deaf, the range of duties enumerated in paragraph 7 of the circular are wider than could be expected of such an officer, and they indicate a need for a specialized social worker.

The Council for Training in Social Work set up in 1962 and the National Institute for Social Work Training are still in their early stages and have not yet had time to evolve patterns of specialized studies.

Certain emphasis was placed on the needs of the young deaf with speech by the Ministry of Health. These young people, because of immaturity, can find the immediate post-school period most disturbing. It is a time in their lives when very special care should be exercised, and there is much to be said for establishing contacts during the last year at school. Teachers also can greatly help by seeking to continue their interest in former pupils. Already many quite successful youth clubs for the deaf are run in conjunction with the missions, but they still fail to cater for all deaf. Where groups are too small and too isolated for separate club activities, studied co-operation with other clubs can achieve quite satisfactory results.

Good placement work brings security and confidence to the deaf person. The records of the deaf in industry is a very satisfactory one—welfare officers already work closely with youth employment officers and disablement re-settlement officers of the Ministry of Labour. Nevertheless, many teachers still feel that more opportunity should be taken of natural and cultivated aptitudes. In areas of full employment the scope is much wider, but great care is still needed—desirable, too, is the continuing contact at work, wherever possible with industrial welfare officers.

Little has so far been said about the religious services for the deaf. Many feel that a faith born of conviction will nurture fortitude to aid a young person to face up to the limitations imposed by his affliction. State schools confine themselves to non-sectarian scripture studies which neither embarrass the education authority nor greatly help the deaf child who leaves school with but the faintest glimmer of the fundamental source of moral responsibility.

Local authorities are advised that they should not involve themselves in spiritual care, but that facilities for this should result from co-operation with the Churches. Many existing missioners for the deaf are ordained, and if these could be relieved of their purely social duties they could devote their un-doubted energies to this really urgent problem.

Managed by local authorities, centres, although secular in character, could offer their facilities to all denominations. In a number of areas separate clubs have been set up for Roman Catholics so small groups are further isolated from wider companionship. Voluntary societies may wish to provide chapels adjoining centres and in doing so help by their act of trust in the statutory authorities to build stronger bonds of co-operation.

Numerically, the greatest majority by far of people suffering loss of hearing are those classified as hard of hearing. It is estimated that there are more than $1\frac{1}{2}$ million throughout the country (only 14,823 were on registers of the local authorities at 31 December 1961). As most become deaf in later life they are, therefore, already fully integrated into the community and command full fluency of speech; their plight cannot, however, be dismissed with the issue of a Medresco hearing aid. How often and how truly has it been said that only those who have experienced deafness can know what it really means. The newly deaf can be helped considerably by audiometric technicians, and by the advice of health visitors and social workers who could be available at centres seeking to improve the management of and perseverance with appliances which at first are neither comfortable to wear nor easy to control. Hearing aids, indeed, are wonderful gadgets, but how unselective they are when compared with the human ear! Up and down the country the British League of the Hard of Hearing has done much to promote clubs and occasions for meeting and receiving lessons in lip-reading. In general there is a strong desire on their part not to be associated with the deaf without speech, but there are one or two missions for the deaf where mutually helpful and successful co-operation exists. The improved facilities which could be offered in the new-type deaf centre may be attractive to the hard of hearing, and the prospects of encouraging periodic reassessment of hearing would undoubtedly be enhanced.

The Younghusband Report called for more research in connection with the welfare of the deaf and hard of hearing. As already stated, much research has been undertaken into the medical aspects and into the process of diagnosis, but in the social field there is both scope and need for well-directed research into the personal living problems of deaf people. It has been a pattern of English life for research projects to be promoted and financed by voluntary effort; usually this has been centralized in some national body. The already well-established Royal National Institute for the Deaf is in an advantageous position to play a leading part.

The realization of the slowness of their progress over the past fifteen years in this sphere of their activities should be a spur to local authorities to take advantage of annual reviews of their Ten Year Plans to reappraise their position relative to the provision of the high standard of service called for in the Younghusband Report.

A final cautionary note—the principle of maintenance of objective is of prime importance in war, it is equally vital in peace. The complexity of this issue, the multiplicity of agencies and services involved, must not allow us to be side-tracked, to be embroiled in personal ideas and prejudices. The true aim is to so help any and all who suffer from deafness to be able to fit themselves into their rightful place in society and to live full and happy lives.

References

1. BALLANTYNE, J. C., *Deafness*, 1960.
2. EWING, A. W. G., *Educational Guidance and the Deaf Child*, 1957.
3. EWING, I. and EWING, A. W. G., *New Opportunities for Deaf Children*, 1961.
4. EWING, I., *The Handicap of Deafness*, 1938.
5. Reports of the National Conferences of the Royal National Institute for the Deaf, 1960 and 1962.
6. Report of the Working Party on Social Workers in the Local Authority Health and Welfare Services (Younghusband Report), 1959.
7. Reports of the Minister of Health for 1951 and 1961.
8. National Assistance Act, 1948.

35. Rehabilitation and Resettlement of the Severely Disabled

W. M. USDANE

Chief, Research Division Vocational Rehabilitation Administration,
Department of Health, Education and Welfare, Washington, D.C.

THE provisions in "The Welfare State" become far more ambiguous when applied to the severely disabled than to the disabled. The great experiments in social service initiated in Great Britain during the past eighteen years, for example, have only pointed up the uncertainty of how to deal appropriately with the multiple problems of the permanently and severely disabled. Professor Titmuss implied a grave question as to whether the performance of welfare with the severely disabled, the aged, the poor and others has more or less fulfilled the promise of welfare.[1]

But it was Eric Fromm who defined uncertainty as the very condition that impels man to unfold his powers. It is this uncertainty which undoubtedly prompted the two trends and the development of a specific type of vocational evaluation which will be discussed in this chapter. The trends were initiated, as will be pointed out later, in the one case by local authorities and in the other by psychiatric hospitals. The unusual vocational evaluation was developed by a voluntary body.

Legislation and Implementation

The rehabilitation and resettlement of the severely disabled are partially taken into account in the Disabled Persons (Employment) Act of 1944 and 1958 through provisions for sheltered employment. But unfortunately, as Lord Beveridge points out in *Voluntary Action*, the Act is not concerned with those who are not seeking employment—in particular, the chronically ill, the emotionally ill and the mentally retarded.[2] The provisions of the Act fail to secure the registration of those who should be registered but who inaccurately judge themselves or are judged wrongly by the officer administering the Act who may decide, along with his Advisory Panel, that the individual is beyond training or suitable employment. Description of the Act itself can be found in *Public Social Services*,[3] *Services for the Disabled*,[4] *The Handicapped Person*,[5] *The Social Services of Modern England*,[6] and *Help for the Handicapped*.[7]

Current provisions for those severely handicapped who are capable of

302

work of limited economic value include sheltered employment. The Disabled Persons (Employment) Act gives the Minister of Labour authority to make arrangements necessary for providing sheltered employment and to defray the resultant expenses or losses out of public funds by making grants to voluntary undertakings or local authorities. The Act can also arrange for one or more non-profit-making public companies to be formed, under the control of the Ministry of Labour or its agents, for the express purpose of providing sheltered employment for the severely disabled. One company of this type was registered in April 1945, and is known as Remploy, Ltd.

But Remploy, Ltd., which employs over 6000 severely disabled persons, is able to accept into each of its ninety factories throughout the United Kingdom only three or four each year per factory. And as of March 1963, the *Ministry of Labour Gazette* listed 5954 unemployed, registered, severely disabled persons classified as unlikely to obtain employment other than under sheltered conditions. In addition, there may be other persons at present, wholly dependent either on public or charitable funds or the support of friends or relatives, who may be capable of work of economic value under sheltered conditions, but for a number of reasons have never taken the first step towards obtaining such employment—*registration* as a disabled person.

For in order to obtain the full benefit of the provisions of the Act, the disabled person must be registered. Main conditions for registration are in line with the definition of disability:

(1) He is substantially handicapped in getting or keeping suitable employment or work on his own account, and
(2) the disablement must be one which is likely to last for at least twelve months after registration.

If there is doubt about the application, it is referred to a Disablement Advisory Committee or panel set up by the committee for a recommendation, and the final decision rests with the Minister who must consider any recommendation made by the committee or panel. A certificate is then issued to every applicant who has been registered and his name is entered in the register that is kept at the Employment Exchange.

Initially organized to provide sheltered employment for the severely handicapped, Remploy, Ltd., sees itself now as "a commercial company in every sense of the word".[8] During a year's study in 1962–3 of sheltered workshops in the United Kingdom with special emphasis upon Remploy, Ltd., the author found that those professional individuals visited in local authorities, mental hospitals and voluntary organizations all had difficulty in obtaining entry into any of the Remploy factories for patients or persons who were already on the National Register at a local Employment Exchange. The approximately 6000 on the waiting list, the fact that from all ninety factories each year only about 250 persons leave for open employment[9] or less than three per factory, and the entry limitations of the Industrial Rehabilitation Units preclude flexible utilization of either Remploy or the I.R.U.

There are sixteen Industrial Rehabilitation Units that provide an average length course of eight weeks. The course is for those who, after illness or accident, need mental and physical toning up to fit them for employment or who need an opportunity of adjusting themselves gradually to normal working conditions. The course also provides occupational assessment to determine the type of work or training for which they are best suited. In visiting eight of these Industrial Rehabilitation Units, the author found that these units reproduce the atmosphere of industrial workshops and engage mainly on production work under the supervision of selected craftsmen. The level of achievement is notably high, and individuals are engaged on sub-contractual work from local business or industry or in the making of products produced and sold by the Units themselves. Of those who complete this course, about 75 per cent are placed in employment or training.[10]

Careful selection is made of those who are sent to the Industrial Rehabilitation Units, and the Ministry of Labour official, the Disablement Resettlement Officer, stationed at the local Employment Exchange, acts as liaison officer between the I.R.U. and the Exchange. Since the I.R.U. strives to attain in its workshops the standards of work and discipline that are practised by normal industry, it is rarely utilized for those whose needs can best be served by sheltered employment. Recommendations, for example, are often for direct placing in industry upon completion of the eight-week period; other individuals are suggested for training. About one in five people passing through an I.R.U. is referred for training in new crafts or skills to one of thirteen Government Training Centres or to a Commercial College. It is essential, obviously, in an I.R.U., to ensure that the disabled person can keep up with an intensive training syllabus. In summary, the I.R.U. does not meet the essentially sheltered needs of the severely disabled for rehabilitation and resettlement. For a few, other sheltered shops are available.

Thirty-five sheltered workshops for the severely disabled are administered by voluntary organizations which are aided by grants from the Ministry of Labour. In addition, local authorities are now providing sheltered employment or training under Section 3 of the Disabled Persons (Employment) Act, 1958, for about 400 severely disabled persons who are not blind. These powers have been made compulsory in the case of the blind but are only permissive in the case of other disabilities. The Ministry of Labour meets the cost of training and pays grants towards the current and capital expenditure incurred by local authorities on these services. Of the voluntary organizations, there are about 800 severely disabled persons in training or employment in workshops receiving deficiency grants. Apart from four of these voluntary organization sheltered employment workshops, the rest receive financial help towards running costs directly from the Ministry of Labour in the form of a "deficiency grant" to offset trading losses.

Occupational Centres: Work Adjustment Programmes by Local Authorities

As mentioned previously, in addition to the 6000 registered unemployed severely handicapped individuals seeking placement in sheltered workshops, there are a great number of others who have never taken that first step towards obtaining employment—i.e. registration as a disabled person.

While local authorities maintain registers of all handicapped people who seek the assistance of the welfare services, there is no compulsory registration. The registers include practically all blind persons and give a fairly reliable picture of the extent of blindness in the population. There is no accurate count of the others, however, since only recently were any rehabilitation and resettlement services for this group developed by local authorities. Without counting the blind, of those between the ages of 16 and 64, there were approximately 90,000 severely disabled including the partially sighted. Of those over the age of 64, apart from the blind but including the partially sighted, there were about another 50,000 persons.[11]

The Ministry of Health and local authorities are responsible for one of the new trends in the rehabilitation and resettlement of the severely disabled. Through imaginative and creative work adjustment programmes, a variety of occupational centres have been started and can be found mainly in miscellaneous premises owned either by local authorities or voluntary bodies or in rented rooms, church halls or other similar accommodations.

As *The Development of Community Care*[12] states, there should be "employment within his capacity and any rehabilitation or training necessary to enable him to engage in it, or failing that, some satisfying occupation".

In Middlesex County, for example, the author observed four occupational centres, two of which were in a church hall, one in a purpose-built adult training centre for the mentally subnormal, and one within a factory estate. Currently there are now 40 purpose-built or specially adapted comprehensive centres, and 17 more are either under construction or are almost completed throughout the United Kingdom.[13] It has been suggested that 185 new centres are to be considered, which goal clearly reinforces the concept of the occupational centre as one of the new trends in the rehabilitation and resettlement of the severely disabled individual.

Strangely enough, some of the individuals in these centres are beginning to move into open employment, even though the vast majority of the group had never registered at the local employment exchange. Initially started as craft and social organizations, many centres are developing purposeful occupations of an industrial type in new comprehensive settings.

The occupational centre is providing the type of transitional phase into possible entry to a sheltered workshop or regular employment that is denied the severely handicapped in the commercialized Remploy factories or in the highly industrialized rehabilitation units. For the severely handicapped with minimal skill possibilities or without work experience, there is the need to (a) develop a "work personality" or an adjustment to work which is meaningful to him, (b) restore work habits and experience successful completion of work, and (c) provide a therapeutic setting in which both (a) and (b) can be accomplished.

The occupational centre affords a reality assessment and evaluation on actual jobs obtained from local industry or business. Here there is a clear attempt to evaluate the whole person by involving him actively in his own occupational adjustment. In addition, there is a personal adjustment training aspect which involves the following: personal health and appearance, ways to get along with fellow workers, ways to travel, personal relationships, means of getting employment, ways to get along with the supervisor, group relationships, and work achievement.

For the mentally subnormal, the new occupational centres are called Adult Training Centres. These provide training in habits of work and social behaviour and have as the goal possible placement in either open or sheltered employment. One of the most creative is an adult training centre in Middlesex County that is closely connected with a large industrial firm. The firm has accepted within its plant fifteen mentally subnormal young adults who occupy space directly on the floor of the factory. The supervisor of the mentally subnormal group is reimbursed by the local authority but is thoroughly familiar with the procedures, products, and training necessary for positions within the factory. The members of his group had originally been trained in work habits, semi-skills and the routine of occupational demands and had merely advanced to the penultimate step to actual placement. The goal, eventually, was to place as many of this small group within the plant as possible. Already two of the original group had moved together into regular jobs on the floor of the factory, doing the same type of work for which they had been given supervised training in the smaller original group.

This approach to rehabilitation and resettlement signifies Havighurst's definition of developmental tasks.[14] A developmental task is ". . . a task which arises at or about a certain period in the life of the individual, successful achievement of which leads to his happiness and to success with later tasks while failure leads to unhappiness in the individual, disapproval by the society, and difficulty with later tasks". Without such a step-by-step developmental approach in the vocational exploration of possible employment objectives for the severely disabled from reality self-imposed goals of the individual, there may be retrogression in the form of inadequate achievement and eventual goal failure.

Another occupational centre was located on the factory estate rather than within the factory itself. Here there was also immediate identity with a work setting. In addition, there was a classroom where simple lessons dealing with the counting of money, travel problems, and reading skills needed in the work of the occupational centre were given immediate attention and related to meaningful problems to which the mentally subnormal were able to respond with high motivation.

This trend, a work-adjustment setting within an occupational centre closely allied with subsequent steps into either actual employment or a sheltered workshop, appears to be increasing. As a positive step in the resettlement of the severely disabled, it counters the growing tendency of both Remploy, Ltd., and the older established sheltered workshops in the United Kingdom to afford a terminal rather than a transitional step to appropriate vocational adjustment within the community.

Mobile Vocational Evaluation Units

The Spastics Society created the Careers and Employment Department in 1957 to co-ordinate counselling, training, schooling and placement problems of the cerebral palsied school leaver and the adult spastic. This Department developed the first Mobile Evaluation Unit in 1958, and the twentieth was completed in 1963. These mobile units are underwritten completely by the Spastics Society with the primary purpose to educate and acquaint the local authorities with the potential training and placement of the severely disabled young adult cerebral palsied. Upon the basis of the mobile unit's evaluation recommendations, the local authority works closely with the results in implementing the findings with support from the Ministries of Health, Labour and Education.

The Mobile Evaluation Unit, a creative development, consists of a 12–day informal course given in various parts of England and Wales, usually in a local small hotel. The course is conducted by a professional team of five members, all with a background in personnel management and psychology. From twenty-five to thirty young adult cerebral palsied are brought by bus to the designated location, and, for a week and a half, live in the hotel with the professional team, away from parents and home and concentrating on practical tests, group discussion and job assignments. Both the professional team and the group assembling are mobile in the sense that both have travelled away from their usual environment, and within a new setting, embark on an opportunity for a fresh look at the group's capacity to undertake a concerted effort towards each member's vocational evaluation.

In addition to the professional team members, local representatives from the Ministry of Labour Employment Exchange are brought in to discuss job opportunities, how to apply for a job and labour market information. The local authority social worker may often be requested to review available resources within the community.

For over 75 per cent of the group, this is the first occasion they have been away from home for as long as a fortnight without parents. Within the hotel, smaller rooms are prepared for vocational evaluations on samples of actual work trials, psychological tests and group discussions of job preparation and job interviewing. Individual vocational counselling sessions occur whenever they are felt to be appropriate by members of the professional team. This approach enables the professional team member to observe the capacities and limitations of the individual within a realistic "living" situation.

The programmes of each evaluation course are flexible, but that one which was observed by the author included the following:

(1) Group discussion (only ten to a group) on various practical subjects covering everyday living. Everyone is encouraged to contribute, and staff members interchange as group leaders along with members of the assessment group themselves.

(2) Talks by specialists on a variety of subjects connected with employment, training and leisure-time activities.

(3) Visits to local factories, offices and other places of occupational interest.

(4) Discussion on hobbies and interests.

(5) Films of an industrial, social and travel nature.

(6) Social events: panel games, concerts, dances, sports.

(7) Practical work: sample tests designed to give indications on ability to absorb instructions, perseverance, concentration, manual dexterity, speed, attitudes, distractability, interests.

(8) Each student has to write a letter (or type) applying for a job which is presented to him and which he thinks he can manage. The letter is then discussed with him by a member of staff and then may be discussed by the group as a whole.

(9) Each student has a trial interview for this job application by his letter, and plays role of both applicant and employer to give himself some awareness of his strengths and weaknesses.

(10) Observation hunts are included to test initiative and ingenuity. Individuals may be paired in order to increase mobility—one may push a wheelchair of a friend, but two items are requested of any team.

(11) Staff may enact sketches demonstrating "wrong" ways to behave in a variety of work settings; these are then used as discussion points by the group.

(12) Concerts or evening programmes are arranged by individuals who are in charge of their own entertainment in the event films are not shown or any assessment programme does not occur in the evening.

Before the group is assembled, however, medical reports, school records, interviews with each individual and his parents, intelligence test reports and any other necessary information are collected on each person and reviewed by members of the professional team. Staff members are billeted in the same hotel, eat in the same dining-room, and have a constant opportunity to observe individual and group behaviour. During the twelve days, in small groups of three or four, work samples are given comprising complex tasks, tool control and speed of movement. Most of the samples are concerned with reality assignments: ballpoint pen assembly, use of the tickopress machine, screw sorting, tying of knots for electronic cable harnessing, and a variety of other tasks for eye–hand co-ordination. It is made clear to each participant that a staff member will follow through with him on any of the recommendations that result from the Assessment Course.

The nature of the complexity of each severely disabled person's problems is seen more clearly by the variety of statutory and voluntary bodies from which the Mobile Evaluation Unit drew the twenty-nine participants.

(a) Statutory bodies were represented by fourteen individuals coming from a variety of Local Authority Schools for Physically Handicapped Children, Secondary Modern Schools, Occupational Centres, and one Old People's Home. Six of these showed unsatisfactory adjustment in material from social workers.

(b) Unsatisfactory employment accounted for three; one of these was on probation for two years for embezzlement in his former position.

(c) Two came from unsatisfactory adjustment to Remploy Factories.

(d) Five came from Special Schools run by the Spastics Society.

(e) Three came from unsatisfactory adjustment to Occupation Centres run by Affiliate Spastics Society organizations.

(f) One came from a Residential Training College run by another Voluntary Body for the Handicapped after failure to make appropriate progress.

(g) One came from a Special School for the Handicapped run by another Voluntary Body after unsatisfactory progress.

The final results of the twentieth Mobile Assessment Unit resulted in the following recommendations for the twenty-nine severely handicapped cerebral palsied ranging from age 16 to 26:

(a) Six were to be placed in regular open employment by the Employment Officers of the Spastics Society, in conjunction with either the Local Authority Youth Employment Officers who work with those 16 to 18, and with the Disablement Resettlement Officers of the Ministry of Labour Employment Exchanges who work with the registered disabled who are over 18.

(b) Eight were referred to Sherrards, a residential sheltered employment training centre in which training for a variety of job families is included. Concurrent vocational counselling towards work attitudes will occur here.

(c) Two were recommended during an interim period for several months for Christmas Card Printing at home under sponsorship of Spastics Society. Small equipment is brought to their home. Both are to be considered for referral to local Remploy Factories in year's time.

(d) Five were to be placed in new Sheltered Workshop opening within a year by Spastics Society—including hostel accommodations. Until this Workshop is opened, two will be placed in Occupational Centres run by Local Authorities who have underwritten the Spastic Society Affiliate Groups' Workshops under provisions of statutory authority.

(e) Two were recommended for homework schemes of jewellery-making run by the Spastics Society since last two years, and in which approximately 144 are involved with a small group doing general handicraft work. Goods are marketed by the Society, and piecework rates prevail. Future consideration for occupation centre placement are to be kept in mind during the relationship of these two to members of the Staff of the Careers and Employment Department.

(f) Three were recommended for commercial training at the Spastics Society Office Training Centre which provides accommodation in suitable local lodgings.

(g) One is being considered for an Occupational Centre where machine adaptation will be necessary before placement is worked out.

(h) One has severe ambulation problems, in wheelchair, and walks only with constant support. Activities of daily living are poor, and little indication that improvement can be accomplished in this sphere; she also lacks confidence. She will be given jewellery-making for half day, and will continue in same occupational centre the other day where she is now.

(i) One will need considerable psychiatric case work prior to any consideration for work; has difficult home background; history of early seizures but now they are under control, and individual is a mild hemiplegic Has had variety of schooling under both statutory and voluntary bodies To be followed closely by the Careers and Employment Departmen regarding progress psychiatrically.

Transitional Industrial Workshops for Patients in Psychiatric Hospitals

There has been a recent important trend for the longer-term patients in specialized psychiatric hospitals; the use of industrial work in psychiatric hospitals is increasing. This approach is not to be confused with work don in occupational therapy units or with some of the craft work accomplished by patients and sold on the hospital grounds. The trend is to undertake work from outside firms, with a minimum of articles manufactured by the hospitals themselves. As an extension of the industrial work accomplished on the hospital grounds in workshops apart from the main hospital buildings, arrangements are also made for some patients to go daily from hospital to outside employment, returning at the end of the day's work.

This new pattern of industrial development includes the Industrial Therapy Organization Ltd., which in a psychiatric hospital in Bristol stands for a non-profit-making organization. This approach provides a training factory and sheltered workshops which form additional intermediate stages between work within the hospital and outside employment. The plans of Dr. Early[15, 16] include a three stage plan to rehabilitate and resettle the long-stay and long-unemployed psychiatric patient with residual disability. It is his finding that long-hospitalized long-unemployed paranoid schizophrenic patients over the age of 40 appear to have the best prognosis. He states further that patients with short unemployment records and less than one year in hospital appear to work out least well in an undertaking such as the Industrial Therapy Organization.[15]

Again the principles quoted from Havighurst apply in this case. For this general trend in transitional industrial workshops for hospitalized mental patients consists of developmental steps. The first stage is an in-patient industrial workshop at Glenside Hospital where the majority of the chronic psychotic patients are hospitalized. The second stage is the Industrial Therapy Organization, a non-profit company with registered offices in York Street, St. Phillips Marsh, Bristol. This stage attempts to offer medically and industrially supervised employment training under conditions approximating ordinary factory conditions. The third stage, after the I.T.O. experience of the patient, will be further training in open industry or open industrial employment. The third stage is currently in process of implementation, but stage two is in process of evaluation after three years of operation.

The major purpose of stage three is to enlist the co-operation of understanding employers to afford the patient an opportunity for further training in regular employment. If the patient is successful, he will either be employed or be recommended by the employer. Trade union representation has been assured of no exploitation on the part of patients, and the Bristol Trades Council is in support of the new trend in aiding the mental patient's return to the community through a graded series of increasing reality work experiences.

It is interesting, in the light of information earlier stated in this chapter, that it is not proposed to establish I.T.O. "as a Remploy-type factory nor as a sheltered workshop, but rather as a training factory, stimulating initiative".[16] The transitional aspects of this new trend in the rehabilitation and resettlement of the severely disabled are constantly reinforced throughout each of the three stages. Workshops hitherto developed on hospital grounds tended to operate mainly with terminal goals.

Subnormal patients and epileptics are not excluded from referral to I.T.O. There have been increasing referrals from psychiatric sources and from non-medical sources other than Glenside Hospital where the inpatient industrial therapy department is located as the first stage. Weekly meetings of staff operating the I.T.O. are arranged, and the local health authority has seconded a health visitor "whose prime duty will be to act as social worker". I.T.O. accepts applications for places in the factory from all consultant psychiatrists in the Bristol clinical area and from doctors in charge of day hospitals and occupation therapy departments as well as from the medical officer of health. Since movement of patients through the factory is the main purpose, the time any patient may remain is curtailed. Should it be considered by staff conference that the patient is no longer making progress and is unlikely to proceed further in industrial training, he is discharged from I.T.O. Consideration of placement in open employment, Remploy or sheltered workshop would be the next step. Careful explanation and review of his progress and goals with the patient are part of his help towards eventual return to the community through work adjustment.

In 1960 the Cheadle Royal Hospital near Manchester presented an exhibition at which over fifty hospitals demonstrated various types of production. Assembly of cardboard or plastic materials and light engineering products predominated in both mental hospitals and mental deficiency institutions. The general trend in psychiatric hospitals during the past five years has been to extend factory-type work within the hospital, again apart from the occupational therapy unit. Highcroft Hall, Birmingham, employs 300 patients, using a delivery van for the sole use of its industrial therapy in light engineering products. A survey of the number of industrial therapy departments in 181 mental hospitals of England and Wales done by Cheadle Royal's psychiatric staff in 1961 reported that industrial units existed in 48 per cent of mental hospitals with a further 15 per cent intending to open them soon. But no attempt was made to evaluate their effectiveness, and many are even yet in a rudimentary stage of development into appropriately industrialized departments. Wadsworth and Wells in the Industrial Unit at Cheadle Royal studied the attitude of patients to industrial therapy.[17] One of the conclusions indicated that the reality orientation of even those with severe illnesses of long duration to the meaningfulness of work is high. It was also found that without doubt patients show a strongly positive attitude to industrial therapy.

It is interesting to note that Cheadle Royal Hospital chooses to produce its own product in contrast to the mental hospital's Industrial Units' performing contract work. But the hospital's assumptions and goals are still based on the use of the Industrial Unit for transitional purposes along with other gains for chronic patients. In 1963 a conference was held to set up a National Advisory Council on Industrial Therapy to advise and help hospitals on every aspect of the development of their Industrial Therapy Units or Re-Employment Training Units.[18]

Two recent trends have been reviewed in the rehabilitation and resettlement of the severely disabled in Great Britain: (1) the increasing use of occupational centres by local authorities for the restoration of work habits and work adjustment, and (2) the increase of organized industrial therapy units for the transition of mental patients from psychiatric hospitals to the community. In addition, an interesting development for the assessment of the severely disabled cerebral palsied has been described in the mobile evaluation unit.

References

1. TITMUSS, R. M., *Essays on "The Welfare State"*, George Allen & Unwin Ltd., 1958.
2. LORD BEVERIDGE, *Voluntary Action*, George Allen & Unwin, London, 1948, p. 252.
3. *Public Social Services*, The National Council of Social Service, 26 Bedford Square, London, 1961.
4. *Services for the Disabled*, Ministry of Labour, H.M.S.O., 1961.
5. MONTGOMERIE, J. F., *The Handicapped Person*, The Scottish Council of Social Service, 10 Alva Street, Edinburgh, 1958.
6. HALL, M., *The Social Services of Modern England*, Routledge and Kegan Paul, London, 1960.
7. *Help for the Handicapped*, The National Council of Social Service, London, 1958.
8. *Remploy*, Remploy House, 415 Edgware Road, Cricklewood, London, 1962.
9. *Report and Accounts*, Year ended 31 March 1962, Remploy, Ltd., London, 1962.
10. "Industrial Rehabilitation Units", *Ministry of Labour Gazette*, August 1953.
11. *The Development of Community Care*, Ministry of Health, C.M.D. 1973, April 1963, p. 30.
12. *Ibid.*, pp. 31–2.
13. *Ibid.*, p. 35.
14. HAVIGHURST, R. J., *Human Development and Education*, New York: Longmans, Green, 1953, p. 2.
15. EARLY, D. F., "The Industrial Therapy Organization (Bristol), The First Two Years", *The Lancet*, 23 February 1963, pp. 435–6.
16. EARLY, D. F., "The Industrial Therapy Organization", *The Lancet*, 1 October 1960, pp. 754–7.
17. WADSWORTH, W. V. and WELLS, B. W. P., "The Attitude of Patients to Industrial Therapy", unpublished manuscript, 1962.
18. Personal Communication from Mr. W. V. WADSWORTH, Medical Superintendent, Cheadle Royal Psychiatric Hospital, 20 June 1963.

36. Housing and Aids for the Disabled*

J. H. BARGH

Barrister-at-Law, Director of Welfare Services, Glamorgan County Council

COMMUNITY responsibility for the provision of suitable housing for the disabled is a relatively new concept, but the problem itself is as old as man. Geographic and climatic characteristics of a country determine fundamentally the pattern of shelter which its people will develop as protection against the elements, and the extent to which refinements are superimposed on the bare essentials depends on the social and economic development of the country.

Housing in undeveloped countries is generally simple and designed to meet minimal requirements. The northern European climate has historically impelled man to provide his shelter using heavy materials such as brick and stone, and the provision of suitable housing for disabled persons in countries such as this must be seen in its context. In coming years, properties purpose-designed for the disabled may become increasingly available, but to alleviate the adverse living conditions which are the lot of thousands of handicapped persons, it is imperative that steps be taken now to adapt to their requirements the older properties in which they live. Handicapped people tend to be housed in the least suitable property: their economic circumstances are usually such that this appears almost to have the mark of inevitability. Mostly, their dwellings are small, squalid, devoid of any semblance of convenience, except the one outside, and their proximity to industrial undertakings.

Housing Problem

What is the problem of housing the disabled? Surely it is the usual one of the physically handicapped; that of helping them to lead a life as nearly normal as possilbe. Their present housing difficulties stem mainly from lack of foresight in design of houses generally, failure to comprehend and provide in physical terms for man's reasonable requirements. These shortcomings continue today in houses of modern design and are perpetuating limitations and defects which can be rectified only laboriously and expensively.

A man stricken by disability becomes conscious only too soon of the

* Reprinted from the *County Councils Gazette*, Vol. 56, No. 1, January 1963, with the permission of the editor and author.

limitations of his house in relation to his new mode of life. His object is now to have the fullest physical expression commensurate with the minimum expenditure of effort. How can he achieve this in a typical home—light that impossible stove or fire, turn on a water tap, go upstairs to a bedroom or down steps to an outside W.C.? To him, the physical effort of taking a single step, stooping, or lifting a hand to the face can be a major physical operation. Who is going to help him, and how? The medical and nursing profession have done their best for him and the State has ensured that he will have enough money to meet his main requirements. But who is to help him to take up the threads of life?

County councils, as welfare authorities, now have a great contribution to make in this field. Under the terms of the National Assistance Act, 1948, they must provide a variety of services designed to alleviate the condition of persons so afflicted.

A Fuller Life

Experience is now growing amongst local authorities of the ways in which a handicapped person may be assisted to live a fuller life. It is not within the scope of this article to refer to the subjective and intangible factors by means of which a handicapped person may be brought back into the community, but to refer to one or two practical ways of assisting him. Assessments can be made of his physical capabilities and a survey undertaken of the extent to which adaptations can be undertaken to his home, and how far the provision of aids and gadgets would help him to attain a measure of normality or independence.

Working relationships between welfare service departments and housing departments have developed to meet his housing problem; architects and welfare workers are applying their specialized knowledge in devising patterns of adaptation and, incidentally, obviating administrative difficulties such as those arising from obtaining planning permission consents and observance of bylaws.

Regarding the cost of adaptations, it is common practice of local authorities to define a policy within which it will operate; to determine what adaptation it will undertake, and generally within what financial limits works will be undertaken. The need for extensive adaptations frequently arises, the cost of which would far exceed the value of the property. Here, of course, re-housing is the only solution and the closest co-operation between the county council and county district council is essential to secure an effective solution for the handicapped person.

Here the law contemplates that some persons may be able to contribute to the cost of the works. Factors secondary to the main purpose may arise; for example, amenities introduced into the house for the handicapped person may appreciate its value or confer benefit on other residents in the house.

Presumably in this light, the National Assistance Act empowered local authorities to recover, where appropriate, the whole or part of the cost of adaptations. One Welsh authority, however, in the light of the very modest sums recovered, has decided that for an experimental period it will make no charge to a handicapped person for this service. In coal-mining areas partnership often exists between the local authority Welfare Department and the Coal Industry Social Welfare Organization under which the latter bears an appreciable proportion of the cost of works undertaken in the home of a disabled miner.

Housing problems of disabled persons have much in common and some broad suggestions are submitted:

Outside Requirements (for persons using a wheelchair or walking aids)

Pathways should be level, slopes non-slippery and be wide enough to take easily a wheelchair. The entrance gateway may also require widening. Handrails may be required, steps may have to be eliminated and a sloping path provided. Steps may be elongated and reduced in height (Plates 18–19).

Doorways

Steps leading to entrance doors may need alteration and handrails provided. Doors may be widened to allow of easier access. Standard key-operated locks may have to be replaced by a level handle type, or keys may be adapted to suit a crippled hand. Locks placed high in a door may need lowering.

Living Rooms and Hallways

Handrails may be necessary in a hall, passage, staircase and/or rooms. Furniture layout may need replanning to allow easy passage and use of a wheelchair. Electric light switches may need re-positioning, and gas and electric meters re-siting. The height of windows, latches, cooking stoves, sinks and cupboards may call for alteration. Some rooms may justify the provision of sliding doors. Where a wheelchair is used, door frames, the bottoms of doors and wall corners should be protected with metal plates.

Bathrooms

The w.c. and wash hand-basin may need alteration in position or level. Ceiling type light switches with cord control may confer benefit. Handrails may be needed, and a hoist over the bath or lavatory pan can promote independence and is good for morale.

Bedrooms

Where possible, the disabled person's bedroom should have good sunlight and a pleasant outlook. Windows should be low enough to be operated from a wheelchair. The position of the bedroom in relation to the bathroom is of importance and often a second bedroom door giving access to the bathroom is advantageous. A sliding bedroom door with cord control often assists a person confined to a wheelchair. Use of an electric light is often facilitated by a two-way cord from a ceiling switch (one switch being placed near the door, the other near the head of the bed). Convector-type heaters, wall electric fires or central heating are suitable.

The problem often arises of lifting a disabled person to and from a bed and wheelchair. A hoist or sling, either fixed or mobile, may be provided and may enable a person to continue living in his own home.

Lack of Foresight

Many difficulties encountered in adapting homes could, undoubtedly, have been obviated—without affecting normal usage—if consideration had been given in design to the possibility of use by elderly or disabled persons. Today the elderly, many of whom are physically handicapped, form an ever-increasing proportion of the community and architects and planners would do well to keep in mind these factors when planning future housing estates. Homes generally should be more flexibly designed and incorporate facilities suitable for the aged.

Welfare authorities are becoming increasingly concerned with social rehabilitation and a major function of social welfare officers is directed in one way or another to this end. Fundamental to this process is the supply of aids and gadgets which promote a wider range of physical activity. Careful thought, and experience in the design and application of physical aids, can materially assist a disabled person to mitigate the effects of his disability and secure full benefit from the adaptations made to his home.

One welfare authority has for some years had in its workshops for the handicapped a department manufacturing aids for disabled persons. Starting modestly six years ago the output of this workshop is nearly 1000 aids per annum, which fall generically into some ninety types. The original conception was that one handicapped person would be so employed, but today four handicapped persons and a working foreman are overtaxed by the ever-increasing demand. The Ministry of Labour are, in this context, to be complimented on their reception of the original proposal and for their continued support and guidance extended to the authority. Aids produced here are "tailored" to suit individual requirements and are issued free of charge to the disabled person. Materials used—wood, light metals and plastic—are inexpensive, but labour costs would tend to be high if the opportunity were not taken to provide sheltered employment for other disabled people.

The development of a scheme of this nature depends on the existence of officers having appropriate social work experience and technical potentiality.

With such a nucleus it is possible for social workers in the field to be taught the value and the technique of aid production.

Principles of operation of the "Aids" scheme are:

(a) Social welfare officers make initial investigation and indicate a disabled person's possible requirements;
(b) "on-the-spot" discussion takes place with a specialist in this work;
(c) design and construction of appropriate aids is agreed;
(d) aids are then manufactured in the workshop, and "tried out" with the disabled person;
(e) the Social Welfare Officer makes "follow-on" visits and submits periodic progress reports.

In recent years this authority's experience has been placed at the disposal of other councils, whose officers have been given a course on the subject of assessing "aids" requirements, undertaking works of adaptation to the home and social rehabilitation.

It is not, however, suggested that all aids need be individually tailored, and where there is no individual connotation standard aids are purchased from the British Red Cross Society or from commercial concerns.

Aids and adaptations are distinctly useful for the purpose they serve but they constitute only one device in rehabilitating a disabled person towards a new life. The mainspring of this humanitarian conception is the local authority's Social Welfare Officer, whose patience, skill, understanding and ability to encourage, lead the handicapped person from despair to endeavour —and, perhaps, to some degree of achievement.

37. Services for the Treatment and Rehabilitation of Spinal Paraplegics and Tetraplegics in Great Britain

L. GUTTMANN

Director, National Spinal Injuries Centre, Stoke Mandeville
Hospital, Aylesbury, Bucks.

The Past

It is only since the Second World War that a comprehensive service for people paralysed as a result of injury or disease of the spinal cord has been organized in Great Britain and indeed in any country. Until that time, the horizon of curative medicine to these people, in particular those suffering from transection or severe injury of the spinal cord as a result of a fracture, gunshot wound or stab wound of the spine, was very limited. Its aim was to relieve the damaged cord from pressure or haemorrhage by conservative or surgical means or remove bullets or other foreign bodies from the cord. It gave little or no thought to compensating the paralysed for their residual paralysis, except by means of corsets of leather and steel and other medical aids. Indeed, the whole attitude of the medical profession was one of defeatism that nothing or very little could be done for these people, as in any case their duration of life was considered to be very limited. Those who managed to survive for longer periods were doomed to lives of uselessness and helplessness, either at home or in crowded institutions for incurables.

During the First World War, the mortality rate of soldiers with spinal cord injuries in the British and American armies was 80 per cent, and Harvey Cushing, the famous American neurosurgeon, in 1927 gave a vivid description of the pitiful fate of these battle casualties: "The conditions were such", he writes, "owing to pressure of work as to make it almost impossible to give these unfortunate men the care their conditions required. Each case demands undivided attention of a nurse trained in the care of paraplegics. Only those cases survive in which the spinal lesion was a partial one."

There was no significant change in this problem during the period after the First World War, and in 1934 Gowland gave the following account of the conditions of those pathetic human wrecks treated at the Star and Garter Home, which was set up after the First World War for disabled ex-Servicemen. He writes: "Two or three times a week, the patient is bathed: this means he must be lifted from his bed to his ward chair and wheeled into the bathroom, where his pyjamas and night-clothes are removed, and he is placed in

319

a very warm bath and washed by an orderly." In discussing the problem of painful reflex spasms and contractures, he points out: "The position is often terrible. I suppose there is more morphia, atropine and hyoscine used in this Home, which I look after, than in any place of the same size in the country."

This defeatist attitude was based on the concept that, as a result of a spinal cord lesion involving such essential functions as voluntary movements, all forms of sensation, control of bladder, bowels and sexual function, as well as blood circulation, certain complications—namely, sepsis from infection of bladder and kidneys on the one hand and pressure sores on the other—are inevitable. Therefore, any attempt to restore such a person to his former social activities seemed to be out of the question. Even in the early stages of the Second World War, when the modern conception of rehabilitation of the disabled was generally accepted for amputees and other crippling disabilities, spinal paraplegia was not included in this concept. The author recalls a Symposium on Rehabilitation following Injuries of the Central Nervous System, held in the Neurological Section of the Royal Society of Medicine in 1941, where four speakers discussed rehabilitation following brain injuries and one (the author) following peripheral nerve injuries. The subject of spinal paraplegia was not even mentioned. Society as a whole remained apathetic to the problem of paraplegia in those years. Most of these unfortunate people were dependent on charity and remained a focus of curiosity.

A fundamental step forwards in a new approach to the problem of management of spinal paraplegia was taken during the Second World War by the Peripheral Nerve Committee of the Medical Research Council, under the leadership of Brigadier George Riddoch, Neurological Consultant to the British Army and the Ministry of Health, when it was decided to congregate spinal cord casualties in special units. There were several reasons for this decision: First of all, it was generally agreed that conditions for a systematic study of the many problems concerned with the treatment and rehabilitation of spinal paraplegics were infinitely more favourable in a spinal unit than when these cases lay scattered in general medical or surgical wards, from which, as a rule, they were transferred to chronic wards or homes for incurables. Even if they were admitted to neurological, neurosurgical, orthopaedic or urological units, the facilities available were limited to the study of specialized problems and short-term treatment only. Above all, these units were so busy with their many other afflictions in their specialities that, as a rule, it was quite impossible for both the medical and nursing staff to give spinal paraplegics, let alone tetraplegics, that meticulous care and attention which these patients need day and night, especially during the acute stages. The spinal units set up during the early stages of the Second World War were those at the mental hospitals in Warrington (Winwick) and Sheffield (Wharncliffe), the Ministry of Pensions Hospitals at Leeds (Chapel Allerton),

Worcester (Ronkswood), Newcastle (Dunstan Hill), Llandrindod Wells, Cardiff (Rookwood), Basingstoke, the National Orthopaedic Hospital, Stanmore, and the Polish Hospital, Wrexham, where most of the 700-odd casualties with spinal cord lesions were collected. However, these early units did not prove satisfactory, for it had not been generally recognized that, in order to prevent their becoming merely an accumulation of doomed cripples, the provision of certain arrangements was indispensable:

(1) Adequate technical facilities for tne specialized care and rehabilitation of these long-term patients, including physiotherapy, occupational therapy and pre-vocational training in workshops. In this connection, the setting up of a special ward for convalescent paraplegics was essential for the final stages of their rehabilitation, in order to facilitate and encourage independence and return of these patients to social and professional activities.

(2) Nursing and auxiliary staff, including orderlies, sufficient in number to cope with the many details involved in the work and in particular avoidance of the usual practice of changing the nursing staff from one department to another at short intervals.

(3) Most important of all, supervision of such a unit by an experienced surgeon or physician, who was prepared to devote his full time to the work, which demands meticulous attention to details, to organize the various details of treatment and lastly, but by no means least, to correlate the sometimes conflicting interests of the various medical and surgical specialities concerned with the rehabilitation of these patients.

(4) Arrangements for domestic and industrial resettlement of paraplegics.

T. B. S. Dick (1949) has given an excellent account of the unsatisfactory conditions prevailing in this period of the war in one of the first spinal units, where some forty cases were treated. Although a neurosurgical team was in charge of the spinal unit, he states: "No one member of that team devoted more than a part of his time to the care of spinal injury cases." In describing two examples of inadequate treatment, which he had chosen at random, he continues: "It was not uncommon at this period on a ward round to find virtually every case of paraplegia with persistent pyrexia. There did not appear as yet to be a definite plan or end in view of the rehabilitation of even the more fit patients."

From my personal observations, conditions were very similar in other units. Moreover, it was little consolation that, at that time, the results in other countries were no better. Even as late as 1944, American authors (Everts and Woodall) were still able to write: "Certainly it cannot be said that any striking advance has been made in the late care of spinal cord injuries."

A New Approach

On 1 February 1944 a new spinal unit was set up at the then Ministry of Pensions' hospital Stoke Mandeville at Aylesbury in Buckinghamshire, as one of the preparations for the Second Front. With the opening of this unit, a new approach was created to this difficult problem. The new concept was that it is not true that the fact that a man has sustained a paraplegia necessarily condemns him to institutional care but that the principles of modern treatment and rehabilitation can be applied to a patient with even such a profound disablement, not only to prolong his life but to make him a useful member of society, in spite of his severe disability. It was at that time quite revolutionary to reject the generally held defeatist attitude that sepsis from pressure sores and infection of the urinary tract are inevitable complications and that not only can these complications, as well as contractures of the paralysed limbs, be successfully treated but even altogether avoided in the majority of these patients. Moreover, it was also quite unorthodox to teach that the treatment of pressure sores and the social rehabilitation of paraplegics can be at least as rewarding as, say, the extirpation of a brain tumour.

The Present

After the war, most of the initial spinal units were dissolved and the majority of the patients transferred to the Stoke Mandeville Unit and the newly-formed units in Southport, Sheffield (Lodge Moor), Wakefield (Pinderfields) and Hexham. Today, apart from the Stoke Mandeville Unit, which developed into a national centre and consists at present of 190 beds, there are the following units set up in Great Britain for the paraplegia service:

Rookwood Hospital, Cardiff	36 beds
Edenhall Hospital, Edinburgh	40 beds
General Hospital, Hexham	15 beds
Lodge Moor Hospital, Sheffield	60 beds
Promenade Hospital, Southport	34 beds
Pinderfields Hospital, Wakefield	28 beds

In the following account, details are given of the activities of the National Spinal Injuries Centre, Stoke Mandeville, which, starting from scratch on 1 February 1944, has gradually developed into the largest centre of its kind in Europe and the British Commonwealth. In fact, with its associated units, it is the largest unified paraplegia service in the world. The Centre itself consists of six male and two female wards, with a small annexe for children and twelve private rooms, where the 190 patients are housed. The develop-

The Development of the Stoke Mandeville Centre since it was taken over by the National Health Service.

ADMISSIONS

Date	1.4.51 to 31.3.52	1.4.52 to 31.3.53	1.4.53 to 31.3.54	1.4.54 to 31.3.55	1.4.55 to 31.3.56	1.4.56 to 31.3.57	1.4.57 to 31.3.58	1.4.58 to 31.3.59	1.4.59 to 31.3.60	1.4.60 to 31.3.61	1.4.61 to 31.3.62	1.4.62 to 31.3.63
New admissions	107	122	185	178	166	194	156	299	245	253	258	259
Re-admissions for routine check-ups or specialized treatment	198	282	255	258	369	402	474	463	504	577	675	685
	305	404	440	436	535	596	630	762	749	830	933	944
Out-patients	63	198	184	229	190	279	332	329	285	363	388	401
Total	368	602	624	665	725	875	962	1091	1034	1193	1321	1345

DISCHARGES

	1.4.51 to 31.3.52	1.4.52 to 31.3.53	1.4.53 to 31.3.54	1.4.54 to 31.3.55	1.4.55 to 31.3.56	1.4.56 to 31.3.57	1.4.57 to 31.3.58	1.4.58 to 31.3.59	1.4.59 to 31.3.60	1.4.60 to 31.3.61	1.4.61 to 31.3.62	1.4.62 to 31.3.63
Discharged	297	393	423	421	525	582	604	662	742	809	899	938
Home or Settlements	206	308	344	351	458	513	525	565	644	732	827	854
Chaseley Convalescent Home	25	9	15	11	8	4	9	18	5	6	4	6
Star and Garter Home	5	10	15	12	11	12	7	10	9	11	9	10
Duchess of Gloucester House	56	53	40	27	27	38	42	40	29	30	23	28
Other institutions	5	13	9	20	21	15	21	29	37	30	36	19
Deaths	5	7	4	8	10	7	13	11	18	19	13	21
Total	302	400	427	429	535	589	617	673	760	828	912	938
Total turnover	670	1002	1051	1094	1260	1464	1579	1764	1794	2021	2233	2283

ment of the Centre since the hospital was taken over by the National Health Service is shown in Table 1, which demonstrates the continuously increasing turnover. The Centre is provided with all facilities for the immediate as well as late stages of paraplegia due to accident and other causes, and it also has all facilities for physical rehabilitation, including sport, and for work, including training in workshops. It has its own swimming pool, garages for cars and tricycles, its own research department for biochemical, physiological and electronic research, and its own secretariat and welfare department. This centre, which has served the whole country for many years, has proved that a spinal unit can and indeed should be a section of a general hospital. For this centre, in spite of its large size, has been no detriment to the units of other surgical and medical specialities. On the contrary, for those units serving the local and regional population, such as the medical, neurological, paediatric, plastic, geriatric and rheumatological units, the existence of the spinal centre, far from being an hindrance for their own development, has afforded facilities which they have been able to utilize most advantageously for their own patients. It can be said, without exaggeration, that Stoke Mandeville as a whole is today one of the most rehabilitation-minded, general hospitals in this country.

Plate 20 gives an aerial view of the hospital, the area marked representing the Spinal Centre, including the swimming pool and the recreation unit. It also shows part of the sports ground, with the two basketball pitches and six huts for accommodation of disabled sportsmen and sportswomen who come to the various sports meetings held during the year. It also shows the "H" of the landing area for helicopters, which in recent years have been used in increasing numbers for the admission of acute traumatic paraplegics and tetraplegics.

Clinical Work

As already pointed out, the turnover of both in-patients and out-patients has steadily increased since 1952, as shown in Table 1. This involves both new patients and re-admission of former patients for check-ups for specialized treatments—in particular, plastic repair of sores and treatment of urinary infection. Particular attention is drawn to the fact that amongst the new admissions there is an increasing number of traumatic paraplegics and tetra-plegics, who are admitted immediately after or within the first forty-eight hours or first few days of accident. This has proved, of course, a very great blessing for these patients, as a spinal unit with its specialist staff and facilities can prevent those complications which, until a few years ago, were considered as inevitable. It is a fact that those patients who are admitted to Stoke Mandeville immediately never develop a sore, and in the majority of patients the paralysed bladder can be kept sterile at least for many weeks and months and in certain cases permanently. It may be stressed that, quite apart from the avoidance of unnecessary human suffering and prolonged stay in hospital, the saving of public money by adequate treatment is quite considerable. Many of the traumatic patients arrive here from general, orthopaedic and accident hospitals in seriously ill conditions, not only on account of their spinal cord injuries but also because of associated injuries to other parts of the body, such as damage to the internal organs, especially the lungs, with haemo- or pneumothorax, head injuries and fractures of the long bones.

The other group of seriously ill, new admissions comprises patients who come from hospitals or from home and are suffering from sepsis due to multiple bedsores and with varying degrees of bladder and renal infections—furthermore, with contractures of joints and varying degrees of spasticity.

As a National Centre, Stoke Mandeville admits patients from all parts of the country and, as far as private patients are concerned, from all over the world. The majority are admitted by road or rail and some, particularly those from abroad, by 'plane. Service personnel of the British Forces, who sustain traumatic paraplegia overseas, have arrived in this country within forty-eight hours of injury from as far away as Singapore, Aden and Germany. In recent years, transport by helicopter has increased and has indeed proved a life-saving measure in some of the patients admitted from this country.

TABLE 2

National Spinal Injuries Centre,
Analysis of 3000 cases

	Servicemen and Pensioners	Civilians	Total	Percentage
Traumatic lesions	753	1210	1963	65·4
Transverse myelitis	34	125	159	5·3
Poliomyelitis	89	63	152	5·1
Vascular processes	11	95	106	3·5
Spina bifida		62	62	2·1
Multiple sclerosis	41	80	121	4·0
Disc lesions	6	27	33	1·1
Miscellaneous	66	338	404	13·5
Total	1000	2000	3000	100·0

Since February 1944, over 3200 paraplegics and tetraplegics have been treated in this Centre. Table 2 gives a statistical analysis of the first 3000 patients admitted by May 1963. From the statistics, it is clear that the majority (65·4 per cent) are traumatic lesions at various levels of the cord. Most of the traumatic civilian patients come from the London area or from the south of England. The column headed "Miscellaneous" in Table 2 consists of non-traumatic patients other than transverse myelitis and polios, such as thrombosis of the spinal artery, haematomyelia, tuberculosis, tumours, syphilis, epidural abscess, degenerative and congenital processes. Special mention may be made of children with spina bifida who have been admitted in increasing numbers in recent years, and in this respect a close co-operation exists between the spinal centre and the paediatric unit of the hospital.

TABLE 3

Traumatic Lesions

	Servicemen and Pensioners	Civilians	Total	Percentage
Cervicals				23·6
complete	36	99	135	6·8
incomplete	86	245	331	16·8
T 1–5				9·8
complete	62	84	146	7·5
incomplete	18	27	45	2·3
T 6–12				43·1
complete	198	419	617	31·4
incomplete	113	115	228	11·7
Cauda Equina	240	221	461	23·5
Total	753	1210	1963	100·0

Table 3 shows an analysis of the 1963 traumatic lesions according to the level and completeness of the cord injury. It may be noted that a relatively high percentage of traumatic lesions affect the cervical portion of the cord, resulting in tetraplegia. An analysis of the number of traumatic lesions at the time of injury shows that the majority occur between the ages of 16 and 30. The tragedy is that, amongst these patients, the number of cervical injuries is relatively high, and diving, motor-car and motor-cycle accidents are the major causes.

The mortality rate amongst the 3000 patients is given in Table 4. It may be noted that these statistics include every patient who died either during treatment in this Centre or after discharge home or to other institutions. The uncorrected figures include causes of death quite independent of those directly relating to paraplegia, such as tuberculosis, cancer, cerebral haemorrhage and fresh accidents. The mortality statistics reveal a very low mortality rate even amongst the traumatic paraplegics from the Second World War. Most of them were initially treated in other hospitals in accordance with the old methods.

It is beyond the scope of this article to describe in detail the medical and surgical methods employed at Stoke Mandeville, and the author refers to his publications elsewhere (1945, 1949, 1953, 1962). However, two statistics on domestic and industrial resettlement are given which demonstrate the results of the treatment and rehabilitation of these patients.

TABLE 4

Mortality Rate

Total Material, 3000 cases
496 deaths	=	16·5%
343 corrected figure	=	11·4%

Traumatic Patients, total 1963
331 deaths	=	16·9%
242 corrected figure	=	12·3%

Servicemen and Pensioners, total 753
180 deaths	=	23·9%
132 corrected figure	=	17·5%

Civilians, total 1210
151 deaths	=	12·5%
110 corrected figure	=	9·0%

Analysis of Servicemen and Pensioners
World War I, total 67
39 deaths	=	58·2%
15 corrected figure	=	22·4%

World War II, total 468
125 deaths	=	26·7%
103 corrected figure	=	22·0%

Post War Period from 1946, total 218
16 deaths	=	7·3%
14 corrected figure	=	6·4%

As soon as a paraplegic is out of bed and in his wheelchair, regular work in our workshops is included in the programme, in concert with all other activities—i.e. physiotherapy, sport, re-education of bladder and bowels, and, in children and young adults, schooling. The Centre has workshops for light engineering, engraving, clock-assembly, and carpentry, as well as facilities for typing, shorthand and computer training. In these workshops, pre-vocational training is given by instructors who work in close contact with the medical staff and report each week on the patient's aptitude and progress. It is the regularity and accuracy of work which has proved most essential in restoring a paraplegic's activity of mind and self-confidence. Arrangements are made with the Disablement Resettlement Officer of the Ministry of Labour and the employers themselves, regarding the patient's future industrial and professional integration whilst the paraplegic is still in hospital, to ensure the least possible delay in his employment after discharge.

Since 1947 the author has published statistics at regular intervals on the

domestic and industrial resettlement of paraplegics, and the number of
paraplegics engaged in remunerative work has varied between 69 and 82 per
cent of those discharged from the Centre and available for employment, the

TABLE 5

Domestic Resettlement of 3000 Patients

Living at home	2059
Living in paraplegic settlements, hostels and homes for the disabled	240
Patients under treatment at Stoke Mandeville	151
Patients under treatment in other hospitals	54
Deaths	496
Total	3000

TABLE 6

Employment Statistics on 3000 Patients

Analysis		
Deceased		496
Retired and over age		103
Physically unfit (including 64 cervicals)		143
Under treatment at Stoke Mandeville		151
Under treatment at other hospitals		54
Not traced		41
Available for employment		2012
Total		3000
Available for Employment 2012		
Full time	1097	54·5%
Part time	222	11·0%
Home occupations	399	19·9%
Not working	294	14·6%
Total	2012	100·0%
Analysis of Employed		
Full time	1097	63·9%
Part time	222	12·9%
Home occupations	399	23·2%
Total	1718	100·0%

majority being full-time employed. The latest statistics were compiled in
May 1963, and concerned survivors out of 3000 paraplegics and tetraplegics
treated since 1944. Table 5 shows the domestic resettlement, and it may be
noted that most of the paraplegics live in their own homes, which is, of course,

the ideal of domestic resettlement. Table 6 gives an analysis of the employment of 2012 patients out of a total of 3000 available for employment at the time of the statistic, from which it is seen that altogether 85·4 per cent are gainfully employed, and of these 54·5 per cent full-time, in a variety of jobs in business, profession and open industry. Many have been working for many years as teachers, accountants, lawyers, doctors, clergymen, architects, film producers, clerical officers, typists, telephonists, draughtsmen, commercial artists, printers, laboratory technicians, watch-repairers, cobblers, radio mechanics, machine operators, workshop instructors, cutters, grinders, welders, assembly and bench workers, and temporary or established civil servants in various Government Departments. Paraplegic women are doing full housework and looking after their families from their wheelchairs, and quite a number of these have married after their paraplegia and about twenty-five have become mothers of normal babies. This clearly shows that paraplegia as such is not a bar to pregnancy, and in fact the great majority of paraplegic women are quite capable of bearing children in the normal way, and only in very exceptional cases was Caesarian section necessary.

Units affiliated to the Centre

(1) *Spinal Unit at Rookwood Hospital, Cardiff.* This unit was started in 1951 and has a complement of 36 beds. It deals with both acute and long-standing paraplegics and tetraplegics. It is to be regretted that full use is not made of the facilities at Cardiff for acute cases, and the co-operation of the accident and orthopaedic hospitals in Wales in sending their cases immediately after injury to a spinal unit is not as satisfactory as in England.

(2) *Spinal Unit at the Star and Garter Home, London.* This unit was set up in 1946 and has a complement of 20 beds. It is a unit for long-term patients only, who, for one reason or another, are not able to return to their own homes. Most of the residents are tetraplegics. This unit is, however, an active one with workshop facilities (clock and watch repair), physiotherapy and sport, and is run on vastly different lines from those of the Home described by Gowland, mentioned previously in this article.

(3) *Chaseley Home, Eastbourne.* This is another after-care unit for paraplegic ex-Servicemen only, which was set up in 1946 with 35 beds. Recently, the Ministry of Health has agreed that six beds be allocated to civilian paraplegics. This is another after-care home with workshop facilities (woodwork), physiotherapy and sport.

(4) *Lyme Green Settlement for paraplegic ex-Servicemen.* This is a settlement set up in Macclesfield, Cheshire, by the Red Cross after the war for paraplegic ex-Servicemen and their families. The married people live in bungalows and single paraplegics in the Hall. This unit has 30 residents and the Settlement is provided with sheltered workshops (clock repair, carpentry and shoe repair).

(5) *Kytes Settlement for paraplegic ex-Servicemen.* This was also set up by the Red Cross, and a former patient of Stoke Mandeville, the Rt. Hon. Julian Holland-Hibbert, C.B.E., was a prime mover in the foundation. In contrast to the Lyme Green Settlement, the majority of residents do full-time work in factories and offices in the Watford area, and most of them have been employed for many years.

(6) *The Duchess of Gloucester House, London.* This is a hostel for paraplegics of 78 beds (72 for men and 6 for women), which was started in 1949 by the Ministry of Pensions in co-operation with the Ministry of Labour and has been administered since 1953 by the Ministry of Labour. This was the first hostel set up in this country for those paraplegics, both civilian and ex-Service, who were able and willing to take up full-time employment in industry under normal, outside working conditions. New residents are selected by a Board comprised of representatives of the Ministry of Labour and myself, as medical consultant. The hostel is provided with a workshop and an instructor in charge (himself a paraplegic), for those few residents whose employment is pending or who are out of work. There are also good facilities for sport. No provision is made for married couples, but the hostel gives male and female paraplegics the opportunity to live in the hostel and be employed so long as their own houses are not ready or if, for one reason or another, they cannot return to live with their families. Since 1949, about 350 paraplegics of various levels have graduated from the hostel. No less than 30 firms within a radius of 12 miles of the hostel at present provide full-time employment for about 100 paraplegics (both residents and former residents), and in general the employers speak very highly of their paraplegic workers. The great majority are engaged in assembly and bench work, as labourers or instructors. Others are doing clerical work, accountancy, shorthand and typing, switchboard operating and engineering work. Many of these residents live in the hostel for many years. Absenteeism of this group of workers during the year is extremely low, which is indeed most gratifying and proves beyond all shadow of doubt that the majority of paraplegics can hold down their jobs in competition with those less disabled as well as with the able-bodied. Their salaries and wages are commensurate with those of able-bodied workers, and as wage-earners they have, of course, to pay income tax and also for their board and lodging at the hostel. Over 40 of the residents or former residents now living at home have bought their own cars from their earnings and have returned their motorized tricycles to the State, which the latter had provided to them free of charge in accordance with welfare regulations in Great Britain.

All these hostels and homes are medically guided by this Centre and visited by the author and senior members of the medical staff, although they have their own medical officers for routine care. The residents are readmitted to Stoke Mandeville for regular check-ups or specialized treatment if necessary.

Routine After-care following Discharge

In 1951, having regard to the increasing number of patients discharged to their homes, a systematic out-patient service was organized to deal with routine clinical check-ups, particularly for those paraplegics who had found employment and were anxious to have as little time off work as possible. This has proved a most essential part of the work of the Centre, in order to detect and treat any deterioration in a paraplegic's condition and thus keep as many of them as possible at their work. Table 1 shows the very great increase in this after-care service over the years, increasing from 63 in 1951 to 401 in 1962. Where distance does not permit an out-patient check-up, the paraplegic or tetraplegic is readmitted for a day or two for the necessary check-up, and the increase in this service too is shown in Table 1.

Teaching

For many years, this Centre has been engaged in teaching undergraduates and postgraduates of the medical profession, as well as of the nursing, physiotherapy and occupational therapy professions, and this activity has greatly increased in recent years:

(1) *Medical Staff, Welfare Officers and Administrators.* The great majority of these were physicians, surgeons and medical students from many hospitals in this country and abroad. The Centre takes part in the regular postgraduate courses arranged by the British Council and organized by the Stanmore Orthopaedic Hospital, as well as those from the National Hospital for Nervous Diseases, Queen Square, London and the medical services of the army and air force. Recently, the Centre has been included in the postgraduate courses of the Royal College of Surgeons in London. Physicians and surgeons from other countries have been sent to this Centre for training ranging from several weeks to many months, and as a result in several countries spinal units have been set up. The same applies to welfare officers, administrators and architects from hospitals and government departments of this and other countries.

(2) *Postgraduate courses for nurses.* Apart from regular visits of groups of nurses who are sent to this Centre for formal lectures through the Royal College of Nursing, three-monthly postgraduate courses have been introduced since 1953, which are attended by nurses from hospitals and institutions in this country and indeed all over the world. They receive regular lectures by the senior members of the medical staff, and this also includes instruction in ward work. Some of these postgraduate nurses continue working in the Centre after the course, to gain more detailed experience. The Centre is included in the training programme of student nurses of the Aylesbury

Nursing School, in their second and third years. Recently the University of Cologne in Germany has, with the agreement of the British Nursing Council, requested to send student nurses in their third year for three months' training in the Centre.

(3) *Physiotherapy and occupational therapy staff.* In addition to full-day visits of individuals and groups of physiotherapists and occupational therapists from their teaching schools, annual postgraduate courses for physiotherapists are held, which have become quite popular and are greatly supported by the Chartered Society of Physiotherapy.

(4) *Teaching outside the Centre.* Throughout the years, members of the medical staff of this Centre, as well as the Lay Administrator and Welfare Officer, have delivered a very great number of lectures to teaching hospitals, training schools and many organizations such as Red Cross, St. John Ambulance Brigade, W.V.S., British Legion, Rotary Clubs, Government Departments, etc. Members of the medical staff have been invited to lecture at international congresses and visit other countries to lecture on the problems of paraplegia.

Research

From the beginning, intensive clinical and experimental research has gone hand in hand with the clinical work, in which the medical officers, both senior and junior, have taken part. In recent years, a special research department has been set up of physiological, biochemical and electronic laboratories. Research workers from this country and abroad have visited this Centre and co-operated in research on certain physiological problems in the spinal man. Recently, the National Polio Research Fund has given a grant to this Centre for setting up an Electro-Mechanical Unit, which is engaged in the development of mechanical aids for severely disabled paraplegics and tetraplegics, by which a person without the use of arms and fingers is able to control a number of devices, including telephone, electric typewriter and a machine by sucking and blowing through a tube, using a special code. The results of the research have appeared in over 100 publications in many leading journals and textbooks.

Meetings of medical and scientific organizations, such as the Neurological and Orthopaedic Sections of the Royal Society of Medicine, the British Biochemical Society and sections of international congresses have been held at the Centre throughout the years. Moreover, regular international scientific meetings on paraplegia have been held since 1954 on the occasion of the annual International Stoke Mandeville Games. As a result of these meetings, the International Medical Society of Paraplegia was founded in 1961 at Stoke Mandeville, which now has its own international journal published by Livingstone's of Edinburgh.

Sport

Since the inception of the Stoke Mandeville Centre, sport has been a very important part of the physical, psychological as well as social rehabilitation of the paralysed. This has proved extremely successful, and the profound value of sport in preventing these patients from retiring into inactivity cannot be exaggerated. Sporting activities are included in the medical treatment, and games, such as archery, table-tennis and swimming, are part of the training of the patients.

In 1948 the author founded the Stoke Mandeville Games as a sports movement for the paralysed, with twenty-six British ex-Servicemen. These Games, which were at first held annually as a national event, soon developed in number as regards both competitors and sports events and became in 1952 the first organized sports festival for severely disabled people in the world. In order to accommodate the many paralysed sportsmen and sportswomen who come to the National and International Games at Stoke Mandeville every year, accommodation huts were built with the help of a Paraplegic Sports Endowment Fund founded from voluntary contributions, which has become responsible for financing the Games. Stoke Mandeville is especially suitable for this sports festival, as an excellent sports ground is attached to the hospital. The idea of sport has spread more and more to many countries, and in 1960 the International Stoke Mandeville Games were held in Rome, immediately after the Olympic Games, where 400 paralysed men and women and 250 escorts were accommodated in the Olympic Village. The late Pope John XXIII gave a special audience to all competitors and escorts in the Vatican City. In 1964 the Games were held in Tokyo after the Olympic Games.

In November 1962 the First British Commonwealth Paraplegic Games were held in Perth, Western Australia, immediately before the British Empire and Commonwealth Games for the able-bodied, when sixty paraplegic men and women and twenty escorts made this epic journey. This alone, apart from the resettlement of paraplegics in employment, proves the dramatic change which has taken place in the whole concept of what was once one of the most depressing and neglected subjects in medicine. The Stoke Mandeville Games for the Paralysed have inspired other disabled people to take up sports activities, and as a result the British Sports Association for the Disabled (B.S.A.D.) was founded at Stoke Mandeville four years ago. Annual Multi-Disabled sports meetings are held at the sports ground of Stoke Mandeville Hospital, where amputees, paralysed and blind compete in various sports events, which include archery, dartchery (a combination of archery and darts), field sports, table-tennis, fencing, bowling, obstacle races, and swimming. The Stoke Mandeville Games for the Paralysed have found recognition by national and international sports organizations of the able-bodied, the most outstanding being the

Award of the Fearnley Cup in 1956 by the International Olympic Committee, during the Olympic Games in Melbourne (Plate 21). This Olympic Award is given for outstanding achievement in the service of the olympic idea, and it was the first time that an Olympic Trophy had been won by a Sports Organ-ization of disabled sportsmen in the history of the Olympic Games.

The Future

However, in spite of great advances made during the last twenty years in the problem of paraplegia, there is no room for complacency, and there are many problems, both medical and social, which still have to be dealt with. These can be summarized as follows:

(1) *Medical Problems*. There is still discrepancy of opinion about the best immediate management of spinal cord injuries as a result of fractures and fracture dislocations of the spine. There are still a considerable number of these patients who are treated in departments which are neither equipped nor have the necessary knowledge and experience for dealing with all the prob-lems of the acute paraplegic. The old attitude still exists to concentrate on the management of the spine and either neglect or treat inadequately the other problems, in particular the paralysis of the bladder and bowels and care of the skin. Alas, it will take some time before it is generally accepted that such a patient deserves the same highly skilled treatment from the start as does any other serious affliction of the body, whether it be brain, chest or abdo-minal injuries. Just as today everyone agrees that fractures of the long bones are best dealt with in orthopaedic departments, the same principle should apply to the patient with a fractured spine and paraplegia or tetraplegia, who should be treated in a spinal unit. There is also the vast problem of the infection of the urinary tract, which depends so much on the adequate initial treatment following paraplegia and which is far from solved. In this connection, the increased duration of life of these patients has brought new problems of late renal and vascular disturbances, which previously did not exist, as the patients died. These are only a few of the medical problems involved.

(2) *Transport*. This can be divided into two parts:

    (a) *Wheelchairs:* Although the provision of wheelchairs by the State has been an established fact in Great Britain since the Health Service came into being, the most suitable wheelchair for the various types of disabled person is still under discussion. This became very evident at a Symposium on Wheelchairs organized by the Polio Research Fund in November 1963, and held under the Chairmanship of the author when representatives of the Ministry of Health, physicians, surgeons, administrators, engineers, manufacturers and users had a joint discussion about this problem.

(b) *Motorized transport:* While ex-Service pensioner paraplegics are privileged in obtaining motor-cars adapted with hand-controls from the State, civilian paraplegics are still using invalid motor-tricycles provided by the State, in which they are unable to carry a passenger —unless, of course, they are able to afford to buy their own cars. However, it must be said that this type of covered-in motor-tricycle is a vast improvement on the former open motor-tricycle, in which the paraplegic had to travel in all elements

(c) *Public transport:* There is a need for adjustment of public transport to the requirements of the paralysed. This applies in particular to the railways. Paraplegics still have difficulty in entering compartments and often find it easier to travel in the guards van—indeed a very unsatisfactory situation. Therefore, some adjustment to the carriages is necessary for paraplegics and other severely disabled people, to facilitate their travel by rail. Moreover, some airlines still have difficulties in accommodating paraplegics, and in particular there is not always a lifting device available at airports to facilitate the carrying of the paraplegic into the aeroplane.

(3) *Buildings.*

(a) *Housing facilities:* This is another important problem. It must be admitted that in recent years the housing authorities have become more aware of the necessity for building special houses of bungalow type for the paralysed, which thus enables them to live a normal life. The authorities are also more co-operative in adjusting the houses of the paralysed by widening the doors, building ramps, providing garages, and adjusting bathrooms and toilets. However, this is still a very slow process, and paraplegics sometimes have to stay in hospital longer than is medically necessary until their houses have been adjusted or they have been re-housed—indeed, a vast expense to the Hospital Service. There is no doubt that the need for proper housing facilities for paraplegics is an ever increasing problem.

(b) *Institutional care with workshop facilities:* There is an increasing number of paraplegics with high lesions, especially tetraplegics who are now surviving for many years but who, for one reason or another, cannot live in their own homes to be looked after by their families. Although there are hostel facilities in Great Britain for ex-Servicemen, there is only one hostel—the Duchess of Gloucester House— as pointed out previously, which deals with civilian paraplegics. However, only those paraplegics can be admitted to that hostel who are capable of doing full-time employment in open industry or commerce. The problem still remains to provide after-care hostels for those who cannot return home or who, having lived at home for a time, can no longer be looked after by their families. There is a

great need to build hostels for this group, and such hostels should
be provided with sheltered workshop facilities, as quite a number of
these severely disabled people could still be useful and even gainfully
employed under these conditions. These hostels should be built
preferably in the neighbourhood of spinal units and set up on a
regional basis. The author has submitted a memorandum to the
Minister of Health, urging that the first pilot scheme should be
started at Stoke Mandeville Hospital, where ideal conditions exist
for such a hostel. One of the great advantages of these hostels would
be the relieving of hospital beds for the admission of urgent cases,
who otherwise deteriorate at home or in hospitals which cannot
deal adequately with these severely disabled people. Such a hostel
is now nearing its completion at Stoke Mandeville.

(c) *Public buildings:* These still present great architectural obstacles to a
paraplegic's return to full social activities, and paraplegics still have
greatest difficulty in visiting theatres, cinemas, restaurants, hotels,
museums, post offices, banks, swimming pools and sports stadiums,
as well as working in some offices and factories. While, from the
architectural point of view, a flight of steps to the entrance of a building may be impressive, for the paraplegic as well as other severely
disabled persons, including amputees and those with vascular and
chest diseases, they present an almost insurmountable barrier.
Moreover, the toilets are very often inaccessible to people in wheel-
chairs. It will take some time before architects in particular and society in general will assist our disabled fellowmen by making such
buildings accessible to them, to assist them in their endeavours to
become full members of society.

References

CUSHING, H., The Med. Dept. U.S. Army in World War I, *Surgery II*, Part 1, 757,
    1927.
DICK, T. B. S., M. D. Thesis, Manchester University, 1949.
EVERTS, W. H. and WOODHALL, B., *J. Amer. med. Ass.*, **126**, 145, 1944; *Brit. Med. J*,
    1, 188, 1934.
GUTTMANN, L., New hope for spinal cord sufferers, *New York Medical Times*, **73**,
    318, 1945.
GUTTMANN, L., Surgical aspects in traumatic paraplegia, *J. Bone & Joint Surg.*,
    31B, 389, 1949.
GUTTMANN, L., Principles of physiotherapy in the treatment of spinal paraplegia,
    Physiotherapy, Oct., **35**, 157, 1949.
GUTTMANN, L., The treatment and rehabilitation of patients with injuries of the
    spinal cord, Monograph in Vol. Surgery, *Medical History of the Second World
    War*, pp. 422–516, Published by H.M.S.O., London, 1953.
GUTTMANN, L., Our paralysed fellowmen at work, *Rehabilitation*, **43**, 9–17, 1962.
GUTTMANN, L., Sport and the disabled, *Sports Medicine*, Arnold, London, pp.
    367–91, 1962.

38. A Doctor Looks at a Disability—Treatment and Welfare Services for Persons Suffering from Arthritis and Rheumatism

Physician to the Rheumatics Unit, St. Stephen's Hospital, Chelsea. Vice-Chairman,
British Rheumatism and Arthritis Association

RHEUMATISM is said to be derived from the Greek term *rheumatismos* which signifies mucus (catarrh), an evil humour which flows from the brain to the joints and other parts of the body giving rise to pain. Arthritis is a term used when the joints are the main seat of the rheumatic disease. The terms "arthritis" and "rheumatism" are now used to embrace a large and miscellaneous group of diseases and disorders of the supporting tissues.

The rheumatoid type of arthritis, the most crippling of the rheumatic diseases, may manifest itself for the first time in childhood, in the young and middle-aged adult, or in the elderly person. The osteo-arthritis type of arthritis affects mainly the hands, spine, hips and knees. It is a common cause of pain and disability in elderly people. Gout may be closely associated with osteo-arthritis. Acute rheumatism is the most common cause of structural heart disease in childhood and early adult life.

Rheumatism includes the relatively rare "collagen" diseases, a term which is applied to an ill-defined group of diseases having as a common feature a disturbance of the connective tissues, with varying degrees of vascular involvement, among which are the conditions of poly-arteritis, systemic lupus erythematosus. Its common form is non-articular rheumatism, commonly termed "fibrositis", which includes the clinical picture of the "rotator cuff", "shoulder-hand", and "carpal tunnel" syndromes, derangements of the cervical spine, and lumbar spine, presenting the clinical picture of brachial neuritis, and sciatica, and "rheumatism", in which psychological factors play the main role. Those of us who are actively interested in the treatment of people suffering from the rheumatic diseases are acutely conscious of the fact that rheumatism and arthritis are terms which are difficult to define and hard to describe, and have quite different meanings for the clinician, the research worker, the statistician, and for the sufferer himself. A study of the general morbidity data on the incidence and prevalence of these diseases obtained by notification and analysing medical sickness records, hospital records, and a survey of sickness based on home-visiting have shown that these diseases are very common. It has been estimated that 2 million people in the British Isles suffer from some type of rheumatic disability.

In a recent survey of the general population in a Lancashire town made by Professor Kellgren and Dr. Lawrence, 40 per cent of those interviewed stated that they had some rheumatic symptoms at the time of the survey. Nearly half of those with such complaints had never consulted a doctor, and only one-fifth had even been in hospital or attended an out-patients' clinic. In 1958 some 15,500 patients suffering from rheumatoid arthritis were admitted to hospital in England and Wales, together with 13,500 suffering from osteo-arthritis, and 12,000 with "displaced intervertebral discs" (Ministry of Health and Registrar-General's officers' report). The "displaced discs" probably include lumbago of many different causes. It was estimated that 2,900,000 patients were treated by general practitioners under the National Health Service for chronic rheumatic diseases in any one year. This represents nearly 10 per cent of the total number of patients treated in general practice during the year. A recent survey quoted by the Royal College of Physicians Committee on Chronic Rheumatic Diseases showed that approximately 1,740,000 of the population were affected with rheumatoid arthritis, and that 3,700,000 of the over-65 age group had disabling osteo-arthritis.

This report noted that an appreciable number of hospital beds are occupied by patients with these rheumatic disorders. The number of out-patients is much larger, and the number of patients treated at home even greater. It stated that a treatment problem of such magnitude required the collaboration of all branches of the medical services. The greatest share of responsibility for the management of these patients falls on the general practitioner. Medical consultants with special experience in the rheumatic diseases are still few in number, and are only available in some parts of the country. There is a scarcity of beds, and adequate out-patient facilities for the care of the more serious and difficult cases.

For many years prior to the introduction in 1948 of the National Health Service, rheumatic units with in-patient facilities and large out-patient departments existed at the West London Hospital, St. Stephen's Hospital, Chelsea, and at the important spas, such as Bath and Buxton. Basic scientific research was increasing our knowledge of these diseases. Considerable advances in the diagnosis and treatment were being made. Controlled therapeutic trials were helping to improve drug treatment.

The establishment of special centres was rightly considered to be the most promising method of advancing the study of the chronic rheumatic diseases. Such centres were gradually developed mainly in close association with teaching hospitals in different parts of the country. These centres were to concern themselves mainly with research and teaching. The training of young specialists should be the responsibility of university authorities, Boards of Governors, or of Regional Boards. At Bath, Bristol, Edinburgh, Hammersmith, Taplow, Manchester, Sheffield and Stoke Mandeville, such centres have been set up. Since the introduction of the National Health Services, the appointment of an increasing number of consultants in physical medicine to the main hospital groups meant that good treatment facilities have been made available for people with these diseases. Physicians with training and experience in the rheumatic diseases are now working with, or as consultants in, physical medicine, in most hospitals in close co-operation with the orthopaedic surgeons.

To a lesser extent efforts are being made to encourage the family doctor to take on the responsibility for the routine care of his rheumatic patients.

Little detailed information is available as to the effects of rheumatoid arthritis on the social and economic status of the individual. The medical profession is only now beginning to realize that the rheumatic diseases are not only a medical problem but also an important social problem, to help in the solution of which persistent medical guidance and direction is essential. Professor Walter Bauer in Boston (U.S.A.) and Dr. John Duthie in Edinburgh have undertaken long-term studies which have suggested that of people with rheumatoid arthritis, one in five leads a normal life, three suffer moderate restriction of their activities but are able to earn their living or run their homes, while the remaining one in five is wholly or partially dependent on others.

It is the family doctor who is the first to be consulted when a man falls ill, and he is usually the first to attach the diagnostic label of arthritis or rheumatism to his patient. Sometimes he has little knowledge or interest in the rheumatic diseases. This is not his fault, it is due to the lack of opportunity in undergraduate training. When he has attached the label to his patient, often he does not know what to do for him. He may feel that he has not got the knowledge and facilities to give his patient adequate care. Even when the facilities are available, sometimes he does not know where to get them.

The hospital physician interested in these diseases has to take a careful history and make a detailed clinical examination, and usually also have X-rays and pathological investigations before he is able to attach a diagnostic label to his patient. The patient may have been examined by every conceivable laboratory test, and X-ray examination, drugs and physical measures may have been prescribed, but too often little interest has been taken in him as a man, and little attention paid to the factors that affect or may have affected his reaction to the disease. Often a patient tells us that no one has had the time to listen to his story or explain the nature of his disability and to plan a line of management with him.

For the hospital physician to complete his clinical picture two other reports are needed, one by the almoner, giving details of the patient's social background, family life, and his daily work, and the other, the activities of daily living chart done by the occupational therapist, to give a picture of how he is able to cope with the things that he needs to do daily in his house, such as washing, dressing, eating and so on. It is only when this additional information has been obtained and put together by the doctor that he knows something about his patient and is able to make a proper diagnosis and plan a line of management.

Those of us who are consultants in the National Health Service tend to have large out-patient clinics, and often following his initial consultation with the physician, the patient is seen at intervals by a series of different registrars or clinical assistants, who do not know him, and apart from reading the short notes in the case-sheet are unfamiliar with his problem. Although everyone in the hospital service is doing his best, and trying to help the patient, in many cases this could be done better by the family doctor, if only he had been taught to recognize and treat rheumatic diseases.

The psycho-social make-up of the patient before the onset of the disease will in great part determine his reaction and ability to adjust himself to the disease. Anxiety, the wearing effect of prolonged pain, constant frustration due to inability to perform even simple routine activities, fear of becoming incapacitated, crippled and dependent on others, a feeling that he has an incurable disease with which he will have to live for the rest of his life, leads to apathy, and may cause friction in family life. Our hospital almoners, and those who work for voluntary organizations, can do a great deal to alleviate and to prevent the suffering caused in this way.

To keep at work when one has arthritis is made more difficult because of persistent and often increasing pain, fatigue, stiffness and disability, requiring increasing drive and determination to do even a routine job in the home or in industry.

It is particularly important to gain as much insight as possible into the adverse influence of domestic, economic and social factors. We have all seen how much of our time and effort is wasted, and how the effects of well-planned and expensive forms of hospital treatment are rapidly lost if we fail to recognize and control these factors. Patients who have done well in hospital go back to uncongenial homes and unsuitable work and immediately relapse. Patients realize that often we are unable to offer them a specific cure for their disease, and are often haunted by this fear of crippling and dependence. A careful and full assessment in hospital by the physician and his team can do a great deal to give the patient moral as well as physical help, and dispel unwarranted fear and give justifiable hope.

This is essential if the patient is to co-operate. Success is dependent on the patient's active co-operation and may have to be carried on for a long time. The patient's family plays a very important part in success or failure. I have found that the patient's mother by over-protection may make successful rehabilitation impossible. An unco-operative wife, or sympathetic but obstructive employer, has been the real cause of someone with rheumatoid arthritis failing to return to work. How to reduce loneliness and a feeling of frustration and a sense of not being wanted are all worthy of sympathetic and detailed study. These problems should at least be appreciated and clearly defined before the patient leaves the hospital. This takes time, much time, and the rheumatologist who does his job properly must be prepared to give as much time to the social as he does to the strictly "scientific" aspect of his work.

Contributions to progress and new advances in our knowledge of arthritis and its management and prevention may come from those arthritic people who study their difficulties and their attitudes towards their disabilities and those of their fellow sufferers, just as it does from those professional people who add to knowledge by recording what they see through the microscope and label "rheumatism". What doctors think and feel about patients and what patients think and feel about doctors are not always similar.

It has been pointed out that medical care of any person or group of people is not the care offered but the care that is accepted and received. Organization is becoming more and more detailed and necessary as more and more people are concerned with the individual patient. Within the hospital service advances have been made mainly in improving diagnosis and in treating "episodes" in the disease. What is needed is what the Americans call "continuous comprehensive care".

If someone who is arthritic is to manage his life successfully, the medical knowledge of his disease needs to be integrated with a proper understanding not only of the facilities available for his treatment, but also those which can enable him to lead as full a life as possible.

> Who learns and learns, but does not what he knows,
> Is one who ploughs and ploughs, but never sows.

Having integrated knowledge it is essential to act on it, to apply it to the individual who needs help. Doctors and patients and medical auxiliaries need to work in close co-operation with members of the various statutory bodies and voluntary organizations. But for their efforts to be successful the rheumatologist must not only integrate but guide and often personally direct the activities of the many members of this team.

Successful rehabilitation of the individual and the prevention of disability and crippling disease depends on the provision and maintenance of an unbroken chain of facilities. The links may be of different shapes and sizes. A link that is missing or broken may be the cause of a person failing to regain his health and not returning to a full and contented life at work and in his home.

The National Health Service provides the family doctor, the rheumatologist, the orthopaedic surgeon, the nursing staff, the physical medicine department, with the staff of almoners and medical auxiliaries, the rehabilitation unit, the local government health and welfare authorities, including the district nurse. The Ministry of Labour and National Service offers the services of the Disablement Rehabilitation Officer and facilities for industrial rehabilitation and vocational training. The Ministry of Pensions and National Insurance is responsible for proper benefits and allowances. Although with the introduction of the Welfare State the early concept of charity has been replaced in part by the more clearly defined functions of doing things for the individual which are not or cannot be done by the State, charitable bodies still have an important part to play. One of their functions is to help to close the gap left by the state services, so that help is given to any rheumatic sufferers in need of it.

The British Rheumatism and Arthritis Association and the Central Council for the Disabled are among the many voluntary bodies which undertake welfare and social research. The Empire Rheumatism Council promotes medical research, which is vital for a better understanding of the rheumatic diseases, which will in time lead to the elimination and prevention of many forms of rheumatism and arthritis.

Let us not forget the importance of studying our patients as well as their diseases. As Lord Horder used to teach us at St. Bartholomew's Hospital, what matters is, "Le malade, toujours le malade" (Trousseau).

39. The Shaftesbury Society

GORDON A. FRANKLIN
Secretary of the Shaftesbury Society

THE LAST decade of the eighteenth century was a formative period both in the realm of philosophy and religion. Humanism, as proclaimed by the revolutionaries on the Continent, and the universality of the Love of God as declared by the founders of our great missionary societies, had their repercussions in the life of our own country, in that Christian people of all denominations felt a new concern for the poor and particularly the children of the poor. Their concern was expressed in gathering groups of children into little improvised schools, primarily to teach the children to read so that they might read the Bible for themselves, but going on to simple instruction in the three R's. For obvious reasons the schools were early dubbed "Ragged Schools". This movement spread through all our great centres of population, and in 1844 the Ragged School Union was formed under the Presidency of Lord Ashley, later the 7th Earl of Shaftesbury, an association that continued until his death in 1885. Thus was created the formative influence in child welfare work of the last century. From the beginning, the voluntary teachers of the Ragged Schools sought to express their Christian teaching in terms of service to the community. It was therefore natural that the children of the slums should be taken out into the country for day or half-day outings, and in 1892 Sir Arthur Pearson, in association with the R.S.U., founded the Pearson's Fresh Air Fund to give financial assistance to this work.

Concurrent with the organization of outings came the establishment of holiday-convalescent homes for children needing a period of recuperation away from the city, and much later permanent holiday camps where groups of children with their leaders could be accommodated.

The Education Act of 1870 brought changes in the work of the Ragged Schools which gradually became inter-denominational missions and youth centres. Continuing the tradition of Christian service, many of these centres included a soup kitchen for free food distribution. By the end of the century the R.S.U. was administering the London School Children's Dinner Fund and the London School Children's Boot Fund. In this century these centres have done pioneer work in the organization of day nurseries, nursery schools and sunray and massage clinics for delicate and handicapped children.

It is hard to discover when the R.S.U. first showed special interest in the care of the physically handicapped, but early in its history it arranged holidays for crippled children. After the 1870 Education Act the mission workers became aware of the loneliness of crippled children who by reason of their disability could not attend the board schools that were being established. To alleviate their plight, simple clubs were formed to which groups of children were brought in their wheeled chairs for games and social intercourse. Because the earliest of these clubs met in people's houses, they were called Cripple Parlours, and the name persisted for fifty years. The whole of Greater London was served by these clubs under the leadership of a small army of voluntary workers. Handbooks for the guidance of workers among the handicapped were published regularly. To give permanent value to this work, a register of case histories was formed of those known to us, and quickly expanded to about 7000. Contact with the people was maintained by a small staff of domiciliary caseworkers and a greater number of voluntary visitors.

For about seventy years this was the only register of its kind in London, and it formed the base of the evacuation of a large number of handicapped people in the Second World War.

It was, perhaps, inevitable that an organization with holiday homes for normal children and this new concern for the handicapped should establish convalescent homes especially for crippled children, and this was begun about 1890. Because children might be in these homes for three months or more, part-time teachers were employed to occupy the children's time constructively and so, by a slow process, the convalescent homes became residential schools, the first one registered with the Board of Education in 1916.

In the course of time six of these schools were established dealing with all types of orthopaedic, muscular and neuro-muscular handicaps. The first school for severely handicapped boys was established in 1943, the primary qualification for admission being a handicap so severe as to preclude entry to any other school. A sister school for severely handicapped girls was established in 1947.

The Present Work of the Shaftesbury Society

Mission Centres

The Society still maintains forty inter-denominational mission centres in the Greater London area. These missions exercise the ministries of a Christian Church with a wide variety of practical expression of their teaching. The uniformed children's organizations and youth clubs have their place, and, for the aged, permanent day centres and luncheon clubs. A very practical service in one or two missions is the provision of chiropody clinics for the aged. Several of the missions have clubs for the physically handicapped.

Holiday Convalescent Centres

The Society maintains one home for babies 0–5 years of age. Originally a convalescent home for post-hospital recuperation it now caters largely for children "in care" because of unsatisfactory home conditions. At the other extreme of the age scale there is one holiday home for old age pensioners heavily subsidized from central funds. Holiday camps in Essex and Kent which originally provided for parties of children from London missions are used increasingly for school journeys and for the physically handicapped.

Domiciliary Casework among the Handicapped

For many years the Society was alone in this field of activity, and in addition to expert advice, helped to provide surgical appliances. This is no longer necessary, but we still keep a large pool of invalid chairs for loan to those people who cannot obtain one through the health scheme. In addition we arrange holidays in our own camps for physically handicapped men, women and children from the Greater London area. The most recent development is the provision of holidays for whole families in which either or both parents are paralysed and who otherwise would have no hope of such relief. Also related to our casework is the organization of Christian social clubs for handicapped adults of which twenty-five are associated with the Society. Where it is necessary we act as sponsors for the loan of wireless sets from the Wireless for the Bedridden Society. Our caseworkers serve on School Care Committees and Disablement Advisory Committees and Panels.

Residential Schools for the Physically Handicapped

In this field of activity the Shaftesbury Society has done and is doing pioneer work. Reference has been made to the first schools for the severely handicapped dealing with all types of physical disability. In recent years the Society has specialized in the care of two groups. There was always a certain proportion of pupils in the schools who by reason of their handicap suffered from incontinence. Encouraged by the great advances in the training and treatment of these conditions, a pioneer establishment was planned and built to provide for their needs. The success of this experiment has been outstanding due to the devoted work of specialists, consultants and staff. It is still the only school of its kind in existence. The other group for which we have especially catered is those suffering from muscular dystrophy. Although at present no remedial treatment is possible for them, and their expectation of life is very short, the Society has been glad to be able to enrich their experience and provide them with the care impossible in their own homes. About sixty pupils in an advanced stage of dystrophy are in the Society's schools. In all these six schools our object, in addition to care, treatment and education, is to provide the happy atmosphere of a Christian home.

Adult Residential Centre for the Handicapped

Because of our natural concern for the welfare of pupils who left our schools at the age of 16 years too severely handicapped to gain admission to any of the existing sheltered workshops, we opened a small home for eighteen severely handicapped young men at Bognor Regis. As our purpose was to provide only for those refused elsewhere it is obvious that it was a social experiment rather than a remedial one. In its own sphere it has been eminently successful. The residents have their own amateur radio club, and within the limits of their physical ability engage in basket work, the making of costume jewellery and water-colour, oil-painting and scraper-board work. Their pictures are of a high standard and much sought after. The community life has enriched them greatly. At present the Society is proposing to extend its work in this field by building two Homes for young men suffering from muscular dystrophy who have reached school-leaving age.

General Welfare Services

In 1895 *The Sunday Companion* founded the "Barefoot Mission" to provide poor children with shoes and stockings in the winter months. This was taken over by the Society, and its work greatly expanded by merging it with "The Guild of the Good Samaritan", founded in 1892 by the Editor of *The Young Women* and also transferred to the Society.

The Guild is still our working auxiliary, making and collecting garments both new and secondhand for the assistance of needy families. Hospital almoners, parish workers, local authority welfare workers and School Care Committees refer to us families in need of clothing or other special help.

General Remarks on the Present Situation

In the field of welfare work generally, and the care of the physically handicapped in particular, the post-war period has seen the emergence of many special groups focusing attention on the needs of particular handicaps. Research is being sponsored to a degree never before known, and only possible in an age of specialization. The development in the 1950's of statutory schemes for the welfare of the handicapped has made possible our partnership between voluntary and statutory bodies that is most encouraging.

The Shaftesbury Society constantly has to find solutions to the problem of how to adapt its work to a changing need without losing sight of the value of its past and its roots in the life of the Christian Church. Its achievements are the best guarantee of its ability to live out the words of its crest "Love—Serve".

40. The Spastics Society

C. P. STEVENS

Director of the Spastics Society

THE NATIONAL SPASTICS SOCIETY was founded in 1952 by three parents of spastics and a social worker. It became The Spastics Society in 1962 on amalgamation with the British Council for the Welfare of Spastics, founded in 1947. It believes that a cerebrally palsied child cannot be seen or helped outside the context of his family, and two of the original aims of the Society's founders—to give practical help and skilled advice and to provide a common meeting ground for spastics and their parents—still guide much of the Society's work.

Social Work Department

The Social Work Department is formed of trained social workers in close contact with the staff of the Society's five schools, its assessment and diagnostic centre, where border-line educable children are observed and assessed over a period of months, and with its adult residential centres and holiday hotels. There is also close liaison with other centres specializing in the care of the cerebrally palsied, and with local authorities, hospitals and voluntary organizations throughout the country. This work can be broken down to three divisions.

Social Work

The medical, educational and social assessment service for children and adults is an important part of this: not only is the child carefully examined by a paediatrician and educational psychologist experienced in the field of cerebral palsy (or in the case of an adult by the educational psychologist only), but considerable time is given to explaining to the parents the Panel's recommendation for the child. In this way much needless worry and misunderstanding can be eliminated. There is also a social worker in this Department who specializes in adult care for those spastics who are too heavily physically or mentally handicapped to enjoy anything but full-time residential care.

Regional Social Work

The Society hopes ultimately to have one social worker in each of its twelve regions, though at the moment only four of these have been appointed.

They will maintain links between the family, local statutory and voluntary services, local parent groups and the Society's Head Office.

Family Help Service

This is the newest and most experimental area of social work, and the first unit providing this service was opened in Nottingham in 1963, eleven more being planned for England and Wales over the next ten years. Spastics and their families within a forty-mile radius of Nottingham will benefit from the centre, which will operate in close co-operation with the local authorities and hospitals concerned. The service will be for spastic children of pre-school age and severely handicapped children of school age who are unable to benefit from statutory services, and will include short-term care, family casework by a trained social worker, nursing and practical help in the home by home visitors, supported by medical and therapeutic services at the centre.

Careers and Employment Department

This consists of a team of trained social workers, many of whom have further qualifications in personnel management. Spastic adults and school-leavers are interviewed, often two or more years before leaving school, and a complete assessment made of the ambitions and potential of each student. Many who will be unable to find jobs or placements in sheltered workshops may be helped in other ways. There are those who are able to take unskilled jobs without training; others enter residential or day-work centres, or spend twelve months at the Society's Further Education Centre, where they take a course designed to help them to gain self-sufficiency and emotional maturity before taking vocational training; and others, sponsored by the Ministry of Labour, may go to the Society's Industrial Training Centre or to one of its Office Training Centres. Special twelve-day assessment and adjustment courses are run by the Department, each taking approximately twenty-five or thirty young spastics who are in some way presenting training or employment problems. During these courses there are intelligence, dexterity and practical tests, visits to factories and other social outings (Plate 22). Discussions, both formal and informal, take place, and the staff are able to observe the young people as complete personalities and as potential employees, and then to make appropriate recommendations for their futures. The Department maintains close links with youth employment officers and disablement resettlement officers in all parts of the country and with training centres and sheltered workshops run by other societies. It has established connections with many well-known firms, some of whom now run special training schemes for spastics. For those who live at home and will never be able to undertake even sheltered employment, there is a Homework Scheme, which provides the raw materials and markets the finished products of jewellery and other handicrafts (Plates 23–25). Further facilities will be available at the Birmingham Sheltered Workshop and Hostel for about 120 spastics, and at the Harlow Work Centre for a smaller number.

Schools and Centres Department

Besides the Society's five boarding schools, this Department administers four adult residential centres. Coombe Farm and Ponds provide for the younger adults. Daresbury for those of lower intelligence and Prested Hall for those between twenty-five and forty. Ponds has recently been extended, and extensions are planned for the other three centres including a special unit at Prested Hall to suit the more intellectually inclined, and facilities at Daresbury for women (at the moment it only provides for men). In addition, three more centres are planned over the next ten years, the first of which has been opened in Buxton. Another centre which will be opening within the next few years is a pioneer unit at Meldreth in Cambridgeshire, where basic training will be provided for 120 severely subnormal spastic children. Fees for all existing national centres are met by the local authorities.

Local Centres Department

This advises the Society's 145 local affiliated societies on the establishment of centres. Approximately seventy local centres are in existence at the moment, providing a wide range of facilities—education, nursery care, short-term care, occupation, treatment, holiday facilities, etc.—and many of the remaining societies are planning to open centres. In deciding what kind of centre to advise a group to open, the Local Centres Department has taken into account existing facilities provided by the local authorities and other local bodies and their plans for the future.

Co-operation with the ministries and local authorities is an integral part of all the Spastics Society's services to spastics. The Society has been able to benefit from the longer experience of local government, and is now in many instances pointing the way ahead. Many theorists have said that with the development of the Welfare State in Great Britain there should be no need for the voluntary organization, and yet the resources and influence of charitable societies in this country continue to increase and have yet to make their full impact on society. The Spastics Society expects to spend at least £7 million over the next seven years on new schools and centres, and £2 million on research of all kinds, and these large sums will be spent after consultation and co-operation with the ministries concerned and, in the case of research, after consultation with the best advice available. It is estimated that there are 75,000 spastics in England, Scotland and Wales. A number of these are so lightly handicapped that they may never need the help of the Spastics Society. There are others who are so badly handicapped that they must be cared for in hospitals, but the vast majority will at some time or the other require help, support or care, and the Spastics Society has accepted the challenge to provide these to the best of its ability.

41. The British Epilepsy Association

GEORGE S. BURDEN

General Secretary of the British Epilepsy Association

THE part played by the social attitudes and the behaviour of all those who come in contact with people who suffer from epilepsy is not always appreciated because advances in the medical field have made it possible to assist, in varying degrees, almost everyone who suffers from the condition, but these advances cannot achieve their full aim without the understanding and support of the rest of the community.

It is difficult to estimate the incidence of epilepsy, and various inquiries have produced figures ranging from 3 or 4 to more than 10 per 1000 of the population. It would appear reasonably certain to assume that one person in every 200 may suffer from some form of epilepsy, which means that there are about a quarter of a million people affected by it in this country. The type of seizure may vary greatly. In some, a brief loss of awareness (or absence)— *petit mal*—may be scarcely noticeable, whilst in others a dramatic fall accompanied by noise and convulsions—*grand mal*—may be frightening to the onlookers, especially if they were not aware that the individual suffered from this condition. Many people have warning of an on-coming attack, but for those who do not, or for whom the warning is too short to enable them to profit by it, the uncertainty of the occurrence of the attacks can be very troublesome. It is probable that this uncertainty is the most disturbing aspect of epilepsy to those around. Once they are aware of the diagnosis, many people are embarrassed at the thought of associating with someone who suffers from this condition. A sensitive person who suffers from epilepsy is aware of the embarrassment, and so, on both sides, there are strong reasons why the epileptic may lead a very lonely existence. It is this factor which makes the provision of social clubs for epileptics more especially a therapeutic necessity than just socially desirable.

Modern methods of investigation and treatment—especially with the aid of new anti-convulsant drugs—enable about half of those subject to epilepsy to achieve complete or near complete control of their seizures. A further quarter will achieve reasonably good control, and fits may occur infrequently or with diminished severity. Sometimes it is possible to keep the fits under control by day, but they may occur at night. In such cases, care must be taken in placing the individual in employment where a shift system does not operate. The remaining quarter may need the help of various services in the

351

community—rather less than half may need institutional care in colonies, mental hospitals or hospitals for the mentally handicapped.

The health and welfare services of the State and of the local authorities are available to help all disabled people, but often those needing assistance do not know where to apply or to whom to go. A recent inquiry from local welfare authorities shows that less than 5 per cent of the estimated number of people suffering from epilepsy have availed themselves of the right to be placed on the register of the substantially and permanently physically handicapped. Probably five times this number need the help of the local authority.

Many who do not need the active assistance of statutory services require the sympathetic understanding of those around them. They are able to follow full-time employment in a wide variety of trades and professions, if they are allowed to do so by employers and fellow employees (Plates 26–9). At times they may be obliged to accept employment beneath their capacities through mistaken ideas which others have of their responsibility or their level of competence.

The British Epilepsy Association therefore has the following aims.

Firstly, to give all the assistance possible to those who suffer from epilepsy and to their families and friends.

Secondly, to improve the understanding of epilepsy by the general public so that those who suffer from this condition shall not also suffer from the ignorance and prejudice of those around them. In addition, by means of pamphlets, lectures, films, etc., to help in the training of nurses, social workers and all those who have to deal with epileptics so that they, too, may have a better understanding of the difficulties which face sufferers and also of their potential contribution to the community in which they live.

Thirdly, to make a positive contribution to the overcoming of epilepsy by means of a research fund from which inquiries into all aspects of epilepsy may be sponsored or supported and to give all possible encouragement to qualified investigators that they may make further inquiries into this condition.

Fourthly, to be a source of information on all questions relevant to the welfare of individuals suffering from epilepsy, to collect information and to share our knowledge and experience with others seeking to help epileptics both in this country and in all parts of the world. In pursuance of this last aim, steps have been taken to establish an International Bureau for Epilepsy which has the active support of the International League against Epilepsy (a medical organization) and the national associations in several countries in Europe and America.

Membership of the Association is open to all who suffer from epilepsy or who wish to support and encourage the activities of the Association on their behalf.

The Association is registered as a charity in accordance with the National

Assistance Act of 1948. The first move to organize a special service for the welfare of epileptics was in 1938 when Miss (later Dame) Evelyn Fox, a pioneer in the mental health field, invited Dr. Tylor Fox (for thirty years Medical Superintendent of Lingfield Epileptic Colony) to join her in planning research into what happened to epileptics discharged as recovered from colonies. Their discussions led to a sub-committee of the National Association for Mental Health which organized a workshop and inaugurated a scheme for after-care with financial support from local authorities. After the passing of the National Assistance Act which gave power to local authorities to provide workshops and to draw up schemes to aid the substantially and permanently physically handicapped, the need for a more general and propaganda service for the epileptic in the community became apparent. With the approval of the Medical Director of the National Association for Mental Health (Dr. Alfred Torrie) the group of interested people and social workers connected with the Epilepsy Sub-Committee decided to form the British Epilepsy Association. Dr. Tylor Fox died shortly before the inaugural meeting in 1950 and hence the new Association adopted the name of Tylor Fox Memorial.

The Association has a Welfare Department under the direction of a Welfare Secretary who is a trained social worker. Club activities are the responsibility of the Club Organizer. Many inquiries are by letter, and an adequate secretarial staff is maintained to deal expeditiously with a substantial correspondence.

The major part of the income of the Association comes from voluntary subscriptions and donations both from private individuals and commercial and industrial concerns. Less than one-tenth of the income of the Association is derived from grants from Hospital Management Committees and from local authorities.

Reference has already been made to the activities of the Welfare Department. In 1962 some 1100 new applications were received for help and advice in connection with a wide variety of difficulties such as employment, accommodation, education and training, questions concerning marriage, children, treatment facilities, institutional care, emigration, etc. At times parents may wish to discuss the social implications of a diagnosis of epilepsy; at others, social worker colleagues may seek advice on handling a particularly complicated situation or perhaps a small grant may be required for a special difficulty. In all such cases the Welfare Department welcomes inquiries and offers the best advice and help in its power. Holidays for individuals and in groups are arranged for children and adults, holiday homes are visited, and up-to-date information on facilities is available from the Department.

In addition to publishing the leaflets and pamphlets previously referred to on many different topics—some prepared for special groups as nurses, ministers of religion, employers and so on—the Association publishes a

Journal three times a year in which many general subjects are discussed. This and examples of literature will willingly be sent to any inquirer.

Addresses and Information

British Epilepsy Association, 27 Nassau Street, London, W. 1.

Branches in Birmingham, Leeds, Liverpool, Newcastle and Sheffield. Social clubs and local groups in Newcastle, Derby, Norwich, Nottingham, Chesterfield, Leicester, Stoke-on-Trent, Bristol, Portsmouth, Brighton and in the Greater London area. Local representatives in Belfast, Birmingham, Bristol, north Wales, Newcastle, Middlesbrough and Leeds.

42. The Cheshire Foundation Homes for the Sick*

BASIL KIERNANDER

Honorary Medical Adviser to the Cheshire Foundation Homes

GREAT advances have been made in the field of physical medicine. Many have been technical ones, but the greatest, perhaps, has been the reorientation of our thinking in terms of the care of the patient as a whole rather than solely of the treatment of disease or injury. The importance of rehabilitation, defined in the Beveridge Report as "a continuous process by which disabled persons should be translated from the state of being incapable under full medical care to the state of being producers and earners", is now fully recognized. Rehabilitation techniques are constantly being improved. Rehabilitation centres, providing temporary homes where the less seriously disabled are helped to return to work in due course, are increasing in number. Yet all this does not solve the problem of dealing with people so handicapped that they cannot be usefully employed or those suffering from a disablement of a progressive nature.

What, then, is the fate of the patient who can do little or nothing unaided; who has, at best, no chance of recovery or who may even face the prospect of a progressively deteriorating condition? In good homes much of the constant care and attention needed may be given by the family. In many cases, however, expert nursing is required; in others, social and economic factors give rise to serious problems. What, too, of the younger permanently disabled person, with the profoundly depressing prospect of a long-drawn-out existence in the chronic sick ward of a hospital, surrounded perhaps by the senile or dying?

One of the most fruitful experiments in the care of people with long-term disabilities—the Cheshire Homes—began as a private enterprise. These homes have now spread not only throughout the United Kingdom but overseas as well. The way in which Group Captain Leonard Cheshire, V.C., D.S.O., D.F.C., was inspired to begin his work for the incurable and homeless sick is described in his biography, but his ideas and certain features of his organization seem particularly apposite to any general consideration of the problem of caring for the chronically disabled.

What are the basic requirements of any home caring for such people? While they must and do vary as individual homes, their general principle

* Based on the Presidential Address given to the Section of Physical Medicine of the Royal Society of Medicine, London, on 8 June 1960.

should be to help the disabled to become (and, more important perhaps, to feel) as independent as possible. It is now widely appreciated that the cardinal need of disabled people is to be helped to consider themselves part of the community at large rather than to be sheltered from it, and it is clear that the normal running of a hospital ward is not always compatible with the freedom and encouragement of activity that is so necessary to them.

It is vitally important that the staff and patients in each of these homes are selected to make the best of the patients' potential activities. Irrespective of class, creed or race, they must all be encouraged to do everything possible to lead a happy and useful life to help each other as integral parts of the community.

The Cheshire Homes are run as homes, not hospitals, and they aim to offer the freedom and affection of normal family life. All the residents are asked to live together as one family group, and they are encouraged to take a very active part in the day-to-day running of the house. It has been found that each home should accommodate, if possible, about thirty to thirty-five patients, with equal numbers of men and women. With appreciably less than thirty beds the home is not an economic proposition; with many more the atmosphere changes subtly and it becomes an "institution". It has also been shown that a preponderance of residents with any one disorder is unwise, tending to lead to temperamental difficulties.

Table 1 is based on information from ten of the thirty-four Cheshire Homes already established in the United Kingdom. It will be seen that it is very similar to Table 2, compiled by Miss A. Whitaker in her study of patients aged between 15 and 55 in chronic sick wards of the local authority accommodation and homes in the North-East Metropolitan Region.

TABLE 1

Representative Pattern of Patients in Typical Cheshire Homes in the United Kingdom

Disease	M.	F.	Total
Multiple sclerosis	29	22	51
Parkinson's disease	13	9	22
Cerebro vascular disorders	8	6	14
Congenital central nervous system disorders	21	19	40
Other central nervous system disorders	20	17	37
Rheumatoid diseases	13	10	23
Musculo-skeletal disorders	21	2	23
Respiratory disorders	1	0	1
Cardio-vascular disorders	0	1	1
Congenital malformations	2	4	6
Other diseases	8	3	11
Total	136	93	229

TABLE 2

After Miss A. Whitaker

Disease	M.	F.	Total
Multiple sclerosis	40	74	114
Parkinson's disease	19	27	46
Cerebro vascular disorders	12	15	27
Congenital central nervous system disorders	13	10	23
Other central nervous system disorders	15	29	44
Rheumatoid diseases	3	18	21
Musculo-skeletal disorders	13	6	19
Respiratory disorders	3	1	4
Cardio-vascular disorders	0	2	2
Multiple disabilities	4	7	11
Other diseases	0	1	1
Total	122	190	312

It may be difficult for those who work in hospitals to realize how artificial an existence is that of the long-stay patient. In a home, for example, it is important to have pleasant rather than functional and aseptic surroundings with attractive decoration, furniture and a garden. The Cheshire Homes vary from converted "stately homes" to modern ones specially built for the purpose, but these requirements are always kept in mind. Mechanical problems are often present—correct width of doors; lay-out of bedrooms; the relevant aids to independence in bathrooms, toilets, lifts, and in the dining rooms and kitchens—but these are by no means insuperable, and it has been found that the most practical advice on these points often comes from the patients themselves. At Le Court, in Hampshire, they gave the local committee and architect invaluable information in planning the new building.

Each Cheshire Home is run autonomously by a Local Committee within the general aims and principles of the Foundation. In each country a central trust is established, owning all the properties, presiding over the homes and constituting the source of the Local Committees' authority. The homes are largely dependent on voluntary help, donations and contributions, administered by the Committees and, in fact, the difficulty inherent in obtaining the sums necessary for both day-to-day running and development projects is the factor which, more than anything else, governs the Foundation's rate of expansion. The running costs are, of course, kept as low as possible; the help given by occasional and by part-time voluntary workers contributes to this result, as does the active part played by many of the residents themselves. Invaluable, too, is the wonderfully dedicated service of the permanent staff, many of whom carry out their rewarding but onerous duties in return for a purely nominal salary. This means that the weekly bed-cost of the homes in England is as low as £8 to £11 compared with £23 in a National Health Service hospital with chronic sick facilities.

The Local Committees play a vital part in the lives of the patients; the members live in the district and bring the outside world into the homes and, more important, take the patients into their own houses. They also arrange, either on their own account or jointly with suitable organizations, outside visits and excursions. Where possible they make contacts with local industry.

The Local Committees are also responsible for dealing with applications for admission to the homes and authorize admissions as and when vacancies occur.

The Matron or the Warden is the administrative head of each home, but the discipline is very different from that essential in a hospital, for it must be stressed that the aim is to create the atmosphere of a family. In many of the homes Welfare Committees drawn from the ranks of the patients have been set up and, among other things, administer the funds for canteens, newspapers and entertainments. At Le Court they also manage a magazine entitled *The Cheshire Smile*, produced quarterly as a journal for residents and supporters of the Foundation. It is edited by Frank Spath, one of Le Court's most gravely disabled residents.

The patients are encouraged to take an active part in the daily running of the homes; many help with cooking, washing-up, the laundry or looking after each other. They are also encouraged to take up activities such as dressmaking, painting, manufacturing handicrafts, printing and so on as serious occupations, since the majority find diversional occupational therapy boring after a short while but useful work-therapy much more satisfying. The proceeds from sales of baskets, leatherwork and handicrafts usually go into the patients' welfare fund.

The backgrounds and capabilities of the residents are as varied as those in any cross-section of the community outside the homes (Plates 30–34). Mr. T., for example, was born in 1909 and employed in hospitals all his working life, rising to the position of Hospital Secretary. Multiple sclerosis was diagnosed in 1949, and by 1955 his illness had progressed so much that he could no longer get round the hospital buildings efficiently. He therefore retired, but his wife died in 1958, leaving him lonely and depressed. Neighbours were good to him, but he realized that it was becoming increasingly impracticable to live on his own and in 1961 he entered one of the Cheshire Homes. Although he is now confined to a wheelchair and his eyesight is failing, Mr. T. is making as much use as possible of his experience as an administrator. He is chairman of the Home's Residents Committee and its representative and spokesman. He does a certain amount of clerical work, keeping the social fund account and the workshop accounts. He spends part of each day helping the other residents with their typing and duplicating.

Mr. D., a young man of 36, was a quantity surveyor when he contracted polio in 1955. This affected his arms, upper trunk and breathing. He is able to propel himself in a wheelchair using his legs and is able to shave and feed himself with the help of mechanical aids, but under physical stress breathing becomes difficult. He then "frog breathes": that is, he swallows air in short gulps, filling his lungs rather as if he were blowing them up with a bicycle pump. After spending over a year in an iron lung he is now able to dispense with it altogether, only sleeping in a rocking-bed. (A rocking-bed aids breathing by pushing the abdominal contents against the diaphragm.) After the first three and a half years of his illness, when he kept himself occupied by learning Russian, Mr. D. was transferred from the Western Hospital to the Nuffield Orthopaedic Centre (Mary Marlborough Lodge). This was in the early days of the Lodge and Mr. D. and the staff there worked together on various devices and experiments, such as the artificial muscle. He now has a "rocker arm" and a "distaff" which were fitted there, and with these he feeds himself, types, writes and plays chess. He is very keen on finding outside work for himself and for the other residents. He has typed four books and also does work for a quantity surveyor, checking figures. He became engaged to another resident in the home and the couple are now married and are living in the home.

A further and most interesting extension of Leonard Cheshire's original idea was initiated when he and his wife Sue Ryder, well known for her work on behalf of war victims and refugees in Europe and her foundation of the Forgotten Allies Trust, formalized an association of their respective organizations by bringing into being the Ryder Cheshire Mission for the Relief of Suffering. Through this they sought to strengthen their existing foundations by making them part of a larger whole; to increase their potentiality by providing the means for joint and concerted action; and to establish a permanent and constitutional way of helping people outside the scope of the other groups. The Raphael Settlements, one at Dehra Dun in India and one near Godalming in Surrey, were among the first of the Mission's projects.

These Settlements, while run on the same lines as the Cheshire Homes, are intended (a) to cater for people (those in higher age groups, for example) who would not normally be admitted to the homes; (b) to care for disabled married couples who might otherwise have to enter separate institutions; and (c) to act as training centres for staff, many of them from overseas, who could later serve in any of the Cheshire organizations and carry Cheshire's aims and ideals all over the world.

The Cheshire Homes, then, occupy a singular place in the field of social welfare in Britain. In the space of twelve years Leonard Cheshire and his helpers have transformed an ideal into an organization which, by drawing on ordinary people, has shown that social welfare on a large scale is not the prerogative or exclusive concern of the State. That people should help each other and themselves is surely the essence of true social welfare.

References

1. BOYLE, A., *No Passing Glory*, Collins, 1955.
2. BRADDON, R., *Cheshire V.C.*, Evans Brothers Ltd., 1954.
3. CHESHIRE, L., *The Face of Victory*, Hutchinsons, 1961.
4. FORREST, A. J., *But Some There Be*, Robert Hale Ltd.
5. HUGHES, G., *Cheshire V.C.*, Living Biographies, Phoenix Publishing House.
6. RUSSELL, W., *New Lives for Old*, Gollancz, 1963.

SECTION VIII
SERVICES IN THE MENTAL HEALTH FIELD

43. Serving the Mentally Ill

MARY PHILLIPS

Tutor in Social Work Training, College of Commerce, Bristol

DURING the past twenty years there has been rapid and widespread development in the mental health field, and we have every reason to believe that we are still only at the beginning of a period of great progress. This continuous process is the result of two main factors. First, a much wider acceptance of the extent to which irrational behaviour is due to a mental illness or psychological disturbance whereas it was formerly attributed to moral or hereditary weakness. This increase of understanding on the part of the public has had the effect of reducing the degree of stigma associated with mental illness except amongst the elderly who still experience strong feelings of shame when they or their relatives become ill.

The second factor has been the increased effectiveness of the treatment of mental illness. Although we are very much at the beginning of this development and as yet know little of the causes and therefore of possible preventive measures, the outlook for patients individually and for those working in this field is very much more hopeful. The enthusiasm and optimism of today relate to what we feel may well take place during the next decade, an attitude which contrasts strongly with the feelings of the patients and staff in the old institutions which in 1930 were renamed hospitals. Today the services for the mentally ill fall far short of those provided for the physically ill, but there are many indications that this situation is no longer acceptable to the man in the street, let alone those who work in the field of mental health.

The greater understanding and the more hopeful prognosis have increased the demands made on those who work in this field, and in spite of better treatment methods, work is severely hindered by a shortage of trained staff both in hospital and in the community. Not only has the tempo of the work increased, and the emphasis moved from hospital care to social rehabilitation, but the study of human behaviour, its irrational manifestations and their social consequences are now of great interest to social workers in other fields. This has meant that at a time when the work itself has been expanding, considerable demands have been made on those working in the mental health field for help with training and in an advisory capacity. No wonder the ground is never adequately covered.

363

Legislation

The social worker in the mental health field operates within the framework of three Acts of Parliament, namely the National Health Service Act, 1946, the National Assistance Act, 1948, and the Mental Health Act, 1959.

Many of the changes in current procedure and policy are attributed by the public and the press to the Mental Health Act, 1959. Whilst this was certainly a great landmark, this is more because it was an official recognition of changes in the attitude towards and in the treatment of the mentally ill that had already taken place but which were hindered by the existing legislation.

At the time of its publication, the Mental Health Act was severely criticized, especially by social workers and voluntary organizations, because it did not make the provision of an aftercare service by the local authorities compulsory. This criticism disregarded one of the main recommendations of the Report of the Royal Commission relating to Mental Illness and Mental Deficiency (1954–7) which was that as far as possible services for the mentally ill should be provided under the same legislation as other types of handicap on the grounds that separate legislation and separate services would increase the segregation that already existed between the mentally ill and the rest of the community. "In our view the aftercare of patients after leaving hospital must be considered part of the general community care for which local authorities are responsible" (Royal Commission Report, para. 675).

It is curious that another recommendation made by the Royal Commission, that the aim should be treatment and care in the community wherever possible (chapter 10) has received so much more attention than the recommendation that services for the mentally ill should as far as possible form an integral part of the existing social services. "In present conditions no one should be excluded from benefiting from any of the general social services simply because his need arises from mental disorder rather than from other causes" (para. 592).

Again, much more publicity has been given to the changes in procedure for compulsory admission to hospital, although these measures are used in a minority of cases only, than to the fact that the Act abolished the "designation" of some hospitals which were compelled to admit mentally ill patients under the previous legislation. It was hoped that this measure would break down the isolation of the psychiatric hospital and encourage the development of alternative hospital facilities. "In particular the Minister hopes that there will be a substantial increase in psychiatric facilities at general hospitals—this applies to existing hospitals as well as to new or redeveloped ones—both to secure the better distribution and siting of psychiatric services and to help to ensure that there is the closest possible contact between psychiatric and other hospital services" (Memorandum on Parts 1, 4–7 of the Mental Health Act, 1959, H.M.S.O.). The significance of this decision will probably only be fully understood when there are more psychiatric units in general hospitals and when more of the existing psychiatric hospitals lose their present function of caring for very large numbers of the mentally ill in isolation. This development, once under way, will do much to reduce the difference in the standard of service for the mentally and the physically ill. (See papers by Dr. William Sargent and Dr. Stanley Smith on this subject at the N.A.M.H. Conference Report, 1961.)

The Minister of Health issued a Circular to local authorities on 4 May 1959 (eighteen months before the Mental Act became law) reminding them that the "main recommendations of the Royal Commission Report affecting local authority services can be adopted under existing powers and need not therefore await the passing of the Mental Health Bill". The powers referred to are, first, those given under Section 28 of the National Health Service Act which states that "a Local Authority may with the approval of the Minister and to the extent as the Minister may direct, make arrangements for the purpose of the prevention of illness, the care of persons suffering from illness or mental defectiveness or the aftercare of such persons". Secondly, powers were given under Sections 21 and 29 of the National Assistance Act to provide residential accommodation for persons who "by reasons of age, infirmity or any other circumstances are in need of care and attention which is not otherwise available to them", and to make arrangements "for the care of the blind, deaf and dumb, and those substantially and permanently handicapped by illness, injury or congenital deformity".

Until 1959 very few local authorities made use of these powers in relation to the mentally ill, thus continuing their exclusion from the improved standards of social service that became available after 1948. The Mental Health Act amended the two Acts already mentioned and the Children's Act of 1948 where necessary to ensure no gaps existed and that wherever possible the mentally disordered should benefit from the social services provided for other types of handicap.

The Ten Year Plans

In February 1962, following the publication of the Hospital Plan for England and Wales, the Minister of Health asked the local authorities to review their health and welfare services and to draw up plans for developing them over the next ten years. "The plan for the development of the hospital service is therefore complementary to the expected development of the service for the prevention and for care in the community and a continued expansion of those services has been assumed in the assessment of the hospital provision to be aimed at." This meant in effect that local authorities were asked not only to take a long look ahead, but to plan over a very wide front and to co-ordinate the efforts of the Health and Welfare Departments to a greater extent than had occurred in the past.

The results of all this planning were published by the Minister in April 1963 (H.M.S.O., Cmnd. 1973) with details of the services provided by each local authority in March 1962 and those planned for 1967 and 1972. The Report is therefore a forward-looking document and is a remarkable achievement particularly in view of the many uncertainties facing the local authorities in relation to staffing and developments in the field of medicine. It is also a recognition by every authority that the health and welfare services have to be substantially increased over the next ten years. In his introduction (para. 4) the Minister emphasizes that each authority has an independent responsibility in its own area and that no attempt was made to indicate common standards. "Nevertheless, it was essential to bring the separate plans together so as to provide a nation-wide picture of these developments as they are at present envisaged and to attempt to set them within the context of national purposes and common standards."

The importance of bringing the plans together is borne out by a study of the wide variation in the standard of service provided and planned by local authorities in different parts of the country, and this applies particularly in the field of mental health. "The total of persons receiving services at the end of 1961 represents ratios of 0·87 mentally ill or psychopathic persons per 1000 population: but in many areas the ratios are as high as about 2 for mental illness. Such large variations cannot be due solely to local differences in the extent of the need or even in the demarcation between hospital and local authority services. It must be assumed that in many areas there are needs that have not yet come to light" (para. 80). In addition it must be said that because so few areas have been able to develop a comprehensive service for the mentally ill, little is really known about what can be achieved once adequate numbers of trained staff are available. However, authorities have been asked to review their plans annually, and on each occasion to carry them forward a further year, "so that plans for the next decade will always be in view" (para. 162). With the publication of the plans for the health and welfare services there is the promise of long-term yet flexible planning in the mental health field which should bring to an end the present situation whereby the standard of help available to those recovering from a mental illness varies according to where they live.

Social Work with the Mentally Ill

"Social work for mentally ill patients started for patients who were receiving hospital treatment and since 1948 has continued to be carried out mainly from hospitals" (Report of the Royal Commission, para. 607). Although this was the situation in most areas until a few years ago, the numbers of social workers employed in psychiatric hospitals was and still is grossly inadequate. In 1953 there were 180 qualified psychiatric social workers employed in hospitals and in 1961, when there were 136,346 people in psychiatric hospital beds, the figure had only risen to 193. Even these figures do not indicate the real nature of the shortage because some of the London and the teaching hospitals employ several psychiatric social workers whereas in the provinces one person will be working in a hospital with 1500–2000 beds and a very large catchment area. (In addition a number of hospitals employ untrained social workers although the figure is not known.)

In spite of the difficulties arising from large numbers of patients and huge geographical areas, the psychiatric social worker has acted as a link not only between the patient and the family, but also between the hospital staff and the community social services at a time when the isolation of the hospitals was being replaced by the "open door policy". Much of the social worker's time is spent visiting the patients' homes, sometimes following a request from the patient himself and sometimes because the medical staff require details of the social and family background in their attempt to diagnose and treat the patient's illness. These visits to the home and family are of great value in providing the social worker with an opportunity of bridging the gap between hospital and home at a time of great anxiety, and from then on of supporting the family in their attempt to come to terms with the patient's disturbed behaviour. As their confidence in the social worker develops, the relatives will be able to discuss their fears as to the possible causes and future prognosis of the illness as well as gain some understanding of what the hospital staff is trying to achieve. These visits also help the social worker prepare for the patient's eventual return home and assess the amount of support that will be needed.

Attempts have been made in recent years to divide social work into two types of activities, one concerned with practical problems and the other with emotional or personal difficulties. Nowhere is this division proved more false than in social work with the mentally ill. The social worker will be involved with many problems relating to property, finance, employment, etc., which may at first sight appear to be straightforward practical matters but as they are unravelled prove to be a fundamental part of the patient's illness or personality disorder.

Mrs. C., an elderly woman who was admitted to hospital in a depressed and agitated condition, recovered sufficiently to leave hospital and go to a small private nursing home. She had sufficient money for this but, in spite of her improved condition, remained convinced that her money had been stolen from the bank. It took a long time to gain her confidence and overcome her suspicions so that the comparatively simple matter of her move to more comfortable conditions could be arranged. Mrs. P. was extremely disturbed on admission to hospital; during her long stay there her husband died and the contents of her home were severely damaged by fire. When, contrary to expectations, she later recovered sufficiently to leave home provided she had a great deal of support, it was necessary to help her replace the contents of her home and at the same time develop her self-confidence again and to overcome the temptation to return to the more sheltered life she had known in hospital. Mr. D., on the other hand, had had a comparatively short illness, but prior to his arrival in hospital he had been confused and had left his property at various addresses which he was unable to recall. As he recovered and became more organized, the social worker was able to help him retrieve his few worldly belongings and, in so doing, overcame his suspicions to the point where he was able to accept help in finding employment and then in settling back into the community.

The tempo of the work in hospitals has greatly altered, but although many patients leave after a stay of 6–8 weeks there is still a great deal of work to be done for those patients who, in spite of every modern treatment, remain in hospital, and for their families who need help in understanding why this is so in spite of what the "papers say about the modern cures". Although the present trend is towards more psychiatric units in general hospitals for short-term patients, the needs of the chronic sick, and especially the elderly, remaining in the large psychiatric hospitals must also be met, especially as the relatives of these patients are themselves an ageing group who need continuous support.

The hospital social worker has also moved out with the medical staff to work in the out-patients' departments in general hospitals, to the neurosis units and day hospitals. Here it has been possible to establish contact at an early stage of breakdown and to give active support to the relatives right through the illness. As the community services develop, close liaison between the hospital staff and the local authority social workers becomes increasingly important, and the quality of the service provided for the mentally ill depends a great deal on this co-ordination. At the present time a great deal is being said and written on the subject of the merits of hospital care or community care. The really important thing is that there should be continuity of care for those whose illness makes it necessary for them to spend periods, long or short, in hospital.

The Local Authority Services

The most striking feature of the local authority services for the mentally ill is that although they all operate under the same legislation, their administration and standard vary enormously from one part of the country to another. In some areas the health and welfare services operate as one department, in others they are separate. The Mental Health Department is a section of the

Health Department, whereas the Welfare Department is responsible for the care of the handicapped, the homeless and the elderly, many of whom may be suffering from some degree of mental disorder. It cannot be said that those who operate these services have all found a way of ensuring that those who use them do not suffer from this administrative division of responsibilities.

The variations in standard of service is closely related to the great shortage of trained staff. It is only since the publication of the Younghusband Working Party Report in 1959 and the official acceptance of its main recommendations (see Ministry of Health Circular 10/361) that the role of the social worker in this field, and the importance of training for those coming into the work, has received widespread support. The establishment of the new training courses at Colleges of Further Education (in January 1963 there were nine in Great Britain) has stimulated some local authorities to recruit young staff with a view to seconding them for training, and now that training and status is more assured there has been no shortage of applicants. Even so, in view of the large numbers of officers nearing retirement age (according to the Working Party Report 45 per cent of mental welfare officers in 1959 were over the age of 50) and the fact that a proportion of new entrants will be away for two years training, it is unlikely that there will be any real increase in numbers for some time to come. In recent years there has been a slowly but steadily growing interest in this field amongst psychiatric social workers, but the number now being trained is quite inadequate to meet the needs of the local authority services.

Casework Service

Although the recruitment and training of staff now shows signs of improving, community care, if it is to mean anything to those leaving hospital, will require more than new hostels, clubs and social centres. Of course, not all patients leaving hospital require the services of a social worker. Many are able to return to their home and their job, and with the help of their general practitioner and sometimes with out-patient attendance at a psychiatric clinic, manage on their own to pick up the threads again. When this is not so, it usually means that the patient lacks self-confidence to the point of not being able to use the advisory services such as those provided by the Ministry of Labour for the rehabilitation of people recovering from illness or injury. As a result the patient will need considerable support from the social worker especially during the period immediately after his discharge from hospital to help him to get back into "normal circulation" again. There are many people leaving hospital who will never get as far as this, but who, if accepted by their families and neighbours and supported at every stage by a social worker, can remain for long periods in their own homes. There is also the group of people who have not been to hospital, but who are referred by officers of the National

Assistance Board to the Mental Health Department because they have with-drawn into their own homes to the point of neglecting themselves, and who may, by means of long-term and careful work, eventually accept treatment at a clinic or in hospital—or even join a social club.

Such was Miss E., an elderly spinster living alone in a large house formerly occupied by her family. As a girl she had stayed at home helping her mother whilst the rest of the family went out to work. She had nursed her elderly parents until their death and continued to look after the home for her sisters, both of whom had recently died. Living alone in the large house she became depressed and blamed herself for her sisters' death. For a time she relied on neighbours to do her shopping, which meant that she did not go out at all, and then she even ceased to dress herself. She began to worry, with good reason, about the state of the house, but felt unable to cope with repairs or to organize the sale of the house and its contents with a view to moving into something smaller or even a home for elderly people. In spite of her money worries she refused to apply for National Assistance because she associated this with the workhouse and charity which she did not deserve. The social worker's first task was to win her confidence, which took many months. It was important to help her make her own decision about the house when the temptation to take over this problem was great because of her poor health. Finally, after many months of visiting, it was possible for her to enter a psychiatric hospital for treatment to which she responded well. As a result of this and the con-tinued support of the social worker who continued to visit her in hospital. Miss E. was able to arrange for the sale of her house and to make an applica-tion for admission to a home for elderly people near to where she had pre-viously lived.

It is characteristic of the work with these and other discharged patients living in the community that progress can only be measured over a long period, and it is difficult for staff who have been previously occupied with the dramatic conditions surrounding compulsory admission to hospital to feel that they are achieving anything by regular visiting over a long period. So far few areas have achieved the conditions necessary for the development of an integrated casework service. These are, first, the opportunity for mental welfare officers to discuss their work with experienced caseworkers or psychiatrists, and the allocation of cases to workers according to ability rather than to chance. It is also essential that there should be close liaison between local authority services and the local psychiatric hospital, including regular case conferences between the mental welfare officers and the hospital staff. This is now happening to a much greater extent. Finally, much will depend on the understanding of the Mental Health Department's function by other social services including other departments of the local authority and those agencies which are often the first to make contact with the mentally ill in the community but will not refer them at an early stage of breakdown.

to the Mental Health Department if they do not understand the type of service it offers.

Hostels

A great deal is now being said and written about hostels as an alternative to hospital care, and, by comparison with a casework service, they offer the satisfying prospect of a tangible result, an indication of work done. In the main, hostels are suggested for two groups of the mentally ill. First, for the elderly and mentally infirm who do not require hospital care. In fact the elderly can be divided into those who need more care and supervision than can be provided in the hostels run by the Welfare Department, and this means employing staff who are trained psychiatric nurses, and, secondly, those who are able-bodied but eccentric and who do not like and do not fit into hostel life. They would be happier in grouped dwellings with a warden near at hand so that they can retain not only their personal belongings but their right to occupy themselves in their own way. If domiciliary services (including meals on wheels, laundry, home help and regular visits from a social worker) could be extended, a great deal of time, money and heartbreak would be avoided because these people do not settle in hospital or hostels.

The other group consists of younger people who are considered fit to leave hospital but who have no home to which they can return and who are not sufficiently independent to find lodgings and work. These people find it difficult to get work from a hospital address, and in any case need time to adjust to living outside hospital before starting a job. It is usually hoped that most of these younger residents will move into lodgings after a period of a few months, but the small number of hostels of this type already in existence have found this difficult to achieve. Dr. P. A. Tyser in his Report on Winston House, Cambridgeshire, given to the 1962 N.A.M.H. Conference, spoke of the danger of "blocking the hostels with people who would remain permanently and whose work pattern would be irregular". Meanwhile many of those who leave hospital with nowhere to go drift from hostel to hostel such as those run by the Salvation Army and other voluntary organizations which cater for those on National Assistance. If they are not well enough to settle in these hostels, they take to the roads and end up in hospital again or, to an increasing extent, in prison. (See Dr. Gray's paper to the N.A.M.H. Conference, 1962.)

Although much is said and written about hostels, in January 1963 there were only thirty-five hostels providing 692 beds, most of which were for mentally subnormal. According to the Minister's Report on Development and Community Care (Cmnd. 1973), many more are planned, 16,000 places (or 0·3 per 1000 population) by 1972. It is probable that most of these will cater for elderly people who are too disturbed for the ordinary residential houses.

Employment

Apart from accommodation the greatest need for the rehabilitation of the mentally ill is the provision of sheltered employment. The importance of satisfying occupation for the recovery of the mentally ill has been recognized for some time in hospitals which have introduced a programme of occupational activities which aim at creating conditions in hospital as near as possible to those in the community. The tragedy is that there are many patients who in hospital enjoy a wide programme of activities but who on return home are faced with long periods of idleness broken by the twice weekly visits to the Employment Exchange, and, if they are lucky, attendance at a social club once a week.

The Ministry of Labour offers a comprehensive service for the rehabilitation of the disabled which includes the help of the Disablement Resettlement Officer at every Exchange, Industrial Rehabilitation Units in every region and the possibility of training courses or employment at a sheltered workshop such as Remploy. Whilst it is certainly true that efforts have been made to include a higher proportion of the mentally disordered at the units and training centres, it must be admitted that these services are not geared to the needs of those recovering from a mental illness.

The local authorities are empowered under the Disabled Persons (Employment) Act, 1944, to establish sheltered workshops for any type of handicapped person, but few have taken advantage of these powers because of the administrative complexities involved. An example of what can be done has been given by the Industrial Therapy Organization (Bristol) Ltd. which developed from the industrial unit in Glenside Hospital, Bristol. In his first Annual Report, February 1961, the chairman wrote: "We were bedevilled with Ministry regulations . . . I think it is true to say that if we had attempted to iron out all the difficulties facing us before we started, I.T.O. would never have been launched." To some extent the difficulties relate to the fact that four Ministries are involved—Health, Labour, Pensions and National Insurance and the National Assistance Board. The fact that in eighteen months seventy-five people who had been in hospital for long periods were placed in employment proves that the efforts made to deal with Ministry regulations were worthwhile. The danger exists, however, that in order to prove these workshops are an economic proposition, production becomes all important to the detriment of the patient.

By 1963 four other industrial therapy organizations had been started along similar lines to the one in Bristol, but the attitude in this country to the needs of the mentally ill in the field of employment contrasts sadly with the positive approach in Holland where there are a large number of sheltered workshops in which the mentally ill and subnormal are employed on a wide variety of contract work of an attractive and colourful nature. Earnings are based on effort as well as results, and are supplemented (not reduced as in this country) by state benefits. Whatever this costs the taxpayer, it is less wasteful than allowing people to deteriorate mentally through inactivity so that they have to return to hospital.

Social and Handicraft Centres

Because of the difficulties experienced in relation to the establishment of sheltered workshops, many local authorities are now providing centres staffed by occupational therapists who continue the work begun in hospital of building up the patient's self-confidence and of encouraging him to express himself in a creative way. These centres usually combine handicrafts with social and cultural activities (such as music and drama) which play a great part in helping people to rediscover their own potential and the interests they share with other people.

Social Clubs

In other areas where it has not been possible to start such a centre social clubs of many kinds have been started by social workers often with the help of voluntary organizations, or the other way round. These are of great value in helping people who have left the comparatively sheltered environment of the hospital feel that they are welcome and that they can in time make their own contribution to the running of the club. Once again the ultimate aim of these clubs should be to act as a bridge between the hospital and the community, and not to remain as segregated units within it.

Voluntary Organizations

As in many other fields of social work, the services provided for the mentally ill today owe a great deal to the efforts of a few voluntary organizations and pioneering individuals. More recently there has been a growing interest in the subject of mental illness and its treatment on the part of the general public, which has been further stimulated by very good radio and television programmes. This interest has now developed into a wish to be of service both to those who are in hospital and to those who are living in the community. The Minister of Health, in the Report of 1963 and in earlier circulars, has made it clear that it is the responsibility of the local authorities and the hospitals to ensure that this goodwill is not wasted, and that the wide range of services offered by the voluntary organizations to other groups of handicapped people should now be extended to the mentally ill. Many individuals and groups are already helping at the social centres and clubs where their contribution is particularly valuable because they can introduce an informal and unofficial atmosphere, and because they are often in touch with many other organizations who can be encouraged to show an interest in the club or individual members. These clubs need a higher proportion of helpers, especially when they first start, because many of the people recovering from a mental illness have some difficulty in forming relationships or participating in group activities. For the same reason it is important that the club's programme should not be over-organized and that there is plenty of time for the members to chat over a cup of tea and to feel their way with each other.

Hospital Friends

Most hospitals now have Associations of Friends which are affiliated to the National League of Hospital Friends. The League acts in an advisory capacity, especially to new associations. The members find endless ways of raising money to provide additional amenities at the hospitals, and in addition send gifts at Christmas and on birthdays to patients who have no relatives or friends. Many of the friends also undertake regular visiting of patients who would otherwise not have anyone to come and see them, sometimes taking them out individually or in groups. In a number of hospitals in the rural areas, Women's Institutes have been started by the members of Institutes from the nearby villages. This has proved of great value because besides providing an interesting programme of activities to those who have to stay for long periods in hospital, it also encourages patients leaving hospital to join their local Institute and helps the ordinary housewife to realize how much she can help those who are suffering from mental illness or who have recently recovered.

Educational Programmes

Some of the Associations of Hospital Friends and voluntary bodies organize meetings and exhibitions in an attempt to interest the general public and increase their understanding of the problems and developments taking place in this field. In this work they receive a great deal of help from the staffs of hospitals and local authorities, and also from the National Association of Mental Health. For many years this Association has acted as a parent figure to individual sufferers who do not know where to turn for help and to all those working in the field of mental illness and subnormality. In particular the Association has done a great deal to fill the many gaps in training facilities and has brought about a greater awareness on the part of the public of the problems, and a greater willingness to co-operate on the part of the many different groups of workers through its annual conference. Both the N.A.M.H. and Mental Aftercare Association have pioneered a wide range of hostels or have helped local groups to do so.

As the statutory services for the mentally ill are extended, the need for the work of the voluntary organizations will increase. Even when all the services are adequately staffed, because of the loneliness and difficulties experienced by the mentally ill in making contact with their fellow men, there will still be a place for the voluntary worker who, without attempting to cure or treat the illness, appreciates the value of the friendly unofficial visitor. Although treatment prospects and hospital conditions are much better and still improving, mental illness is still a very frightening experience for the patient and those who live with him. Those who are fortunate in not having to face this problem themselves can do much by expressing support and sympathy when it happens to their neighbour. And none of us can afford to feel satisfied with the services provided for the mentally ill until we consider them to be adequate for ourselves or our relatives.

44. Serving the Mentally Subnormal

F. Joan Todd

Psychiatric Social Worker

"BACKS were meant to carry burdens." An expression of sympathy evoked this reply from a 70-year-old woman who was still caring for her mentally subnormal son of 50. Too often this attitude has been forced on parents because the stigma attached to having a handicapped child makes them draw in on themselves. Other people are often unhelpful either because they do not realize the problems attendant on caring for a subnormal child or because of the fear which such a handicap arouses, particularly if it is accompanied by physical deformity or abnormality. The term mentally subnormal was introduced in the Mental Health Act, 1959, partly because it was felt that the words idiot, imbecile and feeble-minded person carried emotional overtones hurtful to parents and were likely to perpetuate the lack of understanding. The Report of the Royal Commission on the Law relating to Mental Illness and Mental Deficiency stated: "We consider that the public attitude towards mental disorder has outgrown the terms 'idiot' and 'imbecile' ... and that new terminology is needed to mark a step forward from ancient prejudices and fears and to be an outward sign of a real advance in public sympathy."

The Mental Deficiency Act of 1913

The Mental Deficiency Act of 1913 had used the term "mental defective" to cover four categories—idiots, imbeciles, feeble-minded persons and moral defectives. It was defined as "a condition of arrested or incomplete development of mind, existing before the age of 18 years whether arising from inherent causes or induced by disease or injury". This definition was necessarily wide because of the tremendous range of disability covered, from the helpless bed-ridden child to the anti-social adolescent whose defect might be scarcely more than an educational retardation. The age limit of 18 was intended to separate mental deficiency from mental illness; the latter was broadly regarded as mental disease arising in a person whose development up to that age had been within normal limits. This led to the certification as defective of many children who were suffering from mental illness, since the definitions of the categories of mental deficiency were social rather than clinical in character. Idiots were "unable to guard themselves against common physical dangers", and imbeciles were "incapable of managing their own affairs or in the case of children being taught to do so". The criteria used to define the remaining categories were also social. Feeble-minded persons were those who required "care, supervision, and control for their own protection or for the protection of others", or as far as children were concerned, those who could not benefit from instruction in ordinary schools. Moral defectives were mental defectives who displayed "strongly vicious or criminal propensities". Nowhere in these definitions was intelligence mentioned, and in post-war years it was increasingly thought that mental deficiency was being interpreted too widely and that not only did this make appropriate treatment for all the different categories difficult to obtain but the use of compulsory detention raised questions of the liberty of the subject.

The provisions of the old Act seem inadequate now, but this should not blind us to the fact that it legislated for the care of the defective in the community and made possible the gathering of information about this handicap which led to a new outlook and finally a new Act. It is true that emphasis fell largely on custodial care for defectives, and this is not surprising considered against the background of the social and political ideas of the day. The geneticists of the time forecast a decline in national intelligence if defectives were allowed to beget children. The absence of welfare provisions coupled with recurring unemployment led the less intelligent to break the law in order to survive, and seemed to point to a connection between mental deficiency and crime. Hence the provision providing for the compulsory detention of defectives convicted of criminal offences and of defective women who gave birth to illegitimate children whilst in receipt of poor relief.

Nevertheless, the legislators were alive to the need for preventive measures: the statutory supervision of ascertained defectives living at home; the guardianship orders which allowed for the care of defectives in the community; the duty laid on the local authorities in 1927 to provide occupation and training for defectives; these were the beginnings of our modern community services. Social workers were needed to carry out these provisions, and we owe a great debt to voluntary societies like the Central Association for Mental Welfare for the pioneer work they did in this sphere. Unfortunately, the extent to which the local authorities provided these services varied considerably, and where provision was inadequate the result was a high rate of institutionalization of defectives. Since the institutions thought mainly in terms of custodial care, once these defectives were admitted there was little interest in rehabilitation particularly during the period between the wars when unemployment was high, and defectives often remained in hospital for long periods.

The concern for individual liberty and the realization that outdated ideas about the capabilities of defectives were perpetuated by the inadequate services provided the strongest arguments for the setting up of the Royal Commission of 1954. Studies of the prevalence of mental deficiency and follow-up studies of those classified as defectives had demonstrated that this branch of psychiatry was not so straightforward as it might seem. The Wood Report (1929) showed, for instance, that whereas the incidence of mental deficiency in the age range 10–14 was 25·6 per 1000, in the age range 15–19 it was only 10·8 per 1000. Similar findings were made by other investigators. Follow-up studies of children classified as defective also showed that a high proportion of them grew up into normal adults. These studies revealed the necessity for community services which could give the support enabling this adjustment to adult life to be made without the need for admission to hospital. Many people and Associations gave evidence, among them the National Council for Civil Liberties and the National Association for Mentally Handicapped Children. The final report of the Commission led to the Mental Health Act, 1959.

The Mental Health Act of 1959

This Act has attempted to remedy the limitations of the old Act by creating a unified Mental Health Service and by re-defining the categories subject to compulsory detention. The term "severe subnormality" is defined as "a state of arrested or incomplete development of mind which includes subnormality of intelligence and is of such a nature or degree that the patient is incapable of living an independent life or of guarding himself against serious exploitation, or will be so incapable when of an age to do so". It is intended to include those formerly known as idiots or imbeciles and some of the lower grades of the feeble-minded. The higher grades of the latter now come under the term "subnormality", "a state of arrested or incomplete development of mind (not amounting to severe subnormality) which includes subnormality of intelligence and is of a nature or degree which requires or is susceptible to medical treatment or other special care or training of the patient". It will be noted that in both these definitions actual subnormality of intelligence is required. Many anti-social adolescents who were detained under the old provisions are now excluded because their intelligence is too high, and it was to cater for the more dangerous of these patients that the category of psychopathic disorder was introduced. This is defined as "a persistent disorder or disability of mind (whether or not including subnormality of intelligence) which results in abnormally aggressive or seriously irresponsible conduct on the part of the patient, and requires or is susceptible to medical treatment". This category, which replaces the "moral defective" of the old Act, is now, therefore, quite properly dissociated from mental subnormality.

Perhaps the greatest principle behind the new Act is the emphasis on treatment of the mentally disordered in the community and the stress laid upon the earliest possible return to society of those who are detained compulsorily or who enter hospital informally. It is a tremendous challenge to the local authority services to translate the spirit of the Act into reality. In the sphere of mental subnormality much needs to be done if treatment is to be given outside the hospitals, and only now are people beginning to realize the extent of the problems associated with this handicap. Among the difficulties which arise is that of diagnosis. Unlike many physical disabilities immediate diagnosis is often impossible, and except in severe cases or where the condition is easily recognizable, as in mongolism, there is more often a slow realization over many months or even years. The doubts and anxieties of parents during this period can be very disturbing, and the general practitioner's knowledge is often not specialized enough to enable him to deal with the situation. The National Association for Mental Health set up a diagnostic and counselling service for parents of subnormal children which proved very effective, and special clinics on these lines, incorporated in the ordinary welfare services, would meet a great need. We already have in the hospital medical staffs specialists who could be used as consultants, and in some areas this is already being done. An expansion of this sort of service would be immensely valuable. When the diagnosis is made acceptance of it is often difficult; having a subnormal child is a severe blow to the parents' self-esteem. Even if parents can face up to this they will want to ask questions about the advisability of having another baby, the possibility of improvement or otherwise for the handicapped child, and the services which can be called upon if the child is likely to remain dependent. The problems raised will be different according to the extent of the handicap.

Severe Subnormality

Many parents wish to keep their severely subnormal child as a member of the family. There is no doubt that provided the strain of so doing is not too great, both the child and members of the family can benefit, but it can never be easy even in the best of circumstances. The case of Mrs. C. will illustrate this. This mother brought up Charles, an epileptic son of imbecile level who survived into his 40's. He was a pleasant, obedient, hard-working man who helped his mother in the home, and to all outward appearances caused little dislocation to the family life. Yet this stability in family relationships had been achieved at some cost. When the mother realized that he would never be normal she was very bitter against her husband because she had not been informed that there was epilepsy in his family before she married him. She finally broke off relations with his family completely because of this. A daughter remained unmarried because at the time when she would have left home Charles was in need of such care that she felt that her mother could not manage him on her own. A son who married had no children because of the fear of having an epileptic child. Mrs. C. herself was tied to the home because of Charles's constant need of care, and led a considerably narrowed social life as a result. When he died she was too old to make new contacts, and suffered a tremendous sense of bereavement as a result of her son's continued dependence on her. Yet because this family was a very united group with a strong feeling of independence, none but very close friends knew of the adjustments that they had been obliged to make to come to terms with the situation.

In other cases the problems presented to a family may be greater. A more severely handicapped child may remain a toddler in terms of the care and attention he requires, but he will grow in size, and problems of management may become insuperable. Not every severely subnormal child has the pleasant temperament that Charles had. Some are hyperactive and destructive; some have screaming fits or abnormal sleep rhythms which can completely disrupt family life. The presence of a severely subnormal child can reduce the margin of tolerance for other misfortunes such as a mother's ill health or marital difficulties.

Whatever other problems arise the family is bound to be at a financial disadvantage. A severely subnormal child never becomes a wage-earner, but in many cases the expense of his care is greater than that of the normal boy or girl especially when he is destructive or incontinent. National Assistance Board grants are very small when it is remembered that the liability is permanent. Another factor which is often overlooked is that the presence of a handicapped child in the family will prevent mother from going out to work and thus obtaining supplementary income for the family. The mother of any young family tends to be isolated whilst her children are small, but in the case of the mother of a handicapped child this isolation can be prolonged whilst the child continues to be dependent on her. Where a severely subnormal child is destructive or is unpredictable in behaviour, friends are much less likely to be invited to the home, and to get a sitter-in whilst parents go out together is often well-nigh impossible. This isolation is very difficult for a mother to bear especially when coupled with the physical and mental strain which looking after a severely handicapped child can bring.

The Role of the Social Worker

The social worker whose job it is to help in a situation of this kind must be primarily a family caseworker who can inform the family of the services available and help them to make use of them; this latter function is often the more difficult. Because of the social stigma which parents of handicapped children feel, they may find it very difficult to accept the diagnosis and consequently the help that is available to them. On the other hand, they may be too shocked or depressed to be able to think constructively; where there are already strains in the marriage these will be aggravated. The social worker must build up a relationship with the family, and particularly the mother, so that she can see the problems against the background peculiar to the family concerned and can give support when it is needed. Though the problem is a chronic one it is a mistake to think it remains the same problem. New difficulties will arise as the child grows older and family relationships change, and unless the family look upon the social worker as someone they can call upon whenever there are difficulties, a crisis may arise and the situation be irretrievable before she is consulted. Parents will probably not be aware of the resources in the community which will help in the care of their child as it grows older, and if they have not been able to accept the diagnosis, some parents may even find it difficult to make use of these resources. Where severely handicapped children do not attend training centres, for instance, though it is more often because there is still a shortage of places, it is sometimes because the mother does not want him to mix with the other children whom she thinks may lead him into bad habits. There is frequently little provision for the very severely handicapped child, and only recently are special-care units being set up to care for these children at least for a few hours during the day to enable the mother to cope with normal family demands. With the shortage of housing a family with a handicapped child is often unable to live in conditions which would make a more normal life possible for the rest of the family, and the housing authorities are sometimes unaware of the special needs of these families. It is surprising, too, that very little use seems to have been made of the home help service. The social worker should see her job in part as an educative one, so that the aid of these other services can be enlisted. Parents can also be introduced by the social worker to clubs whose members consist of parents with similar problems. The National Society for Mentally Handicapped Children has branches all over the country, and a family in touch with such a society will often gain a great deal of support from meeting other families with handicapped children. It can also provide the boon of meetings where it is possible to take the handicapped child without his being a source of embarrassment.

With all these resources used to the full it may still be inevitable that the child is admitted to a hospital, but such hospitalization need not necessarily be permanent. Here there is a great need for liaison between the hospital and the local authority social work staff. In urban areas it is often possible for the same social worker to work with a family even after hospitalization, and this continuity of support is the ideal. In rural areas, however, where the catchment area of a hospital may extend over five counties, this is usually impossible. The close liaison mentioned above can do a great deal to maintain continuity of care, but the big institution far removed from the homes of its patients can never be as effective as the small hospital or home serving a local area. Difficulties in visiting, and the consequent estrangement of child and parents, militate against rehabilitation and the happiness of the child who, severely handicapped or not, still needs to feel that he belongs to a family.

Subnormality

A family with a subnormal child will have different problems, and for the social worker the work will be different in that the subnormal child or adult will himself be the focus of casework. At the same time, however, he must be treated as a member of a family. It is from his own family that he will get the support which is of prime importance in his adjustment to his own limitations and to the extra stress that may be caused him by what to others would be normal demands of growing up. If this support is lacking for any reason then he may find difficulties, but it should be remembered that the majority of subnormal people are successful in adapting to adult life.

The social worker will be called upon to help those families whose subnormal member is in some way failing to make the grade, and she will need to understand the complex of family relationships which may be helping or hindering the child. Even in previously stable families the arrival of a subnormal child can cause problems. Where father is a professional or skilled worker, parents may have difficulty in accepting the child's retardation, and if the handicap is ignored excuses for the child's failure will be found elsewhere. For example, parents may think his teacher or his employer has "a down" on him. This leads to over-protection of the child and prevents him from acquiring the self-knowledge and self-discipline which alone will allow him to accept his own handicap but at the same time make full use of the potentialities that he has. Parents who are themselves dull and having to struggle to reach minimum standards may feel threatened by a subnormal child, and put a great deal of pressure on him to conform. This is equally true of older parents who fear for the future of their child and push him beyond his capacity in the hope of making him independent. Quite severe problems can occur when family relationships are disturbed in the first place. The additional stress of a handicapped child can produce strains which seem quite disproportionate, and the child may become a bone of contention between the parents and the focus for their marital disharmony. This will obviously have harmful repercussions on the child himself.

As with severely subnormal children or adults, hospital care may become necessary though it is not likely to be as long-term. Some period away from home to enable the child to gain confidence in his own powers and to give him training which will help him to resettle in the community is often of great value. In these cases there will be problems of helping both child and parents to readjust when he returns home. Parents will have a sense of failure over the initial removal from home, and there may be a fear of confiding problems to the social worker in case this is taken as evidence of a continued inability to care for the child. The adolescent who has received training in hospital will have a considerable effort of adjustment to make. He will be handicapped by his subnormality in intelligence, and since hospitalization often occurs in early adolescence he may have little experience of the adult world. Nevertheless, being older, more will be expected of him, and he will be correspondingly less able to confess his lack of knowledge. An inability to face up to these difficulties may result in frequent changes of jobs or running away from home and he too may have difficulty in accepting help because of his attitudes to authority and his fear of a return to hospital.

The subnormal client without a family will have a double handicap, and the change from school to work is bound to bring with it problems which he can hardly have the experience to deal with unaided. He may react in a variety of ways by exhibiting behaviour problems and hostility to those who are attempting to give him guidance, or by over-dependence on the social worker. Since he will have to face the problem of starting work and that of settling in a new home at the same time, it is particularly useful if this transition can be eased by having hostels available when he leaves the Residential Special School and by the provision of training centres where he can learn to adjust to the demands that work will make upon him. The value of these training centres and hostels as a half-way house to adult independence has been demonstrated by the experiments that have been made in this direction by the National Association for Mental Health and progressive local authorities.

The social worker's role in this situation is to plan with and not for the subnormal client. It may be that it will prove harder to achieve a helpful relationship with him because of his experiences of failure and his suspicion of authority, yet because of his limited intelligence the social worker will have at times to take on more of a parental role than is usual in other forms of casework. To be able to achieve this balance requires a skill which has not always been acknowledged. She must also be able to discuss his problems with him in a way that he can understand and she must be able to work closely with hostel and training centre staffs. Part of her job is to interpret to employers the sort of difficulties that the subnormal person is likely to meet and to enlist his aid and that of other interested persons in the community. She must be able to see the strengths in any situation and bolster these, and she must give support and understanding to hostel staffs or the family without undermining the confidence of the client. She acts in many ways as a liaison officer channelling all sources of help to enable her client to achieve independence.

Community Care

In the term "community care" is implied all that is mentioned above. If we are to have hostels, training centres and special care units, we need staffs to run them and staffs who are trained to appreciate the special problems of the mentally subnormal. If we are to encourage parents to keep their handicapped children in the family we must have the provisions that enable them to do so, and we must have trained social workers who will help these families to solve the difficulties that will inevitably arise. At present many of those working with the mentally subnormal are completely untrained and very few professionally trained psychiatric social workers have been attracted to this field of social work. Its rewards and the skill that it requires are only now beginning to be appreciated. The demand for training has come as much from those working in this sphere as from elsewhere, since these untrained workers have realized how inadequately prepared they have been to deal with the complex emotional problems which they encounter in families with mentally subnormal children. The Younghusband Committee studied the need for training of social workers in the health and welfare fields and following their report the establishment of the Council for Social Work Training and the welcome provision of new training courses will benefit, amongst other services, those for the mentally subnormal.

After the passing of the Mental Health Act in 1959, the Minister of Health asked local authorities to produce a ten-year programme to enable them to make the concept of community care a reality. These programmes include plans for additional social workers and for the training of new entrants and existing staff. Some authorities propose to provide residential homes and hostels for those who need support but do not require hospital care. The importance of social clubs is recognized in many areas, and the provision of junior and adult training centres is a feature of the majority of the plans submitted. Many local authorities have already implemented at least part of their ten-year programme, but a great deal still needs to be done. A recent study (1963) of the place of the hospital in the care of the mentally subnormal in the Manchester Regional Hospital Board Area shows that at present there are very few facilities provided by the local authorities in this area for the very severely handicapped. The study also finds that the three county boroughs with the best training centre facilities have a significantly lower demand for hospital places than other boroughs in the region, demonstrating that given adequate help many families wish to keep their handicapped children at home.

After the emphasis on custodial care for the mentally subnormal which marked the early years of the century, the trend is now towards treating them in the community where this is possible, and there is no doubt that many of these handicapped people can make a useful if limited contribution to society. Where the handicap is very severe, care in the community is still justified if the severely subnormal child and his family are happier as a result. We must remember that the cost of community care cannot be reckoned in purely financial terms. By the same criterion, however, the value of care in the community is to a large extent nullified if it is achieved at too great a sacrifice by the other members of the family in terms of their ability to lead a normal and satisfying life. The need for more hospital facilities is evident, and proposals to increase the number of beds for the mentally subnormal are included in the Ten Year Hospital Plan published by the Minister of Health. At present we have neither sufficient places in hospital nor the services in the community to lower the demand for these places. The gap in our services seems greater because the fuller realization of the needs of the mentally subnormal and their families has led to a demand for improved facilities; but the acknowledgement of the existence of such a gap is in itself progress and in many areas a real start has been made in bridging it.

References

1. ADAMS, M. (Ed.), *The Mentally Subnormal. The Social Casework Approach.*
2. LEESON, J., Place of the hospital in the care of the mentally subnormal, *British Medical Journal*, 16 Mar. 1963.
3. O'CONNOR, N. and TIZARD, J., *The Social Problem of Mental Deficiency.*
4. *Royal Commission on the Law relating to Mental Illness and Mental Deficiency* (1954–7).
5. *Report of the Working Party on Social Workers in the Local Authority Health and Welfare Services* (1959).
6. TIZARD, J. and GRAD, J. C., *The Mentally Handicapped and their Families.*

45. Community Care for the Mentally Disordered

JOHN E. WESTMORELAND

Honorary Secretary, Society of Mental Welfare Officers,
and Mental Health Officer, City of Nottingham

Concepts Ancient and Modern

The trend towards community care is mistakenly thought to be an entirely modern development. This is not quite true. The means of care of the mentally disordered, and particularly the attitudes towards them, have developed slowly over the centuries towards the present concept of care within the community for all those not in acute need of treatment in a hospital. Originally, care within the community was the only form of care since no other was available, and we have, in fact, come a full circle to the starting-point, except that community care today is a positive policy rather than an inescapable situation.

Mental disorder can be presumed to have existed from earliest times, and, lacking means of care or treatment, the sufferers could only be looked after in their own homes or, all too often, rejected to become wanderers on the face of the earth. Some, however, became both violent and dangerous, and places of confinement had to be established, not primarily for the welfare of the mentally disordered person but essentially for the protection of society. Dealing with the mentally disordered has, until comparatively modern times, been conditioned by fear and it was probably fear that inhibited any close inquiry into states of mind when the popular feeling was that the mentally sick were possessed by devils—or misbehaving wilfully. Gradually the fogs of superstition were to some extent dispersed, and asylums were established for the care and protection of the patient and of society, but for little else. Conditions of incarceration became more humane, but little could be done to treat the patient because still little in the way of treatment existed. A spontaneous remission was almost the only hope to bring release to those once admitted.

For too long, mental disorder was almost completely outside the pale of medical practice, but eventually doctors became interested in these conditions, and, very slowly, some insight was gained and limited treatment became possible. During the last fifty years there has been a sudden and almost unbelievable acceleration both in the knowledge of the conditions involved and of treatments that can be applied, until it was possible to draft the Mental

386

Health Act of 1959, establishing that mental disorder must be treated as an illness, dealt with on a medical basis, and even when in an acute phase it is necessary for the patient to be deprived of his liberty against his will, this may only be done on medical recommendation.

The gradual gaining of knowledge has established that in many cases treatment in hospital is only necessary during acute phases of the illness, and that mentally disordered persons can be helped to live reasonably satisfactory lives in the community following comparatively short periods in hospital or between spells of illness. Many sufferers from mental illness, if provided with sufficiently strong social support, can be treated on an outpatient basis without needing to be admitted to hospital at all. Hence the modern concept of community care which contemplates even the quite seriously disturbed remaining at all times in the community except when hospital admission becomes necessary for their own or the public safety or when the illness requires treatment which demands the constant medical and nursing supervision which can only be provided in a hospital.

The Mental Welfare Officer

Community care is a question of socio-medical care with the accent at least as heavily on the social content of the work as on the medical. The mentally ill are people quite frequently bedevilled with social problems, some of which, indeed, may be precipitating factors in the illness and some of which arise because of the illness. Social work of the widest kind is an essential ingredient of community care and, in the main, the social workers in this context are the mental welfare officers of the local health authority. Before discussing, therefore, what these officers do, it may be of interest to see who they are and whence they came.

Mental Welfare Officer first became a statutory title in the Mental Health Act, 1959, which requires local health authorities to appoint officers "to act as mental welfare officers for the purposes of this Act", although workers in this field had adopted the title for themselves long before. These were the persons who, as a result of amendments to the Lunacy Act of 1890 by the National Health Service Act, 1946, became "duly authorized officers". This strangely named animal was not an entirely new creation but was, in fact, the lineal descendant of the Relieving Officer, who was at that time abolished, and the Authorized Officer of the Mental Deficiency Acts, 1913–38.

The Relieving Officer, mainly concerned with the relief of poverty, was really also the first professional community care worker with the mentally disordered. This officer, whose value to the community was appreciated more after his abolition than during his reign, had a vast range of general welfare duties, and certain duties under the Lunacy Act. Although the admission to asylums of persons of unsound mind where compulsory action was required appeared to be his principal duty with the mentally disordered, the fact remained that in his general welfare work he was constantly coping with the problems of the mentally disordered who were unable to maintain themselves unaided in the community and were driven to seek financial support from the Poor Law authorities, and this financial support inevitably called for social support from the responsible officer of the Poor Law authorities, the Relieving Officer. Until the passing of the Mental Deficiency Act in 1913, this officer alone had any responsibilities, statutory or moral, for the care of the mentally subnormal, and many subnormal families and their offspring made great demands on these officers. The first statutory community service for any of the mentally disordered was established by the Mental Deficiency Act, 1913, which required local health authorities to "provide suitable supervision for such persons" living within their area. In the way that things happen, the word supervision was expanded until a social care service of widest application was gradually evolved.

The services for the mentally disordered established in 1948 under the "prevention, care, and after-care" provisions of Section 28 of the National Health Service Act, 1946, were in the main staffed with a mixture of ex-relieving officers and ex-mental deficiency workers. The former were mostly men, whilst the latter had a high proportion of women. From the fusion of their knowledge and experience emerged a philosophy and technique which was so successful as to obscure for a long time the need for formal training to enrich the natural ability of those drawn to this work and to confer an accepted professional status on its practitioners.

No higher praise can be given to the early mental welfare officers than to point out that with little to guide them but their own innate ability and adaptability coupled with compassion and humanity, they were able to evolve a service which, if still imperfect, nevertheless laid the firm foundation on which the modern concept of community care is erected.

The Need for Community Care

The need for community care in some forms of mental disorder would seem to be self-evident, e.g. the severely subnormal and at least some of the subnormal, but the need in cases of mental illness is probably less obvious through, to some extent, changing thought on mental illness. It is perhaps unfortunate that for a long time, in order to combat the stigma attaching to mental illness, it has been preached that "mental illness is an illness like any other illness", whereas the truth is that mental illness *is* an illness but quite *unlike* any other illness. No purely physical illness of itself causes the complete withdrawal from society which is one of the striking features of some forms of mental illness. No form of physical illness creates the difficult social climate so often resulting from the behaviour of the seriously disturbed psychotic patient, and whilst many forms of physical illness leave behind quite serious residual handicaps, these evoke a sympathy which is all too often lacking towards those suffering from permanent handicap or intellectual deterioration as a result of mental illness.

Those recovering from incapacitating mental illness need to re-integrate with society in all ways; they have jobs to find or to return to, to re-enter the home or seek living accommodation, they have to renew personal relationships or build up a new social circle. All too often inhibitions resulting from the illness prevent them from taking on their own account the necessary steps towards reintegration. As a result they need guidance, support and advice on how best to tackle each of the problems with which they are confronted, and sometimes their diffidence is such that action must be taken on their behalf. The community as a whole lacks insight into this problem and shows little spontaneous desire to be enlightened; once, therefore, the social needs of the mentally ill are realized and it is further realized that the required help will not automatically be made available by the community except by individuals in isolated cases, it follows that for these needs to be satisfied properly, an organized community care service is essential.

The Processes of Community Care

The definition of social work by Younghusband—"The process of helping people, with the aid of appropriate social services, to resolve or mitigate a wide range of personal and social problems which they are unable to meet successfully without such help"—is an excellent guide to the processes of community care, but there is an implication that the persons to be helped are part of the community, whereas community care of the mentally disordered is much concerned with those who, as a result of incapacitating illness—whether precipitated by personal and social problems or not—have lost their place in society. The essential first task is to engineer their return to the community.

In social work much is heard nowadays of the casework process, the essence of which is the examination of a problem by a committee of two—the client and the social worker—with the object of enabling the client to see the reason for his own difficulties, and from this point to endeavour to see a possible solution with the ultimate object that the client will then, of his own volition, take the necessary steps to bring the hypothetical solution into reality. This is the operational method of choice over large areas of the social work field and it can be, and indeed is, freely used in the psychiatric field. One of the striking differences between social work with the mentally disordered, different from almost any other field of social work, is that by very reason of the mental disorder the client often is incapable of, or inhibited

from, taking the steps necessary to bring about a solution of his own difficulties. In this field, then, the person of the social worker will obtrude often
quite visibly in the process of resolving or mitigating both personal and
social problems.

The three main headings under which practical assistance to the mentally
disordered could be listed are work, home and personal relationships. The
mentally subnormal frequently require assistance under the first heading—
employment—and occasionally with the other two. The mentally ill very
frequently require assistance under all three headings; it cannot be said that
the process of re-integration with society has been successfully accomplished
until the client is in suitable employment, living under satisfactory conditions
either in the family home or elsewhere, and is enjoying good relationships
with other members of the immediate group.

Employment

Satisfactory employment is an obvious need, not only from the psychological angle but from the sheer inescapable economic need. In many cases,
of course, a person recovering from mental illness is able to return to the
employment held prior to the illness, and the mentally subnormal quite
frequently find work suited to their capacity through ordinary channels.
However, with many of those recovering from mental illness there are special
factors conditioning this question of employment, and better placements for
some of the mentally subnormal can be found by those having understanding
of the person concerned and a wide knowledge of the local labour situation.

The fullest use is made of the services of the Ministry of Labour, and the
Disablement Resettlement Officer is quite often a useful and friendly ally,
but over and above this mental welfare officers need to develop their own
knowledge of the commerce and industry of the area and learn where they
can safely make direct approaches to managements. This is particularly
important in cases where the recovered mentally ill person is diffident about
making personal application. Although the method of choice would be to
ascertain where suitable employment might be available and advise the
client to apply, there are cases where it is necessary for the social worker to
act in the capacity of an agent and seek a post for his client.

The personal contacts established by a mental welfare officer can be of
particular importance for the mentally subnormal. Many of the mentally
subnormal are only capable of work under the right conditions; many are,
in fact, generally regarded as completely unemployable, and yet many of
these latter are given the psychological uplift of becoming self-supporting
units in the community because the social worker is able to introduce them
to an employer who has available work within their capacity under conditions which enable them to settle happily in the job.

Living Accommodation

A satisfactory home, whether it is in fact a place in the family home or a furnished bed-sitter or a flat or lodgings, is an essential requirement. Many of the mentally ill can return and be happily received in the home they left to enter hospital, and most of the mentally subnormal are already units in a family circle when the case first comes to light. Nevertheless, there are those among the mentally ill whose home circle is unwilling to receive them back after the illness. Some, particularly those whose illness has been of a protracted nature, needing a lengthy stay in hospital, find the home has disintegrated whilst they have been away, and some lacked a satisfactory home prior to admission.

With the first class, the Mental Welfare Officer will initially undertake missionary work in the home in an endeavour to spread mental health principles to secure tolerance and reopen the door to the excluded member. Where this technique fails, and in some cases it must, human nature being what it is, the officer will assist the client in the search for suitable accommodation. The client's needs and preferences, which are not always in concert, have to be carefully taken into account when a choice is made as to whether a flat, bed-sitter or lodgings are to be sought. Sometimes it is better for the client to go into lodgings, where he can at least become a member of a synthetic family circle, whilst others may be better suited by becoming tenants of a few cubic feet of space they can call their own. The social worker, therefore, needs an extensive knowledge of the availability of accommodation in the district and a wide knowledge of the varying personalities of those who have lodgings to let, for here again very happy results can accrue from placing the right person in the right environment, a result which the client alone could only achieve by accident.

Personal Relationships

Personal relationships often present difficult problems. Some people develop personality traits which alienate the sympathies of family and friends before the illness has reached a stage where hospital care and treatment becomes necessary, and while in some cases natural sympathy awakens when it is realized that the patient is seriously ill, this is not so in all cases and quite frequently there is a good deal of delicate work to be done by the Mental Welfare Officer to prepare for the discharged patient to be received back into the family circle. Intervention in the work group is necessary on occasions and sometimes it is necessary to assist the clients to create a new system of social contacts.

Personal Service

Apart from those requiring advice and practical assistance in material ways, there are many of those recovering from mental illness who are in great need of a confidant. Despite the marked change in public attitudes towards the mentally ill, the psychiatric patient often suffers from some feelings of shame, and is inclined to be reticent with family and friends although desperately anxious to talk it out with someone. This someone can most usefully be a social worker having some knowledge of mental illness in general and of the patient in particular, and who can offer sympathy and support in the right proportion.

With the subnormal, particularly the severely subnormal, the social worker needs to be a family caseworker in the fullest sense of the word. In these cases, only a minimum of work can be done directly with the subnormal person; the bulk of the work is with the parents and with the family as a group. Not infrequently the first difficulty is for the social worker to gain an entry into the family; often there is resentment that any official action is felt to be necessary with respect to a severely subnormal child about whose condition the parents themselves have feelings of guilt. First, it is necessary to help the parents to adjust to the situation, then to explain what the service can endeavour to do for the child and to gain acceptance of such service. This aspect of the work can be described quite easily in these few lines, but its proper performance calls for skill of a very high degree, inexhaustible patience and deep compassion.

Training Centres

In addition to casework services, training centres are an indispensable part of the pattern for the community care of the mentally subnormal.

Why the education of the severely subnormal should be a responsibility of the local health authority and not of the local education authority is a question to which no good answer has yet been propounded. It seems unjust that parents of the mentally subnormal, as ratepayers, should be mulcted of a contribution towards the costs of the education service but denied benefit from the service they are helping to maintain. To many it seems improper that the education service should be permitted to be selective; services provided for children should be for all children, without differentiation between those intellectually well endowed and those of marked limitation. Too little compassion is shown towards those who have the misfortune to have a child of obvious intellectual inferiority. It is hurtful enough to have such a child, to know that it must be educated in a "special" school, but it is hurtful to a degree that cannot easily be understood for the child to be arbitrarily labelled "unsuitable for education" and curtly cast off. Not only is the child denied a place in the society to which the mere fact of its existence should entitle it to belong, but the parents, too, tend to feel outcasts, to feel that they are being punished for a genetic accident.

To their credit, the local health authorities are making a great effort to remedy the situation in so far as it can be remedied. Through the medium of training centres, which are multiplying rapidly, the severely subnormal child is trained to be less obviously different, to be less of a burden, to be self-helpful to the highest possible degree, to fit into the ordinary pattern of community life as inconspicuously as can be achieved considering the inherent handicap.

Junior Training Centres, catering for severely subnormal children up to the age of 16 years, have been developing over a good many years and the possibilities of training are well understood. The provision of such centres has been rather patchy, some authorities having made better provision than others, but the position is now improving rapidly. There is still not a place available for every child who would benefit from attending a training centre, but prospects are that the situation will be remedied in the near future.

With the adult subnormal, the position is not nearly so good, and ideas need a good deal of clarification. Many of the centres provided for subnormals over the age of 16 years are designated industrial centres, and in many it seems that efforts to provide productive employment overshadow the continued need for training. The subnormal child is not only limited in capacity and slower to learn what he can learn, he is much longer than a normal child coming to his full capacity.

It is arguable whether "junior" training should finish arbitrarily at the age of 16 years or whether the type of curriculum for the older children in the junior training centre ought not to be carried on in the adult training centres until the point has been reached where it is felt the individual has no further skills to learn, even though this process might need to carry on into the early 20's. There is a tendency in adult centres immediately to set the trainee to work at productive employment, utilizing whatever skills he already possesses without thought of further possible development.

In an Adult Training Centre the keyword should be "training", as it is in the junior centres with specially established sheltered workshops available for the employment of those who have reached the limits of training. In the present situation, training and employment are frequently muddled together, with training suffering at the hands of production and the need to complete contract work. There is undoubtedly scope for considerable rethinking here. Quite separate premises should be provided for these quite separate purposes which can so often be in direct conflict if carried on under the same roof.

This criticism can only be advanced because more thought is now being given to the situation in the community of the adult mentally subnormal, and it is confidently hoped that after a period of trial and error a system will be evolved where all those unable to benefit from the ordinary educational system will receive training to the full limit of their capacity, with employment to follow under conditions tempered to meet the needs of those whose abilities are markedly less than normal but who, under such conditions, could become economically self-supporting, thus contributing to the community upon which up to now they have been an unrelieved burden.

Hostels

The value of hostels in certain circumstances, as half-way houses into the community from hospital care, have been well proven. It may be thought that they should have been dealt with under the heading "living accommodation". Hostels are, however, still the subject of considerable controversy.

Although the Mental Health Act empowers local authorities to provide hostels for the mentally disordered, there are many who feel that such establishments are better seen as ancillary departments of hospitals than as a proper field of activity for a local health authority responsible for community care services. Exactly as proceeding from hospital to hostel can be seen as moving half way *into* the community, direct entry into a hostel can equally be seen as moving half way *out* of the community, which to many would seem to be against the principles of community care, which surely are to enable the mentally disordered to live in ordinary circumstances under ordinary conditions in the open community.

There must inevitably be some institutional element about the best-run hostel—good management would be impossible without some regimentation and the imposition of statutory standards would further distort the picture —so that living in a hostel, whilst essentially different from being under treatment in hospital, would still be quite different from ordinary life in the community. It would seem clearly to be the business of community care to help those in the half-way house to take the final step into community living, but not to be concerned in assisting them to take the first step out.

The fact that some hospitals continue to administer hostels, and some local authorities are now establishing similar establishments, demonstrates quite clearly how very vague is the demarcation line between the responsibilities of the two authorities. It is perfectly easy to see what is inescapably a hospital problem, and equally easy to see what is essentially a community problem, but there is an area of "no man's land" between which can equally be everybody's or nobody's problem. For the benefit of the mentally disordered, and indeed for the benefit of the whole community, since in the larger view hospital services are within the total community, a single clear boundary line should be laid down leaving no vague unresolved areas, but ensuring that every person is clearly entitled to the service best suited to his needs. It is submitted that community care should only be concerned with those who with all necessary assistance and social support could live with and among the ordinary individuals of the open community, but those needing care and accommodation beyond this should receive it in some part of an extended hospital service with all the professional and technical resources available.

Community Responsibility

The success or failure of the modern concept of community care depends entirely upon the community itself. There have been periods in history when the mentally disordered were totally rejected by the community; there have been periods when there has been grudging acceptance of some of the mentally disordered in the community. There is undoubtedly now a more enlightened attitude than ever before towards those who suffer from some form of mental disorder.

It often seems, however, that the enlightenment does not go very deep as yet, and it is quite easy to arouse many of the old fears and prejudices towards these unhappy people. There is still need for education on a wide scale to secure the full understanding of those who so far have escaped the misfortune of mental disorder.

It is essential for it generally to be realized that the mentally disordered are fellow citizens, fellow citizens with special problems but, nevertheless, members of the community towards whom all have neighbourly responsibilities. Community care cannot come to full flower merely as a service administered for the community by the local health authority. The community itself has an actual part to play—the community must care. It must care enough to be willing to offer to the mentally disordered the emotional environment in which they can live satisfactorily, must care enough cheerfully to pay the bill for extending the various necessary professional services which at the moment remain woefully inadequate, and care enough to force the pace towards a service from which all can reap full benefit.

46. The National Association for Mental Health

MARY APPLEBEY

General Secretary, National Association for Mental Health

THE FIELD of mental health is probably the most challenging of any in which voluntary bodies are at present working. Mental disorders are so widespread that they have become everybody's business; steps to cure and prevent them have been made possible by advances in knowledge, while new possibilities are always just round the corner. The number of families affected is enormous, probably one family in every five, but there still clings unnecessarily around the word "mental" an aura of fear and superstition.

The National Association for Mental Health is concerned with the mentally disordered—the mentally ill, the subnormal, the severely subnormal and the psychopaths. It tries to concentrate interest on their care and treatment and to encourage research into ways of preventing the disorders arising. It is closely associated with other voluntary bodies interested in some special aspect of this wide range: the Mental After Care Association, the National Society for Mentally Handicapped Children, the National Association of Leagues of Hospital Friends and the Mental Health Research Fund. With the Mental Health Research Fund the Association set up the Mental Health National Appeal to collect money, primarily for the two founder bodies but also for all voluntary bodies concerned with mental health.

The Association has over 300 national bodies affiliated to it, and is supported by over fifty independent local associations for mental health. Its membership includes professional and lay people; doctors, teachers, social workers, nurses, psychologists and members of the general public. It has offices in London and in Leeds.

The N.A.M.H. regarded it as a great step forward when the doors of the hospitals treating mental illnesses were thrown open and the general public began to go inside the high walls. The Association welcomed the development of voluntary admission and discharge, the development of short-stay treatment and community care for the long-term illness. The growing number of people in the community who have been helped by the hospitals are now the best possible advertisement for what is happening inside the hospitals. Fear and superstition have begun to give way, and the phrase "put away" has been replaced by "gone to hospital for treatment". It is not only drugs which have brought about these changes. Doctors have begun to look into the patients' minds and to try to understand how certain conditions arise.

Some, however, remain impervious to treatment of any kind. Some illnesses cannot be treated. There is no cure so far for people suffering from arrested development of mind—the subnormal, or the mentally defective as they used to be called. It is, however, now possible to prevent subnormality from developing in a rare condition known as phenylketonuria provided a special diet is given from within a few weeks of birth, and it is hoped that, as research progresses, prevention may become possible where subnormality has other causes. There are some among the mentally ill with whom the modern treatments fail. For these a whole new theory of work therapy has been devised, and many is the subnormal and the long-stay patient who has responded to the spur of occupation and has returned to his family or been able for the first time to win himself a place in society.

One of the most challenging problems is treatment for the psychopath—the man whose actions seem totally inexplicable and who appears to have no sense of right and wrong. Should he be sent to prison? How far can medicine help him? How far should he be detained for his own good in a hospital setting? These medico-legal arguments have been intensified by clauses in the Mental Health Act, 1959, which for the first time allows compulsory detention in certain circumstances in hospital for such cases.

The mentally disordered fill nearly one-half of our hospital beds, some in special psychiatric hospitals and some in general hospitals. Is their treatment and care as good as it could possibly be? Most people would say No. Psychiatric hospitals were built at a time when treatment was virtually unknown, and only kind custodial care over long periods was possible. For their own good and for that of society, patients were isolated in large buildings with spacious grounds standing far from the towns. Wards were large, supervised by a minimal number of doctors and nurses. In many areas these hospitals remain. Fine work is going on in them, but they were not built for this purpose and, as the Minister of Health has said himself, many of them should come down. Buildings are not the whole story. It will take a long time before doctors and nurses devoting themselves to this work have the same prestige in their own professions as those working in other specialities; a long time before there are enough doctors, enough nurses, and enough money to give the best treatment in ideal surroundings. This leaves out of account anything that might be done in the community by way of prevention, and this means research. Too little money is as yet spent in the mental health field, and too little is known about why certain conditions respond to certain drugs and why certain illnesses happen. All in all, this is a field of work in a constant state of flux where experiment is welcomed, public information essential, and criticism and encouragement vital to an expanding service.

The National Association for Mental Health has these complicated conditions in mind in all that it undertakes. Its broad functions are to act as responsible critic of official action, to be a spur to individual sympathy and effort and to provide supplementary services of a pioneer character.

Among its many activities the Association organizes annual conferences for professional workers where the development of the national services can be reviewed and criticized. It offers refresher courses for doctors, teachers, social workers and others, and seminars for inter-disciplinary discussion of common problems. It keeps a watchful eye on legislation and makes representations to Government Departments as opportunity occurs. At the same time it watches press and Parliament and is in touch with leading journalists and television producers. It publishes a journal, *Mental Health*, and numerous reports and pamphlets.

Through its local and national committees the Association provides a focus for professional and lay people to interest themselves in national and local problems in the mental health field as well as providing opportunities for individual service. Visiting lonely patients, running clubs, hostels and workshops are among the activities undertaken by willing volunteers.

Sometimes the Association itself undertakes new services at the request of Government Departments or because the need for them has been shown. It has started many different trainings which are now part of the national scheme. Until very recently it was the only body training teachers for Training Centres for the Mentally Handicapped.

The Association manages two approved schools for adolescent girls with psychiatric difficulties, one special school for maladjusted boys, three hostels for boys and girls leaving special schools for the educationally subnormal and the maladjusted, a home for mentally frail old ladies, two holiday homes for patients from hospital, and a short-stay home for mentally handicapped children.

Anyone with a mental health problem is welcome to use the Association's services or to support its efforts. A skilled team of advisory workers is available to deal with individual queries, and the Association is always ready to consider national or local problems and to throw in its weight to help the mentally disordered wherever they may be.

47. Alcoholism—The Role of the National Council

RICHARD PERCEVAL

Director of Field Work, National Council on Alcoholism

ALCOHOLISM—what is it? There have been many definitions but perhaps the following is the clearest: "A chronic disease, or disorder of behaviour, characterized by the repeated drinking of alcoholic beverages to an extent that exceeds customary dietary use, or ordinary compliance with the social drinking customs of the community, so that it interferes with the drinker's health, inter-personal relations, or economic functioning."

Alcoholism is recognized by the World Health Organization as a disease and as a serious world social problem, and recently a joint committee of the British Medical Association and Magistrates' Association reported that: "Alcoholism is a problem of a size to merit urgent attention." The committee added that the situation is "unlikely to improve until there is more knowledge of and enthusiasm for the subject".

In many countries, but not in Great Britain until recently, there has been a co-ordinated national effort to do something about alcoholism—not only because it is a serious disease which kills or permanently disables a very large number of people, but also because its repercussions are so vast.

Alcoholism is one of the major causes of broken homes and marriages. It is directly responsible for much instability in the children of alcoholics, and it affects adversely the lives of the many men and women with whom every alcoholic has close social contact.

From a purely economic aspect, alcoholism is a very expensive factor of national life. It is estimated, in America, that about 3 per cent of the nation's industrial workers are alcoholics, and that each of these loses almost four times as many working days through absenteeism as the worker who is not an alcoholic. The cost of incarcerating alcoholics in institutions, some of which cannot provide proper treatment, is alarming, and at the same time the State bears a heavy burden of financial responsibility for the alcoholics' families.

In view of this serious situation it seems surprising that there has not long ago been a real effort in Great Britain to deal with this problem, but this failure has been due largely to a lack of information and, consequently, lack of understanding.

It has been thought that alcoholism is the same thing as the self-indulgent habit of drunkenness—which is not true. It has been thought also that the control of drinking is a matter of will-power—which does not apply to the alcoholics. It has been thought that any attempt to deal with alcoholism implies an interference with the individual's right to act as he or she pleases as regards consumption of alcohol, and the whole subject has sometimes been hopelessly confused with the age-old question of whether alcohol itself is, or is not, an evil thing. This controversy has little or nothing to do with the prevention and arrest of the disease of alcoholism.

A good deal of work has, nevertheless, been going on in many parts of this country on the question of alcoholism, although the need of a co-ordinating body to see that best results are obtained from the various efforts has long been felt. The Churches are beginning to interest themselves in the subject. A number of private clinics and clinics operated by charitable societies have been established. The London School of Hygiene and Tropical Medicine is promoting regular studies of the public health aspects of alcoholism in this country. In 1962 the Ministry of Health, recognizing the inadequacy of its provisions for treatment, issued a memorandum to Regional Hospital Boards recommending the establishment of more in-patient and out-patient facilities, as well as close liaison in aftercare with Alcoholics Anonymous, and steps are being taken in most areas to implement these recommendations. (A directory listing all facilities for the treatment of alcoholism, published by the Steering Group on Alcoholism established by the Rowntree Trust, is available to doctors and others professionally concerned with counselling alcoholics and their families. Applications to the Secretary, National Council on Alcoholism, 212a Shaftesbury Avenue, London, W.C.2.)

Yet all the excellent work outlined above has had, so far, only a limited effect. Because the public is uninformed, the alcoholic, his family, and his employer do not realize that his condition *is* an illness, and that it is treatable: by trying to hide their "shame" they succeed only in worsening his health and prognosis as well as bringing prolonged misery to those closest to him. In addition, many general practitioners have had no specific training in the diagnosis or treatment of alcoholism, nor are they yet universally sympathetic towards this illness.

To try to remedy this obviously unsatisfactory situation a National Council on Alcoholism was formed in September 1962. The character of this Council follows the pattern of the National Council of Alcoholism in the U.S.A., with which the new Council will work in close contact, and its inception was the spontaneous result of a number of meetings at which all who are working in this field were represented.

The programme of the National Council on Alcoholism is based on three concepts:

(1) alcoholism is a disease and the alcoholic a sick person;
(2) alcoholics can be helped and they are worth helping;

(3) alcoholism is a public health problem and therefore a public responsibility.

The objectives of the Council are summarized as follows:

To promote the study of the nature and extent of alcoholism and its treatment as a sickness.

To gather and disseminate information concerning:
the alcoholic himself;
the incidence and progress of his sickness in relation to society;
the medical, social and spiritual agencies which can help him.

To create a new and enlightened public concern about alcoholism.

In every way to encourage and promote research and treatment.

To act as a connecting link, through proposed information centres in large centres of population between the alcoholic, his family and friends and existing treatment centres.

To help all its members by providing facilities for the interchange of the specialized practical knowledge which they are individually acquiring and to place its knowledge and experience at the disposal of all who are seeking to make a serious contribution in any sphere to the recovery of the alcoholic.

To make this knowledge available to the press and radio and television services.

To build up a comprehensive library on the subject of alcoholism.

To promote co-operation with universities, hospitals and theological colleges for the purpose of advancing teaching and training in the medical treatment of alcoholism and the spiritual and social restoration of the alcoholic; also to promote training workshops for physicians, nurses, magistrates and law officers, social workers, clergy, counsellors, and all ancillary helpers.

To arouse the interest and co-operation of civic authorities, community organizations, and large industrial concerns.

To seek association with parallel organizations in other countries and affiliation to recognized international associations in order to benefit from their experience, keep abreast of, and contribute to, international developments, and to invite distinguished workers when they may be of assistance.

Preliminary investigation has shown clearly that the incidence of alcoholism *appears* to be greatest in the areas which have the most enlightened attitude towards this problem. Obviously this curiously deceptive statistical result is brought about by the fact that alcoholics are unwilling to present themselves for treatment if they think they will be ridiculed or not understood.

Consequently where there are doctors or hospitals who have a co-operative attitude towards alcoholics the number of patients will be markedly increased. This seems to show that only a change of public opinion will enable the magnitude of this problem to be objectively assessed.

If, as seems likely, there are at least 400,000 alcoholics in Great Britain, and if, as is *certain*, each alcoholic usually affects adversely the lives of at least five other people, 2 million people would have an opportunity of becoming happier and better citizens if public opinion about this problem could be changed. This is a task in which the National Council of Alcoholism hopes to be the leader. It will, however, obviously need the wholehearted interest of all bodies and individuals who are concerned with public health problems. It is essential that the old moralistic attitude towards alcoholism shall be eliminated. The alcoholic who drinks too much because he or she is literally incapable of stopping or unable to control the consumption of alcohol, needs enlightened under standing rather than punishment or exhortation. It is this fear of criticism and punishment, the underlying conviction that drinking is an adult occupation, and the fallacious dread that to abstain from the use of alcohol is an admission of weakness, that prevents many men and women from recovering.

A significant beginning has been made in this task of educating public opinion and of ensuring a more objective attitude towards alcoholism, but a great deal of hard work has yet to be done in which the co-operation of every doctor, clergyman, social worker and intelligent citizen is vitally necessary.

While it is difficult to assess the damage caused to the community by alcoholism, it is fortunately possible to see the beneficial results which derive from the rehabilitation of alcoholics. The dramatic recoveries achieved through Alcoholics Anonymous and by patients in various hospitals and clinics have shown that the reuniting of families, the salvaging of valuable citizens, and the rescuing from the scrap heap of countless wasted lives, is a task well worth attempting.

48. The Samaritans—Lay People against Suicide

Rev. Chad Varah

Founder of "The Samaritans", Director of the London branch, and Rector
of St. Stephen Walbrook in the City of London

The Samaritans are lay people. They have no professional qualifications of the kind one might expect in the members of an organization specifically to help "those tempted to suicide or despair". They are not doctors or parsons or social workers, though they yield to none in their admiration for the contribution of these professions, and more often than not they supplement their own ministrations by arranging professional counselling or medical treatment for their "clients". A few of them are professional people whose skills are usually irrelevant but occasionally useful, such as lawyers or accountants, and they are the first to recognize that they are accepted as members not because of these qualifications but for their human qualities.

When the social history of the second half of the twentieth century comes to be written, it may be that the outstanding difference between its social services and those of the first half will be seen as the increasing importance of voluntary workers operating alongside trained people in every field, including those where previously the volunteer would have been regarded as useless if not positively harmful. No one was surprised at the nature of the duties entrusted, e.g. to the W.V.S. during the war or at the continuance of this organization in peace-time, for these were tasks requiring the sort of competence and goodwill one expects to find in an experienced housewife; and few eyebrows were raised when during Christian Family Year (1962–3) the Mothers' Union began sending members to help out the hard-pressed staffs of maternity wards on a voluntary part-time basis, for a mother of three or more can be expected to be good at holding the hand of a frightened girl in labour for the first time. But it was a more radical departure from the traditional, and vital, distinction between the expert and the non-expert when the Samaritans began to be the first, and sometimes the only, source of help for large numbers of potential suicides, who included a proportion of mentally ill people needing the attention of a psychiatrist. The medical profession was generously quick to realize that all who required psychiatry were, if they would agree, directed to it, and that those who would not agree would not have sought medical help if the Samaritans had not existed. Far from competing with the mental hospitals and psychiatric clinics, the Samaritans were increasing the use made of these by removing irrational fears of medical

403

treatment. But none of this altered the fact that seriously disturbed persons often unburdened themselves to what might be described as "a well-meaning amateur".

The principle of amateur first aid in cases of physical emergency has long been recognized, and during the war many a man learnt how to apply a tourniquet from his Boy Scout son, but the extension of the principle to mental and emotional emergencies was largely unheard of before 1953, when the Samaritans began to try to do something about London's suicide rate of three a day.

It did not begin as a lay movement, or indeed as a movement at all. It began as the personal ministry of an individual priest of the Church of England who discovered that amongst those who sought his advice on their sexual problems were a proportion of potential suicides, almost all of whom required counselling rather than psychiatric treatment. It seemed to him that once it was clear that suicide was not exclusively a medical problem, non-medical (but still professional) counselling ought to be available to all who were driven to the verge of suicide by their psychological, sexual and spiritual problems. The way to find out whether it would be useful to make the offer of such help was obviously to try it. And since no one could know who the potential suicides were, it would be necessary to inform everyone, and let those who were tempted to destroy themselves respond if they would. This meant using the good offices of the press (and later of radio and television) to keep the service offered before the public, and to do so without the individual case-histories which would make a story really newsworthy but would frighten off the potential clients who rightly demand strict secrecy.

It was not possible to start such a service in one of those south London riverside parishes of 10,000 people described in the *Sunday Times* of Whit Sunday 1963 as the toughest challenge a parson can have, even if it had not had a 500-bed hospital as well. For "specialist ministries" in London it is almost essential to have one of the forty churches in the City of London, which has a huge day-time population but very few residents requiring pastoral care. The most central and also the most beautiful of these, Wren's master-piece, St. Stephen Walbrook, next door to the Mansion House, was offered in 1953 by the Worshipful Company of Grocers, who were anxious to see the experiment tried.

All that was required now was an easily-memorized telephone number, preferably reminiscent of the well-known emergency number 999. The exchange was MANsion House, so MAN 9999 or MAN 9000 would fill the bill. The Post Office was asked what it would cost to have the existing number of the Church telephone changed to MAN 9000. The reply was that such a desirable number would be sure to be in the possession of some business firm, but inquiries would be made. What number should they ring with the

PLATE 35. The Rev. Chad Varah, founder of the Samaritans

PLATE 36. The hand reaching out for the telephone at the Samaritans' headquarters

information? When the dust was cleaned off the telephone which the workmen repairing the bomb damage to the church had had reconnected, it was seen that the number was already MAN 9000.

On 2 November 1953 this number was advertised in the press as the emergency number for those contemplating suicide in the London Telephone Area, and people in despair began to ring it (Plates 35–6). The press continued to regard the service as a "human interest story", thus making the effective operation of the service possible. Most of the national papers gave the kind of coverage which went beyond mere reporting and showed a sympathetic interest and an evident desire for the experiment to succeed. This has continued in national newspapers and magazines and also in local papers. It was the *Daily Mirror* which applied the name "Samaritan" to the priest who answered the telephone, and as the Good Samaritan in the parable was the inspiration of the work and of its no-strings-attached method, the name was accepted without the adjective "good". As things turned out, it soon had to be put in the plural.

The same publicity which attracted the "clients" (the usual term for users of a non-medical social service) also attracted a number of people anxious to help. In addition to people with medical and/or psychological qualifications, there were some who had no qualifications of a kind relevant to this work whatever. Not all were "clients in disguise", though about one in five of those who offer help are really seeking a solution of their own problems, and another two or three have not sufficient stability or maturity or compassion or discretion to be allowed to sit around and come into contact with possibly precariously balanced clients. But there remained some of the unqualified laity whose hearts were evidently in the right place and whose desire to help in whatever humble way was allotted to them was proved to be genuine and lasting. But what could they do?

A parson who has rashly offered to listen to, and try to do something about, the troubles of a place as huge and unhappy as London is soon in no position to refuse any reasonable offer of help. Long before the service becomes a household name he will find himself trying to do five things at once: listen to clients on the telephone, listen to clients who queue up in person, deal with letters from clients, try to organize help (usually by telephone) *for* clients, and sort out the sheep from the goats amongst the volunteers. If he has done eleven one-hour interviews in succession, with the telephone interrupting every few minutes and waiting clients becoming impatient and letters piling up while his secretary goes crazy trying to deal with some of them herself, an unobtrusively helpful man or woman who is not looking for pats on the back can be a godsend. Such a volunteer gets sandwiches that can be eaten whilst interviewing, makes coffee, runs errands, keeps a client from departing in umbrage, and shoos away time-wasting scroungers. But soon he or she decides that rather than have "the boss" crack up, fools must rush in, taking their courage in both hands. So the first "Samaritans" appointed themselves, knowing they had no qualifications to offer but humbly believing they might be better than nobody, especially as they were prepared to obey "the boss" implicitly and would always put a vital decision to him.

From "the boss's" study it was noticeable (a) that clients coming in for a counselling interview were less agitated and more amenable after their "conditioning" by the lay volunteers in the general office, (b) that clients going out with the intention of killing themselves rather than accept psychiatric treatment were usually wheedled by the volunteers into having that treatment arranged for them, and (c) that a proportion of clients who had insisted that they would not talk to anyone but "the boss" had eventually gone away quite happily after a cosy heart-to-heart with one of the volunteers. What has since been christened "befriending" thus emerged and was observed to be of value (a) in supplementing counselling, (b) in picking up some of the failures of counselling in psychiatric cases, such as endogenous depression, and (c) in replacing counselling for those whose real problem is social isolation and friendlessness. As soon as this was recognized, "befriending" was fairly rapidly given priority, and this ministry of a multitude of lay people, the Samaritans, became the principal function, counselling becoming a thing which, like psychiatric treatment, was often needed too and could be organized by a friend whom the client had learned to trust.

At first, the traffic with the mental hospitals was one-way only, but as the value of befriending came increasingly to be recognized by psychiatrists, the Samaritans began to be asked to befriend patients who were having treatment, particularly in out-patient clinics. If and when Christian congregations begin to give priority to a perhaps less specialized form of befriending, it should be possible to clear the decks of the mental hospitals by discharging those who are kept there, occupying beds urgently needed for patients, requiring treatment, simply because the world outside is so callous and so lonely. The spread of the movement throughout the U.K. and Western Europe was greatly expedited by a generous six-year grant from the Gulbenkian Foundation.

From a small and tentative beginning has grown, in just over ten years, "THE SAMARITANS—to help those tempted to suicide or despair", a Company Limited by Guarantee with fifty branches at home and overseas, half as many again in active preparation, and the ambition to add its name to Police, Fire Brigade and Ambulance on the 999 Emergency Call; similar organizations in twenty other countries; and a movement for healing neighbourliness invading the Churches and the community at large. It seems Durkheim was right about suicide being primarily a social problem.

List of Samaritan Branches and Telephone Numbers

Aberdeen
 Tel.: Aberdeen 53000 (emergency).
  Aberdeen 53990 (other calls).

Bedford
 Tel.: Bedford 2200 (emergency).
  Bedford 2317 (other calls).

Belfast
 Tel.: Belfast 246 35 (emergency).
  Belfast 24 636 (other calls).

Bexhill and Hastings
 Tel.: Hastings 666.

Birmingham
 Tel.: Midland 2000 (emergency).
  Midland 1411 (other calls).

Blackpool
 Tel.: Blackpool 20000.

Bournemouth
 Tel.: Bournemouth 21999.

Bradford
 Tel.: Bradford 28282 (emergency).
  Bradford 26987 (other calls).

Brighton
 Tel.: Brighton 63333 (emergency).
  Brighton 65621 (other calls).

Bristol
 Tel.: Bristol 28444 (emergency).
  Bristol 28422 (other calls).

Burnley
 Tel.: Burnley 3000 (emergency).
  Burnley 3061 (other calls).

Cambridge
 Tel.: Cambridge 54545 (emergency).
  Cambridge 56420 (other calls).

Cheltenham
 Tel.: Cheltenham 55777.

Colchester
 Tel.: Colchester 6789 (emergency).
  Colchester 6636 (other calls).

Croydon
 Tel.: Croydon 4545 (emergency).
  Municipal 2905 (other calls).

Derby
 Tel.: Derby 40000 (emergency).
  Derby 48993 (other calls).

Doncaster
 Tel.: Doncaster 3636.

Dundee
 Tel.: Dundee 22955.

Edinburgh
 Tel.: Caledonian 3333 (emergency).
  Caledonian 3334 (other calls).

Exeter
 Tel.: Exeter 77755 (emergency).
  Exeter 77401 (other calls).

Folkestone
 Tel.: Folkestone 55000 (emergency).
  Folkestone 52947 (other calls).

Glasgow
 Tel.: City 4488.

Guernsey
 Tel.: Guernsey Central 3030.

Guildford
 Tel.: Guildford 2345 (emergency).
  Guildford 2346 (other calls).

Halifax
 Tel.: Halifax 62020 (emergency).
  Halifax 66655 (other calls).

Harlow
 Tel.: Harlow 25837

Hull (Kingston-upon-Hull)
 Tel.: Hull 23456.

Ipswich
 Tel.: Ipswich 51000 (emergency).
  Ipswich 58488 (other calls).

Leamington Spa
 Tel.: Leamington Spa 22022 (emergency).
  Leamington Spa 24674 (other calls).

Leicester
 Tel.: Leicester 75000 (emergency).
  Leicester 75330 (other calls).

Liverpool
 Tel.: Maritime 1999.

London
 Tel.: Mansion House 9000 (emergency).
  Mansion House 2277 (other calls).

Manchester
 Tel.: Blackfriars 9000 (emergency).
  Blackfriars 5228 (other calls).

Norwich
Tel.: Norwich 28000 (emergency).
Norwich 21161 (other calls).

Nottingham
Tel.: Nottingham 45000 (emergency).
Nottingham 46464 (other calls).

Oxford
Tel.: Oxford 44044 (emergency).
Oxford 44593 (other calls).

Portsmouth
Tel.: Portsmouth 23432.

Reading
Tel.: Reading 54845 (emergency).
Reading 54846 (other calls).

Salisbury
Tel.: Salisbury 5522.

Scunthorpe
Tel.: Scunthorpe 5555.

Southampton
Tel.: Southampton 25999 (emergency).
Southampton 24466 (other calls).

Stafford
Tel.: Stafford 2121 (emergency).
Stafford 4673 (other calls).

Stoke-on-Trent
Tel.: Stoke-on-Trent 23500.

Surrey (North West)
Tel.: Weybridge 44444 (emergency).
Weybridge 47622 (other calls).

Swansea
Tel.: Swansea 59595.

Woolwich
Tel.: Woolwich 3000 (emergency).
Woolwich 0445 (other calls).

Worcester
Tel.: Worcester 21121 (emergency).
Worcester 28961 (other calls).

SECTION IX
MORAL WELFARE

49. Moral Welfare

MARGARET TILLEY

Formerly Training Secretary, Church of England Council for Social Work

Introduction

The term "moral welfare" came into use in the 1920's and 1930's to describe work formerly called "rescue and preventive". It comprises not only the help given to those in difficulties as the result of their sexual relationships, but also concepts that determine the rights and wrongs of these relationships. The context of moral welfare is the Christian interpretation of life with its belief that every individual is of equal value, and that exploitation of one person by another is always wrong. *Moral*, however, is one of those words which has fallen into disrepute, and because it has acquired a censorious, punitive flavour, it is unacceptable to many social workers. A good deal of thought is therefore being given to a possible alternative name.

The History of Moral Welfare

It is particularly inappropriate that the name should sound punitive when the service originated from local compassionate efforts to meet the needs of unmarried mothers, illegitimate children and others whom society condemned. In the last century, and well into the present one, the unmarried mother found herself in a desperate plight unless her own people rallied round her, and, so far as the State was concerned, her child also was neglected or harshly treated. Among notable pioneers who sought to provide help was Josephine Butler, who not only was deeply moved by the needs of individuals but who had a passionate concern for justice. This made her join issue with the very generally accepted "double standard" in sexual morals, which required women acceptable to society to be chaste but allowed men much greater latitude of conduct. She asserted that this involved a complacent acceptance of prostitution with its section of women outside society, and usually meant that an unmarried woman who had a child took the entire responsibility and bore the brunt of society's ostracism.

It was in this context that local groups of Christians, aware of the hypocrisy and lack of logic underlying society's attitude, and moved by the plight of unmarried mothers, their children, prostitutes who wanted to find their

411

way back to ordinary living, and others in similar difficulties, started homes and shelters to meet immediate needs and to facilitate long-term rehabilitation. Residential work still forms a very important part of the moral welfare service, although its character has changed throughout the years. As a later development there grew up a non-residential service of social workers who are still often described as outdoor workers.

Moral welfare was, therefore, in origin an offer of help by Christians to those whom society rejected. The Church of England eventually accepted particular responsibiltiy for this work, and, as the service grew, co-ordination and planning developed, at first on a diocesan level and then at the centre, until the present arrangement was reached by which the Council for Social Work (formerly called the Moral Welfare Council) became a constituent part of the Church Assembly Board for Social Responsibility. This Council, with a staff housed at Church House, Westminster, has no direct authority over the work done in the dioceses, but its influence is considerable. It plays an important part in framing policy, reviewing and maintaining standards of work, and in public relations with other bodies. It has wider interests and contacts than usually operate on a diocesan level.

The Organization of the Service

Most moral welfare work is still organized on a local basis. Usually the deanery is the autonomous unit, but there is a trend towards diocesan centralization, and some dioceses have gone a long way towards this. The committees which employ the workers and are responsible for the homes are also partly concerned with fund-raising. Throughout England, Wales and Scotland there are about 320 non-residential social workers employed in this way by the Church, and about 120 homes, most of which are for unmarried mothers and their babies, although a small number cater for difficult adolescent girls or children in need of special care. Some of these homes are run by the Church Army, and a number of the non-residential workers are members of the Church Army, usually with further training in moral welfare. Homes and hostels for unmarried mothers are also provided by the Salvation Army. The Roman Catholic Church has organized its own work in this field alongside its other social work with children and with people in matrimonial difficulties, and has about forty-six non-residential workers and sixteen homes in England and Scotland. The Free Churches are responsible for a small number of homes, and in two instances employ a non-residential worker, while Jewish unmarried mothers are helped by Jewish organizations. Some of the committees in the Church of England dioceses are interdenominational and will employ Christians who are not Anglicans, but the non-resident moral welfare workers are usually required to be communicant members of the Church of England. So far as the clients are concerned, help is available to all and no denominational distinctions are made except when it seems appropriate to refer someone to the organization of her particular religious affiliation.

Moral welfare hitherto has had its own training courses, and here again is an interdenominational tradition, as those trained include a number of Roman Catholics and members of the Free Churches. The Josephine Butler Memorial House at Liverpool has provided training since 1920, with a two-year course which can be extended to include a social science certificate at Liverpool University, or reduced for those who are already graduates. Overseas students are welcomed, and special arrangements willingly made for them. Alongside the social work teaching, and integrated with it, is the study of theology and of the Christian way of life. In recent years an additional form of training has developed which is arranged centrally. It is non-residential and much shorter, and caters for the older woman who has had relevant previous experience. Grants from local education authorities and from the Church Assembly are given to students in either form of training. The majority of the non-residential moral welfare workers have taken one of these courses or else have some other social work qualification. A much smaller proportion of residential workers have a specialized social work training though many of those in charge of homes are nurses or are qualified in some other way.

Scope of the Work

What is the present-day scope of the work and what has been the effect of the expanding social services? It is difficult to give a categorical answer without much qualification, for the position varies somewhat from place to place. However, it is true to say that the casework is mainly with unmarried parents and their children, amounting to about 75 per cent of the total work done, and that the remaining 25 per cent relates mostly to problems of disturbed relationships, such as that of the difficult adolescent or the marriage breakdown. Other social workers certainly regard moral welfare workers as dealing particularly with unmarried mothers, and although statistics over this cannot be entirely accurate it is thought that probably about 50 per cent of all unmarried mothers are assisted by moral welfare workers. They are referred by other social workers, clergy, doctors, private individuals, the National Council for the Unmarried Mother and her Child and others. Some local authorities employ staff for this work and have their own mother and baby homes, but most make use of the service provided by the Church, which is grant-aided to a greater or less extent according to the decision of the particular local authority. On the whole there has been a friendly and sound working partnership with the statutory bodies that has strengthened and developed during the last two decades.

Casework Service

It might be assumed that the provisions of the Welfare State, which does not differentiate between the married and the unmarried mother, the legitimate and illegitimate child, would lessen the need for casework help. Also, that social attitudes about these matters are now more tolerant and that the lot of the unmarried mother would be correspondingly easier. Certainly she receives more help and care than formerly, but her position is far from enviable. In some ways her difficulties are those of other unsupported mothers, whether deserted or widows, but she has the added burden and responsibility of deciding whether to keep her baby or not, and society still looks askance at her, even though it often appears to condone the behaviour which has led to her situation. She finds herself, therefore, face to face with an inescapable problem which will arouse in her deep emotions and anxieties, and this may well be at a time when she is antagonized from her family or afraid to confide in them. Alternatively, she may be additionally unhappy because she has caused distress to a family which is affectionate and supportive. Her needs are many and may include, amongst others, practical help, medical care, legal assistance, admission to a home, psychological understanding and spiritual advice.

There are opposing schools of thought about illegitimate pregnancies. Some people see behind this behaviour a neurotic working-out of an unconscious drive, while others emphasize the normality of the average unmarried mother. Moral welfare workers with years of experience are usually impressed by the great diversity of personalities within an age-range stretching from the schoolgirl of 11 or 12 to the middle-aged woman; and the longer they do the work the more cautious they are about generalizations. It is because of this diversity that they try to avoid preconceived ideas as to whether a mother ought or ought not to keep her child, for every person is different and her circumstances vary, and this must be taken into account. Advice and help given to a mother, when making this fundamental decision, requires much sensitivity and skill on the part of the social worker, especially as the needs of the mother and those of the child may not coincide. It is temptingly easy to forget that the child will not for long remain a baby but will become a rampageous toddler, a school-child, an adolescent going out to work. If his mother marries, is her husband going fully to accept him and will his position in the family be equal to that of his half-brothers and half-sisters? If she does not marry, how will his development be affected by the absence not only of a father's presence but often of any familiar image of his father? Growing understanding of the psychological needs of children and of the possible damage done to them when these are not met, has heightened general awareness of these difficulties, and arrangements which only ensure shelter and food for a child, or which involve frequent moves from one home to another, are now known to be quite unsuitable. The mother also has deep psychological needs. No girl or woman with an average capacity for feeling can pass through this experience lightly or untouched. If she keeps her child she will almost certainly be faced with difficulties both practical and emotional. If she allows him to be adopted she will suffer in the parting, either acutely at the time or perhaps more insidiously at a later date. In this crucial moment of her life she needs skilled help if she is to make a right decision, and if she is to emerge better able to cope with life, and not damaged in her personality and in her capacity to make sound and lasting relationships.

It is, of course, not only the mother and child who need help, but also the family of the girl concerned, for most families are deeply shaken when the daughter of the house has a child outside marriage. This is not merely because it is felt to be a social disgrace reflecting on the whole family, but because a great many conflicting feelings are aroused. Some of these are specifically related to the child. Birth is always an important event and it is natural to a family to welcome a new baby, but the illegitimate child is often denied this birthright by his grandparents and others in the family who may, nevertheless, feel great distress that this should be so. Some grandparents willingly become responsible for the upbringing of the child, but although this may work out happily there are particular hazards.

To help people to make plans and decisions when feelings are mixed and strong is always difficult, and a social worker can often play for time. In this situation, however, there may be real urgency for the baby's sake. So, amongst these conflicting pressures, the moral welfare worker has to steer a way and do justice to a variety of needs without losing sight of the main objective. If the mother is very young there may be special difficulties, for her parents will then regard her as a child not yet old enough to make fundamental decisions; and yet the moral welfare worker realizes that this child has become involved in adult responsibilities, and that she may be resentful and harmed if plans are imposed on her regardless of her wishes.

What of the father of the illegitimate child; and does the moral welfare service take his duties and needs into account? A criticism is sometimes made that this is a service by women for women as if the part played by men could be ignored. Certainly there have been at times real and important efforts made to stir the public conscience and to enlist the help of responsible men, but in the main this criticism is justified, at least so far as the casework service is concerned. Inevitably many putative fathers are shadowy figures for the relationship may have been quite transitory, but this is not always so. All workers have some dealings with putative fathers, and a few are particularly skilful in this part of the work, yet the very real difficulties of the situation so often defeat the wish to help. Obviously, the worker often needs to advise the mother about her legal rights with regard to affiliation, and this means that she may easily be seen by the putative father as antagonistic to his interests, which makes him on the defensive from the start. Yet behind his defence he may, indeed, be someone who needs help and advice in his own right; and, just as with unmarried mothers, there is an infinite diversity in age, background and attitude amongst putative fathers. This part of the service needs further thought and development.

Residential Work

The importance of the residential work has already been stressed. Expectant unmarried mothers do not now go to these homes just because they are without shelter or because their families want them out of the way. At its best, the period in a home can provide much more than this. The girl ought to be able to find there a helpful atmosphere where emotional pressures are not so immediate, and where she can talk when inclined to those in charge, more freely and fully perhaps than she could do with her own people. If she has been feeling afraid and isolated, the company of others in the same situation can be consoling. The homes are mostly small so that an institutional atmosphere is avoided. A few are maternity homes which are particularly suitable for very young girls, but generally confinements take place in the local hospital. Some homes concentrate on special groups selected according to age or other factors, while the rest take a more mixed population which often produces its own kind of group stability.

. In the old days the emphasis was on training, for it was assumed that many of the girls were wayward or came from bad homes, and that they would therefore need to stay a long time if their behaviour and attitudes were really to change. Nowadays the usual length of stay is about six weeks before confinement and six weeks after, which is thought to be a reasonable time in most cases to meet a girl's particular needs and for any arrangements to be made for the baby. Some of the girls are, of course, problems, and some do have a bad background, but this is not the case with the majority, and so the old concept of training is no longer appropriate. But though ordinary people in themselves, these mothers are not in an ordinary situation, and it is therefore natural that their reactions to it are often difficult and make considerable demands on the patience and understanding of the staff, who have to deal with fluctuating moods, emotional crises, continual change of plans, and the like. Ideally, these homes should be run with the maximum flexibility, with this applied also to the length of stay, but it must be admitted that shortage of staff and administrative needs are sometimes allowed to restrict this.

A few homes cater for girls in the early stages of pregnancy, and some offer emergency shelter to homeless women and girls. Accommodation for the mother who keeps her baby often presents difficulties, and from time to time hostels have been run for them. Experience, however, tends to show that such an arrangement may work out badly for the child; for the mother who is not really able, willing or capable of taking responsibility for the child can then postpone any decision about adoption, only to come round to it at the end of a year or so. Experiments whereby a very small number of mothers and children have been given individual accommodation in a house divided into flatlets seem to have been more successful.

As these homes and hostels are run by Church committees, consideration is naturally given to the spiritual welfare of those who come. A local clergyman is appointed as Chaplain, some homes have their own chapel, and attendance at prayers and services is encouraged. It is a matter of opinion in what way and to what extent influence of this kind should be implicit or explicit. Usually the staff who achieve most are those who are least rigid and dogmatic, and whose own lives and behaviour convey Christian values and beliefs. It can, of course, too easily be assumed that girls who may be quite unknowledgeable about church practices necessarily benefit from enforced attendance at unsuitable services, and this can have unfortunate results, since it is more likely to antagonize rather than to attract. On the other hand, girls in this situation, even though religion has never previously meant anything to them, may become aware of deep though confused needs which require sensitive handling in words which they can understand. Opportunities for helping people in residential work are very great, but so are the demands made on the staff if these opportunities are to be met.

Adoption

Before there was legal adoption in this country the emphasis in moral welfare work was to enable the mother to keep her child. Since 1926 adoption has become an increasingly familiar practice, and this, combined with the far better provision made nowadays for deprived children, has changed the situation, so that it can no longer be taken for granted that the child will benefit most if he stays with his mother. Much will depend on her circumstances and also on her disposition. Moral welfare workers have taken a great interest in adoption, and several diocesan committees have become registered adoption societies with the object not only of ensuring a good home for the child but also of integrating adoption plans with other aspects of the work so that the welfare of the natural mother is not left out of account.

Education in Personal Relationships

Alongside this casework service the workers and the committees continue to feel some responsibility for educative and preventive work. At one time this was thought of mostly in terms of sex education, and workers when trained were expected to be able to give specific help over this, either in schools or with other groups of young people. Now it is generally recognized that this should only be done by workers who are particularly suited to it, and a much wider interpretation is given to the whole subject. The trend is towards closer co-operation with organizations such as the Marriage Guidance Councils, who are also concerned with helping people with their personal relationships.

This kind of co-operation has been fostered by the Council for Social Work and its central staff. An important part of the latter's work has always been liaison with national bodies of similar interests, and in particular there has been a close and helpful association with the National Council for the Unmarried Mother and Her Child.

Future Trends

How far a voluntary social agency continues to fulfil a real need always depends in the long run on its capacity to recognize and adapt to changing social conditions, and the moral welfare service is no exception to this. The rapid expansion of the local authority social services is bound to change radically the situation in which moral welfare first came into being, and the concern of the service at present is to make a realistic appraisal both of what may be required of it in the fairly distant future, and also what will almost certainly be needed during the next few years. With this in view the Council commissioned a survey of the work, which was carried out by two members of a University Social Science Department. This is now being studied and is to be published.

Many decisions will have to be taken in the future, and probably the most important one is whether the work with unmarried mothers should continue or be gradually undertaken by the local authority social workers. It is generally conceded that no fundamental principle is involved, but that it is a question of what is likely to work out best for the clients, taking their needs as a whole. Changes, in fact, are bound to come, but arrangements will vary from place to place, and it seems certain that for some years at any rate this particular contribution of moral welfare will be required.

If this is so, then other questions arise. For instance, with restricted resources of money and manpower, should the work be spread thinly over the whole country or concentrated in certain areas? Can the service expect to attract staff of sufficiently good quality when there are so many and such varied opportunities in social work employment? Does an increasingly complex service require a greater degree of centralization at a diocesan level? And, with regard to training, ought moral welfare to continue with its own form of training or recruit workers trained outside the service and then provide special courses for them? All these matters are under consideration.

Moral welfare workers are Church workers as well as social workers, and part of their responsibility is to co-operate with the clergy not only in order to enlist the appropriate help for individuals, but so that the clergy may thereby learn more about the social services and are enabled to co-operate better with social workers. Moral welfare workers need also to be in close touch with other Church workers in comparable fields such as youth work and parish work.

The moral welfare service expresses the Church's concern for those in trouble. It is widely agreed that the Church ought to bear witness to the need for compassion, and many think that this should be done in part through projects of its own, and not just through the activities of its members working in secular employment, important though these may be. These projects could, however, take many forms and need not necessarily include the service offered at present for unmarried mothers. Other groups such as discharged prisoners or alcoholics could equally well claim help, and projects of this kind could in fact take place within the present terms of reference, and indeed have done so at different times and in different places. Should it seem the right policy in certain localities to pass over more of the work with unmarried mothers to local authorities, then the church social service could turn its attention elsewhere. Moral welfare workers would, however, want to make certain that the experience and knowledge gained through the years would not be lost and that the work would be done better than they could do themselves. They would also want to ensure that the position of the unmarried mother was seen in all its complexity, and that the spiritual aspect was not overlooked.

Conclusion

It is not, in fact, just an historical accident that the Church became responsible for this particular piece of work. At the heart of the Christian faith is a profound belief in the importance of relationships, and the unmarried mother is faced, often in extreme youth, with a relationship that is usually broken between her and the father of her child, and one between herself and that child which may be impossible to develop or fraught with difficulty. It is on account of this that she is considered to have spiritual needs, not because she is thought to have done more wrong than many others nor because the Church is more concerned with immorality of a sexual nature than with other forms of anti-social activity. She is in difficulties that are inherent in her situation, and because she knows that her child is born at a disadvantage she feels guilty towards it. The attitude of society, so lax and casual in some respects, must seem illogical and unfair to her. If she is to come to terms with her experience she needs special help, and the moral welfare worker believes that the Christian faith can supply an essential part of this, not primarily through evangelization which may be quite inappropriate, but because a Christian ought to be able to help over the fundamental conflict between the claims of oneself and those of others.

Moral welfare, therefore, may change its name or its form, but what it stands for will have a lasting application, for individuals in this form of trouble will continue to need help, and standards of right and wrong will continue to be relevant. They are relevant because relationships are never so private and so personal that society is unaffected by them, since it is the nature of society that all are members one of another.

50. The National Council for the Unmarried Mother and her Child

MARGARET E. BRAMALL

General Secretary, National Council for the Unmarried Mother and her Child

THE National Council for the Unmarried Mother and her Child is unique in the field of illegitimacy. It is a voluntary agency recognized by Government Departments and throughout the country as a national non-denominational authority. It fulfils the function of co-ordinating the organizations concerned and providing them with a common platform. The Council endeavours to educate public opinion so that the problems raised by illegitimacy may be better understood. It presses for legislative reform and the provision of social services to meet the needs of the child born out of wedlock and his parents, and is interested in the welfare of individual unmarried parents and illegitimate persons.

The Extent of the Problem

Children born out of wedlock are numerically quite a sizeable group of the socially handicapped. In 1962, 55,376 of these children were born, representing 6·6 per cent of all live births, and roughly 1 in 15 children born in England and Wales. Their problem is giving public concern because there has been an upward trend both in their numbers and the percentage of all live births since 1955 when the rate was 4·6 per cent. These children are likely to suffer from emotional, psychological and material deprivation as do other children from fatherless families, and to have their own particular difficulties arising from their sense of being "different", and suffering from a feeling of stigma because of the circumstances of their birth.

Attitudes to Illegitimacy

Society is still in a dilemma about the care of the illegitimate child. It is impossible to help him without helping his mother. Unmarried mothers are a difficult group for whom to obtain understanding and social support. People's attitude towards the unmarried mother is influenced by their religious and ethical views, and their own deep feelings about sex and the mother–child relationship. In the past, society tended to avoid facing the implications, and left constructive help of individual unmarried mothers to

a few pioneers who were usually motivated by Christian charity to the afflicted. Even today, when the public attitude has modified, there is still the need
for a voluntary forward-looking agency, such as the Council, which can voice
the needs of illegitimate persons and their parents.

History and Aims

The National Council for the Unmarried Mother and her Child was formed
in 1918. Due to social conscience awakened by the war public concern for
the welfare of all babies and young children was aroused and was expressed
in the Maternity and Child Welfare Act of 1918. Mortality rates among
illegitimate children had always been very high, but under war-time conditions the ratio of illegitimate to legitimate mortality had risen alarmingly
and was commented on by the Registrar-General in his Report for 1916.
The ratio had increased from 170 per cent in 1907 to 201 per cent in 1916.

The Council was founded by interested persons with the support of the
Child Welfare Council of the Social Welfare Association for London. Mrs.
H. A. L. Fisher was its first chairman. Attitudes towards the unmarried
mother were often still harsh and punitive, and her child had little status.
From the first the Council was interested in creating conditions which would
make it possible for the unmarried mother to regain her self-respect and become an accepted member of the community and for her child to be given the
maximum chance of a secure upbringing. Its founders realized that they
must first educate the public to understand the implications of illegitimacy
before a constructive social policy would be acceptable. Unmarried mothers
were either kept with their children in the workhouse so that a mother was
unable to work and support her child, or separated from their children as
soon as possible. The children were sent to foster-mothers and the mothers
to employment. Shocked by this policy, the Council's chief aim was to make
it possible for mother and child to remain together and be treated as one unit
wherever possible. It has encouraged the provision of a suitable variety of
homes and hostels for pregnant girls and women and unmarried mothers
keeping their children, and has urged local authorities to make full use of
their powers. It worked for legal reforms to improve the status of mother
and child, particularly for the reform of the existing Bastardy Acts so that
illegitimate children could be legitimated by the subsequent marriage of
their parents (achieved through the Legitimacy Act, 1926, and the Legitimacy
Act, 1959), and of the existing Affiliation Act so that the maximum amount
payable under affiliation orders was from time to time raised. The Council
supported the introduction of legal adoption in this country (instituted by
the Adoption Act, 1926). An important achievement in 1947 was the provision of a shortened form of the birth certificate available for all citizens
which does not reveal illegitimacy. About 40 per cent of the certificates

issued are the shortened form. The Council acted, and still does, as a watch-dog for the interests of this socially handicapped group which by its very nature was unlikely to speak for itself. From the first the Council received inquiries and requests for help from unmarried mothers from all over the country, and its welfare function still remains a vital part of the Council's work.

Constitution

The Council is composed of between 250–350 members who are individuals with a particular knowledge of illegitimacy, representatives of local authorities and of religious, professional and other bodies which are particularly concerned. The Committee of Management is elected by the Council and includes representatives of Anglican and Catholic agencies and other national bodies working in this field—doctors, lawyers, social workers and lay people. It has observers from the Ministry of Health and the Home Office.

Present-day Functions

The Council's original aims and functions are remarkably relevant today, although sometimes their emphasis has changed as a result of modifications in public opinion and changing needs. For instance, while the Council still believes that the mother should have every support in keeping her child if she wishes, modern knowledge of the needs of young children and the development in skill in adoption placements make it true to say that the Council would feel that not every mother should be persuaded to keep her child. Each case should be considered on its merits. The unmarried mother needs wise counsel from a skilled social worker to help her to decide, with his long-term interests in view, whether to keep her child or have him adopted. There is little value in putting pressure on the responsible mother to keep her child when she feels he would be better adopted, or in encouraging the inadequate or disturbed mother to do so.

The Council still acts as a reformist body, and its Legal and Parliamentary Committee is occupied in considering long-term legal reform as well as immediate changes which might be made in the interests of parents and child. The Homes and Hostels Committee organizes conferences and meetings with the aim of helping those responsible for the provision of residential care to maintain their standards and meet the needs of the twentieth-century girl.

Amongst its other activities the Council publishes a directory of homes and hostels, and from time to time issues booklets on such subjects as adoption and affiliation proceedings.

Welfare Department

The Welfare Department offers a service to individual unmarried mothers. It receives applications for help from pregnant girls, their parents and from unmarried mothers from all over the world and from all sections of society. Deserted wives and other married women who are having an extra-marital pregnancy are also helped. Putative fathers who may wish to help the mother financially, or claim their rights to apply for custody or access to their child under Section 3 of the Legitimacy Act, 1959, also apply to the Council for advice.

Help is sometimes sought by British girls who have become pregnant abroad and wish to return to this country for their confinement so that the child may be born British, or from parents who are working overseas and wish to send their pregnant daughters back to England.

Inquiries come from the unmarried mother who wants her child adopted, or who has kept her child and is in difficulties due to lack of money or accommodation, or who wants to change her name. Illegitimate people sometimes write because they are worried about legal matters, or fear that their status will debar them from a particular career.

The most common reaction of an unmarried woman and her parents on discovering her pregnancy is fear, a sense of isolation, and a desire to conceal her condition. Social help is available, but the girl fears to make inquiries locally, and may prefer to write to the Council. She often finds the address in the telephone directory or the advice column in a woman's magazine. All applications are treated in strict confidence.

Statutory and Voluntary Provision

The Council's policy is to refer an applicant to the social worker in her own area who can best help her. An unmarried mother's difficulty in getting help is increased by the varied pattern of local services. Local authorities have responsibility for the welfare of unmarried mothers and their children under Section 22 of the National Health Service Act as part of their general responsibility for all mothers and young children. Most local authorities have special schemes for their care, usually discharging their responsibilities by using the voluntary denominational agencies which they subsidize in various ways. Some authorities provide all or part of the services direct.

Voluntary agencies provide about 145 of the 170 or so mother and baby homes which exist in England and Wales, and local authorities normally pay the fees of unmarried mothers living in their area on a *per capita* basis. Denominational agencies, of which the Church of England Diocesan and Deanery Associations provide the most widespread service, are in touch with about 50 per cent of the mothers of illegitimate children born each year. Some other unmarried mothers are helped by local authority child-care officers, welfare officers, health visitors, and by hospital almoners. The Council, by its knowledge of all types of provision in each area, is able to save the unmarried mother unhappiness and delay by referring her direct to the most appropriate person. Usually the Council's Welfare Officer is able to persuade a girl to seek local help. There is, however, a small number of unmarried mothers, less than 350 a year, who are helped directly by the Council's own staff because for one reason or another they cannot, or do not agree, to be referred to a social worker.

The Welfare Department is able to assist social workers in statutory or voluntary organizations who need advice on a complicated variety of specialized problems.

The Consultative Grants Committee of the Council has a limited sum at its disposal for grants and the Council administers the Margaret Club and Day Nursery Fund, a charity which helps unmarried mothers in certain London boroughs.

Accommodation is particularly difficult to find for the unmarried mother, especially if she is bringing up the child herself. The Welfare Department is in touch with an increasing number of householders wishing to offer rooms. The Council is a registered employment agency, and finds residential jobs where a mother can take her child.

A number of pregnant girls and women need somewhere to live while waiting to go to a mother and baby home, and many social workers ask the Council to find accommodation with private families, either as paying guests or on an *au pair* basis. A particularly interesting development is the finding of foster-mothers who will accept young unmarried mothers with their children.

European welfare agencies ask the Council to get in touch with British putative fathers and sometimes, with the help of local social workers, these men can be traced and persuaded to make payments for their illegitimate children.

An important welfare function of the Council is to act as a liaison between the Home Office and the foreign pregnant woman in this country. With the co-operation of social workers the Council reports on foreign unmarried girls with their consent. The Home Office, which carefully considers these girls' requests to be allowed to stay in Britain, attaches great importance to these individual assessments.

The Future

It can be seen that the Council has very wide functions. Ways of helping unmarried mothers and their children may change and new needs arise. It is hoped that social attitudes will alter and more long-term social help will be available for mothers who decide to bring up their own children. While improvements may well take place through the possible development of local authority family advice centres, the Minister of Health clearly envisages that for some years to come the voluntary agencies will make the major contribution in this field; thus the Council's co-ordinating function may well be further expanded. Its usefulness and influence as a national authority on all matters regarding illegitimacy will remain in the foreseeable future. Its welfare function and its capacity as watch-dog for the interests of unmarried parents and illegitimate children will still be needed, for the family is the normal unit for the upbringing of children, and the illegitimate child, however well provided for, is therefore potentially socially handicapped.

51. How Do You Tell Right from Wrong in the Welfare State?*

ELEANOR WINTOUR

A part-time social worker, and in private life the wife of a leading London
editor and the mother of four children

IN THE national interest politicians, diplomats and civil servants frequently
bully, lie, open other people's mail and generally behave in a way they would
never dream of doing at home. Patriotism imposes a special code of
ethics on their professional lives. Something of this sort, I suspect, seems to
be happening to the growing band of welfare workers employed by the
Welfare State. Their predecessors in Victorian times, the Lady Bountifuls,
the Charity Organizers, and so on, were indeed very moral in the accepted
sense. They operated from an orthodox Christian, not to say Puritan, viewpoint, recognizing and applying Shaw's distinction between the deserving
and the undeserving poor, and so they often, though quite inadvertently,
visited the sins of the parents upon the children. They gave money to widows
and orphans, to the industrious and thrifty, but refused it to people who
drank or gambled or were careless about the Seventh Commandment. The
result was often a somewhat ludicrous failure. These do-gooders were, nonetheless, amiable people sincerely trying to apply Christianity to social
problems, honestly believing that hanging religious pictures in the local jail
was relevant to the problem of crime. Occasionally, one still meets them, still
at it. At a recent welfare meeting I attended, an elderly lady rose to ask what
we intended to do about the open, barefaced betting going on in the yards of
L.C.C. council flats. It was as if a ghost had spoken. There was a hideous
silence and the chairman rushed us on to other things.

Life has changed, particularly in the large cities such as London, to which
most of the following remarks apply. Deserving or not, the modern Welfare
State is required by law to love all her children equally. She knows no distinctions between good and bad, only between those who "qualify" and those
who do not. Citizens of the Welfare State, provided they do not falsify their
income statements and medical certificates, may commit every crime in the
book and continue to visit the doctor and dentist, draw social benefits and
be born and die with her blessing. Ironically enough, probably in no branch

* Reprinted from *The Twentieth Century*, winter, 1962/3, with the permission of the
editor and the author, previously under the title "How to Tell Right from Wrong in the
Welfare State".

of the Welfare State does the welfare code of morals deviate more markedly from the traditional code than in those myriad agencies devoted to the welfare of children. The L.C.C. alone runs nine Divisional Offices of Child Care, concerned with school children; in addition, there is the far-reaching health service which guards the child's physical and mental health from conception to maturity. Even the lowliest volunteer worker in any of these London agencies, such as myself, rapidly learns that the child's interests are paramount and that the definition of what comprises these interests owes far more to Freud than to Moses or St. Paul. Without a qualm the individual worker finds himself acting on a set of moral principles which, as a churchgoer (and many are), he ought to deplore. Conversely, he bursts with righteous indignation over "sins" of which his vicar has never heard. When the Children's Officer says that Mrs. A. is a "good" woman, he does not mean at all what the Archbishop of Canterbury means: he means that in the face of considerable difficulties Mrs. A. has taken admirable care of her five illegitimate children. On the other hand, Mrs. B. is a bad mother because she will not face the fact that her darling child is appallingly overweight and take it to the Special Investigation Clinic. (It is one of the triumphs of the Welfare State that the under-nourished child has been almost entirely supplanted by the over-nourished one. This applies to both sexes.)

Willingness to attend clinics of any sort is a cardinal virtue with the Welfare State. Whole families are categorized as "good" or "bad" depending on the regularity with which they get their children to the oculist, dentist, psychiatrist, or bed-wetting clinics at the behest of the school doctor. In spite of the fact that all these services are free and do, on the whole, deal with appointments expeditiously and promptly, large numbers of mothers do not go, or, worse still, make appointments and fail to keep them. On the face of it, this might appear to be the responsibility of the parent. But the Welfare State thinks otherwise. Little William cannot be allowed to fail the eleven plus simply because he cannot see the blackboard, and so the welfare worker tramps through the streets, seeks out William's Mum and tries to persuade her to use the health service. In between home visits, he attacks by form and letter. If all else fails, he will probably get her permission to take the child himself. There may be all sorts of valid reasons why a mother is not able to take her child to the dentist, other than just sheer laziness. She may work during clinic hours, or may have four other small children who have to be dragged along too, or, increasingly, she may speak no English and will not understand what the ear, nose and throat surgeons says anyway. None of this counts in her favour. In official eyes she is not looking after her child properly, she is consuming a great deal of everyone's time, she is not only a bad mother, but a very tiresome one.

The excuse that the mother is working is not only unacceptable—it frequently represents another black mark against her. Mothers of small children should not take regular employment outside the home, however badly the father's earnings need supplementing. Mothers who have no male support should apply for National Assistance. Those who refuse to live on the taxpayers' bounty, but put their children into day nurseries or leave them with older children after school hours, are not doing their duty. No matter what additional amenities they are thus able to provide for their children, or however important it may be to their personal pride to refuse "N.A.B.", the welfare worker usually considers them selfish and grasping. The teachers condemn the working mother's inability to turn up for the Christmas play and the doctor curses her absence at the medical inspection, while the Care Committee worker censoriously enters on the records "Medical Inspection —M. Not P." There is a general suspicion that she really goes out to work because it is more fun than staying at home. But whatever her motive, it is axiomatic that the most important thing for a small child is its mother's constant presence and attention and only a bad mother would refuse this while the Welfare State is there to see that her child doesn't starve. This practically rules out the Puritan virtues of industry, pride and self-respect where women are concerned. It also rules out the newer feminist philosophy about women living their own lives. In the Welfare State, mother's place is in the home.

Home is for all categories of mothers with small children ("small", in general, means under 10) whether they are married, divorced, abandoned or unmarried. As far as the welfare worker is concerned, no stigma attaches to the unmarried mother. She may feel very guilty herself but his primary concern must be with her child, not her sin. Her first duty to the child is to "get hold" of the man and obtain a court order on him. She will rarely get enough to support them both, and the rest will have to be made up by the National Assistance Board, but the Welfare State, reversing what traditional morality regards as the order of nature, believes that it's the man who pays. Via the poor man's lawyer, when necessary, it urges the mother on to pursue the unmarried father through the courts in order to wring from him the due percentage of his weekly earnings, sometimes so small an amount that it would seem rather more of a saving in time, trouble and cost to the taxpayer, if the N.A.B. had paid the whole amount themselves. Male responsibility, however, is a strongly cherished principle and welfare workers take a poor view of the unmarried mother who shows any tendency to let him off. Obviously, it is impossible to quote individual cases in any identifiable way, but the following illustrations are all taken from first-hand experience.

One example is Miss C., a soft-hearted girl, who said she couldn't possibly take his money—"he has his own family to support"—and whom the local Child Care Officer consider feckless and silly. The Moral Welfare Officer has had to talk seriously to Miss D., not so much because it is her second illegitimate baby, but because it is the second time she has let the man get away. Clearly Miss D. is not going to get much in the way of a court order on the very young man who is the father of her baby, and no one suggests that she should try to get a wedding ring. There is too much danger that the new stepfather might be an undesirable parent for the child of Miss D.'s first lapse. But in failing to secure a court order, Miss D. is not displaying a sufficiently serious attitude towards maternity, and it is this, rather than her attitude to sex, that the Moral Welfare Officer is trying to change. No Moral Welfare Officer would ever dream of visiting Mrs. P. who has six children and two court orders and is the pin-up girl of her local divisional children's office. Her offspring, happy, intelligent, well-cared for and much loved, move in steady procession through the local primary and grammar schools, past A levels, and into excellent jobs. Mrs. P.'s one failing is that every few years she has to arrange a miscarriage, and everyone is always very happy when this comes off successfully. She even manages it so well that the children do not have to go into the care of the council, even briefly. By every canon known to the Welfare State she is a perfect mother—so perfect that the question of fathers simply never arises.

None the less, in my experience the Welfare State does definitely prefer mothers to be married, and it prefers them to have reached the age of consent. It is constantly on the lookout for signs of "moral danger", particularly among the plainer teen-age girls, because it knows from practical experience that they are more likely to succumb with joyful surprise to the first invitation. The prettier ones can afford to wait, and normally do. The welfare worker also deplores broken homes on the usual psychiatric grounds that it has a bad effect on the children. But views on the sanctity of marriage are heavily qualified by the proviso that women should marry good fathers, and when a woman has made a mistake about this she can and should end the marriage in the interests of her children. Good fathers are men who give their wives most of their earnings (if they do not, they can be visited by a rather terrifying character known as the Special Officer); do not "knock the children about" (if they do, they can be visited by the N.S.P.C.C.); and while sound in mind and body never cease to provide for their families (if they try, they will be pursued by a court order). When a father fails seriously on any of these counts, the social worker, the health visitor and anyone else concerned will very probably urge the mother to get the flat put in her name and throw him out. She may have married him for better or worse, but she had no right to make such a promise on behalf of her children. Given sufficient provocation, then, a mother can escape from an undesirable husband (though he has not quite the same privileges), provided she keeps the children with her. There is as far as I am aware no law on earth that can force a woman to remain with her children, and perhaps it is because the Welfare State is so utterly powerless in a matter so fundamental to their code that the workers unite in regarding the mother who does leave her children as beyond redemption. This is really sin in the religious sense, particularly if the mother deserts the children for love. I cannot imagine any divisional organizer giving Lady Chatterley a second thought, but I shudder to think of a caseworker's report on Anna Karenina.

Fortunately, romantic passion is one problem the Welfare State rarely has to face. Relatively few women ever do desert their children. When a mother leaves home for another man it is understood that if he wants her he has to take the children too. This is usually a cosy arrangement whereby the man gets a housekeeper and companion and the woman gets a better home for herself and the kids, plus continued financial support for the children from her abandoned husband. The Welfare State sanctions it by doing its best to circumvent any legal difficulties. "Don't say you aren't married", a housing official told a woman in this situation, "from our point of view you are." On the other hand, when it came to getting a school uniform grant for one of her daughters the office of child care found it more convenient not to have her married, and unmarried she appeared on the form. In these circumstances, divorce and legal re-marriage may be something that people do not get around to doing.

The mother on her own can count on the Welfare State to keep her and her children alive and together. The father on his own is not so fortunate. If his wife dies, he cannot settle down on N.A.B. simply to be at home with his small children. The councils will do their best to help by providing him with home helps at heavily subsidized rates of pay (but no more reliable than unsubsidized domestic help) and social workers will be found to lead the children to their various medical and educational appointments, but these are very makeshift arrangements, and the father's best hope of holding the family together is re-marriage. Otherwise, the children must go to relatives or into the care of the local council. The councils try to run their homes in the most homelike way possible, but they can never be more than substitutes for the real thing. Councils know this and do their best to avoid taking children into care for long periods. So when Bobby tells the welfare worker on the way to clinic about a nice lady "who sleeps in my Daddy's bed", the news is received with rapture at Divisional Office—possibly Mr. B. has found someone to solve his problems. But there is a decreasing supply of unattached women willing to accept the heart, hand and domestic chores of a middle-aged widower, and if Mr. B. succeeds in getting someone to tie herself permanently to him and his family, he will really be in luck. A more usual solution, and one accepted by child welfare officers only because no one can think of a better, is that the teenage daughter, where there is one, may take over her mother's duties and try to cook, clean and care for the littler ones, and possibly go to school herself at the same time. Very occasionally in cases where the father's mentality is very low, it is discovered that the child has taken her mother's place in every sense. From Oedipus to the Australian aborigine, people in nearly all societies have recoiled in peculiar horror from the sin of incest. The welfare worker is no exception. The second that there is any suspicion, the children are removed from the control of the father and put into the charge of the council as being in need of "care and protection". By the time this happens, as far as the unfortunate girl is concerned, the damage is already done; she is rescued from further contamination, but only at tremendous cost to the other children, who, having already lost their mother, now lose the only home, however undesirable, they have ever known and where, being totally innocent, they have probably been very happy. The welfare worker who enters the house crying Moral Danger and packs the terrified weeping children off to Care is as much outraged by incest as any- one, but, none the less, he's hard put to it to go home, put his hand on his heart and unhesitatingly say "I have done a good day's work". Cases of this sort are, however, really rare. (An experienced worker I know has only seen eight in a fairly long tour of duty in one of London's worst areas.) I mention them not because they are typical, but because they exemplify how even in a situation where the most casual of us is prepared to take a moral stand, a sharp conflict can arise between the aims of social welfare and our traditional moral beliefs.

Very few professional welfare workers feel themselves competent to enter into ethical discussions. Most of them merely try to assist as many people as possible without breaking the rules governing who is eligible for what, and hope for the best. But occasionally as they tramp about their divisions spread- ing welfare, they wonder how those religious and moral leaders, who are so constantly castigating our evil ways and urging a return to morality, find it so easy to tell right from wrong.

SECTION X
FURTHER EXAMPLES OF "ALL-PURPOSE" VOLUNTARY ORGANIZATIONS

PLATE 37. Members of the British Red Cross Society delivering food for the Meals on Wheels Service for sick and aged people

PLATE 38. Chiropody service being given by a detachment of the British Red Cross Society

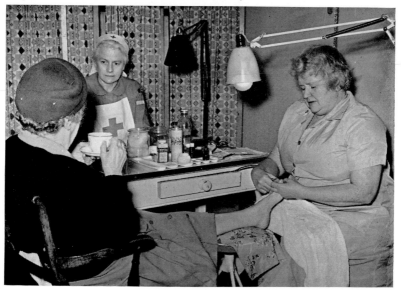

Plate 42. W.V.S. preparing meals on wheels

PLATE 43. The Methodist home for the aged at Bury St. Edmunds

PLATE 44. A glimpse of the kitchen at the above home

52. The National Council of Social Service

DAVID HOBMAN*

Information Officer, National Council of Social Service

THE National Council of Social Service represents a complex structure based upon a simple ideal. Established in 1919 to provide the machinery for co-operation it has played a major part in making the corporate expression of the voluntary movement articulate and effective. It provides a means of consultation between voluntary agencies with both central and local government in the consideration of social policies, which it helps to evolve and implement. The steady expansion of the Council's work and the widening spheres of its influence have stemmed from its application of the theory of joint social action, the concept upon which a welfare society depends for its fulfilment.

Structure

The Council consists of representatives of over 100 voluntary societies, together with its own associated groups, ten Government Departments, professional institutions, and a number of distinguished leaders in public life. Its foundation was an expression of faith with no assurance of an adequate income for its continuance. The fact that this has grown to a figure exceeding £250,000 annually gives some indication of the recognition it has achieved. It is derived from two main sources—voluntary subscriptions and support from charitable foundations for specific projects on one side, and grant-in-aid from a number of Government Departments on the other. By preserving such a balance it is enabled to pursue its objects with the necessary freedom of action and to maintain its capacity to initiate new ventures and pilot experimental projects against a background of reasonable security; two essential factors for an organization with a comprehensive programme, much of which is dependent upon long-term planning for its fruition.

Services

The basis of a great deal of the Council's work lies in the provision of a service of information. One of the most important aspects of this task is

---

* Mr. Hobman is also author of *A Guide to Voluntary Service*, 1964, H.M.S.O., which gives a useful account of the opportunities for voluntary service (Editor).

435

the regular publication of circulars interpreting legislation on matters affecting charities. In recent years these have covered such diverse subjects as grant aid, rating, local government reorganization, fund-raising in relation to the laws of betting and gaming, and the law of charity itself, which has undergone major revision as the result of a series of Acts of Parliament whose drafting reflected many of the views expressed by the N.C.S.S. submitted, in evidence, on behalf of its constituent members.

Other examples of the ways in which it assists voluntary enterprise are to be found in the legal advisory service provided for trustees of community centres and village halls; the publication of handbooks, pamphlets and journals such as *Social Service Quarterly*, *Citizens' Advice Notes*, in the summary of current trends and legislation which comprises *NACOSS News*, as well as in the answers provided for the increasing number of inquirers seeking information about every aspect of social work in this country. The Council's Charities Aid Fund also provides a service of specialized information in addition to distributing more than £1½ million annually in deeds of covenant.

Promotional Work

The process of bringing groups of people together to consider varying aspects of community life has provided the N.C.S.S. with the means of identifying and crystallizing the needs of particular groups, and a number of its informal working parties have eventually become independent voluntary societies in their own right. The National Federation of Young Farmers' Clubs, the National Association of Boys' Clubs and the Youth Hostels Association, set up during the years before the Second World War, or the Social Workers' Pension Fund and the National Bureau for Co-operation in Child Care afterwards, have all been promoted by the N.C.S.S. In each instance the preliminary negotiations took into account the need to ensure that their terms of reference were clearly defined, adequate funds promised and an appropriate administration appointed, in order to secure their ultimate foundation upon a lasting basis.

Associated Bodies

In other cases, where the operation of newly formed associations has been concerned with a general, rather than a limited sector of the community, and where they have been constituted on a representative basis broadly resembling the Council's own, they have continued to remain within the overall framework, whilst having freedom to develop their own programmes which are complementary to those of the N.C.S.S., to whose Executive they are ultimately responsible, upon whom they depend for financial support, and whose common services they share.

Of this category two organizations, the National Old People's Welfare Council and the National Citizens' Advice Bureaux Council, are described separately in this book. Others are the National Federation of Community Associations established in 1945 but which stemmed from the Council's New Estates Committee, formed twenty years earlier in order to study the needs of families being re-housed in the massive suburban building schemes, and the National Association of Women's Clubs which federates and serves a large number of independent self-determining local clubs.

The Council's Central Churches Group formed in 1941 serves as a channel of communication, with the primary object of encouraging the fullest possible participation by church members of all denominations in community organization, as well as helping the clergy to equip themselves with general knowledge about the application of the social services in the course of their pastoral work.

Standing Conferences

Five major Standing Conferences have been initiated by and remain associated with the N.C.S.S. They are the Standing Conference of National Voluntary Youth Organizations (SCANVYO), a consultative body representing nearly fifty organizations covering about one-third of all young people between the ages of 11 and 21, and The Women's Group on Public Welfare which brings together the majority of national women's organizations and the members of its own local Standing Conferences of Women's Organizations throughout the country to consider matters of common interest. This Group has been responsible for the publication of a number of searching inquiries such as its survey on *Loneliness* recently re-published and on the *Education and Training of Girls* in 1962, which helped to focus attention on their important subjects.

The standing conferences of music and drama, both formed in 1946, seek to encourage amateur performers by promotional work as well as by co-ordinating practical schemes of education, and by assisting in training and informing public opinion. The Standing Conference for Local History which followed two years later performs a similar function in stimulating interest and raising standards, and publishes a quarterly magazine, *The Amateur Historian*.

Rural and Urban Development

Whilst the bodies described in the preceding paragraphs are closely integrated with the N.C.S.S., its Rural Committee and the Standing Conference of Councils of Social Service provide the most immediate extension of its work throughout the country in the creation of direct lines of communication with the administrative counties in the case of Rural Community Councils and with the major centres of urban population, through Councils of Social

Service. The Rural Community Council movement was deliberately conceived as a long-term national policy at the time of the National Council's own inception with the primary purpose of promoting the well-being of people living in lightly populated areas, where the drift towards the cities threatened serious social and economic repercussions stemming from insufficient employment opportunities and inadequate resources for communal activities.

It is against this background that the Rural Community Councils, now established in the great majority of counties, have developed. Their responsibilities include the service for rural craftsmen administered in co-operation with the Rural Industries Bureau, advice on the provision of village halls, the development of amateur music and drama, the formation of local history committees, the strengthening of local government through the National Association of Parish Councils, another body which the N.C.S.S. was largely instrumental in founding, as well as the organization of activities for the handicapped, the elderly and other groups with special needs.

The early Charity Organization Societies were established in the second half of the nineteenth century as a manifestation of the desire for co-operative action between philanthropic bodies and family casework agencies, but local Councils of Social Service, as they are now understood, did not begin to take shape until the years immediately preceding and during the First World War, when the need to mobilize all available resources brought voluntary agencies together in joint council. During this period there was a gradual recognition of the wider purpose of community organization dependent upon universal participation as an extension of the limited, although dedicated, action of a minority whose concern was primarily with the plight of social casualties rather than with the total needs of a rapidly changing society.

Although development was sporadic, new councils were formed during the 1930's, but it was not until comparatively recently that the movement gathered momentum until there are now some 150 Councils of Social Service in existence with plans for many more being spontaneously engendered. The closest relationship exists between them and the N.C.S.S., as it does with the Rural Community Councils, but in both cases the local organizations are autonomous with freedom to pursue independent policies reflecting the felt needs of their communities, by the application of a general formula adapted, where necessary, to meet local circumstances.

International

The N.C.S.S. is concerned with a number of aspects of international co-operation. It provides the secretariat for the British National Conference on Social Welfare which acts as the British Committee of the International Conference of Social Work. The British Conference is responsible for recruiting delegates for meetings in different parts of the world, and maintains a close link with the work of the United Nations Social Commission. It has also created a national forum for the study of social questions in this country through the medium of a triennial conference on a topic of current interest.

In addition to its work for the British National Conference, the international department of the N.C.S.S. is responsible for the administration of the work of the British Committee for the International Exchange of Social Workers and Administrators, and is constantly engaged in arranging tours of observation for social workers from abroad as well as advising those who wish to undertake prolonged study or seek employment in the United Kingdom. It also provides the secretariat for the Standing Conference of British Organizations for Aid to Refugees which brings together the principal bodies interested in the welfare of refugees abroad and in this country for the consideration of mutual problems and the stimulation of new projects in areas not already covered by the world-wide network of international relief agencies.

Two recent developments in the Council's work overseas have been the establishment of the Standing Conference of Voluntary Organizations Co-operating in Overseas Social Service (VOCOSS) which provides a consultative service for those organizations with overseas responsibilities and acts as a clearing house for the exchange of information by member organizations in recognition of the fact that if it is to be fully effective there must be agreement upon the broad features of a common strategy of approach. The Committee on Overseas Service by Volunteers was formed to co-ordinate the activities of bodies sending young graduates and others with equivalent training for periods of service in developing countries. With the support of the Ministry of Overseas Development it has been enabled to recruit about 800 young people during its first two years of operation.

Planning and Research

The view that forward planning in the field of social welfare is, by its nature, a complex operation demanding sustained liaison between the theorist and the practitioner has given rise to a number of major research projects. Their wide range can be illustrated by the following three examples. *Help for the Handicapped* was an inquiry into the opportunities of the voluntary services in a particular sphere. *New Communities in Britain* considered the social needs and achievements in new towns and housing estates, and a survey into *the staffing of residential institutions* which will take three years to complete is now being undertaken. Developments in education, health and welfare are making increasing demands upon the full-time services of men and women. The need for careful selection and training of staff is crucial to all of them because each one is a competitor for the limited available labour, and the belief that a general appraisal of the problem will lead to sounder planning has prompted the N.C.S.S. to launch an examination of the existing estimates of staffing needs in particular sectors as they may be expected to develop in the light of current trends. At the same time an inquiry is being undertaken into the recruitment, training and deployment of volunteers, a question which has assumed considerable significance in view of the Minister of Health's Ten Year Plan for the hospital and local authority health and welfare services with its emphasis upon community care.

Pattern for Co-operation

The N.C.S.S. and the parallel Councils of Social Service in Northern Ireland, Scotland and Wales have made a considerable impact upon the lives of countless people throughout the country in establishing a pattern for co-operation which has proved its relevance in contemporary society and which has been adopted in many communities throughout the world as an integral feature of a dynamic social policy.

53. The British Red Cross Society

JEAN BOWDEN

Author, Editor and Journalist, Member of the British Red Cross Society

THE British Red Cross Society takes its inspiration from the work of Henri Dunant, a young Swiss businessman who in 1859 was a horror-stricken spectator at the Battle of Solferino, waged between the forces of France and Austria. After the battle Dunant's book, *Un Souvenir de Solferino*, aroused much interest among those active in the (then) almost Utopian field of "voluntary aid". In 1863, a year after the publication of his book, Dunant, together with Gustave Moynier, organized a preliminary meeting in Geneva to which representatives of the world powers were invited; in the following year came the Geneva Convention.

From that time on Britain was in the forefront of work in the voluntary aid movement. The object of the British Red Cross Society was "to furnish aid to sick and wounded and to co-ordinate in days of peace and war all offers of voluntary assistance". The inclusion of the words "in days of peace and war" was prophetic of the scope of the Society's work; between the two world wars, and particularly since 1945, its nursing and welfare activities both at home and overseas have extended rapidly. Welfare activities in Great Britain are carried out by a membership of 96,000 men and women with the help of 85,000 junior members.

These workers are volunteers who carry out their tasks under the guidance of professional advice and supervision. This is achieved both by the appointment of qualified social workers as advisers to the branches in the U.K. and by a carefully graded series of short and certificated welfare courses and allied courses such as those on mental health.

In the hospital field the Society covers a wide range of services as auxiliary to the almoner. This includes regular visiting, which is important for long-term patients and the elderly. Over 1000 hospitals accept help in nursing duties from Red Cross volunteers, known as V.A.D.s, who also give help with nursing and welfare tasks in convalescent homes and homes for the elderly. These duties are carried out by 45,000 V.A.D. men and women.

Before admission to or discharge from hospital, the almoner often asks the Red Cross to co-operate by visiting the patient and talking over any problems which may have to be faced when leaving or returning home. In the case of a long convalescence, or a long-term illness, a visit is paid to the patient's home at the request of the almoner to ensure that needs are fully understood. The co-operation with the district nurse and the health visitor is very close.

Other services within the hospital include the provision of trolley shops, libraries and a picture library. The picture library provides an exchange scheme whereby good reproductions of paintings, linked with talks on art, are available to long-term patients.

Language cards containing simple basic questions are to be had in many languages to help hospital staffs to communicate with foreign patients, and special maternity and child welfare cards are available in certain languages. In addition the Society has groups of linguists available to translate for the medical staff.

In many hospitals Red Cross members perform reception duties for patients who are either being admitted or attending for out-patient treatment. Care is available for relatives who are visiting the dangerously ill; out-patient canteens and escort services are also on hand in many hospitals.

In the case of invalids, either at home or in hospital, who are worried about missing relatives, the Red Cross can furnish a compassionate tracing and welfare inquiry service, carried out on a world-wide scale if need be through Red Cross Headquarters. This service is particularly valuable where invalids, old people and refugees are worried about relations from whom they have been separated; it is widely used both by hospitals and by the general public, through local Red Cross branches.

In the domiciliary field the Society undertakes many services to the sick and disabled in their homes. These include visiting at the request of the almoner or undertaking personal services such as shopping, teaching of hobbies and handicraft, and the provision of meals on wheels (Plate 37). As agents of the local authority the Red Cross may supply on loan such things as bed rests, bed tables, air beds or wheelchairs. Special services are provided for the handicapped child, designed to be of help to parents and to the child; for instance, the Red Cross will supply a "sitter-in" to release parents for rest, shopping or relaxation, while, on the other hand, a member of the Junior Red Cross may engage the young patient in games and helpful occupations. The Junior Red Cross will also act as companion to the disabled child through one of the many holiday schemes.

A considerable part of Red Cross welfare work is directed towards helping to keep old people in their own homes as long as possible. With the permission of the district nurse, help is given with such personal services as washing and brushing the hair and helping the infirm elderly person to take a bath. Accident prevention is always in mind when Red Cross personnel visit the elderly. Members of the Junior Red Cross can carry out many tasks for them such as errands, shopping, gardening.

The Society's welfare services aim at preventing deterioration through loneliness by regular visiting, nursing aid service under the direction of the district nurse, and the provision of clubs both daily and periodic; escorts to clinics and out-patient departments for treatment, including chiropody (Plate 38); holiday schemes, and the provision of residential and long-stay accommodation in homes and flatlets for frail old people.

The Society has also developed a wide selection of simple aids for daily living. These are available on medical recommendation for handicapped children, adults and old people, for patients at home and in hospital. The aids include writing, drawing and sewing aids for arthritic or spastic patients, and retrieving sticks, shoe grips, stocking puller-ons for patients unable to bend. The Red Cross has been instrumental in having these designed.

In addition special care and help to relatives is an important part of the Red Cross welfare services as it is well-known that many families break down under the strain of caring for handicapped or elderly people. In the relatively new field of mental health, the Society is developing a wide range of welfare activities. A great many mentally ill and severely subnormal patients need and receive special attention and social help. In co-operation with the mental welfare officers and psychiatric social workers, the Society is giving assistance with visiting, clubs and other activities, escort duties and relief to relatives; in the hospital field, special care of the lonely patient and the provision of morale-building services such as beauty treatment (especially important to a long-term woman patient); and group and recreational activities for those able to benefit and particularly requested by medical superintendents.

The Junior Red Cross is an integral part of the adult Society but is particularly suited to working with child patients or invalids. Indeed, invalid or handicapped children can be greatly helped and stimulated by themselves becoming Home Members of the Junior Red Cross. Membership of the three groups which comprise the Junior Red Cross is open to children between 5 years and school-leaving age. The cadet Units are usually attached to V.A.D. detachments; the links are formed in schools, youth clubs, or other independent organizations. The Junior Red Cross motto is "Serve One Another", and with this ideal in mind training courses are given in health, first aid, hygiene, nursing, mothercraft and so on. Practical appliance follows: Junior Red Cross members help in health clinics as messengers, at blood-donor sessions as tea-makers and record-keepers, at first-aid demonstrations as "patients", and with personal services to the old or to the disabled. (Plate 39) These manifold tasks are carried out by about 85,000 young people in the Junior Red Cross units at present.

The British Red Cross Society supplies adult staff for 676 permanent first-aid posts in England, Wales and the Bailiwick of Guernsey. There also are over 5000 temporary first-aid posts staffed by the Red Cross. Infant and Child Welfare Clinics, Pre- and Post-Natal Clinics, Immunization, Orthopaedic, School Medical and Dental Clinics, and Foot Clinics total 3849 at which the Red Cross supplies helpers. In addition, in London there is the Greater

London Red Cross Blood Transfusion Service. This exists to meet the need which is sometimes found, and usually in conditions of urgency, for whole, fresh blood. The hospital contacts the Headquarters of the Greater London Red Cross Blood Transfusion Service in St. Andrews Place, N.W. 1, and a donor is sent as soon as possible. In 1962, 4462 such calls were answered by this service, many of them for rare blood groups. Several donors have given blood more than 80 times, many between 50 and 70 times, and 40 or 30 donations is regarded as quite average.

Under the auspices of the Joint Committee of the Order of St. John and the British Red Cross Society, nine homes and convalescent hospitals are administered. The Red Cross also runs homes for the aged sick, for the young disabled, for crippled girls, and for handicapped women. There are also holiday camps and a holiday home for the disabled (Plates 40–1).

In time of national disaster the Red Cross extends its first aid, relief and welfare work to meet the situation. When disaster strikes abroad, the British Red Cross sends immediate help and then, when subsequently refugees come to these shores, the Red Cross workers are at hand to welcome them. The British Red Cross organized the air lift that brought the Hungarian refugees to this country after the Hungarian Uprising; it was the biggest civilian air lift undertaken up to that time. Once the Hungarians were in this country, the Red Cross helped to settle them into the community in which they had to make a new life. More recently the Red Cross helped with the welfare of the 370 islanders of Tristan da Cunha who were evacuated to Great Britain when their home was overwhelmed by volcanic eruption. The Hampshire branch of the Red Cross met them at Southampton and escorted them to Pendell Camp, near Redhill, where the Surrey Branch had established a sick bay and provided comforts such as blankets and bedding and children's amenities. A Divisional Director of the Society who had spent two years in Tristan was there to welcome them, and the sick-bay staff was supplemented throughout their stay by Red Cross V.A.D.s.

In this way the Red Cross Society pursues the aims set out in its Charters: "the improvement of health, the prevention of disease, and the mitigation of suffering."

Selection of Publications Obtainable from the British Red Cross Society

The Ceaseless Challenge—popular illustrated history of the International and British Red Cross and its work today.
Mental Health Manual.
Welfare Services Manual.
Signpost to Welfare.

54. The St. John Ambulance Brigade

GEORGE W. WOODHILL

Brigade Secretary, St. John Ambulance Brigade

THE Order of St. John of Jerusalem originated in the eleventh century in Jerusalem where sick and needy pilgrims and Crusaders were cared for in the Order Hospice. By 1140 a branch of the Order had been established in England. In 1540 the Order in England was suppressed by Henry VIII.

The English Knights, however, continued to be associated with the charitable work of the Order, which was then based on Malta. In 1831 the Order was revived in England, and with a tradition of nine centuries of charitable and hospitaller service concentrated on the adaptation of this tradition to modern times by the formation of three Foundations, the St. John Ambulance Association, the St. John Ambulance Brigade and the Ophthalmic Hospital in Jerusalem. The St. John Ambulance Brigade was founded in 1887 from among the first certificate holders of the Association which had been founded ten years earlier to teach first aid. It has as its emblem the eight-pointed white cross. The main object of the Brigade is to train and maintain a body of men and women thoroughly efficient in first aid and nursing who can turn out when needed to help the sick and the injured and to supplement the work of professional doctors and nurses in time of national disaster or emergency. Men are trained in first aid and some also in nursing. Women are trained in first aid and nursing. All members receive continuous progressive training with their divisions and are re-examined annually by doctors and state-registered nurses responsible for technical training. Some 3000 medical men are enrolled as surgeons in the Brigade as also are 1500 or more fully qualified state nurses on the General Part of the Register apart from the nurses on the special parts of the Register. From this it will be seen that the Brigade has a strong force of fully qualified professional people among its members.

The St. John cadets are an integral and vital part of the Brigade, consisting of boys and girls who have joined between their 11th and 18th birthdays who are themselves first-aiders, but these cadets do not go on public duty without adults to accompany them. St. John cadets also have a fine record of voluntary service to the public. They help blind people in many ways, and render cheerful and valuable help to disabled and old people by running errands for them, changing library books, shopping and gardening. Thus they help in many ways by which comfort and friendship can be brought to those in need. In these ways they foster the traditions of the Order of St. John and uphold its objects which are, first, the encouragement of all that makes for the moral and spiritual strengthening of mankind in accordance with the first great principle of the Order embodied in its motto *Pro Fide* ("For the Faith"); and, secondly, the encouragement and promotion of all works of humanity and charity for the relief of persons in sickness, distress, suffering and danger, without distinction of race, class or creed, and the extension of the second great principle of the Order, embodied in its motto *Pro Utilitate Hominum* ("For the Service of Mankind").

The Brigade consists wholly of voluntary workers who all have their own individual professions and who do their training when they have finished their normal work, and who do their best to turn out for public duty whenever they are wanted. As part of this duty to the public, each year Brigade members deal with more than half a million cases of first aid and also give over 3 million hours to voluntary attendances at ceremonial parades, sporting events, beach huts, theatres, cinemas and places where crowds congregate and where their services may be needed. The growth and extent of the Brigade's work is well illustrated by the following figures. The first public duty to be performed was at Queen Victoria's Golden Jubilee in 1887 when fifty ambulance men were on duty and 200 cases were treated. At the Coronation of Queen Elizabeth II in 1953 over 8000 members of the Brigade from the United Kingdom and all parts of the Commonwealth were on duty and nearly 6000 cases were treated. More recently, at the wedding of Princess Margaret in 1960, nearly 1400 Brigade members including cadets were on duty, and 1200 casualties were treated. In Greater London, on an average, 365 members are on duty every day of the week, and they treat about 100 casualties daily. The Brigade is organized on a District County basis, and each command has now prepared an emergency scheme for major accidents, such as floods, railway accidents, large fires, etc., to ensure that teams of ambulance and nursing personnel can be readily alerted by day or night and go to the scene of disaster with the minimum of delay. They also carry out escort duties by land, sea and air. Invalids and injured persons travelling long distances sometimes to other countries may need an escort, and this is provided where the cost of the escort's expenses can be covered by the authorities or by the patient.

The scope of the Brigade's service to the public is much wider than may be imagined, as will be seen by the following activities. Services for invalids in their homes include increasing help in domiciliary care of old people and the physically and mentally handicapped. Increased requests for the nursing aid service have been received in recent years; this provides members with an opportunity to gain practical nursing experience under the supervision of the district nurse. This experience is invaluable in time of influenza epidemics, etc., when our nursing members are often asked to help the hospitals when their own staffs are depleted by illness. A very considerable amount of service is given by members to the community as "good neighbours", especially for the lonely and the old. These neighbourly services include helping to make beds and attend to the toilet needs of an invalid, disabled or infirm person; care of the hands and feet, attending to the needs of a sickroom; helping to feed helpless persons and for those living alone, seeing that satisfactory arrangements are made for drinks or meals. For example, arrange for the Meals on Wheels Service to call. Often help is needed to get an invalid in and out of bed and to dress and undress. They also need help when taking exercise. Assistance of this kind is also given by Brigade members at established homes for the elderly or disabled, including many of the Cheshire Homes. In this connection help would be forthcoming for day centres when these are set up. Foot clinics are attached to many clubs for old people where a qualified chiropodist looks after their feet regularly and St. John members assist at these clinics. In some areas St. John members operate the Meals on Wheels Service; run Darby and Joan Clubs and help at recreational clubs for the otherwise more or less house-bound. In this connection they also help with transport.

When there is illness people often need sick-room requisites, and such articles may be obtained on loan from the Brigade Medical Comforts Depots which are to be found in many towns and villages.

The Brigade gives help in accompanying and staffing holiday centres and camps for the handicapped.

Special welfare facilities are provided in conjunction with the B.R.C.S. for Service Hospitals, and for war-disabled ex-Service men and women, the latter being under the aegis of the Joint Committee of St. John and Red Cross, as also are the Hospital Library Department services.

Turning now to the help given in hospitals in addition to auxiliary nursing, this includes help given with the reception of patients, trolley shops, hospital libraries, visiting patients and help to relatives. Assistance is given with the transport and escorts and with the Hospital Car Service (in conjunction with the B.R.C.S. and W.V.S.). When patients leave hospital, Brigade personnel help with visiting and after-care.

The Brigade, together with the British Red Cross Society, undertakes the training of members of the Civil Defence Corps. Many Brigade members have joined the Civil Defence Corps and the Industrial Civil Defence Service, mainly in the Ambulance and First Aid Section, and also in the Welfare and other Sections. The Voluntary Aid Societies may also form units wearing their own uniform and with their own officers and N.C.O.s to work parallel with the Civil Defence Corps. The organization of the Ambulance and First Aid Section has also been revised, so that first-aid parties will form units in the front line, where they will be a vital element in treating casualties. Many members who do not feel able to join the Civil Defence Corps or who are more interested in the nursing work than in first aid join the parallel organization, the National Hospital Service Reserve. At the request of the Ministry of Health, the Brigade and the British Red Cross Society have undertaken the recruitment and training of members of the public who join this Reserve as nursing auxiliaries. The work of the National Hospital Service Reserve is twofold. Under normal conditions its members act as auxiliaries to the regular hospital nursing service whenever they are required; and in the event of emergency they would not only supplement hospital staff, but also help to man Forward Medical Aid Units set up between hospitals and the scene of a disaster.

The Brigade maintains close contact with the Ministries of Health, Pensions, Labour, Education and the Home Office, and also with the Admiralty, the War Office and the Air Ministry. Indeed, one of the objects of the St. John Ambulance Brigade in the United Kingdom is to provide Reserves for the Medical Services of Her Majesty's Armed Forces and to prepare such permanent organization during times of peace as may be at once available in time of emergency.

The Brigade works in close co-operation with many Government Departments, the Statutory and Voluntary Services and the local health and welfare service as well as with other voluntary bodies.

The foregoing is a résumé of the work of the Brigade in the United Kingdom, but it is now established in almost all countries of the Commonwealth and includes members of many different races and creeds, all united by the great traditions of service of the Order of St. John. Subject to the requirements of climatic and other geographical variations, the duties carried out by the Brigade overseas are similar to those performed in the United Kingdom. It should not be forgotten, however, that in many territories overseas the value of training in first aid and nursing is even greater than at home where medical aid is never far away. Even with the development of air transport, in remote regions there may be a delay of several days before the help of a doctor or fully trained nurse can be obtained or the patient removed to hospital. Because of the frequent occurrence of severe hurricanes, the Order of St. John instituted an Emergency Scheme in the Caribbean and North Atlantic area in 1956. This scheme was linked to relief plans prepared by the Government in those areas in which St. John and the Red Cross were asked to participate. Recently it was decided that similar plans would be useful in other countries of the Commonwealth where St. John operates in the event of major disasters or emergencies. An Emergency Scheme of general application has, therefore, been drawn up, and the basis of the plan is that the responsibility for giving direct practical assistance rests with the Brigade people locally. The functions of the Brigade are primarily first aid, nursing and care of sick, helping with inoculations, and the provision of medical comforts. Help will also be given, where necessary, with functions normally dealt with by the Government and other organizations, such as the establishment of rest centres, and the distribution of food, clothes and blankets.

55. The Joint Committee of the Order of St. John of Jerusalem and the British Red Cross Society

T. L. SOMERSCALES

Secretary, Joint Committee of the Order of St. John of Jerusalem
and the British Red Cross Society

THE Joint Committee is the modern representative of a series of Joint Committees established by the British Red Cross Society and Order of St. John from 1914 onwards to carry out certain joint activities, particularly those concerned with war disabled. These are the Committee's main care, but it also administers the St. John and Red Cross Hospital Library Service, and certain St. John and Red Cross other activities, which are convenient subjects for joint action. The Joint Committee and Sub-Committees are comprised of equal numbers of St. John and Red Cross officers. On the latter representatives of other organizations, with which the Joint Committee co-operate, also sit. In the counties the Joint Committee works through County Agencies drawn from the local St. John and Red Cross members. Its area of operation is confined to England, Wales and Northern Ireland. The Joint Committee's finances come from monies handed over at the end of the war, mainly, but not exclusively, for the ex-Service war disabled. Capital and income are spent according to a carefully regulated plan which is constantly reviewed.

The Committee's most important work is centred upon its Ex-Services War Disabled Help Department through which assistance and advice are given to disabled ex-Servicemen individually. This work is de-centralized as far as possible to County Agencies in which members of the Order, Brigade and Red Cross play a full part. The provision of means of independent travel between home and work, grants towards the cost of suitable housing accommodation, help in the establishment of state pensionary rights, the settling of war wounded in appropriate occupations, and the provision of clothing and comforts for those who are now feeling the burden of old age, may be mentioned as illustrating the scope of the department's work.

Other activities of a more recreational nature include the provision of diversional handicraft facilities, general hospital welfare and comforts, and the loan of motor-propelled tricycles.

In more specialized fields the Committee assist the St. John and Red Cross

Paraplegic Settlements for ex-Servicemen, at Lyme Green, near Macclesfield, and at Kytes, near Watford. There is a constant demand for the specially designed bungalow accommodation which is available for some eighty ex-Servicemen and their families in these Settlements. At the Lyme Green Settlement suitable occupations are provided for residents and also a clinic for the care of those needing treatment. The St. John and Red Cross Barrowmore Village Settlement, near Chester, also provides accommodation and work for those ex-Servicemen and others who, because of tuberculosis or other infirmities, need to pursue a gainful occupation under protected conditions. The Committee also established a small St. John and Red Cross settlement at Norwich providing cottages and bungalows for severely disabled ex-Servicemen. All the settlements referred to are administered by local St. John and Red Cross Committees.

Assistance, in the many forms already recited, is given to ex-officers through the Ex-Services War Disabled Help Department. In addition the Committee's Convalescent Hospital at Brighton is available to all ex-officers, and has the medical and nursing facilities to care for a limited number of heavy cases. Patients pay specially reduced fees which, in some cases, are only nominal.

Scio House Hospital, Putney, a residential home for the elderly requiring nursing care, is a further example of the Committee's care for ex-officers. This hospital provides accommodation for twenty-five residents, twenty-one being in single rooms.

The Committee gives much needed help, often in the form of regular weekly grants, to retired nurses and V.A.D. members with war service. Many nurses after a lifetime of service are in urgent need of a permanent home where they can spend their years of retirement in congenial company and surroundings. Such homes are provided by the Committee at Bramshott Lodge, Hindhead, and Ernest Burdon House, Bournemouth. These homes are always fully occupied and together accommodate some sixty residents each in a pleasant bed-sitting room and at a cost within their means.

The Committee is the largest existing dispenser in the country of hospital libraries. Some 1100 hospitals throughout England, Wales and Northern Ireland, having a total of 96,000 beds, make use of the hospital library service, the cost of which is met by a capitation fee payable by the hospital. This service is sustained by the voluntary efforts of over 4500 St. John and Red Cross librarians, who are based on County Library Depots and who in the course of a year issue nearly 4 million books to patients. Out of the Committee's own funds, a library service is provided to patients in service hospitals throughout the world as well as to war-disabled pensioners and to St. John and Red Cross residential and medical institutions.

A feature of the work of the Library Department is the special libraries provided for tubercular patients and the loan libraries, which meet the particular demands of the individual patients.

Microfilm projectors and electric page-turners are supplied to cover the needs of the heavily disabled patient.

56. Citizens' Advice Bureaux

JOAN PRIDHAM

Secretary, National Citizens' Advice Bureaux Council

Present Position and Historical Background

There are at present 439 Citizens' Advice Bureaux in England, Scotland, Wales and Northern Ireland. Their purpose is stated as:

> to make available to the individual accurate information and skilled advice on many of the personal problems that arise in daily life; to explain legislation; to help the citizen to benefit from and to use wisely the services provided for him by the State, and in general to provide counsel to men and women in the many complexities which beset them in an increasingly complex world.

Bureaux are established in nearly all big cities and in many towns where the population is 10,000 or more. The establishment of bureaux in smaller towns is not generally encouraged mainly because the volume of work in such places would not be sufficient to provide the required experience for the workers. It is apparent, however, that people in country areas have as much need for the services of bureaux as those in towns, and efforts are constantly being made to extend the service provided by bureaux at focal points, such as market towns, to the surrounding rural areas by means of publicity of various kinds. The need to provide this service for country people as well as to fill the gaps that exist in towns of moderate size is urgent, especially because of the invitation to bureaux to co-operate with the recently established Consumer Council, set up by the Board of Trade, by providing a source of advice and guidance at local level on consumer problems.

Planned in 1938 at the time of the Munich crisis, the bureaux were designed to meet the needs of a disrupted community, of evacuation, of divided families or those rendered homeless by enemy action. Between two and three hundred opened in the early months of the war and the number rose to 1050 in the peak period.

Some people thought that with the coming of peace the need for the bureaux would disappear, but it soon became clear that this was not the case. C.A.Bx. were obviously needed during what was hopefully called the resettlement period, and soon became taken for granted as a permanent feature of modern society. An editorial comment in the *Local Government Journal* of September 1959 emphasizes their continuing function in a welfare-conscious state:

The report of the Citizens' Advice Bureaux Council reads like a summary of the history of the development of present day social administration, so widespread is the scope of the activities of the movement and so closely does its work reflect the various changes in social conditions which have taken place in the last few years.

C.A.Bx. have won the confidence of the public who use them increasingly and of local authorities and Central Government Departments who seek their aid in interpreting their policies and making their services known to the public.

This partnership between statutory departments, both central and local, and voluntary organizations is a feature of our modern society in which visitors from overseas are especially interested. It is of particular importance to C.A.Bx. who could not do their work effectively without close co-operation with a whole range of statutory officials, but who must at the same time guard their independence of statutory control. In the words of Lord Denning (speaking at a national conference of C.A.Bx. in 1957) this is:

A free service, free to those who receive, voluntary in the most part by those who give; supported indeed by the State but not controlled by it; supported by local authorities but not controlled by them, and I hope, like the law never to be controlled by any public authority.

Individual Bureaux

The volume of work in large towns requires that bureaux be on a full-time basis, whereas in many smaller places part-time opening is all that is required.

Similarly, in some large towns they are staffed by paid workers, sometimes supported by a team of volunteers, whilst in smaller places they may be staffed entirely by voluntary workers who in fact account for 70 per cent of the total C.A.B. force. In addition there is normally a panel of consultants (e.g. the local Probation Officer, a lawyer, moral welfare worker) who support the work of the bureau and are available to give guidance as specialists in their own subjects.

Each bureau is autonomous, under a locally appointed committee representative of the appropriate voluntary and statutory social welfare agencies and of the local authority. They are closely linked to the national service, and represented through county and regional committees on the National (policy-making) Council.

Recruitment and Training

In most areas there is a constant demand for new workers. The work is exacting but immensely rewarding, and whilst a substantial number of people have been with the service since its early days there are many younger people amongst the new recruits. Volunteers are carefully chosen and include retired business and professional people as well as younger women who have run a home and brought up a family. Most are not professional social workers, but have a wide range of experience as well as a fund of knowledge, and the ability to relate this to the problems of those who come to them for help. In addition to their main task of interviewing in the bureau, volunteers must be prepared to spend time and effort in training both when they first enter the service and as a continuous part of their contribution to it, as new legislation is introduced, new techniques are developed and new social approaches to various problems are evolved, for example in the field of mental health.

The syllabus of preliminary training for new workers consists of a course of lectures organized locally by the secretary of the bureau under the guidance of a headquarters officer and supplemented by practical work under supervision and visits of observation to the courts, to sittings of administrative tribunals, to various types of institution and to the offices of local and central government.

The Work of the Bureaux

The work of the bureaux may be summarized as follows:

(a) directing people to the right source of help; helping them to complete forms; reassuring them following decisions by officials; helping them to understand and use appeal machinery;
(b) co-ordinating the various social services both voluntary and statutory which may be needed to solve one complex problem;
(c) interpreting the formal written word;
(d) filling the gaps in the social services and dealing with personal problems; acting as a "safety valve" through the simple act of listening sympathetically; recognizing deep-seated and difficult social problems of which the inquirers themselves may not be aware.

More than a million inquiries are received each year, and monthly returns are made to headquarters under the following main headings: civic, local and national information; communications and travel; education and training; employment; family and personal; health and medical; insurance; property and land; service and ex-service questions and war pensions; trade and manufacture.

This system enables headquarters officers and the National Council to have at any time a clear picture both of the number of inquirers coming to the bureaux and of the changing emphasis on various types of problem.

The variety of work may best be illustrated by a selection from the questions at one bureau in the course of a day:

"The landlord has told me that the new rating revaluation means that my rent will be increased. Is this true?"

"At what age can a girl leave home without her parents' consent?"

"How can I get a home help?"

"Am I entitled to holiday pay?"

"I want to claim retirement pension as I am now 65. The Ministry of Pensions have asked for a copy of my birth certificate but as my birth was not registered I have not got this. What can I do about it?"

And the complexity of some problems by the following illustration:

A married woman, separated from her husband, came to the bureau in great anxiety because she had fallen into arrears with her rent and her landlord was threatening her with eviction. She was employed in domestic work and was also in receipt of a separation allowance but in conversation with her it transpired that she was being required to make unusually large payments of tax under P.A.Y.E. Correspondence with the Inspector of Taxes revealed that there had been arrears of tax payments and that the high rate had been fixed in order to recover these. It seemed to the bureau, however, that the arrears had already been cleared. Moreover, the tax assessment was on the basis of maximum payment under the separation order whereas certificates obtained by the bureau from the county court revealed that the full amount due had rarely been paid. The bureau obtained a temporary loan from a benevolent fund in order to clear the arrears of rent and this loan was repaid when a refund of tax of approximately £45 was obtained. A period of eleven months elapsed before the bureau could regard this case as closed during which time there were numerous interviews with the inquirer and extensive correspondence with the Inspector of Taxes, the Clerk to the County Court, the benevolent fund from which the loan was obtained, as well as numerous telephone calls to all parties concerned.

Relationship with Local Authorities, Government Departments, the Legal Profession and with Other Organizations and Social Workers

Reference has already been made to the relationship with local and central government.

It is one of partnership and mutual understanding which leaves the bureau entirely free of statutory control, able to explain the decisions and point of view of "authority" to the inquirer but able, too, if this seems necessary, to challenge the decisions of either.

Great care is taken in the training of C.A.B. workers to underline the need to refer those requiring legal advice to a solicitor, and this is of particular importance—and presents particular difficulty—in the many cases which have both a legal and a social aspect.

C.A.Bx. both at national and local level work in close contact with The Law Society which is responsible for the administration of schemes for the provision of legal aid in civil actions in the courts and for legal advice. A high proportion of those seeking legal aid or advice are helped to obtain it by the bureaux.

Structure of the Service

A citizens' advice bureau is part of a national voluntary service and is represented through its county and regional organization on the National Citizens' Advice Bureaux Council, which is responsible for the policy of the movement. This Council in turn is closely linked with its parent body, the National Council of Social Service, which provides the secretariat for and meets the main part of the cost of the headquarters service, with the help of grants from two Government Departments.

From headquarters each bureau receives regularly, through the medium of Citizens' Advice Notes and monthly information circulars, information on legislation, and on statutory and other provisions affecting the life of the citizen. Help and guidance in the day-to-day work of the bureaux is given by headquarters and field advisory staff.

Each bureau is, nonetheless, a local self-governing unit. It is organized by the community for the community, and its success depends to a large extent on co-operation with other bodies, statutory and voluntary. The responsibility for financing a bureau rests on its Local Committee, the cost being largely met in most cases by grants from the local authority under powers conferred by the Local Government Act of 1948.

Citizens' Advice Bureaux Overseas

In recent years increasing interest has been shown in C.A.B. by countries overseas and especially by the newly developing countries and those like Israel, which have a problem of changing population and resettlement.

Officers of the National Council have visited Zambia and Southern Rhodesia, the Union of South Africa and Ghana; and a constant stream of social workers and administrators is welcomed at the headquarters office and by local bureaux.

As a result there are now C.A.B. services, modelled on the British pattern, in South and West Australia, British Guiana, Israel, Southern Rhodesia and South Africa.

As a visitor to Southern Rhodesia from a London bureau said recently:

It is a revelation to see a C.A.B. at work in another continent, not because it is different from ones at home, but because it is so much the same. It seems to prove that the citizens' advice bureau is fundamentally sound, yet flexible and versatile—that this practical down to earth service of information, advice, help and support meets as great a need in Salisbury as in Southwark.

57. The Citizens' Advice Bureau Service in Central London—A Service of the Family Welfare Association

ANN HAWKINS

C.A.B. Liaison Officer, Family Welfare Association

THE previous chapter describes more fully the work of Citizens' Advice Bureaux in the whole country, but this chapter directs attention to C.A.Bx. in London.

Another aspect of the work of the Family Welfare Association in London is to provide a Citizens' Advice Bureau Service.

The Unique Service Provided by C.A.B.

"The seeking of information by a person with a problem offers an opportunity to help which is unique in the Citizens' Advice Bureaux Service and from the callers' point of view there is an opportunity for initial consultation free of any special 'label'." These words are quoted from the 1961–2 Report of the Citizens' Advice Bureaux run by the Family Welfare Association in Central London and sum up the very special position which the C.A.Bx. occupy among the social services.

Every year over 100,000 people consult the Bureaux for which the Association is responsible and the public have rightly come to regard the C.A.B. as an essential social service in London. The Association is directly responsible for fifteen C.A.Bx. in twelve metropolitan boroughs, and works very closely with two bureaux in settlements in a further two boroughs. There are at the present time* ten metropolitan boroughs with no C.A.B., and although the public are free to consult any bureau they wish, there is need for expansion of the service in London, so that it is even more readily available for everyone who needs it.

* With effect from 1 April 1965, when, as a result of London Government re-organization, the 28 Metropolitan Borough Councils cease to exist, the present deployment of C.A.Bx. will result in there being at least one Bureau in each of the 12 inner London Boroughs which replace the Metropolitan Boroughs. C.A.Bx. now existing in 6 of the Metropolitan Boroughs are outside the control of the Family Welfare Association and this arrangement will continue. The Association is, however, seeking the necessary Local Authority financial support to open additional Bureaux where these are required.

The Costs of the Service

The major part of the cost of the Central London C.A.B. Service is met by the metropolitan borough councils in whose areas the bureaux are located. The permissive powers given to local authorities by the Local Government Act of 1948 to meet these costs are being used to an increasing extent each year, and in the year up to 31 March 1964 the grants amounted to £31,439. The Family Welfare Association, out of its own voluntary funds, meets the central administrative costs of the service. Though local authorities often have their own information centres to inform the public about local authority services, they are not qualified to advise on family and personal problems; to mediate, for example, in disagreements between people forced to live at too close quarters. Thus local authorities are quick to recognize the supreme importance of the bureaux' independent service, and not only support them financially but give them all possible assistance in their work.

The C.A.Bx. in Central London are staffed by full-time, trained social workers. On joining the Service they undergo up to a year's in-service training, whatever their previous experience, before acceptance on to the Family Welfare Association's C.A.B. staff. The majority of the bureaux can call on the help of members of the legal profession, who give their services voluntarily, and assist in dealing with some of the very many legal problems which are brought to C.A.B. Several bureaux in Central London are fortunate in having the help of part-time voluntary workers, some of whom undertake clerical work, while a few are concerned more directly in the work of advising the public.

Anyone living in a country with no C.A.B. might well wonder how the public know of the existence of the service. That the bureaux are regarded by the British as universally available was illustrated vividly by the Secretary of a C.A.B. in Australia. She described how two English people who had consulted her were found to have looked up the address of their local C.A.B. in the telephone directory as they would have done at home. Most people in fact need no prompting to consult a C.A.B. if they have a problem. If any encouragement to use the bureaux is needed, however, this is readily given by the Police, the clergy, Government Departments, other social workers, and, indeed, by anyone who in the course of their work is consulted by the public on problems outside their own immediate scope.

The variety of problems brought to the bureaux is very great and the constant shift in emphasis of inquiries clearly reflects not only changes in legislation but alterations in social and economic conditions. In London the largest number of inquiries concern housing. In the region of 30,000 difficulties in this field are brought to the C.A.Bx. in Central London in a year and over 20,000 family and personal problems of all kinds are handled annually.

The acute shortage of accommodation in London at moderate rents causes many problems, and some of the increasing number of personal and domestic worries are inevitably linked with housing difficulties.

The Problems of Immigrants

Many areas of London have substantial immigrant populations from the West Indies, Pakistan, Cyprus, West Africa and other parts of the Commonwealth. In 1958, following racial troubles in North Kensington, the Family Welfare Association appointed, with the necessary financial support of the Borough Council, a West Indian Social Worker to assist the C.A.B. in the solution of some of the problems which were seen to exist in the area. This appointment has proved to be of very great value from many points of view. The worker is able to advise and assist in the solution of the problems of individual immigrants, and the presence of a West Indian as a member of a team of social workers is beneficial in educating both the Londoners and the immigrants in race relations.

In order that the specialist social services may operate successfully, the existence of a readily available, independent service of information and advice such as that provided by C.A.B. is clearly essential. The C.A.B. Service in its twenty-five years of existence has shown itself to be able to adapt to meet new needs and changing conditions. It looks forward to an increasingly close working partnership with the local authorities and with the full range of the social services.

Much of the information needed by the bureaux to equip them to deal with citizens' problems, including details of new legislation, is provided by the National C.A.B. Council, in association with the National Council of Social Service. The National C.A.B. Council is actively engaged in expanding and developing the C.A.B. Service; it maintains a close link with the individual organizations responsible for the bureaux, with Government Departments and the wide range of organizations directly or indirectly concerned with the C.A.B. Service. The National Council is thus in a position to make known in appropriate quarters the views of the C.A.B. Service upon social problems.

The Family Welfare Association, with its long tradition of service to the citizens of London, is convinced of the vital need for the C.A.B. movement to be extended. Provided that the local authorities will meet the costs involved, the Association can expand its C.A.B. Service and thus ensure that C.A.Bx. are readily available to advise all members of the London public who need them.

58. The Work of the Women's Voluntary Service

ELSA DUNBAR

Women's Voluntary Service For Civil Defence

PERHAPS one of the most significant trends in social welfare in the post-war years has been the emergence of the volunteer to play an important part in supplementing the work of local authorities and of trained social workers. Today it is universally accepted that volunteers working part-time and on a rota basis, if properly organized, can undertake continuing responsibilities on both a local and a national basis.

A New Service

Voluntary work has always been a tradition in this country, but it is true to say that before the formation of the Women's Voluntary Service in 1938 the opportunities for women without particular skills, training or leisure were few and far between. The original function of the W.V.S. was to inform women about the way in which they could help their families in the event of attack from the air, and to recruit them for the Air Raid Precautions (later Civil Defence) Services. It was soon obvious that there were many women who, although unable to join these services because of home responsibilities, were willing and anxious to do something to help. The W.V.S. was organized on a national basis following the Civil Defence pattern; women were able to offer their help locally and, when evacuation took place, they were soon called upon to help billeting officers, irate householders, homesick and difficult children and overworked school teachers.

The W.V.S. put itself at the service of local authorities to undertake whatever work was required. Within a very short time almost every local authority in the country had asked for a W.V.S. Centre to be opened and, as the war progressed, the requests for the W.V.S. covered an ever broadening field.

Membership

During the war years the call for volunteers was unlimited, and by 1941 W.V.S. membership topped the million mark. For the first time in their lives many women were being asked to give help outside their own home and immediate circle and were finding that, no matter how little time they had, or how little experience, there was a job for them to do. The W.V.S. was learning about the handling of volunteers and appreciating the importance

461

of at all times considering their interests and their welfare and of giving them all possible help with information and equipment to do their work efficiently and well. The uniform was thought out carefully, its wearing optional, its price kept as low as possible. A grey–green colour was chosen which would not show dust or dirt and did not need constant brushing. The red blouse was kind to a white, tired face, important not only to the wearer, but also to the people to whom help was given. The uniform proved an important factor in the welding together of women from every walk of life—no embarrassment over smart hats or fur coats for the woman who had none. And this was essential in a Service where there were no ranks, and the responsibility for the job was vested in the woman who had the ability to do it and not the woman with social position or money.

War-time Work

To assess the scope of the work and the responsibility which was undertaken by volunteers during the early days of the W.V.S., it is worth looking at one or two major operations of very varied types.

The Volunteer Car Pool, the responsibility for which was delegated to the W.V.S., controlled the operation of 20,820 cars from 1942 to 1945, dealt with requests from those authorized to call on the Pool, allocated duties, issued petrol coupons and handled mileage claims from drivers. In three years 60 million miles were driven under this scheme.

On 930 permanent sites and on hundreds of other temporary ones, clubs and canteens were organized for Servicemen, providing as many as 96 million meals in one year. Large-scale voluntary-worked contracts were accepted for the three Services Knitting Associations: 3 million garments a year were repaired for the Army and 129,588 camouflage nets were garnished for the Ministry of Supply.

Agricultural workers could not enjoy the benefits of extra food in factory canteens or British Restaurants, so the W.V.S., under the auspices of the Ministry of Food, organized a scheme to deliver meat pies to them on the farms and in the fields. The W.V.S. baked, collected and distributed an average of 1,324,000 pies weekly!

Peace-time Work

The work of the W.V.S. did not end when peace came, although some members did give up their work when the men in the forces returned home. Many new problems, as well as the continuing ones of housing, resettlement, rationing and shortages had to be tackled. In 1948, when the Civil Defence Corps was formed and the Acts which ushered in the Welfare State came into operation, there was still a wide and opening field for voluntary service.

The Women's Auxiliary to Civil Defence

The Secretary of State for Home affairs announced, in speaking about the continuance of the W.V.S., "whatever the future holds, the need will continue for voluntary helpers to supplement public service, both on occasions of emergency and at other times"; in 1951 the role of the W.V.S. was further ratified as the Women's Auxiliary to the Civil Defence Corps.

How has the W.V.S. fulfilled the obligations laid upon it then and re-affirmed since by subsequent Home Secretaries?

Over the years its members have been encouraged to join the Welfare Section of the Civil Defence Corps of which they now form a substantial part, and in 1962 more than 1000 W.V.S. were qualified instructors. The W.V.S. is responsible for the recruitment, training and staffing of the teams of the Food Flying Squads, the mobile emergency feeding units of the Ministry of Food. In addition the W.V.S. members who are not enrolled in the Civil Defence Corps are given emergency training to enable them to serve as auxiliaries. In any local emergency the W.V.S. is automatically called upon to staff rest centres, to feed and clothe people in distress and every W.V.S. centre has its own emergency plans.

Perhaps one of the most important and difficult jobs undertaken by the W.V.S. in connection with Civil Defence has been the scheme to bring information to women about nuclear warfare and what they should know for the protection of their own homes and families. The One-in-Five Scheme takes its name from the aim to speak to one-in-five of the women of the country—3 million. The speakers, all volunteers, are given special training before being authorized to give the talks, and many women have joined the W.V.S. for this particular work.

Help to the Social Services

In 1948 the Children's Act came into operation and within a few years a close relationship developed between the W.V.S. and the Children's Committees. Volunteers help children's officers in a number of ways, the most important of which is the finding of foster homes. The W.V.S. befriends both the staff and children in homes, organizes a "Godmother" scheme in many homes, and provides escorts for children needing hospital or dental treatment. Since 1951, holidays have been organized for children recommended by medical officers of health, children's officers, education authorities, probation officers and the leading children's organizations, and the W.V.S. also runs its own short-stay home to which these authorities can send children in need of temporary care through family difficulties.

There are many opportunities for volunteers to help with preventive work arising out of the Children's and Young Persons Bill. The woman who distributes welfare foods, or clothing, or has been consulted when a household is in difficulties, is often able to give help and advice which prevents the family reaching the stage where it is regarded as a problem. In serious cases where skilled help has been called in, the W.V.S. can back this up by providing assistance with furniture and helping to rehabilitate the home.

Welfare of Prisoners and Ex-prisoners

The W.V.S. work for the welfare of prisoners and ex-prisoners was started in 1947 at the request of the Prison Commissioners. It has developed to assist the prison welfare authorities in the care and after-care of increasingly large numbers of men and boys as well as women and to meet the special needs of juvenile delinquents. Great care is taken in enlisting aid from the right people, and volunteers are selected with the aim of matching them to individual cases. Many are drawn from those experienced in dealing with problem families or in welfare work for the Services and their families overseas, and this kind of background has proved more successful than any training in enabling volunteers to make the initial approach to a section of the community whose confidence is not easily won.

In all these fields of service—for Civil Defence, for children, for prisoners and ex-prisoners—there is direct contact between the W.V.S. and the various responsible departments.

Health and Hospital Work

Other Government Departments also make calls on W.V.S., notably the Ministry of Health. When the National Health Service came into being, W.V.S. members were working in 267 hospitals as receptionists and guides, providing shopping services by means of trolley shops, visiting the friendless patients and helping with library services, and, at the request of the almoner, visiting patients discharged from the hospital. In 1949 the work was extended to include the organization of canteens for out-patients and visitors. By the end of 1963 the W.V.S. was undertaking a wide variety of non-nursing work in more than 1365 hospitals and operating 484 canteens.

In 101 hospitals for the mentally ill and in 48 for the mentally subnormal, a special effort has been made to develop a bridge between patients and the outside world through volunteers carrying out basically the same work. Volunteers, carefully selected for their care and patience, can be instrumental in hastening recovery and improving the attitude of members of the public towards the mentally ill. A recent major development in W.V.S. work is the provision of purpose-designed shops and canteens in the hospital grounds where patients, visitors and staff can meet in bright and attractive surroundings.

In 1962, when the Ten Year Hospital Plan was announced, the Minister emphasized that he looked to voluntary organizations to make the plan a success. He believed that voluntary help was needed and had not yet reached its potential. The W.V.S. promised its full support.

Volunteers are never lacking for hospital work. They must be accustomed or trained to work as members of a team and to understand hospital rules and, if they have to fall out, must be replaced. The W.V.S. serves the hospitals by organizing a reliable service, no less than by the work of the individual members who bring to the patients a measure of reassurance and understanding and a contact with normal life which even the most humane and expert management could not give. The W.V.S. gives its help to the various health services of local authorities dealing with home helps, blood transfusion services, welfare foods distribution, mass radiology, etc., and with the welfare of the blind and disabled.

Welfare of the Elderly

As more people live longer, there would appear to be no foreseeable end to the demands for volunteers to help local authorities in meeting their responsibility for the welfare of the old. The W.V.S. runs 2000 Darby and Joan Clubs for the lonely, provides accommodation in twenty-four residential clubs for those in need of care and attention, and three nursing homes to which they can go in time of illness. The latest one to be opened is for elderly people who are mentally frail and need special attention. Volunteers help in different ways with many services, such as chiropody or laundry services, organized by local authorities for the welfare of the elderly.

The W.V.S. arranges visits by members, their friends, school children, guides and scouts, to lonely people. Visiting schemes must be well organized as sporadic visits by the well-meaning are not the answer to this problem, for the old people look forward to their regular visit and are bitterly disappointed when it does not take place.

Meals-on-Wheels

The Meals on Wheels Service, which provides a popular meal for the homebound unable to cook for themselves, is perhaps the biggest single W.V.S. service for the domiciliary care of the old (Plate 42). It ensures regular visits by W.V.S. members who can ascertain whether all is well and who can call on the W.V.S. Centre for any help which may be needed. It involves close contact between the W.V.S. Centre and the officers of the local authority, doctors, nurses or others authorized to recommend that the meals be delivered.

The 1962 Amendment to the National Assistance Act empowered local authorities to assist voluntary organizations by providing capital expenditure for this scheme, in addition to the grants previously made to subsidize the provision of the meals, and this should mean even more rapid expansion of the service. In the last six years the number of meals delivered has risen from 1 million to 7 million per year, and new schemes are constantly being started. The heated containers in which the meals are delivered are also being used wherever possible to take hot food to Darby and Joan Clubs which have no kitchen in which to cook, or to any available and conveniently situated room, where a midday meal can be served. The W.V.S., recognizing the importance to the health and morale of lonely old people of eating a nourishing meal in the company of others, is concentrating its efforts on developing this service alongside the meals for the home-bound.

Two new experiments are a mobile kitchen from which meals can be collected by cars and taken to a number of outlying villages, and a mobile diner which can be sited in a particular place until other accommodation is available.

Housing Schemes

The housing of old people has always been of special concern to the W.V.S., which works in close co-operation with the Ministry of Housing in formulating its policy. Some 1000 flats and flatlets in houses converted into individual bed-sitting-rooms with shared kitchen and bathrooms are administered by the W.V.S. on behalf of many housing authorities, the tenants being drawn from local authority housing lists, and others are purchased, converted and managed by the W.V.S. Housing Association. The regular visits to collect rents, deal with fuel bills and repairs, give the W.V.S. visitors an opportunity to know the old people and help them with any problems. Other schemes provide housing for retired professional women, for young women during their first year in a big city, and for refugees.

Clothing

Over 200,000 people are given clothing each year on the recommendation of recognized welfare organizations, the National Assistance Board or the Police. In addition, every W.V.S. Centre is prepared to provide clothing in emergencies. The "national wardrobe" is collected from the public and millions of garments are processed by the W.V.S.—sorted, repaired and made ready for immediate issue. Nothing is wasted. There is always a demand for the victims of disasters or for refugees overseas for anything which may not be needed in Great Britain. As its contribution to World Refugee Year, the W.V.S. collected, processed and baled over 1000 tons of clothing for U.N.R.W.A., a formidable task by any standards.

Welfare for the Services

Since 1944 W.V.S. members have been working overseas, organizing clubs and leisure-time activities for the Services. Under the scheme, sponsored by the N.A.A.F.I., each member receives a small personal allowance and is provided with accommodation. Because of this, it has been possible to select the best people for the job without having to confine the selection to those with an income, and the members at home appreciate the reasons why these facilities are given and realize that the overseas members are only receiving the minimum amount to make it possible for them to undertake the job and are equally giving voluntary help. Close contact is kept between the W.V.S. at home and overseas through the magazine adoption scheme— each W.V.S. Centre collecting and sending books, magazines and games for distribution by the W.V.S. overseas, and to every regiment, base and ship serving overseas.

Contribution of the Volunteer

The W.V.S. offers no inducement to its members beyond the opportunity to give of themselves. It eschews sentimentality and sets a high standard of service, reserving the right to dismiss any volunteer who does not carry out her obligations, no matter how small they may be. It has found that women will always come forward to undertake a job if the need for it is fully explained and the channels are cleared so that they can get on with it without fuss or bother. The belief shown from the beginning by the chairman of the W.V.S., the Dowager Marchioness of Reading, in the capability, resource and staying power of volunteers has been amply justified.

In a changing world the W.V.S. believes that voluntary service is essential to the life of the State and should be integrated into statutory aid. It has a valuable contribution to make in humanizing legislation and helping those responsible for its implementation in a variety of ways by bringing unofficial assistance and understanding to the problems of the people for whom it is designed.

SECTION XI
THE CHURCHES IN WELFARE

59. The Central Churches Group—a Bridge-building Operation

Rev. W. W. Simpson

Advisory Secretary, Central Churches Group, National Council of Social Service

Some names are more inspiring, more exciting, more suggestive even than others. Some are the reverse of any of these things. Among the less inspired is that of the Central Churches Group of the National Council of Social Service. Not even its initials—C.C.G.—spell out any interesting or particularly euphonious sound or message. And yet it stands for one of the most significant developments in the field of modern social service, representing as it does an attempt on the part of the National Council of Social Service to establish a point of contact and consultation between the religious bodies in this country and both the voluntary and the statutory social services.

It is Central in the sense that it operates under the aegis of the National Council of Social Service. In this context the term "Churches" has a wider connotation than is usual in this country, embracing as it does not only the Anglican, Roman Catholic and Free Churches, but also the Jewish community. It is a group, not in the etymological sense of a "lump" or a "mass" but rather in the derivative sense of "a number of persons in a certain relation, as having a certain degree of similarity".

The similarity, the relationship, in this case derives from the growing realization that those who, for the most part quite unwittingly, helped to lay the foundations of the Welfare State by their pioneer activities in the establishment of schools, hospitals and almshouses, have not, by the emergence of the new Society, been rendered either irrelevant or redundant. The formation of the Central Churches Group was announced as long ago as 1941 in the first issue of a bulletin entitled *In the Service of the Community*, where its objects were stated to be:

   (a) To provide for continuous co-operation in matters of importance and urgency in the social field between the Churches and the National Council of Social Service.
   (b) To encourage church members to participate more fully in voluntary community services which are organized outside church life.
   (c) To secure that these community services develop in a way which is not inimical to the life and work of the Churches themselves and that the churches have opportunity to make their distinctive contribution.
   (d) To these ends to promote the appointment of suitable church representatives on national and local committees for various kinds of social service, and to assist in the distribution of essential information for the guidance of those responsible for church action in this field.

Not long afterwards the London Council of Social Service, which today more than ever works in the closest possible collaboration with the National Council, set up its own Churches Groups, similarly constituted and with virtually identical aims.

During the first stage of its existence the Central Group concentrated in the main on the fourth of these objects, particularly from the point of view of "the distribution of essential information for the guidance of those responsible for Church action in this field". Among the bulletins and pamphlets published by the Group during this period were the following: *Religious Ministrations for Munition Workers* (published during the war); *The Churches' Part in Old People's Welfare*; *The Provision of New Centres of Community Life*; *Social Service and Social Justice*; *A Review of the Churches' Work for Charity in the Light of Services Provided by the State*; *Social Service as a Religious Vocation* (perhaps the Group's most substantial contribution towards the fulfilment of its second object); and a *Handbook for Social Workers on the Moral Principles Underlying the Approach to Social Service*.

Similarly, the London Churches Group has also published a number of valuable papers, outstanding among which have been a *Statement on its Policy and Work*; a *Handbook to the Social Services in London*; a pamphlet on *Religion and Old Age*, and, more recently, a leaflet on *Some Opportunities for Voluntary Work in London*.

In the course of time, however, the members of the Central Group began to feel that although their regular meetings were of the greatest possible interest and value to those who were fortunate enough to take part in them, they did not bring the members sufficiently into touch either with church workers or social workers in the field. Nor were pamphlets and papers, however well and authoritatively produced, an adequate substitute for personal contact.

And here the second stage of the Group's life began. Inspired partly by reports of discussions at the centre and partly by growing recognition of need for closer contact in the country between representatives of the Churches and of the voluntary and statutory social services, a number of local Churches Groups began to emerge as if by a process of spontaneous generation. The story of the beginning of what came to be widely known as the "Cornish Experiment" was told, for example, by the then Bishop of Truro in a broadcast talk in December 1953.

> The Church [said the Bishop] need not abdicate from her social responsibilities. Far from it. What we have got to do is to work out new ways of co-operating with the Welfare State. First there is a great need of interpreting the new Social Services to the man in the street and the family in the cottage; to explain what they are out to do, what they actually offer, and how we can take advantage of what they offer. Who is there who can interpret this work? The towns have their Citizens' Advice Bureaux which act as a most useful liaison between the private citizen and the Social Services. But what about the country districts where there are not enough people available to

serve on Advice Bureaux—and if there were, such a set-up might be regarded with suspicion? Some one person is needed who is by tradition part of the pattern of the countryside, who knows the people and is trusted. What about the country parson?

But if the "country parson" was to be cast for this so obviously important role, two things quickly became clear. First, that he would need to be well briefed. And, secondly, that the term "country parson" must be interpreted as covering not only the Anglican clergyman but also ministers of all denominations. In due course the approval of the appropriate authorities in each of these three groups was secured, and a series of meetings arranged at which leading representatives of all the various social and welfare services (statutory and voluntary) in the county were able to explain to and discuss with clergy and ministers the workings of their various departments.

These meetings resulted in one notable discovery and one important piece of practical work. The discovery, not altogether unexpected perhaps, was that the meetings themselves served a dual purpose. The clergy and ministers obviously gained a great deal of information. But those who came to give the information quickly discovered that there were still things which they themselves needed to learn about the needs and problems of the people whose welfare the social services were designed to serve. A two-way traffic resulted of great mutual benefit.

The important piece of practical service quickly followed from recognition of the fact that not only was the information imparted more than any one person could be expected to carry in however well-equipped a memory, but that, if he was to be expected to deal adequately with all the questions which might arise in the course of his pastoral work, he might well find himself landed with a full-time job. A broadsheet was therefore prepared and published by the Cornwall Council of Social Services giving a list of the general social and welfare services available in the county, with, in each case, an address and telephone number to which anyone could apply for further help or information.

Other areas followed suit until in November 1954 it became evident that some consultation was needed at a national level, and a Conference on Co-operation between the Churches and the Social Services with special reference to Rural Areas was held at Friends' House in London.

This Conference, apart from its own inherent interest and value, proved in its turn the prelude to the third stage in the developing influence of the Central Churches Group. A conference on Mental Health—The Churches' Challenge and Opportunity—attracted considerable interest on the part of both voluntary and statutory bodies at work in that particular field and at the same time helped to prepare the way for further conferences of a similar kind on other aspects of the relationship between the Churches and the welfare services.

The first of these was sparked off by a report on Responsibility in the

Welfare State, published in 1961 and containing an account of a survey and a project undertaken by the Social Responsibility Council of the Birmingham Council of Christian Churches in an attempt to assess the ways in which the religious bodies, inspired by the ideal of good neighbourly service, could help to fill some of the already patent gaps in the services rendered to a wide variety of needy people both by the voluntary and the statutory bodies.

From this Conference two things emerged. The first was further evidence of the way in which, again by a process of spontaneous generation, small-scale projects were beginning to operate in many urban as well as rural areas throughout the country. Outstanding among these was the so-called Fish Scheme at Headington which owed its inspiration, as many other local projects have done, to a Stewardship Campaign in a local church, and to the recognition of the church members that when they had begun to solve their financial problems they had only just begun to realize their responsibilities to their immediate neighbourhood. The fish was chosen as having been one of the earliest of Christian symbols.

In this particular case the parish is divided into nine areas each under an area warden, all headed by a central organizer. Each street has one or some-times two street wardens, and all wardens have a metal fish on their gate-posts and a fish badge is worn by all members. A letter was sent to every household in the parish explaining the scheme, which is available to every-body. A card, also bearing its emblem of the fish, was enclosed, with a request that it be displayed in the window in any case of emergency. Ques-tionnaires were circulated inviting people to indicate what they could do in the way of giving time and talents as well as money, and all offers of help were registered both in a central file and in the file of the appropriate area warden. The scheme has been in operation for over a year and has remained active and intact with members of other denominations, agnostics and people of all ages joining in.

The second thing that emerged very clearly was that if the voluntary help which the Churches might reasonably be expected to muster was to be effectively used it must be properly prepared. A further Conference followed on the Training and Preparation of Voluntary Workers, which led in due course to a consultation between a group of experts on ways of initiating training or preparation schemes for members of churches and religious bodies who might volunteer for various forms of good neighbour service. Three basic elements were agreed to be essential to any scheme for good neighbour training; helping the volunteer to adopt a right attitude to those he seeks to serve; encouraging a responsible attitude to any commitment undertaken; and making sure that volunteers are as well informed as possible about the services provided by the statutory and established voluntary organi-zations. Discussion also centred on the recruitment and deployment of volunteers.

There is one further point which must be borne in mind and which takes us back to the third of the objects of the Churches Group as stated in its initial bulletin and quoted earlier in this article.

This point refers to the distinctive contribution the Churches have to make in the field of social service. Over and above the multifarious activities implicit in the acceptance of the bidding to love our neighbours as ourselves, the Churches have a prophetic ministry to fulfil. This arises from the ever-present danger lest in the understandable preoccupation of the Welfare State with the mental, physical and material needs of its members, society may get its priorities wrong and lose sight of those ultimate values which alone can give meaning and purpose to the life of the individual man, woman and child. The interpretation of those values and the clarification of the meaning and purpose of living is, or should be, the distinctive contribution of the churches in this as in all other fields of the life of the community.*

* Further information about continuing activities and publications issued by the Central Churches Group may be had on application to the Advisory Secretary of the Group, c/o National Council of Social Service, 26 Bedford Square, London W.C.1.

60. The Church of England in Welfare Work

RT. REV. MARK A. HODSON

Lord Bishop of Hereford,
Chairman of the Church of England Council for Social Work

WHEN we consider the part played by the Church in social welfare, two prior considerations have to be borne in mind. First, that the Church is where the practising Christian is. Many workers have gone into the social work field through a sense of Christian vocation. Work organized by church authorities is by no means the total contribution of the Church to the pattern of social work in the Welfare Society. And, secondly, that although the Church has a Council for Social Work which is part of the Church Assembly's Board for Social Responsibility, this by no means covers all the social work undertaken by the Church of England.

Let us take a quick glance at the past, then at the present pattern and, finally, see what future trends are discernible.

In the past the Church played a major part in the social care of the poor and aged and sick not merely of her own members but all whom she could reach. As in education, some church schools remain, so in nursing, small areas of work are still undertaken by the Church. In particular the nursing sisters of St. John the Divine have maternity and district visiting in two areas in London whereas the Community at one time was responsible for the nursing of several large general hospitals in London as well as smaller ones elsewhere. The Ranyard Mission similarly in the past had responsibilities for hospital work and now undertakes some district nursing. The Church at one time undertook through its Police Court Mission what has now developed into the Probation Service and still has a part in this field in probation hostels in some eleven dioceses.

It should not be imagined that the Church is clinging for sentimental reasons to these corners of work once undertaken more widely. Looked at in one way it is due to the policy which is manifestly part of the English way of life that statutory and voluntary bodies should remain side by side in social work. Again, from another angle, the Church by its very nature and title-deeds feels the need to demonstrate continually her concern in the welfare of men's bodies as well as souls.

To turn to the present situation. A most striking contribution to the social work by the Church of England in recent times has been through its moral welfare workers. In each diocese there are trained women (in only one place at present is a man undertaking this work) and in the Provinces of Canterbury and York there are at present nearly 500 employed. The Council for Social Work referred to above has half its members elected by the Standing Conference of Diocesan Moral Welfare Councils, but the work is directed by their Diocesan Councils or by local associations. It consists of casework connected with moral problems, notably those of the unmarried mother and her child, and in providing residential help. The Church of England actually provides the greatest amount of residential help in this area of need and in its care are hostels for pregnant mothers who are able to go to work, shelter homes, mother and baby homes and maternity homes.

For this work women are trained at Josephine Butler House in Liverpool or in the shorter London course for older women. There is constant thought being given to the extension of these courses.

No article on the Church of England's contribution to social work could omit the very large part played by the Church Army. Founded over eighty years ago the Church Army now has a large number of men and women engaged in social as well as evangelistic work. There are more than three-quarters of a million beds available for men in hostels where special attention is paid to the rehabilitation of the homeless and unemployed. There are also hostels for women. Missioners are attached to twelve prisons, and prisoners are helped while in prison and especially at the time of their discharge, and their families are cared for by a special department. While not wishing to make a full list of activities of the Church Army, the care of the aged must be noted. A number of homes are run by the Church Army in the south of England for old people.

At the other end of the age groups the Church of England Children's Society, with over 100 homes, has in its care at any one time some 3000 children. About 5000 children are helped every year mostly in small homes and nurseries and nearly 1000 are boarded out in private homes.

The attempt to make a complete list of other ways in which the Church seeks to fulfil the command to "take care of him" which the Good Samaritan gave, must be resisted, but the work of the Royal Association in aid of the Deaf and Dumb, though smaller in size, is one of the best and most effective agencies in this field. And some of the Anglican religious communities undertake work for smaller groups of people needing very special attention in residential care.

What will be the future pattern of social work undertaken by the Church? This depends on many factors. It seems at present that the national policy will be to encourage voluntary bodies to work in close partnership with the statutory services. While the Church must foster vocations to social work carried on by local authorities, there will for a long time be gaps in the social services which need to be filled. The specifically moral welfare work shows no sign of being redundant. If more workers could be provided they would be eagerly welcomed. The caseload of present workers is very heavy indeed. But in common with all branches of social work the recruitment is below the number needed. Older women are being attracted to the work, but there is no sign that in the immediate future the supply will exceed the demand. Particularly is this the case in residential work. Here the Government has shown that it especially welcomes the work of voluntary bodies, but it is just here that the lack of workers is most likely to hold up progress.

Meanwhile a working party on the future policy of the Social Work Council is seeking to find what more is meant by the phrase "caring for the uncared for", which seems to be the aim of the Church for the future. As in so many branches of social work the Church pioneered the way and was then ready and happy to hand over to statutory bodies with greater financial resources, so today she must be thoroughly awake to the tasks that as yet are not being adequately undertaken. It is equally important that a working partnership between statutory and voluntary social organizations be established and that the Church should minister to everyone engaged in social work, whoever employs them. Whilst, in response to human need, the Church might often pioneer a social service, it has the responsibility of maintaining the proper ethos of all service and of shedding the light of the Gospel of God on all human situations. This is the special contribution which the Church alone can make.

There is a growing tendency to professionalize social work, to introduce long and highly technical training courses through which full-time social workers must successfully pass if they are to be qualified to do social work. This is often accompanied by ordinary people contracting out of neighbourly social care on the grounds that they are unskilled and that people are now trained and employed to act for them. Whilst blundering into situations where technical skill is needed is dangerous, contracting out of friendly care is utterly disastrous. The skilled social worker cannot function alone, and it is clearly imperative that a new and fruitful relationship between neighbours and professional social workers be worked out. Here both the ubiquity and nature of the Church place it in a strategic position to act.

And as a last word it must be borne in mind that when the Church is effectively at work there is no gloomy down-town street or forbidding block of flats that is not being visited regularly by the parish priest and his helpers who are thus able to play a valuable part in the social as well as religious care of their people.

61. The Churches and the Welfare Services

REV. D. ALAN KEIGHLEY

Former Secretary, Social Responsibility Department,
British Council of Churches

THIS chapter is contributed out of the experience of the Social Responsibility Department of the British Council of Churches as summarized unofficially by one person who was its Secretary for some years. The British Council of Churches, a product of the twentieth-century oecumenical movement, came of age in 1963. Its members are the Church of England and the Anglican Churches in Wales, Scotland and Ireland, the Church of Scotland, the main Free Churches in the British Isles as well as some of the smaller ones, and bodies like the Salvation Army, the Y.W.C.A. and Y.M.C.A., and the Student Christian Movement. It enables its constituent organizations to work together in those fields in which their common outlook makes this desirable, to discuss their differences, and to create a growing climate of understanding which makes closer relationships and increased co-operation possible. The constant consultation involved has led to much close understanding and a growing body of achievement.

The Social Responsibility Department is made up of official representatives with some co-opted members, and a full-time secretary (though this last is only a recent achievement). It is the channel through which the constituent organizations of the Council operate over a broad field of social (including industrial) questions, producing not only mutual understanding among them, but between them and those with expert knowledge and experience in, for example, social welfare. It helps them to define their contemporary responsibilities, to co-ordinate their activities, to make official representations when necessary, and from time to time it moves on from consultation to the bringing about of specific projects.

The outlook of the Churches it represents is developing against the background not only of the coming of the Welfare State in Great Britain, but of much new theological thinking influenced by the situation of the Churches in what is often called, with rough accuracy, a "post-Christian society". Reference to two of these theological trends is indispensable in the present discussion. There is a new consciousness of the Church as a servant, as the Body of Christ which should play the same role as her Lord. The Church has always enjoined charity and works of mercy beyond its own membership, because without them it could not be the Church, and for the sake of its own spiritual health. But there is a new emphasis on caring for people and help-ing them, for their own sake—because they are part of God's world which He loves indiscriminately whether the love is returned or not. Combined with the impact of modern psychology and the new study of sociology, this leads to a desire to understand peoples' problems and help them in their actual situations rather than to pontificate about ideal solutions, though without being faithless to ultimate ideals.

There is also a deepening of thought about the relation between the com-munity and the individual. Some Protestant thinking has tended to individua-lism, because of its origin, or has in the past tended (in practice at least) to regard the Church as a collection of groups of individual believers. The in-dispensable Christian emphasis on the personal, reflecting on the denial of so much to so many human personalities in the industrial revolution, led to a stress on the value of the individual *per se*. The time for this stress has gone. It is clear that man only fulfils himself, and the purpose of his divine creation, as he works out a fruitful and positive relationship with the community in which he lives. Our problem is to re-discover how to help people to live together in community, so that the individual and the various groups each receive their due but do not dominate, and both make their contributions to human happiness. If there have been defects of excessive individualism in some Christian thinking, other streams within the Church, to which the idea of the Church as the ideal community has always meant much more, and which have never lost this emphasis in their social thinking, have also needed to enrich their understanding in the light of modern psychology and sociology. The texture of society is now so much more complex, and movement within it so much more constant, that a simple approach (based, for example, on outmoded hierarchical ideas) is quite inadequate.

Thus theological currents as well as new opportunities helped the Churches to leave behind fairly quickly the inevitable regrets that some of the services which they had tried to render to the needy were to be dealt with more comprehensively by the State. Two things have become increasingly clear. First, statutory services by their very nature provide rather for general and widespread requirements than particular or unusual needs. Secondly, the nature of the need has changed from the purely physical to those arising from a combination of physical, social and psychological factors, where friendliness and the communication of confidence are often important.

There is scope for a great variety of ancillary activities. These may be of the simplest, like help with a hospital library or trolley shop. They may involve an individual in a personal relationship, like befriending and visiting a long-term mental hospital patient who is lonely, and perhaps taking him out. They may include long-term work by a small group, like running a cripples club on church premises. Sometimes the Churches, acting in their own best tradition, will pioneer where others may follow. Thus the Richmond Fellowship* has set up two small communities which act as half-way houses between the mental hospital and the complicated everyday world from which people can go out to work as they are able and gradually learn to organize their lives against a secure background.

It goes without saying that the Churches are also deeply concerned for the statutory social services and those who work in them, and that many Christians are professional social workers or busily engaged in voluntary activities which are not run by specifically Christian bodies. The total picture may be roughly analysed as follows:

(a) Statutory welfare services whose humanitarian purpose is fully supported by the Churches. Contact with the staff, which happily includes many active Christians, is welcomed, and Christians in search of a vocation can often be directed towards these careers.

(b) Voluntary bodies employing full-time professionally trained staff. Sometimes these are agents of the statutory services and some of them are explicitly Christian, e.g. the large moral welfare organization of the Church of England and the National Children's Home (Methodist).

(c) Voluntary bodies channelling mainly part-time services, like the W.V.S., in which many individual Christians are active.

(d) Smaller church organizations or groups using part-time volunteers, e.g. various efforts to help discharged prisoners, some of which have been directly stimulated by the British Council of Churches. Sometimes these activities are a specialized extension of the pastoral work of a minister or priest, like the work of the Rev. Clifford Hill for West Indians in North London.

The various contributions need to be fitted together smoothly. Clergy and ministers and full-time social welfare workers should each know what the other has to offer. The Churches need to be in touch with people outside their own known members in order to make their own best contribution. Some years ago the British Council of Churches organized a conference in Manchester which was intended to be a pilot scheme for other areas too. Against the background of pastoral work mainly in slum areas of Manchester, there were sessions dealing with the plan of the Welfare State, its general problems, the problem family, the care of old people, deprived children, problems of the health services, community centres and the Churches, and social workers and the clergy. The conference is described and summarized in a small book, *Parsons Meet Welfare Workers.*†

* The Richmond Fellowship, Denbridge House, 2 Wells Road, Bickley, Kent.
† Edited by Harold Lees, John Sherratt & Son, Altrincham, 1956.

The results of another important inquiry by the Churches, entitled *Responsibility in the Welfare State*, were published in 1962.* The subtitle was "A study of relationships between the social services and the Churches in a city suburb". One area of Birmingham was carefully investigated to find out what the relations between Churches and the Welfare State actually were, and what further needs there might be which the Churches should help to fill. The extent of unmet need was explored, and a startling amount of social isolation and need for help was revealed.

> Approximately one in every four households in this area are in a situation where some form of voluntary help—to follow the statutory benefit to which they are entitled— would have added to their well-being. Secondly, it has been demonstrated that senior officers and local authority departments recognized that there are limits beyond which, for various reasons, statutory provision does not reach, and are ready to welcome voluntary co-operation—including more specifically co-operation from the Churches —as a supplement to their work. Thirdly it has been shown that many workers in all grades of the statutory services are anxious for more community contacts and would be glad of a closer working relationship with clergy and lay members of local churches.†

After much preparation one person with a telephone was appointed as a centre of contact who would pass on to the appropriate place all calls for help from the Churches. The suburb was divided into seven areas, and in each of these one church had the primary responsibility for dealing with needs that came to light. Joint enterprises were organized, such as visiting flat tenants as they moved in and gradually drawing them into the local community, and discussion with workers from both statutory and voluntary social services. The activities begun as part of the project are continuing and developing in the light of further experience.

Something should also be said about the relationship between some of the fairly extensive services run mainly on voluntary lines and the possible contribution of local churches or councils of churches. In recent years the Home Office has encouraged local churches (and other voluntary organizations) to try to help with the aftercare of offenders. This obviously involved a satisfactory relationship with the network of Discharged Prisoners' Aid Societies. Much of their work is estimable, but difficulties arise in practice. The adequacy of their coverage and resources is variable. Experience suggests that it is not always easy for one voluntary group, based on a local church —willing but having to find its way in a new venture—to channel its contribution into the existing pattern of another, such as a Discharged Prisoners' Aid Society. The latter will have much longer experience, but may already be fully extended. Yet duplication of networks should be unnecessary, even if it were possible. The Social Responsibility Department of the British

---

* Published by Birmingham Council of Christian Churches, 401 Lodge Road, Birmingham, 18.
 † *Responsibility in the Welfare State*, p. 74.

Council of Churches gave evidence to the recent Sub-Committee on the Rehabilitation of Offenders set up by the Home Secretary's Advisory Council on the Treatment of Offenders. It suggested that there should be statutory provision of a skeleton framework of permanent and dependable sources of aftercare all over the country, to assess the need of those who have been in detention, to deal with the more exacting needs, and to co-ordinate efficiently the efforts of various voluntary groups.

In general it is evident that the Churches are becoming increasingly aware that a comparatively affluent society may well have more social problems rather than less, though they will be of a rather different type from the simple physical needs which the Churches of an older generation mainly tried to meet. Because the nature of the problem has changed it is clear that if the Churches are to help their members to make a useful contribution they will have to persuade them and provide them with some simple training or background for many forms of voluntary work. The texture of society is now so complex that well-meaning ignorance can lead to disastrous results.

There is one question which keeps cropping up in different ways in discussion of these topics—the question of responsibility. We no longer suppose that when a family, or some of its members, cannot cope with its situation in some way, it is simply its own fault. But it may sometimes be at least partly at fault even if the social environment must share the responsibility. Do the welfare services sometimes obscure or discourage personal responsibility? On the other hand, does society sometimes shelve its responsibility, leaving it to "the welfare" and assuming that this is enough? This is relevant both in regard to proper use of social services and to the question of moral accountability. It is too early for a consensus, but the issue will continue to crop up.

62. Welfare Work in the Methodist Church

Rev. Kenneth G. Greet

A Secretary at the Department of Christian Citizenship of the
Methodist Church

RIGHT at the heart of the city of Bristol, surrounded by the bright shops and splendid offices which have replaced the buildings bombed during the Second World War, stands John Wesley's "New Room". It is the oldest Methodist Chapel in the world. The visitor has to cross a quiet courtyard and pass the equestrian statue of the little man who was both evangelist and social reformer and who helped under God to change the face of eighteenth-century England. The building contains many interesting features. There is the stable for the preacher's horse, and the rooms which were used as a dispensary for the sick, and an almonry for the poor. Wesley was a very practical saint, and his book *Primitive Physic* contained scores of homely remedies which he prescribed for those who were ill.

It is not surprising that the great Church which grew out of the work of John and Charles Wesley and which now has a world membership of some 19 million should be devoted, in a variety of ways, to the welfare of the people. The shape of its welfare work, like that of other voluntary agencies, has altered as the State has assumed more and more responsibilities. The impetus towards more comprehensive state-provided facilities has often been accelerated by the pressures which Methodism, in company with other bodies, has exerted. The Central Missions which Methodism erected in the centre of most of the large centres of population around the turn of the present century did an incalculable amount of good in providing relief for the poor and hungry. The present writer served in a mission which provided cheap daily dinners for the members of a depressed mining community. When unemployment was at its height in the area the Mission provided free soup and ran a clothing centre and boot-repairing shop. Though the need is nothing like as great in these days, some Methodist Missions still help the poor with cheap meals and clothing.

It will be convenient to set forth under headings the main forms of welfare work now undertaken by the Methodist Church.

Homes for Unmarried Mothers

There are several homes for unmarried mothers. Two of these in London,

484

run by the Women's Fellowship of the Church (Susanna Wesley House, Stothard Place, London, E.C. 2), receive over 100 young mothers every year.

National Children's Home

This Methodist Institution has thirty-nine branches in various parts of the United Kingdom, and its "family" (at 31 March 1964) was made up as follows: in the Home's normal branches and hostels, 1279; in its medical and remedial branches, 336; in its approved schools, 190; in private homes by boarding-out payments, 197; in private homes by adoption where contact is maintained, 900; children who have left the home but who remain under its supervision, 219; children for whose aftercare the home has taken responsibility under Section 34 of the Children Act, 1948, 220. Help has also been given to more than 200 other children. There were 1529 applications from would-be adopters during the year. There were 1479 applications for admission of children during the year. The total number of women child-care staff (including sisters) was 540. The maintenance of the work reflected in these statistics costs over £1 million a year. (Headquarters office: Highbury Park. London, N. 5.)

Methodist Homes for the Aged

These homes are situated in various parts of the country and provide accommodation for more than 500 elderly people. Further homes are being constructed. Residents have their own private bed-sitting-room (some of the rooms are designed for married couples) (Plates 43–4). The amount paid varies according to means. There is a communal lounge and dining hall and a sick bay for those who are ill or bed-ridden. (Headquarters office: 1, Central Buildings, Westminster, London, S.W. 1).

Methodist International Houses

These are centres for the accommodation of students, the largest being in London (at 4 Inverness Terrace, London, W. 2). In a typical year the London House is used for longer or shorter periods by an average of 1500 students from 95 countries representing all parts of the Christian Church and of other faiths. Social and cultural facilities are provided and an immense amount of work is done in helping students to find accommodation and in solving their many problems. The Methodist Church also helps coloured immigrants in a variety of other ways.

The West London Mission

Reference was made in the introduction to this article of the welfare work undertaken by the Central Missions. The most extensive programme is that of the West London Mission (Headquarters at Kingsway Hall, Kingsway, London, W.C. 2). This was founded by the great Christian social reformer Hugh Price Hughes, who came to west London in 1887. He brought into being numerous centres for the relief of the poor, the sick and the old. Now the Mission, in addition to the worshipful activities at its centre in Kingsway, runs a crèche for children, a hostel for alcoholics, two homes for expectant unmarried mothers, several residences for the aged and for young people in need of care, a holiday centre and a clothing store.

Prison and Hospital Chaplains

The Methodist Church has part-time chaplains at many of the country's prisons and hospitals. They do an incalculable amount of good in helping men and women through times of great difficulty and depression.

The Methodist Relief Fund

This is part of the greater work of relief undertaken by the British and World Councils of Churches. The Fund now administers over £30,000 per annum which comes from voluntary giving. It has assisted in numerous projects for the relief of refugees and has helped to build several villages in Hong-Kong. Increasingly it is able to support long-term relief and rehabilitation projects such as an orphanage in Nigeria for motherless babies whose chance of survival would otherwise not be good. The Fund also provides assistance for some within the United Kingdom who are in distress because of sudden disaster or personal misfortune. (Headquarters office: The Department of Christian Citizenship, 1 Central Buildings, Westminster, London, S.W.1.)

The Department of Christian Citizenship

The Department just referred to is also responsible for "the effective presentation of the Christian Social Witness". This involves the preparation of judgements and the offering of practical guidance on a variety of matters many of which fall within the field of welfare work (e.g. the Department has presented to the Church a comprehensive statement on the housing problem, on suicide and on the care of handicapped children).

It should be said at the conclusion of this brief review of some of the specific ways in which the Methodist Church is involved in welfare work that the normal pastoral work of ministers and deaconesses makes a very great contribution to the varying needs of men and women. This is a matter which can never be reflected in any statistical figures, but, particularly in the case of hospital, prison and industrial chaplaincies, the amount of service rendered is beyond reckoning.

With the increasing provision of state welfare services, some of which were pioneered by the Church and other voluntary agencies, the shape of the Church's responsibility alters. But there remain large opportunities of supplementing the state services and of filling the gaps that statutory organization is always bound to leave.

63. Roman Catholic Welfare Services

Rev. H. O. Waterhouse, s.j.

Priest-Director, Catholic Social Guild, Oxford

THE most highly organized welfare work in the Catholic body in Britain, that which is carried out by the diocesan Rescue Societies acting directly under ecclesiastical authority, is concerned mainly with children and therefore falls outside the scope of this symposium. The activity which is most likely to spring to people's minds when Catholic adult welfare is mentioned is that which is performed by the Society of Saint Vincent de Paul, an autonomous lay society with national and regional organization but which operates mostly at parish level. It is distinguished for the counsel and material assistance given to the poor in the best Christian tradition of hidden generosity.

In addition to this can be found a whole range of welfare work which is done under Catholic auspices though not necessarily coming directly under ecclesiastical authority and control. One cannot, of course, assess the contribution made by public-spirited Catholics (one would call them the best sort of Catholics) to welfare work organized by others.

It would be an impossible task, as well as tedious for the reader, to try to convey a complete picture by way of a catalogue; so much of the work is spasmodic and incidental to other activities engaged in by lay societies and religious orders. There are, for example, in the Archdiocese of Westminster alone (i.e. London north of the Thames, Middlesex and Hertfordshire) 97 orders of women distributed in 175 convents, and while most of the sisters will be engaged in full-time teaching and a good proportion in nursing, it is common to find, even in the case of the teaching orders, that convents seek out welfare work of some sort to help to nourish the spirit of charity amongst their members. Often enough it will be no more than *ad hoc* works of mercy, visits to families in distress and so on, and therefore spasmodic; though it is astonishing with what regularity there can be found still at the doors of some convents a string of tramps enjoying a snack.

Much even of that which is more permanent and organized will have to go unrecorded here: one can only pick out some typical examples in the hope that this will give the reader some idea of what is being achieved.

Of the religious sisters whose main occupation lies in welfare one can mention the Little Sisters of the Poor. These take a vow to practise "hospitality towards the aged poor". They have in Great Britain twenty-four large houses to which people of any religion are admitted.

For the poor who are sick at home it would be hard to find welfare work superior in quality to that done by the Little Sisters of the Assumption. These train as nurses and then give themselves without fee to the care of the sick in workingmen's homes, not only giving them skilled nursing but attending to household tasks and preparing meals for the family. Little wonder that they complain they are too few in number to cope with the calls made upon their services. They have four convents in London and five in various parts of the provinces.

Much more numerous are the Sisters of the Good Shepherd who specialize in caring for problem and delinquent girls and women. They run approved schools, homes for unmarried mothers and their babies, nurseries and training schools, even a "Magdalen Monastery" where women who have been on the streets can take permanent refuge, adopting the life of prayer, penance and work which is normal for communities of nuns. There are 300 Good Shepherd sisters in the English province.

Work for the mentally subnormal and physically handicapped is also undertaken by various congregations of religious sisters. It is not easy to draw the line here between what is welfare and what should be more strictly classed as medical care; but it would be wrong to omit all reference to the institutions listed in the *Catholic Directory* under the title "Hospice for the Dying". These are to be found in Hackney, Liverpool, Clydebank and Airdrie; three of them staffed by the Irish Sisters of Charity and one by the Sisters of Charity of St. Vincent de Paul.

The last-named congregation, whose habit has long been a very familiar sight in the slum areas of many of our large cities, engage in a multitude of charitable works, many of which rank as welfare of a high degree. They care for the blind, the deaf and dumb, mental defectives, cripples, deprived children, delinquents, girls in need of moral welfare and stranded women whom the Police bring to their night shelters. All this in addition to the thousand and one tasks assigned them by the priests of the parishes in which they operate as general social workers.

Less noticed by the outside world is the work done in the "Nazareth Houses". Here are gathered the aged poor of both sexes and orphan and destitute children. There are thirty-two such houses in Great Britain staffed by the Poor Sisters of Nazareth.

If pride of place in Catholic welfare work must be yielded to the religious orders (and not exclusively to the women's congregations: one can instance the Sons of Divine Providence who care for old people and the Brothers Hospitallers of St. John of God who look after mental defectives and the chronic sick) it would be wrong to omit mention of some lay societies which provide welfare work for their members. The widespread Catholic Women's

League expects it from its members, but for the most part leaves the initiative to local groups. The Legion of Mary gives special attention to the provision of hostels for girls who might otherwise be in moral danger; the Marillacs are an association of young women who visit and assist poor and lonely old people. There is a Catholic Housing Society in London, registered as Hearth and Home Ltd., which provides accommodation for the aged and is seeking to add a nursing home to the flats already occupied. A comparative new-comer is the Catholic Handicapped Children's Fellowship, which has already established itself in many dioceses and has a registered national office in Sussex.

Most of this extensive activity has grown haphazardly without following any uniform pattern or having any overall organization imposed from above by ecclesiastical authority to secure the most economic use of the manpower or womanpower available. It has not sprung up as a result of academic researches pointing to some need: it has been the fruit of observation made on the spot by Christians with their eyes open for cases of distress. Although enterprises have often been launched because of the energetic promptings of a priest or bishop, there is little, apart from the rescue work referred to at the beginning of this article, for which ecclesiastical authority has assumed organizing responsibility. If it be a characteristic of Catholicism that in the matter of belief the individual looks to authority in the Church for guidance, in the matter of expressing his Christianity in suitable forms of work for others he is left largely to exercise his private judgement. Exhortation he will receive from above, but not explicit instructions.

One must not, therefore, expect to find in the Catholic body any sort of central board for co-ordinating the welfare work undertaken by Catholic societies or for giving guidance on the training of those who want to do it in a scientific way. Nevertheless, there is increasing recognition that the circumstances of today call for intelligent as well as devoted service, and that those who are to give of their best can only do so by being thoroughly up to date and taking advantage of the findings of scientific research. This is a trend that must be welcomed.

It calls sometimes for adaptations that break long and precious traditions, and when the modifications in methods involve extensive building alterations to large establishments the cost can be very heavy. There is irony in the fact that the breaking up of the large children's homes and orphanages into smaller units which facilitate modern methods of child care is being done under pressure from without because of the more widespread appreciation of the values of family life which Catholics have always held dear.

It may be that even more adaptation will be called for in the treatment of delinquents and the old. The trends made manifest by this book will be a pointer to them. What is quite certain is that Catholics are taught by the highest authority in the Church not to wait passively for social trends to reveal themselves as established practices, to be welcomed or opposed as the case may be; but rather to use their wits and their enthusiasm to give social movements a Christian direction. This, indeed, is the very theme of Pope John XXIII's masterly encyclical *Mater et Magistra*: how to bring into line with Christian precepts modern trends in the social order.

64. The Social Services of the Salvation Army

R. W. BOVAN

Chief Secretary, Salvation Army Men's Social Services

THE Salvation Army was born in 1865 in the East End of London. In its early days men starved to death, and their bodies were found in the streets. In 1866 the cholera epidemic caused more than 8000 deaths in that area; drunkenness was rife and seemed inevitable with all its concomitants of moral degradation and material squalor.

With the disappearance of much primary poverty and the inception and development of the Welfare State much of the social work undertaken by the pioneer voluntary organizations has inevitably changed; indeed, many a "charity" initiated to meet a specific need has long since ceased to be required.

Why then does the Salvation Army persist, and why does the demand for its services not diminish? The answer may well be found to some extent in the foresight and wisdom of its Founder, and in the wide humanitarian warmth of its religion.

William Booth once described himself as "fishing in the sewers for the souls of men". His charge to his soldiers was "go for souls, and go for the worst". In simple words he meant care for people, the more degraded they appear the more they need you, go where the need is greatest.

This wide and wise humanity has meant that for the Salvation Army Officer engaged in its social services, the man is far more important than the machine.

William Booth noted that:

> Most schemes that are put forward for the improvement of the circumstances of the people are either avowedly or actually limited to those whose actual condition least need amelioration. Remedies are propounded which if adopted tomorrow will only affect the aristocracy of the miserable; it is the thrifty, the industrious, the sober, the thoughtful who can take advantage of these plans. No one will ever make even a visible dint on the morass of squalor, who does not deal with the improvident, the lazy, the vicious and the criminal.

The Salvation Army avowedly seeks the social rehabilitation as well as the spiritual salvation of the improvident, the lazy, the vicious and the criminal.

Not by his faith and humanity alone did William Booth build well. He showed also a wisdom in advance of his age, he had an understanding of men

492

and women that is astonishing. One declared object of the National Council for Alcoholism is to make clear that "Alcoholism is a disease".

Nearly seventy years earlier, in *In Darkest England and Way Out*, William Booth wrote:

> While in one case drunkenness may be resolved into a habit, in another it must be accounted a disease; what is wanted in the one case therefore is some method of moving the man out of the sphere of the temptation, and in the other, for treating the passion as a disease, bringing to bear upon it every agency, hygienic and otherwise, calculated to effect a cure.

The term "alcoholic" is of fairly recent origin, but the Salvation Army has been working among those suffering from this disease for many years. In a number of countries the sufferer is assisted by every available means; psychiatric, medical or social as well as by religious means.

The publication of Booth's work in 1890 did not mark the inception of the social services of the Salvation Army; these grew spontaneously as the needs became apparent. When Booth first realized the plight of the homeless he instructed his son to open hostels for them. He said in effect, "get a factory, get any building, put in warmth and light, arrange for food and take these men off the streets". With the "shelters" the need for "lodging houses" became apparent. These have now been in existence for many years; not on a profit-making basis, but as a provision to meet human need. Many of those factories, acquired as a result of William Booth's realization of the urgent need of his day, are still in use, and though in need of replacement they cannot be relinquished. They provide cheap lodgings for 8,000 men nightly in Great Britain—a home for the homeless. This number tends to increase, despite prophesies of some social workers. No longer is the cost of this provision a charge on charitable funds. The population of these hostels is divided roughly:

(1) Forty-five per cent in employment.
   These are men (a) with matrimonial problems; (b) affected by housing clearance schemes or housing shortage; (c) away from home in seasonal employment; (d) who are rootless.
(2) Twenty-five per cent old age pensioners who choose the hostel way of life.
(3) Twenty per cent unemployed or semi-handicapped and often unemployable.
(4) Ten per cent casuals—"problem men" often "running away" from life.

The National Assistance Board meets the basic costs for many men, while others find the needed cash from National Health Insurance payments or unemployment pay. In 1962, however, 18,000 free beds (and breakfasts) were given to needy men. In addition to shelter and food provided these places are designed to encourage thrift and, where necessary, to place men in useful work; here also the man may find helpers competent to advise him on his personal problems. If he will accept it, psychiatric services are at his disposal and, in London, a Chiropody Clinic is available should he require it. In all this social work there is no attempt to compel a man in any way with respect to his religion.

For over half a century the "Army" has been caring for the aged. This need has not diminished with the inception of the National Health Service, for while increasing geriatric skill has enabled hospitals to abolish the old chronic sick wards, there are still a large number of people who, while not ill enough to tie up a hospital bed, are still quite unable to care for themselves. In the Eventide Homes of the Salvation Army many such are finding in their latter days a refuge and a home.

There are many old people, men rather than women, who want no such provision. For them, these places spell loss of freedom. They do not want the small flatlet so eagerly sought by others, they rather desire the unfettered life of the lodging house; a bed and breakfast; adequate hot water; someone to make the bed, and, for the rest, just to do as they please.

This service the Salvation Army Hostel provides, while unobtrusively, in the background, officers watch over the old men in every way.

Domiciliary care, friendly visiting, and practical assistance are given, and club facilities are provided in some 300 centres.

For eighty years the Salvation Army has faced the personal and social problems associated with the unmarried mother and her child. Service in this field has included not only institutional care, but the training of mid-wives, and the provision of hospital care. The Mothers' Hospital and Training School for Midwives has achieved world-wide renown, not only for the excellence of its training, but also for the standard of its "obstetric" and "paediatric" work.

Care for needy and delinquent children is undertaken in children's homes; homes and hostels for working girls and boys; approved schools; approved probation homes and hostels; in these places full facilities are given for training in many practical fields and rehabilitation in good citizenship.

Large numbers of discharged prisoners are assisted; many of them come as a result of the activities of discharged prisoners' aid societies and probation officers.

In a large country mansion ex-prisoners are received, with their families, in order that a new life may be properly begun. This rehabilitation centre is meeting a great need in resolving domestic strain and enabling life-partners to start life afresh.

In the west country a "Harbour Light Residence" provides a home where alcoholics are received and helped; here, with work and food and "group therapy", the medical care of a local practitioner, and the constant watchfulness of the Warden and his wife, men who had long ago given up all hope are gaining new strength and in a number of cases being re-united with their families, "dried out", and with a great hope of living useful lives thereafter.

Unique among social services is the highly successful missing persons work of the Salvation Army. This is undertaken at the Headquarters of the Men's Social Services by an Investigation Department which claims a success rate of 62 per cent in reuniting inquirers with loved ones. The study of the files of this Department will convince any honest inquirer of the immense social problems arising from the disappearance of loved ones, bread-winners and others. The Women's Social Work undertakes the search for missing husbands and putative fathers.

An Anti-suicide Bureau, which has been successful in averting many would-be suicides from their intention, is also based on the Men's Social Services Headquarters.

Officers of the Salvation Army visit more than ninety prisons in Great Britain regularly, and in 1962 held nearly 12,000 interviews. The officers responsible for this service also visit and assist the relatives of prisoners, trying to maintain the often severely strained family ties, and at the same time giving practical help and advice. By this watchful care and the imaginative plan by which many hundreds of prisoners' children receive gifts at Christmas time, the Army is endeavouring to prevent the ill consequences to the future generation of that sense of embitterment which so often comes to the families of those who are in prison.

The Salvation Army looks to the future aware that the charter of its social services is broadly based and sound, seeking only to help wherever there is need.

65. Welfare Work of the Anglo-Jewish Community

MONTAGUE RICHARDSON

Welfare and Youth Officer, Jewish Institute Advisory Centre

THE Biblical injunction "Love thy neighbour as thyself" and the Hebrew word for charity, *Zedakah*, which is derived from the word meaning "justice", have always been the mainspring of Jewish endeavour in the field of social welfare. In most communities it was the religious authorities who were the pioneers in social work, and the Synagogue was no exception. From earliest times it was at the Synagogue that "bread was given to wayfarers and charity to the poor". Although certain specialized institutions were established earlier, it was not until the middle of the nineteenth century that a more systematic approach was made to the whole problem of social welfare, when it was realized that mere alms-giving and the relief of distress without rehabilitation was inadequate.

At all times it was of paramount importance to help the poor of the Jewish community in the fulfilment of their religious responsibilities in the sphere of worship and the Jewish Dietary Laws.

The Jewish Welfare Board

Although most of the large provincial towns had their own arrangements for helping those in need, it was in London that the major Jewish welfare organizations came into being. The principal organization is the Board of Guardians and Trustees for the relief of the Jewish poor (now known as the Jewish Welfare Board), 74a Charlotte Street, London, W.1. This was founded in 1859 and covers a wide field of welfare work including departments for the welfare of old people, welfare and employment of boys and girls, welfare of women and children, convalescence and loans and general welfare. Each department is staffed by professional social workers assisted by committees of voluntary workers. The Board has residential homes for children, catering especially for the needs of those who are homeless or whose home life is unsatisfactory.

Since 1945 there has been a marked expansion in the work for the aged. The first homes to be established were for the able-bodied, but it was soon realized that these did not meet the needs of all the aged. Some were capable of looking after themselves and preparing their own meals, but would benefit from a helping hand in emergencies.

For these, flatlets were the answer as they enabled elderly people to lead independent lives. For others, more nursing attention was necessary than usually provided in a normal home, and for these a home for the infirm aged was established. It was also realized that some elderly people displayed symptoms of senility which made them unsuitable for residence in the ordinary home but did not warrant their admission to a mental hospital, and for these a home for the mentally ageing was opened. New homes and flatlets are at present under construction, which will enable many more elderly Jewish people to be accommodated.

The Jewish Welfare Board has been particularly successful in helping boys and girls enter suitable trades and professions, for not only are introductions given to suitable employers, but also, where necessary, tools are provided and fees paid.

Through its special work for the welfare of boys and girls from unsatisfactory home backgrounds and for those displaying anti-social tendencies, the Board, in co-operation with other organizations, has helped to make the problem of juvenile delinquency of minor significance in the Anglo-Jewish community. (The two Jewish Approved Schools have only a small proportion of Jewish pupils.)

The United Synagogue

The United Synagogue, Woburn House, Upper Woburn Place, London W.C.1, founded in 1870 as an amalgamation of various synagogues, has concentrated especially in the religious aspect of welfare work. Through its Bequests and Trusts Committee it continues to administer the more traditional forms of charity associated with earlier years, such as the distribution of marriage portions, New Year and Passover gifts, bread and coal tickets, etc. Through its Mutual Aid Fund, financial help by the way of a loan or grant is available to the business man in difficulties. The Visitation Committee consisting of representatives of most of the religious sections of the Jewish community is responsible for arranging visits by ministers and laymen to Jewish patients in hospitals and similar institutions, and also those in prisons, remand homes and Borstal institutions, etc.

The Welfare Committee of the United Synagogue, in addition to organizing special religious services for children and young people, helps in the religious and cultural work in Jewish Youth Clubs. It is also responsible for administration of the Jewish Institute Advisory Centre in the East End of London, which was founded in 1905, and is a forerunner of the Citizens' Advice Bureaux, which are now playing such an important role in the general community.

Youth Work

In the latter part of the nineteenth century the social consciences of the more affluent section of the Jewish community—together with so many others—were stirred by the existence of poverty and degradation in the slum areas of the large towns. Clubs were founded to help young people in these areas in their leisure time. The keynote of this work was the personal participation by adults from wealthy and cultured backgrounds who shared their leisure with the youngsters. In the case of the Jewish community it was reinforced by the need to help the children of the more recent immigrants to Great Britain adjust themselves rapidly to life in a new country. The first Girls' Club was established in 1896, and in the same year the first Boys' Club, both of which still continue to flourish. Through the very high quality of the adults, who worked in a voluntary capacity, tremendous progress was achieved and many new clubs were founded, most with their own premises. The clubs co-operated in 1899 to form the Jewish Athletic Association, which subsequently developed into the Association for Jewish Youth, 33 Henriques Street, London, E.1. The aims of these clubs are to foster devotion to Judaism and maintain high standards of citizenship. The Association is actively associated with the work of youth organizations in the general community, and is in constant liaison with the Ministry of Education and with local authorities.

Among the outstanding developments in recent years have been the erection of club buildings incorporating the most up-to-date ideas of layout and décor to permit a wide range of activities—cultural, artistic and physical. Of even greater significance has been the appointment of professional-trained youth leaders, for until the Second World War the conduct of club work was entirely in the hands of volunteers, but now the volunteers, fortunately, still remain, but in partnership with the professionals.

Until the Second World War, the cost of running clubs had to be met entirely from voluntary funds, but since that time the Jewish Club Movement, like the rest of the club movement, has benefited from generous grants made both by the Ministry of Education and local authorities towards capital and other forms of expenditure.

Clubs for the Elderly

In more recent years another club movement has been established, but this time not for the young, but for those reaching retirement age. Under the auspices of the Association of Jewish friendship Clubs, Absa House, 46 Commercial Road, London, E.1, nearly 100 clubs exist in London and the main provincial centres. Noteworthy have been the clubs established in residential homes. This movement developed from the joint sponsorship of the League of Jewish Women and the Welfare Committee of the United Synagogue.

Specialized Agencies

From early days the need for specialized institutions for sections of the community was recognized. As far back as 1795 an orphan asylum was established which subsequently became known as the Jewish Orphanage and is now called the Norwood Home for Jewish Children. For many years housed in a large building, the children are now distributed in small family homes, each with its own house mother or father. The children attend local schools, and the aim is always to help them integrate into the general community.

In 1747 the Spanish and Portugese Jewish Community established its Beth Holim Home for the Aged at 253 Mile End Road, London, E.1.

In 1819 the Jewish Blind Society was founded, 1 Craven Hill, Lancaster Gate, London, W.1. This organization carries out extensive welfare work for Jewish blind throughout the United Kingdom. It has homes for the blind and infirm blind and also a holiday home. In addition it sponsors social clubs for those who continue to live in their homes.

In 1840 the Home for Aged Jews, 105 Nightingale Lane, London, S.W.12, was established, and within recent years extensions have been made to the original building to allow many of the elderly residents to occupy small bedrooms and also to permit the nursing of the infirm in properly equipped infirmary wards.

In 1863 the Residential School for Jewish Deaf Children, 101 Nightingale Lane, London, S.W.12, was founded. Jewish deaf children are admitted as residential pupils from the age of 3, and receive instruction in their faith as well as in the usual deaf-school curriculum.

In 1889 the Home and Hospital for Jewish Incurables, 295 High Road, London, N.15, was established, and is responsible for the care and medical treatment of Jewish persons permanently disabled by disease or deformity.

With the development of welfare services throughout the community, and with the greater financial participation of the State and local authorities, it has become possible to give even greater attention to those in need of specialized care. As a direct result two new associations have been established in post-war years. In 1951 the Jewish Association to Aid Backward Children, 18 Seymour Place, London, W.1, which maintains residential schools and homes for the care of mentally retarded and handicapped children, which has pioneered new educational techniques for helping such children. In 1955 the Jewish Association for the Physically Handicapped, 43 Whitley Court, London, W.C.1, was founded, which provides a holiday home for adults and also for Jewish children and also organizes clubs for them.

Social Work for the General Community

The Jewish Community is not only concerned with the needs of its own members, and through such organizations as the League of Jewish Women and the Association of Jewish Ex-Servicemen, Jewish men and women are encouraged to participate in social welfare work of the wider community and thereby contribute to the national life.

Although many societies continue to support the charitable objects for which they were founded many years ago, there is now a much greater awareness of the need for a more systematic approach to welfare work, and an increasing readiness to appoint trained social workers and to accord them professional status.

66. A Church Settlement in East London*

HELEN M. ROSS
Previously Chairman of the Committee of the Presbyterian Settlement

THE Presbyterian Settlement in East London was founded in 1899.

East London has been a problem area for centuries. Its history has been dominated by two factors—its situation on the River Thames and its nearness to the City of London. Along the river the demands of shipping and ship-building resulted in the growth of riverside hamlets which were notorious for their overcrowding, their filth, their vice and their lawlessness. Inland, the villages took the overflow of the London population: not only the wealthy who wished for country homes within reach of the City but criminals hiding from justice, workmen seeking to evade the strict regulations of the City guilds, and industries unwanted in the City because of their smell, noise or danger. The area also attracted a steady inflow of countrymen seeking their fortune, and a spasmodic invasion of foreign refugees who could find no homes within the City walls. It became the centre of new industries created to meet the needs and opportunities of the City market. Its local government, intended for a rural community, was never either strong enough or flexible enough to cope with the economy or lawlessness of its ever-growing population, and its relations with the City were frequently strained. These factors have been strangely constant, and there has been a remarkable continuity in the problems that have arisen in the area. Reading about conditions in East London today one finds oneself time and again transported back centuries to earlier efforts to deal with similar situations. The river may overflow its banks less frequently, but the flood of 1928 which submerged part of Poplar and Millwall and made many houses uninhabitable was a direct lineal descendant of the "huge flood" of 1352 "occasioned by vehement tempests from the sea . . . which ran over all the said banks and ditches". The housing problem now is on a scale that no sixteenth-century Elizabethan could have conceived to be possible; but the proclamation in 1580 that no more houses were to be built within three miles of the City and that not more than one family should live in one house showed a premonition of things to come. The 1958 newspaper headline "Stepney prostitutes 'worst of the lot' " is a reminder of the fact that the "Tigeresses of Ratcliff Highway" made a considerable figure in East End journalism in the past; while the headline

* Based on an article which appeared under the title "Sixty Years in East London" in the *Journal of the Presbyterian Historical Society of England*, Vol. 11, No. 4, 1959.

501

"Police Sergeant says man 'lunged' at him with knife", though it speaks of an exceptional happening now, would have been a commonplace in the days when no policeman dare venture alone into certain areas in the district.

But if the stage was set in earlier centuries for East London to develop as it did, it was the Industrial Revolution that created the appalling situation with which local government, the social services and the Churches have been struggling ever since. The factors which have made it what it was were just the factors to make it a centre of expansion where trade and industry developed. The building of docks, canals, roads and railways brought workmen in their thousands from all over the British Isles; the transport facilities encouraged the establishment of new factories; and the local government was totally unsuited to deal with the problems arising from the sudden influx of population. The result was chaos. There was never enough accommodation for the people, though speculative builders covered all the available space with houses—buying up the houses of middle-class folk who moved out of the district and squeezing in a group of cottages where there had been a garden, or filling up marsh land with household refuse and building on it. The little four-roomed houses which were the norm were as often as not inhabited by two or three families, and it was not uncommon for a family to have only one room. Sanitation was almost non-existent, and in some places there were open drains in the streets. It was not till 1852 that the provision of water to the houses was made compulsory; but even then the water company had not sufficient equipment to provide it. As late as 1870 there was a street where 250 people shared one water-tap which was put on for twenty-five minutes a day, Sundays excepted. This lack of accommodation and sanitation was accompanied by dire poverty. Wages were a mere pittance and employment insecure, and the people were ill fed and ill clothed. It was small wonder that epidemics devastated the area and that disease, drink, prostitution and lawlessness were a perpetual problem: the wonder is that in spite of it all—and this is the opinion of the majority of observers—the East End of London was fundamentally a respectable and self-respecting area.

The persistence of these problems into the twentieth century is illustrated in the Annual Reports of the Presbyterian Settlement in Poplar. In 1902 it is said: "Many of the babies who used to be brought to the crèche have died during the last two months." We often hear it said: "We cannot grieve. The children are taken away from their misery." In 1904 the warden wrote: "Theoretically we disapprove of relief giving, but when we come face to face with men, women and children well-nigh starving, is it possible to withhold a ticket for milk, groceries or coal? In justice, we must mention that it is in very few cases are we asked for relief, and that when such is bestowed the gratitude is great." In 1906 she wrote: "The majority do not want charity, they want work, and because it is so scarce men, women, and children are starving day after day in this wealthy England of ours." As late as 1913 the Report contains this: "Although we have a warm welcome in the houses of the women it is sometimes difficult not to turn coward and shrink from the evil-smelling streets with tumble-down houses, ragged women gossiping and dirty children playing." Distress, unemployment and housing are recurrent themes in the reports, as also are the accounts of the great numbers of invalid children and cripples, and of the exacting lives led by the factory girls and the temptations with which they were faced. Even today, when the social services and the Welfare State have achieved a transformation which is little less than miraculous, housing, unemployment and vice remain to take their place alongside some of the newer problems of the area; and the majority of the old houses still have only a cold water supply and no inside sanitation.

The Churches in the East End did all they could to evangelize their neighbours, and in this they were supported by their fellow Christians outside the area. A pattern of church life was built up with mothers' meetings, clubs, large Sunday schools and all manner of other agencies which might attract and help, while gifts of money and clothing poured in, and large numbers of voluntary workers came to their assistance. But the churches remained comparatively empty, and as the middle classes moved further and further away from the district it became increasingly difficult to finance the work and find leaders. Moreover the whole area became working-class. As one shocked writer in 1900 described it: "One meets no ladies in the principal thoroughfares; there is not visible anywhere the outward indication of wealth. People, shops, houses, conveyances—all together are stamped with the unmistakable seal of the working class." It was to counteract this that the Settlement Movement sprang into being in the 1880's. The original aim of the movement was to bridge the gap between the working and upper classes by providing centres where people from the upper classes could live in working-class areas and break down the barriers by friendship, service and education. This movement was essentially Christian in origin; and though the prototype Settlement, Toynbee Hall, was non-denominational and primarily concerned with education, and many later settlements were purely philanthropic, the Churches took up the idea and denominational settlements were founded.

But though the Settlement's work for the Churches did not in fact increase church membership as it was hoped, this was not caused by lack of a church-centred policy on the part of the Settlement leaders. It was always their object to integrate the mothers' meetings into the congregations to which they were attached. The mothers' meeting at Bow, for example, was given up when the church at Bow was closed on the ground that a mothers' meeting that was not based on a church had no point. Care was taken to interest the women in the concerns of the Church. Branches of the Women's Missionary Association were formed and, poor though they were, the women were encouraged to make their contributions for church work. Moreover, these meetings were frequently devotional. Looking at them objectively one cannot but feel that they had a very great intrinsic value. They were not only "havens of rest and comfort where trouble may for a time be laid aside", but they provided Christian teaching and services of worship of a kind which the women could understand and which appealed to their emotions in a setting in which they felt at home, thus putting Christian ideals before many a woman who would otherwise never have heard of them. What if these ideals made no appreciable impact on the lives of a considerable number of them; cannot the same be said of church members? And what if many of them were Methodists on Tuesdays, Presbyterians on Wednesdays and Anglicans on Thursdays; thus getting a triple dose of devotion as well as three outings in the summer? To put it at its lowest value, they were better at these meetings than at the public houses. One cannot but feel that the work done by the Settlement for the surrounding congregations had an enduring value which cannot be assessed by the success or failure of its efforts to build up church membership.

But from the very beginning the Settlement found that it had another task beyond that of helping the congregations. As will have been seen from the introduction to this article, the social conditions were an outrage to the Christian conscience. Canon Wilberforce, living outside the area, might say complacently that the state of the poor was, with all its evils, "better than they deserved at the hands of God", and that the existing social order combined "the greatest measure of temporal comforts and spiritual privileges"; but those on the spot could not see the situation as the will of God nor refrain from doing their utmost to help. Moreover, they soon discovered that help needed to be skilled if it was to be effective. The Report of 1909 points out that "many an earnest worker for Christ makes mistakes from ignorance of the social problems of the day, and there is much mis-spent and ill-directed charity. On the other hand, Social Work without religion leads nowhere and has little permanent value. Realizing that these two must go hand in hand, the Committee has arranged a series of conferences on Religious and Social Subjects." Social service came increasingly on the time-table, and in 1908 Health Visitation, Charity Organization Society, Children's Care Committees and Bromley Sick Asylum were added to the activities. To these in 1910 were added visits for the Ragged School Union and Invalid Children's Aid Association, and the Settlement workers began to attend lectures at the School of Sociology. The Children's Country Holiday Fund, which was to play a large part in the life of the Settlement from then on, was added in 1911. Indeed, so many and various did the social activities of the Settlement become that they cannot be enumerated: suffice it to say that work among boys and men was started during the First World War, and that the Citizens' Advice Bureau—now one of the most important of the Settlement activities

—was started during the Second World War. Since 1929 deaconesses have gone to the Settlement for part of their training. In 1934 it was recognized as a club leaders' training centre by the National Council of Girls' Clubs, and it also takes social science students for practical training.

The value of all this social work has to be considered not only in the light of the countless lives that were made easier by the help and friendship of Settlement workers, but for the part it played in the transformation of the district from its squalid chaos at the end of the nineteenth century to its well-ordered and comparatively prosperous state today. The borough councils, on whom lay the main responsibility for establishing order, were created in 1901. What it meant to Poplar to have the Presbyterian Settlement and others like it can be deduced from the Settlement reports. The participation of the Settlement in the various organizations usually started from their inception, and the phrase "the Borough Council asked us to provide" is a recurring one. Sometimes the Settlement was a pioneer, and borough action followed in its wake. Sometimes its function was to point out action that was necessary, sometimes it provided officers or members for committees or workers to undertake tasks sponsored by the council; and sometimes it came to the assistance of individuals whose needs could not be met by the local administration. Not the least of the contributions of the Settlement was the part played by the most notable of its wardens, Miss Helen Mackay, who in 1913 was elected a member of the Board of Guardians. She was also a Justice of the Peace, and in 1921 the Council showed its appreciation of her services by electing her an alderman; this latter position, however, she soon resigned on account of the pressure of her other duties. Her concern for social legislation is reflected in the Settlement reports. When the National Insurance Act in 1912 made it necessary that all wage-earners should be insured, she arranged for a Court of the Ancient Order of Foresters to be opened at the Settlement so that the women might have the opportunity of joining a society whose policy they could help to determine. In 1918, after the passing of the Representation of the People Act, she started a history class to educate women to vote responsibly. In 1924 she advocated the raising of the school-leaving age to 15.

When it is remembered that Poplar was the borough in which George Lansbury played such a prominent part; that the Poplar Board of Guardians were the first to grant outdoor relief and the leaders in the revolt against the shocking conditions in the workhouses; and that the Borough Council was in the forefront—possibly too much in the forefront—in social reform, being the perpetrators of "Poplarism", the importance of the part played by the Settlement becomes clear. The influence of Christians like Lansbury and Miss Mackay helped to create a tradition of good government which has never been lost; Poplar today has the reputation of being one of the best-governed of the London boroughs.

The improved social conditions of East London and the development of the Welfare State have not made the social services of the Settlement unnecessary. Care Committee work, the Children's Country Holiday Fund, the Youth Clubs and the uniformed organizations, the Hospital Savings Association, the Women's Meetings, the Darby and Joan Club, the Young Wives' Club, and all the visiting connected with this work, have continued to be needed. The Citizens' Advice Bureau has dealt with thousands of cases a year—housing problems, matrimonial problems, accident benefit claims, health and psychiatric problems and countless others—and has had help from a Poor Man's Lawyer and a psychiatrist. All this work has been enough to tax the resources of the Settlement to the uttermost. Since the Second World War there have rarely been any full-time voluntary workers, and the work has been carried on by a paid staff with the help of part-time voluntary workers, many of whom are residents who pay for their board and help in the Settlement in their free time, working elsewhere during the day.

The Settlement has sometimes been criticized for devoting its energies too much to social service and too little to religious work. It is undoubtedly true that the social reforms have done nothing to make easier the work of evangelism: the people are even more indifferent to God in their prosperity than they were in their poverty. Nevertheless, the suffering, poverty and disease of the nineteenth century were something no Christian country could tolerate, and it cannot have been the will of Christ that it should be tolerated. It took the concentrated and dedicated efforts of social workers and the co-ordinated work of administrative bodies to bring any order out of the chaos; it would have been more than tragic if the Church had had no part in what was done. It seems as if the growth of the Kingdom of God has two aspects; the bringing of individuals to Christ, and the bringing in of a social order that is governed by Christian principles. The Church cannot afford to neglect either of these tasks. The new arrangements in East London, by which in 1958 the Settlement—now called Poplar House—became the headquarters of the new training centre for evangelistic work in industrial areas, are the beginning of an experiment in the bringing together of these two aspects of Christian work, and the inauguration of the new scheme forms a fitting opening to a new and promising chapter in the history of the Settlement.

Postscript, 1963

The years since 1959 have seen the team of workers at Poplar House, in common with Settlement workers elsewhere, trying to find the right pattern for voluntary work in the Welfare State. Certain principles are beginning to emerge. First, there is the task of discovering and meeting needs which are not covered by the statutory services—the Settlement must still pioneer. For example "meals on wheels" in Stepney, Poplar and Millwall were started and run by the Churches and other voluntary agencies until the local authorities took over. Secondly, there is the responsibility of filling in the inevitable gaps in the welfare services. This includes such things as giving immediate help in emergencies which occur outside office hours; helping people whose problems fall outside the scope of the statutory services; and doing after care work for the social workers. All this means close co-operation with the local authorities; and some of it involves the training of voluntary workers. The Ministry of Health encourages this co-operation. Thirdly, there is the task of encouraging, organizing and training local people to serve the community. The work done for old people by the youth clubs and the church members; the support given to the Residents Association by members of St. Paul's Church, Millwall; and the canteen for dockers, open from 7 a.m., run by members of the same church, are examples of what has been achieved.

Settlement work in the past was done by Settlement residents for the community. It looks as if in the future settlements will be focal points from which members of the community themselves give trained and co-ordinated voluntary service. "Team-work" and "Good neighbourliness" are today's slogans. The Poplar House Centre, where Churches and Settlement are together tackling the problems of the neighbourhood in close co-operation with the local authorities, is typical of what is being done in many areas.

Epilogue

"... just as in a single human body there are many limbs and organs, all with different functions, so all of us, united with Christ, form one body, serving individually as limbs and organs to one another.

"The gifts we possess differ as they are allotted to us by God's grace, and must be exercised accordingly: the gift of inspired utterance, for example, in proportion to a man's faith; or the gift of administration, in administration. A teacher should employ his gift in teaching, and one who has the gift of stirring speech should use it to stir his hearers. If you give to charity, give with all your heart; if you are a leader, exert yourself to lead; if you are helping others in distress, do it cheerfully."

(Romans xii 4–8, from *The New English Bible New Testament*, 1961, by permission of the Oxford and Cambridge University Presses.)

Name Index

Subject Index

513

Date Due